Major Problems in
African-American History
Volume I

MAJOR PROBLEMS IN AMERICAN HISTORY SERIES

GENERAL EDITOR

THOMAS G. PATERSON

Major Problems in African-American History
Volume I
From Slavery to Freedom, 1619–1877

DOCUMENTS AND ESSAYS

EDITED BY
THOMAS C. HOLT
THE UNIVERSITY OF CHICAGO

ELSA BARKLEY BROWN
THE UNIVERSITY OF MARYLAND, COLLEGE PARK

Australia • Brazil • Japan • Korea • Mexico • Singapore • Spain • United Kingdom • United States

WADSWORTH
CENGAGE Learning·

Major Problems in African-American History Volume 1: From Slavery to Freedom, 1619–1877: Documents and Essays
Edited by Thomas C. Holt and Elsa Barkley Brown

Editor in Chief: Jean L. Woy

Senior Associate Editor: Frances Gay

Project Editor: Gabrielle Stone

Editorial Assistant: Heather Hubbard

Associate Production/Design Coordinator: Jodi O'Rourke

Assistant Manufacturing Coordinator: Andrea Wagner

Senior Marketing Manager: Sandra McGuire

Cover Design: Sarah Melhado

Cover Art: Aaron Douglas, *Into Bondage*, 1936 oil on canvas. In the collection of The Corcoran Gallery of Art, Washington, DC, museum purchase and partial gift of Thurlow Evans Tibbs, Jr., The Evans-Tibbs Collection 1996.9.

For product information and technology assistance, contact us at **Cengage Learning Customer & Sales Support, 1-800-354-9706**

For permission to use material from this text or product, submit all requests online at **www.cengage.com/permissions** Further permissions questions can be emailed to **permissionrequest@cengage.com**

Library of Congress Control Number: 99-71961

ISBN-13: 978-0-669-24991-0

ISBN-10: 0-669-24991-2

Wadsworth
20 Channel Center Street
Boston, MA 02210
USA

Cengage Learning is a leading provider of customized learning solutions with office locations around the globe, including Singapore, the United Kingdom, Australia, Mexico, Brazil, and Japan. Locate your local office at **www.cengage.com/global**

Cengage Learning products are represented in Canada by Nelson Education, Ltd.

To learn more about Wadsworth, visit **www.cengage.com/wadsworth**

Purchase any of our products at your local college store or at our preferred online store **www.cengagebrain.com**

Printed in the United States of America
10 11 12 13 14   22 21 20 19 18

Contents

C H A P T E R   3
The Origins of North American Slavery and Racism
Page 82

C H A P T E R   4
The Origins of African America and the
Continuity of African Culture
Page 110

C H A P T E R   5
The Development of a Slave Society in Colonial North America
Page 157

C H A P T E R   6
Subordination and Autonomy: the Dialectics of Master-Slave Relations
Page 195

C H A P T E R   7
The Roots of Resistance: Slave Cultures and Communities
Page 245

C H A P T E R   8
Free Blacks Confront the "Slave Power": The Meaning of Freedom in a Slave Society
Page 294

C H A P T E R   9
Civil War and Emancipation
Page 334

C H A P T E R   1 0
The Work of Reconstruction
Page 368

Preface

African-American history is, paradoxically, both a very old and a very new field. It is very old in the sense that some of its pioneering works appeared in the middle and late nineteenth century. Moreover, those works—by William Wells Brown, George Washington Williams, and Gertrude Bustill Mossell, among others—addressed some of the field's principal issues, ones that have animated the subject to this day: what contributions blacks have made to building and defending the nation; what role blacks might have had in its cultural development and progress; how blacks might lay claim to equal citizenship. African-American history is also very new, in the sense that its widespread emergence as a formal subject of study in colleges and universities dates from the 1970s.

Whether old or new, however, scholars in this field have generally recognized its intimate connection to the most fundamental and contentious political issues of its day—such as slavery, freedom, equality, and social justice. As such, African-American history has itself been a politically contested field and provides an alternative perspective on the character, formation, and destiny of the American nation. Of course, some of the subjects of African-American history—for example, slavery and emancipation—have long been part of the standard American history curriculum. Outside of a very few predominantly black institutions, these subjects were not studied from the perspective of black Americans themselves. Since the 1970s, historians have focused on developing an African-American historiography that centers on black thought, action, and community. Volume I covers the African-American experience from the beginnings of the Atlantic slave trade to the Reconstruction period; Volume II, from Reconstruction to the present.

As part of the *Major Problems in American History* Series, these volumes are intended to provide students and instructors with a framework for thinking about African-American history and with essential, readable, and provocative documents and essays on the issues raised by the African Americans' historical experience. That experience is both intimately linked to American history as a whole and also distinct from that history in innumerable ways. We wanted to acquaint students with the economic, political, and social circumstances in which African Americans have had to function and at the same time to offer students an opportunity to view U.S. history and the African-American experience in the United States through the eyes of African Americans.

As with that of other nonelite groups unable to control the recording of history or the preservation of that record, much of the lived experience of black Americans remains undocumented. In fact, the range and volume of literature and documentation of what has been done to or said about African Americans is much larger than that of the actions and thoughts of African Americans themselves. Even within the records of African Americans, those of men and prominent elites are often more known and available than those of women or of poor and working-class people. This is the reality that has made the choices more difficult for all scholars of the African-American experience; it requires innovation in both the search for and the interpretation of primary sources. In some cases, scholars have found letters and eyewitness accounts by African Americans buried in massive government files, especially those generated at moments of crisis like wars and civil unrest. Others have turned to traditional sources, such as plantation records or the testimony of elite whites, but subjected them to a more searching scrutiny, reading "between the lines." In other cases, scholars have sought out unconventional historical materials, such as folktales, music, photographs, and material objects. The essays and documents in this volume reflect many of these approaches.

Volume I explores the causes and consequences of the slave trade, the origins of slavery and racism, and the development of a slave society and African-American culture in colonial North America in Chapters 2–5. Chapters 6 and 7 cover the dynamics of the master-slave relationship and the roots of resistance within the slave cultures and communities through letters, personal accounts, and folktales. Chapter 8 describes the experience of free blacks in a slave society and the meaning of freedom in that context. And Chapters 9 and 10 cover the Civil War, Emancipation, and the struggles of Reconstruction.

Like the other volumes in this series, *Major Problems in African-American History* is made up of both primary sources (textual and visual documents) and essays interpreting some of the major issues in the field. Every chapter opens with a brief introduction that sets the scene and defines the central issues. The documents and essays that follow suggest the differing perspectives from which historians address those issues, either through posing conflicting interpretations of the same events or offering differing angles of vision on a general theme. Our aim in each chapter is to provide materials that suggest ways of thinking about the African-American experience. This will enable readers to develop their own understanding or assessment of the questions scholars have raised and also allow readers to ask their own, perhaps entirely new, questions about the subject. Each chapter closes with a list of books and articles for further reading.

We would like to thank all the people who helped us in compiling this anthology. We have canvassed a large number of scholars of African-American history for suggestions about the appropriate content of these volumes. We are especially indebted to a number of people who provided us with extraordinarily generous replies, including not only syllabi and helpful advice but in many cases copies of documents and essays: Susan O'Donovan and Leslie Rowland, both of the University of Maryland, College Park; Julie Saville of the University of Chicago; and Stephanie J. Shaw of Ohio State University. We would also like to thank the following people who reviewed our tables of contents at various stages and provided us with thoughtful commentary and challenges: John D. Baskerville, University of Northern Iowa; Richard J. M. Blackett, the University of Houston; David W. Blight, Amherst College; Margaret Washington Creel, Cornell University; Dennis C. Dickerson, Williams College; Lillie J. Edwards, Drew University; Patience Essah, Auburn University; V. P. Franklin, Drexel University; Raymond

Gavins, Duke University; Robert L. Harris, Jr., Cornell University; Evelyn Brooks
Higginbotham, Harvard University; Darlene Clark Hine, Michigan State University; Gerald C. Horne, University of North Carolina, Chapel Hill; James O. Horton,
George Washington University; Rhett S. Jones, Brown University; Earl Lewis, the
University of Michigan, Ann Arbor; Daniel Letwin, Pennsylvania State University;
Daniel C. Littlefield, University of South Carolina; Valinda W. Littlefield, University of Illinois—Urbana; Leon F. Litwack and Waldo E. Martin, Jr., University of
California, Berkeley; Genna Rae McNeil, the University of North Carolina, Chapel
Hill; Peter M. Mhunzi, Pasadena City College; Tiffany L. Patterson, SUNY, Binghamton; Rosalyn Terborg-Penn, Morgan State University; Brenda Gayle Plummer,
the University of Wisconsin at Madison; Linda Reed, the University of Houston;
Joseph P. Reidy, Howard University; Julius Scott, the University of Michigan, Ann
Arbor; Herbert Shapiro, University of Cincinnati; Stephanie J. Shaw, Ohio State University; Gerald Smith, University of Kentucky; Donald Spivey, the University of
Miami; Judith Stein, City College of the City University of New York; Brenda
Stevenson, University of California, Los Angeles; Jeffrey C. Stewart, George Mason
University; Arvarh E. Strickland, University of Missouri—Columbia; Sterling
Stuckey, University of California, Riverside; H. Lewis Suggs, Clemson University;
Joe W. Trotter, Jr., Carnegie Mellon University; Clarence Walker, University of
California, Davis; Juliet E. K. Walker, University of Illinois at Urbana-Champaign;
Randolph Walker, LeMoyne-Owen College; Marli Weiner, University of Maine;
Robert S. Weisbrot, Colby College; and Francille R. Wilson, the University of
Maryland, College Park. Each of us has also incurred debts to student researchers
and editorial assistants along the way. Tom Holt thanks Hannah Rosen, Laurie
Green, and Steven Essig not only for library and clerical assistance but also for
their useful suggestions regarding the content. Elsa Barkley Brown is grateful to
Kelly Quinn, Marya McQuirter, and Doris Dixon.

And, finally, the production of these volumes has been immeasurably aided by
the staffs of both **Cengage Learning** and its predecessor, D.C. Heath. James Miller
and Sylvia Mallory initiated the project. Fran Gay has been indispensably cheerful and determined in seeing that it was completed, and Gabrielle Stone has
been thorough in overseeing the production of the project to bound books. Series
Editor Thomas G. Paterson has nurtured, cajoled, and driven it forward from start
to finish.

T. H.
E. B. B.

Interpreting

African-American History

What has motivated the study of African Americans as a separate topic in American history? What kinds of issues do such studies raise? What, exactly, constitutes the history of people of African descent in the United States? How is the field related to and different from general U.S. history? What are and have been the purposes to which historians and lay people have studied and written this history? What are the material and institutional bases for the development of a study of African Americans?

The question "What is African-American history?" was throughout the nineteenth and twentieth centuries, and continues to be, a political as much as an intellectual question. Most nineteenth- and twentieth-century white historians and social scientists, adopting biological conceptions of racial differences, assumed that black people, in the United States and elsewhere, had no history worth speaking of and no ability to undertake historical or other intellectual scholarship. The very notion that anyone might study the history of black people or that black people themselves might write or teach any subject worth others reading or studying contradicted many of the assumptions of the ordering of human society. Thus the study of African-American history was a contested issue. Additionally, for a people many of whom were newly freed from or only a generation or two removed from slavery, the question of how Americans in general conceptualized the relationship of black people to the national story was crucial in constructing themselves as free people, as citizens with full rights, and as equals. As African Americans, along with allies, struggled to alter their status in U.S. society and in the U.S. academy, history became a battleground.

Throughout the twentieth century various African Americans invested history with the power to transform social institutions. Both whites and blacks, so the argument went, had to overcome ignorance and miseducation about the history of black people. To black men, women, and children, knowledge of African-American history would impart a new sense of themselves and their abilities—an empowerment. To whites, this education would provide an incentive to dismantle the discriminatory legal, educational, economic, and social barriers that have kept black citizens relegated to secondary status or less for the majority of U.S. history. For all Americans, there was, in the arena of African-American history perhaps more than in any other, a recognition of the political power of history. Today we are perhaps less conscious of that, yet contemporary debates about how aspects of African-American experience will be remembered may continue to suggest the political nature of what are often represented as merely intellectual debates.

What are the ways in which and the places where you have been introduced to African-American history? How have your ideas about African-American history in particular and history in general been shaped by the contexts in which you encountered these histories?

 D O C U M E N T S

The first three documents reveal the assumptions that many African Americans had about the ways in which the study of history could reshape the status of African Americans in the United States. Writing in 1920 for the first issue of a children's publication, *The Brownies' Book*, edited by W. E. B. Du Bois, Annette Brown addressed a poem to the subject of this lack of information about black achievements in the United States. Implicit in this poem is an assumption that children need to know the history of their people as much as they need to know the dominant national heroes and heroines. Perhaps it also urges children reading it to take responsibility for their own education, to seek out their history. The second document, a speech given at Hampton Institute in November 1921 by Carter G. Woodson, five years after he founded the *Journal of Negro History,* addresses how historical research and writing will help African Americans gain the respect of others. After receiving a Ph.D. in history from Harvard University in 1912, Woodson founded the Association for the Study of Negro Life and History (ASNLH) in 1915 and initiated Negro History Week in 1926. In the third document, Mary McLeod Bethune, then president of the ASNLH, lays out to the 1937 annual meeting her vision of black history as fundamental to the development of black self-esteem.

The fourth and fifth documents, by historians of the African-American experience, suggest how individual scholars, themselves African American, approach their work. John Hope Franklin, perhaps the premiere historian of the African-American experience in the second half of the twentieth century, discusses his experiences working as a historian in a society that denied him many of what might be seen as the basic necessities of work—a place to sit, a place to eat. In the fifth document, Vincent Harding writes what might be called a manifesto for what he and others saw as a new approach to African-American history and to being African American and a historian in the 1970s. Harding, a veteran of the civil rights movement, positions history frankly as a political undertaking and suggests that historians of his generation have viewpoints on history writing, on the experiences of African Americans, and on the United States radically different from the viewpoints of historians of the African-American experience who preceded them.

In the final document, poet Lucille Clifton offers a way of thinking about the development of history and its radical potential. She juxtaposes the acceptance of a history constructed by others, in which she would be portrayed as a victim, to the discovery of a different relationship to history—one that is more empowering.

1. *The Brownies' Book* Encourages Black Children to Know Their History, 1920

We gathered 'round the fire last night,
Jim an' Bess an' me,
And said, "Now let us each in turn
Tell who we'd rather be
Of all the folks that's in our books."
(Of course, we wouldn't want their looks.)

Bess wished that she'd been Betsy Ross,
The first to make the flag.
She said, "I'd like to so some deed
To make the people brag,
And have the papers print my name,—
If colored girls could rise to fame."

An' I stood out for Roosevelt;
I wished to be like him.
Then Bess said, "We both had our say,
Now tell who you'd be, Jim."
Jim never thinks like me or Bess,
He knows more than us both, I guess.

He said, "I'd be a Paul Dunbar
Or Booker Washington.
The folks you named were good, I know,
But you see, Tom, each one
Of these two men I'd wish to be
Were colored boys, like you and me.

Sojourner Truth was colored, Bess,
And Phyllis Wheatley, too;
Their names will live like Betsy Ross,
Though they were dark like you."
Jim's read of 'em somewhere, I guess,
He knows heaps more than me or Bess.

2. Carter G. Woodson on His Goals for Black History, 1922

We have a wonderful history behind us. We of the *Journal of Negro History* shall have going the rounds soon a lecture on the ante-bellum period, setting forth the stories of Negroes who did so much to inspire us. It reads like the history of people in an heroic age. We expect to send out from time to time books written for the express purpose of showing you that you have a history, a record, behind you. If

---

Annette Brown, "The Wishing Game," *The Brownies' Book*, 1, no. 1 (January 1920), 7.

Carter G. Woodson, "Some Things Negroes Need to Do," *Southern Workman*, 51 (January 1922), 33–36.

you are unable to demonstrate to the world that you have this record, the world will say to you, "You are not worthy to enjoy the blessings of democracy or anything else." They will say to you, "Who are you, anyway? Your ancestors have never controlled empires or kingdoms and most of your race have contributed little or nothing to science and philosophy and mathematics." So far as you know, they have not; but if you will read the history of Africa, the history of your ancestors—people of whom you should feel proud—you will realize that they have a history that is worth while. They have traditions that have value of which you can boast and upon which you can base a claim for a right to a share in the blessings of democracy.

Let us, then, study this history, and study it with the understanding that we are not, after all, an inferior people, but simply a people who have been set back, a people whose progress has been impeded. We are going back to that beautiful history and it is going to inspire us to greater achievements. It is not going to be long before we can so sing the story to the outside world as to convince it of the value of our history and our traditions, and then we are going to be recognized as men.

3. Mary McLeod Bethune Outlines the Objectives of the Association for the Study of Negro Life and History, 1937

If our people are to fight their way up out of bondage we must arm them with the sword and the shield and the buckler of pride—belief in themselves and their possibilities, based upon a sure knowledge of the achievements of the past. That knowledge and that pride we must give them "if it breaks every back in the kingdom."

Through the scientific investigation and objective presentation of the facts of our history and our achievement to ourselves and to all men, our Association for the Study of Negro Life and History serves to tear the veil from our eyes and allow us to see clearly and in true perspective our rightful place among all men. Through accurate research and investigation, we serve so to supplement, correct, re-orient, and annotate the story of world progress as to enhance the standing of our group in the eyes of all men. In the one hand, we bring pride to our own; in the other, we bear respect from the others.

We must tell the story with continually accruing detail from the cradle to the grave. From the mother's knee and the fireside of the home through the nursery, the kindergarten and the grade school, high school, college and university—through the technical journals, studies and bulletins of the Association,—through newspaper, story-book and pictures, we must tell the thrilling story. When they learn the fairy tales of mythical king and queen and princess, we must let them hear, too, of the Pharoahs and African kings and the brilliant pageantry of the Valley of the Nile; when they learn of Caesar and his legions, we must teach them of Hannibal and his Africans; when they learn of Shakespeare and Goethe, we must teach them of Pushkin and Dumas. When they read of Columbus, we must introduce the Africans who touched the shores of America before Europeans emerged from savagery;

Mary McLeod Bethune, "Clarifying Our Vision with the Facts," by Mary McLoud Bethune. From *Journal of Negro History,* 23, (January 1938), 12–15. Reprinted by permission.

when they are thrilled by Nathan Hale, baring his breast and crying: "I have but one life to give for my country," we must make their hearts leap to see Crispus Attucks stand and fall for liberty on Boston Common with the red blood of freedom streaming down his breast. With the *Tragic Era,* we give them *Black Reconstruction;* with Edison, we give them Jan Matzeliger; with John Dewey, we place Booker T. Washington; above the folk-music of the cowboy and the hill-billy, we place the spiritual and the "blues"; when they boast of Maxfield Parrish, we show them E. Simms Campbell. Whatever man has done, we have done—and often, better. As we tell this story, as we present to the world our facts, our pride in racial achievement grows, and our respect in the eyes of all men heightens.

Certainly, too, it is our task to make plain to ourselves the great story of our rise in America from "less than the dust" to the heights of sound achievement. We must recount in accurate detail the story of how the Negro population has grown from a million in 1800 to almost 12 million in 1930. The Negro worker is today an indispensible part of American agriculture and industry. His labor has built the economic empires of cotton, sugar cane and tobacco; he furnishes nearly 12 per cent of all American bread-winners, one-third of all servants, one-fifth of all farmers. In 1930, we operated one million farms and owned 750,000 homes. Negroes operate today over 22,000 business establishments with over 27 million dollars in yearly receipts and payrolls of more than five million dollars. Negroes manufacture more than 60 different commodities. They spend annually for groceries over two billion dollars, a billion more for clothes, with total purchasing power in excess of 4½ billion dollars. Negro churches have more than five million members in 42,500 organizations, owning 206 million dollars' worth of property and spending 43 million dollars a year. Some 360,000 Negroes served in the World War, with 150,000 of them going to France. Negroes are members of legislatures in 12 states; three or more states have black judges on the bench and a federal judge has recently been appointed to the Virgin Islands. Twenty-three Negroes have sat in Congress, and there is one member in the House at present. Under the "New Deal," a number of well qualified Negroes hold administrative posts.

Illiteracy has decreased from about 95 per cent in 1865 to only 16.3 per cent in 1930. In the very states that during the dark days of Reconstruction prohibited the education of Negroes by law, there are today over 2 million pupils in 25,000 elementary schools, 150,000 high school pupils in 2,000 high schools and 25,000 students in the more than 100 Negro colleges and universities. Some 116 Negroes have been elected to Phi Beta Kappa in white Northern colleges, over 60 have received the degree of Doctor of Philosophy from leading American universities and 97 Negroes are mentioned in *Who's Who in America.* It is the duty of our Association to tell the glorious story of our past and of our marvelous achievement in American life over almost insuperable obstacles.

From this history, our youth will gain confidence, self-reliance and courage. We shall thereby raise their mental horizon and give them a base from which to reach out higher and higher into the realm of achievement. And as we look about us today, we know that they must have this courage and self-reliance. We are beset on every side with heart-rending and fearsome difficulties.

Recently, in outlining to the President of the United States the position of the Negro in America, I saw fit to put it this way: "The great masses of Negro workers

are depressed and unprotected in the lowest levels of agriculture and domestic service while black workers in industry are generally barred from the unions and grossly
discriminated against. The housing and living conditions of the Negro masses are
sordid and unhealthy; they live in a constant terror of the mob, generally shorn of
their constitutionally guaranteed right of suffrage, and humiliated by the denial of
civil liberties. The great masses of Negro youth are offered only one fifteenth the
educational opportunity of the average American child."

These things also we must tell them, accurately, realistically and factually.
The situation we face must be defined, reflected and evaluated. Then, armed with
the pride and courage of his glorious tradition, conscious of his positive contribution to American life, and enabled to face clear-eyed and unabashed the situation
before him, the Negro may gird his loins and go forth to battle to return "with
their shields or on them." And so today I charge our Association for the Study of
Negro Life and History to carry forward its great mission to arm us with the facts
so that we may face the future with clear eyes and a sure vision. Our Association
may say again with Emperor Jean Christophe: "While I live I shall try to build that
pride we need, and build in terms white men as well as black can understand! I am
thinking of the future, not of now. I will teach pride if my teaching breaks every
back in my Kingdom."

4. John Hope Franklin Explains the Lonely Dilemma of the American Negro Scholar, 1963

. . . The dilemmas and problems of the Negro scholar are numerous and complex.
He has been forced, first of all, to establish his claim to being a scholar, and he
has had somehow to seek recognition in the general world of scholarship. This has
not been an easy or simple task, for, at the very time when American scholarship
in general was making its claim to recognition, it was denying that Negroes were
capable of being scholars. Few Americans, even those who advocated a measure of
political equality, subscribed to the view that Negroes—any Negroes—had the
ability to think either abstractly or concretely or to assimilate ideas that had been
formulated by others. As late as the closing years of the nineteenth century it was
difficult to find any white persons in the labor or business community, in the pulpit
or on the platform, in the field of letters or in the field of scholarship, who thought
it possible that a Negro could join the select company of scholars in America.

The Negro, then, first of all had to struggle against the forces and personalities
in American life that insisted that he could never rise in the intellectual sphere. . . .

. . . The world of the Negro scholar is indescribably lonely; and he must, somehow, pursue truth down that lonely path while, at the same time, making certain that
his conclusions are sanctioned by universal standards developed and maintained by
those who frequently do not even recognize him. Imagine the plight of a Negro historian trying to do research in archives in the South operated by people who cannot
conceive that a Negro has the capacity to use the materials there. I well recall my

John Hope Franklin, "The Dilemma of the American Negro Scholar," in Herbert Hill, ed., *Soon One Morning: New Writing by American Negroes.* Copyright © 1963 by Alfred A. Knopf, Inc. Reprinted by permission.

first visit to the State Department of Archives and History in North Carolina, which was presided over by a man with a Ph.D. in history from Yale. My arrival created a panic and an emergency among the administrators that was, itself, an incident of historic proportions. The archivist frankly informed me that I was the first Negro who had sought to use the facilities there; and as the architect who designed the building had not anticipated such a situation, my use of the manuscripts and other materials would have to be postponed for several days, during which time one of the exhibition rooms would be converted to a reading room for me. . . .

Many years later, in 1951, while working at the Library of Congress, one of my closest friends, a white historian, came by my study room one Friday afternoon and asked me to lunch with him the following day. I reminded him that since the following day would be a Saturday, the Supreme Court restaurant would be closed, and there was no other place in the vicinity where we could eat together. (This was before the decision in the Thompson restaurant case in April 1953, which opened Washington restaurants to all well-behaved persons.) My friend pointed out that he knew I spent Saturdays at the Library, and he wondered what I did for food on those days. I told him that I seldom missed a Saturday of research and writing at the Library of Congress, by that my program for that day was a bit different from other days. On Saturdays, I told him, I ate a huge late breakfast at home and then brought a piece of fruit or candy to the Library, which I would eat at the lunch hour. Then, when I could bear the hunger no longer during the afternoon, I would leave and go home to an early dinner. His only remark was that he doubted very much whether, if he were a Negro, he would be a scholar, if it required sacrifices such as this and if life was as inconvenient as it appeared. I assured him that for a Negro scholar searching for truth, the search for food in the city of Washington was one of the *minor* inconveniences. . . .

5. Vincent Harding on the Differences Between Negro History and Black History, 1971

. . . [M]uch of the story of Negro History is told [in] its attempt to reveal the "contributions" of blacks to the American saga; its emphasis on black heroism in the wars; its call for racial pride and for continued struggle to enter the mainstream of American life; its claim to be primarily interested in objective truth, while writing history through tears. . . .

Much of Negro History took this tack. It did not intend to threaten the established heroes or the basic values of America. . . . Rather it sought only to guarantee that the black presence was properly acknowledged, assuming that blackness could be contained within the confines of the American saga. It was an obvious parallel to the efforts to include a special minority of "ready" Negroes into an American society which would not be basically changed by their presence.

. . . Almost all of [the] proponents [of Black History] have come into their intellectual maturity under the tutelage of the fathers of Negro History, but unlike

Vincent Harding, "Beyond Chaos: Black History and the Search for the New Land." Reprinted by permission from Vincent Harding.

them we have lived most of our adult lives since 1954. We have lived through the politics of the sixties, through all of the promises and betrayals, through the discomfiting of the West. . . .

We who write Black History cannot track our "bleeding countrymen through the widely scattered documents of American history" and still believe in America. . . . We cannot—do not wish to—write with detachment from the agonies of our people. We are not satisfied to have our story accepted into the American saga. We deal in redefinitions, in taking over, in moving to set our own vision upon the blindness of American historiography. . . .

Black History does not seek to highlight the outstanding contributions of special black people to the life and times of America. Rather our emphasis is on exposure, disclosure, on reinterpretation of the entire American past. . . . [I]t is clear even now that the black past cannot be remade and clearly known without America's larger past being shaken at the foundations. While Negro History almost never questioned the basic goodness and greatness of American society, while it assumed its innate potential for improvement (provided it was ready to read additional volumes on Negro History), Black History has peeped a different card.

Black History suggests that the American past upon which so much hope has been built never really existed, and probably never will. . . .

. . . Black History is clearly more than the study of exclusively black things, for since the days of our slavery we could not be understood in an exclusively black light. So that Black History which seeks to deal with America begins with its European heritage, assesses the "Rise of the West." It asks how much of this ascendancy came at the expense of the death and degradation of our fathers and other nonwhite peoples of the globe. When it is clear that the "greatness" of Europe was built under the shadow of our ancestors' deaths, how shall we view this Western world and its major child—America? Black History . . . is the exposure of the strange foundations of Western power. . . .

Black History looks upon America with little of the affection and admiration which was obviously carried by our Negro History fathers. We look at the paradox of Black indentured-servitude/slavery being introduced into the colony of Virginia at the same time that the House of Burgesses came into being. So slavery and "representative government" were planted together. . . . From the perspective of Black History, the greater freedom which was gained for local government in the English colonies actually turned out to be freedom to embed the slavery of our forefathers deep into freedom's soil. So we are forced to begin to ask whether it was ever freedom's soil.

. . . [B]lacks must read history with Indian eyes as well, and cannot fail to note that many of the New England "fathers" participated not only in the forced migration and decimation of the original inhabitants, but gave full strength to that trade in men which brought other dark men to these shores. The treatment received by both blacks and Indians cannot fail to shape the black approach to New England history. . . .

Indeed Black History is forced to press on to ask about the meaning of America itself. (This raising of questions did not mark Negro History. Perhaps our fathers lived too close to the brutal experiences of black life to allow such a luxury.) When the spirit and institutions of the nation were so fully formed and defined by the leaders of Massachusetts and the rest of New England—slave traders on the one hand, slaveholders on the other—what indeed is the nation's meaning? Whose founding "fathers" were they, and what does their creation mean for the children of their slaves?

Black History is not satisfied with telling how many black men fought in the Revolutionary War. We are not among those who lift the banner of Crispus Attucks, for we are caught in painful dilemmas. While we recognize their heroism, we recognize too that a revolution which ended with more than 700,000 persons still in slavery was perhaps no revolution at all, but essentially a war among colonialist powers. So the children of the slaves who fought might better mourn rather than rejoice and celebrate, for it is likely that our fathers were no different than the millions of non-white pawns who have been pushed about by the military leaders of the colonizers for centuries. (And we save our energies and our wits for the exposing of this delusion and the encouraging of the heirs of the slaves to refuse to be pawns any longer.) In this way the experiences of our forefathers and the developments of this generation coalesce into a totally different reading of America than is usually known. . . .

Such a reading of America presses us to ask whether it was ever a democracy, demands to know whether it is possible for a democracy to exist where one quarter of the population of the land is either in slavery or being steadily driven off its ancient grounds. Black History is not simply "soul food" and "soul music" as some of its misinterpreters have suggested. Black History is the history of the Black Experience in America, which is the history of black and white—and Indian—inextricably, painfully, rarely joyfully, entwined. So Black History explores Henry Adams concerning the American nation at the beginning of the nineteenth century and hears him say that America in 1800 was a healthy organism. Then in the same work we read that the one major problem in America in 1800 was "the cancer" of slavery. In that set of statements America is diagnosed for black eyes: Healthy—except for cancer.

Black History is the constant demand that the cancerous state of America be seen and known. . . .

Black History cannot help but be politically oriented, for it tends toward the total redefinition of an experience which was highly political. Black History must be political, for it deals with the most political phenomenon of all—the struggle between the master and the slave, between the colonized and the colonizer, between the oppressed and the oppressor. And it recognizes that all histories of peoples participate in politics and are shaped by political and ideological views. . . .

6. Lucille Clifton on the Nurturing of History, c. 1990

i am accused of tending to the past
as if i made it,
as if i sculpted it
with my own hands. i did not.
this past was waiting for me
when i came,

Lucille Clifton, "i am accused of tending to the past," copyright © 1991 by Lucille Clifton. Reprinted from *Quilting Poems, 1987–1990* with the permission of BOA Editions, Ltd.

> a monstrous unnamed baby,
> and i took with my mother's itch
> took it to breast
> and named it
> History.
> she is more human now,
> learning language everyday,
> remembering faces, names and dates.
> when she is strong enough to travel
> on her own, beware she will.

E S S A Y S

In the first essay, John Hope Franklin, the leading African-American historian in the post–World War II era, sketches the history of the field since the late nineteenth century. He argues that successive generations of African-American scholars struggled to recover their history in the midst of changing but always politically charged circumstances. To reclaim the history of a stigmatized people was, it seems, an inherently political act, even though the character of the politics changed over time. David W. Blight describes the efforts of an earlier generation to reclaim its true historical legacy. On the twentieth anniversary of the Emancipation Proclamation Frederick Douglass struggled passionately against the white southern myth of the "Lost Cause," which appeared to authorize a national reconciliation from which blacks were excluded. An accurate memory of the war and emancipation, Douglass believed, would better sustain the continuing struggle to realize finally the fruits of the destruction of slavery. The continuing mythic power in our own day of the historical myths embodied in monuments, museums, memorials, and rituals is also the subject of the third essay, by Fath Davis Ruffins. The failed effort to win public support for an African-American museum in the nation's capital reflected many of the competing historical visions and political agendas among blacks as well as between blacks and whites. The materialization of African-American history is a form of political recognition, but the debate over the appropriate form and character of that material representation exposes fierce differences over "the politics of memory."

The History of African-American History

JOHN HOPE FRANKLIN

According to my calculation, there have been four generations of scholarship—of unequal length—in Afro-American history. The first generation began auspiciously with the publication in 1882 of the two-volume *History of the Negro Race in America* by George Washington Williams and ended around 1909 with the publication of Booker T. Washington's *Story of the Negro.* Although it is difficult to characterize this first period of serious scholarship in the field, it is safe to say that the primary concern of the writers was to explain the process of adjustment Afro-Americans

Reprinted by permission of Louisiana State University Press from *The State of Afro-American History: Past, Present, and Future* edited by Darlene Clark Hine. Copyright © 1986 by Louisiana State University Press.

made to conditions in the United States. Whether it was the aggressive integrationism of George Washington Williams or the mild accommodationism of Booker T. Washington, the common objective of the writers of this period was to define and describe the role of Afro-Americans in the life of the nation. . . .

There were no trained, professional historians among them, with the exception of W. E. B. Du Bois. . . . They wrote of "The Progress of the Race," "A New Negro for a New Century," and "The Remarkable Advancement of the American Negro." . . . Obviously their concern was with adjustment, adaptation, and the compatibility of Afro-Americans with the white world in which they were compelled to live.

The second generation was marked by no special fanfare until the publication of Du Bois' *The Negro* in 1915, the founding of the Association for the Study of Negro Life and History also in 1915, the launching of the *Journal of Negro History* in 1916, and the publication in 1922 of Carter G. Woodson's *The Negro in Our History*. Woodson was the dominant figure of the period. He was not only the leading historian but also the principal founder of the association, editor of the *Journal*, and executive director of the Associated Publishers. He gathered around him a circle of highly trained younger historians whose research he directed and whose writings he published in the *Journal of Negro History* and under the imprint of the Associated Publishers. Monographs on labor, education, Reconstruction, art, music, and other aspects of Afro-American life appeared in steady succession, calling to the attention of the larger community the role of Afro-Americans, more specifically the contributions they had made to the development of the United States. The articles and monographs reflected prodigious research and zeal in pursuing the truth that had *not* been the hallmark of much of the so-called scientific historical writing produced in university seminars in this country some years earlier.

Woodson provided the intellectual and practical leadership of the second generation. With his strong sense of commitment, he offered the spirit and enthusiasm of a pioneer, a discoverer. He even provided the principal theme for the period when he said—in his writings and on numerous occasions—that it was the objective of him and his colleagues "to save and publish the records of the Negro, that the race may not become a negligible factor in the thought of the world." Nor should the record of Afro-Americans become a negligible factor in their own thought, Woodson contended. Thus he began doing everything possible to keep the history of Afro-Americans before them and before the larger community as well. Every annual meeting of the Association for the Study of Negro Life and History had several sessions devoted to the teaching of Afro-American history in the elementary and secondary schools. In 1926 Woodson began the annual observance of Negro History Week to raise the consciousness of Afro-Americans regarding their own worth and to draw the attention of others to what Afro-Americans had contributed to American civilization. Shortly thereafter he launched the *Negro History Bulletin,* a magazine for students, teachers, and the general public. Forty years before this country began to observe History Day, there was Negro History Week. Fifty years after the beginning of the *Negro History Bulletin,* the American Historical Association was still wrestling with the idea of a popular history magazine for students and the general public.

. . . Perhaps a convenient place to mark the beginning of the third generation is with the appearance in 1935 of W. E. B. Du Bois' *Black Reconstruction.* . . . In his book on Reconstruction, as the subtitle indicates, he was interested in "the part which black folk played in the attempt to reconstruct democracy in America." . . .

The third generation of Afro-American historical scholarship spanned, roughly, a twenty-five-year period that ended with the close of the 1960s. Most of the members of this generation were, like Du Bois, interested in the role that Afro-Americans played in the nation's history. Their training was similar to that of the second generation, but their interests were different. They looked less to Afro-American achievements and more to the interactions of blacks with whites, and more to the frequent antagonisms than to the rare moments of genuine cooperation. They tended to see Afro-American history in a larger context, insisting that any event that affected the status of Afro-Americans was a part of Afro-American history even if no Afro-Americans were directly involved. Mississippi's Theodore Bilbo, reading Rayford Logan's *What the Negro Wants* (1944) to his colleagues in the United States Senate and interpreting it for their benefit, was as much a part of Afro-American history as was Heman Sweatt's seeking admission to the University of Texas Law School.

The third generation experienced the fire and brimstone of World War II. Its predicament was not one that Adolf Hitler created but one created by the racial bigotry within their own government and in the American community in general. While all Afro-Americans were exposed to this special brand of racial perversion in the form of eloquent, if shallow, pronouncements against worldwide racism, Afro-American historians were especially sensitive to the persistent hypocrisy of the United States from the colonial years right down to World War II. Small wonder that they had difficulty maintaining a semblance of balance in the face of studied racial discrimination and humiliation. One of them declared that the United States government was "guilty of catering to the ideals of white supremacy." Another called on the United States to "address herself to the unfinished business of democracy," adding somewhat threateningly that "time was of the essence." If anyone doubts the impatience and anger of Afro-American historians during those years, he or she should examine the proceedings of the annual meetings of the Association for the Study of Negro Life and History or follow the activities of the historians themselves.

A salient feature of this generation was the increasing number of white historians working in the field. Some years earlier the second generation of historians had indicated that there were numerous areas in which work needed to be done. White historians entered the field to share in the work. One of them published the first extensive study of slavery in almost forty years and another wrote an elaborate work on the antislavery movement. Still another presented the first critical examination of Negro thought in the late nineteenth century. Interestingly enough, hostile white critics called these white historians "neo-abolitionists." Others worked on Afro-Americans in the antebellum North, Afro-American intellectual history, racial discrimination in education, and Afro-Americans in urban settings. Meanwhile, university professors began to assign dissertation topics in Afro-American history to white as well as Afro-American students. They also participated in the annual meetings of the Association for the Study of Negro Life and History and contributed to the *Journal of Negro History*. By the end of the 1960s Afro-American history was no longer the exclusive domain of Afro-Americans.

I believe that Carter G. Woodson would have been pleased with this involvement of white historians in the third generation of scholarship. When he founded the *Journal of Negro History* in 1916, he invited white scholars to sit on the editorial board and to contribute articles. He was, nevertheless, a man of shrewd insights, and I am not suggesting for a moment that he would have approved of or even tolerated whites of the third generation whose motives were more political than scholarly. Even so, he would have welcomed papers for publication in the *Journal of Negro History,* whether submitted by whites or blacks, so long as they were the product of rigorous scholarship and were not contaminated by the venom of racial bias. . . .

In the fourth generation, which began around 1970, there emerged the largest and perhaps the best-trained group of historians of Afro-America that had ever appeared. The Afro-Americans in the group were trained, as were the white historians, in graduate centers in every part of the country, in contrast to those of the third generation, who had been trained at three or four universities in the East and Midwest. No area of inquiry escaped their attention. They worked on the colonial period, the era of Reconstruction, and the twentieth century. They examined slavery, the Afro-American family, and antebellum free blacks. Their range was wide, and they brought educational, cultural, and military subjects, among many others, under their scrutiny.

These new approaches as well as the accelerated intensity in the study of Afro-American history were greatly stimulated by the drive for equality that had already begun in the third period. In their insistence that they be accorded equal treatment in every respect, Afro-Americans summoned the history of the United States to their side. They had been here from the beginning, they argued, and had done more than their share in making the country rich and great. Since history validated their claims, it was important that the entire nation should become familiar with the facts of Afro-American history. Consequently, it should be studied more intensely, written about more extensively, and taught more vigorously. Institutions of higher education came under pressure to add courses in Afro-American history and related fields and to employ specialists in the field. Responses were varied. One dean at a leading predominantly white university said that he had no objection to a course in Afro-American history, but it would be difficult in view of the fact that there was not sufficient subject matter to occupy the teachers and students for a *whole* semester. Another rushed out and persuaded one of the leaders in the black community, who happened to be a Baptist minister, to teach a course in Afro-American history. Despite the intellectual, educational, and political considerations affecting their decisions, many colleges and universities incorporated courses in Afro-American history into their curricula.

. . . There was zeal, even passion, in much that they wrote, for [scholars in the field of Afro-American history] were anxious to correct all the errors and misinterpretations of which earlier historians had been guilty. Thus, they undertook to revise not only the racist historians of an earlier day but the Afro-American historians of an earlier generation as well. . . .

In his *History of the Negro Race in America* (1882), George Washington Williams was extremely critical of Frederick Douglass for various positions he took on slavery and freedom in the years before the Civil War. We could excoriate Williams, as did his contemporaries, but that would be unfair without at least first understanding Williams' impatience with a political party that had betrayed not only the freedmen but Frederick Douglass, their chosen spokesman, as well. Likewise, one could be extremely critical of Carter G. Woodson's preoccupation with the achievements of Afro-Americans, but one should remember that Woodson was hurling historical brickbats at those who had said that Afro-Americans had achieved nothing at all. One could likewise be extremely critical of the historians of the third generation for their preoccupation with what may be called "mainstream history." In the process, some claim, they neglected some cherished attributes of Afro-American life and history, such as race pride and cultural nationalism. Such claims overlook the important fact that the historians of the third generation were compelled by circumstances to fight for the integration of Afro-American history into the mainstream of the nation's history. Their fight to integrate Afro-American history into the mainstream was a part of the fight by Afro-American students to break into the graduate departments of history in every predominantly white university in the southern states and in very many such institutions outside the South. It was also a part of the fight of Afro-Americans to gain admission to the mainstream of American life—for the vote, for equal treatment, for equal opportunity, for their rights as Americans. They pursued that course in order to be able to refute those, including our favorite dean—our favorite whipping boy, incidentally—who argued that Afro-Americans had little or no history. They also did so in order to support their argument that Afro-American history should be recognized as a centerpiece—an adornment, if you will—of the history of the United States.

. . . As a relatively new field, at least only recently recognized as a respectable field of intellectual endeavor, [Afro-American history] is alive and vibrant. This is why it can easily attract and excite a large number of graduate and undergraduate students. It provides, moreover, a very important context in which much, if not the whole, of the history of the United States can be taught and studied. It also provides an important context in which much of the history of the United States can be reexamined and rewritten. In its unique position as one of the most recent areas of intellectual inquiry, it invites the attention of those who genuinely seek new avenues to solve some of the nation's most difficult historical problems. And, if it is a valid area of intellectual inquiry, it cannot be segregated by sex, religion, or race. Historians must be judged by what they do, not by how they look.

I like to think that it was more than opportunism that increased the offerings in Afro-American history in the colleges and universities across the land. I like to believe that it was more than the excitement of the late 1960s that provided new opportunities to teach and learn Afro-American history. I prefer to entertain the thought that in addition to those other considerations there was the valid interconnection between the history of a people and their drive for first-class citizenship. The quest for their history, lost and strayed, was a quest in which black and white alike could and did participate, as both teachers and writers of history. The drive for first-class citizenship was a drive whose immediate benefit could be enjoyed only by those who had been denied it or by those others who at least truly understood the loathsome nature that such denial represented.

Some members of the fourth generation, no doubt, will regard this sentiment as optimistic if not maudlin. I would be the first to say that there is some of both in it. I would only add that when one begins a poem, a hymn, a short story, or even a history, one must be optimistic about its completion and about what it seeks to teach. If one believes in the power of his own words and in the words of others, one must also hope and believe that the world will be a better place by our having spoken or written those words.

The Burden of African-American History: Memory, Justice, and a Usable Past

DAVID W. BLIGHT

In the first week of January 1883, on the twentieth anniversary of the Emancipation Proclamation, a distinguished group of black leaders held a banquet in Washington, D.C., to honor the nineteenth century's most prominent Afro-American intellectual, Frederick Douglass. The banquet was an act of veneration for Douglass, an acknowledgment of the aging abolitionist's indispensable role in the Civil War era, a ritual of collective celebration, and an opportunity to forge historical memory and transmit it across generations. The nearly fifty guests comprised a who's who of black leadership in the middle and late nineteenth century. . . . After a sumptuous dinner, numerous toasts were offered to Douglass, and to nearly every major aspect of black life: to "the colored man as a legislator"; to "the Negro press"; to "the Negro author"; to "the Republican Party"; and so forth. Douglass himself finally ended the joyous round of toasts by offering one of his own: to "the spirit of the young men" by whom he was surrounded. Many of the most distinguished guests had come of age only since the Civil War. For them slavery, abolitionism, and even the war itself were the history beyond memory. Douglass had captured an essential meaning of the occasion; the young had gathered in tribute to the old. As they met to celebrate and to understand the pivotal event in their history—emancipation—the meaning of that event was being passed to a new generation of black leaders.

In his formal remarks at the banquet, Douglass demonstrated that during the last third of his life (he lived from 1818 until 1895), a distinguishing feature of his leadership was his quest to preserve the memory of the Civil War as he believed blacks and the nation should remember it. Douglass viewed emancipation as the central reference point of black history. Likewise the nation, in his judgment, had no greater turning point, nor a better demonstration of national purpose. On the twentieth anniversary, Douglass sought to infuse emancipation and the war with the sacred and mythic qualities that he had always attributed to them. . . . Emancipation day, he believed, ought to be a national celebration in which all blacks—the low and the mighty—could claim a new and secure social identity. But it was also an "epoch" full of lessons about the meaning of historical memory. . . . Douglass challenged his fellow black leaders to remember the Civil War with awe. "The day we celebrate," he said, "affords us an eminence from which we may in a measure survey both the past and the future. It is one of those days which may well count for a thousand years." This was more than mere banquet rhetoric. . . .

"'For Something Beyond the Battlefield': Frederick Douglass and the Struggle for the Memory of the Civil War," by David W. Blight. From *Journal of American History,* 75 (March 1989), 1156–1178. Copyright © 1989 by the Journal of American History. Reprinted by permission.

Douglass's effort to forge memory into action that could somehow save the legacy of the Civil War for blacks—freedom, citizenship, suffrage, and dignity—came at a time when the nation appeared indifferent or hostile to that legacy. The richly symbolic emancipation day banquet of 1883 occurred only months before the United States Supreme Court struck down the Civil Rights Act of 1875, sacrificing the Civil War amendments, as the dissenting Justice John Marshall Harlan put it, and opening the door for the eventual triumph of Jim Crow laws across the South. The ruling in *United States v. Stanley,* better known as the *Civil Rights Cases,* declared that the equal protection clause of the Fourteenth Amendment applied only to states; a person wronged by racial discrimination, therefore, could look for redress only from state laws and courts. In effect, the decision would also mean that the discriminatory acts of private persons were beyond the safeguards of the Fourteenth Amendment. . . .

Douglass interpreted the *Civil Rights Cases* as a failure of historical memory and national commitment. Reflecting on the Supreme Court decision in his final autobiography, Douglass contended that "the future historian will turn to the year 1883 to find the most flagrant example of this national deterioration." White racism, among individuals and in national policy, he remarked, seemed to increase in proportion to the "increasing distance from the time of the war." Douglass blamed not only the "fading and defacing effects of time," but more important, the spirit of reconciliation between North and South. Justice and liberty for blacks, he maintained, had lost ground from "the hour that the loyal North . . . began to shake hands over the bloody chasm." Thus, Douglass saw the Supreme Court decision as part of a disturbing pattern of historical change. Historical memory, he had come to realize, was not merely an entity altered by the passage of time; it was the prize in a struggle between rival versions of the past, a question of will, of power, of persuasion. This historical memory of any transforming or controversial event emerges from cultural and political competition, from the choice to confront the past and to debate and manipulate its meaning.

. . . From the early days of Reconstruction, but especially by the 1870s, Douglass seemed acutely aware that the postwar era might ultimately be controlled by those who could best shape interpretations of the war itself. Winning the peace would not only be a matter of power, but also a struggle of moral will and historical consciousness. In the successful rise of the Democratic party, Douglass saw evidence that the South was beginning to win that struggle. In 1870 he complained that the American people were "destitute of political memory." But as he tried to reach out to both black and white readers with his newspaper, Douglass demanded that they not allow the country to "bury dead issues," as the Democrats wished. "The people cannot and will not forget the issues of the rebellion," Douglas admonished. "The Democratic party must continue to face the music of the past as well as of the present."

Some of Douglass's critics accused him of living in the past. . . . To such criticisms Douglass always had a ready answer: he would *not forgive* the South and he would *never forget* the meaning of the war. At the Tomb of the Unknown Soldier in Arlington National Cemetery in 1871, on one of the first observances of Memorial Day, Douglass declared where he stood.

We are sometimes asked in the name of patriotism to forget the merits of this fearful struggle, and to remember with equal admiration those who struck at the nation's life, and those who struck to save it—those who fought for slavery and those who fought for liberty and justice. I am no minister of malice . . . I may say if this war is to be forgotten, I ask in the name of all things sacred what shall men remember?

. . . By intellectual predilection and by experience, Douglass was deeply conscious that history mattered. As the author of three autobiographies by the 1880s, he had cultivated deep furrows into his own memory. In a real sense, the Frederick Douglass who endures as an unending subject of literary and historical inquiry— because of the autobiographies—is and was the creature of memory. Moreover, Douglass deeply understood that peoples and nations are shaped and defined by history. He knew that history was a primary source of identity, meaning, and motivation. He seemed acutely aware that history was both burden and inspiration, something to be cherished and overcome. Douglass also understood that winning battles over policy or justice in the present often required an effective use of the past. He came to a realization that in the late nineteenth-century America, blacks had a special need for a usable past. "It is not well to forget the past," Douglass warned in an 1884 speech. "Memory was given to man for some wise purpose. The past is . . . the mirror in which we may discern the dim outlines of the future and by which we may make them more symmetrical."

. . . [I]n the 1880s, according to Douglass, blacks occupied a special place in America's historical memory, as participants and as custodians. He understood his people's psychological need not to dwell on the horrors of slavery. But the slave experience was so immediate and unforgettable, Douglass believed, because it was a history that could "be traced like that of a wounded man through a crowd by the blood." Douglass urged his fellow blacks to keep *their* history before the consciousness of American society; if necessary, they should serve as a national conscience. . . . But as Douglass learned, such historical consciousness was as out of date in Gilded Age America as the racial justice he demanded.

. . . Douglass hoped that Union victory, black emancipation, and the Civil War amendments would be so deeply rooted in recent American experience, so central to any conception of national regeneration, so necessary to the postwar society that they would become sacred values, ritualized in memory. . . .

Douglass's pledge to "never forget" the meaning of the Civil War stemmed from at least five sources in his thought and experience: his belief that the war had been an ideological struggle and not merely the test of a generation's loyalty and valor; his sense of refurbished nationalism made possible by emancipation, Union victory, and Radical Reconstruction; his confrontation with the resurgent racism and Lost Cause mythology of the postwar period; his critique of America's peculiar dilemma of historical amnesia; and his personal psychological stake in preserving an Afro-American and an abolitionist memory of the war. Douglass never softened his claim that the Civil War had been an ideological conflict with deeply moral consequences. He abhorred the nonideological interpretation of the war that was gaining popularity by the 1880s. The spirit of sectional reunion had fostered a celebration of martial heroism, of strenuousness and courage, perhaps best expressed by Oliver Wendell Holmes, Jr., and later popularized by Theodore

Roosevelt. Holmes experienced and therefore loathed the horror of combat. But to him, the legacy of the Civil War rested not in any moral cause on either side, but in the passion, devotion, and sacrifice of the generation whose "hearts were touched with fire." To Holmes, the true hero—the deepest memory—of the Civil War was the soldier on either side, thoughtless of ideology, who faced the "experience of battle . . . in those indecisive contests." . . . By the 1880s Holmes's memory of the war became deeply rooted in American culture. . . .

Douglass resisted such an outlook and demanded a teleological memory of the war. His Memorial Day addresses were full of tributes to martial heroism, albeit only on the Union side; but more important, they were testaments to the abolitionist conception of the war. The conflict, Douglass insisted in 1878, "was a war of ideas, a battle of principles . . . a war between the old and new, slavery and freedom, barbarism and civilization." After Reconstruction Douglass was one of a small band of old abolitionists and reformers who struggled to sustain an ideological interpretation of the Civil War. . . .

The second source of Douglass's quest to preserve the memory of the Civil War was his refurbished nationalism. At stake for the former fugitive slave was the sense of American nationhood, the secure social identity that he hoped emancipation and equality would one day offer every black in America. Douglass expressed this connection between nationalism and memory in his famous speech at the unveiling of the Freedmen's Memorial Monument at Abraham Lincoln in Washington, D.C., in April 1876. . . . Attended by President Ulysses S. Grant, his cabinet, Supreme Court Justices, and numerous senators, the ceremony was as impressive as the bright spring day, which had been declared a holiday by joint resolution of Congress. After a reading of the Emancipation Proclamation and the unveiling of the statue (which Douglass later admitted he disliked because "it showed the Negro on his knees"), Douglass took the podium as the orator of the day. . . . Through most of the speech he spoke to and for blacks; the monument had been commissioned and paid for almost entirely by blacks. But the monument was not only to Lincoln; rather, it was to the *fact* of emancipation. . . . Douglass was, indeed, trying to make Lincoln mythic and, therefore, useful to the cause of black equality. But the primary significance of Douglass's Freedmen's Memorial address lies in its concerted attempt to forge a place for blacks in the national memory, to assert their citizenship and nationhood. . . .

The third cause of Douglass's concern over the memory of the Civil War was the resurgent racism throughout the country and the rise of the Lost Cause mentality. . . . Historians have defined the Lost Cause in at least three different ways: as a public memory, shaped by a web of organizations, institutions, and rituals; as a dimension of southern and American civil religion, rooted in churches and sacred rhetoric as well as secular institutions and thought; and as a literary phenomenon, shaped by journalists and fiction writers from the die-hard Confederate apologists of the immediate postwar years through the gentle romanticism of the "local color" writers of the 1880s to the legion of more mature novelists of the 1890s and early twentieth century who appealed to a national audience eager for reconciliation. . . . Led by Jefferson Davis, and especially by the prototypical unreconstructed rebel, Gen. Jubal Early, these former Confederate leaders created veterans' organizations, wrote partisan confederate histories, built monuments, made Robert E. Lee into a romantic icon, and desperately sought justification for their cause and explanations for their defeat. . . . During the 1870s and 1880s they forged an organized movement in print, oratory, and granite, and their influence persisted until World War I.

The "national" Lost Cause took hold during the 1880s primarily as a literary phenomenon propagated by mass market magazines and welcomed by a burgeoning northern readership. . . . They wrote about the Old South, about the chivalry and romance of antebellum plantation life, about black "servants" and a happy, loyal slave culture, remembered as a source of laugher and music. They wrote about colonial Virginia—the Old Dominion—as the source of revolutionary heritage and the birthplace of several American presidents. Northern readers were treated to an exotic South, a premodern, preindustrial model of grace. These writers sought, not to vindicate the Confederacy, but to intrigue Yankee readers. Northern readers were not asked to reconcile Jefferson's Virginia with the rebel yell at the unveiling of a Confederate monument. They were only asked to recognize the South's place in national heritage.

The conditioning of the northern mind in popular literature had its counterpart in veterans' reunions, which in the 1880s and 1890s became increasingly intersectional. Celebration of manly valor on both sides and the mutual respect of Union and Confederate soldiers fostered a kind of veterans' culture that gave the Lost Cause a place in national memory. The war became essentially a conflict between white men; both sides fought well, Americans against Americans, and there was glory enough to go around. Celebrating the soldiers' experience buttressed the non-ideological memory of the war. The great issues of the conflict—slavery, secession, emancipation, black equality, even disloyalty and treason—faded from national consciousness as the nation celebrated reunion and ultimately confronted war with Spain in 1898. . . .

In the midst of Reconstruction, Douglass began to realize the potential power of the Lost Cause sentiment. Indignant at the universal amnesty afforded ex-Confederates, and appalled by the national veneration of Robert E. Lee, Douglass attacked the emerging Lost Cause. "The spirit of secession is stronger today than ever . . . ," Douglass warned in 1871. "It is now a deeply rooted, devoutly cherished sentiment, inseparably identified with the 'lost cause.' which the half measures of the Government towards the traitors have helped to cultivate and strengthen." . . .

As for proposed monuments to Lee, Douglass considered them an insult to his people and to the Union. He feared that such monument building would only "reawaken the confederacy." . . .

Douglass never precisely clarified just how much southern "repentance" or "reformation" he deemed necessary before he could personally extend forgiveness. He merely demanded "justice," based on adherence to the Civil War amendments and to the civil rights acts. . . . He lamented the passing of so many of the old abolitionists like Garrison whose services would be needed in what Douglass called "this second battle for liberty and nation."

. . . [T]he aging Douglass never wavered in his critique of racism. "The tide of popular prejudice" against blacks, Douglass said in 1884, had "swollen by a thousand streams" since the war. Everywhere, he lamented, blacks were "stamped" with racist expectations. Douglass expressed the pain of being black in America: wherever a black man aspired to a profession, "the presumption of incompetence confronts him, and he must either run, fight, or fall before it." The alleged rapes by black men of white women were to Douglass manifestations of the South's invention of a new "crime" to replace their old fear of "insurrection." Lynching, therefore, represented a white, southern invention of new means to exercise racial power and oppression. In a speech in 1884, commemorating the rescue of fugitive slaves in the 1850s, Douglass chastised his Syracuse audience for preferring sectional peace over racial justice. "It is weak and foolish to cry PEACE when there is no peace," he cried. "In America, as elsewhere, injustice must cease before peace can prevail."

The fourth source of Douglass's arguments in the debate over the memory of the Civil War was his conviction that the country had been seduced into "national forgetfulness," a peculiar American condition of historical amnesia. In his numerous retrospective speeches in the 1880s, Douglass discussed the limitations of memory. He knew that memory was fickle and that people must embrace an "ever-changing . . . present." Even his own "slave life," he admitted, had "lost much of its horror, and sleeps in . . . memory like the dim outlines of a half-forgotten dream." But Douglass's greater concern was with collective memory, not merely with personal recollection. Douglass was rowing upstream against a strong current in American thought. As a people, Americans had always tended to reject the past and embrace newness. The overweening force of individualism in an expanding country had ever made Americans a future-oriented people, a culture unburdened with memory and tradition. . . . To Douglass, the individualism that bred indifference and the racism that bred oppression were the twin enemies undercutting efforts to preserve an abolitionist memory of the Civil War. . . .

Most assuredly, . . . Douglass was not one of those Americans who rejected the past. . . . He believed that individualism could coexist with social justice, that getting on in the world released no one from the weight of history. "Well it may be said that Americans have no memories," Douglass said in 1888. "We look over the House of Representatives and see the Solid South enthroned there; we listen with calmness to eulogies of the South and of traitors and forget Andersonville. . . . We see colored citizens shot down and driven from the ballot box, and forget the services rendered by the colored troops in the late war for the Union." More revealing still was Douglass's contempt for northern sympathy with the Lost Cause. He believed northern forgiveness toward the South shamed the memory of the war. "Rebel graves are decked with loyal flowers," Douglass declared, "though no loyal grave is ever adorned by rebel hands. Loyal men are building homes for rebel soldiers; but where is the home for Union veterans, builded by rebel hands? Douglass had never really wanted a Carthaginian peace. But he felt left out of the nation's happy reunion; the deep grievances of his people—both historic and current—were no longer to be heard. At the very last, Douglass demanded that the power to forgive should be reserved for those most wronged.

The debate over the meaning of the war was not merely a question of remembering or forgetting. Douglass worried about historical amnesia because his version of the war, his memory, faltered next to the rival memories that resonated more deeply with the white majority in both North and South. Douglass may never have fully appreciated the complexity of the experience of the Civil War and Reconstruction for whites. The overwhelming number of white northerners who voted against black suffrage shared a bond of white supremacy with southerners who rejected the racial egalitarianism of Radical Reconstruction. The thousands of white Union veterans who remembered the war as a transforming personal experience, but not as the crucible of emancipation for four million slaves, had much in common with white Georgians who had found themselves in the path of Gen William T. Sherman's march to the sea. There were many rival memories of the war and its aftermath, and there was much need for forgetting and healing. As Friedrich Nietzsche suggested, personal happiness often requires a degree of forgetting the past. "Forgetting is essential to action of any kind," wrote Nietzsche, "Thus: it is possible to live almost without memory . . . but it is altogether impossible to live at all without forgetting . . . there is a degree of the historical sense which is harmful and ultimately fatal to the living thing, whether this living thing be a man or a people or a culture." Nietzsche captured elements of both truth and danger in human nature. Douglass focused his efforts on the dangers of collective forgetting, not on its personal or cultural necessity. Douglass knew that his people, confined to minority status and living at the margins of society, could rarely afford the luxury of forgetting. Although he may not have thoroughly discriminated between the rival memories he confronted, he became fully aware of their power and their threat. Thus, with ever fewer sympathetic listeners by the late 1880s, Douglass was left with his lament that "slavery has always had a better memory than freedom, and was always a better hater."

Those were not merely words of nostalgic yearning for a vanished past uttered by a man out of touch with changing times. In a sense, Douglass was living in the past during the last part of his life; for him, the Civil War and Reconstruction were the reference points for the black experience in the nineteenth century. All questions of meaning, of a sense of place, of a sense of future for blacks in America drew upon the era of emancipation. Hence, the fifth source of Douglass's pledge to "never forget": a tremendous emotional and psychological investment in his own conception of the legacy of the conflict. As an intellectual, Douglass had grown up with the abolition movement, the war, and its historical transformations. His career and his very personality had been shaped by those events. So, quite literally, Douglass's effort to preserve the memory of the Civil War was a quest to save the freedom of his people and the meaning of his own life.

Douglass embraced his role in preserving an abolitionist memory of the war with a sense of moral duty. In an 1883 speech in his old hometown of Rochester, New York, he was emphatic on that point.

> You will already have perceived that I am not of that school of thinkers which teaches us to let bygones be bygones; to let the dead past bury its dead. In my view there are no bygones in the world, and the past is not dead and cannot die. The evil as well as the good that men do lives after them. . . . The duty of keeping in memory the great deeds of the past, and of transmitting the same from generation to generation is implied in the mental and moral constitution of man.

But what of a society that did not widely share the same sense of history and preferred a different version of the past? Douglass's answer was to resist the Lost Cause by arguing for an opposite and, he hoped, deeper cultural myth—the abolitionist conception of the Civil War, black emancipation as the source of national regeneration.

In trying to forge an alternative to the Lost Cause, Douglass drew on America's reform tradition and constantly appealed to the Constitution and to the rule of law.

Moreover, reversing a central tenet of the Lost Cause—the memory of defeat—Douglass emphasized the memory of victory, the sacrifices of the Union dead, and the historical progress he believed inherent in emancipation. This is what Douglass meant in an 1878 Memorial Day speech in Madison Square in New York, when he declared that "there was a right side and a wrong side in the late war which no sentiment ought to cause us to forget."

In some of his postwar rhetoric Douglass undoubtedly contributed to what Robert Penn Warren has called the myth of the "Treasury of Virtue." He did sometimes imbue Union victory with an air of righteousness that skewed the facts. His insistence on the "moral" character of the war often neglected the complex, reluctant manner in which emancipation became the goal of the Union war effort. In structuring historical memory, Douglass could be as selective as his Lost Cause adversaries. His persistent defense of the Republican party after Reconstruction caused him to walk a thin line of hypocrisy. Indeed, Douglass's millennialist interpretation of the war forever caused him to see the conflict as a cleansing tragedy, wherein the nation had been redeemed of its evil by lasting grace. Douglass knew that black freedom had emerged *from* history more than from policy deliberately created by human agents. Moreover, he knew that emancipation had resulted largely from slaves' own massive self-liberation. But winning the battle over the legacy of the Civil War, Douglass knew, demanded deep cultural myths that would resonate widely in society. He knew that the struggle over memory was always, in part, a debate over the present. In his view, emancipation and black equality under law were the great results of the war. Hence, while urging old abolitionists not to give up their labors in 1875, Douglass contended that "every effort should now be made to save the result of this stupendous moral and physical contest." Moreover, nine years later Douglass warned that unless an abolitionist conception of the war were steadfastly preserved, America would "thus lose to coming generations a vast motive power and inspiration to high and virtuous endeavor." Douglass labored to shape the memory of the Civil War, then, as a skillful propagandist, as a black leader confident of the virtue of his cause, and as an individual determined to protect his own identity.

In his book *The Unwritten War: American Writers and the Civil War,* Daniel Aaron observes that very few writers in the late nineteenth century "appreciated the Negro's literal or symbolic role in the war." Black invisibility in the massive Civil War fictional literature—the absence of fully realized black characters, even in Mark Twain or William Faulkner—is yet another striking illustration that emancipation and the challenge of racial equality overwhelmed the American imagination in the postwar decades. Slavery, the war's deepest cause, and black freedom, the war's most fundamental result, remain the most conspicuous missing elements in the American literature inspired by the Civil War. Black invisibility in America's cultural memory is precisely what Douglass struggled against during the last two decades of his life. Obviously, Douglass was no novelist himself and was not about to write the great Civil War book. But memories and understandings of great events, especially apocalyptic wars, live in our consciousness like monuments in the mind. The aging Douglass's rhetoric was an eloquent attempt to forge a place on that monument for those he deemed the principal characters in the drama of emancipation: the abolitionist, the black soldier, and the freed people. Perhaps the best reason the Civil War remained, in Aaron's words, "vivid but ungraspable" to literary imagination was that most American writers avoided, or were confounded by, slavery and race, the deepest moral issues in the conflict.

The late nineteenth century was an age when white supremacy flourished amid vast industrial and social change. The nation increasingly embraced sectional reunion, sanctioned Jim Crow, dreamed about technology, and defined itself by the assumptions of commerce. Near the end of his monumental work, *Black Reconstruction* (1935), W. E. B. Du Bois declared himself "aghast" at the way historians had suppressed the significance of slavery and the black quest for freedom in the literature on the Civil War and Reconstruction era. "One is astonished in the study of history," wrote Du Bois, "at the recurrence of the idea that evil must be forgotten, distorted, skimmed over. . . . The difficulty, of course, with this philosophy is that history loses its value as an incentive and example; it paints perfect men and noble nations, but it does not tell the truth." As Du Bois acknowledged, it was just such a use of history as "incentive and example" for which Douglass had labored.

Although his jeremiads against the Lost Cause myth and his efforts to preserve an abolitionist memory of the conflict took on a strained quality, Douglass never lost hope in the regenerative meaning of the Civil War. It was such a great divide, such a compelling reference point, that the nation would, in time, have to face its meaning and consequences. In an 1884 speech, Douglass drew hope from a biblical metaphor of death and rebirth—the story of Jesus' raising Lazarus from the dead. "The assumption that the cause of the Negro is a dead issue," Douglass declared, "is an utter delusion. For the moment he may be buried under the dust and rubbish of endless discussion concerning civil service, tariff and free trade, labor and capital . . . , but our Lazarus is not dead. He only sleeps."

Douglass's use of such a metaphor was perhaps a recognition of temporary defeat in the struggle for the memory of the Civil War. But it also represented his belief that, though the struggle would outlast his own life, it could still be won. Douglass gave one of his last public addresses on the final Memorial Day of his life (May 1894) at Mount Hope Cemetery in Rochester, where he would himself be buried some nine months later. The seventy-six-year-old orator angrily disavowed the sectional reconciliation that had swept the country. He feared that Decoration Day would become an event merely of "anachronisms, empty forms and superstitions." One wonders if the largely white audience in Rochester on that pleasant spring afternoon thought of Douglass himself as somewhat of an anachronism. In a country reeling from an economic depression in 1893, worried by massive immigration, the farmers' revolt, and the disorder of growing cities, Douglass's listeners (even in his old hometown) may not have looked beyond the symbolic trappings of the occasion. One wonders how willing they were to cultivate their thirty-year-old memory of the war and all its sacrifice, to face the deeper meanings Douglass demanded. The aged Douglass could still soar to oratorical heights on such occasions. He asked his audience to reflect with him about their "common memory." "I seem even now to hear and feel the effects of the sights and the sounds of that dreadful period," Douglass said. "I see the flags from the windows and housetops fluttering in the breeze. I see and hear the steady tramp of armed men in blue uniforms. . . . I see the recruiting sergeant with drum and fife . . . calling for men, young men and strong, to go to the front and fill up the gaps made by rebel powder and pestilence. I hear the piercing sound of trumpets." These were more than Whitmanesque pictures of bygone peril and glory. In a nation that now acquiesced in the frequent lynching of his people, that shattered their hopes with disfranchisement and segregation, Douglass appealed to history, to what for him was authentic experience, to the recognition scenes that formed personal and national identity. On an ideological level, where Douglass did his best work, he was still fighting the war. By 1894 he was as harsh as ever in his refusal to concede the Confederate dead any equal place in Memorial Day celebrations. "Death has no power to change moral qualities," he argued. "What was bad before the war, and during the war, has not been made good since the war." A tone of desperation entered Douglass's language toward the end of his speech. Again and again he pleaded with his audience not to believe the arguments of the Lost Cause advocates, however alluring their "disguises" might seem. He insisted that slavery had caused the war, that Americans should never forget that the South fought "to bind with chains millions of the human race."

No amount of nationalism, individualism, or compassion could ever change Douglass's conception of the memory and meaning of the Civil War. His pledge to "never forget" was both a personal and a partisan act. It was an assertion of the power of memory to inform, to inspire, and to compel action. Douglass was one of those nineteenth-century thinkers who by education, by temperament, and especially by experience believed that history was something living and useful. Even in the twilight of his life, there was no greater voice for the old shibboleth that the Civil War had been a struggle for union *and* liberty. "Whatever else I may forget," Douglass told those assembled at Mount Hope Cemetery, "I shall never forget the difference between those who fought for liberty and those who fought for slavery; between those who fought to save the Republic and those who fought to destroy it." The jubilee of black freedom in America had been achieved by heroic action, through forces in history, through a tragic war, and by faith. Among Douglass's final public acts, therefore, was to fight—using the power of language and historical imagination—to preserve that jubilee in memory and in reality. In a Rochester cemetery, he stood with the Union dead, waved the last bloody shirts of a former slave, a black leader, and a Yankee partisan, and anticipated the dulling effects of time and the poet Robert Lowell's vision of "the stone statues of the abstract Union soldier" adorning New England town greens, where "they doze over muskets and muse through their sideburns."

Sites of Memory, Sites of Struggle: The "Materials" of History

FATH DAVIS RUFFINS

Though little noticed by the mainstream press and little discussed within all but a small segment of the museum world, the idea of an African-American museum on the Mall in Washington, D.C., flared and died between 1984 and 1994. Over the course of this decade, there were many debates about the soundness of this concept

"Culture Wars Won and Lost, Part II: The National African-American Museum Project," by Fath Davis Ruffins. From *Radical History Review,* 70 (1998), 78–101. Reprinted with the permission of Cambridge University Press.

within the Smithsonian Institution, within Congress, within professional museum associations such as the American Association of Museums, and within the inbred world of culturally specific Black museums.

Although most Americans are probably unaware of it, museums and archives devoted to what is now called the African-American experience have a long history. The first museum at a historically Black college was founded on paper at Howard University in 1867, and in the flesh at Hampton Institute in 1868. Major collections of archival materials were established before 1900, most famously by Dr. Jesse B. Moorland, a wealthy member of turn-of-the-century Washington's light-skinned elite, at Howard University, and by Arthur Alfonso Schomburg, a Puerto Rican of mixed descent who immigrated to New York City in the 1880s. Both of their collections (with many additions) live in the present as the Moorland-Spingarn Research Center at Howard, and the Schomburg Center for Research in Black Culture, since 1929 part of the vast New York Public Library system. By 1988, the African American Museums Association (AAMA) had documented 108 museums and archives in the U.S. and Canada devoted to the study of African-American life, history, and culture.

Although there have been some significant public and private resources devoted to preserving and interpreting the African experience in America, the larger mythos of Black history is that it has been "lost, stolen, or strayed." This phrase was the title of a widely viewed and well-regarded television special aired in 1968 and narrated by Bill Cosby. Though it seems astonishing today, before about 1970 African Americans were simply missing from most official formulations of American history. The historians who produced the "social history" revolution in scholarship of the 1960s and 1970s wrote to recover the voices of the "voiceless" slaves and put them back into American history in their rightful places. [Their] works . . . changed the landscape of American history and paved the way for more than two generations of inquiry into the lives of many Americans who left neither vast estates nor voluminous letters and diaries, nor were the powerful leaders of their time. In a quite literal way, these scholars recovered some of what had been thought unrecoverable.

How was this possible? When scholars began to ask new questions and search for new sources, they found that actually quite a lot of Black history was there for the analyzing. Church records, court records, published slave narratives, Work Projects Administration oral histories from the 1930s, ethnographic films beginning in the 1890s, photographs, and obscure but published books and articles provided an absolute wealth of material to examine. Although there certainly are important gaps in the nation's collections—such as the relative lack of eighteenth- and nineteenth-century artifacts documenting the lives and world views of rural and enslaved Black folk—there are also many significant resources. Textual, visual, archeological, and, to a lesser extent, artifactual materials have been actively saved for more than a hundred and thirty years, largely by dedicated Afro-American bibliophiles, collectors, and institutions such as the Schomburg Center and Howard, Fisk, and Atlanta Universities. Although much more could have been saved and though many official histories of the U.S. ignore these sources, there actually exist today numerous collections, public and private, which document the diversity of African-American experiences.

It is within this larger climate of the rhetorical loss of Black history, but significant collections holdings, that we must view the initiative for an African-American museum on the Mall. The idea of building a National African-American Museum was not new in 1984. In fact, various proposals to that effect had been circulating around Capitol Hill since the late 1970s at least. In 1981, a National Afro-American Museum was authorized by Congress to be located in Wilberforce, Ohio. Although no federal dollars were ever allocated for the project, the museum was and is largely funded by state resources through the Ohio Historical Society, as part of its general cultural mission within the state thanks to the power of Black state legislators in Ohio. In September 1987 the Wilberforce museum opened to great fanfare. However, that institution clearly did not satisfy the desires of many people to see a national museum in Washington, not in a rural location far from the center of national power and international visibility.

Although numerous people may have discussed the idea of a Black museum on the Mall, Tom Mack was the person who introduced the idea onto the national stage. . . . Mack was and is the president of Tourmobile, Inc., a Washington, D.C., tour bus company with an exclusive contract to ferry tourists along the Mall, past the Smithsonian museums and other monuments. Over the course of doing business, Mack, an African American, became acutely aware of the lack of a Black presence on the Mall. . . . He argued for a clear and positive projection of African Americans in a Black museum on the Mall. Like many Black people, Mack thought that the absence of such a museum represented a tremendous oversight. He felt it was symbolic of the nation's profound and officially sanctioned ignorance of the African-American contribution to U.S. history and culture.

. . . Apparently, Mack first contacted Congressman Mickey Leland (D-Texas) in 1985. Through Leland's work, a *non-binding* House Resolution (H.R. 666) was passed in 1986, which affirmed in principle the idea of an African-American museum on the Mall. . . .

The AAMA is an organization principally comprised of Black museums and, to a lesser degree, Black professionals in the museum world. As a formal organization, AAMA is twenty years old in 1997. . . .

. . . [M]any members of the AAMA were quite opposed to the idea of a Black museum on the Mall. . . .

. . . Many Black museum directors and their staffs feared that an African-American museum on the Mall would suck up all the available public and private funds, leaving nothing for them. Others had similar concerns about collections. Would everyone now wish to donate their collections to the Smithsonian? What would be left for acquisition by smaller institutions without fully up-to-date storage facilities and without the prestige of a Smithsonian connection?

Within the Smithsonian itself, [some] others representing significant centers of Black activity worried that they would be forced to incorporate themselves into the Mall effort, thus risking the hard-won, independent identities of their museums and programs. Still others were concerned that the founding of an African-American museum on the Mall would relieve historically white Smithsonian museums from their responsibilities to include Black people in their narratives. . . .

. . . In 1989, then Smithsonian Secretary Robert McCormick Adams and then Assistant Secretary Thomas Freudenheim hired the well-known New York museum professional Claudine Brown to direct an Institutional Study Project, to investigate the feasibility of a Mall museum. . . .

. . . A key initial question [this committee] had to consider was a sizeable skepticism on the part of a few members of the Smithsonian Board of Regents (and many other Americans) that there were enough artifacts documenting Afro-American experience to justify a museum—on the Mall or anywhere else. The sense that Black history had been lost was enormously powerful. Certainly, many losses in material culture, traditional songs and stories, and documentary evidence have occurred because of the deprivations that slavery and segregation produced. At the same time, an uncounted wealth of historical artifacts, family papers, and the work of self-taught artists remains in private hands, most often those of descendants. In direct contrast to Native peoples, whose artifacts were widely collected from the moment of European contact, most of the objects made and used by Africans in America were routinely discarded or consumed by use. Still, there are two hundred-year-old churches and their records, early manumission papers, nineteenth-century quilts, an abundance of archeological artifacts, and other materials that document the years before about 1890. As for twentieth-century collecting, the process has literally just begun, especially for the years after World War II. Yet there was great doubt in many quarters that the artifactual record was large enough or the artistic production of sufficient quality to justify an entire museum. Eventually, the Institutional Study Project's curator, Deborah Willis, would identify more than 20,000 objects in 150 collections that the Mall museum could acquire. Although her findings silenced critics of the museum, whose doubts were object-based, these findings could not address other, more ideological critics of the museum who had political or pragmatic concerns about issues such as the public financing of the museum.

A second important question had to do with slavery. Would the museum be a memorial to the millions who lived and died in slavery in the way that the Holocaust Museum is a memorial to victims of the Third Reich? Sentiment on behalf of a slavery memorial was particularly reflected in the fact that Tom Mack's original idea was to have a memorial museum on just this subject. Because slavery is "an American holocaust," where more appropriate to have its memorial than among the gleaming white monuments on the Mall?

Though it is little known outside various centers of Afrocentricity, many African Americans interpret their history in the Americas as a holocaust. Focusing extensively on the Atlantic slave trade, this version of American history has replaced nineteenth-century Afro-Americans' biblical millennial claims with twentieth-century claims of intentional genocide and "crimes against humanity." Today, there are multiple interpretations of the "Black Holocaust" far too numerous to detail here. They focus on the horror of capture, the degradation and death of the Middle Passage, and the most brutal aspects of slavery in the United States, and in the American diaspora more generally. For the past decade, Howard University has hosted an annual conference entitled "The Black Holocaust Conference." Indeed, I can recall dozens of conversations with other African-American museum professionals whose "insider" tours of the U.S. Holocaust Museum generated some variant of the following question: "Why can't we have a museum like that, a museum that details what was done to our people and by whom?" This idea did, and still does, have many adherents within African-American museums and cultural institutions.

Further, this interpretation of Africans' history in America as a genocide has become a key aspect of the internal cultural symbolism of most African-American institutions in the 1990s. Just as other communities have their "mythos of origin," most African Americans inhabit a cultural landscape with flags and signposts quite distinct and at odds with many other Americans' views of the national past. A comprehensive cultural history of African Americans since World War II remains to be written. Yet even a cursory look at that subject reveals a set of deep changes that began in the late 1960s and reverberate today. Before 1960, most (though not all) of the positive images of achievement were integration-oriented examples. Afro-American newspapers of the 1950s and 1960s were filled with stories about the "first Negro principal" or the "first fireman" or the "first student" at a locally or nationally known college. But since the 1970s and accelerating in the late 1980s, some African Americans, especially young people, began to turn away from integration as a symbol of success in American society. Increasingly, the symbols of separatism epitomized by Malcolm X for much of his career have become more resonant. Although Malcolm X rejected racial distinctions after a religious trip to Mecca, his longer career flowed back to that of Elijah Muhammad, founder of the separatist Nation of Islam in the 1930s, and eventually back to the crucial work of early Pan-Africanist Marcus Garvey in the 1910s and 1920s. In these versions of African-American history, "doing the self" is the key sign of success. Some examples of this imagery are purely symbolic—such as the flying of a green, black, red, and sometimes gold flag which derives directly from Garveyism. Other examples are the tremendous growth of Black magazines, bookstores, toy companies and other businesses, as well as Afrocentric private schools, publishing companies, and offshoot denominations, such as George Stallings's African-American Catholic Church. Enrollment at historically Black colleges and universities has grown many times over in the 1990s, and the best of them are able to attract some of the best African-American students in the country. It is within this larger African-American cultural framework that the concept of the slave trade and slavery as genocide must be seen. To most African Americans, even those who disagree on political or cultural strategies, this concept is an article of faith, a key element of identity as true as any other clear historical fact.

Yet if we examine the mythos of slavery among other Americans, perceptions immediately shift. From Stone Mountain, Georgia, to Monument Walk in Richmond, from the lovely gardens of Savannah to the white King and Queen of Mardi Gras, the landscape of the South is filled with memorials to the "Lost Cause." From Robert E. Lee and Stonewall Jackson to the Unknown Confederate Soldier, the heroes of, and sacrifices made for, the cause of the Confederacy are still venerated with tremendous zeal in many states. Variations of the Stars and Bars are integral to many southern state flags; and Dixie remains the alternate national anthem in many clubs, schools, and legislatures throughout the South. . . . As is well known to most museum professionals one can tarry a long time in the charming historic houses and beautiful plantation mansions of the antebellum South and hear nary a word about slavery. Though some eighteenth-century sites, such as Mount Vernon and Monticello, have begun to present information about some of the best documented enslaved plantations populations in the early American republic, most of the other historic houses have not done so. In the mid 1980s, Spencer Crew and James Horton surveyed museums across the country and found little change in their presentations of American history. Black participation and contributions were still largely ignored; most museums seemed not to have changed at all.

Affection for the Old South, the Lost Cause, and all of their romantic grandeur and noble tragedy have been a part of American public culture since the late 1870s. From Currier and Ives prints to mass-manufactured greeting cards, from *The Birth of a Nation* to *Gone with the Wind,* from *The Littlest Rebel* to *Jezebel,* the romance of the Old South remains a powerful set of images for many Americans. Of course, Black people are necessary to the scenery of these images. Can a mint julep be as sweet without Old Uncle to serve it? Can the Kentucky Derby be as much fun without a Kentucky colonel and his faithful attendant? Can breakfast pancakes ever be as good without Aunt Jemima's product in our stomachs and our hearts? These images of popular culture are widespread and, unlike direct monuments to the Confederacy, not limited to the South.

From Columbus's era to 1865, slavery was legal in what is now the United States. Although African people were present at the creation of the early colonies and the first states, they could not become citizens until 1868 (with the ratification of the fourteenth amendment to the U.S. Constitution). The end of slavery was seen by many white southerners as a deep attack against the sacred rights of property guaranteed in the Constitution. Southern leaders and intellectuals routinely claimed that emancipation had been the largest confiscation of private property in the history of the world! Unlike the Third Reich, the adherents of slavery never experienced anything like the Nuremberg trials in Germany in the post–World War II years. American slavery was a moot point by the time the United Nations was formed and has never been officially condemned by any international body. Although the Nazis epitomize contemporary visualizations of sadistic criminals and pure evil, the heroes of the American Confederacy remain heroes.

For Americans not from those states where "the Cause" was lost, and especially for that 70 percent of living white Americans who are descendants of turn-of-the-century immigrants from Europe, slavery is not a personal legacy. Indeed, many of these Americans probably view slavery as an unfortunate but distant blot on the land of the free and the home of the brave. Exempt from the pain of the sin of slavery—a pain to which William Faulkner and some other southern novelists gave voice—these northern, midwestern, and western Americans may well view slavery as a historical problem of little direct relevance to them. Indeed, many of the most romantic views of slavery in American popular culture were created by people with no direct ties to the South.

By contrast, the era of legal segregation (1890–1965) is of much greater concern to a wide range of contemporary Americans. Such historical concern seems particularly important to politically emergent groups such as Latinos or Asian Americans whose regional histories also include de jure and de facto segregation. Since the segregated era officially ended only thirty years ago, it is within the living memory of most Americans over forty. In 1944, Swedish sociologist Gunnar Myrdal published his classic two-volume study, *An American Dilemma,* which was commissioned by the Carnegie Foundation of New York. He proposed that segregation and the discriminatory practices that existed throughout American society had produced a functional and essentially emotional problem for many non-Negro Americans. Ambivalent about granting full equality to Afro-Americans, many people also realized that inequality directly violated the essential mythos of America as the land of freedom, where individuals were judged on their own singular terms and merits. Such cultural contradictions were bound, Myrdal felt, to produce a social crisis eventually. Researched and written during America's "Good War," which was fought by segregated armed forces, Myrdal's volumes stand as eloquent testimony to the state of American race relations at the dawning of the modern Civil Rights Movement. The subsequent Supreme Court decisions, demonstrations, boycotts, and marches in the face of massive white Southern resistance, form a central leitmotif in the analysis of the last fifty years of American history. Consequently, the modern era of legal segregation and the movement that dislodged it probably have more emotional salience to many living Americans than the "moonlight and magnolias" of the Confederate South so key to American popular culture in the 1930s and earlier.

This larger, incredibly intricate, and difficult cultural context shaped the work of the Institutional Study Project on the proposed Black museum on the Mall. The advisory committee convened by Claudine Brown was charged with the relatively narrow job of making an internal report to the Smithsonian Board of Regents. Lobbying the board, though difficult, was a lot easier than convincing a majority of white men in the U.S. Congress to agree not only to a piece of legislation but also to the perpetual financial support that is the very foundation of public trusts for national museums. Though the advisory committee struggled with the problem of a new museum on the Mall and made key suggestions regarding the troubling issues of content, its members were unable to resolve questions of control within their own ranks. Preoccupied by a series of internal battles regarding the AAMA National Trust idea, they did not systematically address the perplexing political problems of launching the museum across the bow of some of the most powerful mythos in American life. . . .

There were and still are numerous internal arguments for or against an African-American museum on the Mall. They center on several key issues: Who would control the museum? Who would pay for the museum? Was a free-standing museum necessary? If so, why? These debates permeated the Institutional Study Report. First and perhaps most important, Mack opposed Smithsonian control of the museum. He seemed to feel that the Smithsonian's history of racism and neglect of African Americans made its control inappropriate. Many within the AAMA agreed with him. . . . Mack favored some form of independent control more like that of the National Gallery of Art, or the Kennedy Center. He emphasized the importance of private funding of all or part of the museum. His career as a businessman encouraged him to equate funding with control and management. . . .

. . . However, raising private funds has been quite difficult for Black museums nationwide. Most of the large and successful African-American museums exist today because of city or state allocations, which reflect the political power of Black people in that region. It is no accident that most of these museums are in cities that have had Black mayors for some or all of the past twenty years.

The primary role of public financing in the development of African-American museums is not accidental either. The legacy of twenty generations of slavery and four of segregation has significantly limited the aggregate personal wealth of African Americans. Though currently unfashionable to mention, as it has been for most of American history, slavery and segregation cost Black people the "natural" fruits of their labor that for many white Americans have been the fundamental benefit of the capitalist market economy. This Afro-American history of relative personal poverty is clearly reflected in strategies for funding Black museums—the primary sources are public funds.

. . . [T]he mood of key members of the 101st and 102nd Congresses was one of budget slashing, especially for hard-to-control cultural projects. . . . [The Institutional Study Report] did not take into account conservative efforts at just that time to do away with the NEA and NEH, entities whose primary responsibility was to give away federal money for culture.

Similarly, proponents of a Mall museum of slavery seemed not to recognize that it would be tantamount to a Holocaust Memorial in Auschwitz, not Washington, D.C. Instead of being removed from the "scene of the crime," the proposed museum would be erected within sight of locations where slave pens stood during the 1850s and the early years of the Civil War. Just as the Holocaust Memorial at Auschwitz has been the subject of international controversy and protest, adherents of a slavery museum on the Mall found themselves embroiled in sophisticated controversies in Congress, in part related to a different, non-African-American version of the history of slavery and the American past. . . . [A] museum of slavery located between the sacred white memorials to Founding Fathers George Washington and Thomas Jefferson, whom we all know to have been slaveholders, would privilege a version of American history important to African Americans but unshared by numerous others.

Although the Lost Cause may be a narrow, regional mythos that most Americans outside the South do not really care much about, there are other, more widespread assumptions that are equally problematic. For example, hip Americans of all backgrounds recognize that Black people have contributed something of importance to American life. After all, jazz is America's classical music! African-American musical traditions can be seen as the "Great Mother" of American music. From the spirituals to the blues, from ragtime to free jazz, from gospel to rhythm-and-blues and rock-and-roll, African Americans have been involved in music and other kinds of performance arts from the earliest days of the republic. At the same time, so have a lot of non–Black Americans. Though ragtime may have emerged from Black jook joints at the turn of the century, many of the most popular ragtime composers were white. In any form of jazz, from Dixieland to swing to bebop and so on, there have been extraordinarily talented musicians and composers who were not Black. Though many African Americans regard jazz as a genre wholly invented and most effectively performed by Black people, many others disagree with that perspective, including a number of well-known jazz artists. In fact, some would argue that what makes jazz so great is that, with the right talent and training, anyone anywhere in the world can play it and even contribute to the body of world jazz music. According to this argument, it is precisely the portable quality of jazz that makes it a classical form. The perception of jazz as a classical music is today almost a cliché. Yet Duke Ellington, who died in 1974, did not live to see this sea change in the musical assessment of jazz; it has largely been achieved over the last fifteen years.

The above analysis of ideas about jazz points to a mythopoetic problem in conjoining internal African-American mythos with wider American mythos, even those that give critical meaning to Black contributions. Is jazz truly great because it demonstrates the achievements of African Americans? Or is jazz truly great because it is a world music that can be played by anyone? In real life, both of these concepts can be true simultaneously. But in official cultural institutions, people must make clear and political choices about which narratives to tell. Debates about jazz exemplify larger debates about the telling of African-American history.

Is the story of Black separation, isolation, and achievement against the odds the primary narrative of meaning? In most African-American museums, some version of this narrative is absolutely central; it fulfills African Americans' need for a validating and distinctive history. However, for other Americans troubled by the history of segregation, the great narrative of African-American life has much more to do with integration into and acceptance by the mainstream of American life. The story of the acceptance of talented, well-qualified, deserving Afro-Americans has a lot to do with the modern Civil Rights Movement between 1945 and about 1970. Many civil rights activists were military veterans, college students, housewives, and ministers. They seemed to be precisely the sort of people who should not be discriminated against; no one epitomized them better than the Reverend Doctor Martin Luther King, Jr.

. . . To many non–African Americans, social integration is *the* important African-American story. In this formulation, recognizing Black separateness seems awfully similar to segregation. Celebrating Black inclusion is essential; that is a story of which *all* Americans can be proud.

Consequently, the notion of an African-American museum on the Mall raised serious questions in the "integration vs. separation" debate. This debate was all too straightforward in the 1940s, when Gunnar Myrdal and his integrated staff of Ph.D.s conducted research for the *American Dilemma* volumes. By 1970, desegregation had become the official law of the land, and full integration was the stated ideal of many governmental and corporate institutions. Yet during the late 1980s and 1990s, a number of Americans, some of them African-American, were re-examining the costs and questioning the value of integration as a goal. . . . Two very different mythos about the American past have collided headlong, and debates about the African-American museum occurred within this context.

By 1992, a number of cultural critics of various ethnic backgrounds had begun to doubt that a Black museum on the Mall was a good idea at all. Articles in a number of publications, especially the *Washington Post,* argued that a separate Black museum would be a step backward. Was this museum idea not just a new form of segregation or even "ghettoization"? Was not Black history really just American history with the "real story" put back in? . . .

In different ways, in two different Congresses, debates about the museum's control and financing, and more general arguments about "ghettoization" and overly zealous spending on "revisionist" cultural interpretation, expressed themselves in legislative difficulties. Such problems served to kill the proposed legislation, first in the House during the 102nd Congress, and in the Senate during the 103rd Congress. . . .

Following this defeat, the push for an African-American museum on the Mall lost momentum. . . .

Although certainly a setback, this legislative defeat does not represent the whole story of the African-American presence on the American cultural landscape in this era. In 1983, Ronald Reagan, under threat of congressional override of a veto, reluctantly signed the Martin Luther King, Jr., holiday into law. No other Americans save for former Presidents have ever had their birthdays celebrated as national holidays. The powerful, bipartisan congressional support for the King Day legislation, though not unanimous, was impressive. Although some states, such as Arizona, refused for a long time to go along with this holiday, today King's birthday is observed in virtually all of the states. Schools, religious institutions, clubs, state governments, many large corporations, and the media all participate in constructing and performing this holiday. The only "new" American holiday declared since World War II, this annual evocation of the memory of King's life, and of others who in modern times gave their lives for freedom and justice helps reinterpret and transform some old American mythos. The symbolic importance of the holiday cannot be overestimated.

The King holiday points unmistakably to the profound meaning of the Civil Rights Movement and its "success" for most living Americans of all ethnic backgrounds. In his profound speeches and sermons, King was uniquely able to articulate a truly mythopoetic version of the American past that could unite people of different colors by calling them to America's highest purpose. During his life, King was a far more controversial figure than young people today may realize. Many, many people did not agree with him. Inside Black communities, some felt that pacifism was a ridiculous position to take in the face of white violence. Many traditionalists within the Baptist Convention and many longtime southern leaders felt that King and his bunch were stirring things up much too much. Others began to follow the lead of Malcolm X, national spokesperson for the Nation of Islam, into a Black separatist vision. Still others abandoned America for a new life in the Caribbean or "returned" to Africa, especially to newly independent nations such as Ghana.

Within white communities, even outside the South, there were many people who opposed desegregation, whether actively or passively. For them, King was an irritant and the epitome of a Black man who had stepped out of his place. Indeed, King and his associates were subjected to relentless surveillance and many "dirty tricks" under at least three presidents. When King began to criticize the Vietnam War as early as 1966, he lost significant support from many Americans who had been brought up during the "Good War" and felt that criticism of the government during wartime was treasonous. . . .

In the face of all this, King . . . continued to voice freedom and justice for all as the nation's highest goal. . . . King articulated a dream of a new America that became the most powerful restatement of the American dream in the twentieth century.

His public assassination made King a martyr. But his crusade for a desegregated America resulted in the Civil Rights Act of 1964 and the Voting Rights Act of 1965. Although we may not yet live in "the promised land" that he saw over the mountaintop, King was clearly a Moses of modern times. Given this powerful overlay of the African-American search for justice and the wider "American Creed" Gunnar Myrdal identified, it is not accidental that King's life and the "success" of the Civil Rights Movement have come to be celebrated in a national holiday.

Over the past ten years, several large and publicly funded museums of African-American history have been built in the South. There is no museum devoted to slavery, but in Memphis, Birmingham, Atlanta, and other cities there are civil rights museums. Clearly, it is this modern freedom movement in which most Americans feel that they can share. As with all mythos, some elements are forgotten or downgraded in importance. . . . Although there may be no African-American museum on the Mall in the foreseeable future, the institution of the King holiday and the widespread celebration of the Civil Rights Movement point to a meeting place between African-American and wider American mythos—perhaps the only meeting place possible today.

. . . The United States exists not only in the North American continent but also in the hearts and minds of its citizens (not to mention those of film and television viewers worldwide). In our minds, however, we do not all live in the same America. In fact, some of our Americas directly contradict one another. For ethnic museums, this dilemma is peculiarly complicated, for it is difficult to reconcile internal ethnic visions with the larger narratives of nationhood that almost inevitably elide culpability in favor of celebration.

At the same time, however, there appear to be some versions of an American dream that can be voiced beyond any specific ethnic experience. . . . Without question, Martin Luther King articulated a complicated but nonetheless pluralistic and inclusive statement of the American dream for which he made the greatest sacrifice. We know the name of King, but we do not know the names of all the others who were murdered trying to vote in the South. . . . To remember them, all nations build memorials and sometimes even museums.

Werner Sollers argues in *Beyond Ethnicity* that the new mythos of America is a narrative about immigration. . . . If Sollers is correct, is it not surprising that the symbolic descendants of John Smith, of Pocahontas, and of some of the millions welcomed by Emma Lazarus's poem have had and will have their narratives celebrated on the Mall. And it is also not surprising that the symbolic descendants of those unknown nineteen Africans taken from a Dutch ship in Jamestown harbor in 1619 do not. The presence of certain buildings, the memorials to certain events, and the absence of others speak eloquently, though with great ambiguity, about the vast structure of national recollection that is mythos.

 # FURTHER READING

Elsa Barkley Brown, "'What Has Happened Here': The Politics of Difference in Women's History and Feminist Politics," *Feminist Studies,* 18 (Summer 1992), 295–312.

Douglas Henry Daniels, "African American Intellectual and Vernacular History," *Journal of American Ethnic History,* 16 (1997), 69–76.

John Hope Franklin, "Afro-American History and the Politics of Higher Education," *Bulletin of the American Academy of Arts and Sciences,* 40 (1986), 26–42.

John Hope Franklin, *George Washington Williams: A Biography* (1985).

Jesus Garcia and David E. Tanner, "The Portrayal of Black Americans in U.S. History Textbooks," *Social Studies,* 76 (1985), 200–204.

Jacqueline Goggin, *Carter G. Woodson: A Life in Black History* (1993).

Jacqueline Goggin, "Countering White Racist Scholarship, Carter G. Woodson and the *Journal of Negro History,*" *Journal of Negro History,* 68, no. 4. (1983), 355–375.

Lorenzo J. Greene, *Working with Carter G. Woodson, the Father of Black History: A Diary, 1928–1930,* ed. Arvarh E. Strickland (1989).

Vincent Harding, "Power from Our People: The Sources of the Modern Revival of Black History," *Black Scholar,* 18 (1987), 40–51.

Darlene Clark Hine, "Black Women's History, White Women's History: The Juncture of Race and Class," *Journal of Women's History,* 4 (1992), 125–133.

Darlene Clark Hine, ed., *The State of Afro-American History: Past, Present, and Future* (1986).

Kenneth Robert Jankin, *Rayford W. Logan and the Dilemma of the African-American Intellectual* (1993).

Linda McMurry, *Recorder of the Black Experience: A Biography of Monroe Nathan Work* (1985).

August Meier and Elliott Rudwick, *Black History and the Historical Profession, 1915–1980* (1986).

Clarence E. Walker, *Deromanticizing Black History: Critical Essays and Reappraisals* (1991).

Francille Rusan Wilson, "Racial Consciousness and Black Scholarship: Charles H. Wesley and the Construction of Negro Labor in the United States," *Journal of Negro History,* 81, nos. 1–4 (1996), 72–88.

Francille Rusan Wilson, " 'The past was waiting for me when I came': The Contextualization of Black Women's History," *Feminist Studies,* 22 (1996), 345–361.

CHAPTER

2

Africans and the Slave Trade: Causes and Consequences

If African-American history is the experience of African-descended peoples in the Americas, then that experience could be said to begin with the Atlantic slave trade. Of course, one might also begin with the "African background," the political character and cultural features of the societies from which African slaves were drawn. But whatever possible virtues such an approach might have for tracing some aspects of African-American culture to their ostensible sources, it also risks a static, ahistorical picture of those African societies and cultures. The Atlantic slave trade spanned three and a half centuries; different African societies not only were affected at different times during that span, they also changed over the course of the contact with Europe and America. And since more than half of all Africans landed in the Americas arrived in the eighteenth century, they came not from "traditional" African societies but from worlds already transformed by that trade. Thus the more salient question about the African societies from whence American slaves derived may be, What was their relationship to that trade? Who was enslaved and how they were enslaved may well have shaped decisively the human resources and capacities of those landed in the New World.

Many earlier histories of this era cast these questions of origins in highly moralistic terms. On the one hand, well into the twentieth century some white apologists for slavery argued that since Africans were enslaved in their native lands, the European slavers merely performed a Christian duty in rescuing them from a heathen and bringing them to a more enlightened slavery, one that would school them for a civilized existence. Some African Americans, on the other hand, have worried about how to respond to the charge: "You were sold by your brothers." In the first instance, then, there is concern to absolve or mitigate the guilt of Europeans in a human disaster many have called a Holocaust. In the second instance, the concern is to absolve Africans from complicity in that crime, as well as deny the apparent mitigation of European guilt that such complicity is thought to offer.

Although most modern scholars begin from different premises—that is, from attempts to discern the cultural and social origins of African-descended Americans—even they are haunted by these earlier formulations of the question. What is the psychological and social base line for the African-American experience if the enslaved merely exchanged one master for another? What were the consequences for the melding of a diverse set of ethnic groups into a single African-American people if some ethnic groups were the victims of others? What was the nature of the African societies affected by the trade?

What emerges from contemporary scholarship is a portrait of fairly sophisticated African societies that dealt with Europeans on an equal footing, militarily and politically. The later image of a subjugated Africa under colonial rule does not apply to the earlier era of the slave trade. The question remains, however, as to the extent to which the slave trade was an unequal exchange that ultimately would undermine African self-determination. And if some Africans held their own with Europeans while others slipped onto slave ships bound for American mines and plantations, what were the consequences of the difference? What historical memory did the latter group bring with them to American shores?

 ## DOCUMENTS

The first and second documents, by a Portuguese chronicler, describe the almost random raids along the West African coast and the kidnapping of Africans for the Lisbon slave markets. These early expeditions, transpiring about a half-century before Columbus's first voyage to America, were authorized by Portugal's Prince Henry, known as "the Navigator." The third item is a portrait by Albert Eeckhout, a Dutch artist employed by the West India Trading Company, of one of the diplomats sent in the 1640s by King Dom Garcia II, the Christian ruler of the Congo, as his representative to Portugal's Governor Johan Maurits of Brazil at the port of Recife. Such missions were not unusual in the seventeenth century and indicate the relative equality between some African and European rulers in the early stages of the Atlantic slave trade. The fourth and fifth documents, coming from the early eighteenth century, describe the slave trade during its peak years, after it had become a more systematic procurement of millions of laborers for mines and plantations in the Americas. First, Willem Bosman, a Dutch trader, describes in detail the practices of slave traders and suggests something of the motives for the African participants in the trade. In the next document, William Snelgrave, an English trader, describes slave-trading transactions in the court of the king of Whydah, in which the power relations between European traders and African rulers is clearly one of African parity, if not control. He goes on, however, to describe two instances of resistance by the African captives. In one of the rare first-person accounts by an African victim of enslavement, Olaudah Equiano describes the kidnapping of himself and his sister in the late 1750s. The final document is an illustration of the British slaver, *Brookes,* which demonstrates the infamous practice of "tight-packing," a way to maximize the number of slaves a ship could carry.

1. A Portuguese Trader Describes a Kidnapping, c. 1440s

"O how fair a thing it would be if we who have come to this land for a cargo of such petty merchandise, were to meet with the good luck to bring the first captives before the face of our Prince. And now I will tell you of my thoughts that I may receive your advice thereon. I would fain go myself this next night with nine men of you (those who are most ready for the business), and prove a part of this land along the river, to see if I find any inhabitants; for I think we of right ought to meet with some, since 'tis certain there are people here, who traffic with camels and other animals that bear their freights. Now the traffic of these men must chiefly be to the seaboard; and since they have as yet no knowledge of us their gathering cannot be too large for us to try their strength; and, if God grant us to encounter them, the very least part of our victory will be the capture of one of them, with the which the Infant will feel no small content, getting knowledge by that means of what kind are the other dwellers of this land. And as to our reward, you can estimate what it will be by the great expenses and toil he has undertaken in years past, only for this end." "See what you do," replied the others, "for since you are our captain we needs must obey your orders, not as Antam Gonçalvez but as our lord; for you must understand that we who are here, of the household of the Infant our lord, have both the will and desire to serve him, even to the laying down of our lives in the event of the last danger. But we think your purpose to be good, if only you will introduce no other novelty to increase the peril, which would be little to the service of our lord." And finally they determined to do his bidding, and follow him as far as they could make their way. And as soon as it was night Antam Gonçalvez chose nine men who seemed to him most fitted for the undertaking, and made his voyage with them as he had before determined. And when they were about a league distant from the sea they came on a path which they kept, thinking some man or woman might come by there whom they could capture; but it happened otherwise; so Antam Gonçalvez asked the others to consent to go forward and follow out his purpose; for, as they had already come so far, it would not do to return to the ship in vain like that. And the others being content they departed thence, and, journeying through that inner land for the space of three leagues, they found the footmarks of men and youths, the number of whom, according to their estimate, would be from forty to fifty, and these led to the opposite way from where our men were going. . . . And, returning towards the sea, when they had gone a short part of the way, they saw a naked man following a camel, with two assegais [javelins or spears] in his hand, and as our men pursued him there was not one who felt aught of his great fatigue. But though he was only one, and saw the others that they were many; yet he had a mind to prove those arms of his right worthily and began to defend himself as best he could, shewing a bolder front than his strength warranted. But Affonso Goterres wounded him with a javelin,

---

"How Antam Gonçalvez brought back the first captives . . . ," in *Documents Illustrative of the History of the Slave Trade to America,* ed. Elizabeth Donnan (New York: Octagon Books, 1969), 1:18–20.

and this put the Moor in such fear that he threw down his arms like a beaten thing. And after they had captured him, to their no small delight, and had gone on further, they espied, on the top of a hill, the company whose tracks they were following, and their captive pertained to the number of these. And they failed not to reach them through any lack of will, but the sun was now low, and they wearied, so they determined to return to their ship considering that such enterprise might bring greater injury than profit. And, as they were going on their way, they saw a black Mooress come along (who was slave of those on the hill), and though some of our men were in favor of letting her pass to avoid a fresh skirmish, to which the enemy did not invite them—for, since they were in sight and their number more than doubled ours, they could not be of such faint hearts as to allow a chattel of theirs to be thus carried off—despite this, Antam Gonçalvez bade them go at her; for if (he said) they scorned that encounter, it might make their foes pluck up courage against them. And now you see how the word of a captain prevaileth among men used to obey; for, following his will, they seized the Mooress. And those on the hill had a mind to come to the rescue, but when they perceived our people ready to receive them, they not only retreated to their former position, but departed elsewhere, turning their backs to their enemies. . . .

2. Slave Raiding on the West African Coast, 1448

. . . And when the ship had been provisioned, they made their voyage straight to Cape Verde, whereat in the past year they had captured the two Guineas of whom we have spoken in another place, and thence they passed on to the Cape of Masts. . . .

And so journeying along the sea coast, in a few days they went on shore again, and came upon a village, and its inhabitants issued forth like men who showed they had a will to defend their houses, and among them came one armed with a good buckler and an assegai [javelin or spear] in his hand. And Alvaro Fernandez seeing him, and judging him to be the leader of the band, went stoutly at him, and gave him such a great wound with his lance that he fell down dead, and then he took from him his shield and assegai; and these he brought home to the Infant along with some other things, as will be related further on.

Now the Guineas, perceiving that man to be dead, paused from their fighting, and it appeared to our men to be neither the time nor the place to withdraw them from that fear. But rather they returned to their ship and on the next day landed a little way distant from there, where they espied some of the wives of those Guineas walking. And it seemeth that they were going nigh to a creek collecting shellfish, and they captured one of them, who would be as much as thirty years of age, with a son of hers who would be of about two, and also a young girl of fourteen years, who had well-formed limbs and also a favorable presence for a Guinea; but the strength of the woman was much to be marvelled at, for not one of the three men who came

"Of how Alvaro Fernandez returned again to the land of the Negroes . . . ," in *Documents Illustrative of the History of the Slave Trade to America*, ed. Elizabeth Donnan (New York: Octagon Books, 1969), 1:39–41.

upon her but would have had a great labour in attempting to get her to the boat. And so one of our men, seeing the delay they were making, during which it might be that some of the dwellers of the land would come upon them, conceived it well to take her son from her and to carry him to the boat; and love of the child compelled the mother to follow after it, without great pressure on the part of the two who were bringing her. From this place they went on further for a certain distance until they lighted upon a river, into the which they entered with the boat, and in some houses that they found they captured a woman, and after they had brought her to the caravel, they returned once more to the river, intending to journey higher up in order to try and make some good booty. And as they were pursuing their voyage thus, there came upon them four or five boats of Guineas prepared like men who would defend their land, and our men in the boat were not desirous to try a combat with them, seeing the great advantage their enemies had, and especially because they feared the great peril that lay in the poison with which they shot. And so they began to retreat to their ship as well as they could, but seeing how one of those boats was much in front of the others, they turned round upon it, but it retired towards its companions, and as our men were trying to reach it before it escaped (for it seemeth that it was already distant a good way from the company) their boat came so near that one of those Guineas made a shot at it and happened to hit Alvaro Fernandez with an arrow in the leg. But since he had already been warned of its poison, he drew out that arrow very quickly and had the wound washed with urine and olive oil, and then anointed it very well with theriack, and it pleased God that it availed him, although his health was in very troublous case, for during certain days he was in the very act of passing away from life. The others on the caravel, although they saw their captain thus wounded, desisted not from voyaging forward along that coast until they arrived at a narrow strip of sand stretching in front of a great bay, and here they put out their boat and went inside to see what kind of land they would find; and when they were in sight of the beach they saw coming toward them full 120 Guineas, some with shields and assegais, others with bows. And as soon as they came near the water these began to play and dance like men far removed from any sorrow; but our men in the boat, wishful to escape from the invitation to that festival, returned to their ship. And this took place 110 leagues beyond Cape Verde, and all that coast trendeth commonly to the south. And this carvel went further this year than all the others, wherefore with right good will a guerdon of 200 doubloons was granted unto it, that is to say 100 which the Infant Don Pedro, who was then Regent, ordered to be given, and another 100 which it obtained from the Infant Don Henry. And had it not been for the illness of Alvaro Fernandez, by which he was much disabled, the caravel would have gone further still, but it was obliged to return from that last place I have mentioned, and it came straight to the Isle of Arguim, and thence to the Cape of the Ransom. . . . And although they did not carry an interpreter, yet by making signs they obtained a negress, whom the Moors gave them in exchange for some cloths they brought with them, and had they not brought so little they could have obtained much more, judging by the desire that the Moors showed. And thence they made their voyage towards the Kingdom, where they received the doubloons as I have already said, together with many other guerdons from the Infant their lord, who was very joyful at their coming on account of the advance they had made in their expedition. . . .

3. A Congolese Envoy to Brazil, c. 1643

This man is one of three envoys whom King Dom Garcia II of the Congo sent as his embassy to Governor Johan Maurits in Recife, Brazil, in 1643. This subject is wearing a black velvet coat trimmed in gold and silver, and a plumed, beaver felt hat with a gold and silver band, and he carries a silver-plated saber. These were all gifts from the Brazilian governor to the Congolese king.

Reprinted from Allison Blakely, *Blacks in the Dutch World: The Evolution of Racial Imagery in a Modern Society* (Bloomington: University of Indiana Press, 1993), 122. Copyright Allison Blakely, 1993. Courtesy of The National Museum of Denmark, Department of Ethnography, Copenhagen.

4. Willem Bosman, a Dutch Trader, Describes the
Details of Bargaining for Slaves, 1701

. . . Till within these two last years the chief factors [merchants or agents] of Mouree and Cormantyn had also the advantage of the slave trade of Fida and Ardra, which turned to some account, and was indeed more advantageous to them than the gold trade; the commerce there being at so low an ebb, that without the mentioned slave-traffick they could not live up to the part which the dignity of their posts required, without suffering by it. But since some ill-meaning men have prepossessed the directors of the company in prejudice of them, by urging that by this means they became too rich; for which reason, they have thought fit to entrust the slave trade to the masters of the ships, which they send thither: the consequence of which time will discover; but for my part I don't expect they will find it conduce much to their interest; for the commanders of ships, though very expert in all sea affairs, yet being unacquainted with the negroes, will not be able to succeed very well: besides that some of them are of such a boorish nature, that they hardly know how to preserve the honour of the company amongst the negroes. I would not here be understood to speak of them all, for there are several men of very good parts amongst them: but the difference occasioned by this new practice will clearly appear with respect to the other Europeans trading hither; and I cannot believe it will turn to the advantage of the company. . . .

The remaining trade of these people consists in slaves; which are also bought up by the mentioned negroes: but most of them are transported thence by the English, French and Portuguese ships. Sometimes the slave trade here proves very advantageous, especially about the village Lay.

It sometimes happens that when the in-land countries are at peace, here are no slaves to be got: So that the trade of this place is utterly uncertain; and it only serves to touch at in our passage this way, without depending on any thing from it. . . .

The inhabitants of Popo, as well as those of Coto, depend on plunder and the slave trade; in both of which they very much exceed the latter; for being endowed with a much larger share of courage, they rob more successively [successfully] and consequently by that means encrease their trade: Notwithstanding all which, to fraight a ship with slaves, requires some months attendance. . . .

The first business of one of our factors when he comes to Fida, is to satisfie the customs of the king and the great men, which amounts to about 100 pounds in Guinea value, as the goods must yield there. After which we have free licence to trade, which is published throughout the whole land by the cryer.

But yet before we can deal with any person, we are obliged to buy the King's whole stock of slaves at a set price; which is commonly one third or one fourth higher than ordinary. After which we obtain free leave to deal with all his subjects of what rank soever. But if there happen to be no stock of slaves, the factor must then resolve to run the risque of trusting the inhabitants with goods to the value of

"Description of the Coast of Guinea," in *Documents Illustrative of the History of the Slave Trade to America,* ed. Elizabeth Donnan (New York: Octagon Books), 1969, 1:438–439, 441–443, 352–356.

one or two hundred slaves; which commodities they send into the inland country, in order to buy with them slaves at all markets, and that sometimes two hundred miles deep in the country: For you ought to be informed that markets of men are here kept in the same manner as those of beasts with us.

Not a few in our country fondly imagine that parents here sell their children, men their wives, and one brother the other; but those who think so deceive themselves; for this never happens on any other account but that of necessity, or some great crime. But most of the slaves that are offered to us are prisoners of war, which are sold by the victors as their booty.

When these slaves come to Fida, they are put in prison all together, and when we treat concerning buying them, they are all brought out together in a large plain; where, by our chirurgeons, whose province it is, they are throughly examined, even to the smallest member, and that naked too both men and women, without the least distinction or modesty. Those which are approved as good are set on one side; and the lame and faulty are set by as invalides, which are here called mackrons. These are such as are above five and thirty years old, or are maimed in the arms, legs, hands, or feet, have lost a tooth, are grey-haired, or have films over their eyes; as well as all those which are affected with any veneral distemper, or with several other diseases.

The invalides and the maimed being thrown out, as I have told you, the remainder are numbred, and it is entred who delivered them. In the mean while a burning iron, with the arms or name of the companies, lyes in the fire; with which ours are marked on the breast.

This is done that we may distinguish them from the slaves of the English, French or others; (which are also marked with their mark) and to prevent the negroes exchanging them for worse; at which they have a good hand.

I doubt not but this trade seems very barbarous to you, but since it is followed by meer necessity it must go on; but we yet take all possible care that they are not burned too hard, especially the women, who are more tender than the men.

We are seldom long detained in the buying of these slaves, because their price is established, the women being one fourth or fifth part cheaper than the men. The disputes which we generally have with the owners of these slaves are, that we will not give them such goods as they ask for them, especially the boesies (as I have told you, the money of this country;) of which they are very fond, though we generally make a division on this head in order to make one sort of goods help off another, because those slaves which are paid for in boesies cost the company one half more than those bought with other goods. . . .

When we have agreed with the owners of the slaves, they are returned to their prison; where from that time forwards they are kept at our charge, cost us two pence a day a slave; which serves to subsist them, like our criminals, on bread and water: So that to save charges we send them on board our ships with the very first opportunity; before which their masters strip them of all they have on their backs; so that they come aboard stark-naked as well women as men; in which condition they are obliged to continue, if the master of the Ship is not so charitable (which he commonly is) as to bestow something on them to cover their nakedness.

You would really wonder to see how these slaves live on board; for though their number sometimes amounts to six or seven hundred, yet by the careful management of our masters of ships, they are so regulated that it seems incredible: And in this particular our nation exceeds all other Europeans; for as the French, Portuguese and English slave-ships, are always foul and stinking; on the contrary ours are for the most part clean and neat.

The slaves are fed three times a day with indifferent good victuals, and much better than they eat in their own country. Their lodging-place is divided into two parts; one of which is appointed for the men the other for the women; each sex being kept apart: Here they lye as close together as is possible for them to be crowded.

We are sometimes sufficiently plagued with a parcel of slaves, which come from a far in-land country, who very innocently persuade one another, that we buy them only to fatten and afterwards eat them as a delicacy.

When we are so unhappy as to be pestered with many of this sort, they resolve and agree together (and bring over the rest of their party) to run away from the ship, kill the Europeans, and set the vessel a-shore; by which means they design to free themselves from being our food.

I have twice met with this misfortune; and the first time proved very unlucky to me, I not in the least suspecting it; but the up roar was timely quashed by the master of the ship and my self, by causing the abettor to be shot through the head, after which all was quiet.

But the second time it fell heavier on another ship, and that chiefly by the carelessness of the master, who having fished up the anchor of a departed English ship, had laid it in the hold where the male slaves were lodged; who, unknown to any of the ships crew, possessed themselves of a hammer; with which, in a short time, they broke all their fetters in pieces upon the anchor: after this they came above deck and fell upon our men; some of whom they grievously wounded, and would certainly have mastered the ship, if a French and English ship had not very fortunately happened to lye by us; who perceiving by our firing a distress'd-gun, that something was in disorder on board, immediately came to our assistance with chalops [shallups] and men, and drove the slaves under deck: Not withstanding which before all was appeased about twenty of them were killed.

The Portuguese have been more unlucky in this particular than we; for in four years time they lost four ships in this manner. . . .

5. William Snelgrave, an English Trader, Describes the Business of Slave Trading and Two Slave Mutinies, 1734

For the better understanding of the following Relation it is necessary to prefix some Account of the late State of the Country of Whidaw; before the terrible Destruction and Desolation therein in the Month of March 1726–7.

The Reader then is to observe, That the Sea-Coast this Kingdom lies in 6 Degrees 40 Minutes North Latitude. Sabee, the chief Town of the Country, is situate

"William Snelgrave's Account of Guinea," in *Documents Illustrative of the History of the Slave Trade to America*, ed. Elizabeth Donnan (New York: Octagon Books, 1969), 2:342–344, 352–356.

about seven Miles from the Seaside. In this Town the King allowed the Europeans convenient Houses for their Factories and by him we were protected in our Persons and Goods, and when our Business was finished, were permitted to go away in Safety. The Road where Ships anchored was a free Port for all European Nations trading to those Parts for Negroes. And this Trade was so very considerable, that it is computed while it was in a flourishing State, there were about twenty thousand Negroes yearly exported from thence, and the neighbouring Places by the English, French, Dutch, and Portuguese. As this was the principal Part of all the Guinea Coast for the Slave Trade, the frequent Intercourse that Nation had for many Years carried on with white People had rendered them so civilized, that it was a Pleasure to deal with them. . . .

It so happen'd, that in the Evening of the Day we came into the Camp, there were brought above eighteen hundred captives, from a Country called Tuffoe, at the distance of six days Journey. . . .

The King, at the time we were present, ordered the Captives of Tuffoe to be brought into the Court: Which being accordingly done, he chose himself a great number out of them, to be sacrificed to his Fetiche or Guardian Angel; the others being kept for Slaves for his own use; or to be sold to the Europeans. There were proper Officers, who received the Captives from the Soldiers hands, and paid them the value of twenty Shillings Sterling for every Man, in Cowries, (which is a Shell brought from the East Indies, and carried in large quantities to Whidaw by the Europeans, being the current Money of all the neighbouring Countries far and near) and ten Shillings for a Woman, Boy, or Girl. . . .

About three a Clock that Afternoon, a Messenger came from the great Captain, to inform us, the King had appointed immediately to give us an Audience. . . .

On our coming into the Court, where we had seen the King at our former Audience, we were desired to stay a little, till the Presents were carried into the House, that his Majesty might view them. Soon after we were introduced into a small Court, at the further end of which the King was sitting cross-legg'd on a Carpet of Silk, spread on the Ground: He was himself richly dress'd, and had but few Attendants. When we approached him, his Majesty enquired in a very kind manner, How we did? ordering we should be placed near him; and accordingly fine Mats were spread on the Ground for us to sit on. Tho' sitting in that Posture was not very easy to us, yet we put a good Face on the matter, understanding by the Linguist, that it was their Custom.

As soon as we were placed, the King ordered the Interpreter to ask me, What I had to desire of him? To which I answered, "That as my Business was to trade, so I relied on his Majesty's Goodness, to give me a quick dispatch, and fill my Ship with Negroes; by which means I should return into my own Country in a short time; where I should make known how great and powerful a King I had seen." To this the King replied by the Linguist, "That my desire should be fulfilled: But the first Business to be settled was his Custom." Thereupon I desired his Majesty to let me know what he expected? There was a Person then present (I believe on purpose) whose name was Zunglar, a cunning Fellow, who had formerly been the King's Agent for several Years at Whidaw; where I had seen him in my former Voyages. To him I was referred to talk about the Affair. So Zunglar told me, "his Master being resolved to encourage Trade, tho' he was a Conqueror, yet he would not impose a greater Custom than used to be paid to the King of Whidaw." I answered, "As his Majesty was a far greater Prince, so I hoped he would not take so much." This Zunglar not replying readily to, and the King observing it, (for the Linguist told him every word that pass'd between us) His Majesty himself replied, "That as he was the greater Prince, he might reasonably expect the more Custom; but as I was the first English Captain he had seen, he would treat me as a young Wife or Bride, who must be denied nothing at first." Being surprized at this turn of Expression, I told the Linguist, "I was afraid he imposed on me, and interpreted the King's words in too favourable a manner." His Majesty observing I spoke with some Sharpness, asked what I said? Which the Linguist having told him, his Majesty smiled, and expressed himself again to the same purpose: Adding, "I should find his Actions answerable to his Words." Being greatly encouraged by the King's gracious Expressions towards me, I took the Liberty to represent to his Majesty, "That the best way to make Trade flourish, was to impose easy Customs, and to protect us from the Thievery of the Natives, and the Impositions of great Men; which the King of Whidaw not doing, had greatly hurt the Trade. For the ill usage the Europeans had met with of late from him and his People, had caused them to send fewer Ships than formerly they did. And tho' a large Custom might seem at first for his Majesty's Advantage, yet it would soon be found, that a great number of Ships would thereby be hindred from coming to trade; so that in this respect he would lose far more in General, than he would gain by that Particular."

The King took what I said in good part, telling me, "I should name my own Custom," which I at first declined: But being prest to do it a second time, I told the Linguist to ask his Majesty, "Whether he would be pleased to take one half of what we used to pay at Whidaw?" To this the King readily agreed; adding, "He designed to make Trade flourish; and I might depend upon it, he would prevent all Impositions, and Thievery, and protect the Europeans that came to his Country, saying, that his God had made him the Instrument to punish the King of Whidaw, and his people, for the many Villanies they had been guilty of towards both Whites and Blacks: That the Embassadors now in his Camp from the said King, had informed him of me and my Character, and that by the account they had given him of my former dealings in their Country, he could put much Confidence in me." Then his Majesty having asked me divers Questions concerning our former ill usage in the Country of Whidaw, to which I answered as I thought proper . . .

I come now to give an Account of the Mutinies that have happened on board the Ships where I have been.

These Mutinies are generally occasioned by the Sailors ill usage of these poor People, when on board the Ship wherein they are transported to our Plantations. Wherever therefore I have commanded, it has been my principal Care, to have the Negroes on board my Ship kindly used; and I have always strictly charged my white People to treat them with Humanity and Tenderness; In which I have usually found my Account, both in keeping them from mutinying, and preserving them in health.

And whereas it may seem strange to those that are unacquainted with the method of managing them, how we can carry so many hundreds together in a small Ship, and keep them in order, I shall just mention what is generally practiced.

When we purchase grown People, I acquaint them by the Interpreter, "That, now they are become my Property, I think fit to let them know what they are bought for, that they may be easy in their Minds: (For these poor People are generally under terrible Apprehensions upon their being bought by white Men, many being afraid that we design to eat them; which, I have been told, is a story much credited by the inland Negroes;) So after informing them, That they are bought to till the Ground in our Country, with several other Matters; I then acquaint them, how they are to behave themselves on board towards the white Men; that if anyone abuses them, they are to complain to the Linguist, who is to inform me of it, and I will do them Justice; But if they make a Disturbance, or offer to strike a white Man, they must expect to be severely punished."

When we purchase the Negroes, we couple the sturdy Men together with Irons; but we suffer the Women and Children to go freely about: And soon after we have sail'd from the Coast, we undo all the Mens Irons.

They are fed twice a day, and are allowed in fair Weather to come on Deck at seven a Clock in the Morning, and to remain there, if they think proper, till Sun setting. Every Monday Morning they are served with Pipes and Tobacco, which they are very fond of. The Men Negroes lodge separate from the Women and Children: and the places where they all lye are cleaned every day, some white Men being appointed to see them do it. . . .

The first Mutiny I saw among the Negroes, happened during my first Voyage, in the Year 1704. It was on board the *Eagle* Gallery of London, commanded by my Father, with whom I was as Purser. We had bought our Negroes in the River of Old Callabar in the Bay of Guinea. At the time of their mutinying we were in that River, having four hundred of them on board, and not above ten white Men who were able to do Service: For several of our Ship's Company were dead, and many more sick; besides, two of our Boats were just then gone with twelve People on Shore to fetch Wood, which lay in sight of the Ship. All these Circumstances put the Negroes on consulting how to mutiny, which they did at four a clock in the Afternoon, just as they went to Supper. But as we had always carefully examined the Mens Irons, both Morning and Evening, none had got them off, which in a great measure contributed to our Preservation. Three white Men stood on the Watch with Cutlaces in their Hands. One of them who was on the Forecastle, a stout fellow, seeing some of the Men Negroes take hold of the chief Mate, in order to throw him over board, he laid on them so heartily with the flat side of his Cutlace, that they soon quitted the Mate, who escaped from them, and run on the Quarter Deck to get Arms. I was then sick with an Ague, and lying on a Couch in the great Cabbin, the Fit being just come on. However, I no sooner heard the Outcry, That the Slaves were mutinying, but I took two Pistols, and run on the Deck with them; where meeting with my father and the chief Mate, I delivered a Pistol to each of them. Whereupon they went forward on the Booms calling to the Negroe Men that were on the Forecastle; but they did not regard their Threats, being busy with the Centry, (who had disengaged the chief Mate,) and they would have certainly killed him with his own Cutlace, could they have got it from him; but they could not break the Line wherewith the Handle was fastened to his Wrist. And so, tho' they had seized him, yet they could not make use of his Cutlace.

Being thus disappointed, they endeavoured to throw him overboard, but he held so fast by one of them that they could no do it. My Father seeing this stout Man in so much Danger, ventured amongst the Negroes to save him; and fired his Pistol over their Heads, thinking to frighten them. But a lusty Slave struck him with a Billet so hard, that he was almost stunned. The Slave was going to repeat his Blow, when a young Lad about seventeen years old, whom we had been kind to, interposed his Arm, and received the Blow, by which his Arm-bone was fractured. At the same instant the Mate fired his Pistol, and shot the Negroe that had struck my Father. At the sight of this the Mutiny ceased, and all the Men-negroes on the Forecastle threw themselves flat on their Faces, crying out for Mercy.

Upon examining into the matter, we found, there were not above twenty Men Slaves concerned in this Mutiny; and the two Ringleaders were missing, having, it seems, jumped overboard as soon as they found their Project defeated, and were drowned. This was all the Loss we suffered on this occasion: For the Negroe that was shot by the Mate, the Surgeon, beyond all Expectation, cured. And I had the good Fortune to lose my Ague, by the fright and hurry I was put into. Moreover, the young Man, who had received the Blow on his Arm to save my Father, was cured by the Surgeon in our Passage to Virginia. At our Arrival in that place we gave him his Freedom; and a worthy Gentleman, one Colonel Carter, took him into his Service, till he became well enough acquainted in the Country to provide for himself.

I have been several Voyages, when there has been no Attempt made by our Negroes to mutiny; which, I believe, was owing chiefly, to their being kindly used, and to my Officers Care in keeping a good Watch. But sometimes we meet with stout stubborn People amongst them, who are never to be made easy; and these are generally some of the Cormantines, a Nation of the Gold Coast. I went in the year 1721, in the *Henry* of London, a Voyage to that part of the Coast, and bought a good many of these People. We were obliged to secure them very well in Irons, and watch them narrowly: Yet they nevertheless mutinied, tho' they had little prospect of succeeding. I lay at that time near a place called Mumfort on the Gold-Coast, having near five hundred Negroes on board, three hundred of which were Men. Our Ship's Company consisted of fifty white People, all in health: And I had very good Officers; so that I was very easy in all respects. . . .

After we had secured these People, I called the Linguists, and ordered them to bid the Men-Negroes between Decks be quiet; (for there was a great noise amongst them.) On their being silent, I asked, "What had induced them to mutiny?" They answered, I was a great Rogue to buy them, in order to carry them away from their own Country, and that they were resolved to regain their Liberty if possible." I replied, "That they had forfeited their Freedom before I bought them, either by Crimes or by being taken in War, according to the Custom of their Country; and they being now my Property, I was resolved to let them feel my Resentment, if they abused my Kindness: Asking at the same time, Whether they had been ill used by the white Men, or had wanted for any thing the Ship afforded?" To this they replied, "They had nothing to complain of." Then I observed to them, "That if they should gain their Point and escape to the Shore, it would be no Advantage to them, because their Countrymen would catch them, and sell them to other Ships." This served my purpose, and they seemed to be convinced of their Fault, begging,

"I would forgive them, and promising for the future to be obedient, and never mutiny again, if I would not punish them this time." This I readily granted, and so they went to sleep. When Daylight came we called the Men Negroes up on Deck, and examining their Irons, found them all secure. So this Affair happily ended, which I was very glad of; for these People are the stoutest and most sensible Negroes on the Coast: Neither are they so weak as to imagine as others do, that we buy them to eat them; being satisfied we carry them to work in our Plantations, as they do in their own Country.

However, a few days after this, we discovered they were plotting again, and preparing to mutiny. For some of the Ringleaders proposed to one of our Linguists, If he could procure them an Ax, they would cut the Cables the Ship rid by in the night; and so on her driving (as they imagined) ashore, they should get out of our hands, and then would become his Servants as long as they lived.

For the better understanding of this I must observe here, that these Linguists are Natives and Freemen of the Country, whom we hire on account of their speaking good English, during the time we remain trading on the Coast; and they are likewise Brokers between us and the black Merchants.

This Linguist was so honest as to acquaint me with what had been proposed to him; and advised me to keep a strict Watch over the Slaves: For tho' he had represented to them the same as I had done on their mutinying before, That they would all be catch'd again, and sold to other Ships, in case they could carry their Point, and get on Shore, yet it had no effect upon them.

This gave me a good deal of Uneasiness. For I knew several Voyages had proved unsuccessful by Mutinies; as they occasioned either the total loss of the Ships and the white Mens Lives; or at least by rendring it absolutely necessary to kill or wound a great number of the Slaves, in order to prevent a total Destruction. Moreover, I knew many of these Cormantine Negroes despised Punishment, and even Death it self: It having often happened at Barbadoes and other Islands, that on their being any ways hardly dealt with, to break them of their Stubbornness in refusing to work, twenty or more have hang'd themselves at a time in a Plantation. . . .

6. Olaudah Equiano, an Ibo, Describes His Capture, 1756

. . . I was born, in the year 1745, in a charming fruitful vale, named Essaka. The distance of this province from the capital of Benin and the sea coast must be very considerable; for I had never heard of white men or Europeans, nor of the sea; and our subjection to the king of Benin was little more than nominal; for every transaction of the government, as far as my slender observation extended, was conducted by the chiefs or elders of the place. . . .

We practised circumcision like the Jews, and made offerings and feasts on that occasion in the same manner as they did. Like them also, our children were named from some event, some circumstance, or fancied foreboding at the time of their

The Interesting Narrative of Olaudah Equiano, or Gustavus Vassa, the African (2 vols., London, 1789), 1:32, 41, 46–48.

birth. I was named *Olaudah,* which, in our language, signifies vicissitude, or fortunate also; one favoured, and having a loud voice and well spoken. . . .

. . . My father, besides many slaves, had a numerous family, of which seven lived to grow up, including myself and a sister, who was the only daughter. As I was the youngest of the sons, I became, of course, the greatest favourite with my mother, and was always with her; and she used to take particular pains to form my mind. I was trained up from my earliest years in the arts of agriculture and war: my daily exercise was shooting and throwing javelins; and my mother adorned me with emblems, after the manner of our greatest warriors. In this way I grew up till I was turned the age of eleven, when an end was put to my happiness in the following manner—Generally, when the grown people in the neighbourhood were gone far in the fields to labour, the children assembled together in some of the neighbours' premises to play; and commonly some of us used to get up a tree to look out for any assailant, or kidnapper, that might come upon us; for they sometimes took those opportunities of our parents' absence, to attack and carry off as many as they could seize. One day, as I was watching at the top of a tree in our yard, I saw one of those people come into the yard of our next neighbour but one, to kidnap, there being many stout young people in it. Immediately, on this, I gave the alarm of the rogue, and he was surrounded by the stoutest of them, who entangled him with cords, so that he could not escape till some of the grown people came and secured him. But, alas! ere long it was my fate to be thus attacked, and to be carried off, when none of the grown people were nigh. One day, when all our people were gone out to their works as usual, and only I and my dear sister were left to mind the house, two men and a woman got over our walls, and in a moment seized us both; and, without giving us time to cry out, or make resistance, they stopped our mouths, tied our hands, and ran off with us into the nearest wood: and continued to carry us as far as they could, till night came on, when we reached a small house, where the robbers halted for refreshment, and spent the night. We were then unbound, but were unable to take any food; and, being quite overpowered by fatigue and grief, our only relief was some sleep, which allayed our misfortune for a short time. The next morning we left the house, and continued travelling all the day. For a long time we had kept the woods, but at last we came into a road which I believed I knew. I had now some hopes of being delivered, for we had advanced but a little way before I discovered some people at a distance, on which I began to cry out for their assistance; but my cries had no other effect than to make them tie me faster, and stop my mouth, and then they put me into a large sack. They also stopped my sister's mouth, and tied her hands; and in this manner we proceeded till we were out of the sight of these people.—When we went to rest the following night they offered us some victuals; but we refused them; and the only comfort we had was in being in one another's arms all that night, and bathing each other with our tears. But, alas! we were soon deprived of even the smallest comfort of weeping together. The next day proved a day of greater sorrow than I had yet experienced; for my sister and I were then separated, while we lay clasped in each other's arms. It was in vain that we besought them not to part us: she was torn from me, and immediately carried away, while I was left in a state of distraction not to be described. I cried and grieved continually; and for several days I did not eat any thing but what they forced into my mouth. . . .

7. An Illustration Showing "Tight-Packing" for the Middle Passage, c. 1790s

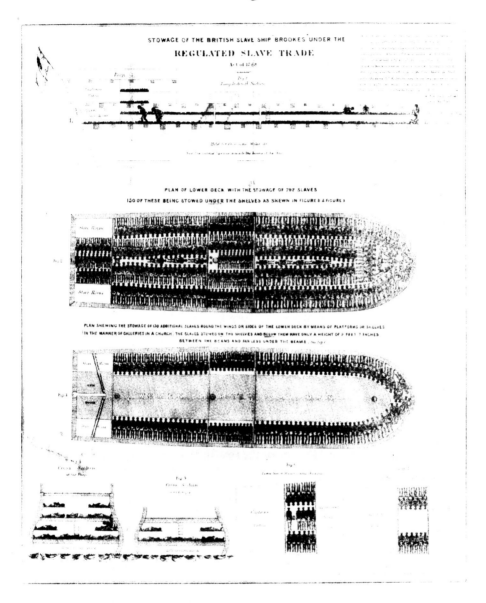

The Plan of the *Brookes.*

"The Plan of the *Brookes,* in *Documents Illustrative of the History of the Slave Trade to America,* ed. Elizabeth Donnan (New York: Octagon Books, 1969), 2:592.

E S S A Y S

Both of the essayists that follow agree that the Atlantic slave trade relied on trading partnerships between Africans and Europeans and was not the product of European control over African societies. In the first essay, however, the late Walter Rodney, an African historian and Guyanese political activist, argues that the Atlantic slave trade produced a "protocolonial" relationship between Europeans and Africans. At first, interethnic wars were a primary but incidental source of slaves for the Atlantic trade, but as demand increased, warfare was pursued for the sole purpose of capturing slaves for sale to the Europeans. The villains of Rodney's story are the increasingly venal African ruling classes that corrupted traditional African legal and social systems to produce more and more slaves for sale. In the second essay, John Thornton, of Millersville University in Pennsylvania, argues that the slave trade was governed largely by factors and needs internal to African social and political systems. The most important factor was that people, not land, were the major source of wealth and security in African societies and, consequently, slavery was an important institution; thus the shift from a domestic slave economy to supplying the trans-Atlantic slave trade was a natural one. Lacking a monopoly of the arms trade and unable consistently to defeat Africans militarily, European traders could not force Africans to undertake the slave trade or even dictate the terms of trade.

African Societies Were Transformed by the Slave Trade

WALTER RODNEY

Together with the Senegambia, the Upper Guinea Coast was being exploited for slaves in the 1460s, even before the southern sections of the West African coast had been charted by the Portuguese. Four hundred years later, the Atlantic slave trade was still being prosecuted in the area. Over this span of centuries, the Upper Guinea Coast was involved in all the phases of the slave trade. It supplied Europe, the mines of Central and South America, and the plantations of the Caribbean and North America. In the late eighteenth century, it was Sierra Leone that was chosen as the site for the first settlement of freed slaves in West Africa; yet in spite of this memorial to freedom, and in spite of the British Navy, the slavers were still present in the neighbouring estuaries and rias until the second half of the nineteenth century. Thus, though the Upper Guinea Coast was not as notorious and unfortunate as Angola and the Bight, it is in many ways a classic region for the study of the Atlantic slave trade.

Fifty years after these shores had been seen by the Portuguese, the latter were shipping abroad, "when the trade of the country was well ordered," more than 3,500 Africans every year. Captives taken were mainly destined for the nearby Cape Verde islands and the Iberian peninsula, with Madeira and the Canary Islands providing secondary markets. Sometimes captives from this section of the coast were procured by passing ships and became galley slaves—as, for example, in 1504, when the East Indies fleet of Alfonso de Albuquerque obtained seventy Negroes at Santiago. This may also have applied to ships bound for the Americas. The Cape Verde islands were situated on the route of the sailing vessels proceeding from Portugal to Brazil, and it is not unlikely that small numbers of Africans from Upper Guinea were carried as slaves to Brazil at an early date.

It was the Spanish market which held out the greatest prospects. . . .

The close connection with the Spanish Indies can be seen from the Spanish records of the registration of slave ships. The principal administrative device which the Spanish developed to organize the importation of slaves into the Americas was the register or licence (*registro*) which, on payment of a fee, was issued to a ship's captain, authorizing him to transport an agreed number of slaves from a given point in West Africa to a specific port in the Americas. . . .

During the height of the register system up to 1595, there seems to have been no standard annual issue, and the number of slaves which each captain was allowed to carry varied considerably. Some licences authorized the transport of more than 600 slaves, others less than 100. Nevertheless it is possible to arrive at some conception of the over-all volume of slave exports in this period. Both de Almada and André Dornelas left the firm impression that the years of trade in their experience from the 1560s and 1570s to the end of the century were years of boom and prosperity for the slave traders. . . .

The size of the vessels used in the Atlantic slave trade was quite small. Even in the eighteenth century they seldom went above 300 tons, while craft of only sixty tons were known to make the Atlantic crossing. However, the size of the ships belied the number of slaves transported. Dornelas remarked that it was not unusual to find 200 "pieces" of humanity packed into a small coastal boat, and the ships which made the Atlantic journey carried at least twice that amount. At the onset of the register system, the ships to the Spanish Indies carried 400 to 500 slaves each, and this was later increased. Under these circumstances, it is not surprising that the average annual export of Guinala alone was close to 3,000 slaves.

On the other side of the Atlantic, the Spanish authorities were having great difficulties in regulating the influx of slaves in such a way as to collect revenue. In 1590, the House of Trade in Seville, having received reports that the customs of Cartagena were being systematically defrauded by the arrival of vessels with large numbers of slaves beyond the amount authorized by the registers, demanded a complete account of slaves entering the port for the preceding five years. The Cartagena officials were bent on denying their own complicity, and tried to convince the House of Trade that ships licensed to carry, say, 139 or 311 slaves arrived in America with exactly that number on board. Not only were these claims false, but whatever numbers arrived in the New World represented a considerable reduction of those who were embarked. In 1569, the mortality of slaves shipped from the Cape Verde islands to Spanish America was estimated to be at least 20 per cent on each ship, and much higher in some individual cases.

It is clear that the register system was not being complied with in terms of the numbers of captives taken on board on the African coast, ships being packed with cargoes of 800, 1,000 or more slaves. The object of the ships' captains was to defeat the revenue provisions on both sides of the Atlantic, robbing the Portuguese coffers in Guinea and the Spanish coffers in the Americas, because they paid duty only on the number inscribed on their registers. Furthermore, ever since the 1560s there were ships which obtained slaves even without registers.

. . . It is probable that as many as 5,000 slaves per annum were exported from the Upper Guinea Coast between 1562 and 1640; that is to say during the period of *registros,* corresponding to a substantial Spanish interest in African slaves, but preceding both the extension of plantation slavery in the Americas and the full development of the *asiento* agreements. . . .

According to another Spaniard, the Jesuit Alonso de Sandoval, who was in close contact with slavers and slave-owners in Cartagena in the early seventeenth century, the slaves of Upper Guinea were the most popular in the Spanish Indies, and were known as *escravos de ley.* This expression probably stemmed from the fact that the slaves were brought under special contract, but it came to mean they were slaves of the highest quality. They were said to have been diligent, keen, intelligent, and good-natured, and they never lost an opportunity to play their instruments, sing, and dance. They were also quick to learn the Spanish language, adopt the Spanish dress, and follow the *fiesta a la Española.* To this already imposing list of "virtues," the Conselho Ultramarino added that the slaves of Cacheu were know for their fidelity. These dubious compliments belong mainly to the realm of myth, though it is possible that, in adapting themselves to the New World situation, Upper Guinea Africans placed a noticeably greater emphasis on forms of amusement than did others of their countrymen. In any case, the resort to song and dance constitutes one of the most important survival techniques of Africans enslaved in the Americas.

Some scholars have felt that the specific provenance of the slaves has some significance for New World studies. However, quite apart from the likelihood that many of the alleged tribal characteristics were misleading stereotypes, what is relevant from an African viewpoint is whether the reputation of a given tribe or locality was sufficiently decisive to affect the conduct of the trade with respect to that tribe or locality. De Sandoval held that the preference for the Negroes of Upper Guinea meant that the Spanish American buyers paid more for them. Later writers, like Barbot and Ogilby, made similar claims; while a local report was provided by the English chief factor in the Gambia in 1678 that he was unable to buy slaves at Cacheu, because of the excessive price offered by his Spanish competitors.

One must therefore consider the possibility that the Spanish preference for *escravos de ley* was affecting the volume of slaves exported from the Upper Guinea Coast. This was implied by the Conselho Ultramarino when it stressed the importance of preserving Cacheu, because of the quality of the slaves, and because "it was from there that the greater part of the slaves needed in the Spanish Indies and the mines of Potosi were obtained. Furthermore, its loss would ruin the sugar estates of Bahia and Rio de Janeiro." The mention of Bahia and Rio de Janeiro is misleading, since Angola and Congo were supplying those markets. It could be that the element of preference affected the destination and consequently the numbers of Africans taken from their homes. Certainly, since the total of victims was not as tremendous in the sixteenth and early seventeenth centuries, then the few thousands per annum transported from Upper Guinea were relatively more significant in the Spanish Indies.

. . . Of the 6,884 slaves said to have been imported between 1585 and 1590, all but 507 originated from Cape Verde-Guinea. At the same time, the Upper Guinea Coast was also exporting slaves to Nueva España (Mexico), Tierra Firme (Panama), La Guira (Venezuela), and Rio de la Plata (Argentina).

To obtain even a few thousand captives per year from this small stretch of coast was a major undertaking, providing a clear example of the organization which went into slaving activities on African soil and the disorganization which resulted within African society. How were such numbers of Africans made available for shipment? A modern history of the Atlantic slave trade states:

> African natives became merchantable slaves in any one of five ways. They were criminals sold by the native chiefs as punishment; or they were individuals sold by themselves or their families in time of famine; or they were persons kidnapped either by European slavers or, more often, by native gangs; or they had been slaves in Africa and sold by their masters; or else they were prisoners of war.

This list can serve as a basis for the discussion of the conduct of the slave trade on the Upper Guinea Coast, with the exception of the category who were supposedly slaves in Africa, since that will require fuller attention at a later stage.

Up till the end of the era of slave trading, a ship's captain would occasionally risk kidnapping Africans from the shore (as Hawkins and the Portuguese before him had done), but such forays did not really pay, since they entailed casualties to the ship's crew. Besides, no regular or seasoned trader would resort to man-stealing, because it damaged future prospects. At the time of de Almada's writing, the Nalus on the Cogon had for several years been hostile to all Europeans, because a ship, which was loading ivory at the Cogon, sailed away with a dozen Nalus. The ship was manned by "individuals who had no experience of trade in those parts."

Given that for the most part the Europeans paid for their African cargoes, then the main issue relates to the methods by which Africans were made available for purchase. In times of famine, it is said that they volunteered themselves. Occasionally, such instances are documented, usually with reference to the Senegambia, where famine was produced by locust plagues. However, to cite famine as a major contributor to the slave trade is a gross distortion, and to add that "most of the tribes had no means of storing food for long periods" is to obscure the issue. Food shortages did occur among certain tribes on the Upper Guinea Coast, and those who were not rich enough to have food stocks all the year round had other means of meeting their wants until the main grain crop had been reaped. Famine could be said to have struck only when the staple crop failed and other supplementaries were simultaneously affected. Only a serious locust plague did this, and, for most of the West African coast, they were rarities.

The first record of a locust attack on the Upper Guinea Coast is provided by a captain-major of Cacheu, who reported that locusts caused a famine in the area in 1639–41. In 1750, fears were expressed that since locusts were swarming the hinterland they would descend to the coast. Shortly afterwards, the locusts were at the estuary of the Gambia, spreading desolation, and they may conceivably have visited the coast farther south. Of course these may not have been the only instances, but from 1750 onwards the chronicling of events was more continuous and more complete, and yet one does not hear of another locust swarm until 1841–3, and then again in 1893. Furthermore, even in these rare instances, there was no allegation that Africans proceeded to sell themselves or their children, so that the original proposition that such were the consequences of famine is itself extremely dubious.

Africans, in the main, were not captured by Europeans nor did individuals rush to sell themselves—they were forcibly brought to the European buyers by other Africans. "Wars" are admittedly the most prolific agency for the recruiting of captives. When the Manes led the invasion into Sierra Leone in 1545, they sparked off a period of unprecedented slaving. The Portuguese seized the opportunity to profit from the rout of the Sapes. The ocean-going slavers remained in the coastal bays and estuaries, while the boats of the *lançados* [local slave dealers] hovered like vultures in every river, waiting to take hold of the victims of the struggles. So numerous were the unfortunates, that the boats sometimes rejected further offers of slaves after they had gorged themselves until full.

After recruiting some Sape youths as soldiers, the Manes sold as many as possible to make the restless population manageable. Whenever a ship needed slaves, the Sapes were the ones to be sold. Farma, the first Mane overlord, died in 1606, and during his long regime it was not unusual to have twenty or thirty vessels loading slaves at any given time in the ports of Sierra Leone. . . .

The Mane example illustrates one extreme of the relationship between tribal wars and the slave trade. The origins of the Mane wars were entirely independent of the presence of the Europeans but, as a by-product, they filled the holds of the slave ships. Yet it is significant that the Mane invasions coincided with the activities of European slavers. Inevitably the Manes came to look upon the supply of slaves to the Europeans as an end in itself. English slave traders in the 1580s reported that Farma would obtain 300 or 400 slaves on request, by embarking on a campaign. This was one indication of what was largely true of Upper Guinea in the era of slave trading; namely that most of the inter-group hostilities were motivated by and orientated towards the Atlantic slave trade. The mêlée of peoples on the river Cacheu—Banhuns, Casangas, Djolas, Papels, and Balantas—was regarded by the slave traders as a paradise. Indeed, the whole of the Upper Guinea offered ample opportunities for conflicts between ethnic groups, localized wars being fought specifically to procure slaves for export.

One small but dependable source of slaves in Upper Guinea lay in the antagonism between the Bijagos islanders and the residents of the adjacent mainland. Bijagos society was geared towards the conduct of war. While the women cultivated the land, built the houses, gathered sea-food, and fished, the men dedicated themselves to building *almadias* and waging war. They attacked indiscriminately all the peoples of the nearby mainland; and the inhabitants of one island preyed upon those of another, once they were at sea—for the sea, they said, had no king. The Bijagos were excellent sailors and swimmers, and disciplined soldiers. Their weapons were handled with a dexterity born of assiduous practice, and tremendous prestige resulted from success in the use of arms. Women took the initiative in choosing their husbands, and they sought warriors with fine reputations. A successful combatant acquired many wives and *almadias,* and this in turn led to more wealth, especially since the owner of the *almadia* was entitled to one-third of the spoils from any expedition.

Bijagos assaults on the mainland had all the elements of cinematographic spectacle. The warriors anointed their bodies with red ochre, coal, and white clay, stuck feathers in their hair, and hung horses' tails on their breasts, attaching little bells to them. An elaborate ceremony was presided over by a priestess, whose final duty was the breaking of an addled egg on the stern of each *almadia*. Then, with a dip of paddles, they went scudding off at a rate that the Europeans found amazing. Their journey was timed so that they landed during the hours of darkness. Surrounding a given village, they quickly set fire to the thatched huts. If the occupants came out fighting, they were cut to pieces by the expert Bijago warriors; and, more often than not, they were prepared to surrender.

The sordid reality behind these bizarre episodes was that the Bijago activities had been considerably stimulated and enlarged on account of European slave traders. It is true that some Portuguese opposed the Bijago tactics. Sebastiao Casao, a prominent merchant in the Geba–Ria Grande area, was in the forefront of a move to enlist the aid of the Portuguese government to put down the Bijagos, because they were harassing the Beafadas, among whom he traded. However, the more important consideration for the Portuguese was that they could buy slaves from the Bijagos, and the more frequent and ferocious were the attacks, the better were the slave merchants pleased. Up to 1594, de Almada seems to have been quite happy with the fact that the Bijago attacks yielded large numbers of Beafadas and Papels as slaves. In an account of 1669, another Cape Verde trader with long experience on the coast waxed ecstatic over the capacity of the small Bijagos islands to provide slaves. In twenty-five trips over a period of years in his own small boat, Coelho had personally acquired well over 1,000 slaves, apart from large quantities of other merchandise.

Bijago response to the European demand for slaves can be measured by the development of unity among the different islanders, with respect to the pursuit of slaves. By the early seventeenth century each island decided to put aside insular jealousies in favour of joint campaigns against the mainland, amassing fleets of *almadias* for this purpose. As the century progressed, Portuguese talk of defending the coast from the Bijagos was no longer heard. They (and other Europeans) concentrated wholeheartedly on exploiting the potential of the Bijago market. When slavers found few or no slaves, they would reproach the islanders, insisting that this was a stain on the latter's good name. Other Europeans, they said, would ignore the Bijagos on hearing that these famous warriors had become decadent. Such appeals, accompanied by the liberal distribution of alcohol, usually achieved the purpose of inciting the Bijagos to go out and bring in more victims for the slave merchants.

The Beafadas were particularly exposed to the Bijago attacks, but they in turn were active slave raiders, who spread terror in the hinterland. The same was true of the Papels, especially those on Bissau who had the direct assistance of the European traders. Like the ships' captains, the resident traders did not usually undertake raiding on their own initiative. However, there were exceptions, the most important being the *lançados* and *grumetes* on the island of Bissau. In 1686, three Spanish Capuchins carrying out missionary work in Upper Guinea prepared a description of the conduct of the slave trade. They reported aggrievedly that the Bissau *lançados* and their descendants not only engineered hostilities, but had also demanded of the missionaries that they should bless the slaving expeditions—threatening to hang them if they did not comply.

No tribe was free from involvement in these hostilities. Some did not take an aggressive stand, but were liable to attack from other tribes: the Nalus from the Beafadas, Papels, and Bijagos; the Balantas from the Papels and Bijagos; and the Djolas from the Mandingas. This last instance—that of the Djola-Mandinga confrontation—had the same piratical overtones as the Bijago attacks. Sailing south of the estuary of the Gambia, the Mandingas fell upon the Djolas as they gathered seafood in large parties upon the coast. At first, the Djolas were taken unawares, but obviously they soon began to prepare for these attacks, and many Mandingas were in turn made captive.

None of these "wars" was fought to gain territory or political dominance. Few of them arose out of tribal animosities. This was the view consistently maintained by observers like de Mercado in 1569, the Bishop of Cape Verde at the end of the sixteenth century, and the Jesuits in the early seventeenth century. Even though their eyewitness accounts of slaving in the era of the "registers" were usually as brief as they were condemnatory, the picture can legitimately be filled in with evidence taken from later in the seventeenth century. For instance, the three Capuchins mentioned above had nearly forty years of intermittent Capuchin activity in Upper Guinea behind them, and they fully corroborated comments made in the previous century and earlier in the seventeenth, and added further details.

One of the things about which the Capuchins were quite definite was that all the conflicts which they heard termed "wars" were nothing more than robberies and manhunts; and the coastal *lingua franca* was rich in terms denoting the violent seizure of persons for sale into slavery.

With the incentive of European goods, slave raiding became a profession, with persons dedicating themselves entirely to the service of the slave trade. The heir to the throne of Bissau in 1606 was one such individual. In 1663 the Franciscan, André de Faro, encountered (and baptized) a noble on the river Nunez, who had a retinue of over sixty servants, all employed in manhunting. His name was Salim, but the Portuguese nicknamed him "The Highwayman." Such professional slave hunters were called *gampisas* by the Beafadas. It was their custom to acquire with the purchase price of their captives some wine or food, which was offered to the captives. This, apparently, was a sop to the consciences of the *gampisas*. The Portuguese found it cheaper to baptize the slaves.

By the end of the sixteenth century, the individuals who could be deprived of their freedom by process of law were those condemned to death, those who administered poison to or placed a fatal fetish on others, adulterers with a king's wife, and those who solicited war against the king or asked the *xinas* to bring about his death. To these it must be added that debts often led to slavery, and the same can be said for the variety of offences which came under the term *chai*: namely the failure to comply with prohibitions or taboos. The slaves obtained in these several ways could be considered in one sense as criminals, since they were duly convicted by the law of the land. At the same time, it is clear that customary law in Upper Guinea was functioning in a radically different way during the slave trade era than it did before and afterwards.

Many of the charges which resulted in enslavement were complete fabrications. Adultery, as many observers realized, was one of the charges which offered great scope for fraud. Marital infidelity was a common affair in the polygamous societies of the area, especially since many of the wives of kings, chiefs, and nobles were simply domestic servants. If in the normal course of things enough accusations were not made, traps were set by husbands with the complicity of their wives, so that "woman palavers" could be raised.

Above all, the allegations relating to the deaths of individuals were the ones which gave opportunities for chicanery. Crimes were essentially of two sorts: those which were discoverable by physical proof (such as murder, theft, or adultery), and those which were discoverable only because sickness or death had come about. Many deaths were attributable to evil influences, emanating from a *feticeiro.* He was sought out and charged with the offence of "eating the spirit" of the deceased. Sometimes the evil was conceived of as residing in the deceased himself. The Africans were prone to come to this latter conclusion when death resulted from accident.

Clearly, offences in the latter category had to be detected in a manner that was quite different from ordinary crimes. It was the interrogation of the dead person by the priest which yielded information as to whether a given person had died because of a fatal "fetish" being placed upon him; and it was the priest who ferreted out the guilty party, though ostensibly it was the dead man who acted as accuser. The possibilities for fraud in these cases were infinite. It was not that every death was attributed to witchcraft—at least, things had not deteriorated to that extent before the end of the sixteenth century—but when the interrogation led to someone being branded a *feticeiro,* this had all the appearances of a deliberate plot, with the slave trade as the incentive. Travelling in 1822 in a section of Temne country where the slave trade had been stamped out, Major Laing was witness to the interrogation of a dead girl. On that occasion, the answer was that nobody was responsible for her death, but, as Laing remarked, "had the slave trade existed, some unfortunate individual might have been accused and sold into captivity."

When anyone was successfully arraigned on a charge, his family and dependants often followed him into slavery—as though he had committed Adam's original sin, reported the Capuchins. This was always so in witchcraft cases, and sometimes an extended family could be wiped out in one sale. In part, this was a safeguard for the enslavers, since they were freed from the vengeance of the victim's family. In some cases, however, it was the family alone who were sold, because the supposed *feticeiro* was already dead. If, as outlined above, accidental death was held to be proof of evil dealings, then the person's family was also liable to penalties. *Lançados* were at the court of Masatamba, the Casanga king, in 1570, when a man fell from a palm tree and died. Immediately the officials of the king went to the house of the dead man, seized his wives, children, and relatives, and sold them all. This was not an isolated instance. By the end of the sixteenth century, a fatal fall from a palm tree seems to have become a "crime," the punishment for which was that the deceased's family was automatically sold.

From the example given above, it can be discerned that not only was there scope for fraud on the basis of the pre-existing law, but that the customary laws were themselves changing, especially with respect to the penalties imposed. This is the aspect of the situation which stands in need of greatest emphasis. Sale into slavery was becoming the punishment meted out for an ever-increasing number of crimes, descending to the most trivial, so that even when a charge was not spurious, there was a ludicrous disparity between crime and punishment.

Perhaps the assumptions of savagery which were long current in relation to the "Dark Continent" may lead to the belief that, slavery or no slavery, the system of law on the Upper Guinea Coast may have been unenlightened. This is far from the truth. In the opening years of the sixteenth century, murder alone was punishable by death among the Bulloms, while the Temnes had no capital offences. Indeed, on the whole West African coast, capital punishment was a rarity, in distinct contrast to Europe. The principal penalties were in the form of fines. Adultery, for instance, was easily resolved by the offending male paying agreed damages. Deprivation of liberty seems to have been entirely unknown, but with the advent of the Atlantic slave trade Africans were led to become parties in plots which resulted in the life-long deprivation of the liberty of their fellows.

When the *lançados* violated local taboos, they were subject to fines, and they claimed that every pretext was used to mulct them. Some of the Africans themselves were open to the same kind of exploitation, with the vital difference that they suffered slavery as a consequence. Another example of the severity and ruthlessness introduced by the slave trade is seen in the treatment of debtors. To borrow and fail to repay the most trifling item in the seventeenth century was sufficient warrant for arrest, conviction, and execution by sale. That people should have been sold for debts may seem plausible in the light of the imprisonment of debtors in Europe, but it must be reiterated that it was by indigenous standards that the punishment of offences by slavery was lopsided and vicious.

The Djolas and the Balantas were hostile to the slave trade, and did not indulge in the various dodges and stratagems just outlined. On the other hand, the Casangas and the Beafadas were prolific producers of criminals for the benefit of the Portuguese *lançados* and the slave ships. Perhaps this may lie at the basis of the charge which the neighbours of the Beafadas levelled at them—that it was the Beafadas who introduced slavery into the world. On the Upper Guinea Coast taken as a whole, during the period of intensive trade with the Spanish Indies, the victims produced as alleged criminals were substantial in number. No lengthy list of slaving methods is required. The two forms of conducting the slave trade were force of arms (wielded by Africans) and the chicanery of a warped system of customary law.

From the methods of slave trade there arose certain consequences. Since some tribes were more predatory than others, it is possible very broadly to assess the results of slaving on individual tribes. The small Bijagos Islands appear to have been relatively immune to enslavement. To begin with, the mainland peoples could not counter-attack the Bijagos in their island homes; and, in the second place, the Bijagos were not favoured as slaves by the Europeans. It was claimed that Bijago children made good slaves, but adults (especially males) were not good bargains as they were able to wish death upon themselves, and frequently did so. Lemos Coelho pinpointed the Bijagos of the island of Fermosa as being prone to committing suicide, because of the belief that their spirits would return home. It is indeed true that the inhabitants of Fermosa believe that the spirits of the initiated find rest in an adjacent islet. In any event, the Portuguese steered clear of the Bijagos as far as securing slaves for service on the coast was concerned, and the Bijago reputation in the Americas was equally discouraging. Labat, a well-informed commentator on the American scene, said that the Bijagos were noted for rebellion on the slave ships and were sold with great difficulty in the Caribbean, because of their ferocity and tendency to escape. They would not work except under the whip, they wounded themselves, and they frequently committed suicide. . . .

A few other tribes may also have escaped with relatively slight losses in the period under discussion. De Almada thought that the Djolas were increasing in

number because they did not indulge in slave trading. This is not difficult to believe, because from all accounts the Djolas did a good job of defending themselves.
The same can be said of the Balantas, so that comparatively few of these tribes
must have appeared on the market.

The Upper Guinea Coast was unfortunate in that it comprised so many petty
politics, offering scope for inter-group conflicts; and it was doubly unfortunate in
having the powerful Mande peoples as its neighbours. When the Portuguese
reached the Gambia in 1455, their reputation as dealers in human kind had already
preceded them from the Senegal, and the Mandingas would have nothing to do
with them. However, the very next year, the Mandingas accorded a friendly welcome to the Portuguese, and for the remainder of the long period of pre-colonial
trade they were the chief collaborators with the Europeans in Upper Guinea. In the
light of the Mande inclination towards trade (particularly the Muslim element), it
was not surprising that the Europeans and the Mande should have forged strong
trading relations. If human beings were the most saleable objects, then the Mande
were willing to provide them; and they could exploit the vestiges of military and
political control which they still maintained over several littoral groups in the sixteenth and seventeenth centuries. . . .

Tribes who had come closely under Mandinga influence also took the initiative in raiding their neighbours for slaves. The Casangas were outstanding in this
respect—their ready supply of slaves and exceptionally favourable treatment of the
lançados made Casanga territory a haven for the Portuguese. That the Casanga
king should have been in the habit of bestowing on his Cape Verde friends gifts of
ten or a dozen slaves attests to the amicable relations with the Portuguese, as well
as his ability to produce this particular merchandise. . . .

Unlike the Mandingas, the Susus and the Fulas did not wield political or military dominance over the coastal people in the sixteenth century, but one effect of the
Mane invasion was to set the Bulloms, Temnes, and Lokos at odds with the Susus
and Fulas. Once conflicts flared, the captives invariably found their way into the
holds of the slave ships. The Susus themselves began to move closer to the sea after
routing the Manes. By the mid eighteenth century they had found an outlet on the
Atlantic between the Pongo and the Scarcies, largely at the expense of the Bagas.
By this time, the Susus and the Fulas had joined the Mandingas as the most active
agents of the trade in Upper Guinea; but long before that, the Susus and Fulas had
taken to raiding. During the second half of the seventeenth century the majority of
the slaves shipped from Sierra Leone were provided by these two tribes.

The greatest victims of the slave trade may not have been people of the littoral
fringe, but rather the Paleo-Negritics, who occupied the interior plateau and parts of
the Futa Djalon. The Tenda country, as described by Mungo Park, was a vast tract
of land along the Gambia between 10 degrees and 14 degrees longitude West. All
this was under the rule of Mandinga chiefs and Farims from the earliest European
reports, but discerning observers noticed that the supposed Mandinga population
was not homogeneous. Jobson, for example, found that above Barracunda on the
Gambia the men wore hides instead of cloth, the women were heavily tattooed, and
a different language was spoken—though Mandinga was understood by the "better
sort." Lemos Coelho was also able to point out that the population of the Gambia
and Cabo was Mandinga only in the sense that this tribe had come to dominate the

inhabitants in every cultural sphere. The Mandingas had become "naturalized," and the indigenous people had taken the name of the Mandingas. Thus many of the slaves who may have been described as Mandingas must have been Tendas or Paleo-Negritics in the process of assimilation. Apart from these, Coelho also specified that the Bassarels, a distinct Tenda group, were the principal captives sold by the Mandingas; and some years later de la Courbe found that the slaves on the Gambia had become merchantable because of war, crimes, sorcery, or the fact of belonging to a "subject race." The latter could hardly have been other than the Paleo-Negritics.

For the period 1562–1640, the great slave-raiding tribes on the Upper Guinea Coast were the Manes, the Mandingas, the Casangas, the Cocolis, and (to a lesser extent) the Susus and Fulas. It is therefore accurate to represent the littoral non-Mande peoples as being to a considerable degree encircled and exploited by their Mande neighbours of the interior. One principal result of slave raiding was to emphasize and prolong the harassment of those ethnic groups who had sought the coast as a refuge, following political turmoil in the Western Sudan. When the *lançados* met the Mande on the mangrove line of farthest river travel they forged a trading partnership which boded ill for the peoples of the coast.

With respect to intra-tribal slaving operations, it is equally imperative to seek out the aggressors and the aggrieved parties. The slave trade exacerbated personal rivalries of all sorts, and no section of the society was exempted from these. There must have been conflicts among nobles, and among individuals in the lesser ranks of society, bearing in mind the fact that every act of violence and every piece of chicanery perpetrated in the interests of the slave trade often brought on its own train of vengeance and retribution. But superimposed upon these personal struggles, and indeed upon the inter-tribal conflicts also, there was a definite pattern of class exploitation, with the ruling class as the offending party.

The "ruling class" must be taken to mean the kings, chiefs and nobles. At times it appears possible to draw a dividing line between the king and his nobles. The slave ship offered a most convenient vehicle for the disposal of rivals to the king's authority, and the noble was obviously a profitable target for plots leading to the sale of his numerous family and dependents. De Almada stated that the persons who died after submitting to the "red-water" ordeal in Casanga territory were the rich ones whom the king wished to kill. But the king of Casanga was unusually autocratic. The typical king or chief of the Upper Guinea Coast was simply *primus inter pares* [first among equals] as far as the other nobles were concerned. The possibility did not exist for the kings or chiefs to victimize their principal subjects at will. Only with the substantial support of the nobles themselves can one envisage the king taking measures against one of their number. In the latter sixteenth and the early seventeenth century, the ruling class in Sierra Leone was not ethnically homogeneous, and the Mane element was bent on the extermination of the Sape nobility. Elsewhere, however, there is no evidence to suggest divisions between king and noble or between noble and noble leading to any significant export of the privileged class.

It must be borne in mind that when the Europeans arrived they dealt with the Africans through the ruling class. Only the ruler of a given area could grant the *lançados* permission to reside and trade there, and only he could extend protection to them subsequently. The responsibility for the slave trade, as far as Africans themselves bear part of this responsibility, lies squarely upon the shoulders of the tribal rulers and élites. They were in alliance with the European slave merchants, and it was upon the mass of the people that they jointly preyed.

The law of the land was the king's law, administered by himself and the nobility. When this law was made into the handmaid of the slave trade, this came about because the ruling class so desired, knowing that it was they who stood to benefit from the perversion of justice. Another examination of the question of adultery will illustrate this. Though polygamy was theoretically possible for all, it was wealth which determined how many wives a man possessed. The nobles had dozens of wives, and thus plenty of opportunity to encourage "woman palavers." Besides, the very definition of adultery depended upon class considerations. Actual copulation constituted adultery when the wife of a Beafada commoner was involved; when the wife of a nobel was concerned, physical attempt was sufficient for a charge; while an indelicate proposal to one of the king's wives was enough for conviction.

As with adultery, so with every other charge—the ruling class were the ones who instituted them, and the common people were the victims. Contemporary European observers had no difficulty in discerning this. Ogilby, for example, affirmed that individuals became slaves either through war "or else under the pretext of some imperious and arbitrary laws by the kings and great men of the country." The Capuchins were very explicit on this latter point.

> The crimes for which innumerable men, women and children are condemned to slavery usually consist of deceits, frauds and acts of violence of the powerful men; these latter are the judges, plaintiffs and witnesses, and in the end the unfortunate poor who cannot resist them are enslaved.

The same observers added that

> the rich and powerful enjoy the privilege of making captives, because there is nobody to resist them. They [the nobles] look upon so many persons with dislike, and when they feel so inclined, they easily exercise their privilege, because their own interests are not harmed by their greed. The king proceeds with the same licence.

Apart from the unlikely possibility of being sold by the king, the noble could be certain that the law offered him protection. In Sierra Leone in the mid eighteenth century, the rich still only paid fines if they were guilty of crimes, except where the offender transgressed any basic rule of the Poro. Where slave raiding was concerned, the noble remained to a large extent inviolate because, if captured, he was almost always returned to his own people on payment of a ransom. Even the fearsome Bijagos were prepared to offer captured nobles for ransom in return for two commoners or five oxen. Up to the end of the eighteenth century, the ruling class on the Upper Guinea Coast continued to follow this practice of ransom for their own security.

If a noble was actually sold to the Europeans, he still had an excellent chance of recovering his freedom. In June 1622 the residents of Cacheu complained to the Governor of Cape Verde that the trade factor in Cacheu had been so foolhardy as to export a Negro related to the king. The consequences were not stated, but other instances of a similar nature indicate that the Cacheu traders had good cause for complaint. For example, in June 1680 the chief factor of the Royal African Company in Sierra Leone reported that two English private traders had stolen a noble from the Nunez, and the residents had threatened to kill all the Englishmen who fell into their power. Fortunately the private traders carried the noble to the Company's factory at Sherbro, and the chief factor purchased the individual in question and returned him to his homeland. It therefore seems to have been the convention that nobles were not to suffer servitude, and that every effort should be made to secure the release of any noble who inadvertently fell into the hands of the slave traders.

The noble suffered a minimum of disadvantages through the degeneration of the customary law and the rise of slave trading, and if he was sold he stood a very good chance of regaining his freedom; the commoner was the target of all the abuses of the law, he was the victim of slave raids, and when he was sold his position was desperate. . . .

. . . [T]he *lançados* could purchase any captive without inquiring after the title by which he had been acquired, and with the assurance that they were not to be perpetually challenged to return purchases on the grounds that the individuals concerned had been stolen. This arrangement was essential if the Europeans were to trade simultaneously in the territories of the Casangas, Banhuns, Papels, Beafadas, and Bijagos—all within a limited compass, and each one selling its neighbours. When de Almada said that the river Cacheu was a slaver's delight, it must have been made so by the conjoint action of the ruling groups in each tribe to allow the *lançados* to buy persons freely, irrespective of how they were acquired. In the second place, Barreira's report that the kings did not challenge a sale when any of their subjects was involved implies that the several tribal rulers on the coast had come to a reciprocal understanding to equalize their greed. One king was not afraid to turn a blind eye when he saw his subjects being sold by another king, because perhaps the very next day their positions would be reversed.

There was another reciprocal agreement between the *lançados* and the African ruling class which militated against the ordinary individual who sought to escape after being sold. When a captive escaped from a *lançado,* the latter turned to the nearest chief or noble (with a "gift") and asked him to announce on his *bombalon* that such and such a person had fled. Such communications were the exclusive preserve of the ruling class, and without their co-operation the *lançados* could not have coped with the frequent escape of captives for whom they had already paid. Later the Royal African Company also found it necessary to pay neighbouring *fidalgos* to return fugitive slaves.

It is an obvious and well-recognized fact that the African chiefs and kings were actively engaged in partnership with the European slavers all along the coast, but the impression given of inter-tribal conflicts has usually seemed to outweigh that of internal struggles. On the Upper Guinea Coast at least, one is forced to give much more attention to the way that victims were produced for the slave ships from within individual tribes. As Basil Davidson points out, throughout the history of slaving all over the world the distinction between selling people within a group (such as an ethnic group or religious community) and those who were outsiders was not rigidly maintained. The same applied on the Upper Guinea Coast, where the kings were just as likely to rob their own people as to attack their neighbours. The isolated exceptions only serve to reinforce this generalization; because it could scarcely have been simple coincidence that the Djolas and the Balantas, who produced the least slaves either by raiding or by preying upon each other, were the very tribes with an amorphous state structure from which a well-defined ruling class was absent.

Tribal divisions were not, then, the most important. When the line of demarcation is clearly drawn between the agents and the victims of slaving as it was carried on among the littoral peoples, that line coincides with the distinction between the privileged and the unprivileged in the society as a whole. The Atlantic slave trade was deliberately selective in its impact on the society of the Upper Guinea Coast, with the ruling class protecting itself, while helping the Europeans to exploit the common people. This is of course the widespread pattern of modern neo-colonialism; and by the same token the period of slave trading in West Africa should be regarded as protocolonial. Though on the one hand there was no semblance of European political control over the African rulers, on the other it was the Europeans who were accumulating capital.

In the midst of lamenting the trials and tribulations of the *lançados,* Barreira related that one day a Mandinga arrived at Cacheu, having journeyed there to resolve a doubt which was besetting him. He asked the Moslem *imam* of Cacheu: "Why is it that the whites are free, and the blacks are their slaves?" The reply was that God made the whites first and the blacks afterwards, and he decreed that the latter should serve their elder brothers. This was an imaginative portrayal of the colonial relationship.

Indirectly, via European testimony, the African rulers made it manifest that they regarded the slave trade as an imposition, but were prepared to pay that price for European goods. On this point, the Capuchins offered evidence which they elicited by questioning the African rulers on their attitude to the Atlantic slave trade. They found, as Barreira before them had done, that the African slavers recognized their profession for the evil it was, but contended that they indulged in man-stealing because the whites would purchase no other goods. In the long run, the terrible logic of this situation caused the African chiefs to cling to the Atlantic slave trade as their staple economic activity, even after it had become an anachronism within the capitalist system. . . .

African Societies Voluntarily Participated in the Slave Trade

JOHN THORNTON

Warfare and Slavery

We have established so far that Africans were not under any direct commercial or economic pressure to deal in slaves. Furthermore, we have seen not only that Africans accepted the institution of slavery in their own societies, but that the special place of slaves as private productive property made slavery widespread. At the beginning, at least, Europeans were only tapping existing slave markets. Nevertheless, one need not accept that these factors alone can explain the slave trade. There

Africa and Africans in the Making of the Atlantic World, 1400–1680 by John Thornton 98–125. Copyright © 1992, 1998 by John Thornton. Reprinted by permission of Cambridge University Press.

are scholars who contend that although Europeans did not invade the continent and take slaves themselves, they did nevertheless promote the slave trade through indirect military pressure created by European control of important military technology, such as horses and guns. In this scenario—the "gun-slave cycle" or "horse-slave cycle"—Africans were compelled to trade in slaves, because without this commerce they could not obtain the necessary military technology (guns or horses) to defend themselves from any enemy. Furthermore, possession of the technology made them more capable of obtaining slaves, because successful war guaranteed large supplies of slaves.

Hence, through the operation of their control over the "means of destruction," to use Jack Goody's descriptive term, Europeans were able to influence Africans indirectly. They could direct commerce in ways that helped them and also compel Africans to wage wars that might otherwise not have been waged. This would cause Africans to seek more slaves than they needed for their own political and economic ends and depopulate the country against their wishes. The quantitative increase would exceed Africans' own judgment of a proper level of exports. In the end, this not only might increase economic dependence but could result in large-scale destruction of goods, tools, and ultimately development potential. Hence, in the end, Africans would be helpless, exploited junior partners in a commerce directed by Europe.

However, this argument will ultimately not be any more sustainable than the earlier commercial and economic ones. Certainly in the period before 1680, European technology was not essential for warfare, even if Africans did accept some of it. Likewise, it is much easier to assert than to demonstrate that Africans went to war against their will or solely to service the slave trade. Indeed the more we know about African warfare and resulting enslavement, the less clear and direct the connections between war and the export slave trade become.

The contemporary evidence strongly supports the idea that there was a direct connection between wars and slavery, both for domestic work and for export. This did not mean that there was no nonmilitary enslavement, of course. Judicial enslavement was one common way of obtaining slaves and judges, moreover, were not above distorting the law to provide more captives or enslaving distant relatives of guilty parties. Jesuit observers believed that this was common in Ndongo as early as 1600, and missionary travelers often commented on it in the seventeenth-century Upper Guinea region. But however scandalous this may have been, it is unlikely that judicial enslavement accounted for more than a few percent of the total exports from Africa.

Thus the fact that military enslavement was by far the most significant method is important, for it means that rulers were not, for the most part, selling their own subjects but people whom they, at least, regarded as aliens. The fact that many exported slaves were recent captives means that they were drawn from those captured in the course of warfare who had not yet been given an alternative employment within Africa. In these cases, rulers were deciding to forgo the potential future use of these slaves. Some of the exports were slaves whom local masters wished to dispose of for one reason or another and those who had been captured locally by brigands or judicially enslaved.

This is exactly the situation described by da Mosto in his account of Jolof in 1455. After a description of the use of the slaves in the domestic economy, da Mosto noted that most slaves were captured in wars with neighboring countries and the civil wars. Many of these captives were integrated into the domestic economy, but the rest were sold to the "Moors" for horses (i.e., they entered the Saharan trade), although "Christians" had recently entered the trade on the coast. This account focuses on two aspects of African societies that predisposed them to participate in the slave trade. The first is the regular use of slaves in the domestic economy and particularly as revenue for centralizing states, and the second is the role of warfare.

The causes and motivations behind these wars are crucial for understanding the slave trade. Philip Curtin has examined the Senegambian slave trade of the eighteenth century and has proposed a schema for viewing African warfare that resulted in slave captures that can be fruitfully applied to the earlier period as well. He proposes that wars be classified as tending toward either an economic or a political model. In the economic model the wars were fought for the express purpose of acquiring slaves and perhaps to meet demands from European merchants; in the political model wars were fought for mostly political reasons, and slaves were simply a by-product that might yield a profit. Both models are seen as "ideal types," and individual wars might contain a mixture of motives, of course. On the whole, however, Curtin believes that the eighteenth-century Senegambian data support a political, rather than the economic, model.

Actually, discerning between an economic and a political model is not easy in practice. Consider the case of Portuguese Angola, a state seemingly founded on the premise of exporting slaves. Angola's wars ought to fit the economic model if any state's would. Yet many of Angola's wars, and the majority of the most lucrative ones in terms of acquiring slaves, had more or less clear-cut political motives. Portugal's early wars in Angola, for example, were as much for establishing a foothold in the area as for capturing slaves. In 1579, after all, the Portuguese were nearly driven out by the forces of Ndongo, and the wars between then and about 1595 were defensive as much as offensive.

When the Portuguese at last went on the offensive against Ndongo, their series of wars in the early seventeenth century also resulted in gains in territory, and after 1624 they became embroiled in a long series of wars that might be called the War of the Ndongo Succession, in which Portuguese officials hoped to place a pliant king on Ndongo's throne and met with the resistance of Queen Njinga (1624–63). This war, almost continuous from 1624 until 1655, can account for most of the activities of the Portuguese army in the period, and the expansion of the war to the east can account for the appearance of many eastern Angolan slaves in the New World during this time. Of course, this does not mean that all of Angola's wars fit the political model, but only that we should keep in mind that in Africa, as elsewhere, wars could always be multivalent, even defensive or strategic ones. . . .

The Jolof and Angolan models we have just examined suggest that the solution to the problem of the nature of African wars will not be easy to assess. In theory, wars with objectives that Europeans might see as political, such as annexing territory (or defending territory) or acquiring and strengthening political rights, should be classed as political, whereas raids conducted solely to acquire loot or trade goods should be classed as economic. In practice, however, as we have already seen from our previous examination of Jolof politics, capturing slaves made political sense to Jolof rulers as well as economic sense. Slaves were sources of wealth, and even in a hit-and-run operation that did not envision political conquest (although Jolof certainly did make conquests as well), the slaves could be made to produce wealth in the same way that a conquest would. Likewise, Jolof's rulers might employ the slaves to generate private revenue for them or to act as personal servants, soldiers, and administrators and thus raise them up against their rivals for power within Jolof. Hence, even a war that simply resembles a raid with no political objectives would have major political consequences if slaves were taken—and the fact that some were sold to outside parties should not lead us to the conclusion that the war had no political motives.

These considerations thus make it difficult to evaluate testimony about the motivations of warfare by European observers, who thought of wars that netted simply booty, even if this meant slaves, as being economic ventures (i.e., ventures aimed at securing slaves for export). Surely some of the ventures conducted by African rulers seem to have had no other purpose. Edward Fenton believed that his request for slaves in 1580 in Sierra Leone led the ruler to conduct a war merely to fill his requests—a war he thought would net 3,000–4,000 slaves. De Almada, likewise, recalled that once the ruler of Kayor waged a war in 1576 solely to obtain slaves to pay a debt he owed the Cape Verdian merchant. Similarly, several contemporary observers believed that many of the wars waged by the Angolan governor Mendes de Vasconcellos in the early seventeenth century had the acquisition of slaves as their only motive.

Such wars, however, may well have been waged solely in order to acquire slaves even without the demands of Atlantic traders. One example of this comes from Fernandes's late fifteenth-century informants. According to them, the Sanhaja of the desert made war against the people south of them "more for pillage than for power." Likewise, Jannequin de Rochefort argued on the experience of his observations in 1639 that the wars were not for conquest but to raid for people and cattle.

This issue goes to the heart of the unusual nature of African politics and one of the matters that makes it different from Eurasian politics. Just as slavery took the place of landed property in Africa, so slave raids were equivalent to wars of conquest. For this reason, one must apply a different logic to African wars than the equations of political motives equals war of conquest and economic motives equals slave raid. This analysis changes our understanding of the objectives of war and must ultimately change our assessment of African warfare.

Lovejoy, for example, has proposed that warfare was endemic in Africa as a result of political fragmentation. In other words, the very fact that Africa had few large-scale political units meant that wars would be more frequent, and thus enslavement increased. As fragmentation increased (a situation that he believes took place during the period of the slave trade), war naturally increased. Underlying this is the assumption that a political situation of small states would naturally lead to a movement to consolidate them into larger, Eurasian-style polities. Thus, although African politics actually determined the course of warfare, the intrinsic structure of those politics created more wars. Furthermore, one need not consider most wars as being explained by the economic model but by the political model, in which wars were an attempt to remedy the fragmentation by consolidating power. The failure to consolidate was thus the fuel that fired the slave trade.

Lovejoy's solution would be more helpful if it were true that there is a correlation between political centralization and peace, but unfortunately this does not seem to have been the case. This emerges clearly from an examination of the policies of the empire of Songhay, which controlled a huge area in the sixteenth century—larger than any other state at the time and on a scale that rivals most European states. Songhay was an expanding empire and thus waged wars of territorial conquest, capturing slaves along the way. According to the *Tarikhs,* local chronicle sources, for example, Sonni Ali, who ruled from 1468 to 1492 (about the same time as the Atlantic trade developed), conducted some sort of war or campaign in every year of his reign. The campaigns varied in length, size, and complexity, and not all were conducted by the king himself. The chroniclers who described these wars commented often on the motivations of their ruler (which were usually to extend territory, punish insults, retaliate for attacks on his territory, and the like) but never specifically mentioned the capture of slaves as one of the goals, nor did they take the trouble to enumerate or boast of the slaves captured, clearly implying that the Songhay expansion was politically rather than economically motivated.

The exploits of his successor, Askia Muhammed, are less clear, because a different chronicler discussed them, but he too conducted many large expeditions, although perhaps somewhat less frequently than his predecessor. As in the case of Sonni Ali, the acquisition of slaves was never mentioned or the number of captives discussed, and moreover, Askia Muhammed's motivations were similar to those of his predecessor.

But the warfare of an expanding Songhay was perhaps the exception in Africa. This is because most of Africa was, as Lovejoy argues, fragmented. However, this fragmentation was not simply the result of a failure of politics, nor did it increase appreciably during the time in question. Instead, it appears as a constant feature of African society, characteristic of the entire precolonial period.

As a measure of African fragmentation, consider the normal size of African states, based on the boundaries of these states. . . . There was no African state as large as the larger Asian or Euro-American empires of the period. . . .

In all, only perhaps 30 percent of Atlantic Africa's area was occupied by states with surface areas larger than 50,000 square kilometers, and at least half of that area was occupied by states in the medium-sized (50,000–150,000 square kilometers) range. The rest of Atlantic Africa was occupied by small, even tiny, states. Of this group, a few states in the southeastern part of modern Ghana and Benin-Togo—including Allada, the core of the later kingdom of Dahomey, and the larger Akan states (Akim, Denkyira, Akwamu, and the core of the later Asante kingdom)—each controlled perhaps 5,000 square kilometers in the late seventeenth century. But they too occupied a relatively small part of the total, and certainly more than half the area of Atlantic Africa was ruled by ministates whose surface area ranged from 500 to 1,000 square kilometers. If this were not dramatic enough, one should consider that if these statistics were broken down by population, a portion considerably greater than half of all of the people in Atlantic Africa lived in the ministates, because these states were found in the most densely populated parts of the region.

Thus, one can say with confidence that political fragmentation was the norm in Atlantic Africa. By this account, the "typical Atlantic African probably lived in a state that had absolute sovereignty but controlled a territory not exceeding 1,500 square kilometers (smaller than many American counties, perhaps the area occupied by a larger city). Populations might vary considerably; in the sparsely inhabited areas of central Africa, such a state might have 3,000–5,000 inhabitants, but on the densely inhabited Slave and Gold coasts it could control as many as 20,000–30,000 people. Virtually all the land from the Gambia River along the coast to the Niger delta was in states of this size, and much of the land stretching into the interior. In areas like Angola ministates like these occupied the mountainous land between Kongo and Ndongo and the area of the Kwanza River between Ndongo and the larger states of the central highlands.

In short, enlargement of scale does not seem to have been a priority for leaders. Historians, anxious to assert that Africans did build large states, have to some extent focused too much attention on the empires and the medium-sized states, and thus the point is often overlooked. But the reasons for Africa's small states were probably not the result of some sort of backwardness that prevented them from seeing the advantages of larger units.

One reason for the smallness of scale (not necessarily the only one) may derive from the legal system, which did not make land private property, and may also explain why the Americas, the other world area without landed property, was also the home of small and even tiny states (outside its own few dramatic empires). In Eurasia, control over large areas of land was essential, because it was through grants of land that one rewarded followers, and this land was normally worked by tenants of one kind or another. Eurasians were relatively less interested in controlling people, for without land, the people's labor could not be assigned or its reward collected by landowners. African states were not concerned with land—for as long as there was no population pressure on the land, more people could always be accommodated. Hence, African wars that aimed at acquiring slaves were in fact the exact equivalent of Eurasian wars aimed at acquiring land. The state and its citizens could increase their wealth by acquiring slaves and did not need to acquire land, unless they were short of land at home (which was not the case, as far as we can tell).

The acquisition of slaves instead of land in wars had other advantages. Whereas conquest of land necessarily required administration of larger areas and expansion of military resources, the acquisition of slaves only required a short campaign that need not create any new administrative conditions. Moreover, conquest of land and its subsequent government usually required sharing the proceeds of land with existing landlords, state officials, and other wealthy member of the defeated state, who might be defeated but usually still had to be co-opted. Slaves, on the other hand, were unable to bargain as wealthy landlords might have and could be integrated individually or in small groups into existing structures.

We can see these processes in operation in the case of Sierra Leone. The Sapes, as the early Sierra Leone inhabitants were called in documents of the time, were not creating empires or even larger states. They seem to have exported many slaves, however, for although the Sapes did not apparently enter into the trade immediately, by 1500 they accounted for a large proportion of the slaves imported into Europe. If the frequency of the ethnonym in bills of sale is any guide to relative volume, early sixteenth-century port records have them as the third most common group, behind Jolofs (which probably also includes exports from Songhay and some from Mali) and Mandinkas (Mali exports). The Sape slaves, according to Fernandes's informant Alvaro Velho, were the result of "constant wars" of the region.

These wars do not appear to have been waged for territorial expansion; although we lack the chronicle sources of the Sudanese region to confirm this, certainly there was no consolidation in Sierra Leone as a result of warfare. But as Velho also testified, slaves were used in the domestic economy to increase the ruler's personal income, and perhaps this in itself can explain the propensity for wars that did not increase wealth by the annexation of territory but by the annexation and transport of people.

This feature can also explain the existence, already in Velho's time (1499), of small raids being conducted in the "Rivers" region, composed, according to Fernandes, of Falup raiding parties in canoes penetrating all the rivers of the region. In the sixteenth century the Falup were joined by the Bissagos Islanders, who were soon renowned for their naval attacks on the mainland. This type of war was very common in that region in the sixteenth and seventeenth centuries, where a host of visitors describe canoe-based parties that would move silently and strike suddenly (sometimes at night) and carry off people.

In these instances, the slaves could well have been used either by the rulers of the small states of the area to increase their personal dependents and thus strengthen their power base or by private citizens, merchants, or aristocrats to increase their wealth or to increase their power vis á vis the rulers. Although some of these raids may also have been undertaken to supply European demand, this demand was in addition to the greater African demand for slaves to be used domestically as well as for export.

Many Africans retained females from the raids and sold off males, because the Atlantic trade often demanded more males than females. The Bissagos Islanders held many female slaves, and observers believed that virtually all the productive labor was done by women. Lemos Coelho, a Cape Verdian merchant, believed that many societies held large reserves of slaves who could be sold but who would work for their owners in the meantime. Naturally enough, the Portuguese in Angola fell into the same pattern, retaining many slaves on their plantations along the major river, and still selling off many, especially males.

Increasing wealth through warfare and enslavement was of course a cheap way of increasing power. Slaves could be captured in wars and in raids and carried back to the home territory by the victors and put to work, without the attacking armies having to conquer and occupy territory. For small states with small armies, this was a logical way to become richer. But of course, in the medium-sized states and empires, territorial expansion also took place. We have already discussed the wars of expansion in Songhay and Jolof and noted that in addition to increasing territory, their wars also resulted in capturing slaves. For the expanding empire, enslavement of the conquered population allowed the rulers of the expanding state to increase their personal wealth and also to build armies and administrative corps of direct dependents, just as the revenues from the conquered territories provided continuous new income. Thus, external expansion could also increase wealth, and the slaves that were a by-product of the wars of expansion could increase centralization at home.

All these factors resulted in an enormous slave population in Africa at the time of the arrival of the first Europeans and during the whole era of the slave trade. They meant that the necessary legal institutions and material resources were available to support a large slave market, one that anyone could participate in, including Europeans and other foreigners. Those who held slaves and did not intend to use them immediately could also sell them, and indeed, this is why the number of African merchants who dealt in slaves was large.

Central African data corroborate this process very well. Although there were few useful records for the pre-1483 period, it is clear that Kongo was expanding territorially during the initial period of Portuguese contact, because it was regularly cited as fighting frequent wars. However, we have also already seen that one of the most important aspects of Kongo's centralization was the development of a large urban center with numerous slaves, giving the ruler an advantage over other members of the coalition that began the kingdom. Political motives such as increasing territory, revenues and a loyal power base played a role in Kongo as in Jolof.

Thanks to Portuguese participation in some of Kongo's wars, we can find out how slaves were used. As in the other areas, the ostensible motive for wars was quite strictly political. For example, Kongo made war against islands in the mouth of the Zaire River in 1491 to bring them back to obedience. The instructions of the king of Portugal to Gonçalo Rodrigues in 1509 strongly support the idea that slaves were captured in such wars. Rodrigues was given orders concerning how to sell whatever slaves the king of Kongo might choose to grant him for participation in the campaign. A still better description concerns a campaign conducted in 1513 or 1514 against Munza, an enemy south of Kongo. This war was apparently a defensive war, for Munza was said to have attacked Afonso's son, the Mweni Mbamba, and the war was to relieve him and punish Munza. King Afonso and the Portuguese in his service sent at least 600 slaves back to the capital during the war (and when the army returned, they brought at least 190 more), of which 510 were diverted to the Atlantic trade. Of all these slaves at least 90 remained in Kongo, and Afonso complained that the Portuguese whom he had entrusted with disposal of the slaves in the war had done so improperly, leaving too few in Kongo and, moreover, among them only those who were "old and thin." Afonso was clearly concerned with both domestic use and foreign exports and, at least in this case, believed that his interests were not served by the export of too many, but he was also clearly willing to allow a substantial number to be sold outside the country.

Perhaps one of the reasons that the central African region was a rich source of slaves was that there were several states like Kongo for whom slaves were both a by-product of wars of expansion and useful in themselves for increasing centralization and loyalty. Beginning around 1520, Kongo ran into the growing power of Ndongo, which like Kongo was expanding and using slaves to support centralization. That such wars as developed in the mid-1520s worked in this way is suggested by several letters of complaint written by Afonso in 1526; in one of his bitterest he deplores the (unofficial) help that the Portuguese gave the ruler of Ndongo, which resulted in the capture and sale of Afonso's subjects, even the nobility. A similar struggle seems to have been waged earlier against the Nziko kingdom, which continued exporting slaves itself, becoming a major exporter by the 1530s. Even the countries that were not leading the expansion might export slaves as a result of this warfare; the inhabitants of the islands in the mouth of the Zaire River called "Pamzelungos" in sixteenth-century sources, also exported slaves, perhaps taken in unsuccessful attempts by Kongo to suppress their revolts. On the basis of the available evidence it is possible to make a very strong case for a simple political explanation of slave-producing wars, even when these wars did not have expansion as a goal and in spite of the Portuguese involvement and the Africans' own strong interests in exporting slaves. . . .

African Warfare and European Military Technology

Although I have shown the African wars led to enslavement on a large scale and that African politics can explain even slave raids that seem to have no political motive, the hypothesis that Europeans influenced African behavior through control over military resources must still be addressed. Given the significance of warfare for expansion of wealth in Africa, the military case must be carefully examined.

Certainly, Europeans did participate, wherever possible, in African politics, often as "military experts" or advisors, occasionally as armed mercenaries. They did this both officially through government-sponsored assistance programs such as the aid that Portugal gave to Kongo in 1491, 1509, 1512, and 1570, or unofficially and without authorization, as in the support for Ndongo in the 1520s, the help that gunners gave to the Mane in the 1550s, and perhaps the assistance to Benin in the 1510s and 1520s. Other foreigners of European origin also provided assistance—Hawkins's help in Sierra Leone and Ulsheimer's in Benin are two more sixteenth- and early seventeenth-century examples. Acceptance of this assistance might simply be seen as the desire of centralizers to make use of foreign, rather than local, officials and dependents as a means of keeping local political debts to a minimum and of creating a dependent bureaucracy. But it is also clear that Europeans provided new military techniques and technology as well, perhaps at the price of demanding more vigorous participation in the slave trade than their patrons wished.

However, the kind of military assistance that Europeans in the sixteenth and seventeenth centuries could render in Africa was not as decisive as much of the writing on the "gun-slave" and "horse-slave" cycles implies. For example, Elbl has examined records of Portuguese horse imports into Senegambia and found that they can scarcely be considered numerous enough to be crucial to the military survival or even success of Jolof cavalries. Moreover, as Law has pointed out in a detailed study of the horse problem, much of the Sudanese region was capable of breeding fairly large numbers of horses by the fourteenth century. Thus, the Atlantic trade coincided with a period when demands for horses were declining, and perhaps the trade must be seen in much the same light as the trade in other commodities—as supplementing or even complementing an existing trade and production.

Firearms and other personal weapons (as in the gun-slave cycle) are even more problematic. European firearms and crossbows, the missile weapons that differed most from those in use in Africa, were designed to counteract armored cavalry or for naval warfare in Europe. Although they had great range and penetrating power (capabilities that developed out of a long-standing projectile-versus-armor contest), they had a very slow rate of fire. For Africans, who generally eschewed armor, the advantages of range (penetrating power being relatively unimportant) were more than offset by the disadvantages of the slow rate of fire, except in special circumstances.

Such circumstances were found in naval warfare, for example. . . . [I]n the initial encounters between da Mosto's ships and Mandinga craft in the Gambia, the crossbowmen in the tops were able to fire to good effect against the attacking forces, protected as they were by the high sides of their ships. This particular feature of the ship may be one of the reasons Kongo favored Portuguese assistance in its wars with the Zaire islands, where African craft, Portuguese ships, and the long-range weapons of the Europeans could be used to good effect.

Likewise, artillery would be useful for attacking fortified locations. European artillery was used in Sierra Leone in the 1560s and in Benin, probably in 1514, when the king of Benin seized a Portuguese bombard, but certainly in 1601, when Ulsheimer joined Dutch sailors who used a gun to blast down the gate of a rebel town. In these cases, as in those of the naval engagements, however, the new weapons were hardly of such overwhelming decisiveness that they tipped the scales of warfare strongly.

European ships could be employed only as a supplementary force, for . . . unsupported European ships were helpless close in to shore. Only slight changes in fortifications could greatly reduce the effectiveness of artillery. In the Benin area, artillery was not effective, because most of the fortifications were largely earthworks. Indeed, it is only because they could not defend their gate that the defenders of the town that Ulsheimer helped attack were defeated. The stockades of Sierra Leone were perhaps more vulnerable, but earthworks could render them much safer. The common use of earthworks and hedges of living trees in fortifications probably explains why the cannon had such little value as a siege engine in the Angolan wars of the sixteenth and seventeenth centuries.

In this instance the Portuguese operations in Angola after 1575 are especially informative, for here the Portuguese attempted direct conquest with their own weapons and, at least in some instances, with their own soldiers. If European military technology and techniques were of special merit, surely this would be demonstrated in Angola. Portuguese operations might then be of the simple slave-raiding model that many scholars prefer, in which an all-powerful state conducts systematic wars on its weaker and ill-organized neighbors to gather slaves, relying on the strength of its weapons and the organization and size of its armies to ensure victory and minimize losses. If European weaponry or military organization were indeed superior, given their strong motivations to acquire slaves for export, one would surely expect this model to describe the Portuguese attacks in Angola.

Certainly, the early exports of slaves from Angola were clearly linked to the operations of the Portuguese army. This can be seen in customs data from Luanda covering the period 1579–85, when great surges of exports in 1579–80 and lesser ones in 1581 and 1583 are correlated with wars (described in great detail by contemporary Jesuit observers), and the periods of relative peace in 1580 and 1584–5 show almost no exports. Similarly, Beatrix Heintze has estimated that the wars promoted by Mendes de Vasconcellos, Portuguese governor from 1617 to 1622, resulted in the export of over 50,000 slaves in just a few years—though this ferocious rate of export was not kept up.

But the documentation cannot support the idea that the Portuguese wars in Angola were simply raids of a militarily dominant European power against its weaker neighbors. Cadornega, the chronicler of the Angolan wars of the seventeenth century, was quick to point this fact out. His campaign and battle descriptions are lengthy and show a soldier's eye for military detail. He often records fairly small-scale Portuguese operations conducted, one might easily say, simply for obtaining slaves, that ended in failure and disaster. After recounting one particularly difficult campaign, he asserts that this was far too difficult to be simply a "guerra de negros" (war for slaves). Although one can discount this comment in part as simply a reply to critics who believed that all the Angolan wars were just slave raids, with no political or diplomatic gains in mind (and perhaps running counter to such gains), the detail of his documentation does confirm that whoever conducted war to capture slaves was in no way guaranteed success and might well be killed by his quarry. Cadornega reports an apt saying in this context: "He who would singe another man's whiskers had better look out for his own."

Portugal's African enemies often possessed skilled and well-equipped armies and very often constructed strong fortifications. Cavazzi described in detail the complicated operations needed to attack one of these fortified locations during a campaign that he accompanied in 1659. This particular campaign, moreover, continued after taking the town, only to lose badly in another battle, with the result that virtually all its Portuguese members were killed.

Likewise, although the Portuguese played the role of a heavily armored infantry in many of the campaigns, their presence was not decisive, and in most respects their tactics were identical to those of their enemies. Portuguese soldiers could not win unsupported by Africans and were regularly massacred when they tried to do so. If Angola was a major participant in the Atlantic slave trade and the source of export for many thousands of people, it was not through the superiority of European arms.

In summary, we can say that although European arms may have assisted African rulers in war in some cases, they were not decisive. It is unlikely that any European technology or assistance increased the Africans' chances of waging successful war (as the Portuguese in Angola could surely have attested) or that it made the attackers suffer fewer losses. Therefore, Europeans did not bring about some sort of military revolution that forced participation in the Atlantic trade as a price for survival.

The Rapid Growth of Slave Exports and Innovations in Military Technology and Warfare

It is possible to conclude that European influence over the slave trade may not have been significant in the first century and a half of the trade simply by acknowledging that Africans had slaves and a slave trade already, and that early forms of European military technology and organization were not critical to the success of African armies. But it might still be possible to argue that ultimately Europeans forced Africans to exceed their capacity to deliver slaves at a later period when high demands for slaves and improved military technology played a more important role.

One potential piece of evidence is the dramatic increase in slave exports after 1650. This increase is roughly correlated both with the explosion of growth of plantation economies under northern European control in the Caribbean and with the large-scale arrival of northern Europeans on the African coast. These newcomers brought with them improved weapons technology and a generally greater industrial capacity than Portugal had. Could these events have signaled the arrival of a new and potentially more disruptive group of merchants and resulted in Africans being forced to expand the existing trade against their will? My research suggests, however, that the changes were more of quantity than quality, and that although the increased demand (and subsequent rise in prices) may have persuaded more Africans to part with their slaves, it did not force them to do so against their will.

African exports of slaves expanded dramatically beginning in the mid-seventeenth century, to the point where the number of exported slaves grew from being a relatively small number relative to the total population of the African regions from which they were taken to having a major demographic impact. Virtually all the work on the volume of the slave trade shows that the total number of slaves exported increased relative to the total areas or to the (estimated) African populations involved. The negative demographic impacts, although somewhat apparent in the beginning of the period in some areas (such as central Africa), intensified and spread to virtually the whole of Atlantic Africa. In the late eighteenth century much of Africa reached demographic exhaustion.

It is possible to trace the growth in slave exports in considerable detail for most of the seventeenth century. Even allowing for a fair margin of error, it is obvious that exports did indeed grow significantly. Thanks to the detailed data on shipping available in the archives of Seville and the union of the Spanish and Portuguese crowns in 1580, which brought much of Portuguese trade in Africa under Spanish supervision, we have a detailed picture of trade in the last years of the sixteenth century to 1640, when the ending of the union once again clouds the picture. . . .

Several points are worthy of note. First of all, it is clear that there was dramatic growth, increasing from a rate of 0.6 percent per annum in the sixteenth century to well over 1.5 percent per annum by the second half of the seventeenth century, with exports nearly doubling between 1650 and 1700. However, this growth was uneven, for some regions exported more slaves, while others maintained more or less the same level.

For example, the trade of the western regions, such as Senegambia, hardly grew at all throughout the period. Angolan trade grew more, but still modestly, during the same period. Angola's total exports moved from something on the order of 2,000–3,000 slaves in the early sixteenth century to 4,500 by century's end, continuing to 8,000 by 1650 and eventually 11,000 by century's end. The growth increased the Angolan share of the trade from approximately half in 1500 to better than 65 percent by 1650.

But Angolan growth was eventually eclipsed by the dramatic rise of exports from the Gulf of Guinea. In 1500 most slaves from this area came from Benin, but by the end of the sixteenth century Benin had ceased selling slaves in any appreciable number. This loss was more than compensated for by the rapid growth of the slave trade of Allada in the last half of the sixteenth century and throughout the seventeenth century. Slaves from this area first appear in American inventories about 1550: a "Lucumi" (Yoruba) slave first appears on Hispaniola in 1547, and "Ardras" (Allada) first appear in Peru in the 1560s. All such groups become increasingly numerous in the seventeenth century, both in absolute terms and relative to slaves from other areas in American data.

Continued growth from the region of Allada and its immediate neighbors eventually earned the area the title of "Slave Coast" in the late seventeenth century.

From virtually no exports in 1500, this region was exporting over 19,000 slaves per year, more than half the entire African total, by 1700. But the seventeenth-century growth of slavery in Lower Guinea (Gold Coast to Cameroon) was also enhanced by the entry of the Gold Coast states into the slave trade after 1630, and especially after 1650. This growth is particularly dramatic because the Gold Coast began the seventeenth century as a net importer of slaves and exporter of gold and ended it as a net exporter of slaves and was even importing gold.

Thus, in order to understand why the numbers of slaves increased so dramatically in the seventeenth century, we really need to focus on Angola and the Lower Guinea region. For Angola we must seek the causes of the continued growth of slave trading, and for Lower Guinea the reasons for its people's decision to participate in the trade and expand their exports toward the end of the century.

There are several possible explanations for the growth of the slave trade in these areas. Both Curtin and Lovejoy have suggested that increases in the price of slaves, which can be documented for the period, might have enticed more slaves from their owners. It may have encouraged more "economic model" wars, and it may have persuaded owners that it would be better to forgo domestic use in exchange for the higher price available from the Atlantic trade. Also, owners of slaves living far from the coast might be willing to bear the transport costs of moving slaves to the coast if a higher price were offered. This explanation does give European merchants a role in the growth of enslavement in Africa, but it clearly places the economic decisions in the hands of Africans.

Other explanations focus simply on the increase in wars caused by African political dynamics, discounting the role of trade. The connection between African trade, control over the trade, and politics is a complex and controversial one, but for our purposes, such an explanation still rules out European coercion.

Finally, of course, there is the idea that European coercion, either direct or indirect, is responsible for the increase in warfare, which resulted in more slaves for the Atlantic. In the late seventeenth century the musket was developed into a more effective weapon. Moreover, very large numbers of such weapons were produced as European armies re-armed into bodies in which every infantryman carried a musket. Naturally enough, larger quantities of the improved weapons were also available to ship to Africa, where, it is argued, they may have revolutionized warfare. Thus, by directing weapons selectively to those willing to supply slaves, European merchants may have been able to effect the gun-slave cycle.

A detailed examination of both Angola and the Gulf of Guinea can shed some light on probable causes for the transformation of slave exports. In both cases, however, it seems clear that economic motives and political motives not directly connected to the slave trade were far more important than European coercion or influence.

In Angola, the growth can be explained in large measure by the fact that the same areas continued supplying slaves, and slaves whose capture took place farther and farther east joined the exodus from central Africa. For example, the war of the Ndongo succession really only ended in 1627, though hostilities between Matamba, Angola, and Kasanje (in various combinations, not always involving Portuguese participation) continued sporadically, as, for example, in 1679–85. If supplies of slaves captured in the wars of the Ndongo succession were lost with the ending of the war, the Kongo civil wars (1665–1718) surely contributed more than Kongo had earlier in the century, for all the central African slaves in the Remire plantation in Cayenne (French Guiana) acquired from Dutch traders between 1685 and 1690 were baptized Christians from Kongo.

But, as we have already seen, the big wars were not the only source of Angolan slaves, for smaller campaigns (which some thought were no more than slave raids) also continued in the same areas as before. Cadornega's chronicle, which provides detailed documentation on the operations of the Portuguese army up to 1681, mentions several such wars directed against the usual enemies: the Ndembu and Mbwila region to the north; Kisama, Benguela, and the central highlands to the south; and the lands bordering Matamba on the east. The effects of these eastern wars and similar operations by Matamba's army were noted by several late seventeenth-century travelers. The absence of comprehensive chronicles, like Cadornega's, for the period after 1681 obscures the exact direction and nature of these wars, but they surely seem to have continued.

If improved musketry was somehow a factor in the conduct of any of these wars, great or small, it is not visible in these records. Portuguese military success seems no better in 1680 or even 1700 than it was a century earlier, whatever rearmament or reorganization may have taken place as a result of the entry of muskets.

To these sources, which supplied much of the earlier slave trade, came others from far in the interior. It seems reasonable to suggest that the motive for the capture and transport of these slaves, who often came from hundreds of kilometers east of the positions of the Portuguese, may well have been the higher prices paid for slaves in the late seventeenth century. Cadornega mentions contacts between Kasanje and the emerging Lunda state of the far interior that took place before 1680 but does not mention slaves as among Lunda's exports. Nevertheless, Lunda did begin exporting slaves soon afterward, soon contributing a large supply, and capturing many during its wars of expansion and consolidation. It is interesting to note in this regard that Lunda's armies were not reliant on guns from the Atlantic, for as late as the mid-eighteenth century they still eschewed muskets as cowards' weapons.

We have much less information about the causes of the sudden surge of slave exports from Lower Guinea. The region around Allada, first of the states of the Slave Coast to begin large-scale exports, is very poorly documented by sixteenth- and early seventeenth-century sources, and it is not really until well into the seventeenth century that this situation is remedied. Oral traditions collected in the nineteenth century suggest that this period was characterized by the rise of the powerful Oyo Empire, which is perhaps in some way correlated with the surge of exports. That many of Allada's exports were slaves captured during Oyo expansion is suggested by the fact that Capuchin visitors of the 1660s believed that many of the slaves Allada exported came from the interior and were purchased at markets. Allada and its subject states and neighbors fought numerous wars during the later seventeenth century, even as the kingdom of Dahomey came to dominate the interior and then the coast.

The local African politics of the Gold Coast, the second region to enter the slave trade from Lower Guinea, involved a complicated series of wars between the local states, whose motives are not clear to us and were equally unclear to the Europeans, although the more perceptive observers, such as Willem Bosman, the Dutch factor, provided detailed historical background for some. In total, however, the complexities of local politics and the steady rise of the interior kingdoms of Denkyira, Akwamu, and ultimately Asante overwhelmed the petty politics of the area—the result of deep-seated social changes in the interior kingdoms that owed little to coastal influences. . . .

The military reorganization of Lower Guinea that led to the rise of the great interior powers, such as Asante and Dahomey (and perhaps even the late seventeenth-century expansion of Oyo), has often been blamed on imports of European firearms. But Kea, whose study of this period for the Gold Coast takes such military factors seriously, notes that although the methods of warfare were revolutionized by the interior kingdoms, it was mainly by their use of mass-recruited armies, and firearms had very little effect. The development of these mass armies was the product of social changes and was not determined by the availability of new military technology. Indeed, he argues that the early expansion of Asante was accomplished by mass armies armed with missile weapons, but these were bows and arrows in the crucial early phases, and only later were the troops re-armed with muskets.

It is worth noting that the creation of mass armies and their subsequent re-arming with firearms may have done a great deal to increase the numbers of people enslaved. If earlier wars involved relatively small professional armies, and the majority of the slaves were taken from the military captives, then obviously the group of people vulnerable to enslavement would be fairly small. But with the rise of mass armies, battles were likely to involve more soldiers, thus increasing the number of potential slaves accruing to the victor. However, the simple correlation between imports of firearms and exports of slaves is not a causal relationship. It is more likely that African demands for guns increased simply because they were creating larger armies, which itself had complicated internal, social causes. The availability of European weapons did not provoke an increase in warfare.

As African armies re-armed and became accustomed to the tactics of musket warfare it became harder to go back to some other "art of war," thus ensuring continued demand. This certainly helped European business in general, but it did not deliver to any European power the capacity to engage in weapons blackmail against states that might wish to refuse to sell slaves. This is because no European country or group of merchants came close to having control over the supply of arms to any African state, at least in any but the very shortest run. Europeans could therefore not freely decide to supply arms or not to supply them to force Africans into any decisions. In any case, the only real form of influence available to merchants would be withholding the very means to make war, and such a strategy would be more likely to inhibit than encourage warfare.

As historians learn more about warfare in Africa in this period, and as they probe more deeply into the political and social structures of African states, they realize that warfare needs to be explained in terms of the internal dynamics of the state or state system. As such dynamics are understood, the role of Europeans in causing war (as opposed to benefiting from it, either as a vehicle to sell arms or to buy slaves) begins to diminish. Thus, for example, the study of the Kongo civil wars of the late seventeenth century yields explanations for the wars that lie in the politics of the country and not in Portuguese machinations, as was previously believed.

The same conclusions can be drawn from the study of the Slave Coast and Gold Coast, where the explosion of slave exports and growth of arms imports are the clearest. The numerous surviving letters of Dutch and English factors on the Gold Coast from about 1680 onward certainly tell of a willingness to buy slaves, at least "if the price is right," as one factor wrote in 1683, but there is nothing to suggest that they could or did exercise actual pressure to get the local people to sell them. They did certainly encourage and occasionally bribe local rulers in the multistate system of the coast to fight, including supplying them with arms and even soldiers, but it was normally to get military help in driving other European rivals from their posts and not simply to get slaves. One of the best examples of such an event was the Komenda war of the 1690s, detailed in several contemporary sources. Its origins lay in the complicated politics of African trade, or, as the Dutch factor Bosman said, in "bad government and absurd customs." All sides obtained mercenaries from the Europeans. The relatively small size of African states and the prevalence of professional armies along the coast (it was only in the interior that the mass armies were forming) made small bodies of mercenaries potentially effective, and consequently Europeans frequently hired themselves out in this way. The practice of acting as mercenaries was not restricted to Europeans; several states on both the Gold Coast and the Slave Coast routinely supplied mercenaries in the wars of the period. Robin Law has recently proposed that the kingdom of Dahomey served first as a sort of mercenary state. Their role as suppliers of mercenaries did not give the Europeans much power on the coast; rather, one gets a much stronger impression of European weakness and helplessness in the face of local African politics.

African rulers continued to engage in wars, not unlike those of previous centuries, and naturally, as the new weapons figured more prominently in warfare, acquiring supplies of the weapons became important. Thus, in the late seventeenth century and into the eighteenth century, civil wars troubled the Senegambian states, and often pretenders sought and acquired weapons in order to make their claims. But it would be incorrect to say that somehow Europeans had persuaded the potential candidates to seek power in order to get slaves, even if they did delight in the prospect of increased slaves as a result. Senegalese state leaders built up substantial armies of slave soldiers, and often these armies engaged in local raiding (frequently without royal permission), which proved quite disruptive, but neither the origin of these armed forces nor their kings' lack of ability or desire to control them was the result of European policies or pressures.

In conclusion, then, we must accept that African participation in the slave trade was voluntary and under the control of African decision makers. This was not just at the surface level of daily exchange but even at deeper levels. Europeans possessed no means, either economic or military, to compel African leaders to sell slaves.

The willingness of Africa's commercial and political elite to supply slaves should be sought in their own internal dynamics and history. Institutional factors predisposed African societies to hold slaves, and the development of Africa's domestic economy encouraged large-scale trading and possession of slaves long before Europeans visited African shores. The increase in warfare and political instability in some regions may well have contributed to the growth of the slave trade from those regions, but one cannot easily assign the demand for slaves as the cause of the instability, especially as our knowledge of African politics provides many more internal causes. Given the commercial interests of African states and the existing slave market in private hands in Africa, it is not surprising that Africans were able to respond to European demands for slaves, as long as the prices attracted them.

F U R T H E R   R E A D I N G

Basil Davidson, *Black Mother: The Years of the African Slave Trade* (1961).
J. E. Inikori, "Measuring the Atlantic Slave Trade: An Assessment of Curtin and Anstey," *Journal of African History,* 17 (1976), 197–223.
Robert July, *A History of the African People* (1980).
Paul Lovejoy, "The Impact of the Atlantic Slave Trade on Africa: A Review of the Literature," *Journal of African History,* 30 (1989), 365–394.
Joseph C. Miller, *Way of Death: Merchant Capitalism and the Angolan Slave Trade, 1730–1830* (1988).
Walter Rodney, *A History of the Upper Guinea Coast, 1545–1800* (1970).
Walter Rodney, *How Europe Underdeveloped Africa* (1981).
Barbara L. Solow, ed., *Slavery and the Rise of the Atlantic System* (1991).
Hugh Thomas, *The Slave Trade: The Story of the Atlantic Slave Trade, 1440–1870* (1997).
Eric Williams, *Capitalism and Slavery* (1944).

The Origins of
North American Slavery
and Racism

The causal relationship between racism and slavery figures prominently in most efforts to explain not only the evolution of slavery in North America but the fate of the slaves and their descendants after slavery as well. Which came first, racism or slavery? Did seventeenth-century Englishmen choose to enslave Africans because they were already racially prejudiced. Or was the turn to slave labor primarily an economic decision, with prejudice toward that degraded status developing later?

The paucity of documentary evidence and its seemingly contradictory nature have made for a lively, if largely inconclusive, debate. There is evidence of invidious distinctions between black and white laborers from a relatively early date. There also is evidence that all blacks were not treated as inferiors in civil status. Indeed, they claimed many rights—to property, to the right to sue and testify in courts of law—that would be the envy of later generations of free African Americans. How do we evaluate the relative weight of racial prejudice in a society in which at least some black men could successfully defend their rights in court against white men, including claims to property in other black men as slaves?

It is also clear that by the late seventeenth century the possibilities for free status and equal civil status was being rapidly diminished. By the end of the century, certainly, black *and* slave *had become almost legally synonymous. Some historians argue that even this seeming change over time is illusory, that there is no evidence that Africans were treated better earlier in the century, that the absence of laws or comment cannot be taken as proof of whites' indifference to race. As the essays in this chapter suggest, this debate remains a lively one because it resonates so deeply with contemporary racial issues. If racism is understood to be a product of specific historical and social developments, then one might envision historical and social conditions evolving so as to mitigate or eliminate it. But if racism is taken to be somehow timeless and ineffable, the prospects for ever overcoming it are diminished considerably.*

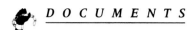

D O C U M E N T S

The first document marks the earliest recorded instance of Africans arriving in a permanent English settlement in North America. The momentous occasion is noted almost offhandedly by John Rolfe, one of the leaders of the Virginia settlement, amid his diverse protestations against English insults to American settlers, the hardships and opportunities of cultivating colonial staples, and diplomatic relations with Native Americans. In the second document, Anthony Johnson, himself either a former slave or an indentured servant, successfully defends his claim to his slave property, John Casar, who claims in turn to have been an indentured servant and not a slave. The document illustrates among other things, the fact that in the seventeenth century Africans could be indentured servants as well as slaves, and that a few of them acquired considerable property themselves, including slaves. In the case of Elizabeth Key, the third document, we witness the successful claim to free status by the mulatto child of a deceased slaveholder. The fourth document is a 1664 Maryland law declaring Negroes slaves for life and regulating the status of children of interracial sexual unions. During the 1660s several laws and judicial decisions in Maryland and Virginia sought to codify the slave's status. The fifth document, the will and testament of a black freeman, Francis Payne, shows the ownership of property by black men and their capacity to pass it on to the next generation, a basic civil right in seventeenth-century Virginia. The final document illustrates the concrete ways in which Virginia law distinguished between white servants and black slaves.

1. John Rolfe Records the Arrival of African Slaves to Virginia, August 1619

For to begin with the yeere of our Lord, 1619. there arriued a little Pinnace priuatly from *England* about Easter [*Easter Sunday O.S. was 28 Mar. in* 1619] for Captaine *Argall*; who taking order for his affaires, within foure or fiue daies returned in her, and left for his Deputy, Captaine *Nathaniel Powell.*

On the eighteenth of *Aprill,* which was but ten or twelue daies after, arriued Sir *George Yearley,* by whom we vnderstood Sir *Edwin Sand[y]s* was chosen Treasurer, and Master *Iohn Farrar* his Deputy; and what great supplies was a preparing to be sent vs, which did rauish vs so much with ioy and content, we thought our selues now fully satisfied for our long toile and labours, and as happy men as any in the world. Notwithstanding, such an accident hapned Captaine *Stallings,* [that] the next day his ship was cast away, and he not long after slaine in a priuate quarrell.

Sir *George Yearly* to beginne his gouernment, added to be of his councell, Captaine *Francis West,* Captaine *Nathaniel Powell,* Master *Iohn Pory,* Master *Iohn Rolfe,* and Master *William Wick[h]am,* and Master *Samuel Macocke,* and propounded to haue a generall assembly with all expedition.

Vpon the twelfth of this Moneth [*April* 1619], came in a Pinnace of Captaine *Bargraues*; and on the seuenteenth [*April* 1619] Captaine *Lownes,* and one Master *Euans,* who intended to plant themselues at *Waraskoyak*: but now *Ophechankanough* will not come at vs, that causes vs [to] suspect his former promises.

Captain John Smith, *Works, 1608–1631,* Part II, ed. Edward Arber (Westminster, U.K.: Archibald Constable and Co., 1895), 540–543.

In May [1619] came in the *Margaret of Bristoll*, with foure and thirty men, all well and in health; and also many deuout gifts: and we were much troubled in examining some scandalous letters sent into *England*, to disgrace this Country with barrennesse, to discourage the aduenturers, and so bring it and vs to ruine and confusion. Notwithstanding, we finde by them of best experience, an industrious man not other waies imploied, may well tend foure akers of Corne, and 1000. plants of Tobacco; and where they say an aker will yeeld but three or foure barrels, we haue ordinarily foure or fiue, but of new ground six, seuen, and eight, and a barrell of Pease and Beanes, which we esteeme as good as two of Corne, which is after thirty or forty bushels an aker, so that one man may prouide Corne for fiue; and apparell for two by the profit of his Tobacco. They say also English Wheat will yeeld but sixteene bushels an aker, and we haue reaped thirty: besides to manure the Land, no place hath more white and blew Marble [? *marl*] than here, had we but Carpenters to build and make Carts and Ploughs, and skilfull men that know how to vse them, and traine vp our cattell to draw them; which though we indeuour to effect, yet our want of experience brings but little to perfection but planting Tobaco. And yet of that, many are so couetous to haue much, they make little good; besides there are so many sofisticating Tobaco-mungers in *England*, were it neuer so bad, they would sell it for *Verinas*, and the trash that remaineth should be *Virginia*: such deuilish bad mindes we know some of our owne Country-men doe beare, not onely to the businesse, but also to our mother *England* her selfe; could they or durst they as freely defame her.

The 25. of *Iune* [1619] came in the *Triall* with Corne and Cattell all in safety, which tooke from vs cleerely all feare of famine; then our gouernour and councell caused Burgesses to be chosen in all places, and met at a generall Assembly, where all matters were debated [that were] thought expedient for the good of the Colony, and Captaine *Ward* was sent to *Monahigan* in new *England*, to fish in May, and returned the latter end of May, but to small purpose, for they wanted Salt. The *George* also was sent to *New-found-land* with the Cape Merchant: there she bought fish, that defraied her charges, and made a good voyage in seuen weekes.

About the last of August [1619] came in a dutch man of warre that sold vs twenty Negars: and *Iapazous* King of *Patawomeck*, came to *Iames* towne, to desire two ships to come trade in his Riuer, for a more plentifull yeere of Corne had not beene in a long time, yet very contagious, and by the trechery of one *Poule*, in a manner turned heathen, wee were very iealous the Saluages would surprize vs.

The Gouernours haue bounded foure Corporations; which is the Companies, the Vniuersity, the Gouernours and Gleabe land: Ensigne *Wil. Spencer,* and *Thomas Barret* a Sergeant, with some others of the ancient Planters being set free, weare the first farmers that went forth; and haue chosen places to their content: so that now knowing their owne land, they striue who should exceed in building and planting. . . .

Now you are to vnderstand, that because there haue beene many complaints against the Gouernors, Captaines, and Officers in *Virginia*: for buying and selling men and boies, or to bee set ouer from one to another for a yeerely rent, was held in *England* a thing most intolerable; or that the tenants or lawfull seruants should be put from their places, or abridged their Couenants, was so odious, that the very report thereof brought a great scandall to the generall action. The Councell in *England* did send many good and worthy instructions for the amending [of] those abuses, and appointed a hundred men should at the Companies charge be allotted and prouided to serue and attend the Gouernour during the time of his gouernment, which number he was to make good at his departure, and leaue to his Successor in like manner; fifty to the Deputy-Gouernour of the College land, and fifty to the Deputy of the Companies land, fifty to the Treasurer, to the Secretary fiue and twenty, and more to the Marshall and Cape merchant; which they are also to leaue to their successors; and likewise to euery particular Officer such a competency, as he might liue well in his Office, without oppressing any vnder their charge: which good law I pray God it be well obserued, and then we may truly say in *Virginia*, we are the most happy people in the world.

2. Anthony Johnson, a Former Slave, Claims His Slave Property, 1655

The deposition of Captain Samuel Goldsmith taken (in open court) 8th of March Sayth, That beinge at the howse of Anthony Johnson Negro (about the beginninge of November last to receive a hogshead of tobacco) a Negro called John Casar came to this Deponent, and told him that hee came into Virginia for seaven or Eight yeares (per Indenture) And that hee had demanded his freedome of his master Anthony Johnson; And further said that Johnson had kept him his servant seaven yeares longer than hee ought, And desired that this deponent would see that hee might have noe wronge, whereupon your Deponent demanded of Anthony Johnson his Indenture, hee answered, hee never sawe any; The said Negro (John Casor) replyed, hee came for a certayne tyme and had an Indenture Anthony Johnson said hee never did see any But that hee had him for his life; Further this deponent saith That mr. Robert Parker and George Parker they knew that the said Negro had an Indenture (in on Mr. Carye hundred on the other side of the Baye) And the said Anthony Johnson did not tell the negro goe free The said John Casor would recover most of his Cowes of him; Then Anthony Johnson (as this deponent did suppose) was in a feare. Upon this his Sonne in lawe, his wife and his 2 sonnes perswaded the said Ar.thony Johnson to sett the said John Casor free. more saith not

Samuel Goldsmith

This daye Anthony Johnson Negro made his complaint to the Court against mr. Robert Parker and declared that hee deteyneth his servant John Casor negro (under pretence that the said Negro is a free man). The Court seriously consideringe and maturely weighinge the premises, doe fynde that the said Mr. Robert Parker most unjustly keepeth the said Negro from Anthony Johnson his master as appeareth by the deposition of Captain Samuel Goldsmith and many probable circumstances. It is therefore the Judgement of the Court and ordered That the said John Casor Negro forthwith returne unto the service of his said master Anthony Johnson, And that mr. Robert Parker make payment of all charge in the suit, also Execution.

From Warren M. Billings, ed., *The Old Dominion in the Seventeenth Century: A Documentary History of Virginia, 1660–1689* (Chapel Hill: University of North Carolina Press 1975), 155–156. Copyright © 1975 by The University of North Carolina Press.

3. Interracial Sexual Relations and Their Consequences: The Case of Elizabeth Key, 1655–1656

The Court doth order that Col. Thomas Speke one of the overseers of the Estate of Col. John Mottrom deceased shall have an Appeale to the Quarter Court next att James Citty in a Cause depending betweene the said overseers and Elizabeth a Moletto hee the said Col. Speke giving such caution as to Law doth belong.

Wee whose names are underwritten being impannelled upon a Jury to try a difference between Elizabeth pretended Slave to the Estate of Col. John Mottrom deceased and the overseers of the said Estate doe finde that the said Elizabeth ought to be free as by severall oathes might appeare which we desire might be Recorded and that the charges of Court be paid out of the said Estate. [names of the jury omitted]

Memorandum it is Conditioned and agreed by and betwixt Thomas Key on the one part and Humphrey Higginson on the other part [word missing] that the said Thomas Key hath put unto the said Humphrey one Negro Girle by name Elizabeth for and during the [term?] of nine yeares after the date hereof provided that the [said?] Humphrey doe find and allow the said Elizabeth meate drinke [and?] apparrell during the said tearme And allso the said Thomas Key that if that if [*sic*] the said Humphrey doe dye before the end of the said time above specified that then the said Girl be free from the said Humphrey Higginson and his assignes Allsoe if the said Humphrey Higginson doe goe for England with an Intention to live and remaine there that then hee shall carry [the?] said Girle with him and to pay for her passage and likewise that he put not of [f] the said Girle to any man but to keepe her himselfe In witness whereof I the said Humphrey Higginson. Sealed and delivered in the presence of us Robert Booth Francis Miryman. 20th January 1655 this writing was Recorded.

Mr. Nicholas Jurnew aged 53 yeares or thereabouts sworne and Examined Sayth That about 16 or 17 yeares past this deponent heard a flying report at Yorke that Elizabeth a Negro Servant to the Estate of Col. John Mottrom deceased was the Childe of Mr. Kaye but the said Mr. Kaye said that a Turke of Capt. Mathewes was Father to the Girle and further this deponent sayth not   signed Nicholas Jurnew
20th January 1655 Jurat in Curia [i.e., "sworn in court"]

Anthony Lenton aged 41 yeares or thereabouts sworne and Examined Sayth that about 19 yeares past this deponent was a servant to Mr. Humphrey Higginson and at that time one Elizabeth a Molletto nowe servant to the Estate of Col. John Mottrom deceased was then a servant to the said mr. Higginson and as the Neighbours reported was bought of mr. Higginson with the said servant both himself and his

From Warren M. Billings, ed., *The Old Dominion in the Seventeenth Century: A Documentary History of Virginia, 1660–1689* (Chapel Hill: University of North Carolina Press 1975), 165–169. Copyright © 1975 by The University of North Carolina Press.

Wife intended a voyage for England and at the nine yeares end (as the Neighbours reported) the said Mr Higginson was bound to carry the said servant for England unto the said mr. Kaye, but before the said mr. Kaye went his Voyage hee Dyed about Kecotan, and as the Neighbours reported the said mr. Higginson said that at the nine yeares end hee would carry the said Molletto for England and give her a portion and lett her shift for her selfe And it was a Common report amongst the Neighbours that the said Molletto was mr Kays Child begott by him and further this deponent sayth not   the marke of Anthony Lenton   20th January 1655 Jurat in Curia

Mrs. Elizabeth Newman aged 80 yeares or thereabouts sworne and examined Sayth that it was a common Fame in Virginia that Elizabeth a Molletto nowe servant to the Estate of Col. John Mottrom deceased was the Daughter of mr. Kay; and the said Kaye was brought to Blunt-point Court and there fined for getting his Negro woman with Childe which said Negroe was the Mother of the said Molletto and the said fine was for getting the Negro with Childe which Childe was the said Elizabeth and further this deponent sayth not   the marke of Elizabeth Newman   20th January 1655 Jurat in Curia

John Bayles aged 33 yeares or thereabouts sworne and Examined Sayth That at the House of Col. John Mottrom Black Besse was termed to be mr Kayes Bastard and John Keye calling her Black Bess mrs. Speke Checked him and said Sirra you must call her Sister for shee is your Sister and the said John Keye did call her Sister and further this deponent Sayth not   the marke of John Bayles   20th January 1655 Jurat in Curia

The deposition of Alice Larrett aged 38 yeares or thereabouts Sworne and Examined Sayth that Elizabeth which is at Col. Mottroms is twenty five yeares of age or thereabouts and that I saw her mother goe to bed to her Master many times and that I heard her mother Say that shee was mr. Keyes daughter and further Sayth not   the marke of Alice Larrett Sworne before mr. Nicholas Morris   19th Jan. 1655.   20th January this deposition was Recorded

Anne Clark aged 39 or thereabouts Sworne and Examined Sayth that shee this deponent was present when a Condition was made betweene mr. Humphrey Higginson and mr. Kaye for a servant called Besse a Molletto and this deponents Husband William Reynolds nowe deceased was a witness but whether the said Besse after the Expiration of her time from mr Higginson was to be free from mr Kaye this deponent cannot tell and mr Higginson promised to use her as well as if shee were his own Child and further this deponent Sayth not   Signum Ann Clark   20th January 1655. Jurat in Curia

Elizabeth Newman aged 80 yeares or thereabouts Sworne and Examined Sayth that shee this deponent brought Elizabeth a Molletto, Servant to the Estate of Col. John Mottrom deceased to bed of two Children and shee layd them both to William Grinsted and further this Deponent Sayth not   Elizabeth Newman her marke   20th January 1655 Jurat in Curia

A Report of a Comittee from an Assembly
Concerning the freedome of Elizabeth Key

It appeareth to us that shee is the daughter of Thomas Key by severall Evidences and by a fine imposed upon the said Thomas for getting her mother with Child of the said Thomas That she hath bin by verdict of a Jury impannelled 20th January 1655 in the County of Northumberland found to be free by severall oathes which the Jury desired might be Recorded That by the Comon Law the Child of a Woman slave begott by a freeman ought to bee free That shee hath bin long since Christened Col. Higginson being her God father and that by report shee is able to give a very good account of her fayth That Thomas Key sould he onely for nine yeares to Col. Higginson with severall conditions to use her more Respectfully then a Comon servant or slave That in case Col. Higginson had gone for England within nine yeares hee was bound to carry her with him and pay her passage and not to dispose of her to any other For theise Reasons wee conceive the said Elizabeth ought to bee free and that her last Master should give her Corne and Cloathes and give her satisfaction for the time shee hath served longer than Shee ought to have done. But forasmuch as noe man appeared against the said Elizabeths petition wee thinke not fitt a determinative judgement should passe but that the County or Quarter Court where it shall be next tried to take notice of this to be the sence of the Burgesses of this present Assembly and that unless [original torn] shall appear to be executed and reasons [original torn] opposite part Judgement by the said Court be given [accordingly?]

Charles Norwood Clerk Assembly

James Gaylord hath deposed that this is a true coppy

James Gaylord

21th July 1656 Jurat in Curia
21th July 1656 This writeing was recorded

Att a Grand Assembly held at James Citty 20th of March 1655 Ordered that the whole business of Elizabeth Key [and?] the report of the Comittee thereupon be returned [to the?] County Court where the said Elizabeth Key liveth

This is a true copy from the book of Records of the Order granted the last Assembly

Teste Robert Booth
21th July 1656 This Order of Assembly was Recorded

Upon the petition of George Colclough one of the overseers of Col. Mottrom his Estate that the cause concerning a Negro wench named Black Besse should be heard before the Governor and Councell Whereof in regard of the Order of the late Assembly referring the said caise to the Governor and Councell at least upon Appeale made to them These are therefore in his Highness the Lord Protector his name to will and require the Commissioners of the County of Northumberland to Surcease from any further proceedings on the said Cause and to give notice to the parties interested therein to appear before the Governor at the next Quarter Court on the fourth day for a determination thereof. Given under my hand this 7th of June 1656. Edward Digges 21th 1656 This Writeing was Recorded.

Whereas mr. George Colclough and mr. William Presly overseers of the Estate of Colonell John Mottrom deceased were Summoned to theis Court at the suite of Elizabeth Kaye both Plaintiffe and Defendant being present and noe cause of action at present appearing The Court doth therefore order that the said Elizabeth Kaye shall be non-suited and that William Grinsted Atturney of the said Elizabeth shall by the tenth of November next pay fifty pounds of tobacco to the said overseers for an non-suite with Court charges else Execution. Whereas the whole business concerning Elizabeth Key by Order of Assembly was Referred to this County Court. According to the Report of a Comittee at an Assembly held at the same time which upon the Records of this County appears, It is the judgment of this Court that the Said Elizabeth Key ought to be free and forthwith to have Corne Clothes and Satisfaction according to the said Report of the Comittee. Mr. William Thomas dissents from this judgment.

These are to Certifie whome it may concerne that William Greensted and Elizabeth Key intends [sic] to be joyned in the Holy Estate of Matrimony. If any one can shew any Lawfull cause why they may not be joyned together lett them Speake or ever after hold their tongues Signum William Greensted Signum Elizabeth Key

21th July 1656 this Certificate was Published in open Court and is Recorded

I Capt. Richard Wright administrator of the Estate of Col. John Mottrom deceased doe assigne and transfer unto William Greensted a maid servant formerly belonging unto the Estate of the said Col. Mottrom commonly called Elizabeth Key being nowe Wife unto the said Greensted and doe warrant the said Elizabeth and doe bind my Selfe to save here [i.e., her] and the said Greensted from any molestation or trouble that shall or futurely arise from or by any person or persons that shall pretend or claime any title or interest to any manor of service [original torn] from the said Elizabeth witness [my ha]nd this 21th of July 1659

Test   William Th[omas] Richard Wright
        James Aust[en]

4. An Act to Discriminate Between Africans and Others in Maryland, 1664

An Act Concerning Negroes & other Slaues

Bee itt Enacted by the Right Hon[ble] the Lord Proprietary by the aduice and Consent of the upper and lower house of this present Generall Assembly That all Negroes or other slaues already within the Prouince And all Negroes and other slaues to bee hereafter imported into the Prouince shall serue Durante Vita And all Children born of any Negro or other slaue shall be Slaues as their ffathers were for the terme of their liues And forasmuch as divers freeborne English women forgettfull of their

"An Act Concerning Negroes & Other Slaves," *Archives of Maryland: Proceedings and Acts of the General Assembly of Maryland, January 1637/8–September 1664*, ed. William Hand Browne (Baltimore: Maryland Historical Society 1883), 533–534.

free Condicōn and to the disgrace of our Nation doe intermarry with Negro Slaues by which alsoe diuers suites may arise touching the Issue of such woemen and a great damage doth befall the Masters of such Negros for preuention whereof for deterring such freeborne women from such shamefull Matches Bee itt further Enacted by the Authority advice and Consent aforesaid That whatsoever free borne woman shall inter marry with any slaue from and after the Last day of this present Assembly shall Serue the master of such slaue dureing the life of her husband And that all the Issue of such freeborne woemen soe marryed shall be Slaues as their fathers were And Bee itt further Enacted that all the Issues of English or other freeborne woemen that haue already marryed Negroes shall serve the Masters of their Parents till they be Thirty yeares of age and noe longer.

5. Francis Payne, a Free Negro Property Owner in Colonial Virginia, Bequeaths His Property, 1673

In the Name of god Amen I Francis Payne of Northampton County in Virginia beinge sick of body but of perfect knowledge and understanding and being willinge to ease my minde of all worldly care Doe make this my last will and Testament as follows

Imprimis I bequeath my soule to my loveing Father my creator and to Jesus Christ who by his blood and passion suffered for my sinns and all the world trustinge through his meritt to injoy that heavenly portion prepared for mee and all true beleevers And as for my body I bequeth it unto the ground from whence it came there to receive a Christian buriall And as for my worldly Estate I doe give and bequeath itt unto my loveing wife Agnes Payne my whole Estate reall and personall moveables and immoveables makinge her my Indubitable Executrix of this my last will and Testament. And Doe here declare that by vertue of these presents all former wills by mee made and signed are rebuked and made void and this is to bee my last will and Testament. And desire that my debts may in the first place bee paid. In Testimony whereof I have subscribed my hand and putt my seale this 9th day of May Anno Domini 1673.

Unto each of our god children a Cow Calfe a peece when they attaine to lawfull age. but as for [Deura?] Driggins he is to have nothinge by this will

Francis X paine
his marke

Signed sealed and delivered in the presence of us
Nathaniel Wilkins
the marke of
Elizabeth X Pettit

The 29th day of September 1673. This day the last will and Testament of Francis Paine Negro was proved in open Court by the Corporall oath of Nathaniel Wilkins

---

From Warren M. Billings, ed., *The Old Dominion in the Seventeenth Century: A Documentary History of Virginia, 1660–1689* (Chapel Hill: University of North Carolina Press 1975), 156–157. Copyright © 1975 by The University of North Carolina Press.

and allowed of and ordered to be Recorded (Provided that Elizabeth Pettitt the other evidence appeare at the next Court and Confirme the probate thereof if livinge and of ability to owne then or otherwise as sure as shee can)

Teste Daniel Neech Deputy Clerk

Recorded the 4th of October 1673. Daniel Neech Deputy Clerk

6. Distinguishing Slaves from Indentured Servants in Virginia, 1705

Of the Servants and Slaves in Virginia

Their Servants they distinguish by the Names of Slaves for Life, and Servants for a time.

Slaves are the Negroes, and their Posterity, following the Condition of the Mother, according to the Maxim, *partus sequitur ventrem*. They are call'd Slaves, in Respect of the Time of their Servitude, because it is for Life.

Servants, are those which serve only for a few Years, according to the time of their Indenture, or the Custom of the Country. The Custom of the Country takes place upon such as have no Indentures. The Law in this Case is, that if such Servants be under nineteen Years of Age, they must be brought into Court, to have their Age adjudged; and from the Age they are judg'd to be of, they must serve until they reach four and twenty: But if they be adjudged upwards of nineteen, they are then only to be Servants for the Term of five Years.

The Male-Servants, and Slaves of both Sexes, are imployed together in tilling and manuring the Ground, in sowing and planting Tobacco, Corn, &c. Some Distinction indeed is made between them in their Cloaths, and Food; but the Work of both is no other than what the Overseers, the Freemen, and the Planters themselves do.

Sufficient Distinction is also made between the Female-Servants, and Slaves; for a white Woman is rarely or never put to work in the Ground, if she be good for any thing else: And to discourage all Planters from using any Women so, their Law makes Female-Servants working in the Ground Tithables, while it suffers all other white Women to be absolutely exempted: Wheraes on the other hand, it is a common thing to work a Woman Slave out of Doors: nor does the Law make any Distinction in her Taxes, whether her Work be Abroad, or at Home.

 E S S A Y S

The two essays that follow take somewhat different approaches to the complex question "Which came first, slavery or racism?" Winthrop D. Jordan, professor of history at the University of Mississippi, reviews the long historiography on this question, noting in passing its resonance with contemporary views of race relations. Rejecting both the view that slavery gave rise to racial prejudice and the view that racism was the motive for enslavement, Jordan argues that the debasement of Africans' status and the perception of low status developed simultaneously. Edmund S. Morgan, professor emeritus at Yale University, asked a some-what different but related question: How could so many Americans be devoted to both free-dom and slavery? In Virginia he discovers the source for both racism and slavery in the material, especially demographic, and political transformations in the late seventeenth century, which made enslavement of blacks the ideological basis for a more elevated status for white freemen.

"The Mutual Causation" of Racism and Slavery

WINTHROP D. JORDAN

Thanks to John Smith we know that Negroes first came to the British continental colonies in 1619. What we do not know is exactly when Negroes were first en-slaved there. This question has been debated by historians for the past seventy years, the critical point being whether Negroes were enslaved almost from their first importation or whether they were at first simply servants and only later re-duced to the status of slaves. The long duration and vigor of the controversy sug-gest that more than a simple question of dating has been involved. In fact certain current tensions in American society have complicated the historical problem and greatly heightened its significance. Dating the origins of slavery has taken on a striking modern relevance.

During the nineteenth century historians assumed almost universally that the first Negroes came to Virginia as slaves. So close was their acquaintance with the problem of racial slavery that it did not occur to them that Negroes could ever have been anything but slaves. Philip A. Bruce, the first man to probe with some thoroughness into the early years of American slavery, adopted this view in 1896, although he emphasized that the original difference in treatment between white servants and Negroes was merely that Negroes served for life. Just six years later, however, came a challenge from a younger, professionally trained historian, James C. Ballagh. His *A History of Slavery in Virginia* appeared in the *Johns Hopkins University Studies in Historical and Political Science*, an aptly named series which was to usher in the new era of scholarly detachment in the writing of institutional history. Ballagh offered a new and different interpretation; he took the position that the first Negroes served merely as servants and that enslavement did not begin until around 1660, when statutes bearing on slavery were passed for the first time.

There has since been agreement on dating the statutory establishment of slav-ery, and differences of opinion have centered on when enslavement began in actual practice. Fortunately there has also been general agreement on slavery's distinguishing characteristics: service for life and inheritance of like obligation by any offspring. Writing on the free Negro in Virginia for the Johns Hopkins series, John H. Russell in 1913 tackled the central question and showed that some Negroes were indeed servants but concluded that "between 1640 and 1660 slavery

"Modern Tensions and the Origins of American Slavery," by Winthrop D. Jordan. *Journal of Southern History*, 28 (February 1962), 18–30. Copyright © 1962 by the Southern Historical Association. Reprinted by permission of the Managing Editor.

was fast becoming an established fact. In this twenty years the colored population was divided, part being servants and part being slaves, and some who were servants defended themselves with increasing difficulty from the encroachments of slavery." Ulrich B. Phillips, though little interested in the matter, in 1918 accepted Russell's conclusion of early servitude and transition toward slavery after 1640. Helen T. Catterall took much the same position in 1926. On the other hand, in 1921 James M. Wright, discussing the free Negro in Maryland, implied that Negroes were slaves almost from the beginning, and in 1940 Susie M. Ames reviewed several cases in Virginia which seemed to indicate that genuine slavery had existed well before Ballagh's date of 1660.

All this was a very small academic gale, well insulated from the outside world. Yet despite disagreement on dating enslavement, the earlier writers—Bruce, Ballagh, and Russell—shared a common assumption which, though at the time seemingly irrelevant to the main question, has since proved of considerable importance. They assumed that prejudice against the Negro was natural and almost innate in the white man. It would be surprising if they had felt otherwise in this period of segregation statutes, overseas imperialism, immigration restriction, and full-throated Anglo-Saxonism. By the 1920's, however, with the easing of these tensions, the assumption of natural prejudice was dropped unnoticed. Yet only one historian explicitly contradicted that assumption: Ulrich Phillips of Georgia, impressed with the geniality of both slavery and twentieth-century race relations, found no natural prejudice in the white man and expressed his "conviction that Southern racial asperities are mainly superficial, and that the two great elements are fundamentally in accord."

Only when tensions over race relations intensified once more did the older assumption of natural prejudice crop up again. After World War II American Negroes found themselves beneficiaries of New Deal politics and reforms, wartime need for manpower, world-wide repulsion at racist excesses in Nazi Germany, and growingly successful colored anticolonialism. With new militancy Negroes mounted an attack on the citadel of separate but equal, and soon it became clear that America was in for a period of self-conscious reappraisal of its racial arrangements. Writing in this period of heightened tension (1949) a practiced and careful scholar, Wesley F. Craven, raised the old question of the Negro's original status, suggesting that Negroes had been enslaved at an early date. Craven also cautiously resuscitated the idea that white men may have had natural distaste for the Negro, an idea which fitted neatly with the suggestion of early enslavement. Original antipathy would mean rapid debasement.

In the next year (1950) came a sophisticated counterstatement, which contradicted both Craven's dating and implicitly any suggestion of early prejudice. Oscar and Mary F. Handlin in "Origins of the Southern Labor System" offered a case for late enslavement, with servitude as the status of Negroes before about 1660. Originally the status of both Negroes and white servants was far short of freedom, the Handlins maintained, but Negroes failed to benefit from increased freedom for servants in mid-century and became less free rather than more. Embedded in this description of diverging status were broader implications: Late and gradual enslavement undercut the possibility of natural, deep-seated antipathy toward Negroes. On the contrary, if whites and Negroes could share the same status of half freedom for forty years in the seventeenth century, why could they not share full freedom in the twentieth?

The same implications were rendered more explicit by Kenneth M. Stampp in a major reassessment of Southern slavery published two years after the Supreme Court's 1954 school decision. Reading physiology with the eye of faith, Stampp frankly stated his assumption "that innately Negroes *are*, after all, only white men with black skins, nothing more, nothing less." Closely following the Handlins' article on the origins of slavery itself, he almost directly denied any pattern of early and inherent racial antipathy: ". . . Negro and white servants of the seventeenth century seemed to be remarkably unconcerned about their visible physical differences." As for "the trend toward special treatment" of the Negro, "physical and cultural differences provided handy excuses to justify it." Distaste for the Negro, then, was in the beginning scarcely more than an appurtenance of slavery.

These views squared nicely with the hopes of those even more directly concerned with the problem of contemporary race relations, sociologists and social psychologists. Liberal on the race question almost to a man, they tended to see slavery as the initial cause of the Negro's current degradation. The modern Negro was the unhappy victim of long association with base status. Sociologists, though uninterested in tired questions of historical evidence, could not easily assume a natural prejudice in the white man as the cause of slavery. Natural or innate prejudice would not only violate their basic assumptions concerning the dominance of culture but would undermine the power of their new Baconian science. For if prejudice was natural there would be little one could do to wipe it out. Prejudice must have followed enslavement, not vice versa, else any liberal program of action would be badly compromised. One prominent social scientist suggested in a UNESCO pamphlet that racial prejudice in the United States commenced with the cotton gin!

Just how closely the question of dating had become tied to the practical matter of action against racial prejudice was made apparent by the suggestions of still another historian. Carl N. Degler grappled with the dating problem in an article frankly entitled "Slavery and the Genesis of American Race Prejudice." The article appeared in 1959, a time when Southern resistance to school desegregation seemed more adamant than ever and the North's hands none too clean, a period of discouragement for those hoping to end racial discrimination. Prejudice against the Negro now appeared firm and deep-seated, less easily eradicated than had been supposed in, say, 1954. It was Degler's view that enslavement began early, as a result of white settlers' prejudice or antipathy toward the first Negroes. Thus not only were the sociologists contradicted but the dating problem was now overtly and consciously tied to the broader question of whether slavery caused prejudice or prejudice caused slavery. A new self-consciousness over the American racial dilemma had snatched an arid historical controversy from the hands of an unsuspecting earlier generation and had tossed it into the arena of current debate.

Ironically there might have been no historical controversy at all if every historian dealing with the subject had exercised greater care with facts and greater restraint in interpretation. Too often the debate entered the realm of inference and assumption. For the crucial early years after 1619 there is simply not enough evidence to indicate with any certainty whether Negroes were treated like white servants or not. No historian has found anything resembling proof one way or the other. The first Negroes were sold to the English settlers, yet so were other English-men. It can be said, however, that Negroes were set apart from white men by the word *Negroes*, and a distinct name is not attached to a group unless it is seen as different. The earliest Virginia census reports plainly distinguished Negroes from white men, sometimes giving Negroes no personal name; and in 1629 every commander of the several plantations was ordered to "take a generall muster of all the inhabitants men woemen and Children as well *Englishe* as Negroes." Difference, however, might or might not involve inferiority.

The first evidence as to the actual status of Negroes does not appear until about 1640. Then it becomes clear that *some* Negroes were serving for life and some children inheriting the same obligation. Here it is necessary to suggest with some candor that the Handlins' statement to the contrary rests on unsatisfactory documentation. That some Negroes were held as slaves after about 1640 is no indication, however, that American slavery popped into the world fully developed at that time. Many historians, most cogently the Handlins, have shown slavery to have been a gradual development, a process not completed until the eighteenth century. The complete deprivation of civil and personal rights, the legal conversion of the Negro into a chattel, in short slavery as Americans came to know it, was not accomplished overnight. Yet these developments practically and logically depended on the practice of hereditary lifetime service, and it is certainly possible to find in the 1640's and 1650's traces of slavery's most essential feature.

The first definite trace appears in 1640 when the Virginia General Court pronounced sentence on three servants who had been retaken after running away to Maryland. Two of them, a Dutchman and a Scot, were ordered to serve their masters for one additional year and then the colony for three more, but "the third being a negro named John Punch shall serve his said master or his assigns for the time of his natural life here or else where." No white servant in America, so far as is known, ever received a like sentence. Later the same month a Negro was again singled out from a group of recaptured runaways; six of the seven were assigned additional time while the Negro was given none, presumably because he was already serving for life. After 1640, too, county court records began to mention Negroes, in part because there were more of them than previously—about two per cent of the Virginia population in 1649. Sales for life, often including any future progeny, were recorded in unmistakable language. In 1646 Francis Pott sold a Negro woman and boy to Stephen Charlton "to the use of him . . . forever." Similarly, six years later William Whittington sold to John Pott "one Negro girle named Jowan; aged about Ten yeares and with her Issue and produce duringe her (or either of them) for their Life tyme. And their Successors forever"; and a Maryland man in 1649 deeded two Negro men and a woman "and all their issue both male and Female." The executors of a York County estate in 1647 disposed of eight Negroes—four men, two women, and two children—to Captain John Chisman "to have hold occupy posesse and inioy and every one of the afforementioned Negroes forever[.]" The will of Rowland Burnham of "Rapahanocke," made in 1657, dispensed his considerable number of Negroes and white servants in language which clearly differentiated between the two by specifying that the whites were to serve for their "full terme of tyme" and the Negroes "for ever." Nor did anything in the will indicate that this distinction was exceptional or novel.

In addition to these clear indications that some Negroes were owned for life, there were cases of Negroes held for terms far longer than the normal five or seven years. On the other hand, some Negroes served only the term usual for white servants, and others were completely free. One Negro freeman, Anthony Johnson, himself owned a Negro. Obviously the enslavement of some Negroes did not mean the immediate enslavement of all.

Further evidence of Negroes serving for life lies in the prices paid for them. In many instances the valuations placed on Negroes (in estate inventories and bills of sale) were far higher than for white servants, even those servants with full terms yet to serve. Since there was ordinarily no preference for Negroes as such, higher prices must have meant that Negroes were more highly valued because of their greater length of service. Negro women may have been especially prized, moreover, because their progeny could also be held perpetually. In 1645, for example, two Negro women and a boy were sold for 5,500 pounds of tobacco. Two years earlier William Burdetts inventory listed eight servants (with the time each had still to serve) at valuations ranging from 400 to 1,100 pounds, while a "very anntient" Negro was valued at 3,000 and an eight-year-old Negro girl at 2,000 pounds, with no time-remaining indicated for either. In the late 1650's an inventory of Thomas Ludlow's large estate evaluated a white servant with six years to serve at less than an elderly Negro man and only one half of a Negro woman. The labor owned by James Stone in 1648 was evaluated as follows:

	lb tobo
Thomas Groves, 4 yeares to serve	1300
Frances Bomley for 6 yeares	1500
John Thackstone for 3 yeares	1300
Susan Davis for 3 yeares	1000
Emaniell a Negro man	2000
Roger Stone 3 yeares	1300
Mingo a Negro man	2000

Besides setting a higher value on the two Negroes, Stone's inventory, like Burdett's, failed to indicate the number of years they had still to serve. It would seem safe to assume that the time remaining was omitted in this and similar documents simply because the Negroes were regarded as serving for an unlimited time.

The situation in Maryland was apparently the same. In 1643 Governor Leonard Calvert agreed with John Skinner, "mariner," to exchange certain estates for seventeen sound Negro "slaves," fourteen men and three women between sixteen and twenty-six years old. The total value of these was placed at 24,000 pounds of tobacco, which would work out to 1,000 pounds for the women and 1,500 for the men, prices considerably higher than those paid for white servants at the time.

Wherever Negro women were involved, however, higher valuations may have reflected the fact that they could be used for field work while white women generally were not. This discrimination between Negro and white women, of course, fell short of actual enslavement. It meant merely that Negroes were set apart in a way clearly not to their advantage. Yet this is not the only evidence that Negroes were subjected to degrading distinctions not directly related to slavery. In several ways

Negroes were singled out for special treatment which suggested a generalized debasing of Negroes as a group. Significantly, the first indications of debasement appeared at about the same time as the first indications of actual enslavement.

The distinction concerning field work is a case in point. It first appeared on the written record in 1643, when Virginia pointedly recognized it in her taxation policy. Previously tithable persons had been defined (1629) as "all those that worke in the ground of what qualitie or condition soever." Now the law stated that all adult men and *Negro* women were to be tithable, and this distinction was made twice again before 1660. Maryland followed a similar course, beginning in 1654. John Hammond, in a 1656 tract defending the tobacco colonies, wrote that servant women were not put to work in the fields but in domestic employments, "yet some wenches that are nasty, and beastly and not fit to be so imployed are put into the ground." Since all Negro women were taxed as working in the fields, it would seem logical to conclude that Virginians found them "nasty" and "beastly." The essentially racial nature of this discrimination was bared by a 1668 law at the time slavery was crystallizing on the statute books:

> Whereas some doubts, have arisen whether negro women set free were still to be accompted tithable according to a former act, *It is declared by this grand assembly* that negro women, though permitted to enjoy their ffreedome yet ought not in all respects to be admitted to a full fruition of the exemptions and impunities of the English, and are still lyable to payment of taxes.

Virginia law set Negroes apart in a second way by denying them the important right and obligation to bear arms. Few restraints could indicate more clearly the denial to Negroes of membership in the white community. This action, in a sense the first foreshadowing of the slave codes, came in 1640, at just the time when other indications first appear that Negroes were subject to special treatment.

Finally, an even more compelling sense of the separateness of Negroes was revealed in early distress concerning sexual union between the races. In 1630 a Virginia court pronounced a now famous sentence: "Hugh Davis to be soundly whipped, before an assembly of Negroes and others for abusing himself to the dishonor of God and shame of Christians, by defiling his body in lying with a negro." While there were other instances of punishment for interracial union in the ensuing years, fornication rather than miscegenation may well have been the primary offense, though in 1651 a Maryland man sued someone who he claimed had said "that he had a black bastard in Virginia." There may have been nothing racial about the 1640 case by which Robert Sweet was compelled "to do penance in church according to laws of England, for getting a negroe woman with child and the woman whipt." About 1650 a white man and a Negro woman were required to stand clad in white sheets before a congregation in Lower Norfolk County for having had relations, but this punishment was sometimes used in ordinary cases of fornication between two whites.

It is certain, however, that in the early 1660's when slavery was gaining statutory recognition, the colonial assemblies legislated with feeling against miscegenation. Nor was this merely a matter of avoiding confusion of status, as was suggested by the Handlins. In 1662 Virginia declared that "if any christian shall committ ffornication with a negro man or woman, hee or shee soe offending" should pay double the usual fine. Two years later Maryland prohibited interracial marriages:

> forasmuch as divers freeborne English women forgettfull of their free Condicōn and to the disgrace of our Nation doe intermarry with Negro Slaves by which alsoe divers suites may arise touching the Issue of such woemen and a great damage doth befall the Masters of such Negros for prevention whereof for deterring such freeborne women from such shamefull Matches . . . ,

strong language indeed if the problem had only been confusion of status. A Maryland act of 1681 described marriages of white women with Negroes as, among other things, "always to the Satisfaccōn of theire Lascivious and Lustfull desires, & to the disgrace not only of the English butt allso of many other Christian Nations." When Virginia finally prohibited all interracial liaisons in 1691, the assembly vigorously denounced miscegenation and its fruits as "that abominable mixture and spurious issue."

One is confronted, then, with the fact that the first evidences of enslavement and of other forms of debasement appeared at about the same time. Such coincidence comports poorly with both views on the causation of prejudice and slavery. If slavery caused prejudice, then invidious distinctions concerning working in the fields bearing arms, and sexual union should have appeared only after slavery's firm establishment. If prejudice caused slavery, then one would expect to find such lesser discriminations preceding the greater discrimination of outright enslavement.

Perhaps a third explanation of the relationship between slavery and prejudice may be offered, one that might fit the pattern of events as revealed by existing evidence. Both current views share a common starting point: They predicate two factors, prejudice and slavery, and demand a distinct order of causality. No matter how qualified by recognition that the effect may in turn react upon the cause, each approach inevitably tends to deny the validity of its opposite. But what if one were to regard both slavery and prejudice as species of a general debasement of the Negro? Both may have been equally cause and effect, constantly reacting upon each other, dynamically joining hands to hustle the Negro down the road to complete degradation. Mutual causation is, of course, a highly useful concept for describing social situations in the modern world. Indeed it has been widely applied in only slightly altered fashion to the current racial situation: Racial prejudice and the Negro's lowly position are widely accepted as constantly reinforcing each other.

This way of looking at the facts might well fit better with what we know of slavery itself. Slavery was an organized pattern of human relationships. No matter what the law might say, it was of different character than cattle ownership. No matter how degrading, slavery involved human beings. No one seriously pretended otherwise. Slavery was not an isolated economic or institutional phenomenon; it was the practical facet of a general debasement without which slavery could have no rationality. (Prejudice, too, was a form of debasement, a kind of slavery in the mind.) Certainly the urgent need for labor in a virgin country guided the direction which debasement took, molded it, in fact, into an institutional framework. That economic practicalities shaped the external form of debasement should not tempt one to forget, however, that slavery was at bottom a social arrangement, a way of society's ordering its members in its own mind.

The Paradox of Slavery and Freedom

EDMUND S. MORGAN

American historians interested in tracing the rise of liberty, democracy, and the common man have been challenged in the past two decades by other historians, interested in tracing the history of oppression, exploitation, and racism. The challenge has been salutary, because it has made us examine more directly than historians have hitherto been willing to do, the role of slavery in our early history. Colonial historians, in particular, when writing about the origin and development of American institutions have found it possible until recently to deal with slavery as an exception to everything they had to say. I am speaking about myself but also about most of my generation. We owe a debt of gratitude to those who have insisted that slavery was something more than an exception, that one fifth of the American population at the time of the Revolution is too many people to be treated as an exception.

We shall not have met the challenge simply by studying the history of that one fifth, fruitful as such studies may be, urgent as they may be. Nor shall we have met the challenge if we merely execute the familiar maneuver of turning our old interpretations on their heads. The temptation is already apparent to argue that slavery and oppression were the dominant features of American history and that efforts to advance liberty and equality were the exception, indeed no more than a device to divert the masses while their chains were being fastened. To dismiss the rise of liberty and equality in American history as a mere sham is not only to ignore hard facts, it is also to evade the problem presented by those facts. The rise of liberty and equality in this country was accompanied by the rise of slavery. That two such contradictory developments were taking place simultaneously over a long period of our history, from the seventeenth century to the nineteenth, is the central paradox of American history.

The challenge, for a colonial historian at least, is to explain how a people could have developed the dedication to human liberty and dignity exhibited by the leaders of the American Revolution and at the same time have developed and maintained a system of labor that denied human liberty and dignity every hour of the day.

The paradox is evident at many levels if we care to see it. Think, for a moment, of the traditional American insistence on freedom of the seas. "Free ships make free goods" was the cardinal doctrine of American foreign policy in the Revolutionary era. But the goods for which the United States demanded freedom were produced in very large measure by slave labor. The irony is more than semantic. American reliance on slave labor must be viewed in the context of the American struggle for a separate and equal station among the nations of the earth. At the time the colonists announced their claim to that station they had neither the arms nor the ships to make the claim good. They desperately needed the assistance of other countries, especially France, and their single most valuable product with which to purchase assistance was tobacco, produced mainly by slave labor. So largely did

"Slavery and Freedom: The American Paradox," by Edmund S. Morgan. From *Journal of American History,* 59 (1972), 5–29. Reprinted by permission from the Organization of American Historians.

that crop figure in American foreign relations that one historian has referred to the activities of France in supporting the Americans as "King Tobacco Diplomacy," a reminder that the position of the United States in the world depended not only in 1776 but during the span of a long lifetime thereafter on slave labor. To a very large degree it may be said that Americans bought their independence with slave labor.

The paradox is sharpened if we think of the state where most of the tobacco came from. Virginia at the time of the first United States census in 1790 had 40 percent of the slaves in the entire United States. And Virginia produced the most eloquent spokesmen for freedom and equality in the entire United States: George Washington, James Madison, and above all, Thomas Jefferson. They were all slaveholders and remained so throughout their lives. In recent years we have been shown in painful detail the contrast between Jefferson's pronouncements in favor of republican liberty and his complicity in denying the benefits of that liberty to blacks. It has been tempting to dismiss Jefferson and the whole Virginia dynasty as hypocrites. But to do so is to deprive the term "hypocrisy" of useful meaning. If hypocrisy means, as I think it does, deliberately to affirm a principle without believing it, then hypocrisy requires a rare clarity of mind combined with an unscrupulous intention to deceive. To attribute such an intention, even to attribute such clarity of mind in the matter, to Jefferson, Madison, or Washington is once again to evade the challenge. What we need to explain is how such men could have arrived at beliefs and actions so full of contradiction.

Put the challenge another way: how did England, a country priding itself on the liberty of its citizens, produce colonies where most of the inhabitants enjoyed still greater liberty, greater opportunities, greater control over their own lives than most men in the mother country, while the remainder, one fifth of the total, were deprived of virtually all liberty, all opportunities, all control over their own lives? We may admit that the Englishmen who colonized America and their revolutionary descendants were racists, that consciously or unconsciously they believed liberties and rights should be confined to persons of a light complexion. When we have said as much, even when we have probed the depths of racial prejudice, we will not have fully accounted for the paradox. Racism was surely an essential element in it, but I should like to suggest another element, that I believe to have influenced the development of both slavery and freedom as we have known them in the United States. . . .

The story properly begins in England with the burst of population growth there that sent the number of Englishmen from perhaps three million in 1500 to four-and-one-half million by 1650. The increase did not occur in response to any corresponding growth in the capacity of the island's economy to support its people. And the result was precisely that misery which Madison pointed out to Jefferson as the consequence of "a high degree of populousness." Sixteenth-century England knew the same kind of unemployment and poverty that Jefferson witnessed in eighteenth-century France and Fletcher in seventeenth-century Scotland. Alarming numbers of idle and hungry men drifted about the country looking for work or plunder. The government did what it could to make men of means hire them, but it also adopted increasingly severe measures against their wandering, their thieving, their roistering, and indeed their very existence. Whom the workhouses and prisons could not swallow the gallows would have to, or perhaps the army. When England had military expeditions to conduct abroad, every parish packed off its most unwanted inhabitants to the almost certain death that awaited them from the diseases of the camp.

As the mass of idle rogues and beggars grew and increasingly threatened the peace of England, the efforts to cope with them increasingly threatened the liberties of Englishmen. Englishmen prided themselves on a "gentle government," a government that had been releasing its subjects from old forms of bondage and endowing them with new liberties, making the "rights of Englishmen" a phrase to conjure with. But there was nothing gentle about the government's treatment of the poor; and as more Englishmen became poor, other Englishmen had less to be proud of. Thoughtful men could see an obvious solution: get the surplus Englishmen out of England. Send them to the New World, where there were limitless opportunities for work. There they would redeem themselves, enrich the mother country, and spread English liberty abroad. . . .

Virginia from the beginning was conceived not only as a haven for England's suffering poor, but as a spearhead of English liberty in an oppressed world. That was the dream; but when it began to materialize at Roanoke Island in 1585, something went wrong. . . . [T]he English settlers whom Raleigh sent there proved unworthy of the role assigned them. By the time Drake arrived they had shown themselves less than courteous to the Indians on whose assistance they depended. The first group of settlers murdered the chief who befriended them, and then gave up and ran for home aboard Drake's returning ships. The second group simply disappeared, presumably killed by the Indians.

What was lost in this famous lost colony was more than the band of colonists who have never been traced. What was also lost and never quite recovered in subsequent ventures was the dream of Englishman and Indian living side by side in peace and liberty. When the English finally planted a permanent colony at Jamestown they came as conquerors, and their government was far from gentle. The Indians willing to endure it were too few in numbers and too broken in spirit to play a significant part in the settlement.

Without their help, Virginia offered a bleak alternative to the workhouse or the gallows for the first English poor who were transported there. During the first two decades of the colony's existence, most of the arriving immigrants found precious little English liberty in Virginia. But by the 1630s the colony seemed to be working out, at least in part, as its first planners had hoped. Impoverished Englishmen were arriving every year in large numbers, engaged to serve the existing planters for a term of years, with the prospect of setting up their own households a few years later. The settlers were spreading up Virginia's great rivers, carving out plantations, living comfortably from their corn fields and from the cattle they ranged in the forests, and at the same time earning perhaps ten or twelve pounds a year per man from the tobacco they planted. A representative legislative assembly secured the traditional liberties of Englishmen and enabled a larger proportion of the population to participate in their own government than had ever been the case in England. The colony even began to look a little like the cosmopolitan haven of liberty . . . first envisaged. Men of all countries appeared there: French, Spanish, Dutch, Turkish, Portuguese, and African. Virginia took them in and began to make Englishmen out of them.

It seems clear that most of the Africans, perhaps all of them, came as slaves, a status that had become obsolete in England, while it was becoming the expected condition of Africans outside Africa and of a good many inside. It is equally clear that a substantial number of Virginia's Negroes were free or became free. And all of them, whether servant, slave, or free, enjoyed most of the same rights and duties as other Virginians. There is no evidence during the period before 1660 that they were subjected to a more severe discipline than other servants. They could sue and be sued in court. They did penance in the parish church for having illegitimate children. They earned money of their own, bought and sold and raised cattle of their own. Sometimes they bought their own freedom. In other cases, masters bequeathed them not only freedom but land, cattle, and houses. Northampton, the only county for which full records exist, had at least ten free Negro households by 1668.

As Negroes took their place in the community, they learned English ways, including even the truculence toward authority that has always been associated with the rights of Englishmen. Tony Longo, a free Negro of Northampton, when served a warrant to appear as a witness in court, responded with a scatological opinion of warrants, called the man who served it an idle rascal, and told him to go about his business. The man offered to go with him at any time before a justice of the peace so that his evidence could be recorded. He would go with him at night, tomorrow, the next day, next week, any time. But Longo was busy getting in his corn. He dismissed all pleas with a "Well, well, Ile goe when my Corne is in," and refused to receive the warrant.

The judges understandably found this to be contempt of court; but it was the kind of contempt that free Englishmen often showed to authority, and it was combined with a devotion to work that English moralists were doing their best to inculcate more widely in England. As England had absorbed people of every nationality over the centuries and turned them into Englishmen, Virginia's Englishmen were absorbing their own share of foreigners, including Negroes, and seemed to be successfully moulding a New World community on the English model.

But a closer look will show that the situation was not quite so promising as at first it seems. It is well known that Virginia in its first fifteen or twenty years killed off most of the men who went there. It is less well known that it continued to do so. If my estimate of the volume of immigration is anywhere near correct, Virginia must have been a death trap for at least another fifteen years and probably for twenty or twenty-five. In 1625 the population stood at 1,300 or 1,400; in 1640 it was about 8,000. In the fifteen years between those dates at least 15,000 persons must have come to the colony. If so, 15,000 immigrants increased the population by less than 7,000. There is no evidence of a large return migration. It seems probable that the death rate throughout this period was comparable only to that found in Europe during the peak years of a plague. Virginia, in other words, was absorbing England's surplus laborers mainly by killing them. The success of those who survived and rose from servant to planter must be attributed partly to the fact that so few did survive.

After 1640, when the diseases responsible for the high death rate began to decline and the population began a quick rise, it became increasingly difficult for an indigent immigrant to pull himself up in the world. The population probably passed 25,000 by 1662, hardly what Madison would have called a high degree of populousness. Yet the rapid rise brought serious trouble for Virginia. It brought the engrossment of tidewater land in thousands and tens of thousands of acres by speculators, who recognized that the demand would rise. It brought a huge expansion of tobacco production, which helped to depress the price of tobacco and the earnings of the men who planted it. It brought efforts by planters to prolong the terms of servants, since they were now living longer and therefore had a longer expectancy of usefulness.

It would, in fact, be difficult to assess all the consequences of the increased longevity; but for our purposes one development was crucial, and that was the appearance in Virginia of a growing number of freemen who had served their terms but who were now unable to afford land of their own except on the frontiers or in the interior. In years when tobacco prices were especially low or crops especially poor, men who had been just scraping by were obliged to go back to work for their larger neighbors simply in order to stay alive. By 1676 it was estimated that one fourth of Virginia's freemen were without land of their own. And in the same year Francis Moryson, a member of the governor's council, explained the term "freedmen" as used in Virginia to mean "persons without house and land," implying that this was now the normal condition of servants who had attained freedom.

Some of them resigned themselves to working for wages; others preferred a meager living on dangerous frontier land or a hand-to-mouth existence, roaming from one county to another, renting a bit of land here, squatting on some there, dodging the tax collector, drinking, quarreling, stealing hogs, and enticing servants to run away with them.

The presence of this growing class of poverty-stricken Virginians was not a little frightening to the planters who had made it to the top or who had arrived in the colony already at the top, with ample supplies of servants and capital. They were caught in a dilemma. They wanted the immigrants who kept pouring in every year. Indeed they needed them and prized them the more as they lived longer. But as more and more turned free each year, Virginia seemed to have inherited the problem that she was helping England to solve. Virginia, complained Nicholas Spencer, secretary of the colony, was "a sinke to drayen England of her filth and scum."

The men who worried the uppercrust looked even more dangerous in Virginia than they had in England. They were, to begin with, young, because it was young persons that the planters wanted for work in the fields; and the young have always seemed impatient of control by their elders and superiors, if not downright rebellious. They were also predominantly single men. Because the planters did not think women, or at least English women, fit for work in the fields, men outnumbered women among immigrants by three or four to one throughout the century. Consequently most of the freedmen had no wife or family to tame their wilder impulses and serve as hostages to the respectable world.

Finally, what made these wild young men particularly dangerous was that they were armed and had to be armed. Life in Virginia required guns. The plantations were exposed to attack from Indians by land and from privateers and petty-thieving pirates by sea. Whenever England was at war with the French or the Dutch, the settlers had to be ready to defend themselves. In 1667 the Dutch in a single raid captured twenty merchant ships in the James River, together with the English warship that was supposed to be defending them; and in 1673 they captured eleven more. On these occasions Governor William Berkeley gathered the planters in arms and at least prevented the enemy from making a landing. But while he stood off the Dutch he worried about the ragged crew at his back. Of the able-bodied men in the colony he estimated that "at least one third are Single freedmen (whose Labour will hardly maintaine them) or men much in debt, both which wee may reasonably expect upon any Small advantage the Enemy may gaine upon us, wold revolt to them in hopes of bettering their Condicion by Shareing the Plunder of the Country with them."

Berkeley's fears were justified. Three years later, sparked not by a Dutch invasion but by an Indian attack, rebellion swept Virginia. It began almost as Berkeley had predicted, when a group of volunteer Indian fighters turned from a fruitless expedition against the Indians to attack their rulers. Bacon's Rebellion was the largest popular rising in the colonies before the American Revolution. Sooner or later nearly everyone in Virginia got in on it, but it began in the frontier counties of Henrico and New Kent, among men whom the governor and his friends consistently characterized as rabble. As it spread eastward, it turned out that there were rabble everywhere, and Berkeley understandably raised his estimate of their numbers. "How miserable that man is," he exclaimed, "that Governes a People wher six parts of seaven at least are Poore Endebted Discontented and Armed."

Virginia's poor had reason to be envious and angry against the men who owned the land and imported the servants and ran the government. But the rebellion produced no real program of reform, no ideology, not even any revolutionary slogans. It was a search for plunder, not for principles. And when the rebels had redistributed whatever wealth they could lay their hands on, the rebellion subsided almost as quickly as it had begun.

It had been a shattering experience, however, for Virginia's first families. They had seen each other fall in with the rebels in order to save their skins or their possessions or even to share in the plunder. When it was over, they eyed one another distrustfully, on the lookout for any new Bacons in their midst, who might be tempted to lead the still restive rabble on more plundering expeditions. When William Byrd and Laurence Smith proposed to solve the problems of defense against the Indians by establishing semi-independent buffer settlements on the upper reaches of the rivers, in each of which they would engage to keep fifty men in arms, the assembly at first reacted favorably. But it quickly occurred to the governor and council that this would in fact mean gathering a crowd of Virginia's wild bachelors and furnishing them with an abundant supply of arms and ammunition. Byrd had himself led such a crowd in at least one plundering foray during the rebellion. To put him or anyone else in charge of a large and permanent gang of armed men was to invite them to descend again on the people whom they were supposed to be protecting.

The nervousness of those who had property worth plundering continued throughout the century, spurred in 1682 by the tobacco-cutting riots in which men roved about destroying crops in the fields, in the desperate hope of producing a shortage that would raise the price of the leaf. And periodically in nearby Maryland and North Carolina, where the same conditions existed as in Virginia, there were tumults that threatened to spread to Virginia.

As Virginia thus acquired a social problem analagous to England's own, the colony began to deal with it as England had done, by restricting the liberties of those who did not have the proper badge of freedom, namely the property that government was supposed to protect. One way was to extend the terms of service for servants entering the colony without indentures. Formerly they had served until twenty-one; now the age was advanced to twenty-four. There had always been laws requiring them to serve extra time for running away; now the laws added corporal punishment and, in order to make habitual offenders more readily recognizable, specified that their hair be cropped. New laws restricted the movement of servants on the highways and also increased the amount of extra time to be served for running away. In addition to serving two days for every day's absence, the captured runaway was now frequently required to compensate by labor for the loss to the crop that he had failed to tend and for the cost of his apprehension, including rewards paid for his capture. A three weeks' holiday might result in a year's extra service. If a servant struck his master, he was to serve another year. For killing a hog he had to serve the owner a year and the informer another year. Since the owner of the hog, and the owner of the servant, and the informer were frequently the same man, and since a hog was worth at best less than one tenth the hire of a servant for a year, the law was very profitable to masters. One Lancaster master was awarded six years extra service from a servant who killed three of his hogs, worth about thirty shillings.

The effect of these measures was to keep servants for as long as possible from gaining their freedom, especially the kind of servants who were most likely to cause trouble. At the same time the engrossment of land was driving many back to servitude after a brief taste of freedom. Freedmen who engaged to work for wages by so doing became servants again, subject to most of the same restrictions as other servants.

Nevertheless, in spite of all the legal and economic pressures to keep men in service, the ranks of the freedmen grew, and so did poverty and discontent. To prevent the wild bachelors from gaining an influence in the government, the assembly in 1670 limited voting to landholders and householders. But to disfranchise the growing mass of single freemen was not to deprive them of the weapons they had wielded so effectively under Nathaniel Bacon. It is questionable how far Virginia could safely have continued along this course, meeting discontent with repression and manning her plantations with annual importations of servants who would later add to the unruly ranks of the free. To be sure, the men at the bottom might have had both land and liberty, as the settlers of some other colonies did, if Virginia's frontier had been safe for Indians, or if the men at the top had been willing to forego some of their profits and to give up some of the lands they had engrossed. The English government itself made efforts to break up the great holdings that had helped to create the problem. But it is unlikely that the policy makers in Whitehall would have contended long against the successful.

In any case they did not have to. There was another solution, which allowed Virginia's magnates to keep their lands, yet arrested the discontent and the repression of other Englishmen, a solution which strengthened the rights of Englishmen and nourished that attachment to liberty which came to fruition in the Revolutionary generation of Virginia statesmen. But the solution put an end to the process of turning Africans into Englishmen. The rights of Englishmen were preserved by destroying the rights of Africans.

I do not mean to argue that Virginians deliberately turned to African Negro slavery as a means of preserving and extending the rights of Englishmen. Winthrop Jordan has suggested that slavery came to Virginia as an unthinking decision. We might go further and say that it came without a decision. It came automatically as Virginians bought the cheapest labor they could get. Once Virginia's heavy mortality ceased, an investment in slave labor was much more profitable than an investment in free labor; and the planters bought slaves as rapidly as traders made them available. In the last years of the seventeenth century they bought them in such numbers that slaves probably already constituted a majority or nearly a majority of the labor force by 1700. The demand was so great that traders for a time found a better market in Virginia than in Jamaica or Barbados. But the social benefits of an enslaved labor force, even if not consciously sought or recognized at the time by the men who bought the slaves, were larger than the economic benefits. The increase in the importation of slaves was matched by a decrease in the importation of indentured servants and consequently a decrease in the dangerous number of new freedmen who annually emerged seeking a place in society that they would be unable to achieve.

If Africans had been unavailable, it would probably have proved impossible to devise a way to keep a continuing supply of English immigrants in their place. There was a limit beyond which the abridgement of English liberties would have resulted not merely in rebellion but in protests from England and in the cutting off of the supply of further servants. At the time of Bacon's Rebellion the English commission of investigation had shown more sympathy with the rebels than with the well-to-do planters who had engrossed Virginia's lands. To have attempted the enslavement of English-born laborers would have caused more disorder than it cured. But to keep as slaves black men who arrived in that condition *was* possible and apparently regarded as plain common sense.

The attitude of English officials was well expressed by the attorney who reviewed for the Privy Council the slave codes established in Barbados in 1679. He found the laws of Barbados to be well designed for the good of his majesty's subjects there, for, he said, "although Negros in that Island are punishable in a different and more severe manner than other Subjects are for Offences of the like nature; yet I humbly conceive that the Laws there concerning Negroes are reasonable Laws, for by reason of their numbers they become dangerous, and being a brutish sort of People and reckoned as goods and chattels in that Island, it is of necessity or at least convenient to have Laws for the Government of them different from the Laws of England, to prevent the great mischief that otherwise may happen to the Planters and Inhabitants in that Island." In Virginia too it seemed convenient and reasonable to have different laws for black and white. As the number of slaves increased, the assembly passed laws that carried forward with much greater severity the trend already under way in the colony's labor laws. But the new severity was reserved for people without white skin. The laws specifically exonerated the master who accidentally beat his slave to death, but they placed new limitations on his punishment of "Christian white servants."

Virginians worried about the risk of having in their midst a body of men who had every reason to hate them. The fear of a slave insurrection hung over them for nearly two centuries. But the danger from slaves actually proved to be less than that which the colony had faced from its restive and armed freedmen. Slaves had none of the rising expectations that so often produce human discontent. No one had told them that they had rights. They had been nurtured in heathen societies where they had lost their freedom; their children would be nurtured in a Christian society and never know freedom.

Moreover, slaves were less troubled by the sexual imbalance that helped to make Virginia's free laborers so restless. In an enslaved labor force women could be required to make tobacco just as the men did; and they also made children, who in a few years would be an asset to their master. From the beginning, therefore, traders imported women in a much higher ratio to men than was the case among English servants, and the level of discontent was correspondingly reduced. Virginians did not doubt that discontent would remain, but it could be repressed by methods that would not have been considered reasonable, convenient, or even safe, if applied to Englishmen. Slaves could be deprived of opportunities for association and rebellion. They could be kept unarmed and unorganized. They could be subjected to savage punishments by their owners without fear of legal reprisals. And since their color disclosed their probable status, the rest of society could keep close watch on them. It is scarcely surprising that no slave insurrection in American history approached Bacon's Rebellion in its extent or in its success.

Nor is it surprising that Virginia's freedmen never again posed a threat to society. Though in later years slavery was condemned because it was thought to compete with free labor, in the beginning it reduced by so much the number of freedmen who would otherwise have competed with each other. When the annual increment of freedmen fell off, the number that remained could more easily find an independent place in society, especially as the danger of Indian attack diminished and made settlement safer at the heads of the rivers or on the Carolina frontier. There might still remain a number of irredeemable, idle, and unruly freedmen, particularly among the convicts whom England exported to the colonies. But the numbers were small enough, so that they could be dealt with by the old expedient of drafting them for military expeditions. The way was thus made easier for the remaining freedmen to acquire property, maybe acquire a slave or two of their own, and join with their superiors in the enjoyment of those English liberties that differentiated them from their black laborers.

A free society divided between large landholders and small was much less riven by antagonisms than one divided between landholders and landless, masterless men. With the freedman's expectations, sobriety, and status restored, he was no longer a man to be feared. That fact, together with the presence of a growing mass of alien slaves, tended to draw the white settlers closer together and to reduce the importance of the class difference between yeoman farmer and large plantation owner.

The seventeenth century has sometimes been thought of as the day of the yeoman farmer in Virginia; but in many ways a stronger case can be made for the eighteenth century as the time when the yeoman farmer came into his own, because slavery relieved the small man of the pressures that had been reducing him to continued servitude. Such an interpretation conforms to the political development of the colony. During the seventeenth century the royally appointed governor's council, composed of the largest property-owners in the colony, had been the most powerful governing body. But as the tide of slavery rose between 1680 and 1720 Virginia moved toward a government in which the yeoman farmer had a larger share. In spite of the rise of Virginia's great families on the black tide, the power of the council declined; and the elective House of Burgesses became the dominant organ of government. Its members nurtured a closer relationship with their yeoman constituency than had earlier been the case. And in its chambers Virginians developed the ideas they so fervently asserted in the Revolution: ideas about taxation, representation, and the rights of Englishmen, and ideas about the prerogatives and powers and sacred calling of the independent, property-holding yeoman farmer—commonwealth ideas.

In the eighteenth century, because they were no longer threatened by a dangerous free laboring class, Virginians could afford these ideas, whereas in Berkeley's time they could not. Berkeley himself was obsessed with the experience of the English civil wars and the danger of rebellion. He despised and feared the New Englanders for their association with the Puritans who had made England, however briefly, a commonwealth. He was proud that Virginia, unlike New England, had no free schools and no printing press, because books and schools bred heresy and sedition. He must have taken satisfaction in the fact that when his people did rebel against him under Bacon, they generated no republican ideas, no philosophy of rebellion or of human rights. Yet a century later, without benefit of rebellions, Virginians had learned republican lessons, had introduced schools and printing presses, and were as ready as New Englanders to recite the aphorisms of the commonwealthmen.

It was slavery, I suggest, more than any other single factor, that had made the difference, slavery that enabled Virginia to nourish representative government in a plantation society, slavery that transformed the Virginia of Governor Berkeley to the Virginia of Jefferson, slavery that made the Virginians dare to speak a political language that magnified the rights of freemen, and slavery, therefore, that brought Virginians into the same commonwealth political tradition with New Englanders. The very institution that was to divide North and South after the Revolution may have made possible their union in a republican government.

Thus began the American paradox of slavery and freedom, intertwined and interdependent, the rights of Englishmen supported on the wrongs of Africans. The American Revolution only made the contradictions more glaring, as the slaveholding colonists proclaimed to a candid world the rights not simply of Englishmen but of all men. To explain the origin of the contradictions, if the explanation I have suggested is valid, does not eliminate them or make them less ugly. But it may enable us to understand a little better the strength of the ties that bound freedom to slavery, even in so noble a mind as Jefferson's. And it may perhaps make us wonder about the ties that bind more devious tyrannies to our own freedoms and give us still today our own American paradox.

 F U R T H E R   R E A D I N G

Warren M. Billings, "The Law of Servant and Slaves in Seventeenth-Century Virginia," *Virginia Magazine of History and Biography*, 99 (1991), 45–62.

Warren M. Billings, "The Cases of Fernando and Elizabeth Key: A Note on the Status of Blacks in the Seventeenth Century," William and Mary Quarterly, 3rd ser. 30 (1973). 467–74.

T. H. Breen and Stephen Innes, *Myne Owne Ground: Race and Freedom on Virginia's Eastern Shore, 1640–1676* (1980).

Kathleen M. Brown, *Good Wives, Nasty Wenches, and Anxious Patriarchs: Gender, Race, and Power in Colonial Virginia* (1996).

J. Douglas Deal, *Race and Class in Colonial Virginia: Indians, Englishmen, and Africans on the Eastern Shore During the Seventeenth Century* (1993).

Barbara Jeane Fields, "Slavery, Race, and Ideology in the United States of America," *New Left Review,* 181 (Spring 1990), 95–118.

David Theo Goldberg, ed., *Anatomy of Racism* (1990).

A. Leon Higginbotham, Jr., *In the Matter of Color: Race and the American Legal Process: The Colonial Period* (1978).

Martha Hodes, *White Women, Black Men: Illicit Sex in the Nineteenth Century South* (1997).

Winthrop D. Jordan, *The White Man's Burden: Historical Origins of Racism in the United States* (1974).

Duncan J. MacLeod, *Slavery, Race and the American Revolution* (1974).

Russell Menard, "From Servants to Slaves," *Southern Studies,* Winter, vol. 16, no. 4 (1977), 355–390.

Edmund S. Morgan, *American Slavery, American Freedom: The Ordeal of Colonial Virginia* (1975).

Thomas D. Morris, *Southern Slavery and the Law, 1619–1860* (1996).

Carole Shammas, "Black Women's Work and the Evolution of Plantation Society in Virginia," *Labor History,* 26 (1985), 5–28.

Alden T. Vaughan, "The Origins Debate: Slavery and Racism in Seventeenth-Century Virginia," *Virginia Magazine of History and Biography,* 97 (1989), 311–354.

William M. Wiecek, "The Statutory Law of Slavery and Race in the Thirteen Mainland Colonies of British America," *William and Mary Quarterly,* 3rd series 34 (1977), 258–280.

Betty Wood, *The Origins of American Slavery: Freedom and Bondage in the English Colonies* (1997).

Peter H. Wood, *Black Majority: Negroes in Colonial South Carolina from 1670 Through the Stono Rebellion* (1974).

Peter H. Wood, *Strange New Land: African Americans, 1617–1776* (1996).

The Origins of African America and the Continuity of African Culture

Ever since the debate between Melville Herskovits and E. Franklin Frazier, scholars have sought appropriate ways of characterizing the relationship between African and African-American culture. Did the Middle Passage and slavery obliterate the cultural heritage of the African captives, as Frazier contended? Or did some cultural traits survive in the New World, as Herskovits claimed? Although few contemporary historians would take either side of that stark dichotomy, the debate lingers on in efforts to characterize and account for culturally influenced practices such as the slaves' family life, personality, religion, and resistance.

As with most such dichotomies the opposition may be a false one. As Herskovits himself observed, some cultural traits were better able to survive the harsh slave regime than others. For example, song, dance, and religion did not require the material resources, the careful apprenticeship in skills, or the master's consent to the same extent as would the decorative arts, artisanry or marriage rites. But even the cultural traits most subject to pressure and change might be "reinterpreted" so that African cultural values and practices reemerged in new American forms—among whites as well as blacks. For example, Catholic saints could become associated with African deities and Christian baptism with African river spirits.

More important still, other historians have argued, the concept of culture itself must not be imagined as a fixed trait or characteristic to be passed unchanged from one generation to the next. All living cultures are influenced by social and historical developments; change and adaptation is part of their very nature. The necessity for change and adaptation was especially pertinent for the ethnically diverse African population in America. Coming from sometimes strikingly different cultures, Africans began the process of cultural change and creativity on board the slave ships and continued that process throughout the three centuries of North American slavery. Most pressing of all were the need to fashion a language that made slaves intelligible to each other as well as to their masters, and the need to fashion a religion that made the harsh new world of slavery intelligible to themselves. In these processes, perhaps, change and continuity were but two sides of the same coin.

DOCUMENTS

In the first document Olaudah Equiano, traded from one ethnic group to another along his journey to the West African coast, describes the cultural diversity of West Africa that he witnesses. The second document consists of five advertisements placed in Virginia newspapers to retrieve runaway slaves. Their meticulous descriptions inadvertently reveal the cultural diversity of the eighteenth-century slave population in physical appearance, language skills, and general knowledge and acculturation. The ads also expose, almost casually, the brutality of slavery. In the third document, Dr. Francis Le Jau describes his cautious efforts to convert slaves to Anglicanism. Notably, he requires that they obtain their master's consent, and he is reticent to entrust them with literacy skills, all of which apparently limits the effectiveness of these early conversion attempts. Although not challenging slavery directly, English evangelist George Whitefield is much less circumspect, as the fourth document reveals. Preaching to thousands at a time, he welcomes slaves and free blacks into his fold and makes the education of orphaned black children his special project. The fifth and sixth documents reveal something of Whitefield's influence on American blacks. The celebrated black poet Phyllis Wheatley pays homage to Whitefield's labors on behalf of her people, and John Marrant, a free black, describes his conversion by Whitefield. Landon Carter's diary entries, the seventh document, show the anxieties as well as the derision of a slaveholder at the conversion of his slaves and fellow slaveowners. Two letters from black converts during the first post–Revolutionary War decade show the steady institutionalization of the Baptist faith among American blacks. The final document is a twentieth-century photograph of a grave in Mt. Olivet Cemetery in Washington, D.C. Although Mt. Olivet was a white cemetery when this photo was taken, the white shells decorating the mound reflect an African style of burial and, possibly, the continuity of African influences in American culture.

1. Olaudah Equiano, an Ibo, Discovers the Cultural Diversity of West Africa, 1789

. . . I was again sold, and carried through a number of places, till, after travelling a considerable time, I came to a town called Tinmah, in the most beautiful country I had yet seen in Africa. It was extremely rich, and there were many rivulets which flowed through it; and supplied a large pond in the center of the town, where the people washed. Here I first saw and tasted cocoa nuts, which I thought superior to any nuts I had ever tasted before; and the trees, which were loaded, were also interspersed amongst the houses, which had commodious shades adjoining, and were in the same manner as ours, the insides being neatly plastered and whitewashed. Here I also saw and tasted for the first time sugar-cane. Their money consisted of little white shells, the size of the finger nail: they are known in this country by the name of *core* [cowries]. I was sold here for one hundred and seventy-two of them by a merchant who lived and brought me there. I had been about two or three days at his house, when a wealthy widow, a neighbour of his, came there one evening and brought with her an only son, a young gentleman about my own age and size. Here they saw me; and, having taken a fancy to me, I was bought of the merchant, and

---

The Interesting Narrative of Olaudah Equiano, or Gustavus Vassa, the African (2 vols., London, 1789), 1:52–54.

went home with them. Her house and premises were situated close to one of those rivulets I have mentioned, and were the finest I ever saw in Africa: they were very extensive, and she had a number of slaves to attend her. The next day I was washed and perfumed, and when meal-time came, I was led into the presence of my mistress, and ate and drank before her with her son. This filled me with astonishment: and I could scarce help expressing my surprise that the young gentleman should suffer me, who was bound, to eat with him who was free; and not only so, but that he would not at any time either eat or drink till I had taken first, because I was the eldest, which was agreeable to our custom. Indeed every thing here, and all their treatment of me, made me forget that I was a slave. The language of these people resembled ours so nearly, that we understood each other perfectly. They had also the very same customs as we. There were likewise slaves daily to attend us, while my young master and I, with other boys, sported with our darts and bows and arrows, as I had been used to do at home. In this resemblance to my former happy state I passed about two months, and I now began to think I was to be adopted into the family, and was beginning to be reconciled to my situation, and to forget by degrees my misfortunes, when all at once the delusion vanished; for, without the least previous knowledge, one morning early, while my dear master and companion was still asleep, I was awakened out of my reverie to fresh sorrow, and hurried away even amongst the uncircumcised.

Thus, at the very moment I dreamed of the greatest happiness, I found myself most miserable: and it seemed as if fortune wished to give me this taste of joy only to render the reverse more poignant. The change I now experienced was as painful as it was sudden and unexpected. It was a change indeed from a state of bliss to a scene which is inexpressible by me, as it discovered to me an element I had never before beheld, and till then had no idea of, and wherein such instances of hardship and cruelty continually occurred as I can never reflect on but with horror.

All the nations and people I had hitherto passed through resembled our own in their manners, customs and language: but I came at length to a country, the inhabitants of which differed from us in all those particulars. I was very much struck with this difference, especially when I came among a people who did not circumcise, and eat without washing their hands. They cooked also in iron pots, and had European cutlasses and cross bows, which were unknown to us, and fought with their fists amongst themselves. Their women were not so modest as ours, for they eat, and drank, and slept with their men. But, above all, I was amazed to see no sacrifices or offerings among them. In some of those places the people ornamented themselves with scars, and likewise filed their teeth very sharp. They wanted sometimes to ornament me in the same manner, but I would not suffer them; hoping that I might some time be among a people who did not thus disfigure themselves, as I thought they did. At last, I came to the banks of a large river, which was covered with canoes, in which the people appeared to live with their household utensils and provisions of all kinds. I was beyond measure astonished at this, as I had never before seen any water larger than a pond or a rivulet; and my surprise was mingled with no small fear when I was put into one of these canoes, and we began to paddle and move along the river. We continued going on thus till night; and when we came to land, and made fires on the banks, each family by themselves, some dragged their canoes on shore, others staid and cooked in theirs, and laid in them all night.

Those on the land had mats, of which they made tents, some in the shape of little houses: In these we slept; and after the morning meal we embarked again, and proceeded as before. I was often very much astonished to see some of the women, as well as the men, jump into the water, dive to the bottom, come up again, and swim about. Thus I continued to travel, sometimes by land, sometimes by water, through different countries, and various nations, till, at the end of six or seven months after I had been kidnapped, I arrived at the sea coast. . . .

2. Six Advertisements for Virginia Slave Runaways, 1736, 1767

Virginia Gazette (Parks), October 29 to November 5, 1736.

RAN away Two Negro Men Slaves; One of them called Poplar, from my House in King William County, some Time in June last; He is a lusty well-set likely Fellow, of a middle Stature, upwards of 30 Years old, and talks pretty good English: The other called Planter, from my Plantation in Roy's Neck, in the County of King and Queen, about the Month of August following. He is a young Angola Negro, very black, and his Lips are remarkably red. He is supposed to be in Company with an old Negroe Fellow belonging to Col. Corbin, of a yellowish Hue, his Hair is like a Madagascar's, and to be gone towards Spotsylvania. Whoever brings the said Negroes, or either of them to my House aforesaid, shall be paid a Pistole Reward for each: Or if already apprehended, any Person giving Notice thereof, so as they, or either of them, may be had again, shall be reasonably rewarded by

Benjamin Needler.

N.B. the Negroe Poplar is Outlaw'd.

Virginia Gazette (Purdie & Dixon), April 16, 1767.

RUN AWAY from the subscriber in Norfolk, about the 20th of October last, two young Negro fellows, viz. WILL, about 5 feet 8 inches high, middling black, well made, is an outlandish fellow, and when he is surprized the white of his eyes turns red; I bought him of Mr. Moss, about 8 miles below York, and imagine he is gone that way, or some where between York and Williamsburg. PETER, about 5 feet 9 inches high, a very black slim fellow, has a wife at Little Town, and a father at Mr. Philip Burt's quarter, near the half-way house between Williamsburg and York; he formerly belonged to Parson Fontaine, and I bought him of Doctor James Carter. They are both outlawed; and TEN POUNDS a piece offered to any person that will kill the said Negroes, and bring me their heads, or THIRTY SHILLINGS for each if bought home alive.

JOHN BROWN.

Lathan A. Windley, comp., *Runaway Slave Advertisements: A Documentary History from the 1730s to 1790* (Westport, Conn.: Greenwood Press, 1983), 1:50, 56. Copyright © 1983 by Flossie E. Windley.

Virginia Gazette (Purdie & Dixon), May 7, 1767.

KING WILLIAM, April 29, 1767.

RUN away from the subscriber, on Monday the 20th of this Instant, a Mulatto slave, named DAVID GRATENREAD; he is an arch fellow, very well known by most people, plays the fiddle extremely well, has a wide mouth, a little piece bit out of one of his ears, has a large bump upon one of his shins, about 37 years of age, 5 feet 6 or 7 inches high, and may perhaps change his name, and pretend to pass as a free man; he carried with him a new brown cloth waistcoat, lappelled, lined with white taminy, and yellow gilt buttons, a new pair of buckskin breeches, gold laced hat, a fine Holland shirt, brown cut wig, and several old clothes that I cannot remember, except an old lappelled kersey waistcoat. I believe he has carried his fiddle with him. He may endeavour to get on board some vessel, and make his escape out of the colony; I therefore forewarn all masters of vessels, or others, from harbouring him. Whoever apprehends the said runaway, and brings him to me, or commit him to any goal, so that I get him again, shall have FIVE POUNDS reward if taken in this colony, if out thereof TEN POUNDS.

RICHARD KING.

Virginia Gazette (Purdie & Dixon), December 17, 1767.

RUN away from the subscriber, a Mulatto fellow named AARON, about 5 feet 10 inches high, about 19 years old, and marked on each cheek IR. Whoever brings the said fellow to the subscriber, in Chesterfield, shall have Forty Shillings reward, besides what the law allows.

HENRY RANDOLPH.

Virginia Gazette (Purdie & Dixon), January 28, 1768.

NORTHHAMPTON, Dec. 14, 1767.

RUN away from the subscriber, a very white Mulatto wench, named ANNAS. She is thick, well made, about 5 feet high, and had on when she went away a country cloth jacket, black with white stripes, branded on the right cheek E, and on the left R, but cannot be discerned except near to her; and observing her nicely there are several cuts on the back part of her neck, and a scar upon her left side. I expect she will try to get on board some vessel, therefore forewarn all Captains from receiving her on board. Whoever takes her up, and brings her to me in Northampton county, shall have Forty Shillings reward, besides what the law allows.

EDWARD RUTLAND.

Virginia Gazette (Purdie & Dixon), October 1, 1767.

RUN AWAY from the subscriber, the 22nd of this instant, three slaves, viz. JUPITER, alias GIBB, a Negro fellow, about 35 years of age, about 6 feet high, knock kneed, flat footed, the right knee bent in more than the left, has several scars on his back from a severe whipping he lately had at Sussex court-house, having been tried there for stirring up the Negroes to an insurrection, being a great

Newlight preacher. ROBIN, about 25 years of age, a stout fellow, about 6 feet high, has a film over one of his eyes, a sore on one of his shins, and is brother to Gibb. DINAH, an old wench, very large, near 6 feet high; she has a remarkable stump of a thumb, occasioned by a whitlow, by which the bones of the first joint came out, and is mother to the two fellows. They carried with them a variety of clothes, among the rest an old blue duffil great coat, one bearskin do, a scarlet jacket, and a fine new linen shirt. It is supposed they will endeavour to make their escape to the Southward. Whoever takes up, and conveys to me the above slaves, shall have a reward of 50 s. for each of the fellows and 20 s. for the wench, if taken in Virginia; if in any other government, 5 1. for each of the fellows, and 40 s. for the wench, paid by

GEORGE NOBLE.

3. Early Slave Conversion Attempts of Francis Le Jau, an Anglican Minister, 1706–1717

. . . As for the Spiritual State of my Parish this is the Account I can give of it for the present.

The extent of it is 20 Miles in length, and from 7 to 14 in breadth. Number of families 80, of the Church of England. Dissenting families 7, if so many, I find but 4 very strict. Baptised this half year past a Marryed Woman and 17 Children. Actual Communicants in all about 50: Constant Communicants every two Months near 30, among whom are two Negroes.

Since I came I baptised in all 2 Adults & 47 Children. Our Congregation is generally of about 100 Persons, sometimes more, several that were inclinable to some of the dissenting partys shew themselves pritty constant among us, and I do what possible to edify them and give them satisfaction in their doubts. On Sunday next I design God willing to baptise two very sensible and honest Negro Men whom I have kept upon tryal these two Years. Several others have spoken to me also; I do nothing too hastily in that respect. I instruct them and must have the consent of their Masters with a good Testimony and proof of their honest life and sober Conversation: Some Masters in my parish are very well satisfyed with my Proceedings in that respect: others do not seem to be so; yet they have given over opposing my design openly; it is to be hoped the good Example of the one will have an influence over the others. I must do the Justice to my Parishioners that tho' many Young Gentlemen are Masters of Great Estates, they and almost all the heads of all our Neighbouring families are an Example of Sobriety, honest & Zeal for the Service of the Church to all the province.

To remove all pretence from the Adult Slaves I shall baptise of their being free upon that Account, I have thought fit to require first their consent to this following declaration *You declare in the Presence of God and before this Congregation that you do not ask for the holy baptism out of any design to ffree yourself from the Duty and Obedience you owe to your Master while you live, but merely for the good of Your Soul and to partake of the Graces and Blessings promised to the Members of the Church of Jesus Christ.* One of the most Scandalous and common Crimes of

From Francis Le Jau, *The Carolina Chronicles of Dr. Francis Le Jau, 1706–1717*, ed. Frank V. Klingberg (reprint; Berkeley: University of California Press, 1956), 60–61, 70, 102.

our Slaves is their perpetual Changing of Wives and husbands, which occasions great disorders: I also tell them whom I baptise, *The Christian Religion does not allow plurality of Wives, nor any changing of them: You promise truly to keep to the Wife you now have till Death dos part you.* I[t] has been Customary among them to have their ffeasts, dances, and merry Meetings upon the Lord's day, that practice is pretty well over in this Parish, but not absolutely: I tell them that present themselves to be admitted to Baptism, they must promise they'l spend no more the Lord's day in idleness, and if they do I'l cut them off from the Comunion.

These I most humbly Submit to the judgment of my Superiors whose Commands and instructions I will follow while I live: I see with an incredible joy the fervor of several of those poor Slaves. Our free Indians our Neighbours come to see me, I admire the sense they have of Justice, and their patience; they have no Ambition; as for their sense of God, their Notions are obscure indeed, but when we take pains to Converse with them, in a jargon they are able to understand: We perceive their Souls are fit Materials which may be easily polish't, they agree with me about the duty of praying, & doing the good & eschewing the evil. The late Colonel Moore and our present Governor have in a great measure put a Stop to their perpetual murdering one another which some of them cannot to this day conceive to be evil. Some of them to whom the Devil has formerly appeared, as they coldly declared to myself, say that evil Spirit never incites them to any thing more than hatred, revenge, and Murder of those that offend them.

I am told still that if anything opposes the publishing of the Gospel among the Indians it shall be the manner how our Indian Trade is carryed on, chiefly the fomenting of War among them for our people to get Slaves. I am so told in general but know no particulars; but it is too true interest has a great power here and dos occasion injustices too visibly to my great sorrow, and thro' misfortune I see no remedy but to be patient and pray and labour as much as I am able in the place I am sent to.

. . . We want a Schoolmaster in my parish for our White peoples Children but as for the Negroes or Indians with all submission I wou'd desire that such a thing shou'd be taken into Consideration as the importance of the matter and the Consequences wch. may follow do deserve. The best Scholar of all the Negroes in my Parish and a very sober and honest Liver, thro' his Learning was like to Create some Confusion among all the Negroes in this Country; he had a Book wherein he read some description of the several judgmts. that Chastise Men because of their Sins in these latter days, that description made an Impression upon his Spirit, and he told his Master abruptly there wou'd be a dismal time and the Moon wou'd be turned into Blood, and there wou'd be dearth of darkness and went away: When I heard of that I sent for the Negroe who ingeniously told me he had read so in a Book; I advised him and Charged him not to speak so, which he promised to me but yet wou'd never shew me the Book; but when he spoke those few Words to his Master, some Negroe overheard a part, and it was publickly blazed abroad that an Angel came and spake to the Man, he had seen a hand that gave him a Book, he had heard Voices, seen fires &c. As I had opportunities I took care to undeceive those who asked me about it; now it is over. I fear that these Men have not judgment enough to make good use of their Learning; and I have thought most convenient not to urge too far that Indians and Negroes shou'd be indifferently admitted to learn to read, but I leave it to the discretion of their Masters whom I exhort to examine well their Inclinations. I have often observed and lately hear that it had been better if persons of a Melancholy Constitution or those that run into the Search after Curious matter had never seen a Book: pardon me if I disclose my thoughts wth too much freedome. . . .

. . . A few days ago I heard of some strange reasoning of my Neighbours. what, sd a Lady Considerable enough in any other respect but in that of sound knowledge; Is it Possible that any of my slaves could go to Heaven, & must I see them there ? a young Gent had sd sometime before that he is resolved never to come to the Holy Table while slaves are Recd there. I really believe they speak so unwisely through Ignorance, and will fail to take proper opportunities to Instruct 'em—there are two poor Negroe Slaves born & brought up among the Portuguese that are very desirous to Abjure the popish heresy's and be Recd. to the Communion among us. I have kept 'em about two years upon tryall, as to their life & behaviour & have taught them as diligently as I could; one of 'em has an Admirable sense and is a pattern of faithfulness & Sobriety to all the slaves in the Parish; the other has not so much wit but is very honest; I intend God willing to receive 'em both in some short time and to do it in Publick in the best & most solemn manner I can contrive. . . .

4. George Whitefield, a Religious Revivalist, Encourages Conversion and Education, 1740

Newborn Town

Wednesday, Dec. 26. Set out early, and rode very pleasantly till dinner time. Had some refreshment at an ordinary on the road, and lodged at a little house in the woods, about thirty-five miles from where we lay last night. I had a good deal of discourse with the people of the house, and after much previous and suitable conversation, I baptised two children of strangers, who lay at the same house that night. I believe there may be hundreds of children in this province unbaptised, for want of a minister. Oh, that the Lord would send forth some who, like John the Baptist, might preach and baptise in the wilderness! I believe they would flock to him from all the country round about.

Thursday, Dec. 27. Set out about eight in the morning; crossed Trent River, a ferry about half a mile wide, and got to an ordinary a little way out of the road, and about thirty-three miles distant, before six at night. As soon as I came in, a young man welcomed me to America, who, upon enquiry, I found had been one of my parishioners at Savannah; this gave me an immediate opportunity of falling into religious conversation, and afterwards I went, as my usual custom is, among the negroes belonging to the house. One man was sick in bed, and two of his children said their prayers after me very well. This more and more convinces me that negro children, if early brought up in the nurture and admonition of the Lord, would make as great proficiency as any white people's children. I do not despair, if God spares my life, of seeing a school of young negroes singing the praises of Him Who made

From *George Whitefield's Journals* (London: Banner of Truth Trust, 1960), 379, 382–383, 419–420, 422.

them, in a psalm of thanksgiving. Lord, Thou hast put into my heart a good design to educate them; I doubt not but Thou wilt enable me to bring it to good effect. . . .

South Carolina

Wednesday, Jan. 2. Rose very early, prayed, sang a hymn, and gave a sharp reproof to the dancers, who were very attentive, and took it in good part. At break of day, we mounted our horses, and, I think, never had a more pleasant journey. For nearly twenty miles we rode over a beautiful bay as plain as a terrace walk, and as we passed along were wonderfully delighted to see the porpoises taking their pastime, and hear, as it were, shore resounding to shore the praises of Him Who hath set bounds to the sea that it cannot pass, and hath said, "Here shall your proud waves be stayed." At night we intended to call at a gentleman's house, where we had been recommended, about forty miles distant from our last night's lodging; but the moon being totally eclipsed, we missed the path that turned out of the road, and then thought it most advisable, as we were in the main road, to go on our way, trusting to the Almighty to strengthen both our beasts and us. We had not gone far when we saw a light. Two of my friends went up to it, and found a hut full of negroes; they enquired after the gentleman's house whither we had been directed, but the negroes seemed surprised, and said they knew no such man, and that they were newcomers. From these circumstances, one of my friends inferred that these negroes might be some of those who lately had made an insurrection in the province, and had run away from their masters. When he returned, we were all of his mind, and therefore, thought it best to mend our pace. Soon after, we saw another great fire near the roadside, and imagining there was another nest of such negroes, we made a circuit into the woods, and one of my friends at a distance observed them dancing round the fire. The moon shining brightly, we soon found our way into the great road again; and after we had gone about a dozen miles, (expecting to find negroes in every place), we came to a great plantation, the master of which gave us lodging, and our beasts provender. Upon our relating the circumstances of our travels, he satisfied us concerning the negroes, informed us whose they were, and upon what occasion they were in those places in which we found them. This afforded us much comfort, after we had ridden nearly threescore miles, and, as we thought, in great peril of our lives. Blessed be Thy Name, O Lord, for this, and all other Thy mercies, through Jesus Christ! . . .

Philadelphia

Thursday, May 8. . . .

I conversed . . . with a poor negro woman, who has been visited in a very remarkable manner. God was pleased to convert her by my preaching last autumn; but being under dejections on Sunday morning, she prayed that salvation might come to her heart, and that the Lord would be pleased to manifest Himself to her soul that day. Whilst she was at meeting, hearing Mr. M......n, a Baptist preacher, the Word came with such power to her heart, that at last she was obliged to cry out; and a great concern fell upon many in the congregation. The minister stopped, and several persuaded her to hold her peace; but she could not help praising and blessing God. Many since this have called her mad, and said she was full of new wine;

but the account she gave me was rational and solid, and, I believe in that hour the Lord Jesus took a great possession of her soul. Such cases, indeed, have not been very common; but when an extraordinary work is being carried on, God generally manifests Himself to some souls in this extraordinary manner. I doubt not, when the poor negroes are to be called, God will highly favour them, to wipe off their reproach, and shew that He is no respecter of persons, but that whosoever believeth in Him shall be saved. . . .

Pennypack and Philadelphia

Friday, May 9. Preached at Pennypack, about three miles' distance from the house where I lay, to about two thousand people, and came back to Philadelphia, about two in the afternoon. Agreed to build my Negro Schools on the land which I have lately purchased. Preached in the evening, and afterwards began a Society of young men, many of whom I trust, will prove good soldiers of Jesus Christ. Amen. . . .

The poor people were much concerned at my bidding them farewell; and, after I had taken my leave, many came to my lodgings, sorrowing that they were to see my face no more for a long season. Near fifty negroes came to give me thanks for what God had done to their souls. How heartily did those poor creatures throw in their mites for my poor orphans. Some of them have been effectually wrought upon, and in an uncommon manner. Many of them have begun to learn to read. One, who was free, said she would give me her two children, whenever I settle my school. I believe masters and mistresses will shortly see that Christianity will not make their negroes worse slaves. I intended, had time permitted, to have settled a Society for negro men and negro women; but that must be deferred till it shall please God to bring me to Philadelphia again. I have been much drawn out in prayer for them, and have seen them exceedingly wrought upon under the Word preached. I cannot well express how many others, of all sorts, came to give me a last farewell. I never saw a more general awakening in any place. Religion is all the talk; and, I think I can say, the Lord Jesus hath gotten Himself the victory in many hearts. I have scarce had time to eat bread from morning to evening; some one or other was generally applying to me under deep soul-concern, and others continually pressing upon me to baptise their infants. I did comply with as many as I could; but I was obliged sometimes to say, "The Lord sent me not to baptise, but to preach the Gospel." . . .

5. Phyllis Wheatley's Homage to George Whitefield, 1770

We hear no more the music of thy tongue,
Thy wonted auditories cease to throng.
Thy lessons in unequal'd accents flow'd!
While emulation in each bosom glow'd;

From Dorothy Porter, ed., *Early Negro Writing, 1760–1837* (Boston: Beacon Press 1971), 532–534.

Thou didst, in strains of eloquence refin'd,
Inflame the soul, and captivate the mind.
Unhappy we, the setting Sun deplore!
Which once was splendid, but it shines no more;
He leaves this earth for Heaven's unmeasur'd height:
And worlds unknown, receive him from our sight;
There WHITEFIELD wings, with rapid course his way,
And sails to Zion, through vast seas of day.

When his AMERICANS were burden'd sore,
When streets were crimson'd with their guiltless gore!
Unrival'd friendship in his breast now strove:
The fruit thereof was charity and love
Towards *America*—couldst thou do more
Than leave thy native home, the *British* shore,
To cross the great Atlantic's wat'ry road,
To see *America's* distress'd abode?
Thy prayers, great Saint, and thy incessant cries,
Have pierc'd the bosom of thy native skies!
Thou moon hast seen, and ye bright stars of light
Have witness been of his requests by night!
He pray'd that grace in every heart might dwell:
He long'd to see *America* excell;
He charg'd its youth to let the grace divine
Arise, and in their future actions shine;
He offer'd THAT he did himself receive,
A greater gift not GOD himself can give:
He urg'd the need of HIM to every one;
It was no less than GOD's co-equal SON!
Take HIM ye wretched for your only good;
Take HIM ye starving souls to be your food.
Ye thirsty, come to this life-giving stream:
Ye Preachers, take him for your joyful theme;
Take HIM, "my dear AMERICANS," he said,
Be your complaints in his kind bosom laid;
Take HIM ye *Africans,* he longs for you;
Impartial SAVIOUR, is his title due;
If you will chuse to walk in grace's road,
You shall be sons, and kings, and priests to GOD.

Great COUNTESS! we *Americans* revere
Thy name, and thus condole thy grief sincere:
We mourn with thee, that TOMB obscurely plac'd,
In which thy Chaplain undisturb'd doth rest.
New-England sure, doth feel the ORPHAN'S smart;
Reveals the true sensations of his heart:
Since this fair Sun, withdraws his golden rays,
No more to brighten these distressful days!
His lonely *Tabernacle,* sees no more
A WHITEFIELD landing on the *British* shore:
Then let us view him in yon azure skies:
Let every mind with this lov'd object rise.

No more can he exert his lab'ring breath,
Seiz'd by the cruel messenger of death.
What can his dear AMERICA return?
But drop a tear upon his happy urn,
Thou tomb, shalt safe retain thy sacred trust,
Till life divine re-animate his dust.

6. The Conversion Experience of John Marrant, 1802

A Narrative, &c.

I, JOHN MARRANT, born June 15th, 1755, in New York, in North America wish these gracious dealings of the Lord with me to be published, in hopes they may be useful to others, to encourage the fearful, to confirm the wavering, and to refresh the hearts of true believers. My father died when I was little more than four years of age, and before I was five my mother removed from New York to St. Augustine, about seven hundred miles from that city. Here I was sent to school, and taught to read and spell; after we had resided here about eighteen months, it was found necessary to re-move to Georgia, where we remained; and I was kept to school until I had attained my eleventh year. The Lord spoke to me in my early days, by these removes, if I could have understood him, and said, "Here we have no continuing city." We left Georgia, and went to Charlestown, where it was intended I should be put apprentice to some trade. Some time after I had been in Charlestown, as I was walking one day, I passed by a school, and heard music and dancing, which took my fancy very much, and I felt a strong inclination to learn the music. I went home, and informed my sister, that I had rather learn to play upon music than go to a trade. She told me she could do nothing in it, until she had acquainted my mother with my desire. Accordingly she wrote a letter concerning it to my mother, which, when she read, the contents were disapproved of by her, and she came to Charlestown to prevent it. She persuaded me much against it, but her persuasions were fruitless. Disobedience either to God or man, being one of the fruits of sin, grew out from me in early buds. Finding I was set upor. it, and re-solved to learn nothing else, she agreed to it, and went with me to speak to the man, and to settle upon the best terms with him she could. He insisted upon twenty pounds down, which was paid, and I was engaged to stay with him eighteen months, and my mother to find me everything during that term. The first day I went to him he put the violin into my hand, which pleased me much, and, applying close, I learned very fast, not only to play, but to dance also; so that in six months I was able to play for the whole school. In the evenings after the scholars were dismissed, I used to resort to the bottom of our garden, where it was customary for some musicians to assemble to blow the French horn. Here my improvement was so rapid, that in a twelve-month's time I became master both of the violin and of the French horn, and was much re-spected by the gentlemen and ladies whose children attended the school, as also by my master. This opened to me a large door of vanity and vice, for I was invited to all the balls and assemblies that were held in the town, and met with the general applause

John Marrant, *Narrative* (London: Plummer, 1802). This document is also available in Dorothy Porter, ed., *Early Negro Writing, 1760–1837* (Boston: Beacon Press, 1971), 429–432.

of the inhabitants. I was a stranger to want, being supplied with as much money as I had any occasion for; which my sister observing, said, "You have now no need of a trade." I was now in my thirteenth year, devoted to pleasure, and drinking in iniquity like water; a slave to every vice suited to my nature and to my years. The time I had engaged to serve my master being expired, he persuaded me to stay with him, and offered me anything, or any money, not to leave him. His entreaties proving ineffectual, I quitted his service, and visited my mother in the country; with her I staid two months, living without God or hope in the world, fishing and hunting on the Sabbathday. Unstable as water I returned to town, and wished to go to some trade. My sister's husband, being informed of my inclination, provided me with a master, on condition that I should serve him one year and a half on trial, and afterwards be bound, if he approved of me. Accordingly I went, but every evening I was sent for to play on music, somewhere or another; and I often continued out very late, sometimes all night, so as to render me incapable of attending my master's business the next day; yet in this manner I served him a year and four months, and was much approved of by him. He wrote a letter to my mother to come and have me bound [as an apprentice] and whilst my mother was weighing the matter in her own mind, the gracious purposes of God, respecting a perishing sinner, were now to be disclosed. One evening I was sent for in a very particular manner to go and play for some gentlemen, which I agreed to do, and was on my way to fulfill my promise; and passing by a large meetinghouse I saw many lights in it, and crowds of people going in. I enquired what it meant, and was answered by my companion, that a crazy man was hallooing there; this raised my curiosity to go in, that I might hear what he was hallooing about. He persuaded me not to go in, but in vain. He then said, "If you will do one thing I will go in with you." I asked him what that was? He replied, "Blow the French horn among them." I liked the proposal well enough, but expressed my fears of being beaten for disturbing them; but upon his promising to stand by and defend me, I agreed. So we went, and with much difficulty got within the doors. I was pushing the people to make room, to get the horn off my shoulder to blow it, just as Mr. Whitefield was naming his text, and looking round, and, as I thought, directly upon me, and pointing with his finger, he uttered these words, "Prepare to meet thy God, O Israel." The Lord accompanied the word with such power that I was struck to the ground, and lay both speechless and senseless near half an hour. When I was come a little too, I found two men attending me, and a woman throwing water in my face, and holding a smelling-bottle to my nose; and when something more recovered, every word I heard from the minister was like a parcel of swords thrust into me, and what added to my distress, I thought I saw the devil on every side of me. I was constrained in the bitterness of my spirit to halloo out in the midst of the congregation, which disturbing them, they took me away; but finding I could neither walk or stand, they carried me as far as the vestry, and there I remained till the service was over. When the people were dismissed Mr. Whitefield came into the vestry, and being told of my condition he came immediately, and the first word he said to me was, "Jesus Christ has got thee at last." He asked where I lived, intending to come and see me the next day; but recollecting he was to leave the town the next morning, he said he could not come himself, but would send another minister; he desired them to get me home, and then taking his leave of me, I saw him no more. When I reached my sister's house, being carried by two men, she was very uneasy to see me in so distressed a condition. She got me to bed, and sent for a doctor, who came immediately, and after looking at me, he went home, and sent me a bottle of mixture, and desired her to give me a spoonful every two hours; but I could not take anything the doctor sent, nor indeed keep in bed; this distressed my sister very much, and she cried out, "The lad will surely die." She sent for two other doctors, but no medicine they prescribed could I take. No, no; it may be asked, a wounded spirit who can cure? as well as who can bear? In this distress of soul I continued for three days without any food, only a little water now and then. On the fourth day, the minister Mr. Whitefield had desired to visit me came to see me, and being directed upstairs, when he entered the room, I thought he made my distress much worse. He wanted to take hold of my hand, but I durst not give it to him. He insisted upon taking hold of it, and I then got away from him on the side of the bed; but being very weak I fell down, and before I could recover he came to me and took me by the hand, and lifted me up, and after a few words desired to go to prayer. So he fell upon his knees, and pulled me down also; after he had spent some time in prayer he rose up, and asked me now how I did; I answered much worse; he then said, "Come, we will have the old thing over again," and so we kneeled down a second time, and after he had prayed earnestly we got up, and he said again, "How do you do now?" I replied worse and worse, and asked him if he intended to kill me? "No, no," said he, "you are worth a thousand dead men, let us try the old thing over again," and so falling upon our knees, he continued in prayer a considerable time, and near the close of his prayer, the Lord was pleased to set my soul at perfect liberty, and being filled with joy I began to praise the Lord immediately; my sorrows were turned into peace, and joy, and love. The minister said, "How is it now?" I answered, all is well, all happy. He then took his leave of me; but called every day for several days afterwards, and the last time he said, "Hold fast that thou hast already obtained, till Jesus Christ come." I now read the Scriptures very much. . . .

7. Landon Carter, a Slavemaster, Confronts the Problem of Slave Conversion, 1776

I think my man Tony is determined to struggle whether he shall not do as he pleases. He has with McGinis been 2 days only pailing in the dairy and henhouse yard with the posts ready hewed and morticed for him. I told him when I rode out this morning he would certainly get another whipping. He was ranging the pales at least one pannel above another full a foot pretending the ground was uneven. I asked him if he could not pare the ground away. He stoopt down like falling but I imagined it was the Negroe's foolish way of hearing better. I rode out. When I came home the pales were all laid slanting. I asked him why he did that. He still laid the fault on the ground and as his left shoulder was to me I gave him one small rap upon it. He went to breakfast afterwards and no complaint. This evening I walked there and then he pretended he could not drive a nail, his arm was so sore. I made Nassau strip his Cloaths off and examined the whole arm. Not the least swelling upon it and every now and then he would tremble. I asked him if I hit him upon the legs he said his stroke was in his bone which made all his body ach. At last, looking full upon him, I

Jack P. Greene, ed., *The Diary of Colonel Landon Carter of Sabine Hall, 1752–1778,* vol. 1 (Charlottesville: University of Virginia Press 1965), 378, 1056–1057. Copyright © 1965 by the Virginia Historical Society.

discovered the Gentleman compleatly drunk. This I have suspected a great while. I then locked him up for monday morning's Chastisement for I cannot bear such a rascal. I thought this a truly religious fellow but have had occasion to think otherwise and that he is a hypocrite of the vilest kind. His first religion that broke out upon him was new light and I believe it is from some inculcated doctrine of those rascals that the slaves in this Colony are grown so much worse. It behoves every man therefore to take care of his own. At least I am determined to do what I can. Mine shall be brought to their [p]iety though with as little severity as [possible]. . . .

News just come John Self at Rings Neck turned a Baptist, and only waits to convert my People. He had two brethren Preachers and two others with him; and says he cannot serve God and Mammon, has just been made a Christian by dipping, and would not continue in my business but to convert my people.

This a strange year about my overseers; some, horrid hellish rogues and others religious villains. Came here after dinner Mr. John Selden, who told us Capt. Burgess Ball wrote from Hampton that Patrick Henry, the late elected Governor, died last tuesday evening, So that being the day of our battery's beginning to Play on Dunmore's gang and they being routed we ought to look on those two joined as two glorious events. Particularly favourable by the hand of Providence.

8. Two Letters from Savannah, Georgia, on the Progress of Baptist Churches, 1792, 1800

SAVANNAH, Dec. 22, 1792.

Dear Brother Rippon,

By return of Capt. Parrot in the ship Hannah, opportunity offers to acknowledge receipt of your kind favour with two boxes of books agreeable to invoice, which were very thankfully acceptable to our Brother Andrew, as well as to myself, and were delivered agreeable to your request. Within a month past a few of our Christian friends providentially collected at my house, when it was thought necessary we should commence a subscription for the building of a Baptist Meetinghouse in this city, as the corporation has given us a lot for that purpose. Mr. Ebenezer Hills and myself were appointed trustees, and we have subscribed £35. 6s. if we can get as much more, we intend to begin the work, please God to smile on our weak endeavours, and the place will be made sufficiently large to accommodate the black people: they have been frowned upon of late by some despisers of religion, who have endeavoured to suppress their meeting together on Thursday evening in the week which was their custom, but is now set aside; so that they only continue worship from the sun rise to sun set on Sabbath days.

I copied brother Andrew's last return of members for brother Silas Mercer, who was here since the association of Coosawhatchie, which is as follows: Return made to the Georgia Association,

---

"Letters Showing the Rise and Progress of the Early Negro Churches of Georgia and the West Indies," *Journal of Negro History,* 1 (January 1916), 82–83, 86–87.

Supposed to be two or three years past	250	
Baptized since (say 80 in this year 1792)	159	409
Excommunicated	8	
Dead	12	20
Total remaining Nov. 26, 1792		389

Brother Andrew lately brought me a letter from brother George Liele, of Jamaica, expressive of the great increase of his church in that island. Andrew is free only since the death of his old master, and purchased his freedom of one of their heirs at the rate of 50 l[£]. He was born at Goose Creek, about 16 miles from Charleston, South Carolina; his mother was a slave, and died in the service of his old master: his father, a slave, yet living, but rendered infirm by age for ten years past. Andrew was married nine years since, which was about the time he and his wife were brought to the knowledge of their wretched state by nature: His wife is named Hannah and remains a slave to the heirs of his older master; they have no children; He was ordained by our Brother Marshall: he has no assistant preacher but his Brother Sampson, who continues a faithful slave, and occasionally exhorts. Some white ministers from the country preach in his church. Jesse Peter, another Negro (whose present master is Thomas Galphin), is now here, and has three or four places in the country where he attends preaching alternately; a number of white people admire him. While he is here, I propose to be informed more particularly of his situation, etc. Although a slave his master indulges him in his profession and gives him uncommon liberty. To return to Andrew, he has four deacons appointed, but not regularly introduced. He supports himself by his own labour. There are no white people that particularly belong to his church, but we have reason to hope that he has been instrumental in the conviction and converting of some whites. Amos, the other Negro minister, mentioned by Brother George, resides at one of the Bahama Islands, which is called New Providence, and is about four days sail towards the southeast. There is one white church at Ogeechee, and another at Effingham; each of these are about twenty miles from this, which are the nearest and only ones. Perhaps fifty of Andrew's church can read, but only three can write.

For the present, accept of the sincere love and kind respects of the Black Society, with Andrew's particular thanks. My ears have heard their petitions to the throne of grace for you particularly, which no doubt they will continue; and let me entreat your prayers for them, and for the connected societies of this State.

Your brother in the Lord Jesus,

Jonathan Clarke.

Savannah-Georgia, U. S. A., Dec. 23, 1800.

My Dear and Reverend Brother,

After a long silence occasioned by various hindrances, I sit down to answer your inestimable favour by the late dear Mr. White, who I hope is rejoicing, far above the troubles and trials of this frail sinful state. All the books mentioned in your truly condescending and affectionate letter, came safe, and were distributed according to your humane directions. You can scarcely conceive, much less than I describe, the gratitude excited by so seasonably and precious a supply of the means of knowledge and grace, accompanied with benevolent proposals of further assistance. Deign, dear sir, to accept our united and sincere thanks for your great kindness to us, who have been so little accustomed to such attentions. Be assured that our prayers have ascended, and I trust will continue to ascend to God, for your health and happiness, and that you may be rendered a lasting ornament to our holy Religion, and a successful Minister of the Gospel.

With much pleasure, I inform you, dear sir, that I enjoy good health, and am strong in body, tho' sixty-three years old, and am blessed with a pious wife, whose freedom I have obtained, and an only daughter and child who is married to a free man, tho' she, and consequently, under our laws, her seven children, five sons and two daughters, are slaves. By a kind Providence I am well provided for, as to worldly comforts, (tho' I have had very little given me as a minister) having a house and lot in this city, besides the land on which several buildings stand, for which I receive a small rent, and a fifty-six acre tract of land, with all necessary buildings, four miles in the country, and eight slaves; for whose education and happiness, I am enabled thro' mercy to provide.

But what will be infinitely more interesting to my friend, and is so much more prized by myself, we enjoy the rights of conscience to a valuable extent, worshiping in our families and preaching three times every Lord's-day, baptizing frequently from ten to thirty at a time in the Savannah, and administering the sacred supper, not only without molestation, but in the presence, and with the approbation and encouragement of many of the white people. We are now about seven hundred in number, and the work of the Lord goes on prosperously.

An event which has had a happy influence on our affairs was the coming of Mr. Holcombe, late pastor of Euhaw Church, to this place at the call of the heads of the city, of all denominations, who have remained for the thirteen months he has been here among his constant hearers and his liberal supporters. His salary is 2000 a year. He has just had a baptistery, with convenient appendages, built in his place of worship, and has commenced baptizing.

Another dispensation of Providence has much strengthened our hands, and increased our means of information; Henry Francis, lately a slave to the widow of the late Colonel Leroy Hammond, of Augusta, has been purchased by a few humane gentlemen of this place, and liberated to exercise the handsome ministerial gifts he possesses amongst us, and teach our youth to read and write. He is a strong man about forty-nine years of age, whose mother was white and whose father was an Indian. His wife and only son are slaves.

Brother Francis has been in the ministry fifteen years, and will soon receive ordination, and will probably become the pastor of a branch of my large church, which is getting too unwieldy for one body. Should this event take place, and his charge receive constitution, it will take the rank and title of the 3rd Baptist Church in Savannah.

With the most sincere and ardent prayers to God for your temporal and eternal welfare, and with the most unfeigned gratitude, I remain, reverend and dear sir, your obliged servant in the gospel.

(signed) ANDREW BRYAN.

9. A Grave Decorated in African Style, 1944

Reprinted from Mechal Sobel, *The World They Made Together: Black and White Values in Eighteenth-Century Virginia* (1987), 220. Copyright Princeton University Press, 1987. Photo courtesy of the Library of Congress.

E S S A Y S

It is clear that African cultural traits both changed and endured in the Americas. The question is which traits and why. The two essays that follow focus on spiritual traits, a cultural domain that is relatively independent of material support or the master's authority. Sterling Stuckey of the University of California at Los Angeles argues that the powerful symbolism of the circle was common to many of the West and Central African peoples brought to the Americas and that values associated with its mystical rites endured in African-American folktales and rituals. By contrast, Mechal Sobel of the University of Haifa in Israel emphasizes the ways in which black and white cultures intertwined, especially evident in the religious values and practices created by the Great Awakening in eighteenth-century Virginia.

How Africans Preserved Their Culture: Culture as Spirit

STERLING STUCKEY

The final gift of African "tribalism" in the nineteenth century was its life as a lingering memory in the minds of American slaves. That memory enabled them to go back to the sense of community in the traditional African setting and to include all Africans in their common experience of oppression in North America. It is greatly ironic, therefore, that African ethnicity, an obstacle to African nationalism in the twentieth century, was in this way the principal avenue to black unity in antebellum America. Whether free black or slave, whether in the North or in the South, the ultimate impact of that development was profound.

During the process of their becoming a single people, Yorubas, Akans, Ibos, Angolans, and others were present on slave ships to America and experienced a common horror—unearthly moans and piercing shrieks, the smell of filth and the stench of death, all during the violent rhythms and quiet coursings of ships at sea. As such, slave ships were the first real incubators of slave unity across cultural lines, cruelly revealing irreducible links from one ethnic group to the other, fostering resistance thousands of miles before the shores of the new land appeared on the horizon—before there was mention of natural rights in North America. . . .

The majority of Africans brought to North America to be enslaved were from the central and western areas of Africa—from Congo-Angola, Nigeria, Dahomey, Togo, the Gold Coast, and Sierra Leone. In these areas, an integral part of religion and culture was movement in a ring during ceremonies honoring the ancestors. There is, in fact, substantial evidence for the importance of the ancestral function of the circle in West Africa, but the circle ritual imported by Africans from the Congo region was so powerful in its elaboration of a religious vision that it contributed disproportionately to the centrality of the circle in slavery. The use of the circle for religious purposes in slavery was so consistent and profound that one could argue that it was what gave form and meaning to black religion and art. It is understandable that the circle became the chief symbol of heathenism for missionaries, black and white, leading them to seek either to alter it or to eradicate it altogether. That they failed to do so owes a great deal to Bakongo influence in particular, but values similar to those in Congo-Angola are found among Africans a thousand or more miles away, in lands in which the circle also is of great importance. Thus scholarship is likely to reveal more than we now know about the circle in Africa, drawing West and Central Africa closer together culturally than they were previously thought to be.

The circle is linked to the most important of all African ceremonies, the burial ceremony. As Talbot shows, in discussing dance in southern Nigeria. "The Ekoi also in some of their dances imitate the actions of birds, but the most solemn of them all is perhaps the Ejame, given at the funeral of great chiefs, when seven men dance in the centre of an immense circle made by the other performers." In that ceremony, the men keep their eyes to the ground and the songs they sing are said to be "so old that their meaning has long since been forgotten," which suggests the ancient quality of dance within the circle, the immemorial regard for the ancestral spirits in a country in which dance exists mainly as a form of worship and appears to have developed as a means of achieving union with God, of "exerting an influence *with his help* on the fertility of men and of crops." Talbot notes the prime importance of rhythm to dance, and his description of "one variety" of dance parallels descriptions of dance in the ancestral circle in the Congo and in America since "the main object appears to be never to lift the feet off the ground and to leave a clear, even, continuous track." The ordinary method of dancing among the people of Southern Nigeria—among them Ibos, Yorubas, Ibibios, and Efiks—appears monotonous and unattractive

> since it consists of slowly moving round in a circle—always in the opposite direction to the hands of a clock, widdershins—with apparently little variation in the few steps employed. It takes time to appreciate the variety and detail in the different movements and the unceasing, wave-like ripple which runs down the muscles of the back and along the arms to the finger-tips. Every part of the body dances, not only the limbs.

In Bakongo burial ceremonies, according to art historian Robert F. Thompson, bodies were sometimes laid out in state in an open yard "on a textile-decorated bier," as bare-chested mourners danced to the rhythms of drums "in a broken counter-clockwise circle," their feet imprinting a circle on the earth, cloth attached to and trailing on the ground from their waists deepening the circle. Following the direction of the sun in the Southern Hemisphere, the mourners moved around the body of the deceased in a counterclockwise direction. If the deceased lived a good life, death, a mere crossing over the threshold into another world, was a precondition for being "carried back into the mainstream of the living, in the name and body of grandchildren of succeeding generations." From the movement of the sun, Kongo people derive the circle and its counterclockwise direction in a variety of ways. "Coded as a cross, a quartered circle or diamond, a seashell's spiral, or a special cross with solar emblems at each ending—the sign of the four moments of the sun is the Kongo emblem of spiritual continuity and renaissance. . . . In certain rites it is written on the earth, and a person stands upon it to take an oath, or to signify that he or she understands the meaning of life as a process shared with the dead below the river or the sea—the real sources of earthly power and prestige."

Wherever in Africa the counterclockwise dance ceremony was performed—it is called the ring shout in North America—the dancing and singing were directed to the ancestors and gods, the tempo and revolution of the circle quickening during the course of movement. The ring in which Africans danced and sang is the key to understanding the means by which they achieved oneness in America. Knowledge of the ancestral dance in Dahomey contributes to that understanding and helps explain aspects of the shout in North America that are otherwise difficult to account for. For instance, the solo ring shouts noted by Lydia Parrish in Virginia and North Carolina are in the ring dances of Dahomey done in group *and* solo forms, the two being combined at times. Thus, as the drums sounded, a woman held a sacrifice under her left arm, slowly dancing in a "cleared space three times in a counter-clockwise direction, ending with a series of shuffling steps in front of the drums, while the young women who followed her cried out a shrill greeting to the spirits." Solo dance combined with other patterns of dance:

> With the drums sounding they formed a line of twos, and one couple behind the other they danced in the customary counter-clockwise direction about the edge of the cleared space, finally forming a single line in front of the drums, which they faced as they danced vigorously. Retreating in line to their place on the South side, before the ancestral temple they remained standing there, while one after another of their number danced singly, moving toward the drums and then retreating before circling the dance-space.

An impressive degree of interethnic contact, representing large areas of black Africa, at times took place at such ceremonies in Dahomey. F. E. Forbes, who spent two years in Dahomey and kept a journal of his observations, reports that one such instance of ethnic cross-play involved "groups of females from various parts of Africa, each performing the peculiar dance of her country." When not dancing a dance with elements unique to a given country, they performed dances common to many different countries of Africa: "the ladies would now seize their shields and dance a shield-dance; then a musket, a sword, a bow and arrow dance, in turns." Finally, "they called upon the king to come out and dance with them, and they did not call in vain." The king's response had its own unifying influence and was understood by the women from the various countries of Africa, just as the response of Daha, the chief observed by Herskovits almost a century later, would have been understood by them as he "twice circled the space enclosed by the 'bamboos' in a counterclockwise direction before he retired to the portico, where several of his wives solicitously wiped the perspiration from his face and otherwise attended him."

A Kongo ancestral ritual that is profoundly related to counterclockwise dance among the Kongo people occurs, according to Thompson, when they place a cross in a circle to derive the four moments of the sun. While counterclockwise dance in itself achieved as much, the graphic representation does so in more explicit terms, marking off in precise ways the important stages or moments along the way: "In each rendering the right hand sphere or corner stands for dawn which, in turn, is the sign of life beginning. Noon, the uppermost disk or corner, indicates the flourishing of life, the point of most ascendant power. Next, by the inevitable organic process as we know it, come change and flux, the setting of the sun, and death, marked by the left-hand [median] point or disk."

The horizontal line of the cross, referred to as the Kalunga line, deserves attention, for we shall later encounter it in American slavery—associated, as in the Congo, with those who lived long and were generous, wise and strong "on a heroic scale." Such people, in the imagination of the Kongo people, "die twice . . . once 'here,' and once 'there,' beneath the watery barrier, the line Bakongo call *Kalunga.*" According to Thompson, "This is a line marked by the river, the sea, or even dense forestation, a line which divides this world from the next." When that line, which extends from dawn to sunset, is evoked by the Kongo staff-cross, it symbolizes the surface of a body of water beneath which the world of the ancestors is found, and this casts additional light on why water immersion has had such a hold on blacks in America and why counterclockwise dance is often associated with such water rites.

The art historian Suzzane Blier has written that the circle is the most frequently employed linear mode of movement in Togo: "In the funeral, circular lines are formed as clockwise movements when linked to women, but are counter-clockwise motion sequences when employed for men." In the funeral, circular movement is used to represent themes of togetherness and containment. For example, when the deceased is carried around the house before being taken to the cemetery, the act "is said to call together the house ancestors so that they will come to the cemetery for the ceremonies to be performed there." The clockwise movement of women in Togo is a significant departure from the counterclockwise movement indigenous to much of Central and West Africa and does not appear to have an analogue in North America. The most likely explanation for its failure to survive in North America is that Africans from Togo who might have continued the clockwise movement in slavery yielded to the overwhelming preference of other Africans for counter-clockwise movement.

An indication of the complex rites to which people other than the Bakongo put the circle is found in ethnic groups from Sierra Leone. The connection of the circle to the ancestors and to the young is so various in that country, from which Africans were imported to American markets, that one better understands the strength and varying patterns of the circle in North America by understanding its antecedents in Sierra Leone. The Sierra Leonian Earl Conteh-Morgan's scholarship illuminates the relationship of the circle to the storyteller as dancing in a counterclockwise direction occurs: "Instances of dancing in a circle occur during storytelling time in the villages as the storyteller sits in the middle while the listeners sit around him and listen attentively." Since storytellers, or griots, focus mainly on the history of their people, ancestors are usually the principal subject of a particular chronicle of the past—the ceremony framed, as it were, by the listeners gathered around the story-teller. Depending on the demands of the narration, they either listen or, on signal from the storyteller, become active participants.

> Clapping and dancing usually occur in stories with a song that takes the form of a re-frain. The refrain is repeated by the listeners at a signal from the storyteller. Although it may not involve physical touching of the storyteller, it nonetheless gives the whole exercise an air of celebration. It also adds an air of vivid drama in the whole process of storytelling.

Such singing of refrains and clapping of hands as dance occurs in a counter-clockwise direction are similar to those of the dance described by Thompson in the Kongo funeral scene. Conteh-Morgan observed counterclockwise dance among the Bundu in Sierra Leone during a burial ceremony, and such dancing around the deceased, given the prominence of sacred dance in traditional societies, would seem to be widespread in Sierra Leone.

The Sierra Leoneans reveal much about the circle in relation to the life process; indeed, the circle may well be the principal African metaphor for it. Among Mende and Temne secret societies, dancing in a circle with people in the center is a common practice on sacred occasions, for example, during rites of passage for young girls. When they are eligible to be selected for marriage by young men, they go through rites in "the secret house, usually in the bush, or in huts specifically built for that. A couple of days are set aside, or one big day, when they are brought out into the open for all to see as they participate in final ceremonies." At this time, the women stand around the girls, who are generally teenagers, clapping and singing as the girls sit in the middle of the circle. "From time to time, dancing in a circle takes place either by the girls themselves or by the women surrounding them. Touching of the heads or shoulders of those in the center and many types and styles of dancing take place as the music varies in rhythm and tempo."

The circle, among Mende and Temne, is the chief symbol of a ceremony that leads to marriage and the renewal of the life process with the birth of children. Although counterclockwise dance of the Mende and Temne continued in North America as a function primarily of religious activity, it is highly unlikely, considering the mockery that was made of slave marriage in America, that the associated institution of preparation for marriage in the secret house survived even in secrecy in slavery.

Nevertheless, other African institutions and African priests were brought to America in large numbers and, unrecognized by whites, found their places in the circle and elsewhere. Some were among the first and last slave preachers. Herskovits tells us that a variety of them came to the New World, which greatly encouraged the preservation of African values in slavery:

> . . . the river spirits are among the most powerful of those inhabiting the supernatural world, and . . . priests of this cult are among the most powerful members of tribal priestly groups. It will be . . . recalled how, in the process of conquest which accompanied the spread of the Dahomean kingdom, at least (there being no data on this particular point from any other folk of West Africa), the intransigeance of the priests of the river cult was so marked that, more than any other group of holy men, they were sold into slavery to rid the conquerors of troublesome leaders. In all those parts of the New World where African religious beliefs have persisted, moreover, the river cult or, in broader terms, the cult of water spirits, holds an important place. All this testifies to the vitality of this element in African religion, and supports the conclusion, to be drawn from the hint in the Dahomean data, as to the possible influence such priests wielded even as slaves.

Priests were present on the plantations of the South, but whether they were, in specific instances, African-born or products of African influence in America is usually difficult to determine. This distinction is mainly theoretical, since at times one finds their practices, irrespective of the period of slavery, to be of nearly pristine purity and highly esoteric, as when they surface in the folktale. There, as in life, they gathered on the principal occasions of worship, above all at ancestral ceremonies, the most important of which in North America was the ring shout, which often was but one aspect, however important, of multifaceted African religious observance. The ring shout was the main context in which Africans recognized values common to them. Those values were remarkable because, while of ancient African provenance, they were fertile seed for the bloom of new forms. . . .

The most stunning illustration of the trickster's involvement in ancestral ceremonies is contained in the tale "Bur Rabbit in Red Hill Churchyard," collected in
South Carolina by Adams. In this tale, Rabbit is trickster in ways never before associated with him (except in the work of the great collector and storyteller William
John Faulkner): he is keeper of the faith of the ancestors, mediator of their claims on
the living, and supreme master of the forms of creativity. As presented in "Red Hill
Churchyard," Brer Rabbit is shown as a man of God, and new possibilities are
opened for understanding him as a figure in Afro-American folklore heretofore un-
appreciated for religious functions. In the Adams tale, ancient qualities of African
culture, some of the most obscure kind, appear to yield new and original artistic
forms within the circle of culture and are directly related to Anansi and Akan priests
in the Suriname bush. More precisely, the tale reveals African tradition and the future
flowing from it, the ground of spiritual being and the product of its flowering.

But the Red Hill ceremony seems, on its face, just one of the many in which
Brer Rabbit uses his fiddle as a kind of magic wand—for example, to realize his will
against predators or in competition for the hand of a maiden. What seems equally
obvious, though inexplicable, is the strong convergence of the world of the living
and that of the dead as a function, it seems, of nothing more than Brer Rabbit's
genius with his instrument. That a deeper meaning lies beneath the surface of the
tale is suggested, even to one without a command of the African background, by
slave folklore, which holds that all sorts of things, under the right conditions, are
possible in the graveyard. Headless horsemen race about, a rabbit is seen walking
"on he hind legs wid a fiddle in he hands," and the sacred and the secular are one in
moments of masterly iconography as the "buck and wing" is danced "on a tombstone." "It look lik in de Christmas ef de moon is shinin' an' dere's snow on de
ground, dat is de time when you sees all kind er sights." At such times, day appears
to light up the night, but the glow is from the moon and "every star in de element . . .
geeing light." The "diff'ence been it ain' look as natu'al." The real seems unreal, the
unreal real as the story unfolds in the depths of winter in the South.

> De ground was kiver all over wid snow, an' de palin's on de graveyard fence was crack-
> lin; it been so cold. . . . An' I look an' listen . . . an' I seen a rabbit settin' on top of a
> grave playin' a fiddle, for God's sake.

The dance of the community of animals occurred:

> All kind 'er little beasts been runnin' round, dancin'. . . . An' dere was wood rats an'
> squirels cuttin' capers wid dey fancy self, and diff'ent kind er birds an' owl. Even dem
> ole Owl was sachayin' 'round look like dey was enjoying' dey self.

Brer Rabbit got up from his seat on the tombstone, stopped playing and "put
he fiddle under he arm an' step off de grave." Then he gave "some sort er sign to de
little birds and beasts, an' dey form dey self into a circle 'round de grave." Within
that setting, several forms of music were heard:

> Well, I watch an' I see Br'er Rabbit take he fiddle from under he arm an' start to fiddlin'
> some more, and he were doin' some fiddlin' out dere in dat snow. An' Br'er Mockin'
> Bird jine him an' whistle a chune dat would er made de angels weep. . . .

Probably a spiritual, the song whistled by Brer Mockingbird is made sadder as Brer
Rabbit accompanies him on the violin, the ultimate instrument for the conveying of

pathos. But sadness gives way to a certain joy as Brer Rabbit, with all the subtlety of his imagination, leads Brer Mockingbird as they prefigure a new form of music:

> Dat mockin' bird an' dat rabbit—Lord. dey had chunes floatin' all 'round on de night air. Dey could stand a chune on end, grab it up an' throw it away an ketch it an' bring it back an' hold it; an' make dem chunes sound like dey was strugglin' to get away one minute, an' de next dey sound like sump'n gittin' up close an' whisperin'.

The music of Brer Rabbit and Brer Mockingbird resembles the improvisational and ironic flights of sound that characterize jazz, especially on Fifty-second Street in New York in the mid-twentieth century. The close relationship between the music in Red Hill Churchyard and jazz finds further support in the behavior of Brer Rabbit, whose style calls to mind Louis Armstrong's:

> An' as I watch, I see Bur Rabbit lower he fiddle, wipe he face an' stick he han'k'ch'ef in he pocket, an' tak off he hat an' bow mighty nigh to de ground.

That scene and the others recall the broader context of Louis Armstrong's musical environment in New Orleans, where jazz was sacred in funeral ceremonies and where African secret societies were important to its sustenance and definition. A further consideration of the tale reveals its irreducible foundation in Africa.

The Herskovitses' discussion in *Suriname Folklore* of the drum harks back to the Akans of the Gold Coast and enables us, by transferring the power of the drum to the fiddle, to understand the central mystery of the ritual, which at first glance seems inexplicable. The drums have a three-fold power in the mythology of the bush Negro. Of the first power, the Herskovitses write, "Tradition assigns to them the . . . power of summoning the gods and the spirits of the ancestors to appear." After Brer Rabbit stopped fiddling, wiped his face, and with the other animals bowed in a circle before the grave, the storyteller tells us,

> de snow on de grave crack an' rise up, an' de grave open an' I see Simon rise up out er dat grave. I see him an' he look jest as natu'al as he don 'fore dey bury him.

The second power of the drums of the Akans is that of "articulating the message of these supernatural beings when they arrive." A flesh-and-blood character capable of speech, rather than a disembodied spirit, appears as the ancestor in the tale. Consequently, the other characters are able to communicate directly with him, and he is greatly interested in them:

> An' he [Simon] look satisfy, an' he look like he taken a great interest in Bur Rabbit an' de little beasts an' birds. An' he set down on de top of he own grave and carry on a long compersation wid all dem animals.

The third power of the drum is to send the spirits of the gods or ancestors "back to their habitats at the end of each ceremony."

> But dat ain't all. Atter dey wored dey self out wid compersation, I see Bur Rabbit take he fiddle an' put it under he chin an' start to playin'. An' while I watch, I see Bur Rabbit step back on de grave an' Simon were gone.

The intensity of the dancing in the circle, to the music of Brer Rabbit and Brer Mockingbird, was great, as indicated by the pace of the music and the perspiration of the performers, though snow covered the ground. From internal evidence alone—

and a large body of external data also suggest as much—we know the dancers fairly whirled in counterclockwise movement. To them dance was sacred, as in Suriname, where "one of the most important expressions of worship is dancing." There the dancers "face the drums and dance toward them, in recognition of the voice of the god within the instruments." The Gold Coast myth, it appears, was elegantly applied in Red Hill Churchyard, but descriptions of the ceremony there and elsewhere in North America make no mention of dancers facing percussionists as a necessary aspect of ritual. This is not surprising, for drums were rarely available to slaves.

Since the functions of the drum in Suriname and of the violin in South Carolina slavery are the same, on the evidence of the tale and the work of the Herskovitses, it is very tempting to conclude that South Carolina slaves, not having access to the drum, simply switched to the violin to express the threefold power. But a case can be made for another explanation of why slaves in South Carolina, and almost certainly elsewhere, used the violin on so sacred an occasion. In this context, David Dalby's assertion that some understanding of "the history and culture of the great medieval empire of Mali" is crucial to an understanding of slave culture is particularly relevant.

> The civilization of Mali included a rich musical culture, based on an elaborate range of string, wind and percussion instruments and on a long professional training for its musicians. This musical culture has survived in West Africa for at least a thousand years and, by its influence on American music, has enabled the United States to achieve an independence from European musical traditions and to pioneer new forms. A bitter aspect of the American slave trade is the fact that highly trained musicians and poets from West Africa must frequently have found themselves in the power of slaveowners less cultured and well educated than themselves.

Dalby's thesis takes on added significance when one looks at slave culture and discovers the extraordinary degree to which slaves, at gathering after gathering, relied on the fiddle. When one takes into account that the one-string violin was used in the Mali Empire, and is used today among the Songhai of Upper Volta, which is within the boundaries of the old empire, to summon the ancestral spirits, new light is cast on "Bur Rabbit in Red Hill Churchyard," revealing a vital Songhai component in the tale and among South Carolina slaves. The presence of the old Mali Empire, then, is felt in a way that could scarcely be more important—in the ancestral ceremony directed by Brer Rabbit with his fiddle.

Among the ethnic groups of the empire, the violin was widespread, in contrast to the banjo, which was used to accompany the griot's declamation or recitation of stories. Where one had to be apprenticed to griots to learn to master the banjo—in Upper Volta and, possibly, elsewhere in West Africa—a nonprofessional could pick up and, after long practice, achieve mastery of the violin without being apprenticed. The violin was a democratic rather than an aristocratic instrument for the Songhai; this helps explain, together with its use elsewhere in West Africa before and through the centuries of the slave trade, its widespread use by American slaves. In fact, the violin was the most important instrument of slave musicians and important among Northern slaves as well. It is small wonder that in "Bur Jonah's Goat" the storyteller says, "Ef you was to take dat fiddle 'way from him [Brer Rabbit], he would perish 'way and die."

Missionaries in Georgia attempted to eradicate the widespread use of the fiddle on the Hopeton plantation, where five hundred slaves, very large numbers of whom were children and some "old and superannuated," formed a slave community. Sir Charles Lyell, who visited the plantation in the 1840s, wrote about efforts of Methodists to rid slave culture of that instrument even though nothing raucous was associated with ceremonies in which it was played. So pervasive was the use of the fiddle at Hopeton that the Malian tradition of string instruments to which Dalby makes reference is the background against which Lyell's remarks should be placed.

> Of dancing and music negroes are passionately fond. On the Hopeton plantation above twenty violins have been silenced by the Methodist missionaries, yet it is notorious that the slaves were not given to drink or intemperance in their merry-makings.

Even when we include the large numbers of children and the very old, we find the astonishing average, on Hopeton, of approximately one fiddle for every twenty slaves in a population of five hundred. When we exclude the young and old, our calculations show that about one in every ten slaves played the fiddle, which makes it difficult to conceive of any ceremony, especially burial rites, in which not even one fiddle was present. And since slaves from Upper Volta were represented on so large a plantation, there was probably a Songhai presence, with ancestral spirits and gods being called forth with the fiddle, as in Red Hill Churchyard, at least until the campaign against its use was launched. It is a study in contrasting cultures that missionaries thought the fiddle profane in religious ceremonies and the African thought it divine in that context.

The ceremony Brer Rabbit directed in Red Hill Churchyard was one with which great numbers of Africans in North America could identify because it involved a burial rite common in enough particulars to West African ethnic groups as a whole. Whatever their differences in language, slaves from many different ethnic groups might easily, at such a ceremony, assume their places in the circle, dancing and singing around the deceased, whether in Virginia, South Carolina, North Carolina, Georgia, Louisiana, Pennsylvania, Maryland, the District of Columbia, or elsewhere. What is certain is that African customs in a more openly expressed form in the North were more likely to occur secretly and in the inscrutable language of the tale in the South. Since the fear of slave insurrections was much less there than in the South, slaves in Philadelphia, for example, were permitted to come together in large numbers for ceremonies.

> Many [in 1850] can still remember when the slaves were allowed the last days of the fairs for their jubilee, which they employed ("light hearted wretch!") in dancing the whole afternoon in the present Washington Square, then a general burying ground—the blacks joyful above, while the sleeping dead reposed below!

The burial ground provided an ideal setting, under the conditions of enslavement, for Africans from different ethnic groups to relate to one another, to find shared religious values that must have been an enormous source of satisfaction as they struggled to prevent their numbers from being smaller still as a result of ethnic allegiances. When customs vital to West Africa as a cultural complex were indulged, such as the relationship and obligations of the living to the ancestors, bonds among Africans of different ethnic groups, if before unknown to them, were recognized and strengthened in America despite differences in language and despite certain differences in burial ceremonies. Occasions for such discoveries were not infrequent, since slaves, permitted to participate in the last days of the fairs, decided that a collective ancestral rite would become an annual event. That meant scores of first-generation members of a particular ethnic group chose to participate in a ceremony practiced in Central Africa and all over West Africa as well. The choice of the graveyard for the setting did not prevent white onlookers from concluding that the slaves were carefree, because they did not understand that African dance was a form of worship essential to sacred ceremony or how painful it was for Africans to practice such a ceremony in an alien land, and as slaves.

> In that field could be seen at once more than one thousand of both sexes, divided into numerous little squads, dancing, and singing, "each in their own tongue," after the customs of their several nations in Africa.

If they had been preserved, the lyrics of what was sung would tell us much about the impact of slavery on the consciousness of first-generation Africans and much about African religious ceremonies generally. But given the context of the songs, the overall meaning is clear enough: they were songs concerning the ancestors, songs some notes of which, like those of Brer Mockingbird in Red Hill Churchyard, conveyed the pain of being on the ground of the dead in an alien land far from the ancestral home. Under those conditions, the degree of musical improvisation must have been exceptional, even for a people noted for improvisational brilliance. Their annual movement to the burial ground in Philadelphia meant a continuing affirmation of their values, so they sang and danced in a circle "the whole afternoon," the ground beneath them being common ground.

But when African languages were sung, the requirements of ethnicity at times made random scatterings of singers unrealistic, which guaranteed the ethnic patterns of behavior in the Philadelphia graveyard. As the English language became more their property, it was easier for the mixture of ethnic peoples to occur in myriad circles in that graveyard and in others. There was, inevitably, some unevenness of movement toward cultural oneness because of the language factor alone; some years in the New World were required before those from different ethnic backgrounds achieved cultural oneness by being able to use the same language. Ironically, it was a degree of harmony that could not be reached through African languages. But from the start of the ceremonies in the graveyard, complementary characteristics of religion, expressed through song, dance, and priestly communication with the ancestors, were organic to Africans in America and their movement in a counterclockwise direction in ancestral ceremonies was a recognizable and vital point of cultural convergence.

Though the number of Africans brought into Pennsylvania in the eighteenth century was small—they accounted for just 2 percent of the state's 333,000 people in 1790—their influence on their descendants for generations determined the nature of most of black religion in the state, and with it sacred song and dance style. This raises a question regarding the relationship of slave culture to demography that deserves an answer different from the one offered until now. From what we know of black religion in Pennsylvania, small numbers of Africans were sufficient to constitute the "critical mass" for the retention of essentials of African religion in slavery. Moreover, what is true of black African culture is true of any culture rich in artistic and spiritual content: initiation into it in youth guarantees its presence in consciousness, and to a considerable extent in behavior for a lifetime.

Fortunately for the slave, the retention of important features of the African cultural heritage provided a means by which the new reality could be interpreted and spiritual needs at least partially met, needs often regarded as secular by whites but as often considered sacred to blacks. The division between the sacred and the secular, so prominent a feature of modern Western culture, did not exist in black Africa in the years of the slave trade, before Christianity made real inroads on the continent. Consequently, religion was more encompassing to the African in slavery than before, the ring shout being a principal means by which physical and spiritual, emotional and rational, needs were fulfilled. This quality of African religion, its uniting of seeming opposites, was perhaps the principal reason it was considered savage by whites. It was the source of creative genius in the slave community and a main reason that whites and free blacks thought the slaves lacked a meaningful spiritual life. Opposition to African religion, therefore, was limited in effectiveness because the African was thought to have a religion unworthy of the name, when, in fact, his religious vision was subtle and complex, responsible for the creation of major—and sacred—artistic forms.

For decades before and generations following the American Revolution, Africans engaged in religious ceremonies in their quarters and in the woods unobserved by whites. From the time of the earliest importation of slaves to the outbreak of the Civil War, millions of slaves did the ring shout, unobserved, with no concern for white approval. But the possibility that whites might discover the guiding principles of African cults kept blacks on guard and led them, to an astonishing degree, to keep the essentials of their culture from view, thereby making it possible for them to continue to practice values proper to them. Such secretiveness was dictated by the realities of oppression and worked against whites acquiring knowledge of slave culture that might have been used to attempt to eradicate that culture. While Lydia Parrish fails to appreciate that political consideration, she effectively draws on African tradition to explain her difficulty in securing certain types of cooperation:

> It took me three winters on St. Simon's to hear a single slave song, three times as many winters to see the religious dance called the ring-shout, still more winters to unearth the Buzzard Lope and similar solo dances, and the game songs known as ring-play. . . . The secretiveness of the Negro is, I believe, the fundamental reason for our ignorance of the race and its background, and this trait is in itself probably an African survival. Melville J. Herskovits . . . quotes a Dutch Guiana Bush Negro as saying: "Long ago our ancestors taught us that it is unwise for a man to tell anyone more than half of what he knows about anything." It is amusing to question Southerners as to the number of times they remember hearing Negroes volunteer information. Not one so far has recalled an instance in which something has been told that was not common knowledge.

For the African, dance was primarily devotional, like a prayer, "the chief method of portraying and giving vent to the emotions, the dramatic instinct and religious fervour of the race." That whites considered dance sinful resulted in cultural polarization of the sharpest kind since dance was to the African a means of establishing contact with the ancestors and with the gods. Because the emotions of slaves were so much a part of dance expression, the whole body moving to complex rhythms, what was often linked to the continuing cycle of life, to the divine, was thought to be debased. But a proper burial, not what whites thought, was what mattered, unless they were present on so sacred an occasion. A proper burial, for the great majority of slaves throughout slavery, was one in accordance with African tradition. "Wen one uh doze Africans die, it wuz bery sad," an old man recalled of slave days in Georgia. "Wen a man's countryman die, he sit right wid um all night. . . . You know . . . doze Africans ain got no Christianity. Dey, ain had no regluh religion." After praying, before leaving the "settin' up," the countrymen "put deah han on duh frien and say good-bye." The placing of hands on the dead was an African custom practiced in West Africa and elsewhere in the Americas, including Dutch Guiana, just as drumming was practiced in Africa and, when permitted, in slave America. But the drummer's tempo apparently varied from place to place in Africa, ranging from the rapidity of some tribes in the Congo area to the slow beat of the Africans who influenced some of the drumming in Georgia graveyards: "We beat duh drum agen at duh fewnal. We call it duh dead mahch. Jis a long slow beat. Boom-boom-boom. Beat duh drum. Den stop. Den beat it agen." On such occasions, there was at times the singing of African lyrics but more often the new lyrics of the spirituals.

Spirituals were born as the religious vision of the larger society was caught, as by centripetal force, drawn to the innermost regions of black spiritual consciousness and applied to what blacks were experiencing in slavery. In an African ritual setting on one such occasion, a black man got on his knees, his head against the floor, and pivoted as members of the group around him moved in a circle, holding his head "down to the mire," singing "Jesus been down to de mire." The arms of those circling "reached out to give a push" and from overhead looked somewhat like spokes in a wheel—a continuation of a tradition centuries old in Sierra Leone and one maintained well over a century in America, which argues a significant Mende and Temne presence in slavery in Georgia. As descendants of Temnes and Mendes in America sang in this century, inspiration was drawn from awareness that Jesus knew despair. This confronting of tragedy was somehow strangely comforting, the throwing of one's whole being into the performance a possible source of the blues in the song sang—the sacred side of the blues, what they owe to the spirituals:

> You must bow low
> Jesus been down
>   to de mire
> Jesus been down
>   to de mire
> Jesus been down
>   to de mire
> You must bow low
>   to de mire
> Honor Jesus
>   to de mire
> Lowrah lowrah
>   to de mire
> Lowrah lowrah
>   to de mire

Lowrah lowrah
    to de mire
Jesus been down
    to de mire
You must bow low
    to de mire
low
    to de mire

"The refrain—repeated relentlessly—corresponds in its character and rhythmic beat to that of drums," the words so filled with emotion that, after a while, they dissolve into moans and cries.

For all her merits as a student of folklore, Parrish, who observed that particular shout, never understood the depths of its spirituality. She considered the shout "a kind of religious dance," and this has been the going thesis for well over a century. Nevertheless, she concluded that "Sperrichels were most often sung at night on the plantations when the 'shout'" was held, a context that should have deepened the meaning of the shout for her, as the relationship between the shout and the spirituals deepens the meaning of the latter for us: "The people, young and old would gather in the praise house, or, if there was none, in one of the larger cabins, where the ceremonies were usually prolonged till after midnight, sometimes till 'day clean.'" Thus, slave youths were introduced to the circle and to the singing of spirituals within it—all the while dancing in ways scholars acknowledge to be little different from black "secular" dance of today.

How White and Black Cultures Merged: Culture as Social Relations

MECHAL SOBEL

After 1750, spiritual revival was widespread in Virginia. It began in response to the needs of the lower class, to their conflicts in values, and to their longings for coherence. Almost invariably, when it came, *it came when and where whites were in extensive and intensive contact with blacks.* Awakenings in Virginia were a shared black and white phenomenon, in which each world view stimulated, permeated, and invigorated the other. For over half a century blacks and whites shared spiritual experiences, and the effect was deep and lasting in both communities. Virtually all eighteenth-century Baptist and Methodist churches were mixed churches, in which blacks sometimes preached to whites and in which whites and blacks witnessed together, shouted together, and shared ecstatic experiences at "dry" and wet christenings, meetings, and burials. A long period of intensive mass interaction ensued.

In the nineteenth century, black and white churches were to go essentially separate ways, but the joint experience of the eighteenth century altered the world views of each. They emerged far more coherent than at the outset of the experience, with their understandings of death and afterlife changed as a result.

The new religious experiences of the Great Awakening of the mid-eighteenth century took place either outside or in very small church buildings, which in themselves were symbolically significant. As Rhys Isaac has so well demonstrated, the churches of the Anglican establishment made a statement through their shape and form: with their grand size and fine orderly finish, most were reflections of the elites' self-image. Blacks *and poor whites* did not feel welcome there. The small wooden churches of the new sects invited the poor to a new homecoming. Most of the rough new meetinghouses of Baptist and later Methodist congregations were very like the simple cabins of both whites and blacks. They were small, plain wooden structures, often earthfast, built of logs or planks, with few doors or windows. Methodists, in fact, often used windowless barns.

Blacks were at the early meetings in fields, barns, and small wooden churches, and contemporary whites understood their appeal. The Rev. Samuel Davies, commenting in 1757, recognized blacks' spiritual confusion and existential need: "Many of them only seem to desire to be, they know not what: they feel themselves uneasy in their *present* condition, and therefore desire a *change.*" From the outset, blacks warmed up many revival proceedings. They "desired a change," recognized spirit and spirit power, and were ready to participate in ceremonies of rebirth and renewal. Ecstasy and spirit travels were an integral part of their tradition, and blacks welcomed this first appeal to their participation.

Their participation deeply affected George Whitefield and the mood of his revival. His journal reported their emotional participation in his meetings; by 1740, he was ready to oppose the strongly held local aversion to conversionary efforts, acquiesced to by most Anglican ministers, and to challenge slaveholders publicly. His challenge was not based on abstract rights but on experience: "As I lately passed through your provinces, I was touched with a fellow-feeling of the miseries of the poor negroes." Negroes attended his meetings, pressed into his room, and touched his person. They began to experience rebirth and to receive the right hand of fellowship. In response, Whitefield specifically challenged whites in Virginia to reconsider their views of blacks and of themselves:

> Think you, your children are in any way better by nature than the poor negroes? No! In no wise! Blacks are just as much, and no more, conceived and born in sin, as white men are; and both, if born and bred up here, I am persuaded, are naturally capable of the same improvement. And as for the grown negroes, I am apt to think, that whenever the Gospel is preached with power among them, many will be brought effectually home to God.

Perhaps Whitefield too had thought himself better by nature than the negroes. Now he knew he was not.

Whitefield rejoiced with the black converts and apparently came to new insights and found new strength. He took on the slave masters in this major attack (reprinted by Franklin and many colonial presses) . . . and warned the Southerners, "Although I pray God the slaves may never be permitted to get the upper hand, yet should such a thing be permitted by Providence, all good men must acknowledge the judgement would be just."

Whitefield met with blacks wherever he went. He went *to* them when he visited plantations: "I went, as my usual custom is, among the negroes belonging to the house." Slaves flocked to hear him wherever he preached. He became convinced

God would show them a particular providence. "God will highly favour them," he wrote in his journal, "to wipe off their reproach, and shew that He is no respector of persons," He now began to add a special address to "the poor negroes" at the end of every sermon, promising that Christ Jesus "will wash you in his own blood." "Shew them, O Shew them," he cried, "the necessity of being deeply wounded before they can be capable of healing by Jesus Christ." In a radical turnabout, he bid the Christian slaves *"to pray for me."* His was a call for both deep ritual involvement and reciprocal aid. Blacks who had been ready for a new birth responded immediately and emotionally.

Whitefield's success with blacks became an important part of his followers' folklore. His ardent supporter, William Seward, recorded in his journal that a black servant, requested to mimic Whitefield at a club, refused and instead preached, "'I speak the truth in Christ; I lie not; except you repent you will all be damned!!' This unexpected speech broke up the club, which has not met since." Seward too found "one Negroe brought to Jesus Christ is peculiarly sweet to my soul."

John Marrant, the black missionary whose autobiography later made famous his conversion by Whitefield, was "struck to the ground and lay both speechless and senseless near half an hour" in response to a Whitefield sermon. He felt challenged by the call to "Prepare to meet thy God, O Israel." Whitefield came to him personally and told him, "Jesus Christ has got thee at last."

Whitefield's sermons were simple and repetitive and very powerful. He graphically pictured damnation and hell, with its eternal fires melting every bone, and the inner experience of the Holy Spirit, which he claimed he had felt and now sought for his audience. His audiences, both blacks and whites, were alternately agitated and soothed, and many "melted" in their midst: they had an experience with spirit, often marked by tears, moans, and fainting.

"Black countenances, eagerly attentive to every word they heard, and some of them washed with tears," played an important role in the emotional response that met Samuel Davies's preaching. In the late 1740s this Presbyterian became minister to seven churches in Hanover County and soon became "the primary instrument in the Great Awakening throughout the entire colony." Davies appealed to the blacks, they responded, and he too was apparently affected by the interaction. By 1757, some 300 were attending each Sunday service, and he had baptized 150. Baptism was given only

> after they had been Catechumens for some time, and given credible evidence, not only of their acquaintance with the important doctrines of the Christian Religion, but also of a deep sense of these things upon their spirits, and a life of the strictest Morality and Piety. As they are not sufficiently polished to dissemble with a good grace, they express the sensations of their minds so much in the language of simple nature, and with such genuine indications of Sincerity, that it is impossible to suspect the possession of some of them, especially when attested by a regular behaviour in common life.

Davies recorded the direct influences of blacks on his own spiritual life:

> March 2, 1756. Sundry of them [the Negroes] have lodged all night in my kitchen; and, sometimes, when I have awaked about two or three a-clock in the morning, a torrent of sacred harmony poured into my chamber, and carried my mind away to Heaven. In this seraphic exercise, some of them spend almost the whole night.

He came to believe that "the *Negroes* above all the human species that ever I knew, have an ear for Music, and a kind of extatic [*sic*] delight in Psalmody." He spent much time teaching blacks to read the Bible and listening to their songs and prayers. He expected that the "*poor African Slaves* will be made the Lord's free men."

Davies's colleague, John Wright, of Cumberland County, reported that "one hundred and thirty persons got under very hopeful religious impressions, among whom were about twenty Ethiopians who spoke to me about their souls concerns." Wright was "transported" by the "exercises [*sic*] of the most savage boy of them."

Classes to teach slaves to read the Bible became acceptable in Hanover in the 1750s. Rev. John Todd, who had some 600 slaves in his three Hanover County churches, claimed that by 1760, "hundreds of *Negroes* beside *white* people, can read and spell, who a few years since did not Know one letter."

> The poor *Slaves* are now commonly engaged in learning to read; some of them can read the Bible, others can only spell; and some are just learning their letters.—But there is a general alteration among them for the better. The sacred hours of the *Sabbath,* that used to be spent in frolicking, dancing, and other profane courses, are now employed in attending upon public ordinances, in learning to read at home, or in praying together, and singing the praises of GOD and the Lamb.

With "joy," Todd noted that at the communal table "these poor *Africans*" were "not like frozen formalists," and they did not rise "with dry eyes."

The diary of James Gordon, an Irish Presbyterian who had settled on a substantial plantation in Lancaster County in 1738, and was a member of one of John Todd's congregations, confirms that in 1759, "religion seems to increase among us." He was referring to a small new congregation that had just grown to fifty-three members. Blacks were already members, and many more were to join. Gordon himself played a role in this excitement and in its interracial aspects, and on at least one occasion he "read a sermon to the negroes." Blacks here sometimes met separately, as they had in Davies's and Todd's other congregations, but they were often together with whites. When in late September of 1759 there was a prolonged meeting [probably at Harvest Home time], Gordon simply recorded, "Our negroes have attended Sermons these four days." In May of 1760, Gordon attended "a pretty large company of the common people and negroes, but very few gentlemen. The gentlemen that even incline to come are afraid of being laughed at."

This Presbyterian revival was in the Northern Neck, a section in which the Anglican Church was in a most "lamentable state of decline." The lower classes there, blacks and whites, were "ripe" for harvesting together. Although Davies addressed an appeal to slaveowners to educate "all of their family members," including slaves, he did not have to appeal to his congregants, mostly "common people," to accept blacks in their midst. They were already doing so.

Gordon estimated that from seventy to eighty blacks attended the 1760 Christmas service, and when Whitefield came through Virginia in 1762, so many blacks and whites came, there was not nearly enough room for all to sit in the chamber. "September 4, 1762. Mr. Whitefield preached to a crowdeed house. Mr. Whitefield was obliged to make the negroes go out to make room for the white people. Several, white and black, could not get room." Although these Presbyterians *were* accepting blacks and were sharing experiences with them, there was no question about who came first. They sat together inside until there was no more room, and then the blacks had to rise to make room for whites, although they joined other whites standing at the windows.

Gordon's diary suggests the very common involvement he had with his slaves. He too cared for them, was cared for by them, and eventually became disillusioned with their work patterns. On June 2, 1760, he lamented, "Went about the plantation, found everything amiss almost; the things of this life much disquiet me, my people are so careless." Whether they were careless or not, Gordon did not come to hate his black family, as Landon Carter did, and the spiritual life of his people continued to interest him. He kept track of their market value as slaves, but he also shared in their religious experiences. On February 24, 1762, he noted, "Frank, a daughter of Betsy and old Jack, died. A few hours before, she told her mother she was dying and hoped to see her in heaven." James Gordon no doubt believed that he too would meet them both there.

Davies had drawn the picture of their joint salvation very graphically:

—And O! When all these warriors meet at length from every corner of the earth, and, as it were, pass in review before their General in the fields of heaven, with their robes washed in his blood, with palms of victory in their hands and crowns of glory on their heads, all dressed in uniform with garments of salvation, what a glorious army will they make! and how will they cause heaven to ring with shouts of joy and triumph!

Gordon shared his spiritual life with poor whites and with slaves. He had apparently taken Davies's admonition to slaveholders very much to heart.

What are you? What being of mighty importance are you? Is not another as dear to himself as you are to yourself? Are not his rights as sacred and inviolable as yours? How come you to be entitled to an exemption from the common laws of human nature? Be it known to you, you are as firmly bound by them as any of our species.

While Whitefield's enthusiasm had begun a revival in 1740, and Davies's Presbyterian awakening affected a limited number in the Northern Neck in the 1750s, it was the Separate Baptists under the leadership of Shubal Stearns who sparked an extraordinary awakening that affected the masses over a much longer period. Stearns, a New Englander who had been deeply influenced by Whitefield but had become a Baptist, journeyed south to do "the Lord's work," living at Opequon Creek and Cacapon, in Berkeley and Hampshire Counties, (West) Virginia, from the summer of 1754 until the summer of 1755. In the fall of 1755, he established himself at Sandy Creek, North Carolina, and from there influenced, and was influenced by, the developments in Virginia. Stearns had come from Connecticut with a small band of about fifteen devoted followers. In Virginia and South Carolina he soon had hundreds and then thousands of active believers, many missionaries in the field. Clearly the "chemistry" of the interaction had been important. He found a large black and white population very receptive to his message and his medium.

Stearns called for personal and communal experience, commitment, and ritual. He was concerned with each and every soul, demanded dedication, and promised personal salvation as well as a rich communal life. He offered a coherent world view with rich personal and communal rewards. His demands were high, encompassing virtually all of an individual's life, but his promises were exciting, both in their means and in their ends.

Stearns proposed replacing the aristocratically run institution of the "other," the Anglican Church, with a consensus community of equals. A Baptist church is its members. No outside body can dictate any aspect of policy or belief. A church calls a person to preach and makes that person a "preacher" by virtue of that call, not by education or outside authority. All the poor white and black members would be brothers and sisters in Christ in this consensus-run community of equals. Each individual should have an equal voice, as together they would establish discipline and judge one another. The church was to be made up of the regenerate: those whom God had saved and who had experienced God's "precious dealing with their souls" in ways they could recount to others. This experience of being "born again" was central and was a sign of the spiritual equality of the highest and lowest. A slave could certainly experience saving grace, even when his owner had not. And all those who were saved could be assured of life everlasting: God in heaven awaited the lambs, all the same and all equal.

Stearn's fellowship replaced the formal baptism of infants with the highly emotional testimony and often ecstatic immersion of those old enough to recognize and recount their experience with spirit. They replaced the learning of the catechism with the yearning for ecstatic spiritual experience, and the celebration of the Lord's Supper at Christmas, Easter, and Whitsunday with very frequent "love feasts" when the bread and wine were brought to the people. As Donald Mathews has noted, the Separate Baptists emphasized physical contact. Babies were dry christened; adults were held while they went under water and often while they "shouted" for joy. After baptism there was the "laying on of hands," when the preacher prayed for the candidate, and the extending of "the right hand of fellowship" to the new brother or sister. The brethren washed each other's feet, anointed the ill with "holy oil," and gave each other the "kiss of charity." At all services they sang vigorously and most often found that some of their number experienced spiritual "travels" or ecstasy that had them shouting and moving.

Stearns and his small congregation formally introduced this polity to Virginia. The almost immediate response and excitement it generated, and the long-term growth that ensued, suggest that the Virginians wanted and needed an all-encompassing emotional and spiritual experience. They needed to take control of their own lives, to impose limits and taboos, and to share both discipline and ecstatic experience with their neighbors, thereby creating a new community.

Blacks and whites were together in virtually every new congregation in Virginia. In this, the Baptist phase, and later in the 1770s and 1780s when the Methodists instituted many of the same or similar practices, racially mixed groups responded, and no participant seems to have questioned seriously the propriety of these "promiscuous" gatherings. White and black, male and female, new converts created new churches.

The Baptist excitement began as a mixed black-white phenomenon, and whites who had lifetimes of intimate association with blacks did not regard it as strange that this new religious experience was a shared one. Blacks were singing and shouting and "having a Christ" right along with whites. In fact, from the outset, it was recognized that their emotional response and spiritual sensitivity helped whites to "come through."

Baptist churches really were independent and were somewhat different from each other in practice. The records that have come down to us seem to reflect such differences in relation to black-white interaction. Some forty Virginia Baptist Church record books are extant from the eighteenth century. Virtually all the records indicate that both blacks and whites were members, in widely varying proportions, such as the 150 blacks and 50 whites in the Burruss or Carmel Church in Caroline County in 1800, or the reverse relationship of 71 blacks and 126 whites in the Buck Marsh or Berryville Church in Clarke County in 1772–1788. There were only 26 white men in this second congregation, whereas there were 40 black men. Generally, black men represented a much larger percentage of the churched blacks than white men did of the churched whites.

Although many blacks began to hold informal all-black meetings on their plantations, a few of the early formal churches were all black as well, such as the Williamsburg "African" Church of Gowan Pamphlet, 1776, and the church on William Byrd III's plantation in Lunenburg County, begun in the late 1750s, in the wake of a revival conducted by whites William Murphey and Philip Mulkey, who organized the mixed Dan River Church. There was an independent "Negro Baptist Church" in King and Queen County by 1782, and in 1788 the Davenport congregation in Petersburg was "mostly people of color" but did have "a few white members." By 1803 it had become the Church of the Lord Jesus Christ (later Gillfield Church), and there were no white congregants. Blacks, on the other hand, were in virtually all eighteenth-century Baptist churches, and in most they were usually a very large block.

Churches followed very different patterns of registering their black members: Some never noted color, some occasionally did, and others had separate listings of slaves from the outset. The Water Lick Baptist Church in Shenandoah County was founded in 1787 by a group of Baptists that left a church at South River. They were already experienced in the faith. Seven men and nine women signed the original covenant; the sixth man was Negro Joseph and the seventh Negro Daniel, and the ninth woman was Negro Jeanny. Clearly, as at Gordon's Presbyterian meeting, they were the last among equals, but they were definitely recognized in this egalitarian church that gave women the vote in 1787. Blacks appear regularly in the church records. There we learn that Brother Daniel was a slave "intrusted with the management of his quarter upon the river" and that he was suspected of theft because he sold some meat. Daniel's own spiritual growth as a result of this incident seems apparent from the record. At first he denied the fact that he sold the meat, but then, in "owning" his own sin (of lying) he found new strength:

> Bro. Thos. Buck entered a complaint against Br. Daniel (negro) for uttering a falsity about selling some bacon. Br. Daniel (a slave to Mr. Peter Catlett and intrusted with the management of his quarter upon the river) sold a few pounds of bacon and being questioned therefor by some of the members denied it. But in a short time returned to the same person owned the fact and the crime of uttering a falsity in denying it, with such evident marks of repentance as gave full satisfaction to those members withal informing them that what he sold was his own property given him by his master for his own private use. That he sold it in pity to the buyer. That his denial was owing to

his fear his master might be displeased with him as he had given him meat to use and not to sell.

As was usual, the church appointed a committee to investigate, and in this case they went to Daniel's owner, Peter Catlett, who was not a member of their church. They reported back that Catlett thought Daniel had "done nothing but what he thought just." Daniel was *not* cowed or broken by this incident. On the contrary he immediately "appointed meetings for the public exhortation of negroes," an act that met with a mixed reaction. Daniel was clearly an "actor" in this scene. A slave, he voluntarily chose to contribute to the church fund, although only heads of households were expected to do so. His opinions were also heard, and although we do not have the details, later, when he showed "partiality in the church," it was "a cause for distress" and dissension, and the community tried to work up a consensus.

Blacks and whites in one congregation had to be at peace with one another, or "in fellowship." Disagreements had to be aired, and forgiveness extended, by all parties. Daniel's is not a unique case. Blacks appear in these church records as individuals, and their interaction with whites can be documented. Again, there is no doubt but that black opinions were being heard and counted in many matters, not only in defense of charges made against them.

Blacks were part of the covenanting "inner group" that formed many of the churches, signing the covenants with their white brothers and sisters. Of the 74 original members at the Dan River Church, 11 were black. Of the 158 who were in the Hartwood Church at its origin in 1771, 24 were black. Lower Banister, organized in July of 1798, then had 31 whites and 11 blacks. The church that Robert Carter and Hannah Ludwell Lee Corbin joined, the Morattico Church, had more blacks in it than whites, including 29 of Carter's own slaves. In the church they were his equals, able to bring criticism of their master as the proper "business" of the church.

Slaves *did* bring criticism of whites to communal sessions. It was not simply an abstract right, although it is most likely that they were careful and concerned in their use of this privilege. The slaveowner could simply leave the church and continue or intensify his behavior. (He could not join another Baptist church without a letter of dismissal showing that he was not under censure.) It should be emphasized that in William Warren Sweet's term, Baptist and later Methodist churches were "courts" for their members. All issues of behavior and misbehavior were to be brought before them. They dealt with issues between whites and whites, blacks and blacks, and *whites and blacks.* They concerned themselves with relations between wives and husbands (condemning wife beating) and parents and children (demanding that parents instruct children and servants in proper behavior), and they condemned "immoral acts" in everyone.

In Virginia, in the last third of the eighteenth century, Baptists found a large range of activities immoral, strictly delimiting proper behavior. It was immoral to play the violin or banjo or sing worldly songs or to dance, to dress "gaudily," to go to horse races, to bet, to drink to excess, to swear, to talk spitefully, or to disturb the consensus in a church family. In 1785, "Joseph Dinry was deeply cencured [*sic*] for whipping his wife." The Broad Run Church found his behavior

An action in or esteem, not a little scandalous For a husband to beat his wife, we judge to be a practice contrary both to Scripture & Reason; to the law & the Gospel. And as

such, not to be once named among Christians. Not to be tolerated in the Church of
Christ, on any pretense whatever.

In 1780, the Upper King and Queen County Church took

into consideration the many superfluous forms and modes of Dressing, and condemned
the Following, viz. Cock't hatts, curl'd and powdered hair, also tied hair by manr [*sic*]
likewise two stocks the one white and the other Black at the same time. Gold to be worn
by none—High Crown'd Caps—Rolls—Necklaces, Ruffles, Stays & Stomagers.

Upper King and Queen excommunicated Davise's Jack (a slave) and

agreed that any member who takes the liberty to go to a horse race or any other such
unnecessary, unprofitable and sinful Assemblies or Gatherings of People are Directed
to come to the next succeeding church meeting and there to be answerable to the
church for such conduct.

Excommunication was the usual punishment for violation of clear-cut taboos. Sin-
ners could return, exhibit contrition, and ask for reinstatement, but until then they
could not participate in the life of the church or the community, nor could they be
buried by the church or expect God to welcome them to heaven.

Blacks and whites were widely excluded for these same faults. White Henry
Watkins was excommunicated "for playing the violin and associating in the company of wicked men," and "Negro Jedia" for "stealing from a brother." Blacks as
well as whites used these church forums to settle disputes among themselves. In
1799, George and Ben brought a dispute to the Buck Marsh meeting over how
much money had changed hands between them (to buy potatoes) and who had
called whom a liar. There was "a black sister wishing the advice of the Church in a
certain [matter] on her mind [about] Marrying a man who has formally had a wife."
One Brother Ned brought charges "against Sister Sarah (servant to Wm. Larue)
that Sarah had taken some Meat from her Master which he conceiv'd was not hon-
estly come by." The church investigated and decided the charges were due to the
animosity Ned held against Sarah and "that it proceeded from other matters which
happen'd Between them some time before." Whites brought very much the same
range of issues for discussion, although the blacks' concern with their own
monogamy (and the whites' concern with black monogamy) was a major issue.

Sexual behavior played an important role in the new morality of these church
families. Fornication and adultery were anathema, and the church set out to
counter the laxity of social norms in Virginia, in which black-white interaction had
played a role. Blacks were adjured to marry other blacks, to regard their marriages
as permanent, and to refrain from sex prior to marriage, outside of marriage, and/or
with whites. Whites were given the same admonitions and adjured to refrain from
sex with blacks. Their power and position as owners and overseers was recognized
as a very dangerous one.

In 1799, "Theo Coleman's Guice [was] Excommunicated for keeping two
wives." The next year Guice was accepted back "by repentance," which no doubt
included his putting aside one wife. Mulatto Charles, on the other hand, was excommunicated for "putting away" his one wife. Divorce was not allowed for
whites or blacks (except if one partner was guilty of adultery), nor was a white
(slaveowner) allowed to "separate" (a euphemism for selling) a slave from his

marriage partner. In Upper King and Queen Church they made this plain: "Query: Is it agreeable to scripture for any member to part man & wife? Answer: No. And any member who Shall be guilty of such crimes shall be dealt with by the church for such crimes [*sic*] misconduct." The Buck Marsh Church reached a similar conclusion in 1791, holding both slaves and slaveowners accountable. They then embarked on a serious evaluation of their black members' marital lives and charged many blacks with "sinfull parting from their spouces" with both whites and blacks bringing charges.

Whites were also widely censured for sexual misconduct. In 1795, Occoquan Church excluded two white women, one for being "previously married" and the other for "a disorderly way of life." Both blacks and whites were commonly charged with "adultery," but only black "Dunn's Peggy [was] excommunicated for keeping a White man as husband unlawfully."

Although "disobedience and Aggrevation" to a master were recognized as cause to excommunicate Negro Nemney, and "Negro Lemon was excommunicated for lying and disobedience to his master," charges involving blacks and whites usually revolved around thefts by the black slaves, violence of the white slaveowners, or sexual misbehavior of both races.

Thefts, as we have seen, were simple cases. Investigative committees were established, often including blacks, and their findings were discussed by the whole church. Consensus was sought, and there was no question but that when a slave "took" something from a master, it was theft. Negro Isaac was "reported" to have taken a "horse, bridle and saddle" belonging to one James Mason. Isaac had already been "tryed for the offense" by his owner and by the Justices of the Peace for Northumberland County. Nevertheless his church, Morattico, concluded that it would investigate the charge, and if they thought it were "true," he would be excommunicated.

Violence to slaves involved questions of both fact and theory. The church had to establish not only what the master had done but what he had a right to do. In June of 1772, the Meherrin Church discussed the question, "Is it Lawful to punish our servants by burning them & in any case whatsoever?" They resolved the issue with a unanimous "No" and immediately moved to suspend Brother Charles Cook "for burning one of his Negroes." In July, Cook, who owned three slaves and at least 150 acres of land, came to a small business meeting to "acknowledge his sin in unlawfully burning one of his Negroes." He was requested to appear before the whole congregation, blacks and whites together, "to give the Church satisfaction." This incident appears to have been traumatic for Charles Cook. There is no evidence of his having had any call to preach prior to his punishment, but by September of 1772, Cook was preaching. Several of his own slaves joined the church, perhaps due to his conversionary efforts. By June of 1775, the church called this former slave burner "Our beloved Charles Cook," as he was "unanimously chosen as a Teaching Elder" for the Sandy Creek branch, a congregation with a very large black membership. In 1777, Cook was given a commission to "Itinerate" or preach around the countryside where, once again, blacks were an important part of his audience. Cook's interaction with blacks and the church had apparently changed his values and his life: From a slaveburner he had become virtually a missionary to the blacks.

Cook's church, Meherrin Church, also moved further in its concern with black welfare. In May of 1773, they considered

> Whether it is lawful for a Bro. or Sister to whip or beat one of their servants or children, members of the Church, before the method that Christ has prefered [*sic*] & laid down in the 18th Mathew, Solved No. [By a] Majority.

The eighteenth verse in Matthew calls for a private verbal confrontation with a wrongdoer and then, if necessary, criticism by a group. The final punishment suggested is shunning:

> Moreover if thy brother shall trespass against thee, go and tell him his fault between thee and him alone: if he shall hear thee, thou hast gained thy brother. But if he will not hear thee, then take thee with one or two more, that in the mouth of two or three witnesses every word may be established. And if he shall neglect to hear the church, let him be unto thee as a heathen man and a publican.

Slaveowners did bring charges against their slaves in church, whereas blacks made more sparing use of this forum. Charges against whites could backfire, but they could also play a role even if proved false. "Negro Abigel, belonging to Brother Hunton," was excommunicated "for slandering & false accusing her Master to other Brethern [*sic*] and then denying it before the Church."

In 1772, Sister Rebekah Johnson of the Meherrin Church was accused "by two of the Black Brethren of the sin of anger and unchristian language, also [of] offering something like parting of a black Bro. & Sister (Man and Wife)." She "own'd . . . part of their allegations" and "seem'd penitent," but the blacks would not accept this. Their charges were apparently far more extensive than what she "own'd." The church appointed a committee of four whites *and two blacks* (Brothers Dick and Sam) to interview all those concerned. The committee succeeded in establishing peace, and although no details were recorded, Sister Rebekah Johnson and Sister Esther (her servant) gave each other the right hand of fellowship. Although we cannot know what happened to Estis, the black husband involved, it appears most likely he was sold away, and that Esther had to make her peace with this, perhaps recognizing that Joseph Johnson, husband and master (and not a church member), was responsible.

Brother Sherwood Walton, an active member of the Meherrin Church in the 1770s, was accused of sin by one of his slaves who was not a member of the church. There ensued a fascinating story, recorded in great detail by the church clerk, that indicates above all else how ready the white brethren were to believe that their brother in good standing (who served on disciplinary committees) could himself be guilty of a sexual sin, as well as to what lengths a slave would go to besmirch a master's "good name."

> September 1775. Bro. Sherwood Walton accused by some of the Brethren for being guilty of, or at least offering the Act of uncleaness to a Mulatto Girl of his own—The circumstances are as follows. 1st the Girl proved with Child. She often hinted to his Daughters that her Master was the Father of it (if she was with child). Upon that he took to correct her for it, she found him in it, and declared she believed he was the father of it, if any one was; Tho she knew not that any person had carnal knowledge of her but supposed it might be done while she was asleep but that she knew of his coming

& offering such things at times to her. This she affirmed, and would not relinquish at the expense of being well drubbed for it several times, this was prov'd to us. At the time of her extremity in childbearing she was charged by the Midwives then to own the truth & clear her Master, if clear, and as her extremity was more than common they told her it might be a judgement of God upon her, and that she might die; but all could not prevail upon her—she confidently affirmed what she had said she then said, but behold when the child was born, it proved to be a remarkable black child, a Negro without any doubt proved by the Midwives & other people who saw the child which gave satisfaction to all the church but 4 . . . [listed by name]. Some of the Brethren neighbours declared her to be of a remarkable wicked Temper & disposition, & did believe she accused him in order to revenge (inso) [?] that it was proved he was always very severe to her & upon closely question him, Bro. Walton, he denied the fact, 2 of the Brethren relinquish'd their scruples . . . the other 2 yet [held out].

The last two individuals who objected to reinstating Walton were "worked on" to bring the community back into harmony, and finally, some time after the black baby was born, all those attending church offered Walton the right hand of fellowship. (One sister, Old Sister Rivers, absolutely refused and absented herself from meetings.)

Walton's slave woman had used the church and church rules to put Walton through a great deal of distress. His behavior had been investigated, his violence to his slaves exposed, and his morals seriously questioned. His daughters had heard the charges as had his neighbors and, in fact, the whole community. Although he was exonerated of "fathering" her child, he certainly emerged with a different public image from what he had before.

Charges against other slaveowners were upheld by Baptist churches: Nero, a slave, charged his owner, John Lawrence, with "misconduct," and the South Quay Church expelled Lawrence. James Johnson was excommunicated by the Black Creek Church as were a Brother Tines and his wife for "using Barbarity toward their Slaves." If the white brother or sister remained strong in the faith and wanted to return, as Lawrence and Cook did, the church could serve as a moral guardian of a black's human rights. But in other cases, as in those of Johnson and Tines, there is no record of white contrition, and it is certainly possible that the punished slaves were punished even more barbarously after these incidents. Other whites in the churches, however, were affected by the bravery and courage of these blacks and were brought to a new consciousness of the realities of slavery.

Slavery per se began to be an issue in the Baptist churches. Again, it was not ideology but the reality of contact and shared spiritual lives that brought whites to this changed perception. Now, too, they had a view of themselves as moral agents, living in a godly way, and criticizing their own behavior. Church after church asked, "Is it a Rituous [sic] thing for a Christian to hold or cause any of the human race to be held in slavery?" After serious consideration they answered, "Unrighteous!!" It is important to emphasize that inasmuch as consensus had been worked up, this was the church as a whole speaking. These were not leadership decisions or a bowing to directives from above.

As whites and blacks shared church life, more whites came to see the institution of slavery as evil. John Poindexter, a successful slaveowner who originally was enraged by his wife's 1788 conversion to the Baptists, was himself converted and rebaptized in 1790. He began to preach in 1791, and soon became very popular, establishing churches and converting hundreds. He himself was also "converted" in regard to slavery. In 1797, he called for prayers for

> the Poor Slaves, who are groaning under grevious oppression in this part of the Lord's Vineyard; I have been an advocate for Slavery, but thanks be to God, My Eyes have been Opened to see the impropriety of it, and I long for the Happy times to Come, when the Church of Christ shall loose the Bands of Wickedness, undo the Heavy burdens, and let the oppressed go free, that her light may Spring forth in the Morning—and her Righteousness go before her—

Many other Baptists were moved to recognize the unrighteousness of slavery. David Barrow, born in 1753 to a farm family in Brunswick County, was "reborn" in 1770. He preached successfully at Mill Swamp Church, Isle of Wight, 1774; fought in the Revolution; and returned to Virginia to preach to growing numbers. In 1784, he freed his slaves, feeling "The Spirit of the Lord is upon me . . . to preach deliverance [emancipation] to the captives."

Robert Carter, one of the few of the top elite to join the Baptists in this period (1777), had become a Swedenborgian by the time he began to free his slaves in 1791, but Leland and other Baptists had influenced him deeply. He too had come to see slaveowning as a sin. Most white Baptists, however, continued to live with slaves, as owners, managers, or neighbors, and most black Baptists continued to be slaves.

New Baptist John Self, Landon Carter's overseer at his Rings Neck plantation, stayed at his job so that he might do God's work, as Carter recorded:

> News just came John Self at Rings Neck turned a Baptist, and only waits to convert my people. He had two brethren Preachers and two other with him; and says he cannot serve God and Mammon, has just been made a Christian by dipping, and would not continue in my business but to convert my people.

Although Self and Poindexter continued to live with slaves and slavery, out of moral responsibility, their shared new faith probably helped some new black Baptists to find the inner strength to risk running away. Owners certainly seemed to think this was so. It was noted that Runaway Hannah "pretends much to the religion the Negroes of late have practiced," and George Noble felt constrained to describe his former slave, Jupiter, "alias Gibb," as having scars on his back from a recent whipping at Sussex courthouse, "having been tried there for stirring up the Negroes to an insurrection, being a great Newlight preacher." In other words, it was his preaching of the word that stirred rebellion both in him and in his audience.

In 1789, the sheriff of King William County complained to the governor that blacks and whites were meeting together, often until two or three in the morning, and that the whites had prevented the patrollers from carrying out their duty by throwing them out of the window of the meeting house. That they were willing to defy the law indicates how important it was to those whites to have blacks at their meetings.

Baptist preacher John Williams (1747–1795), who owned twenty-two slaves, kept a journal of his journey to churches, outdoor meetings, and "revivals" held in the summer of 1771, when hundreds generally came; it was reported that from four to five thousand had assembled for the largest meeting. Christians were "shouting," there was "a good deal of exercise among the people," and Williams found himself with "some liberty and a feeling sense of souls." It is particularly interesting that he did not fear the Devil but spirits.

There were "six preaching gifts among us," he recounts.

> I immediately seem'd to have the greatest impression I have ever had, though did not know from what spirit, therefore, waited some time for some of the rest. All seem'd to be backward which made me conclude mine was from God, but He only Knows whether it was. I was so constrained I could not forbear. I got up & sung & preached to the people from Revelations, 21st chap. & 7th & 8th verses.

These chapters in the Bible deal with salvation and with hellfire in graphic terms; they may have seemed particularly addressed to both the Afro-American and the unchurched white Virginian, given their references to "sorcerers and idolators."

That same summer William Lee adjured his overseer to try to keep his slaves from having contact with the "New Light Preachers" who "have put most of my people [*sic*] Negroes crazy with their new Light and their new Jerusalem." But Lee, and other owners frightened by the new developments, did not succeed in stopping blacks from attending the mass meetings.

At these meetings blacks shared spiritual experiences with whites. Here, as at baptisms and at funerals, blacks had ecstatic vision experiences and recounted "God's precious dealing with their souls." The conversion experience was seen as an experience with death and ecstasy—the hellfire and balm that Whitefield, Williams, and Davies had brought news of. Blacks and whites both knew that to come to Christ was to *die* to the old life, as the old self, and to be reborn in a new spiritual growth. The baptism experience was graphically one of death, of going under the waters, where only the spirit can find nourishment, and rebirth in ecstasy. Whites and blacks were regularly baptized together and "came through" shouting and singing at the same time.

Blacks began recounting their experiences by placing their spiritual journeys in a matrix of African time. One former slave reported, "One day while in the field plowing I heard a voice." Another heard God when "I was about grown." "When the voice first spoke to me I was in the cotton patch." "After I got married," God struck. This voice had to be "checked out" or validated, and it was a sign of just how important white time was becoming that God occasionally brought the magical knowledge of whites' reckoning of age as the gift-proof of true prophecy. A little girl was told "O ye generation of vipers, who had warned you to flee from the wrath to come? My little one, you are now eight years old. Go and ask the Lord to have mercy on your dying soul." The mother accepted the vision as a true one because it gave her daughter white calendar-wisdom.

Blacks regarded this God as a "time God," but this meant a God who came in his own time and who let everyone know that he could not be hurried. He came in visions at his own will and taught patience. "I saw, as it were, a ladder. It was more like a pole with rungs on it let down from heaven, and it reached from heaven to earth." Man had to climb this ladder, slowly.

These black visions converted white Christian concern with the end of days into visions of time past and of forefathers. In vision travels blacks traveled to heaven and saw God as well as their mothers and fathers and other dead relations. The reality of forefathers' power, believed in by Africans, was reinforced by these

"Christian" vision travels. And in the visions, time past was seen as part of the present and of the future.

> I wonder where's my dear mother
> she's been gone so long
> I think I hear her shouting
> Around the Throne of God.

Heaven was home and blacks sang: "I'm going there to see my mother'n, fathr'n," and family. And they "visited" them there from time to time in ecstatic trances.

In these visions blacks also saw new fictive kin: Jacob, Moses, Gabriel, and Jesus were met with and talked to. They became common ancestors, new generations in the genealogical tables, regarded as common to whites and blacks alike. In accepting Christianity, Jacob, Moses, Daniel, Gabriel, and Jesus became spiritual forefathers, as they did in Africa. "When Tiv encountered Europeans and heard the creation story, they immediately accepted 'Adam and Ife' as part of their cosmic doctrine."

For Africans, the "living are reflections of the dead and vice versa." Similarly, American black Christians compared themselves to Adam in his marital troubles with Eve, and to Jonah, who tried to evade responsibility and God's call. They expected to "wrassle" the Lord like Jacob and to find a Moses to lead them from slavery. When black mourners lay moaning on the floor, waiting for the spirit to come to them, the Christians around them sang:

> Rassal Jacob, rassal as you did in the days of old
> Gonna rassal all night till broad day light
> And ask God to bless my soul.

In these vision tales blacks recounted that when they were converted they had to die. God struck them dead:

On Thursday Morning, the sun was shining bright, I was chopping corn in the garden, when a voice "hollered" and said, "Oh, Nancy, you got to die and can't live." I started to run because it scared me but I got weak and felt myself dying from my feet to my head. . . . I cried, "I am dying; I am dying; I am dying. Lord, have mercy on my soul." As quick as a flash I felt a change.

After seeing hell, heaven, and God, Nancy Williams, a slave in Virginia, recounted that she "started to shouting in the spirit and haven't stopped yet. I died the sinner death and ain't got to die no more. I am fixed up for the building." Black after black was called by name and then "was killed dead to sin and made alive again in Jesus Christ." The dying and death were experienced as very real. When God struck Nancy Williams, she claimed her owner was ready to have her buried. She was "put on de bench whar dey laid out de daid." The ensuing trip down to the fires of hell and up to the white glory of heaven—where a true home, a "building," awaited and where eternal life would really be lived—was also very real. Slaves believed they had truly been to these places. They had seen and felt the fires of hell, and their inner essence, part of their being or one of their souls, had been taken on a perilous journey, through trials, up to heaven. The "little me" that was in the "big me," the little Mary in the big Mary, had been taken by a spirit guide to the blazing white of God's throne. There,

I was told that I was one of the elected children and that I would live as long as God lives. I rejoice every day of my life for I know that I have another home—a house not made with human hands. A building is waiting for me way back in eternal glory and I have no need to fear.

Black vision experiences repeated these themes over and over. God knew the sinner by name—the name used in baptism and on the church books. Miles, Patience, Peter, James, Esther, Quamina, Clocy, Anika, Moses, Fanny, Aggy, Bristol, they are all "called by name." God knows their inner essence and they have an eternal name that symbolizes it. No slaveowner could take away or change this name. These people knew that their souls came from God and would return to God, much as Africans believed that their souls were from spirit and would return to spirit. These black Baptists believed that God *killed them dead.* Encounters with God were not mild or gentle affairs. God struck them down, gave them harsh spiritual experiences, and only then brought them to a rebirth.

Consider the parallels of the slave experiences with this description of the experience of an Azande woman-diviner in Africa as recorded by E. E. Evans-Pritchard:

Nambua said that, "she died and . . . [her co-villagers] dug a grave for her and everyone wailed. Her soul went forth and appeared at the place of ghosts. She was just looking about when all her [deceased] relatives collected and made a circle around her. It was her mother who said to her, 'What have you come here for? Get up and go whence you came. Go away quickly.' She departed from amongst these people and her eyes at once opened. Everyone ceased wailing and she began immediately to wake from death and recovered completely."

Similarly at the initiation of a medium along the Lulua, BaSonge, or BaLuba of Zaire, the initiate is also "believed to have been dead, to have traveled to the land of the souls, and to have then returned to life."

In Africa most mediums had died and been reborn during their initiations. In addition, most young people had also undergone initiations into "manhood" and "womanhood," and these near-universal ceremonies also involved a symbolic rebirth. Africans had wide experience both with symbolic death and rebirth as well as with ecstatic joy. A high percentage of African ethnic groups followed ritual that aroused religious ecstasy, although only special mediums served the gods directly.

Afro-American Christianity gave every individual the opportunity to die and be reborn. It amalgamated African understandings of death and spirit travel to the world of forefathers, with Christian visions of God and heaven. Every Christian could find a "home" with God and with kin. Jacob would be there, and Moses, and Jesus, and grandmothers, grandfathers, wives, husbands, and children. A building was waiting, a Big House for all the saved.

The new Christianity changed the African linkage of close kin and unique afterworld, which had excluded the stranger and the slave from the afterlife of an ethnic group, to a linkage of all Christians to one Heaven. In Africa, even a married couple might expect to be separated after death. The Igbo, for example, sent a wife's body, and presumably her soul, to stay with her father's clan. Now all God's children could expect to be in the Christian heaven; certainly status as a slave was not a barrier. On the contrary, "the last would be first." The cause of death and the age of the deceased would not keep an individual out. A slave, beaten to death, could expect to view his master in hell while he was in heaven. Black understandings of immortal places as well as time, while maintaining important continuities with African values, had altered significantly.

Whites too changed their values and understandings. They became more "open" to ecstasy and spiritual life, ready and willing to have "experience," and to share their experience with others. They opened themselves to communal criticism, something Africans may have had more experience with, among co-wives, secret society members, and at the chief's court. And they came to accept death as the gateway to the continuation of the vision world they had already experienced, where their families awaited them, rather than as a terrifying unknown.

FURTHER READING

Roger D. Abrahams, *Singing the Master: The Emergence of African American Culture in the Plantation South* (1992).

Ira Berlin and Ronald Hoffman, eds., *Slavery and Freedom in the Age of the American Revolution* (1983).

W. Jeffrey Bolster, *Black Jacks: African American Seamen in the Age of Sail* (1997).

Alan Dundes, "'Jumping the Broom': On the Origin and Meaning of an African American Wedding Custom," *Journal of American Folklore,* 109 (1996), 324–329.

Douglas R. Egerton, *Gabriel's Rebellion: The Virginia Slave Conspiracies of 1800 and 1802* (1993).

William Ferris, ed., *Afro-American Folk Arts and Crafts* (1983).

Joseph E. Holloway, *Africanisms in American Culture* (1990).

Charles W. Joyner, "The Creolization of Slave Folklife: All Saints Parish, South Carolina, as a Test Case," *Historical Reflections* [Canada], 6 (1979), 435–453.

Daniel Littlefield, *Rice and Slaves: Ethnicity and the Slave Trade in Colonial South Carolina* (1981).

Sidney W. Mintz and Richard Price, *The Birth of African-American Culture: An Anthropological Perspective* (1992).

William D. Pierson, *Black Yankees: The Development of an Afro-American Subculture in Eighteenth-Century New England* (1988).

Albert J. Raboteau, *Slave Religion: The "Invisible Institution" in the Antebellum South* (1978).

Robert Farris Thompson, *Flash of the Spirit: African and Afro-American Arts and Philosophy* (1984).

R. L. Watson, "American Scholars and the Continuity of African Culture in the United States," *Journal of Negro History,* 63 (1978), 375–386.

Donald Yacovone, "The Fruits of Africa: Slavery, Emancipation, and Afro-American Culture," *American Quarterly,* 40 (1988), 569–576.

CHAPTER
5

The Development of a
Slave Society in
Colonial North America

A central theme of African-American history is the process by which slaves from disparate African ethnic groups forged a single African-American people. That process was simultaneous with and interrelated with the transformation of the southern colonies from societies with slaves to slave societies. The American Revolution was an important turning point in that process as it marked the beginning of the end of slavery in the northern states and, by contrast, its intensification in most of the southern states. How did colonial slavery evolve into the mature system of the antebellum South? What impact did its evolution have on the formation of African Americans as a people?

Demographic, social, and political developments shaped this dual transformation. Although most of the slaves brought to North America arrived in the eighteenth century, during that century the slave population also became predominantly American-born. As we saw in Chapter 4, this was also the century in which for the first time African Americans converted to Christianity in large numbers. But it was also a century marked by several slave revolts and aborted conspiracies to revolt, including major scares or uprisings in New York City (1712 and 1741), South Carolina (1739), Virginia (1800), and the still-French colony of Louisiana (1791). Meanwhile, the maturing of staple cultivation for export (tobacco, rice, and indigo) consolidated a wealthy, self-confident planter ruling class in key southern colonies. A series of colonial wars, culminating with the American Revolution, steadily reduced the European colonial rivalries that slaves could sometimes exploit to resist or escape enslavement.

DOCUMENTS

Arguably the beginning points for the process of cultural change that would culminate with a new people—African Americans—were the sites of contact and interaction between Africans and Europeans on the West African coast and the Atlantic islands. In the first document, William Snelgrave, a British trader, relates the story of Tom, one of the interpreters, facilitators, voyagers, and sometime diplomats that historian Ira Berlin has called "Atlantic creoles." The second document provides an account of one of the major slave rebellions of the colonial era. Slaves rebelled at Stono, South Carolina, and then marched to seek refuge in Spanish-controlled Florida. Even in this highly biased account one can discern the influence of the recently arrived Angolan slaves, but it is possible that prior experience and contact with the Portuguese in Africa also influenced the rebels' decisions. The Stono Rebellion suggests the impact of inter-European rivalries in shaping slaves' options for resistance. The third document, Lord Dunmore's invitation to slaves to join the British side in the American War of Independence, shows the last moments when such rivalries would open large-scale opportunities for slaves to alter their status. Eventually both sides competed for black loyalty and military service, as the petition by Saul, the fourth document, illustrates. The fifth document, however, shows that blacks not only could appeal for rewards for military service but also could deploy in their cause the fundamental tenets of the Revolution itself—to wit, "no taxation without representation." But Hector St. John de Crèvecoeur's terrifying encounter in a Carolina forest, the sixth document, suggests the limits of appeals to revolutionary idealism.

1. The Story of Tom, an African Creole, 1727

After this his Majesty fell into a variety of Discourse, and amongst other things complained of Mr. Lambe, (who, as I have related in the beginning of this Book, had been taken Prisoner in the Ardra War) saying, "That tho' he had given him, at his leaving the Court, three hundred and twenty ounces of gold, with eight[y] Slaves, and made him promise with a solemn Oath to return again in a reasonable time, yet twelve Moons had now pass'd, and he had heard nothing from him: Adding, "He had sent a black Person with him, whose name was Tom, one who had been made a Prisoner at the same time, being a *Jaqueenman*, who spoke good English; and this Man he had ordered to return again with Mr. Lambe, that he might be informed, whether what that Gentleman had reported concerning our King, Customs, and manner of Living was true." To this I replied "That I had no personal Knowledge of Mr. Lambe, but had been informed, before I left England, that he went from Whidaw to Barbadoes, which is a Plantation where the English employ their Slaves in making Sugar, and which is a great distance from our own Country; But I hoped he would prove an honest Man, and return again to his Majesty, according to his Promise and Oath." To this the King replied, "Tho' he proved not as good as his Word, other white Men should not fare the worse on that account; for as to what he had given Lambe, he valued it not a Rush; but if he returned quickly, and came with never so large a Ship, she should be instantly filled with Slaves, with which he might do what he thought proper."

It may not be improper here to give a short account of the black Man the King mentioned to me, because he was in England last year, and that Affair was brought before the Lords of Trade, by whom I was examined about him.

"William Snelgrave's Account of Guinea," *Documents Illustrative of the History of the Slave Trade to America,* ed. Elizabeth Donnan (New York: Octagon Books, 1969), 2:345–48.

Mr. Lambe carried this Person to Barbadoes, and several other Places, but at last left him with a Gentleman in Maryland. Afterwards Mr. Lambe trafficked for some Years, from one place to another in the Plantations; and coming to the Island of Antegoa, where I had been in the year 1728, and told the foregoing story to some Gentlemen, and how kindly the King of Dahomè had express'd himself with regard to the said Mr. Lambe, being by them informed of it, this induced him to return to Maryland; and the Gentleman who had Tom in his Custody was so good, as to deliver him again to Mr. Lambe, who came with him to London, the beginning of the year 1731.

Mr. Lambe, soon after his arrival, came to see me at my house, enquiring particularly about what I had related at Antegoa; which I confirmed to him. Then he desired my Advice about his going back to the King of Dahomè. To this I frankly answered, "It was my opinion, he had miss'd the opportunity, by not returning in a reasonable time, according to his promise; several years being now pass'd since he came from thence, and the State of Affairs much altered for the worse: Besides, he might justly fear the King's resentment, as Mr. Testehole had experienced lately to his cost, for abusing his Goodness; for tho' he was Governour for the African Company at Whidaw, yet he had been put to death in a cruel manner."

On this he left me; and the next news I heard, was, That Mr. Lambe had delivered a Letter to his Majesty King George as from the King of Dahomè, which being referred to the Lords of Trade, the Merchants trading to the Coast of Guinea were sent for; and I being ordered to attend, informed their Lordships of what I knew of the matter.

The report from the Lords of Trade was to this Purpose, "That the Letter in their opinion was not genuine, but that the black Man ought to be taken care of, and returned to his King:" Accordingly he was put into the hands of the African Company, who took care of him for many Months; but he growing impatient, applied to their Graces the Dukes of Richmond and Montague, who procured him a Passage on board his Majesty's Ship the *Tiger* Captain Berkeley, then bound to the Coast of Guinea.

Moreover, their Lordships having shewed him great Kindness most generously sent by him several rare Presents to his King, which, no doubt, will make a good impression on him in favour of our Nation; and I have lately heard, that on his being put on Shore at Whidaw, he was forthwith sent to the King, who was then in his own Country of Dahomè, and was received graciously by him: That his Majesty sent down handsome Presents for Captain Berkeley, but before the Messengers got to Whidaw, he was sailed, not having patience to wait so many days, as the return from so far inland a place required.

I had not made this Digression, but only to set this Affair in a true light; and undeceive those that may read this Book, and were so far imposed upon, as to suppose the Black Man to have been an Embassador from the King of Dahomè, to his Majesty King George. I met with several that believed so, till I satisfied them of the contrary; for the jest was carried on so far, that several Plays were acted on the Account, and it was advertised in the News-Papers, that they were for the Entertainment of Prince Adomo Oroonoko Tomo, etc. these jingling Names being invented to carry on the Fraud the better.

This black Person was born at Jaqueen, and being from a Boy conversant with the English trading there, learned so well our Language, that he was employed by them, when grown up, as an Interpreter.

He happen'd to be at Ardra on some business, at the time that Country was conquered, and so became Prisoner to the King of Dahomè. But 'tis time to have done with this Story, and go on where I left off. . . .

2. Description of a Slave Rebellion in Stono, South Carolina, 1739

Sometime since there was a Proclamation published at Augustine, in which the King of Spain (then at Peace with Great Britain) promised Protection and Freedom to all Negroes Slaves that would resort thither. Certain Negroes belonging to Captain Davis escaped to Augustine, and were received there. They were demanded by General Oglethorpe who sent Lieutenant Demere to Augustine, and the Governour assured the General of his sincere Friendship, but at the same time showed his Orders from the Court of Spain, by which he was to receive all Run away Negroes. Of this other Negroes having notice, as it is believed, from the Spanish Emissaries, four or five who were Cattel-Hunters, and knew the Woods, some of whom belonged to Captain Macpherson, ran away with His Horses, wounded his Son and killed another Man. These marched f [sic] for Georgia, and were pursued, but the Rangers being then newly reduced [sic] the Countrey people could not overtake them, though they were discovered by the Saltzburghers, as they passed by Ebenezer. They reached Augustine, one only being killed and another wounded by the Indians in their flight. They were received there with great honours, one of them had a Commission given to him, and a Coat faced with Velvet. Amongst the Negroe Slaves there are a people brought from the Kingdom of Angola in Africa, many of these speak Portugueze [which Language is as near Spanish as Scotch is to English,] by reason that the Portugueze have considerable Settlement, and the Jesuits have a Mission and School in that Kingdom and many Thousands of the Negroes there profess the Roman Catholic Religion. Several Spaniards upon diverse Pretences have for some time past been strolling about Carolina, two of them, who will give no account of themselves have been taken up and committed to Jayl in Georgia. The good reception of the Negroes at Augustine was spread about, Several attempted to escape to the Spaniards, & were taken, one of them was hanged at Charles Town. In the latter end of July last Don Pedro, Colonel of the Spanish Horse, went in a Launch to Charles Town under pretence of a message to General Oglethorpe and Lieutenant Governour.

On the 9th day of September last being Sunday which is the day the Planters allow them to work for themselves, Some Angola Negroes assembled, to the number of Twenty; and one who was called Jemmy was their Captain, they suprized a

"The Stono Insurrection, South Carolina, 1739," in *The Colonial Records of the State of Georgia,* ed. Allen D. Chandler (26 vols., Atlanta: Charles P. Byrd, 1913), 22:232–236 (Part II).

Warehouse belonging to Mr. Hutchenson at a place called Stonehow [sic - - -]; they there killed Mr. Robert Bathurst, and Mr. Gibbs, plundered the House and took a pretty many small Arms and Powder, which were there for Sale. Next they plundered and burnt Mr. Godfrey's house, and killed him, his Daughter and Son. They then turned back and marched Southward along Pons Pons, which is the Road through Georgia to Augustine, they passed Mr. Wallace's Tavern towards day break, and said they would not hurt him, for he was a good Man and kind to his Slaves, but they broke open and plundered Mr. Lemy's House, and killed him, his wife and Child. They marched on towards Mr. Rose's resolving to kill him; but he was saved by a Negroe, who having hid him went out and pacified the others. Several Negroes joyned them, they calling out Liberty, marched on with Colours displayed, and two Drums beating, pursuing all the white people they met with, and killing Man Woman and Child when they could come up to them. Collonel Bull Lieutenant Governour of South Carolina, who was then riding along the Road, discovered them, was pursued, and with much difficulty escaped & raised the Countrey. They burnt Colonel Hext's house and killed his Overseer and his Wife. They then burnt Mr. Sprye's house, then Mr. Sacheverell's, and then Mr. Nash's house, all lying upon the Pons Pons Road, and killed all the white People they found in them. Mr. Bullock got off, but they burnt his House, by this time many of them were drunk with the Rum they had taken in the Houses. They increased every minute by new Negroes coming to them, so that they were above Sixty, some say a hundred, on which they halted in a field, and set to dancing, Singing and beating Drums, to draw more Negroes to them, thinking they were now victorious over the whole Province, having marched ten miles & burnt all before them without Opposition, but the Militia being raised, the Planters with great briskness pursued them and when they came up, dismounting; charged them on foot. The Negroes were soon routed, though they behaved boldly several being killed on the Spot, many ran back to their Plantations thinking they had not been missed, but they were there taken and [sic] Shot, Such as were taken in the field also, were after being examined, shot on the Spot, And this is to be said to the honour of the Carolina Planters, that notwithstanding the Provocation they had received from so many Murders, they did not torture one Negroe, but only put them to an easy death. All that proved to be forced & were not concerned in the Murders & Burnings were pardoned, And this sudden Courage in the field, & the Humanity afterwards hath had so good an Effect that there hath been no farther Attempt, and the very Spirit of Revolt seems over. About 30 escaped from the flight, of which ten marched about 30 miles Southward, and being overtaken by the Planters on horseback, fought stoutly for some time and were all killed on the Spot. The rest are yet untaken. In the whole action about 40 Negroes and 20 whites were killed. The Lieutenant Governour sent an account of this to General Oglethorpe, who met the advices on his return from the Indian Nation He immediately ordered a Troop of Rangers to be ranged, to patrole through Georgia, placed some Men in the Garrison at Palichocolas, which was before abandoned, and near which the Negroes formerly passed, being the only place where Horses can come to swim over the River Savannah for near 100 miles, ordered out the Indians in pursuit, and a Detachment of the Garrison at Port Royal to assist the

Planters on any Occasion, and published a Proclamation ordering all the Constables &c. of Georgia to pursue and seize all Negroes, with a Reward for any that should be taken. It is hoped these measures will prevent any Negroes from getting down to the Spaniards.

3. Lord Dunmore, a British General, Entices Slaves of Colonial Rebels to Flee, 1775

Tuesday, 7 November 1775

Royal Chief Magistracy

A Most Disagreeable but Absolutely Necessary Step

By His Excellency the Right Honorable JOHN Earl of DUNMORE, His MAJESTY'S Lieutenant and Governor General of the Colony and Dominion of VIRGINIA, and Vice Admiral of the same.

A PROCLAMATION.

As I have ever entertained Hopes, that an Accommodation might have taken Place between GREAT-BRITAIN and this Colony, without being compelled by my Duty to this most disagreeable but now absolutely necessary Step, rendered so by a Body of armed Men unlawfully assembled, firing on His MAJESTY'S Tenders, and the formation of an Army, and that Army now on their March to attack His MAJESTY'S Troops and destroy the well disposed Subjects of his Colony. To defeat such treasonable Purposes, and that all such Traitors, and their Abettors, may be brought to Justice, and that the Peace, and good Order of this Colony may be again restored, which the ordinary Course of the Civil Law is unable to effect; I have thought fit to issue this my Proclamation, hereby declaring, that until the aforesaid good Purposes can be obtained, I do in Virtue of the Power and Authority to ME given, by His MAJESTY, determine to execute Martial Law, and cause the same to be executed throughout this Colony and to the end that Peace and good Order may the sooner be restored, I do require every Person capable of bearing Arms, to resort to His MAJESTY'S STANDARD, or be looked upon as Traitors to His MAJESTY'S Crown and Government, and thereby become liable to the Penalty the Law inflicts upon such Offences; such as forfeiture of Life, confiscation of Lands, &c. &c. And I do hereby further declare all indented Servants, Negroes, or others, (appertaining to Rebels,) free that are able and willing to bear Arms, they joining His MAJESTY'S Troops as soon as may be, for the more speedy reducing this Colony to a proper Sense of their Duty, to His MAJESTY'S Crown and Dignity. I do further order, and require, all his MAJESTY'S Liege Subjects, to retain their Quitrents, or any other Taxes due or that may become due, in their own Custody, till such Time as Peace may be again restored to this at present most unhappy

"Lord Dunmore's Proclamation," in Robert L. Scribner, ed., *Revolutionary Virginia: The Road to Independence,* vol. 1 (1976), 334. Copyright © 1976 by the Rector and Visitors of the University of Virginia [The University of Virginia Press].

Country, or demanded of them for their former salutary Purposes, by Officers properly authorized to receive the same.

4. Saul, a Slave Revolutionary Veteran, Petitions for Freedom, 1792

To the Honorable, the Speaker, and Members of the general Assembly.

The petition of Saul, a black slave, the property of Geo. Kelly, Esqr. Humbly sheweth.—In the beginning of the late War, that gave America Independence, Your Petitioner Shouldered his Musket and repaired to the American Standard. Regardless of the Invitation, trumpeted forth by British Proclamations, for slaves to Emancipate themselves, by becoming the Assassins of their owners, Your Petitioner avoided the rock, that too many of his colour were Shipwrecked on.—He was taught to know that War was levied upon America, not for the Emancipation of Blacks, but for the Subjugation of Whites, and he thought the number of Bond-men ought not to be augmented; Under those impressions, your Petitioner did actually Campaign it in both Armies,—in the American Army, as a Soldier,—In the British Army as a Spy, which will more fully appear, reference being had to certificates of Officers of respectability. In this double Profession, Your Petitioner flatters himself that he rendered essential service to his Country, and should have rendered much more had he not, in the Campaign of 1781, been betrayed by a Negro whom the British had employed upon the same business in Gen. Mulinburg's Camp. Your Petitioner was at the time, in Portsmouth, a British Garrison, collecting Information for Colonel Josiah Parker, and his heels saved his neck.—He flew to the advance Post, commanded by Col Parker, and that very night led down the party, as a guide, who took off the British Picquett.—

Your Petitioner will trouble Your Honorable Body no further, with enumeration his different species of services, but begs a reference may be had to his certificates, and to the Honorable Thomas Matthews Esquire.—Hoping the Legislatures of a Republick will take his case in consideration and not suffer him any longer to remain a transferable property. And as in duty bound Your Petitioner will ever Pray.

Saul   X   (his mark)

5. Free Blacks in South Carolina Petition for Equal Rights, 1791

To the Honorable David Ramsay Esquire President and to the rest of the Honorable New Members of the Senate of the State of South Carolina.

The Memorial of Thomas Cole Bricklayer P. B. Mathews and Mathew Webb Butchers on behalf of themselves & others Free-Men of Colour.

Willie Lee Rose, ed., *A Documentary History of Slavery in North America* (1976), 61–62. Copyright © 1976 by Oxford University Press, Inc.

"Eighteenth-Century Petition of South Carolina Negroes," *Journal of Negro History,* 31 (January 1946), 98–99.

Humbly Sheweth

That in the Enumeration of Free Citizens by the Constitution of the United States for the purpose of Representation of the Southern States in Congress Your Memorialists have been considered under that description as part of the Citizens of this State. Although by the Fourteenth and Twenty-Ninth clauses in an Act of Assembly made in the Year 1740 and intitled an Act for the better Ordering and Governing Negroes and other Slaves in this Province commonly called The Negro Act now in force Your Memorialists are deprived of the Rights and Privileges of Citizens by not having it in their power to give Testimony on Oath in prosecutions on behalf of the State from which cause many Culprits have escaped the punishment due to their atrocious Crimes, nor can they give their Testimony in recovering Debts due to them, or in establishing Agreements made by them within the meaning of the Statutes of Frauds and Perjuries in force in this State except in cases where Persons of Colour are concerned, whereby they are subject to great Losses and repeated Injuries without any means of redress.

That by the said clauses in the said Act, they are debarred of the Rights of Free Citizens by being subject to a Trial without benefit of a Jury and subject to Prosecution by Testimony of Slaves without Oath by which they are placed on the same footing.

Your Memorialists shew that they have at all times since the Independence of the United States contributed and do now contribute to the support of the Government by chearfully (sic) paying their Taxes proportionable to their Property with others who have been during such period, and now are in full enjoyment of the Rights and Immunities of Citizens Inhabitants of a Free Independent State.

That as your Memorialists have been and are considered as Free-Citizens of this State they hope to be treated as such, they are ready and willing to take and subscribe to such Oath of Allegiance to the States as shall be prescribed by this Honorable House, and are also willing to take upon them any duty for the preservation of the Peace in the City [Charleston?] or any other occasion if called on.

Your Memorialists do not presume to hope that they shall be put on an equal footing with the Free white citizens of the State in general they only humbly solicit such indulgence as the Wisdom and Humanity of this Honorable House shall dictate in their favor by repealing the clauses the act aforementioned, and substituting such a clause as will efectually (sic) Redress the grievances which your Memorialists humbly submit in this their Memorial but under such restrictions as to your Honorable House shall seem proper.

May it therefore please your Honors to take your Memorialists case into tender consideration, and make such Acts or insert such clauses for the purpose of relieving your Memorialists from the un-remitted grievance they now Labour under as in your Wisdom shall seem meet.

And as in duty bound your Memorialists will ever pray.

Signed 1st July 1791.

> Thos Cole
> Peter Bassnett Mathewes
> Matthew Webb

6. Hector St. John de Crèvecoeur, a Traveler, Encounters the Continuing Horror of Slavery in the New Republic, 1782

. . . I was not long since invited to dine with a planter who lived three miles from ———, where he then resided. In order to avoid the heat of the sun, I resolved to go on foot, sheltered in a small path, leading through a pleasant wood. I was leisurely travelling along, attentively examining some peculiar plants which I had collected when all at once I felt the air strongly agitated; though the day was perfectly calm and sultry. I immediately cast my eyes toward the cleared ground, from which I was but at a small distance, in order to see whether it was not occasioned by a sudden shower; when at that instant a sound resembling a deep rough voice, uttered, as I thought, a few inarticulate monosyllables. Alarmed and suprized, I precipitately looked all round, when I perceived at about six rods distance something resembling a cage, suspended to the limbs of a tree; all the branches of which appeared covered with large birds of prey, fluttering about, and anxiously endeavouring to perch on the cage. Actuated by an involuntary motion of my hands, more than by any design of my mind, I fired at them; they all flew to a short distance, with a most hideous noise: when, horrid to think and painful to repeat, I perceived a negro, suspended in the cage, and left there to expire! I shudder when I recollect that the birds had already picked out his eyes, his cheek bones were bare; his arms had been attacked in several places, and his body seemed covered with a multitude of wounds. From the edges of the hollow sockets and from the lacerations with which he was disfigured, the blood slowly dropped, and tinged the ground beneath. No sooner were the birds flown, than swarms of insects covered the whole body of this unfortunate wretch, eager to feed on his mangled flesh and to drink his blood. I found myself suddenly arrested by the power of affright and terror; my nerves were convulsed; I trembled, I stood motionless, involuntarily contemplating the fate of this negro, in all its dismal latitude. The living spectre, though deprived of his eyes, could still distinctly hear, and in his uncouth dialect begged me to give him some water to allay his thirst. Humanity herself would have recoiled back with horror; she would have balanced whether to lessen such reliefless distress, or mercifully with one blow to end this dreadful scene of agonizing torture! Had I had a ball in my gun, I certainly should have despatched him; but finding myself unable to perform so kind an office, I sought, though trembling, to relieve him as well as I could. A shell ready fixed to a pole, which had been used by some negroes, presented itself to me; filled it with water, and with trembling hands I guided it to the quivering lips of the wretched sufferer. Urged by the irresistible power of thirst, he endeavored to meet it, as he instinctively guessed its approach by the noise it made in passing through the bars of the cage. "Tankè, you whitè man, tankè you, putè some poyson and givè me." How long have you been hanging there? I asked him. "Two days, and me no die; the birds, the birds; aaah me!" Oppressed with the reflections

---

"The Charleston Letter," in Hector St. John de Crèvecoeur, *Letters from an American Farmer* (London, 1782), 242–245.

which this shocking spectacle afforded me, I mustered strength enough to walk away, and soon reached the house at which I intended to dine. There I heard that the reason for this slave being thus punished, was on account of his having killed the overseer of the plantation. They told me that the laws of self-preservation rendered such executions necessary; and supported the doctrine of slavery with the arguments generally made use of to justify the practice; with the repetition of which I shall not trouble you at present.

 E S S A Y S

In the first essay Ira Berlin of the University of Maryland paints a striking portrait of the what he calls "the charter generation" of Africans in the Americas; this first cohort of slaves arrived with linguistic skills and a broad knowledge of the Atlantic world. Allan Kulikoff of Northern Illinois University argues that the process by which a distinctive African-American identity emerged was governed largely by demographic and ecological factors—namely the ratio of new African imports to American-born slaves, the ratio of adult women to men, and the size of plantation communities.

Historicizing the Slave Experience

IRA BERLIN

In 1727, Robert "King" Carter, the richest planter in Virginia, purchased a handful of African slaves from a trader who had been cruising the Chesapeake. The transaction was a familiar one to the great planter, for Carter owned hundreds of slaves and had inspected many such human cargoes, choosing the most promising from among the weary, frightened men and women who had survived the transatlantic crossing. Writing to his overseer from his plantation on the Rappahannock River, Carter explained the process by which he initiated Africans into their American captivity. "I name'd them here & by their names we can always know what sizes they are of & I am sure we repeated them so often to them that every one knew their name & would readily answer to them." Carter then forwarded his slaves to a satellite plantation or quarter, where his overseer repeated the process, taking "care that the negros both men & women I sent . . . always go by the names we gave them." In the months that followed, the drill continued, with Carter again joining in the process of stripping newly arrived Africans of the signature of their identity.

Renaming marked Carter's initial endeavor to master his new slaves by separating them from their African inheritance. For the most part, he designated them by common English diminutives—Tom, Jamey, Moll, Nan—as if to consign them to a permanent childhood. But he tagged some with names more akin to barnyard animals—Jumper, for example—as if to represent their distance from humanity, and he gave a few the names of some ancient deity or great personage like Hercules

"From Creole to African: Atlantic Creoles and the Origins of African-American Society in Mainland North America," by Ira Berlin. *William and Mary Quarterly,* 3rd Series, 53 (April 1996), 251–288. Reprinted by permission from the Omohundro Institute of Early American History and Culture.

or Cato as a kind of cosmic jest: the most insignificant with the greatest of names. None of his slaves received surnames, marks of lineage that Carter sought to obliterate and of adulthood that he would not admit.

The loss of their names was only the first of the numerous indignities Africans suffered at the hands of planters in the Chesapeake. Since many of the skills Africans carried across the Atlantic had no value to their new owners, planters disparaged them, and since the Africans' "harsh jargons" rattled discordantly in the planters' ears, they ridiculed them. Condemning new arrivals for the "gross bestiality and rudeness of their manners, the variety and strangeness of their languages, and the weakness and shallowness of their minds, "planters put them to work at the most repetitive and backbreaking tasks, often on the most primitive, frontier plantations. They made but scant attempt to see that slaves had adequate food, clothing, or shelter, because the open slave trade made slaves cheap and the new disease environment inflated their mortality rate, no matter how well they were tended. Residing in sex-segregated barracks, African slaves lived a lonely existence, without families or ties of kin, isolated from the mainstream of Chesapeake life.

So began the slow painful process whereby Africans became African-Americans. In time, people of African descent recovered their balance, mastered the circumstances of their captivity, and confronted their owners on more favorable terms. Indeed, resistance to the new regime began at its inception, as slaves clandestinely maintained their African names even as they answered their owner's call. The transition of Africans to African-Americans or creoles—which is partially glimpsed in the records of Carter's estate—would be repeated thousands of times, as African slavers did the rough business of transporting Africa to America. While the transition was different on the banks of the Hudson, Cooper, St. Johns, and Mississippi rivers than on the Rappahannock, the scenario by which "outlandish" Africans progressed from "New Negroes" to assimilated African-Americans has come to frame the history of black people in colonial North America.

Important as that story is to the development of black people in the plantation era, it embraces only a portion of the history of black life in colonial North America, and that imperfectly. The assimilationist scenario assumes that "African" and "creole" were way stations of generational change rather than cultural strategies that were manufactured and remanufactured and that the vectors of change moved in only one direction—often along a single track with Africans inexorably becoming creoles. Its emphasis on the emergence of the creole—a self-sustaining, indigenous population—omits entirely an essential element of the story: the charter generations, whose experience, knowledge, and attitude were more akin to that of confident, sophisticated natives than of vulnerable newcomers. Such men and women, who may be termed "Atlantic creoles" from their broad experience in the Atlantic world, flourished prior to the triumph of the plantation production on the mainland—the tobacco revolution in the Chesapeake in the last third of the seventeenth century, the rice revolution in the Carolina lowcountry in the first decades of the eighteenth century, the incorporation of the northern colonies into the Atlantic system during the eighteenth century, and finally, the sugar revolution in the lower Mississippi Valley in the first decades of the nineteenth century. Never having to face the cultural imposition of the likes of Robert "King" Carter, black America's charter generations took a different path—despite the presence of slavery and the vilification of slave masters and their apologists. The Atlantic creole's unique experience reveals some of the processes by which race was constructed and reconstructed in the early America.

Black life in mainland North America originated not in Africa or America but in the netherworld between the continents. Along the periphery of the Atlantic—first in Africa, then in Europe, and finally in the Americas—African-American society was a product of the momentous meeting of Africans and Europeans and of their equally fateful encounter with the peoples of the Americas. Although the countenances of these new people of the Atlantic—Atlantic creoles—might bear the features of Africa, Europe, or the Americas in the whole or in part, their beginnings, strictly speaking, were none of those places. Instead, by their experiences and sometimes by their persons, they had become part of the three worlds that came together along the Atlantic littoral. Familiar with the commerce of the Atlantic, fluent in its new languages, and intimate with its trade and cultures, they were cosmopolitan in the fullest sense.

Atlantic creoles originated in the historic meeting of Europeans and Africans on the west coast of Africa. Many served as intermediaries employing their linguistic skills and their familiarity with the Atlantic's diverse commercial practices, cultural conventions, and diplomatic etiquette to mediate between African merchants and European sea captains. In so doing, some Atlantic creoles identified with their ancestral homeland (or a portion of it)—be it African, European, or American—and served as its representatives in negotiations with others. Other Atlantic creoles had been won over by the power and largesse of one party or another, so that Africans entered the employ of European trading companies and Europeans traded with African potentates. Yet others played fast and loose with their diverse heritage, employing whichever identity paid best. Whatever strategy they adopted, Atlantic creoles began the process of integrating the icons and ideologies of the Atlantic world into a new way of life.

The emergence of Atlantic creoles was but a tiny outcropping in the massive social upheaval that accompanied the joining of the peoples of the two hemispheres. But it represented the small beginnings that initiated this monumental transformation, as the new people of the Atlantic made their presence felt. Some traveled widely as blue-water sailors, supercargoes, shipboard servants, and interpreters—the last particularly important because Europeans showed little interest in mastering the languages of Africa. Others were carried—sometimes as hostages—to foreign places as exotic trophies to be displayed before curious publics, eager for firsthand knowledge of the lands beyond the sea. Traveling in more dignified style, Atlantic creoles were also sent to distant lands with commissions to master the ways of newly discovered "others" and to learn the secrets of their wealth and knowledge. A few entered as honored guests, took their places in royal courts as esteemed councilors, and married into the best families.

Atlantic creoles first appeared at the trading *feitorias* or factories that European expansions established along the coast of Africa in the fifteenth century. Finding trade more lucrative than pillage, the Portuguese crown began sending agents to oversee its interests in Africa. These official representatives were succeeded by private entrepreneurs or *lançados*, who established themselves with the aid of African potentates, sometimes in competition with the crown's emissaries.

European nations soon joined in the action, and coastal factories became sites of commercial rendezvous for all manner of transatlantic traders. What was true of the Portuguese enclaves (Axim and Elmina) held for those later established or seized by the Dutch (Fort Nassau and Elmina), Danes (Fredriksborg and Christiansborg), Swedes (Karlsborg and Cape Apolina), Brandenburgers (Pokoso), French (St. Louis and Gorée), and English (Fort Kormantse and Cape Coast) . . . .

Established in 1482 by the Portuguese and captured by the Dutch in 1637, Elmina was one of the earliest factories and an exemplar for those that followed. A meeting place for African and European commercial ambitions, Elmina—the Castle São Jorge da Mina and the town that surrounded it—became headquarters for Portuguese and later Dutch mercantile activities on the Gold Coast and, with a population of 15,000 to 20,000 in 1682, the largest of some two dozen European outposts in the region.

The peoples of the enclaves—both long-term residents and wayfarers—soon joined together genetically as well as geographically. European men took African women as wives and mistresses, and, before long, the offspring of these unions helped people the enclave. Elmina sprouted a substantial cadre of Euro-Africans (most of them Luso-Africans)—men and women of African birth but shared African and European parentage, whose combination of swarthy skin, European dress and deportment, knowledge of local customs, and multilingualism gave them inside understanding of both African and European ways while denying them full acceptance in either culture. By the eighteenth century, they numbered several hundred in Elmina. Farther south along the coast of Central Africa, they may have been even more numerous. . . .

. . . Of necessity, Atlantic creoles spoke a variety of African and European languages, weighted strongly toward Portuguese. From the seeming babble emerged a pidgin that enabled Atlantic creoles to communicate widely. In time, their pidgin evolved into creole, borrowing its vocabulary from all parties and creating a grammar unique unto itself. Derisively called *"fala de Guine"* or *"fala de negros"*—"Guinea speech" or "Negro speech—by the Portuguese and "black Portuguese" by others, this creole language became the lingua franca of the Atlantic.

Although jaded observers condemned the culture of the enclaves as nothing more than "whoring, drinking, gambling, swearing, fighting, and shouting," Atlantic creoles attended church (usually Catholic), married according to the sacraments, raised children conversant with European norms, and drew a livelihood from their knowledge of the Atlantic commercial economy. In short, they created societies of their own, *of* but not always *in*, the societies of the Africans who dominated the interior trade and the Europeans who controlled the Atlantic trade.

Operating under European protection, always at African sufferance, the enclaves developed governments with politics as diverse and complicated as the peoples who populated them and a credit system that drew on the commercial centers of both Europe and Africa. Although the trading castles remained under the control of European metropoles, the towns around them often developed independent political lives—separate from both African and European domination. Meanwhile, their presence created political havoc, enabling new men and women of commerce to gain prominence and threatening older, often hereditary elites. Intermarriage with established peoples allowed creoles to construct lineages that gained them full membership in local elites, something that creoles eagerly embraced. The resultant political turmoil promoted state formation along with new class relations and ideologies.

New religious forms emerged and then disappeared in much the same manner, as Europeans and Africans brought to the enclaves not only their commercial and political aspirations but all the trappings of their cultures as well. Priests and ministers sent to tend European souls made African converts, some of whom saw Christianity as both a way to ingratiate themselves with their trading partners and a new truth. Missionaries sped the process of christianization and occasionally scored striking successes. At the beginning of the sixteenth century, the royal house of Kongo converted to Christianity. Catholicism, in various syncretic forms, infiltrated the posts along the Angolan coast and spread northward. Islam filtered in from the north. Whatever the sources of the new religions, most converts saw little cause to surrender their own deities. They incorporated Christianity and Islam to serve their own needs and gave Jesus and Mohammed a place in their spiritual pantheon. New religious practices, polities, and theologies emerged from the mixing of Christianity, Islam, polytheism, and animism. Similar syncretic formations influenced the agricultural practices, architectural forms, and sartorial styles as well as the cuisine, music, art, and technology of the enclaves. Like the stone fortifications, these cultural innovations announced the presence of something new to those arriving on the coast, whether they came by caravan from the African interior or sailed by caravel from the Atlantic. . . .

Village populations swelled into the thousands. In 1669, about the time the English were ousting the Dutch from the village of New Amsterdam, population 1,500, a visitor to Elmina noted that it contained some 8,000 residents. During most of the eighteenth century, Elmina's population was between 12,000 and 16,000, larger than Charleston, South Carolina—mainland North America's greatest slave port at the time of the American Revolution.

The business of the creole communities was trade, brokering the movement of goods through the Atlantic world. Although island settlements such as Cape Verde, Príncipe, and São Tomé developed indigenous agricultural and sometimes plantation economies, the comings and goings of African and European merchants dominated life even in the largest of the creole communities, which served as both field headquarters for great European mercantile companies and collection points for trade between the African interior and the Atlantic littoral. Depending on the location, the exchange involved European textiles, metalware, guns, liquor, and beads for African gold, ivory, hides, pepper, beeswax, and dyewoods. The coastal trade or cabotage added fish, produce, livestock, and other perishables to this list, especially as regional specialization developed. Everywhere, slaves were bought and sold, and over time the importance of commerce-in-persons grew. . . .

Knowledge and experience far more than color set the Atlantic creoles apart from the Africans who brought slaves from the interior and the Europeans who carried them across the Atlantic, on one hand, and the hapless men and women on whose commodification the slave trade rested, on the other. Maintaining a secure place in such a volatile social order was not easy. The creoles' genius for intercultural negotiation was not simply a set of skills, a tactic for survival, or an attribute that emerged as an "Africanism" in the New World. Rather, it was central to a way of life that transcended particular venues. . . .

Like other people in the middle, Atlantic creoles profited from their strategic position. Competition between and among the Africans and European traders bolstered their stock, increased their political leverage, and enabled them to elevate their social standing while fostering solidarity. Creoles' ability to find a place for themselves in the interstices of African and European trade grew rapidly during periods of intense competition among the Portuguese, Dutch, Danes, Swedes, French, and English and as equally diverse set of African nationals.

At the same time by the same token, the Atlantic creoles' liminality, particularly their lack of identity with any one group, posed numerous dangers. While their middling position made them valuable to African and European traders, it also made them vulnerable: they could be ostracized, scapegoated, and on occasion enslaved. Maintaining their independence amid the shifting alliances between and among Europeans and Africans was always difficult. Inevitably, some failed.

Debt, crime, immorality, or official disfavor could mean enslavement . . . —at least for those on the fringes of the creole community. Placed in captivity, Atlantic creoles might be exiled anywhere around the Atlantic—to the interior of Africa, the islands along the coast, the European metropoles, or the plantations of the New World. In the seventeenth century and the early part of the eighteenth, most slaves exported from Africa went to the sugar plantations of Brazil and the Antilles. Enslaved Atlantic creoles might be shipped to Pernambuco, Barbados, or Martinique. Transporting them to the expanding centers of the New World staple production posed dangers, however, which American planters well understood. The characteristics that distinguished Atlantic creoles—their linguistic dexterity, cultural plasticity, and social agility—were precisely those qualities that the great planters of the New World disdained and feared. For their labor force they desired youth and strength, not experience and sagacity. Indeed, too much knowledge might be subversive to the good order of the plantation. Simply put, men and women who understood the operations of the Atlantic system were too dangerous to be trusted in the human tinderboxes created by the sugar revolution. Thus rejected by the most prosperous New World regimes, Atlantic creoles were frequently exiled to marginal slave societies where would-be slaveowners, unable to compete with the great plantation magnates, snapped up those whom the grandees had disparaged as "refuse" for reasons of age, illness, criminality, or recalcitrance. In the seventeenth century, few New World slave societies were more marginal than those of mainland North America. Liminal peoples were drawn or propelled to marginal societies.

During the seventeenth century and into the eighteenth, the Dutch served as the most important conduit for transporting Atlantic creoles to mainland North America. Through their control of the sea, they dominated the commerce of the Atlantic periphery. . . .

The Dutch transported thousands of slaves from Africa to the New World, trading with all parties, sometimes directly, sometimes indirectly through their base in Curaçao. Most of these slaves came from the interior of Angola, but among them were Atlantic creoles whose connections to the Portuguese offended the Dutch. Following the Portuguese restoration, those with ties to the Dutch may have found themselves in similar difficulties. During the Dutch invasions, the subsequent wars, and then civil wars in which the Portuguese and the Dutch fought each other directly and through surrogates, many creoles were clapped into slavery. Others were seized in the Caribbean by Dutch men-of-war, privateers sailing under Dutch letters of marque, and freebooting pirates. While such slaves might be sent any-where in the Dutch empire between New Netherland and Pernambuco, West India Company officers in New Amsterdam, who at first complained about "refuse" slaves, in time made known their preference for such creoles—deeming "Negros who had been 12 or 13 years in the West Indies" to be "a better sort of Negroes." A perusal of the names scattered through archival remains of New Netherland reveals something of the nature of this transatlantic transfer: Paulo d'Angola and Anthony Portuguese, Pedro Negretto and Francisco Negro, Simon Congo, and Jan Guinea, Van St. Thomas and Francisco Cartagena, Claes de Neger and Assento Angola, and—perhaps most telling—Carla Criole, Jan Creoli, and Christoffel Crioell.

These names trace the tumultuous experience that propelled their owners across the Atlantic and into slavery in the New World. They suggest that whatever tragedy befell them, Atlantic creoles did not arrive in the New World as deracinated chattel stripped of their past and without resources to meet the future. Unlike those who followed them into slavery in succeeding generations, transplanted creoles were not designated by diminutives, tagged with names more akin to barnyard ani-mals, or given the name of an ancient notable or a classical deity. Instead, their names provided concrete evidence that they carried a good deal more than their dig-nity to the Americas.

To such men and women, New Amsterdam was not radically different from Elmina or Luanda, save for its smaller size and colder climate. A fortified port con-trolled by the Dutch West India Company, its population was a farrago of petty traders, artisans, merchants, soldiers, and corporate functionaries, all scrambling for status in a frontier milieu that demanded intercultural exchange. On the tip of Man-hattan Island, Atlantic creoles rubbed elbows with sailors of various nationalities, Native Americans with diverse tribal allegiances, and pirates and privateers who professed neither nationality nor allegiance. In the absence of a staple crop, their work—building fortifications, hunting and trapping, tending fields and domestic animals, and transporting merchandise of all sorts—did not set them apart from workers of European descent, who often labored alongside them. Such encounters made a working knowledge of the creole tongue as valuable on the North American coast as in Africa. Whereas a later generation of transplanted Africans would be linguistically isolated and de-skilled by the process of enslavement, Atlantic creoles found themselves very much at home in the new environment. Rather than losing their skills, they discovered that the value of their gift for intercultural negotiation appreciated. The transatlantic journey did not break creole communities; it only transported them to other sites.

Along the edges of the North American continent, creoles found slaves' cultural and social marginality an asset. Slaveholders learned that slaves' ability to negotiate with the diverse populace of seventeenth-century North America was as valuable as their labor, perhaps more so. While their owners employed creoles' skills on their own behalf, creoles did the same for themselves, trading their knowledge for a place in the still undefined social order. In 1665, when Jan Angola, accused of stealing wood in New Amsterdam, could not address the court in Dutch, he was ordered to return the following day with "Domingo the Negro as interpreter," an act familiar to Atlantic creoles in Elmina, Lisbon, San Salvador, or Cap Français.

To be sure, slavery bore heavily on Atlantic creoles in the New World. As in Africa and Europe, it was a system of exploitation, subservience, and debasement that rested on force. Yet Atlantic creoles were familiar with servitude in forms ranging from unbridled exploitation to corporate familialism. They had known free people to be enslaved, and they had known slaves to be liberated; the boundary between slavery and freedom on the African coast was permeable. Servitude generally did not prevent men and women from marrying, acquiring property (slaves included), enjoying a modest prosperity and eventually being incorporated into the host society; creoles transported across the Atlantic had no reason to suspect they could not do the same in the New World. If the stigma of servitude, physical labor, uncertain lineage, and alien region stamped them as outsiders, there were many others—men and women of unblemished European pedigree prominent among them—who shared those taints. That black people could and occasionally did hold slaves and servants and employ white people suggested that race—like lineage and religion—was just one of many markers in the social order. . . .

The black men and women who entered New Netherland between 1626 and the English conquest in 1664 exemplified the ability of people of African descent to integrate themselves into mainland society during the first century of settlement, despite their status as slaves and the contempt of the colony's rulers. Far more than any other mainland colony during the first half of the seventeenth century, New Netherland rested on slave labor. The prosperity of the Dutch metropole and the opportunities presented to ambitious men and women in the far-flung Dutch empire denied New Netherland its share of free Dutch immigrants and limited its access to indentured servants. To populate the colony, the West India Company scoured the Atlantic basin for settlers, recruiting German Lutherans, French Huguenots, and Sephardic Jews. These newcomers did little to meet the colony's need for men and women to work the land, because, as a company officer reported, "agricultural laborers who are conveyed thither at great expense . . . sooner or later apply themselves to trade, and neglect agriculture altogether." Dutch officials concluded that slave labor was an absolute necessity for New Netherland. Although competition for slaves with Dutch outposts in Brazil (whose sugar economy was already drawing slaves from the African interior) placed New Netherland at a disadvantage, authorities in the North American colony imported all the slaves they could, so that in 1640 about 100 blacks lived in New Amsterdam, composing roughly 30 percent of the port's population and a larger portion of the labor force. Their proportion diminished over the course of the seventeenth century but remained substantial. At the time of the English conquest, some 300 slaves composed a fifth of the population of New Amsterdam, giving New Netherland the largest urban slave population on mainland North America.

The diverse needs of the Dutch mercantile economy strengthened the hand of Atlantic creoles in New Netherland during the initial period of settlement. Caring only for short-term profits, the company, the largest slaveholder in the colony, allowed its slaves to live independently and work on their own in return for a stipulated amount of labor and an annual tribute. Company slaves thus enjoyed a large measure of independence, which they used to master the Dutch language, trade freely, accumulate property, identify with Dutch Reformed Christianity, and—most important—establish families. During the first generation, some twenty-five couples took their vows in the Dutch Reformed Church in New Amsterdam. When children arrived, their parents baptized them as well. Participation in the religious life of New Netherland provides but one indicator of how quickly Atlantic creoles mastered the intricacies of life in mainland North America. In 1635, less than ten years after the arrival of the first black people, black New Netherlanders understood enough about the organization of the colony and the operation of the company to travel to the company's headquarters in Holland and petition for wages.

Many slaves gained their freedom. This was not easy in New Netherland, although there was no legal proscription on manumission. Indeed, gaining freedom was nearly impossible for slaves owned privately and difficult even for those owned by the company. The company valued its slaves and was willing to liberate only the elderly, whom it viewed as a liability. Even when manumitting such slaves, the company exacted an annual tribute from adults and retained ownership of their children. The latter practice elicited protests from both blacks and whites in New Amsterdam. The enslavement of black children made "half-freedom," as New Netherland authorities denominated the West India Company's former slaves who were unable to pass their new status to their children, appear no freedom at all.

Manumission in New Netherland was calculated to benefit slave owners, not slaves. Its purposes were to spur slaves to greater exertion and to relieve owners of the cost of supporting elderly slaves. Yet, however compromised the attainment of freedom, slaves did what was necessary to secure it. They accepted the company's terms and agreed to pay its corporate tribute. But they bridled at the fact that their children's status would not follow their own. Half-free blacks pressed the West India Company to make their status hereditary. Hearing rumors that baptism would assure freedom to their children, they pressed their claims to church membership. A Dutch prelate complained of the "worldly and perverse aims" of black people who "wanted nothing else than to deliver their children from bodily slavery, without striving for piety and Christian virtues." Although conversion never guaranteed freedom in New Netherland, many half-free blacks secured their goal. By 1664, at the time of the English conquest, about one black person in five had achieved freedom in New Amsterdam, a proportion never equaled throughout the history of slavery in the American South.

Some free people of African descent prospered. Building on small gifts of land that the West India Company provided as freedom dues, a few entered the landholding class in New Netherland. A small group of former slaves established a community on the outskirts of the Dutch settlement on Manhattan, farmed independently, and sold their produce in the public market. Others purchased farmsteads or were granted land as part of the Dutch effort to populate the city's hinterland. In 1659, the town of Southampton granted "Peeter the Neigro" three acres. Somewhat later John Neiger, who had "set himself up a house in the street" of Easthampton, was given "for his own use a little quantity of land above his house for him to make a yard or garden." On occasion, free blacks employed whites.

By the middle of the seventeenth century, black people participated in almost every aspect of life in New Netherland. They sued and were sued in Dutch courts, married and baptized their children in the Dutch Reformed Church, and fought alongside Dutch militiamen against the colony's enemies. Black men and women—slave as well as free—traded on their own and accumulated property. Black people also began to develop a variety of institutions that reflected their unique experience and served their special needs. Black men and women stood as godparents to each others' children, suggesting close family ties, and rarely called on white people—owners or not—to serve in this capacity. At times, established black families legally adopted orphaned black children, further knitting the black community together in a web of fictive kinship. The patterns of residence, marriage, church membership, and godparentage speak not only to the material success of Atlantic creoles but also to their ability to create a community among themselves.

To be sure, the former slaves' prosperity was precarious at best. As the Dutch transformed their settlement from a string of trading posts to a colony committed to agricultural production, the quality of freedpeople's freedom deteriorated. The Dutch began to import slaves directly from Africa (especially after the Portuguese retook Brazil), and the new arrivals—sold mostly to individual planters rather than to the company—had little chance of securing the advantages earlier enjoyed by the company's slaves.

The freedpeople's social standing eroded more rapidly following the English conquest in 1664, demonstrating the fragility of their freedom in a social order undergirded by racial hostility. Nonetheless, black people continued to enjoy the benefits of the earlier age. They maintained a secure family life, acquired property, and participated as communicants in the Dutch Reformed Church, where they baptized their children in the presence of godparents of their own choosing. When threatened, they took their complaints to court, exhibiting a fine understanding of their legal rights and a steely determination to defend them. Although the proportion of the black population enjoying freedom shrank steadily under English rule, the small free black settlement held its own. Traveling through an area of modest farms on the outskirts of New York City in 1679, a Dutch visitor observed that "upon both sides of this way were many habitations of negroes, mulattoes and whites. These negroes were formerly the property of the (West India) company, but, in consequence of the frequent changes and conquests of the country, they have obtained their freedom and settled themselves down where they thought proper, and thus on this road, where they have ground enough to live on with their families."

Dutch vessels were not the only ones to transport Atlantic creoles from Africa to North America. The French, who began trading on the Windward Coast of Africa soon after the arrival of the Portuguese, did much the same. Just as a creole population grew up around the Portuguese and later Dutch factories at Elmina, Luanda, and São Tomé, so one developed around the French posts on the Senegal River. The Compagnie du Sénégal, the Compagnie des Indes Occidentales, and their successor, the Compagnie des Indes—whose charter, like that of the Dutch West India Company, authorized it to trade in both Africa and the Americas—maintained headquarters at St. Louis with subsidiary outposts at Galam and Fort d'Arguin.

As at Elmina and Luanda, shifting alliances between Africans and Europeans in St. Louis, Galam, and Fort d'Arguin also ensnared Atlantic creoles, who found themselves suddenly enslaved and thrust across the Atlantic. One such man was Samba, a Bambara, who during the 1720s worked for the French as an interpreter—*maître de langue*—at Galam, up the Senegal River from St. Louis. "Samba Bambara"—as he appears in the records—traveled freely along the river between St. Louis, Galam, and Fort d'Arguin. By 1722, he received permission from the Compagnie des Indes for his family to reside in St. Louis. When his wife dishonored him, Samba Bambara called on his corporate employer to exile her from St. Louis and thereby bring order to his domestic life. But despite his reliance on the company, Samba Bambara allegedly joined with African captives in a revolt at Fort d'Arguin, and, when the revolt was quelled, he was enslaved and deported. Significantly, he was not sold to the emerging plantation colony of Saint Domingue, where the sugar revolution stoked a nearly insatiable appetite for slaves. Instead, French officials at St. Louis exiled Samba Bambara to Louisiana, a marginal military outpost far outside the major transatlantic sea lanes and with no staple agricultural economy.

New Orleans on the Mississippi River shared much with St. Louis on the Senegal in the 1720's. As the headquarters of the Compagnie des Indes in mainland North America, the town housed the familiar collection of corporate functionaries, traders, and craftsmen, along with growing numbers of French *engagés* and African slaves. New Orleans was frequented by Indians, whose canoes supplied it much as African canoemen supplied St. Louis. Its taverns and back alley retreats were meeting places for sailors of various nationalities, Canadian *coureurs de bois,* and soldiers—the latter no more pleased to be stationed on the North American frontier than their counterparts welcomed assignment to an African factory. Indeed, soldiers' status in this rough frontier community differed little from that on the coast of Africa.

In 1720, a French soldier stationed in New Orleans was convicted of theft and sentenced to the lash. A black man wielded the whip. His work was apparently satisfactory, because five years later, Louis Congo, a recently arrived slave then in the service of the Compagnie des Indes, was offered the job. A powerful man, Congo bargained hard before accepting such grisly employment; he demanded freedom for himself and his wife, regular rations, and a plot of land he could cultivate independently. Louisiana's Superior Council balked at these terms, but the colony's attorney general urged acceptance, having seen Congo's *"chef d'oeuvre."* Louis Congo gained his freedom and was allowed to live with his wife (although she was not free) on land of his own choosing. His life as Louisiana's executioner was not easy. He was assaulted several times, and he complained that assassins lurked everywhere. But he enjoyed a modest prosperity, and he learned to write, an accomplishment that distinguished him from most inhabitants of the eighteenth-century Louisiana.

Suggesting something of the symmetry of the Atlantic world, New Orleans, save for the flora and fauna, was no alien terrain to Samba Bambara or Louis Congo. Despite the long transatlantic journey, once in the New World, they recovered much of what they had lost in the Old, although Samba Bambara never escaped slavery. Like the Atlantic creoles who alighted in New Netherland, Samba Bambara employed on the coast of North America skills he had learned on the coast of Africa; Louis Congo's previous occupation is unknown. Utilizing his knowledge of French, various African languages, and the ubiquitous creole tongue, the rebel regained his position with his old patron, the Compagnie des Indes, this time as an interpreter swearing on the Christian Bible to translate faithfully before Louisiana's Superior Council. Later, he became an overseer on the largest "concession" in the colony, the company's massive plantation across the river from New Orleans. Like his counterparts in New Amsterdam, Samba Bambara succeeded in a rugged frontier slave society by following the familiar lines of patronage to the doorstep of his corporate employer. Although the constraints of slavery eventually turned him against the company on the Mississippi, just as he had turned against it on the Senegal River, his ability to transfer his knowledge and skills from the Old World to the New, despite the weight of enslavement, suggests that the history of Atlantic creoles in New Amsterdam—their ability to escape slavery, form families, secure property, and claim a degree of independence—was no anomaly. . . .

Atlantic creoles were among the first black people to enter the Chesapeake region in the early years of the seventeenth century, and they numbered large among the "twenty Negars" the Dutch sold to the English at Jamestown in 1619 as well as those who followed during the next half century. Anthony Johnson, who was probably among the prizes captured by a Dutch ship in the Caribbean, appears to have landed in Jamestown as "Antonio a Negro" soon after the initial purchase. During the next thirty years, Antonio exited servitude, anglicized his name, married, began to farm on his own, and in 1651 received a 250-acre headright. When his Eastern Shore plantation burned to the ground two years later, he petitioned the county court for relief and was granted a substantial reduction of his taxes. His son John did even better than his father, receiving a patent for 550 acres, and another son, Richard, owned a 100-acre estate. Like other men of substance, the Johnsons farmed independently, held slaves, and left their heirs sizable estates. As established members of their communities, they enjoyed rights in common with other free men and frequently employed the law to protect themselves and advance their interests. When a black man claiming his freedom fled Anthony Johnson's plantation and found refuge with a nearby white planter, Johnson took his neighbor to court and won the return of his slave along with damages from the white man.

Landed independence not only afforded free people of African descent legal near-equality in Virginia but also allowed them a wide range of expressions that others termed "arrogance"—the traditional charge against Atlantic creoles. Anthony Johnson exhibited an exalted sense of self when a local notable challenged his industry. Johnson countered with a ringing defense of his independence: "I know myne owne ground and I will worke when I please and play when I please." Johnson also understood that he and other free black men and women were different, and he and his kin openly celebrated those differences. Whereas Antonio a Negro had anglicized the family name, John Johnson—his grandson and a third-generation Virginian—called his own estate "Angola."

The Johnsons were not unique in Virginia. A small community of free people of African descent developed on the Eastern Shore. Their names, like Antonio a Negro's suggest creole descent: John Francisco, Bashaw Ferdinando (or Farnando), Emanuel Driggus (sometimes Drighouse; probably Rodriggus), Anthony Longo (perhaps Loango), and "Francisco a Negroe" (soon to become Francis, then Frank, Payne and finally Paine). They, like Antonio, were drawn from the Atlantic littoral and may have spent time in England or New England before reaching the Chesapeake. At least one, "John Phillip, A negro Christened in *England* 12 yeeres since," was a sailor on an English ship that brought a captured Spanish vessel into Jamestown; another, Sebastian Cain or Cane, gained his freedom in Boston, where he had served the merchant Robert Keayne (hence probably his name). Cain also took to the sea as a sailor, but, unlike Phillip, he settled in Virginia as a neighbor, friend, and some-times kinsman of the Johnsons, Drigguses, and Paynes.

In Virginia. Atlantic creoles ascended the social order and exhibited a sure-handed understanding of Chesapeake social hierarchy and the complex dynamics of patron-client relations. Although still in bondage, they began to acquire the property, skills, and social connections that became their mark throughout the Atlantic world. They worked provision grounds, kept livestock, and traded inde-pendently. More important, they found advocates among the propertied classes—often their owners—and identified themselves with the colony's most important institutions, registering their marriages, baptisms, and children's godparents in the Anglican church and their property in the county courthouse. They sued and were sued in local courts and petitioned the colonial legislature and governor. While relations to their well-placed patrons—former masters and mistresses, landlords, and employers—among the colony's elite were important, as in Louisiana, the creoles also established ties among themselves, weaving together a community from among the interconnections of marriage, trade, and friendship. Free blacks testified on each other's behalf, stood as godparents for each other's children, loaned each other small sums, and joined together for after-hours conviviality, creating a community that often expanded to the larger web of interactions among all poor people, regardless of color. According to one historian of black life in the seventeenth-century Virginia, "cooperative projects . . . were more likely in rela-tions between colored freedmen and poor whites than were the debtor-creditor, tenant-landlord, or employee-employer relations that linked individuals of both races to members of the planter class." The horizontal ties of class developed alongside the vertical ones of patronage.

Maintaining their standing as property-holding free persons was difficult, and some Atlantic creoles in the Chesapeake, like those in New Netherland, slipped down the social ladder, trapped by legal snares—apprenticeships, tax forfeitures, and bastardy laws—as planters turned from a labor system based on indentured Europeans and Atlantic creoles to raw Africans condemned to perpetual slavery. Anthony Johnson, harassed by white planters, fled his plantation in Virginia to establish the more modest "Tonies Vineyard" in Maryland. But even as they were pushed out, many of the Chesapeake's charter generations continued to elude slav-ery. Some did well, lubricating the lifts to economic success with their own hard work, their skills in a society that had "an unrelenting demand for artisanal labor," and the assistance of powerful patrons. A few of the landholding free black fam-ilies on Virginia's Eastern Shore maintained their propertied standing well into the eighteenth century. In 1738, the estate of Emanuel Driggus's grandson—including its slaves—was worth more than those of two-thirds of his white neighbors.

Atlantic creoles also entered the lowcountry of South Carolina and Florida, carried there by the English and Spanish, respectively. Like the great West Indian planters who settled in that "colony of a colony," Atlantic creoles were drawn from Barbados and other Caribbean islands, where a full generation of European and African cohabitation had allowed them to gain a knowledge of European ways. Prior to the sugar revolution, they worked alongside white indentured servants in a variety of enterprises, none of which required the discipline of plantation labor. Like white servants, some exited slavery, as the line between slavery and freedom was open. An Anglican minister who toured the English islands during the 1670s noted that black people spoke English "no worse than the natural born subjects of that Kingdom." Although Atlantic creole culture took a different shape in the Antilles than it did on the periphery of Africa or Europe, it also displayed many of the same characteristics.

On the southern mainland, creoles used their knowledge of the New World and their ability to negotiate between the various Native American nations and South Carolina's European polyglot—English, French Huguenots, Sephardic Jews—to become invaluable as messengers, trappers, and cattle minders. The striking image of slave and master working on opposite sides of a sawbuck suggests the place of blacks during the early years of South Carolina's settlement.

Knowledge of their English captors also provided knowledge of their captors' enemy, some two hundred miles to the south. At every opportunity, Carolina slaves fled to Spanish Florida, where they requested Catholic baptism. Officials at St. Augustine—whose black population was drawn from Spain, Cuba, Hispaniola, and New Spain—celebrated the fugitives' choice of religion and offered sanctuary. They also valued the creoles' knowledge of the countryside, their ability to converse with English, Spanish, and Indians, and their willingness to strike back at their enslavers. Under the Spanish flag, former Carolina slaves raided English settlements at Port Royal and Edisto and liberated even more of their number. As part of the black militia, they, along with other fugitives from Carolina, fought against the English in the Tuscarora and Yamasee wars.

Florida's small black population mushroomed in the late seventeenth and early eighteenth centuries, as the small but steady stream of fugitives grew with expansion of lowcountry slavery. Slaves from central Africa—generally deemed "Angolans"—numbered large among the new arrivals, as the transatlantic trade carried thousands of Africans directly to the lowlands. Although many were drawn from deep in the interior of Africa, others were Atlantic creoles with experience in the coastal towns of Cabinda, Loango, and Mpinda. Some spoke Portuguese, which, as one Carolinian noted, was "as near Spanish as Scotch is to English," and subscribed to an African Catholicism with roots in the fifteenth-century conversion of Kongo's royal house. They knew their catechism, celebrated feasts of Easter and All Saint's Day or Hallowe'en, and recognized Christian saints.

These men and women were particularly attracted to the possibilities of freedom in the Spanish settlements around St. Augustine. They fled from South Carolina in increasing numbers during the 1720s and 1730s, and, in 1739, a group of African slaves—some doubtless drawn from the newcomers—initiated a mass flight. Pursued by South Carolina militiamen, they confronted their owners' soldiers in several pitched battles that became known as the Stono Rebellion. Although most of Stono rebels were killed or captured, some escaped to Florida, from where it became difficult to retrieve them by formal negotiation or by force. The newcomers were quickly integrated into black life in St. Augustine, since they had already been baptized, although they prayed—as one Miguel Domingo informed a Spanish priest—in Kikongo.

Much to the delight of St. Augustine's Spanish rulers, the former Carolina slaves did more than pray. They fought alongside the Spanish against incursions by English raiders. An edict of the Spanish crown promising "Liberty and Protection" to all slaves who reached St. Augustine boosted the number of fugitives—most from Carolina—especially after reports circulated that the Spanish received runaways "with great Honors" and gave their leaders military commissions and "A Coat Faced with Velvet." In time, Spanish authorities granted freedom to some, but not all, of the black soldiers and their families. . . .

Meanwhile, members of the fugitive community around St. Augustine entered more fully into the life of the colony as artisans and tradesmen as well as laborers and domestics. They married among themselves, into the Native American population, and with slaves as well, joining as husband and wife before their God and community in the Catholic church. They baptized their children in the same church, choosing godparents from among both the white and black congregants. Like the Atlantic creoles in New Amsterdam about a century earlier, they became skilled in identifying the lever of patronage, in this case royal authority. Declaring themselves "vassals of the king and deserving of royal protection," they continually placed themselves in the forefront of service to the crown with the expectations that their king would protect, if not reward, them. For the most part, they were not disappointed. When Spain turned East Florida, over to the British in 1763, black colonists retreated to Cuba with His Majesty's other subjects, where the crown granted them land, tools, a small subsidy, and a slave for each of their leaders.

In the long history of North American slavery, no other cohort of black people survived as well and rose as fast and as high in mainland society as the Atlantic creoles. The experience of the charter generations contrasts markedly with what followed: when the trauma of enslavement, the violence of captivity, the harsh conditions of plantation life left black people unable to reproduce themselves: when the strange language of their enslavers muted the tongues of newly arrived Africans: and when the slaves' skills and knowledge were submerged in the stupefying labor of plantation production. . . .

The charter generations' experience derived not only from who they were but also from the special circumstances of their arrival. By their very primacy, as members of the first generation of settlers, their experience was unique. While they came as foreigners, they were no more strange to the new land than were those who enslaved them. Indeed, the near simultaneous arrival of migrants from Europe and Africa gave them a shared perspective on the New World. At first, all saw themselves as outsiders. That would change, as European settlers gained dominance, ousted native peoples, and created societies they claimed as their own. As Europeans became European-Americans and then simply Americans, their identification with—and sense of ownership over—mainland society distinguished them from the forced migrants from Africa who continued to arrive as strangers and were defined as permanent outsiders.

The charter generations owed their unique history to more than just the timing of their arrival. Before their historic confrontation with their new owner, the men and women Robert Carter purchased may have spent weeks, even months, packed between the stinking planks of slave ships. Atlantic creoles experienced few of the horrors of the Middle Passage. Rather than arriving in shiploads totaling into the hundreds, Atlantic creoles trickled into the mainland singly, in twos and threes, or by the score. Most were sent in small consignments or were the booty of privateers and pirates. Some found employment as interpreters, sailors, and *grumetes* on the very ships that transported them to the New World. Although transatlantic travel in the seventeenth and eighteenth centuries could be a harrowing experience under the best of circumstances, the profound disruption that left the men and women Carter purchased physically spent and psychologically traumatized was rarely part of the experience of Atlantic creoles.

Most important, Atlantic creoles entered societies-with-slaves, not, as mainland North America would become, slave societies—that is, societies in which the order of the plantation shaped every relationship. In North America—as in Africa— Atlantic creoles were still but one subordinate group in societies in which subordination was the rule. Few who arrived before the plantation system faced the dehumanizing and brutalizing effects of gang labor in societies where slaves had become commodities and nothing more. Indeed, Atlantic creoles often worked alongside their owners, supped at their tables, wore their hand-me-down clothes, and lived in the back rooms and lofts of their houses. . . . The regimen imposed the heavy burdens of continual surveillance, but the same constant contact prevented their owners from imagining people of African descent to be a special species of beings, an idea that only emerged with the radical separation of master and slave and the creation of the worlds of the Big House and the Quarters. Until then, the open interaction of slave and slaveowner encouraged Atlantic creoles, and others as well, to judge their enslavement by its older meaning, not by its emerging new one.

The possibility of freedom had much the same effect. So long as some black people, no matter how closely identified with slavery, could still wriggle free of bondage and gain an independent place, slavery may have carried the connotation of otherness, debasement, perhaps even transgression, iniquity, and vice, but it was not social death. The success of Atlantic creoles in rising from the bottom of mainland society contradicted the logic of hereditary bondage and suggested that what had been done might be undone.

The rise of plantation slavery left little room for the men and women of the charter generations. Their efforts to secure a place in society were put at risk by the new order, for the triumph of the plantation régime threatened not inequality— which had always been assumed, at least by Europeans—but debasement and permanent ostracism of the sort Robert "King" Carter delivered on that Virginia wharf. With the creation of a world in which peoples of African descent were presumed slaves and those of European descent free, people of color no longer had a place. It became easy to depict black men and women as uncivilized heathens outside the bounds of society or even humanity.

Few Atlantic creoles entered the mainland after the tobacco revolution in the Chesapeake, the rice revolution in lowcountry Carolina, and the sugar revolution in Louisiana. Rather than being drawn from the African littoral, slaves increasingly derived from the African interior. Such men and women possessed little understanding of the larger Atlantic world: no apprenticeship in negotiating with Europeans, no knowledge of Christianity or other touchstone of Europe culture, no acquaintance with western law, and no open fraternization with sailors and merchants in the Atlantic trade—indeed, no experience with the diseases of the Atlantic to provide a measure of immunity to the deadly microbes that lurked everywhere in the New World. Instead of speaking a pidgin or creole that gave them access to the Atlantic, the later arrivals were separated from their enslavers and often from each other by a dense wall of language. Rather than see their skills and knowledge appreciate in value, they generally discovered that previous experience counted for little on the plantations of the New World. Indeed, the remnants of their African past were immediately expropriated by their new masters. . . .

The relentless engine of plantation agriculture and the transformation of the mainland colonies from societies-with-slaves to slave societies submerged the charter generations in a régime in which African descent was equated with slavery. For the most part, the descendents of African creoles took their place as slaves alongside newly arrived Africans. Those who maintained their freedom became part of an impoverished free black minority, and those who lost their liberty were swallowed up in an oppressed slave majority. In one way or another, Atlantic creoles were overwhelmed by the power of the plantation order.

Even so, the charter generations' presence was not without substance. During the American Revolution, when divisions within the planter class gave black people fresh opportunities to strike for liberty and equality, long-suppressed memories of the origins of African life on the mainland bubbled to the surface, often in lawsuits in which slaves claimed freedom as a result of descent from a free ancestor, sometimes white, sometimes Indian, sometimes free black, more commonly from some mixture of these elements. The testimony summoned by such legal contests reveals how the hidden history of the charter generations survived the plantation revolution and suggests the mechanisms by which it would be maintained in the centuries that followed. It also reveals how race had been constructed and reconstructed in mainland North America over the course of two centuries of African and European settlement and how it would be remade.

How Africans Became African Americans

ALLAN KULIKOFF

Although the eighteenth-century Chesapeake planter looked upon newly enslaved Africans as strange and barbaric folk, he knew that American-born slaves could be taught English customs. Hugh Jones, a Virginia cleric, commented in 1724 that "the languages of the new Negroes are various harsh jargons," but added that slaves born in Virginia "talk good English, and affect our language, habits, and customs." How readily slaves in Maryland, Virginia, and other British colonies accepted English ways is currently a subject of controversy. Some scholars hold that the preponderance of whites in the population was so large, and the repressive power of whites over blacks so great, that slaves in the Chesapeake colonies were forced to accept Anglo-American beliefs, values, and skills. Other writers maintain that slave migrants and their descendents created indigenous social institutions within the framework of white rule. This essay supports the second position by describing how slaves living in Maryland and Virginia during the eighteenth century developed their own community life. . . .

Allan Kulikoff, "The Origins of Afro-American Society in Tidewater Maryland and Virginia, 1700–1790," *William and Mary Quarterly,* 3rd Series, 35 (April 1978), 226–259. Reprinted by permission from Allan Kulikoff.

Data from tidewater Maryland and Virginia suggest that African and Afro-American slaves developed a settled community life very slowly. Three stages of community development can be discerned. From roughly 1650 to 1690, blacks assimilated the norms of white society, but the growth of the number of blacks also triggered white repression. The period from about 1690 to 1740 was an era of heavy black immigration, small plantation sizes, and social conflicts among blacks. The infusion of Africans often disrupted newly formed slave communities. Finally, from 1740 to 1790, immigration declined and then stopped, plantation sizes increased, the proportion of blacks in the population grew, and divisions among slaves disappeared; consequently, native blacks in the tidewater formed settled communities.

Between 1650 and 1690 two demographic patterns shaped black life. Tobacco was the region's cash crop, and most planters were men of moderate means who could afford few slaves. Therefore, blacks constituted a very small percentage of the Chesapeake population—only about 3 percent (or 1,700) of the people in 1650 and 15 percent in 1690 (or 11,500). Most slaves lived on small plantations of fewer than eleven blacks. Moreover, almost all slaves were immigrants, and most came to the Chesapeake from the West Indies. Some had recently arrived in the islands from Africa; others had lived there a long time or had been born there.

These characteristics led blacks toward assimilation in the Chesapeake colonies. Natives of the islands and long-time residents knew English and were experienced in slavery; new African slaves soon learned English in order to communicate with masters and most other blacks. Blacks and whites worked together in the fields, and blacks learned to imitate the white servants by occasionally challenging the masters authority. Seventeenth-century Englishmen perceived Africans as an alien, evil, libidinous, and heathen people, but even they saw that their slaves did not fit this description, and whites treated many blacks as they did white servants. Some black residents became and remained free.

After 1660 the lot of blacks deteriorated; stringent racial laws were passed in Virginia each year between 1667 and 1672, and in 1680, 1682, and 1686. The timing of these laws was due in part to the growth and changing composition of the black population. The number of blacks in the Chesapeake colonies doubled in every decade but one from 1650 to 1690, while white population grew more slowly. African slaves began to be imported directly from Africa for the first time around 1680; from 1679 to 1686, seven ships with about 1,450 slaves arrived in Virginia from Africa. These blacks seemed to Englishmen to be the strange, libidinous, heathenish, and disobedient people they believed typical of Africans.

Africans continued to pour into the Chesapeake: from 1700 to 1740, roughly 43,000 blacks entered Virginia, about 39,000 of whom were Africans. The proportion of Africans among all slave immigrants rose from about 73 percent between 1710 and 1718 to 93 percent between 1727 and 1740. Over half, and perhaps three quarters, of the immigrant slaves went to a few lower tidewater counties, while some of the rest worked in the upper tidewater. The proportion of recent immigrants among black slave adults fluctuated with trade cycles: about one-half in 1709, one-third in 1720, one-half in 1728, and one-third in 1740 had left Africa or the West Indies within ten years. This immigration affected every facet of black life in tidewater, for every few years native blacks and earlier comers had to absorb many recently imported Africans into their ranks.

The demographic composition of slave cargoes suggests that Africans had a difficult time establishing a regular family life after their arrival in the Chesapeake. The slave ships usually carried two men for every women. Children composed less than one-fifth of imported slaves, and there was a similar surplus of boys over girls. Very young children were infrequent in these cargoes; perhaps three-quarters of them were aged ten to fourteen, and nearly all the rest were eight or nine.

Nonetheless, newly enslaved Africans possessed a few building blocks for a new social order under slavery. Many shared a similar ethnic identity. Data from Port York for two periods of heavy immigration show that about half the African migrants were Ibos from Nigeria, while another one-fifth came from Angola. From 1718 to 1726, 60 percent came from Biafra; between 1728 and 1739, 85 percent migrated from Biafra or Angola. Most immigrants spoke similar languages, lived under the same climate, cultivated similar crops, and shared comparable kinship systems. When they arrived in the Chesapeake, they may have been able to combine common threads in their societies and cultures into new Afro-American structures with some ease. . . .

Once they entered the plantation world, African immigrants had to begin to cope with their status. The absolute distinction between slavery and freedom found in the Chesapeake colonies did not exist in West African societies. African communities and kin groups possessed a wide range of rights-in-persons. A captive in war might end up as anything from a chattel, who could be sold, to the wife of one of the victorious tribesmen; he might become a soldier, domestic servant of agricultural laborer. At first, such outsiders would be strangers, but eventually they or their children could move from marginality to partial or full membership in a kin group or community.

When they reached their new homes, Africans were immediately put to work making tobacco. Most were broken in on the most routine tasks of production. Nearly two-thirds of them arrived between June and August, when the tobacco plants had already been moved from seed beds and were growing rapidly. The new slaves' first task was weeding between the rows of plants with hands, axes, or hoes. These jobs were similar to those that Ibos and other Africans had used in growing other crops in their native lands. After a month or two of such labor, slaves could be instructed in the more difficult task of harvesting. Some Africans refused to accept this new work discipline, either not understanding or pretending not to understand their masters. Edward Kimber, a visitor to the Eastern Shore in 1747, wrote that "a new Negro" (a newly enslaved African) "must be broke. . . . You would be supriz'd at their Perseverance; let an hundred Men shew him how to hoe, or drive a Wheelbarrow, he'll still take the one by the Bottom, and the Other by the Wheel."

Under these conditions, Africans were often struck with loneliness and illness. For example, Ayuba (Job) Suleiman was brought to Maryland's Eastern Shore in 1730. He was "put . . . to work making tobacco" but "every day showed more and more uneasiness under this exercise, and at last grew sick, being no way able to bear it; so that his master was obliged to find easier work for him, and therefore put him to tend the cattle." A new slave might become so ill that he could not work. Thomas Swan, a planter in Prince George's County, Maryland, bought two Africans in the summer of 1728; in November of that year he asked the county court to refund one poll tax because "one of them has been sick ever since he bought him and has done him little or no Service."

One in four new Negroes died during their first year in the Chesapeake; in some years—1711, 1727, 1737, 1743—mortality seems to have been especially high. In 1727 Robert Carter lost at least seventy hands—perhaps a quarter of all his slaves born abroad and more than half his new Negroes. Because Africans possessed some native immunities against malaria, most survived the malarial attacks of their first summer in the region, but respiratory illness struck them hard the following winter and spring. Planters considered late spring "the best time of buying them by reason they will be well season'd before the winter." Blacks living in New Kent County, Virginia, between 1714 and 1739 died infrequently in the summer, but deaths rose somewhat in the fall, increased from December to February, and peaked in March and April. The county undoubtedly included many Africans. Whites in the same parish died more frequently in autumn, and less often in spring, than their slaves.

Despite disease and death, new Negroes soon began to develop friendships with other slaves, and to challenge the authority of their masters by attempting to make a new life for themselves off their quarters. They were able to oppose their masters because so many of their fellow workers were also recent immigrants who shared their new experiences under slavery. In the mid-1700s, late-1710s, mid-1720s, and mid-1730s, when unusually large numbers of blacks entered Virginia, these Africans, united by their common experiences and able to communicate through the heavily African pidgin they probably created, ran off to the woods together, formed temporary settlements in the wilderness, and several times conspired to overthrow their white masters.

First, Africans had to find or create a common language because there were few speakers of any single African tongue in any neighborhood. Some new slaves may have devised nonoral means of communication soon after arrival, but the large concentration of Ibos and Angolans among the Africans suggests that many spoke similar languages and that others could have become bilingual. Others probably spoke some West African pidgin that they had learned in Africa in order to communicate with Europeans. A new creole language may have emerged in the Chesapeake region combining the vocabulary of several African languages common among the immigrants, African linguistic structures and the few English words needed for communication with the master.

Almost as soon as Africans landed, they attempted to run away together. Seven of Robert Carter's new Negroes did so on July 17, 1727. They took a canoe and may have crossed the Rappahannock River. Carter sent men "sev[era]l ways" for them, and on July 15 they were returned to him. Enough new Negroes ran away to convince the Virginia assembly to pass laws in 1705 and 1722 detailing procedures to follow when Africans who did not speak English and could not name their master were recaptured.

A few Africans formed communities in the wilderness in the 1720s, when black immigration was high and the frontier close to tidewater. In 1725 the Maryland assembly asserted that "sundry" slaves "have of late Years runaway into the Back-Woods, some of which have there perished, and others . . . have been entertained and encouraged to live and inhabit with the Shewan-Indians." Other slaves, who heard of their success, were "daily making Attempts to go the same Way." Any slave who ran beyond the Monocacy River, at the edge of white settlement, was to have an ear cut off and his chin branded with an "R." The assembly, recognizing that Africans habitually ran away, withheld this punishment for new Negroes during their first year in the colony.

At least two outlying runaway communities were established during the 1720s. Fifteen slaves began a settlement in 1729 on the frontier near present-day Lexington, Virginia. They ran from " a new Plantation on the head of the James River," taking tools, arms, clothing, and food with them. When captured, "they had already begun to clear the ground." Another small community evidently developed on the Maryland frontier in 1728 and 1729. Early in 1729, Harry, one of the runaways, returned to southern Prince George's Country to report on the place to his former shipmates. He told them that "there were many Negroes among the Indians at Monocosy" and tried to entice them to join the group by claiming that Indians were soon going to attack the whites.

As soon as Africans arrived in the Chesapeake colonies in large numbers, government officials began to complain about their clandestine meetings. In 1687 the Virginia Council asserted that masters allowed their blacks to go "on broad on Saturdays and Sundays . . . to meet in great Numbers in makeing and holding of Funneralls for Dead Negroes." Governor Francis Nicholson of Maryland wrote in 1698 that groups of six or seven slaves traveled thirty or forty miles on weekends to the sparsely inhabited falls of the Potomac.

Whites suppressed clandestine meetings primarily because they feared slave rebellions. Africans pushed to suicidal actions might revolt against the slave system. Revolts were rare in the Chesapeake colonies, where whites heavily outnumbered slaves, but Africans apparently participated in conspiracies in Surry, James City, and Isle of Wight counties in Virginia in 1710, and in Prince George's County, Maryland, in 1739 and 1740. The 1739–1740 conspiracy, which is the best documented, was organized by slaves who lived in St. Paul's Parish, an area of large plantations, where numerous slaveholders had recently bought Africans. The Negroes spent eight months in 1739 planning to seize their freedom by killing their masters and other white families in the neighborhood. Their leader, Jack Ransom, was probably a native, but most of the conspirators were Africans, for it is reported that the planning was done by slaves in "their country language." The revolt was postponed several times, and finally the white authorities got wind of it. Stephen Boardley, an Annapolis lawyer, reported that whites believed that two hundred slaves planned to kill all the white men, marry the white women, and then unite both shores of Maryland under their control. Ransom was tried and executed; four other slaves were acquitted; and the furor died down.

Every attempt of Africans to establish an independent social life off the plantation failed because whites, who held the means of terror, insisted that their slaves remain at home. Running to the woods, founding outlying communities, or meeting in large groups challenged work discipline and cost the planter profits. Nevertheless, substantial numbers of Africans probably participated in activities away from the plantation. Slaves from many different African communities proved that they could unite and live together. Others, though unable to join them, must have heard of their exploits and discovered that a new social life might be possible. Sooner or later, however, Africans had to turn to their plantation to develop communities.

But as late as the 1730s, plantations were not very conducive places in which to create a settled social life. A major determinant was the small size of the slave populations of the plantation quarters. On quarters of fewer than ten slaves, completed families of husbands, wives, and children were uncommon and the slaves, who lived in outbuildings, did not control enough space of their own to run their own lives apart from the master. Only 28 percent of the slaves on Maryland's lower Western Shore before 1711 lived on plantations of over twenty slaves, and some of these lived in quarters distant from the main plantation. The rest lived on smaller farms. Quarters were similarly small in York and Lancaster counties in the 1710s. From 1710 to 1740, plantation sizes in Prince George's and Lancaster counties increased, while those in York and St. Mary's stayed the same. If these four counties were typical of tidewater in the 1730s, then 46 percent of the slaves lived on quarters of ten or fewer and only 25 percent resided on units of over twenty (but usually under thirty).

African social structures centered on the family, but slaves in the Chesapeake had difficulty maintaining family life. Men who lived on small quarters often had to find wives elsewhere, a task made more difficult by the high ratio of men to women in much of tidewater. As long as adult sex ratios remained high, men had to postpone marriage, while women might be forced to marry early. Along the lower Western Shore of Maryland, the sex ratio was about 150 in the 1690s and 1700s, but by the 1710s it was under 150 in York County and under 120 in Lancaster County, remaining at those levels until 1740. Even on large plantations men could not count on living in family units, for sex ratios there were higher than on small quarters. During the 1730s the adult sex ratio in Prince George's was 187, but on nine large plantations in that county, each having ten or more adult slaves, it stood at 249. A similar pattern has been found in both York and Lancaster counties at times between 1710 and 1740.

Since most slaves lived on small plantations, the development of settled black community life required visiting between quarters. Sometimes slaves met on larger plantations, getting "drunke on the Lords Day beating their Negro Drums by which they call considerable Numbers of Negroes together." On one Sunday in 1735, Edward Pearson's Negroes with some of his "Neighbours Negroes was Beating a Drum and Danceing but by my Consent" in Prince George's. Slaves probably did not regularly visit friends on nearby plantations, however. Visiting networks could develop only where blacks were densely settled and constituted a larger part of the population. The population in tidewater was never over half slave except in a few counties between the James and York rivers before 1740. Only 16 percent of the people in the Chesapeake colonies were black in 1690, but this proportion grew to 25 percent in 1710 and 28 percent in 1740.

The large plantations in tidewater housed masters, overseers, native blacks, new Negroes, and less recent immigrants, while smaller units, with only few natives or immigrants, tended to be more homogeneous. The concentration of men on large plantations suggests that most African adults were bought by the gentry—a pattern documented by the composition of John Mercer's and Robert Carter's plantations. Mercer bought sixty-nine slaves between 1731 and 1746. These purchases included six seasoned Africans or natives in 1731 and 1732, twenty-five new Negroes from 1733 to 1739, and twenty new Negroes and fifteen seasoned slaves in the 1740s. By 1740 Mercer owned a mixed group of new Negroes, seasoned immigrants, and native children and adults. The composition of Carter's quarters in 1733 shows the culmination of this process. Over half of Carter's 734 slaves lived on plantations where one-fifth to one-half were recent immigrants, and another third resided on quarters composed predominantly of natives or older immigrants. Only one-seventh of his slaves lived on quarters dominated by new Negroes. About one-half (6/13) of the quarters of over twenty slaves, and natives formed a majority of the rest. Most of the farms (11/18) with eleven to twenty slaves included Africans and natives, but five others were peopled by natives. Nine of the eleven quarters where new Negroes formed a majority were small units of fewer than ten slaves.

Most new Negroes learned to be slaves on such diversified plantations. Nearly two-thirds (64 percent) of Carter's recent immigrant slaves lived on plantations with numerous native adults and children, and white overseers resided at almost every quarter. Africans had to learn some English in order to communicate with masters, overseers, and native slaves, and they were put into fields with other slaves who had already learned that they had to work to avoid punishment and that resistance had to be indirect. Africans saw that a few slaves were given responsibility—and power—over other slaves or were taught new skills. Slaves born in Africa apparently were well acculturated on Robert Carter's quarters. While the great majority of his adult slaves were agricultural laborers, some Africans (who had probably been in the country for a number of years) joined their native friends as foremen who worked under white overseers. Perhaps nineteen of the thirty-three foremen on these plantations were born in Africa. Four other men—possibly Africans—became sloopers (boatmen) on Carter's main plantation.

Nevertheless, Africans and native slaves quarrelled on occasion because of the great differences between their respective experiences. Natives had not been herded into ships and sold into bondage. They were probably healthier than immigrants. Many of them were baptized Christians, and some became believers. To immigrants, by contrast, Christianity was an alien creed, and they sometimes tried to maintain their own Islamic or African religions in opposition to it. Ben, for example, was brought from Africa to Charles County, Maryland, about 1730. According to his grandson, Charles Ball, Ben "always expressed great contempt for his fellow slaves, they being . . . a mean and vulgar race, quite beneath his rank, and the dignity of his former station." Ben never attended a Christian service but held that Christianity was "altogether false, and indeed no religion at all."

The most significant difference between recent immigrants and native blacks can be seen in their family life. A native-born slave on Robert Carter's plantations in 1733 usually lived in a family composed of husband, wife, and children, whereas new Negroes were placed in sex-segregated barracks, and seasoned immigrants often lived in conjugal units without children. Though polygamy was common in some African societies, only one of Carter's slaves managed to keep two wives. Conditions at Carter's plantations were optimal; elsewhere, high sex ratios severely limited the marriage opportunities of African men. At first, older slaves could become "uncles" to younger Africans, and Africans of the same age could act as brothers, but African men had to find wives in order to begin a Chesapeake genealogy. They had to compete with natives for the available women; native women may well have preferred native men, who were healthy, spoke English, and knew how to act in a white world, to unhealthy or unseasoned Africans. Furthermore, newly enslaved African women often waited two or three years before taking a husband, thereby reducing the supply of prospective wives even further.

The reluctance of Afro-American women to marry Africans may have been one of the grievances of the Prince George's conspirators in 1739–1740.

Several incidents on Edmund Jening's plantations in King William County, Virginia, in 1712–1713, suggest that Africans competed among themselves for wives, sometimes with tragic results. George, who lived at Beaverdam Quarter, complained in November 1712 that "his country men had poysened him for his wife," and he died the following February from the poison. Roger, Silsdon Quarter, apparently wanted more than one wife. In December 1712 or January 1713, he "hanged himselfe in ye old 40 foot Tob. house not any reason he being hindred from keeping other negroes men wifes besides his owne." The overseer "had his head cut off and stuck on a pole to be a terror to the others."

Slaves in the Chesapeake colonies failed to establish a settled community life in the times of heavy immigrations in the 1710s, 1720s, and 1730s. Conflicts among Africans and between African and native slaves could never be fully resolved as long as substantial numbers of Africans were forced into slavery in the two colonies. On the other hand, the rate of immigration, the proportion of Africans in the slave population, and the percentage of blacks in the population were never great enough to permit successful communities based mostly upon African institutions and values to develop either on the plantation or away from it.

The demographic conditions that prevented blacks from developing a cohesive social life before 1740 changed during the quarter century before the Revolution, as the immigration of Africans to tidewater Maryland and Virginia declined sharply. Only 17 percent of Virginia's adult black population in 1750 and 15 percent in 1755 had arrived within the previous ten years, and these newcomers went in relatively greater numbers to newer piedmont counties than had their predecessors. The proportion of adult blacks in 1755 who had entered Virginia since 1750 ranged from 4 percent in Lancaster County and 8 percent in York County in tidewater Virginia to 15 percent in Caroline County and 21 percent in Fairfax County, both near the fall line. After 1755, almost all of Virginia's black immigrants went to piedmont counties.

As the number of African immigrants in tidewater declined, the internal division among blacks diminished. These immigrants were under greater pressure than their predecessors to acquire the language, values, and beliefs of the dominant native majority. Like new Negroes before them, they sometimes ran away but with less success. On arrival, they found themselves isolated and alone. Olaudah Equiano, for example, was brought to Virginia in 1757 at age twelve. "I was now exceedingly miserable," he wrote, "and thought myself worse off than any . . . of my companions; for they could talk to each other, but I had no person to speak to that I could understand. In this state I was constantly grieving and pining, and wishing for death." But once slaves like Equiano learned English, they became part of the Afro-American community. Bob, twenty-nine, and Turkey Tom, thirty-eight, were new Negroes who lived on the home plantation of Charles Carroll of Carrollton in 1773. Since Bob and Tom were apparently the only two recent immigrant slaves on any of Carroll's many plantations, they both could participate fully in plantation life. Bob was a smith, a position usually reserved for natives; he married the daughter of a carpenter, and lived with her and their two children. Tom, a laborer, also found a place in the plantation's kinship networks: his wife was at least a third-generation Marylander. Very few Africans probably ever became artisans, but most lived on plantations where they could find wives among the native majority.

The size of quarters increased after 1740 throughout tidewater, providing greater opportunities for slaves to develop a social life of their own. The proportion who lived on units of over twenty slaves doubled in St. Mary's County, increased by half in York County, and grew, though more slowly, in Prince George's. In the 1780s one-third to two-thirds of the slaves in nine tidewater counties lived on farms of more than twenty slaves, and only a sixth to a tenth lived on units of fewer than six. If these counties were typical, 43 percent of tidewater's blacks lived on farms of over twenty slaves, and another 25 percent lived on medium-sized units of eleven to twenty. The number of very large quarters also grew. Before 1740 few quarters housed over thirty slaves, but by the 1770s and 1780s the wealthiest gentlemen ran home plantations with over one hundred slaves and quarters with thirty to fifty.

Because plantation sizes increased, more Afro-Americans lived on quarters away from the master's house and his direct supervision. On small plantations the quarter could be located in an outbuilding or in a single dwelling. On large plantations "a Negro Quarter, is a Number of Huts or Hovels, built some Distance from the Mansion-House; where the Negroes reside with their Wives and Families, and cultivate at vacant Times the little Spots allow'd them." Slave houses and the yards surrounding them were centers of domestic activity. The houses were furnished with straw bedding, barrels for seats, pots, pans, and usually a grindstone or hand-mill for beating corn into meal. Agricultural tools and livestock were scattered outside the house, and the quarter was surrounded by plots of corn and tobacco cultivated by the slaves.

Afro-Americans made the quarters into little communities, usually organized around families. Because African immigration largely ceased, the adult sex ratio decreased throughout tidewater until it reached about one hundred by the time of the Revolution. Almost all men and women could marry, and by the 1770s many slaves had native grandparents and great-grandparents. Smaller quarters contained a family or two, and larger quarters were populated by extended families in which most residents were kinfolk. Domestic activities such as eating, playing in the yard, or tending the garden were organized by families, and each family member had a part in them. The quarter was the center of family activity every evening and on Sundays and holidays, for except during the harvest, slaves had these times to themselves. Nonresident fathers visited their wives and children, runaways stayed with friends or kinfolk. In the evenings native men sometimes traveled to other quarters where they passed the night talking, singing, smoking, and drinking. On occasional Sundays they held celebrations at which they danced to the banjo and sang bitter songs about their treatment by the master. . . .

After 1740, the density of the black population and the proportion of slaves in the population of tidewater both increased, and as a result, the area's slave society gradually spread out to embrace many neighboring plantations in a single network. Ironically, masters provided slaves with several tools they could use to extend these cross-quarter networks. As masters sold and transferred their slaves, more and more kinfolk lived on neighboring quarters, and naturally they retained ties of affection after they were separated. Whites built numerous roads and paths to connect their farms and villages, and their slaves used these byways to visit friends or run away and evade recapture. By the 1770s and 1780s, Afro-Americans numerically dominated many neighborhoods and created many cross-plantation social networks.

The density of black population and the proportion of slaves in the population increased in both Chesapeake colonies. The number of slaves per square mile increased by more than one-third between 1755 and the early 1780s in three tidewater areas. Slaves composed 26 percent of the population of the lower Western Shore of Maryland in 1710, 38 percent in 1755, and 46 percent in 1782. A similar change occurred on the Eastern Shore, and by 1775, the results were visible in tidewater Virginia. In that year, nearly every county between the Rappahannock and the James rivers as far west as the heads of navigation was more than one-half black; over half of Virginia's slaves lived in these counties. Between 40 and 50 percent of the people were black in 1775 in the Northern Neck and in piedmont counties adjacent to tidewater. . . .

Even on large plantations, social life was often insecure. Some slaves were sold or forced to accompany their masters to the piedmont, far away from family and friends: about 20 percent of all slaves in southern Maryland left the region between 1755 and 1782. Even when a slave remained the property of the same white family, he might not live on the same farm for more than a few years. For example, after the Revolution large planters in Elizabeth City County, Virginia, tended to hire out their slaves to tenants and small landowners. A slave might live on a different plantation every year, suffering separation from spouse, children, and friends.

Nevertheless, one-half to three-quarters of the Afro-Americas who lived in tidewater in the 1780s enjoyed some sort of social life not controlled by their masters. Perhaps 43 percent lived on large quarters, and another 4 percent were men who lived in the neighborhoods with many large quarters and could visit nearby farms. Another 25 percent lived on farms of eleven to twenty blacks and could participate in the family and community activities of their quarters. The remaining one-fourth of the slaves were women and children who lived on small plantations. They usually did not travel from quarter to quarter but waited for husbands and fathers to visit them.

The Afro-Americans made good use of these opportunities to create their own society. In the years before the Revolution, they developed a sense of community with other slaves both on their own plantations and in the neighborhood. This social solidarity was shown in several ways. In the first place, Afro-Americans often concealed slaves from the neighborhood on their quarters. Since masters searched the neighborhood for runaways and placed notices on local public buildings before advertising in a newspaper, many runaways were not so advertised. The increasing appearance of such advertisements in the *Maryland Gazette* during the thirty years before the Revolution suggests that slaves were becoming more successful in evading easy recapture. The number of runaways in southern Maryland rose in each five-year period between 1745 and 1779, except the years 1765 and 1769, and the increase was especially great during the Revolution, when some escaped slaves were able to reach British troops.

Most runaways required help from other blacks. Only a small minority were helped by whites, and about three-quarters (22/29) of those so helped in southern Maryland were artisans, mulattoes, or women. Women infrequently ran away, and there were few slave mulattoes and artisans. The majority of runaways traveled from plantation to plantation through a quarter underground. Some joined family members or friends on nearby or even distant plantations; others attempted to pass as free in small port towns, find employment, or leave the region. About one-half of southern Maryland runaways and nearly one-third (29 percent) of Virginia's advertised runaways before 1775 stayed with friends or kinfolk. They hid on quarters or in surrounding woods for a few days or weeks, and then returned voluntarily or were recaptured. Many of the other slaves, who wanted to pass as free, also had to use the plantation underground to reach their destinations, and at least half of them stayed within visiting distance of their family and friends. Only one runaway in four in southern Maryland and one in three in Virginia before 1775 left his home province and tried to begin a new life as a free person. . . .

Afro-American slaves had developed strong community institutions on their quarters and in their families and kin groups by the 1760s and 1770s, but the values and beliefs held by members of this community are difficult to determine. Since blacks in the Chesapeake region did not achieve a settled social life until after heavy African immigration stopped and since whites continued to live in even the most densely black areas, one would expect slave culture in the region to reflect white values and beliefs. Even native-born slaves had little choice either about their work or about the people who lived with them in their quarters. Nevertheless, they had a measure of self-determination in their family life, in their religion, and in the ways they celebrated or mourned. The skimpy surviving evidence suggests that when they could choose, tidewater Afro-Americans simultaneously borrowed from whites and drew on the values and beliefs their ancestors brought from West Africa to form a culture not only significantly different from that of Anglo-Americans but also different from the culture of any West African group or any other group of North American slaves.

The way Afro-Americans organized their family life indicates most clearly how they used both African and Euro-American forms to create a new institution compatible with their life under slavery. By the time of the Revolution, most slaves lived in families, and slave households were similar to those of their white masters. About as many Afro-Americans as whites lived in two-parent and extended households. Whites all lived in monogamous families, and only scattered examples of the African custom of polygamy can be found among blacks. Slavery forced the kinfolk of extended families to live very close to one another on large plantations where they played and worked together. By contrast, whites only occasionally visited their extended kinfolk and worked their fields only with their children, not with adult brothers and sisters. This closeness fostered a sense of kin solidarity among Afro-Americans. They named their children after both sides of the family (but interestingly enough, daughters were not often named for their mothers). And they sometimes refused to marry within the plantation even when sex ratios were equal: many of the available potential partners were first cousins, and blacks refused to marry first cousins. This may have represented a transformation of African marriage taboos that differed from tribe to tribe but tended to be stricter than those of Chesapeake whites, who frequently married first cousins.

Native slaves occasionally accepted the outward signs of Christian belief. Their children were baptized and sometimes received religious instruction. All three Anglican clergymen of Prince George's County reported in 1724 that they baptized slave children and adults and preached to those who would listen. In 1731 one Prince George's minister baptized blacks "where perfect in their Catechism" and "visit[ed] them in their sickness and married them when called upon." Similar work continued in both Maryland and Virginia in the generation before the Revolution.

Afro-Americans may have superimposed Christianity upon the beliefs, values, and ceremonies learned from African forebears and from each other. Thomas Bacon, a Maryland cleric and publisher of a compendium of the colony's laws, preached to blacks on Maryland's Eastern Shore in the 1740s at services they directed, "at their *funerals* (several of which I have attended)—and to such small congregations as their *marriages* have brought together." Bacon felt that the slaves he saw were "living in as profound Ignorance of what Christianity really is, (except as to a few outward Ordinances) as if they had remained in the midst of those bar-barous Heathen Counties from whence their parents had been first imported."

Native slaves retained folk beliefs that may have come from Africa. Some African medicine men, magicians, and witches migrated and passed on their skills to other slaves. Medicine men and magicians were spiritual leaders in many African communities, including those of the Ibos, and they continued to practice among Afro-Americans who still believed in their powers. William Grimes was born in King George County, Virginia, in 1784; his narrative of his life as a run-away suggests that he was terrified of a woman he thought was a witch, that he feared sleeping in the bed of a dead man, and that he consulted fortune tellers.

Slave music and dance displayed a distinctly African character. In 1774 Nicholas Cresswell, a British visitor, described slave celebrations in Charles County, Mary-land. On Sundays, he wrote, the blacks "generally meet together and amuse them-selves with Dancing to the Banjo. This musical instrument . . . is made of a Gourd something in imitation of a Guitar, with only four strings." "Their poetry," Cress-well reported, "is like the music—Rude and uncultivated. Their Dancing is most violent exercise, but so irregular and grotesque. I am not able to describe it." The banjo was probably of African origin, and Cresswell's reaction to the dancing sug-gests that it contained African rhythms unknown to European dance. If the form was African, it was placed in an American context: the slave songs Cresswell heard "generally relate the usage they had received from their Masters and Mistresses in a very satirical stile and manner."

Although these little pieces of data do not add up to a complete description of slave culture in the Chesapeake on the eve of the Revolution, some tentative conclu-sions can nonetheless be drawn. In several areas, where slaves could choose how to behave, they did not follow white norms but combined African memories with frag-ments of white culture. The result, however, does not seem to have been heavily African, at least on the surface, and blacks in Maryland and Virginia preserved far less African content in their culture than did slaves in the British West Indies.

African and Afro-American slaves developed their own social institutions in the generations preceding the Revolution, and probably formed their own indigenous culture as well. A period of great disruption among blacks early in the century was followed in the pre-Revolutionary years by a time of settled communities. Newly enslaved Africans came to the Chesapeake colonies in large enough numbers to cause conflicts between native slaves and new Negroes, but the migration was too small to allow Africans to develop syncretistic African communities successfully. Africans were forced by their masters to stay on the quarter, where natives also lived and where unit sizes were small and sex ratios high. As a result, slaves could not transform individual friendships into community institutions. It was only when native adults began to predominate that the earlier conflicts among blacks were contained, and families and quarter communities began to emerge throughout tidewater. At the same time as immigration of Africans declined, the proportion of natives among blacks grew, the sex ratio declined, and the number of slaves per unit increased. These demographic changes made the development of communal institutions easier.

As slaves responded to the demographic and economic environment of the Chesapeake colonies, they developed indigenous institutions. This essay confirms the overall argument made by Mintz and Price, but further suggests the crucial importance of slave immigration, the destiny of slave population, the size of units, and the adult sex ratio in the development of slave communities in the Chesapeake colonies. Because demographic and economic conditions in the Chesapeake were not favorable to black cultural autonomy until nearly the middle of the eighteenth century, the development of distinctive social institutions among the slaves of the region was a long process. . . .

Finally, this essay deals with only a portion of older settled tidewater areas. In the 1730s and 1740s proportionately more black immigrants went to the piedmont than to tidewater, and after 1755 nearly every African found his new home in a piedmont county. How much of the history of tidewater was repeated in the piedmont? If the population of the piedmont was heavily African, perhaps the characteristics of slave society in tidewater in the 1720s and 1730s were replicated in the piedmont in the 1750s and 1760s. But if enough black migrants from tidewater entered the piedmont, the story of the 1750s and 1760s may have been much the same in the two regions. Of course, it is possible that the relationships between slave demography and slave society documented here did not exist in the piedmont. If that is proven, then the basic patterns described here might be called into question. . . .

 ## FURTHER READING

Ira Berlin, *Many Thousands Gone: The First Two Centuries of Slavery in North America* (1998).

Robin Blackburn, *The Making of New World Slavery: From the Baroque to the Modern, 1492–1800* (1997).

Sylvia Frey, *Water from the Rock: Black Resistance in a Revolutionary Age* (1991).

Gwendolyn Midlo Hall, *Africans in Colonial Louisiana: The Development of Afro-Creole Culture in the Eighteenth Century* (1992).

Peter Kolchin, *American Slavery, 1619–1877* (1993).

Allan Kulikoff, *Tobacco and Slaves: The Development of Southern Cultures in the Chesapeake, 1680–1800* (1986).

Jean Butenhoff Lee, "The Problem of Slave Community in the Eighteenth-Century Chesapeake," *William and Mary Quarterly,* 3rd Series, 43 (1986), 333–361.

Philip. D. Morgan, *Slave Counterpoint: Black Culture in the Eighteenth-Century Chesapeake and Low Country* (1998).

Joseph P. Reidy, *From Slavery to Agrarian Capitalism in the Cotton Plantation South, Central Georgia, 1800–1880* (1992).

John K. Thornton, "African Dimensions of the Stono Rebellion," *American Historical Review,* 96 (1991), 1101–1113.

Subordination and Autonomy: The Dialectics of Master-Slave Relations

Scholars often have assumed that to understand the slave's life depends first on how accurately one characterizes the relations between masters and slaves. In what ways and to what extent is that proposition valid? By what criteria does one grasp the meaning of the master-slave relationship—laws, eyewitness testimony, behavior? In theory and in practice, what were the extent and limits of the master's hegemony? To what extent does the logic of slavery predict its actuality?

Certainly the logic of slavery suggests that the master must have absolute power over the slave, who could assert his or her personal will only through the master. Some scholars claim that the slave could not exist as an independent personality, that his or her primary referent was the master, that a meaningful family and community life independent of the master was unlikely if not impossible. Moreover, absent the possibility for developing an autonomous personality, resistance to the institution of slavery was impossible.

Yet slaves did resist and even rebel. Were all the rebels and resisters somehow exceptional, or did systematic fissures, cracks within the ostensibly absolute hegemony of the master, allow some space for resistance to develop? The fact that slaves, who according to the logic of slavery were chattel property, could in some instances own property themselves suggests one such anomaly in the logic of slavery. Slave property claims were only "customary." Without legal status, they relied on the master's goodwill. But was the fact that masters felt compelled or that it was to their benefit to recognize such "rights" an indication of the limits of their hegemony over the slave?

 D O C U M E N T S

In the first document Thomas Cobb, an antebellum legal scholar, reviews the development of jurisprudence and statute law defining and governing the civil status of slaves. In theory the logic of slavery requires that the slave be under the absolute power of the master, but in practice both the security of slavery and the preservation of the master's property rights required legal qualifications of that logic. In the second document, however, North Carolina jurist Thomas Ruffin declares that the absolute dominion of the master must be respected. On large slave plantations the actual dominion over slaves had to be delegated to surrogates, leading some owners like Governor James Henry Hammond of South Carolina to commit their slave management preferences to writing, as in the third document. These rules suggest the minute details of the management of a slave labor force, and they hint at the possible tensions produced by the division of authority among the owner, his overseer, and the black drivers. In the fourth document Frederick Douglass describes his successful manipulation of such divided authority in his violent confrontation with one such surrogate master, the slavebreaker Covey. Resistance by slave women, especially the mothers of enslaved children, was much more complicated, as indicated in the fifth document. Here Harriet Jacobs describes her successful flight, aided by family and friends, from a predatory master and his sadistic wife. The sixth and seventh documents reflect the surprising phenomenon of chattel slaves themselves being able to hold property. In the sixth a slave woman leaves household goods, money, and livestock to her master and her clothing to whoever cares for her in her last days. The seventh is one of hundreds of claims filed by ex-slaves after the Civil War seeking reimbursement for property damaged or destroyed by Union troops during the war, suggesting further the capacity of slaves to accumulate property even though they themselves were legal chattels.

1. Thomas Cobb, an Antebellum Scholar, Describes the Legal Basis for Slavery, 1858

§ 84 *a.* In the Roman law, a slave was a mere chattel (*res*). He was not recognized as a person. But the negro slave in America, protected . . . by municipal law, occupies a double character of person and property. . . .

§ 86. Of the three great absolute rights guaranteed to every citizen by the common law, viz., the right of personal security, the right of personal liberty, and the right of private property, the slave, in a state of pure or absolute slavery, is totally deprived, being, as to life, liberty, and property, under the absolute and uncontrolled dominion of his master, so that infringements upon these rights, even by third persons, could be remedied and punished only at the suit of the master for the injury done him in the loss of service or the diminution in value of his slave. As before remarked, however, no such state of slavery exists in these States. And so modified is the slavery here, partly by natural law, partly by express enactment, and more effectually by the influence of civilization and Christian enlightenment, that it is difficult frequently to trace to any purely legal sources many of those protecting barriers, the denial of whose existence would shock an enlightened public sense.

§ 87. Statute law has done much to relieve the slave from this absolute dominion, and the master from this perilous power, more especially so far as regards the first great right of personal security. In all of the slaveholding States, the homicide of a slave is held to be murder, and in most of them, has been so expressly declared by law. In Georgia, Alabama, Texas, and Arkansas, the provisions for the protection of the person of the slave are inserted in their respective Constitutions, thus making it a

Thomas Reade Root Cobb, *An Inquiry into the Law of Negro Slavery in the United States of America* (Philadelphia, 1858), 1:82–86, 92–94, 99–100, 105–109.

part of the fundamental law, and beyond the reach of ordinary legislation. Nor has the legislation of the States stopped at the protection of their lives, but the security of limbs and the general comfort of the body are, in most of the States, amply provided for, various penalties being inflicted on masters for their cruel treatment. . . .

§ 88. The question has been much mooted, whether in the absence of statute laws, the homicide of a slave could be punished under the general law prescribing the penalty for murder. By some courts it has been held, that so soon as the progress of civilization and Christian enlightenment elevated the slave from the position of a mere chattel, and recognized him for any purpose as a person, just at that moment, the homicide of him, a human being, in the peace of the State, with malice afore-thought, was murder. So long as he remained purely and unqualifiedly property, an injury upon him was a trespass upon the master's rights. When the law, by providing for his proper nourishment and clothing, by enacting penalties against the cruel treatment of his master, by providing for his punishment for crimes, and other sim-ilar provisions, recognizes his existence as a person, he is as a child just born, brought for the first time within the pale of the law's protecting power; his existence as a person being recognized by the law, that existence is protected by the law.

§ 89. It has been objected to this conclusion, that if the general provision of the law against murder should be held to include slaves, why would not all other penal enactments, by the same course of reasoning, be held to include similar offences when committed on slaves, without their being specifically named? The reply made is twofold. 1st. The law, by recognizing the existence of the slave as a person, thereby confers no rights or privileges except such as are necessary to protect that existence. All other rights must be granted specially. Hence, the penalties for rape would not and should not, by such implication, be made to extend to carnal forcible knowledge of a slave, the offence not affecting the existence of the slave, and that existence being the extent of the right which the implication of the law grants. 2d. Implications of law will always be rebutted by the general policy of the law, and it is clearly against the policy of the law to extend over this class of the community, that character of protection which many of the penal statutes are intended to provide for the citizen. . . .

§ 95. Statutes having declared and affixed penalties to the offences affecting the personal security of slaves, it behooves us to inquire, how far the peculiar relation of the slave may affect the defences of those charged with a violation of these statutes. It would seem that from the very nature of slavery, and the necessarily degraded social position of the slave, many acts would extenuate the homicide of a slave, and reduce the offence to a lower grade, which would not constitute a legal provocation if done by a white person. Thus, in The State v. Tackett, it was held competent for one charged with the murder of a slave to give in evidence that the deceased was tur-bulent, and insolent, and impudent to white persons. And an assault or striking by a slave would, in many cases, amount to a justification of a homicide, which, in a white person, would only mitigate the offence. If the slave is in a state of insurrec-tion, the homicide is justifiable, in most of the States, by statute. And if a slave is killed, who, being found at an unlawful assembly, combining to rebel, refuses to surrender and resists by force, the homicide is justifiable.

§ 96. But while the law, from the necessity of the case, will thus subject the slave to the partial control of all the freemen of the country, yet it will not sanction any wanton violation of the person of the slave. Thus, it has been held, that a white citizen is not justified in shooting a negro who he orders to stop, and who refuses to do so, even though the negro be a fugitive or runaway. And in the case of Witsell v. Earnest and another, it was held, that even though the negro be suspected of a felony, and be a fugitive, a person not clothed with the authority of law to apprehend him, cannot lawfully kill such slave while flying from him; nor would an overseer be justified in shooting a negro who fled from punishment.

And so, also, the mere fact that the party committing the homicide was a patrolman, and in the exercise of his duties as such, will not justify the killing of a slave flying from him.

§ 97. No settled rule can be laid down as to the extent of the justification which the circumstances of each case may unfold. This we may say, the law looks favorably upon such conduct as tends to the proper subordination of the slave; but at the same time looks with a jealous eye upon all such conduct as tends to unnecessary and cruel treatment.

§ 98. The personal security of the slave being thus protected by express law, becomes *quasi* a right belonging to the slave as a person. How far may the slave go to protect that right? Subordination on the part of the slave is absolutely necessary, not only to the existence of the institution, but to the peace of the community. The policy of the law, therefore, requires that the slave should look to his master and the courts to avenge his wrongs. The rule, therefore, that justifies the freeman in repelling force by force, applies not to the slave.

If, however, the life or limb of the slave is endangered, he may use sufficient force to protect and defend himself, even if in so doing he kills the aggressor. Such seems to have been the civil law. . . .

§ 107. Another consequence of slavery is, that the violation of the person of a female slave, carries with it no other punishment than the damages which the master may recover for the trespass upon his property. Among the Romans there was also given the master, an action for the corruption of his slave, in which double damages were given. This however, was founded also upon the idea of the injury to the property. Among the Lombards, if a master debauched his slave's wife, the slave and his wife were restored to their freedom. The laws of King Alfred provided a pecuniary compensation to the master for the ravishment of his slave. These laws are suggestive of defects in our own legislation.

It is a matter worthy the consideration of legislators, whether the offence of rape, committed upon a female slave, should not be indictable; and whether, when committed by the master, there should not be superadded the sale of the slave to some other master. The occurrence of such an offence is almost unheard of; and the known lasciviousness of the negro, renders the possibility of its occurrence very remote. Yet, for the honor of the statute-book, if it does occur, there should be an adequate punishment. . . .

§ 111. The right of personal liberty in the slave is utterly inconsistent with the idea of slavery, and whenever the slave acquires this right, his condition is *ipso facto* changed. Hence, the enjoyment of it for a number of years has been held to be strong presumptive evidence of former emancipation.

§ 112. Blackstone defines this personal liberty to "consist in the power of locomotion, of changing situation or moving one's person to whatsoever place one's own inclination may direct, without imprisonment or restraint, unless by due course of law." The slave, while possessing the power of locomotion, moves not as his own inclination may direct, but at the bidding of his master, who may, of his own will, imprison or restrain him, unless he thereby infringes some provision of statute law. So utterly opposite is the position of the slave from that of the freeman in respect to this right, that we could not better define his condition, than to say it is the reverse of that of the freeman.

§ 112*a*. But while the slave's power of locomotion is thus within the absolute control of the master, no third person has any right to restrain or imprison him, except by order of the master, or in cases provided by law. Hence, disobedience of a slave to the order of a person who has no right to control him, in the absence of statute law, would be no justification to such person for a battery or other injury committed on the slave.

§ 113. Reasons of policy and necessity, however, require that so long as two races of men live together, the one as masters and the other as dependents and slaves, to a certain extent, *all* of the superior race shall exercise a controlling power over the inferior. If the slave feels that he is solely under the power and control of his immediate master, he will soon become insolent and ungovernable to all others. If the white man had, then, no right by law to control, the result would be, the excitement of angry passions, broils, and bloodshed. Hence have arisen, in the States, the various police and patrol regulations, giving to white persons other than the master, under certain circumstances, the right of controlling, and, in some cases, correcting slaves. But if the white person exceeds the authority given, and chastises a slave who has given no provocation, he is liable for the trespass.

§ 114. Necessarily, much of the time of the slave is not employed in his master's service. The long hours of the night, the Sabbath day, and the various holidays, are times when, by the permission of masters, slaves enjoy a *quasi* personal liberty. At such times, it cannot be expected that the watchful eye of the master can follow them. Frequent and large collections of them would necessarily occur, and, having no business to occupy their thoughts and conversation, mischief and evil would be the consequence of their assemblage. It has been found expedient and necessary, therefore, in all the slaveholding States, to organize, in every district, a body of men, who, for a limited time, exercise certain police powers, conferred by statute, for the better government of the slave, and the protection of the master. Upon these policemen or patrol, for the time, greater powers and privileges are necessarily conferred, for the execution of their office, in controlling the liberty and movements of the slave.

§ 115. The power and authority of the patrol, however, are limited by the statutes prescribing them, and they are not at liberty to overleap these bounds. Hence, in South Carolina, it was held, that under the authority to disperse unlawful assemblies of negroes, the patrol had no right to interfere with an open assemblage, for the purpose of religious worship, where white persons were also assembled. Nor with an orderly meeting of slaves, with the consent of their masters, upon the premises of a slaveholder, with his permission and occasional presence. Nor can the patrol correct a slave giving no provocation, who is without his master's inclosure, with a permit or ticket authorizing it.

If the patrol inflict excessive punishment upon a slave, they will be liable to the master for the trespass. Some degree of discretion, however, is necessarily allowed them.

§ 116. The necessity for patrol regulations being to control slaves when not under the control of their masters, it would seem that the patrol, upon principle, could never interfere with the master's control of his own slave, and upon his own premises. It would require very express enactment to justify such interference.

§ 117. Yet the master's privilege extends only to his own slaves, and he cannot so act towards them as to interfere or injure his neighbors. Hence, the enactments in many States, against persons permitting assemblages of the slaves of others upon their premises, without the consent of their owners. Hence, also, a master, in many States, is prohibited from furnishing spirituous liquors to his own slaves in such quantities as to enable them to furnish others. Hence, also, in almost all the States, the penalties against the master for permitting his slaves to hire their own time, or to go at liberty, to the injury of others.

§ 118. To restrain the slave altogether from leaving his master's premises, during the time that he is not employed in his master's business, would be unnecessarily harsh towards that dependent class. Hence, by the permission of the master, the slave may be allowed to travel the highway, or to visit and remain at other places; in which event, he is not subject to be controlled or corrected by the patrol, unless found violating some provision of law. The evidence of such permission is called a *permit* or *pass*. The particularity with which it should be written, and what it should contain, must necessarily depend upon the requisition of the statutes regulating patrols. A substantial compliance with the statute is sufficient. On the other hand, the master is not permitted to violate the whole policy of the legislation of a State by giving his slave a "permit" or "pass" for an indefinite or unreasonable period of time, especially if it professes to allow the slave privileges forbidden to the slave, and penal in the master.

§ 119. From this *quasi* liberty of the slave, during the Sabbath and other holidays, flow many interesting questions as to the liability of the master or hirer for the acts of the slave at such times, which will be considered hereafter.

2. Thomas Ruffin, a Judge, Struggles with the Illogic of Slaves as Property and as Persons, 1829

RUFFIN, J.   A Judge cannot but lament when such cases as the present are brought into judgment. It is impossible that the reasons on which they go can be appreciated, but where institutions similar to our own exist and are thoroughly understood. The struggle, too, in the Judge's own breast between the feelings of the man and the duty of the magistrate is a severe one, presenting strong temptation to put aside such questions, if it be possible. It is useless, however, to complain of things inherent in our political state. And it is criminal in a Court to avoid any responsibility which the laws impose. With whatever reluctance, therefore, it is done, the Court is compelled to express an opinion upon the extent of the dominion of the master over the slave in North Carolina.

The State v. John Mann, 1829, in *Reports of the State Supreme Court of North Carolina, December Term, 1828–1830,* 168–171.

The indictment charges a battery on Lydia, a slave of Elizabeth Jones. . . . Here the slave had been hired by the defendant, and was in his possession; and the battery was committed during the period of hiring. With the liabilities of the hirer to the general owner for an injury permanently impairing the value of the slave no rule now laid down is intended to interfere. That is left upon the general doctrine of bailment. The inquiry here is whether a cruel and unreasonable battery on a slave by the hirer is indictable. The Judge below instructed the jury that it is.

He seems to have put it on the ground that the defendant had but a special property. Our laws uniformly treat the master or other person having the possession and command of the slave as entitled to the same extent of authority. The object is the same—the services of the slave; and the same powers must be confided. In a criminal proceeding, and indeed in reference to all other persons but the general owner, the hirer and possessor of a slave, in relation to both rights and duties, is, for the time being, the owner. This opinion would, perhaps, dispose of this particular case; because the indictment, which charges a battery upon the slave of Elizabeth Jones, is not supported by proof of a battery upon defendant's own slave; since different justifications may be applicable to the two cases. But upon the general question whether the owner is answerable *criminaliter* for a battery upon his own slave, or other exercise of authority or force not forbidden by statute, the Court entertains but little doubt. That he is so liable has never yet been decided; nor, as far as is known, been hitherto contended. There have been no prosecutions of the sort. The established habits and uniform practice of the country in this respect is the best evidence of the portion of power deemed by the whole community requisite to the preservation of the master's dominion. If we thought differently we could not set our notions in array against the judgment of everybody else, and say that this or that authority may be safely lopped off. This had indeed been assimilated at the bar to the other domestic relations; and arguments drawn from the well-established principles which confer and restrain the authority of the parent over the child, the tutor over the pupil, the master over the apprentice, have been pressed on us. The Court does not recognize their application. There is no likeness between the cases. They are in opposition to each other, and there is an impassable gulf between them. The difference is that which exists between freedom and slavery—and a greater cannot be imagined. In the one, the end in view is the happiness of the youth, born to equal rights with that governor, on whom the duty devolves of training the young to usefulness in a station which he is afterwards to assume among freemen. To such an end, and with such a subject, moral and intellectual instruction seem the natural means; and for the most part they are found to suffice. Moderate force is superadded only to make the others effectual. If that fail it is better to leave the party to his own headstrong passions and the ultimate correction of the law than to allow it to be immoderately inflicted by a private person. With slavery it is far otherwise. The end is the profit of the master, his security and the public safety; the subject, one doomed in his own person and his posterity, to live without knowledge and without the capacity to make anything his own, and to toil that another may reap the fruits. What moral considerations shall be addressed to such a being to convince him what it is impossible but that the most stupid must feel and know can never be true—that he is thus to labor upon a principle of natural duty, or for the sake of his own personal happiness, such services can only be expected from one who has no will of his own; who surrenders his will in implicit obedience to that of another. Such obedience is the consequence only of uncontrolled authority over the body. There is nothing else which can operate to produce the effect. The power of the master must be absolute to render the submission of the slave perfect. I most freely confess my sense of the harshness of this proposition; I feel it as deeply as any man can; and as a principle of moral right every person in his retirement must repudiate it. But in the actual condition of things it must be so. There is no remedy. This discipline belongs to the state of slavery. They cannot be disunited without abrogating at once the rights of the master and absolving the slave from his subjection. It constitutes the curse of slavery to both the bond and free portion of our population. But it is inherent in the relation of master and slave.

That there may be particular instances of cruelty and deliberate barbarity where, in conscience, the law might properly interfere, is most probable. The difficulty is to determine where a Court may properly begin. Merely in the abstract it may well be asked, which power of the master accords with right? The answer will probably sweep away all of them. But we cannot look at the matter in that light. The truth is that we are forbidden to enter upon a train of general reasoning on the subject. We cannot allow the right of the master to be brought into discussion in the courts of justice. The slave, to remain a slave, must be made sensible that there is no appeal from his master; that his power is in no instance usurped; but is conferred by the laws of man at least, if not by the law of God. The danger would be great, indeed, if the tribunals of justice should be called on to graduate the punishment appropriate to every temper and every dereliction of menial duty. No man can anticipate the many and aggravated provocations of the master which the slave would be constantly stimulated by his own passions or the instigation of others to give; or the consequent wrath of the master, prompting him to bloody vengeance upon the turbulent traitor—a vengeance generally practiced with impunity by reason of its privacy. The Court, therefore, disclaims the power of changing the relation in which these parts of our people stand to each other.

We are happy to see that there is daily less and less occasion for the interposition of the Courts. The protection already afforded by several statutes, that all-powerful motive, the private interest of the owner, the benevolences towards each other, seated in the hearts of those who have been born and bred together, the frowns and deep execrations of the community upon the barbarian who is guilty of excessive and brutal cruelty to his unprotected slave, all combined, have produced a mildness of treatment and attention to the comforts of the unfortunate class of slaves, greatly mitigating the rigors of servitude and ameliorating the condition of the slaves. The same causes are operating and will continue to operate with increased action until the disparity in numbers between the whites and blacks shall have rendered the latter in no degree dangerous to the former, when the police now existing may be further relaxed. This result, greatly to be desired, may be much more rationally expected from the events above alluded to, and now in progress, than from any rash expositions of abstract truths by a judiciary tainted with a false and fanatical philanthropy, seeking to redress an acknowledged evil by means still more wicked and appalling than even that evil.

I repeat that I would gladly have avoided this ungrateful question. But being brought to it the Court is compelled to declare that while slavery exists amongst us in its present state, or until it shall seem fit to the legislature to interpose express enactments to the contrary, it will be the imperative duty of the Judges to recognize the full dominion of the owner over the slave, except where the exercise of it is forbidden by statute. And this we do upon the ground that this dominion is essential to the value of slaves as property, to the security of the master, and the public tranquility, greatly dependent upon their subordination; and, in fine, as most effectually securing the general protection and comfort of the slaves themselves.

3. South Carolina Governor James Henry Hammond, Slaveowner, Instructs His Overseer on the Ideal Disciplinary Regime, c. 1840s

Crop

1 A good crop means one that is good taking into consideration every thing—negroes, land, mules, stock, fences, ditches, farming utensils, &c., &c., all of which must be kept up & improved in value. The effort therefore must not be merely to make *so many* cotton bales or such an amount of other produce, but as much as can be made without interrupting the steady increase in value of the rest of the property.

Remarks.—There should be an increase in number, & improvement in condition & value of negroes; abundant provisions of all sorts for every thing, made on the place, carefully saved & properly housed; an improvement in the productive qualities of the land, & general condition of the plantation; mules, stock, fences & farming utensils in fine order at the close of the year; as much produce as could possibly be made under these circumstances, ready for market in good season, & of prime quality.

Overseer

. . . 5 The Overseer must see that all the negroes leave their houses promptly after hornblow in the morning. Once, or more, a week he must visit every house after horn blow at night to see that all are in.

Remarks.—He should not fall into a regular day or hour for night visit but should go so often and at such times that he may be expected at anytime.

6 The Overseer will be expected not to degrade himself by charging any negro with carrying news to the Employer. There must be no news to carry. The Employer will not encourage tale-bearing, but will question every negro indiscriminately whenever he thinks proper about all matters connected with the plantation, & require him to tell the truth. Whenever he learns anything derogatory to the Overseer he will immediately communicate it to him.

"Governor Hammond's Instructions to His Overseer," in Willie Lee Rose, ed., *A Documentary History of Slavery in North America* (1976), 345–353. Copyright © 1976 by Oxford University Press, Inc.

Remarks.—The Overseer must show no favoritism among negroes. . . .

10 The Overseer must keep the plantation Diary regularly & carefully, note the number of hands engaged each day in various operations under proper heading, the number of sick, weather, allowances & implements given out, articles received at or sent from the plantation, births, deaths & whatever other information or remarks which may be valuable, together with an accurate summary of every thing on the plantation once a month. He must also inform the Employer, without being asked, of every thing going on that may concern or interest him.

11 The negroes must be made to obey & to work, which may be done by an Overseer, who attends regularly to his business, with very little whipping. Much whipping indicates a bad tempered, or inattentive manager, & will not be allowed. The Overseer must never on any occasion—unless in self defence—kick a negro, or strike with his hand, or a stick, or the butt-end of his whip. No unusual punishment must be resorted to without the Employer's consent.

Remarks.—He must never threaten a negro, but punish offences immediately on knowing them; otherwise he will soon have run-aways. . . .

Allowances

1 Allowances are given out once a week. No distinction is made among work-hands, whether they are full-hands or under, field hands or adjuncts about the yard, stables, &c.

Remarks.—Negroes are improvident with a longer interval between allowances many will consume, waste or barter their provisions before it closes & must commit thefts, or have insufficient & unwholesome food during a portion of the time; demoralyzing & rendering them physically incapable of doing full work, if not producing sickness. They should, also, be brought into that contact with the master, at laest [least] once a week, of receiving the means of subsistence from him. . . .

Children

9 There is a separate building [in] the charge of a trusty nurse, where the children are kept during the day. Weaned children are brought to it at the last horn-blow in the morning—about good day light. The unweaned are brought to it at sun rise, after suckling, & left in cradles in charge of the nurse. . . .

Sucklers

13 Sucklers are not required to leave their houses until sun-rise, when they leave their children at the children's house before going to field. The period of suckling is 12 mos. Their work lies always within ½ mile of the quarter. They are required to be cool before commencing to suckle—to wait 15 minutes, at laest [sic], in summer, after reaching the children's house before nursing. It is the duty of the

nurse to see that none are heated when nursing, as well as of the Overseer & his wife occasionally to do so. They are allowed 45 minutes at each morning to be with their children. They return 3 times a day until their infants are 8 mos. old—in the middle of the forenoon, at noon, & in the middle of the afternoon: till the 12th mo. but twice a day, missing at noon: during the 12th mo. at noon only. On weaning, the child is removed entirely from its Mother for 2 weeks, & placed in charge of some careful woman without a child, during which time the Mother is not to nurse it at all.

Remarks.—The amount of work done by a Suckler is about ⅗ of that done by a full-hand, a little increased toward the last.

Old & Infirm

15 Those, who from age & infirmities are unable to keep up with the prime hands, are put in the suckler's gang.

Pregnant

16 Pregnant women, at 5 mos. are put in the suckler's gang. No plowing or lifting must be required of them.

Sucklers, old, infirm & pregnant, receive the same allowances as full-work hands.

Confinement

17 The regular plantation midwife shall attend all women in confinement. Some other woman learning the art is usually with her during delivery. The confined woman lies up one month, & the midwife remains in constant attendance for 7 days. Each woman on confinement has a bundle given to her containing articles of clothing for the infant, pieces of cloth & rag, & some extra nourishment, as sugar, coffee, rice & flour for the Mother.

Sickness

18 No negro will be allowed to remain at his own house when sick, but must be confined to the hospital. Every reasonable complaint must be promptly attended to, & with any marked or general symptom of sickness, however trivial, a negro may lie up a day or so at laest [least]. Homeopathy is exclusively practiced. As no physician is allowed to practice on the plantation—there being no Homoeopathist convenient—each case has to be examined carefully by the master or overseer to ascertain the disease. The remedies next are to be chosen with the utmost discrimination. The vehicles, (tumblers & aprons) for preparing & administering with, are to be thoroughly cleansed. The directions for treatment, diet, &c. most implicitly followed; the effects & changes cautiously observed, & finally the medecines [sic] securely laid away from accidents & contaminating influences. In cases, where there is the slightest uncertainty, the books must be taken to the bed-side, &

a careful & thorough examination of the case, & comparison of remedies, made before administering them. The Overseer must record in the prescription book every dose of medecine [sic] administered.

Hours

19 The first morning horn is blown an hour before day-light. All work-hands are required to rise & prepare their cooking, &c. for the day. The second horn is blown just at good day-light, when it is the duty of the driver to visit every house & see that all have left for the field. The plow hands leave their houses for the stables, at the summons of the plow driver, 15 minutes earlier than the gang, the Overseer opening the stable doors to them. at 11 ½ M. the plow hands repair to the nearest weather house. At 12 M. the gang stop to eat dinner. At 1 P.M. through the greater part of the year, all hands return to work. In summer the intermission increases with the heat to the extent of 3 ½ hours. At 15 minutes before sun-set the plowhands, & at sun-set the rest, knock off work for the day. No work must ever be required after dark. No negro will be allowed to go hunting at night. The negroes are allowed to visit among themselves until the night horn is blown, after which no negro must be seen out of his house, & it is the duty of the driver to go around & see that he is in it. The night horn is blown at 8 ½ P.M. in winter, & at 9 P.M. in summer. The head driver has charge of & blows the horn.

Driver

20 The head driver is the most important negro on the plantation, & is not required to work like the other hands. He is to be treated with more respect than any other negro by both master & overseer. He is on no occasion to be treated with any indignity calculated to lose the respect of the other negroes, without breaking him. He is required to maintain proper discipline at all times. To se[e] that no negro idles or does bad work in the field & to punish it with discretion on the spot. The driver must never be flogged, except by the master, but in emergencies that will not admit of delay. Of this, however, he is to be kept in entire ignorance. He is permitted to visit the master at any time without being required to get a card, though, in general, he is expected to inform the Overseer when he leaves the place, & present himself on returning. He is expected to communicate freely whatever attracts his attention, or he thinks information of interest to the master. He is a confidential servant & may be a guard against any excuses or omissions of the Overseer.

Marriage

21 Marriage is to be encouraged as it adds to the comfort, happiness & health of those who enter upon it, besides insuring a greater increase. Permission must always be obtained from the master before marriage, but no marriage will be allowed with negroes not belonging to the master. When sufficient cause can be shewn on either side, a marriage may be annulled, but the offending party must be severely punished. Where both are in wrong both must be punished, & if they insist on separating must have 100 lashes apiece. After such a separation neither can marry

again for 3 years. For first marriage a bounty of $5.00 to be invested in household articles, shall be given. If either has been married before, the bounty shall be $3.50. A third marriage shall not be allowed but in extreme cases, & in such cases, or where both have been married before, no bounty will be given.

Church

22 All are privileged & encouraged to go to Church on Sundays, but no religious meeting is allowed on the plantation beyond singing & praying, & at such times as will not conflict with the plantation hours, & always with the permission of the Master or Overseer. Church members are privileged to dance on all holyday occasions, & the class leader or deacon who may report them shall be reprimanded or punished at the discretion of the master.

Visiting

23 All visiting with strange negroes is positively forbidden. Negroes living at one plantation & having wives at the other can visit them only between Saturday night & Monday morning, & must get a pass card at each visit. The pass consists of a card with the full name of the place of destination on it & the first letter of the place of leaving below. The card must be delivered to the Overseer immediately on reaching the place named on it, & a return card asked for just before returning. The card is the recognized & required permit in all visiting & any negro leaving the plantation without it, or off the most direct route, shall be punished on detection by the Overseer, & is liable to punishment from any one meeting him. No more than 6 ordinarily at a time can leave the quarter, except for Church. Negroes are subject to the regulations of the place they are at any moment upon, & it is as much the duty of the Overseer & driver to observe them as those under their ordinary charge.

Town

24 Each work-hand is allowed to go to Town once a year (the women always selecting some of the men to go for them) on a Sunday between crop gathering & Christmas. Not more than 10 shall be allowed to go the same day. The head driver may have a cart some Saturday after Christmas that it is convenient for him to go to Town.
    This rule is objectionable & must be altered.

Negro Patches

Adjoining each negro house is a piece of ground convenient for a fowl-yard & garden. No fowl-yard or garden fence shall reach nearer than 60 feet to the negro houses. Negroes may have patches in various parts of the plantation (always getting permission from the master) to cultivate crops of their own. A field of suitable size shall be planted in pindars [peanuts], & cultivated in the same manner as the general crop, the produce of which is to be divided equally among the work-hands. Negroes are not allowed to grow crops of corn or cotton for themselves, nor to have any cattle or stock of any kind of their own.

4. A Slave Man Resists, 1845

My master and myself had quite a number of differences. He found me unsuitable to his purpose. My city life, he said, had had a very pernicious effect upon me. It had almost ruined me for every good purpose, and fitted me for every thing which was bad. One of my greatest faults was that of letting his horse run away, and go down to his father-in-law's farm, which was about five miles from St. Michael's. I would then have to go after it. My reason for this kind of carelessness, or carefulness, was, that I could always get something to eat when I went there. Master William Hamilton, my master's father-in-law, always gave his slaves enough to eat. I never left there hungry, no matter how great the need of my speedy return. Master Thomas at length said he would stand it no longer. I had lived with him nine months, during which time he had given me a number of severe whippings, all to no good purpose. He resolved to put me out, as he said, to be broken; and, for this purpose, he let me for one year to a man named Edward Covey. Mr. Covey was a poor man, a farm-renter. He rented the place upon which he lived, as also the hands with which he tilled it. Mr. Covey had acquired a very high reputation for breaking young slaves, and this reputation was of immense value to him. It enabled him to get his farm tilled with much less expense to himself than he could have had it done without such a reputation. Some slaveholders thought it not much loss to allow Mr. Covey to have their slaves one year, for the sake of the training to which they were subjected, without any other compensation. He could hire young help with great ease, in consequence of this reputation. Added to the natural good qualities of Mr. Covey, he was a professor of religion—a pious soul—a member and a class-leader in the Methodist church. All of this added weight to his reputation as a "nigger-breaker." I was aware of all the facts, having been made acquainted with them by a young man who had lived there. I nevertheless made the change gladly; for I was sure of getting enough to eat, which is not the smallest consideration to a hungry man. . . .

I lived with Mr. Covey one year. During the first six months, of that year, scarce a week passed without his whipping me. I was seldom free from a sore back. My awkwardness was almost always his excuse for whipping me. We were worked fully up to the point of endurance. Long before day we were up, our horses fed, and by the first approach of day we were off to the field with our hoes and ploughing teams. Mr. Covey gave us enough to eat, but scarce time to eat it. We were often less than five minutes taking our meals. We were often in the field from the first approach of day till its last lingering ray had left us; and at saving-fodder time, midnight often caught us in the field binding blades.

Covey would be out with us. The way he used to stand it, was this. He would spend the most of his afternoons in bed. He would then come out fresh in the evening, ready to urge us on with his words, example, and frequently with the whip. Mr. Covey was one of the few slaveholders who could and did work with his hands. . . .

If an [at] any one time of my life more than another, I was made to drink the bitterest dregs of slavery, that time was during the first six months of my stay with

From *Narrative of the Life of Frederick Douglass* (Boston, 1845), 86–88, 91, 94–95, 97–99, 103–105.

Mr. Covey. We were worked in all weathers. It was never too hot or too cold; it could never rain, blow, hail, or snow, too hard for us to work in the field. Work, work, work, was scarcely more the order of the day than of the night. The longest days were too short for him, and the shortest nights too long for him. I was some-what unmanageable when I first went there, but a few months of this discipline tamed me. Mr. Covey succeeded in breaking me. I was broken in body, soul, and spirit. My natural elasticity was crushed, my intellect languished, the disposition to read departed, the cheerful spark that lingered about my eye died; the dark night of slavery closed in upon me; and behold a man transformed into a brute! . . .

I have already intimated that my condition was much worse, during the first six months of my stay at Mr. Covey's, than in the last six. The circumstances leading to the change in Mr. Covey's course toward me form an epoch in my humble history. You have seen how a man was made a slave; you shall see how a slave was made a man. On one of the hottest days of the month of August, 1833, Bill Smith, William Hughes, a slave named Eli, and myself, were engaged in fanning wheat. Hughes was clearing the fanned wheat from before the fan, Eli was turning, Smith was feed-ing, and I was carrying wheat to the fan. The work was simple, requiring strength rather than intellect; yet, to one entirely unused to such work, it came very hard. About three o'clock of that day, I broke down; my strength failed me; I was seized with a violent aching of the head, attended with extreme dizziness; I trembled in every limb. Finding what was coming, I nerved myself up, feeling it would never do to stop work. I stood as long as I could stagger to the hopper with grain. When I could stand no longer, I fell, and felt as if held down by an immense weight. The fan of course stopped; every one had his own work to do; and no one could do the work of the other, and have his own go on at the same time.

Mr. Covey was at the house, about one hundred yards from the treading-yard where we were fanning. On hearing the fan stop, he left immediately, and came to the spot where we were. He hastily inquired what the matter was. Bill answered that I was sick, and there was no one to bring wheat to the fan. I had by this time crawled away under the side of the post and rail-fence by which the yard was enclosed, hoping to find relief by getting out of the sun. He then asked where I was. He was told by one of the hands. He came to the spot, and, after looking at me awhile, asked me what was the matter. I told him as well as I could, for I scarce had strength to speak. He then gave me a savage kick in the side, and told me to get up. I tried to do so, but fell back in the attempt. He gave me another kick, and again told me to rise. I again tried, and succeeded in gaining my feet; but, stooping to get the tub with which I was feeding the fan, I again staggered and fell. While down in this situation, Mr. Covey took up the hickory slat with which Hughes had been striking off the half-bushel measure, and with it gave me a heavy blow upon the head, making a large wound, and the blood ran freely; and with this again told me to get up. I made no effort to comply, having now made up my mind to let him do his worst. In a short time after receiving this blow, my head grew better. Mr Covey had now left me to my fate. . . .

. . . Long before daylight, I was called to go and rub, curry, and feed, the horses. I obeyed, and was glad to obey. But whilst thus engaged, whilst in the act of throw-ing down some blades from the loft, Mr. Covey entered the stable with a long rope; and just as I was half out of the loft, he caught hold of my legs, and was about tying me. As soon as I found what he was up to, I gave a sudden spring, and as I did so, he holding to my legs, I was brought sprawling on the stable floor. Mr. Covey seemed now to think he had me, and could do what he pleased; but at this moment—from whence came the spirit I don't know—I resolved to fight; and, suiting my action to the resolution, I seized Covey hard by the throat; and as I did so, I rose. He held on to me, and I to him. My resistance was so entirely unexpected, that Covey seemed taken all aback. He trembled like a leaf. This gave me assurance, and I held him uneasy, causing the blood to run where I touched him with the ends of my fingers. Mr. Covey soon called out to Hughes for help. Hughes came, and, while Covey held me, attempted to tie my right hand. While he was in the act of doing so, I watched my chance, and gave him a heavy kick close under the ribs. This kick fairly sickened Hughes, so that he left me in the hands of Mr. Covey. This kick had the effect of not only weakening Hughes, but Covey also. When he saw Hughes bending over with pain, his courage quailed. He asked me if I meant to persist in my resistance. I told him I did, come what might; that he had used me like a brute for six months, and that I was determined to be used so no longer. With that, he strove to drag me to a stick that was lying just out of the stable door. He meant to knock me down. But just as he was leaning over to get the stick, I seized him with both hands by his collar, and brought him by a sudden snatch to the ground. By this time, Bill came. Covey called upon him for assistance. Bill wanted to know what he could do. Covey said, "Take hold of him, take hold of him!" Bill said his master hired him out to work, and not to help to whip me; so he left Covey and myself to fight our own battle out. We were at it for nearly two hours. Covey at length let me go, puffing and blowing at a great rate, saying that if I had not resisted, he would not have whipped me half so much. The truth was, that he had not whipped me at all. I considered him as getting entirely the worst end of the bargain; for he had drawn no blood from me, but I had from him. The whole six months afterwards, that I spent with Mr. Covey, he never laid the weight of his finger upon me in anger. He would occasionally say, he didn't want to get hold of me again. "No," thought I, "you need not; for you will come off worse than you did before."

This battle with Mr. Covey was the turning-point in my career as a slave. It rekindled the few expiring embers of freedom, and revived within me a sense of my own manhood. It recalled the departed self-confidence, and inspired me again with a determination to be free. The gratification afforded by the triumph was a full compensation for whatever else might follow, even death itself. He only can understand the deep satisfaction which I experienced, who has himself repelled by force the bloody arm of slavery. I felt as I never felt before. It was a glorious resurrection, from the tomb of slavery, to the heaven of freedom. My long-crushed spirit rose, cowardice departed, bold defiance took its place; and I now resolved that, however long I might remain a slave in form, the day had passed forever when I could be a slave in fact. I did not hesitate to let it be known of me, that the white man who expected to succeed in whipping, must also succeed in killing me.

From this time I was never again what might be called fairly whipped, though I remained a slave four years afterwards. I had several fights, but was never whipped.

It was for a long time a matter of surprise to me why Mr. Covey did not immediately have me taken by the constable to the whipping-post, and there regularly whipped for the crime of raising my hand against a white man in defence of myself. And the only explanation I can now think of does not entirely satisfy me; but such as it is, I will give it. Mr. Covey enjoyed the most unbounded reputation for being a first-rate overseer and negro-breaker. It was of considerable importance to him. That reputation was at stake; and had he sent me—a boy about sixteen years old—to the public whipping-post, his reputation would have been lost; so, to save his reputation, he suffered me to go unpunished.

5. A Slave Woman Resists, 1861

Mr. Flint was hard pushed for house servants, and rather than lose me he had restrained his malice. I did my work faithfully, though not, of course, with a willing mind. They were evidently afraid I should leave them. Mr. Flint wished that I should sleep in the great house instead of the servants' quarters. His wife agreed to the proposition, but said I mustn't bring my bed into the house, because it would scatter feathers on her carpet. I knew when I went there that they would never think of such a thing as furnishing a bed of any kind for me and my little one. I therefore carried my own bed, and now I was forbidden to use it. I did as I was ordered. But now that I was certain my children were to be put in their power, in order to give them a stronger hold on me, I resolved to leave them that night. I remembered the grief this step would bring upon my dear old grandmother; and nothing less than the freedom of my children would have induced me to disregard her advice. I went about my evening work with trembling steps. Mr. Flint twice called from his chamber door to inquire why the house was not locked up. I replied that I had not done my work. "You have had time enough to do it," said he. "Take care how you answer me!"

I shut all the windows, locked all the doors, and went up to the third story, to wait till midnight. How long those hours seemed, and how fervently I prayed that God would not forsake me in this hour of utmost need! I was about to risk every thing on the throw of a die; and if I failed, O what [would] become of me and my poor children? They would be made to suffer for my fault.

At half past twelve I stole softly down stairs. I stopped on the second floor, thinking I heard a noise. I felt my way down into the parlor, and looked out of the window. The night was so intensely dark that I could see nothing. I raised the window very softly and jumped out. Large drops of rain were falling, and the darkness bewildered me. I dropped on my knees, and breathed a short prayer to God for guidance and protection. I groped my way to the road, and rushed towards the town with almost lightning speed. I arrived at my grandmother's house, but dared not see her. She would say, "Linda, you are killing me;" and I knew that would unnerve me. I tapped softly at the window of a room, occupied by a woman, who had lived in the house several years. I knew she was a faithful friend, and could be trusted with my secret. I tapped several times before she heard me. At last she raised the window, and I whispered, "Sally, I have run away. Let me in, quick." She opened the door softly, and said in low tones, "For God's sake, don't. Your grandmother is

From Harriet Jacobs, *Incidents in the Life of a Slave Girl* (1988), 145–49, 179–81. Copyright © 1988 by Oxford University Press, Inc.

trying to buy you and de chillern. Mr. Sands was here last week. He tole her he was going away on business, but he wanted her to go ahead about buying you and de chillern, and he would help her all he could. Don't run away, Linda. Your grandmother is all bowed down wid trouble now."

I replied, "Sally, they are going to carry my children to the plantation tomorrow; and they will never sell them to any body so long as they have me in their power. Now, would you advise me to go back?"

"No, chile, no," answered she. "When dey finds you is gone, dey won't want de plague ob de chillern; but where is you going to hide? Dey knows ebery inch ob dis house."

I told her I had a hiding-place, and that was all it was best for her to know. I asked her to go into my room as soon as it was light, and take all my clothes out of my trunk, and pack them in hers; for I knew Mr. Flint and the constable would be there early to search my room. I feared the sight of my children would be too much for my full heart; but I could not go out into the uncertain future without one last look. I bent over the bed where lay my little Benny and baby Ellen. Poor little ones! fatherless and motherless! Memories of their father came over me. He wanted to be kind to them; but they were not all to him, as they were to my womanly heart. I knelt and prayed for the innocent little sleepers. I kissed them lightly, and turned away.

As I was about to open the street door, Sally laid her hand on my shoulder, and said, "Linda, is you gwine all alone? Let me call your uncle."

"No, Sally," I replied, "I want no one to be brought into trouble on my account."

I went forth into the darkness and rain. I ran on till I came to the house of the friend who was to conceal me.

Early the next morning Mr. Flint was at my grandmother's inquiring for me. She told him she had not seen me, and supposed I was at the plantation. He watched her face narrowly, and said, "Don't you know anything about her running off?" She assured him that she did not. He went on to say, "Last night she ran off without the least provocation. We had treated her very kindly. My wife liked her. She will soon be found and brought back. Are her children with you?" When told that they were, he said, "I am very glad to hear that. If they are here, she cannot be far off. If I find out that any of my niggers have had any thing to do with this damned business, I'll give 'em five hundred lashes." As he started to go to his father's, he turned round and added, persuasively, "Let her be brought back, and she shall have her children to live with her."

The tidings made the old doctor rave and storm at a furious rate. It was a busy day for them. My grandmother's house was searched from top to bottom. As my trunk was empty, they concluded I had taken my clothes with me. Before ten o'clock every vessel northward bound was thoroughly examined, and the law against harboring fugitives was read to all on board. At night a watch was set over the town. Knowing how distressed my grandmother would be, I wanted to send her a message; but it could not be done. Every one who went in or out of her house was closely watched. The doctor said he would take my children, unless she became responsible for them; which of course she willingly did. The next day was spent in searching. Before night, the following advertisement was posted at every corner, and in every public place for miles round:—

"$300 REWARD! Ran away from the subscriber, an intelligent, bright, mulatto girl, named Linda, 21 years of age. Five feet four inches high. Dark eyes, and black hair inclined to curl; but it can be made straight. Has a decayed spot on a front tooth. She can read and write, and in all probability will try to get to the Free States. All persons are forbidden, under penalty of the law, to harbor or employ said slave. $150 will be given to whoever takes her in the state, and $300 if taken out of the state and delivered to me, or lodged in jail.

DR. FLINT."

. . . Christmas was approaching. Grandmother brought me materials, and I busied myself making some new garments and little playthings for my children. Were it not that hiring day is near at hand, many families are fearfully looking forward to the probability of separation in a few days, Christmas might be a happy season for the poor slaves. Even slave mothers try to gladden the hearts of their little ones on that occasion. Benny and Ellen had their Christmas stockings filled. Their imprisoned mother could not have the privilege of witnessing their surprise and joy. But I had the pleasure of peeping at them as they went into the street with their new suits on. I heard Benny ask a little playmate whether Santa Claus brought him any thing. "Yes," replied the boy; "but Santa Claus ain't a real man. It's the children's mothers that put things into the stockings." "No, that can't be," replied Benny, "for Santa Claus brought Ellen and me these new clothes, and my mother has been gone this long time."

How I longed to tell him that his mother made those garments, and that many a tear fell on them while she worked!

Every child rises early on Christmas morning to see the Johnkannaus. Without them, Christmas would be shorn of its greatest attraction. They consist of companies of slaves from the plantations, generally of the lower class. Two athletic men, in calico wrappers, have a net thrown over them, covered with all manner of bright-colored stripes. Cows' tails are fastened to their backs, and their heads are decorated with horns. A box, covered with sheepskin, is called the gumbo box. A dozen beat on this, while others strike triangles and jawbones, to which bands of dancers keep time. For a month previous they are composing songs, which are sung on this occasion. These companies, of a hundred each, turn out early in the morning, and are allowed to go round till twelve o'clock, begging for contributions. Not a door is left unvisited where there is the least chance of obtaining a penny or a glass of rum. They do not drink while they are out, but carry the rum home in jugs, to have a carousal. These Christmas donations frequently amount to twenty or thirty dollars. It is seldom that any white man or child refuses to give them a trifle. If he does, they regale his ears with the following song:—

> "Poor massa, so dey say;
> Down in de heel, so dey say;
> Got no money, so dey say;
> Not one shillin, so dey say;
> God A'mighty bress you, so dey say."

Christmas is a day of feasting, both with white and colored people. Slaves, who are lucky enough to have a few shillings, are sure to spend them for good eating; and many a turkey and pig is captured, without saying, "By your leave, sir." Those who cannot obtain these, cook a 'possum, or a raccoon, from which savory dishes can be made. My grandmother raised poultry and pigs for sale; and it was her established custom to have both a turkey and a pig roasted for Christmas dinner.

On this occasion, I was warned to keep extremely quiet, because two guests had been invited. One was the town constable, and the other was a free colored man, who tried to pass himself off for white, and who was always ready to do any mean work for the sake of currying favor with white people. My grandmother had a motive for inviting them. She managed to take them all over the house. All the rooms on the lower floor were thrown open for them to pass in and out; and after dinner, they were invited up stairs to look at a fine mocking bird my uncle had just brought home. There, too, the rooms were all thrown open, that they might look in. When I heard them talking on the piazza, my heart almost stood still. I knew this colored man had spent many nights hunting for me. Every body knew he had the blood of a slave father in his veins; but for the sake of passing himself off for white, he was ready to kiss the slaveholders' feet. How I despised him! As for the constable, he wore no false colors. The duties of his office were despicable, but he was superior to his companion, inasmuch as he did not pretend to be what he was not. Any white man, who could raise money enough to buy a slave, would have considered himself degraded by being a constable; but the office enabled its possessor to exercise authority.

6. The Last Will and Testament of Patty Cooke, a Virginia Slave, 1821

The Last Will & Testament of Patty Cooke

In the name of God [unclear] I Patty Cooke of sound mind, but in bad health, and wishing to provide against sudden death, do make this my last will and testament.

Art. 1—I give to my kind master all my household furniture, all money, and debts, and stock to him and his heirs forever.

Art. 2—I give to the person who waits on me while sick all my clothes.

Given under my hand this 20th day of July 1821

her

Patty   ✕   Cooke

mark

[witnessed]
C H Edloe?
Elijah Brown

From Will of Patty Cooke, Eppes Family Papers. Courtesy, Virginia Historical Society.

7. Samuel Elliot, an Ex-Slave, Claims Property Lost in the Civil War, 1873

[McIntosh, Ga. July 17, 1873]

Testimony of Claimant

My name is Samuel Elliott   I was born in Liberty County a Slave and became free when the Army came into the County. I belonged to Maybank Jones. I am 54 years old. I reside at Lauralview in Liberty County. I am a farmer. I am the Claimant in this Case.

2 I resided from the 1st of April 1861 to the 1st of June 1865 where I live now at Lauralview. I worked for my master all the time. I changed my business at one time when I was with my master as a waiter—in the rebel service   I was with him Eleven month. I came home with him. I told my son what was going on— he with 11 more ran off and joined the Army (the Yankee Army) on St Catherine Island. I dont remember the Year but it was soon after the battle at Williamsburgh Va, and before the 7 days battle near Chickahomony. I mean that was the time I came home with my master. I was with him at Yorktown— Soon after I came home My son with 11 others ran away & joined the Union Army. My master had me taken up tied me and tried to make me tell "What made them ran off"   I had to lie about it to keep from getting killed. the 11 slaves belonged to My Master Jones that stoped the slave owners from sending or taking slave into the Army as waiters or anything else. it stoped it in our neighborhood . . .

25 The rebels took all of my turkeys   they did not pay me a cent

26 I was threatened at the time My Master tied me up

27 I was molested as above stated because as my master stated I was the cause of all the slaves leaving the County and joining the Yankees . . .

40 At the begining of the rebellion I did not know any thing about the war   Mrs Somersall boys told me the War had commenced and we would all be free   that was soon after they fired on Fort Sumpter. they said the South would get whipped that they better not try, it was a sorry day when they fired on Fort Sumpter—   When the boys told we coloured people would all be free I felt happy   I told Mr Somersall "Glory be to God"   I could not feel it would come through   it was so long I began to think it would not come to pass but I felt happy and prayed for the time to come till it did come. . . .

43 At the beginning of the war I was a slave and became free when the Yankee Army came through. I continued farming after I became free and farming now—   When my Father died he had 20 head of cattle about 70 head of hogs— Turkeys Geese Ducks and Chicken a plenty—   he was foreman for his master and had been raising such things for Years   When he died the property was divided among his children and we continued to raise things just as he had been raising.

"Testimony by a Georgia Freeman Before the Southern Claims Commission," in *Freedom: A Documentary History of Emancipation, 1861–1867, Series 1, Vol. 1: The Destruction of Slavery*, ed. Ira Berlin et al. (Cambridge, U.K.: Cambridge University Press, 1985), 146–150. Copyright © 1985 by Cambridge University Press.

My Father has been dead about 30 years   I continued to raise stock and that was the way I got the property the Yankees took from me   My Master was Maybank Jones. My Father belonged to old Mr Elliott. Mr Jones bought the Elliott Estate out and he allowed us the same priviledge that Mr Elliott did. I live on the same land yet but it belongs to Suiton Stevens   I do not owe my master any thing not a-red-cent—   I am the only person interested in the claim presented by me against the Government. . . .

2 I saw all this property taken, the hogs pork, rice & ducks, were taken in my own wagon.

3 They asked me where all the rebels were. I told them they gone since day before yesterday gone to meet the Army. They asked about the horses, I told them they took them all off the place & cary them off too: they asked me where's the money & silver   I told them they carry them all off. They asked me where the camp was   I told them it was near by Dorchester. They went right on then shooting chickens. They come right into the house & when they find the meat was there they whoop. They hollered good living boys & began to take out the meat.

4 These things were taken at Laurel-view. this is near by Sunbury on the Seaboard in Liberty Co Ga. This property was taken in Dec between the first & the middle of the month & when the Army came. About 40 or 50 came the first time & then they kept coming & going in gangs as hard as they can. They belonged to Col. Baldwin's regiment. When they came there & begun to take my things I asked them "Massa" you going to take all, & leave me nothing to live on, & they said we are obliged to, we come to set you free, & we must have something to eat, but you must go to *"Uncle Sam"*   Uncle Sam's pockets drag on the ground. This property was all or pretty much all taken in one day.

5 Clarissa Monroe & Sue, & William, & Crawford, & Augustus Smith & myself were present at the taking of this property.

6 I dont know if there were any officers there or not I dont know them. I didn't hear any orders given for the taking of the property. The Soldier who spoke to me had straps on his shoulder & on his arm, he was on his horse & staid on his horse & looked on while the others took the things.

7 They just drove the cows right out of the yard   they were just done milked. They took my wagon & put one of their horses to it, my horse they didn't take because he had fistula on his shoulders. They took my harness. They shoot some of the hogs & those in the pen 2 bacon hogs I left in the pen to kill again they tied them. They took the pork from the table in the house & tied it to their saddles. They tied the ducks to the horse & said they were going to fatten them for me. They took the rice off in the wagon. The rice was in the room clean rice.

8 They drove the cattle off & the other things they moved off in wagon & on horses & in an oxcart.

9 They moved this property to Medway Church. I followed them till I got into the main road   they made me go to help drive the cattle about a mile this way, then I came back home & they went on towards the Church.

10 They took this property for the soldiers. They must have taken the things to use   I don't believe they would a took em from me & then throw away. I did not see them use anything there except some rice I had cooked when they came, & that they ate.

11 I made no complaint when they took the property but when they took my money I complained to an officer who had Mr Anderson & Rowe, & [Leuck?] & Mr Billy King prisoners. I told him some of the soldiers had taken my money   I told them I had $65.00 in old bank bills, this officer spoke to another & sent him to go & follow the soldiers & see if they could get the money but I never get the money. The day after they took my property I went down to Mr Delegals & on my return some soldiers asked me if I could change some money for them   I told them Yes & took out my pocket-book & they grabbed it out of my hand in the road.

12 I did not ask for any voucher or receipt for the property.

13 They took the property in the day time   they never come about in the night. I would not have felt so bad if they had not took my money but that was the last thing I had in the world. they took my pants & coat & all   they did not leave me a thing.

14 They were encamped at Medway Church when they took my property & at Sunbury. Midway was 8 or 9 miles from my house & Sunbury 2 or 3 miles. The whole Army was called Sherman's army & Kilpatricks company, & they said it was Col Baldwins company too was there. They took the property the 3rd day after they came there into camp. They staid there about 3 weeks as near as I can tell. They had a little skirmish between Dorchester & Sunbury, they fired & scattered in the woods that was all. I did not know the quartermasters nor any of the other officers.

15 This property was all in good order when taken.

16 *Item No 1.* I had 7 head of cattle. 2 of these were very fine steers & the rest cows except one calf. I am a poor judge of weight I could not say   2 of the steers were 7 years old. I bought one of the steers from Mr John Mallard; a black steer. I don't know how much they would weigh. They made me go along with them to help drive them a mile out to the big road.

Item No 2. One Jersey Wagon   A bran new wagon only built 3 weeks & a new harness. They took one of their own horses & hitched to the wagon & took it off. I saw them use the wagon to haul poultry & rice away in.

Item No 3. I had 15 head of live hogs all sizes. I had 9 good big ones   the 2 in the pen would weigh 200 lbs   they were very fat & large & 2 ft & a half high. The other 6 were small shoats. They shot some of these & the 2 fat ones in the pen they put in my wagon & took off & they put in the other hogs in this wagon & the oxcart, but the oxcart did not belong to me.

Item No 4. I had 4 hogs salted down   I think one of these would weigh very near 300 lbs & the other 3—240 or 250 lbs apiece. I have been used to weighing & selling hogs all the days of my life & am still raising & I own over 200 head of hogs now & a 100 head of sheep.

Item No 5. I had 3 bus & a half of clean rice. I can tell how much it would weigh I am used to measuring it not to weighing it. (A bus of clean rice weighs 64 lbs)

Item No 6. I had 30 head of ducks & some chickens, the chickens I did not put down at all. I had more things than I have stated here   I have only told of those things I saw taken. I had 9 head of cows but I only helped drive away 7. I had 30 head of hogs but only saw 15 of them taken.

17 & 18 passed.

19 They did not pay me a red on this property. This is the first & only account I have ever presented against the Government. I did not see any of this property

wasted. they took it all off carefully & they whooped when they see the meat so I think they were glad to get it. They took all my things out of my house, all my clothing they took too. Two men at Thunderbolt who owned a vessel & went out trapping mink named Stokes & Strickland told me it was only a trap to get me into trouble, putting in my claim. I had property left me by my Father in stock. After he died the property was divided between us, the children & I went right on raising & selling. I had been raising ever since my Father died 31 years ago & I continued raising all the time & up to the time the Army came here & since them.

his

HDSr   Samuel   ✕   Elliot

mark

E S S A Y S

For many analysts the most distinctive defining characteristic of slavery is the fact that slaves were chattel property that could be bought and sold or used to secure a personal debt. As Harvard sociologist Orlando Patterson points out in the first essay, however, this property status was not and is not unique to slaves; at various times in history wives and children have been treated as property, and contemporary professional athletes are still bought and sold against their wills. The distinctive status of slaves must be sought, Patterson argues, in the slavemaster's total power over their fate and in their complete alienation from countervailing sources of power, such as might be found in kin and community. Yet, as Eugene D. Genovese argues, the slaveholder's power also derived from a community, but one riven with competing class interests among whites despite being committed to an ideology that fostered a myth of white racial solidarity. Under certain circumstances slaves could appeal to that larger community for protection; more frequently they had to appeal to their masters for protection from other whites. In either instance social space was opened in an ostensibly closed system that enabled slaves to assert their claims to humanity and even to customary "rights." According to Philip D. Morgan, professor of history at the College of William and Mary, among those customary rights was the right to own property; under the conditions of cultivation in the lowlands of South Carolina, many slaves were able to exercise that right.

The Riddle of Property Rights in Human Beings

ORLANDO PATTERSON

We must now focus all of this discussion on the problem of slavery. The first danger to which our analysis alerts us is the error of all attempts to define slavery in modern legalistic terms. Yet the vast majority of works employ just such an approach. It would be tedious to give a long list of such definitions;[1] we note only a few of the better known. For J. K. Ingram "the essential character of slavery may be regarded as lying in the fact that the master was owner of the person of the slave."[2] H. J. Nieboer, perhaps the most prominent author on the subject, also emphasizes property.[3] Perhaps the most frequently cited definition is that given by the League of Nations committee on slavery: "the status or condition of a person over whom any or all the powers attaching to the right of ownership are exercised."[4] More recently, James L. Watson has deliberately rejected anthropological advances in the definition of the subject by harking back to Nieboer, claiming "that the property aspect of slavery must be accepted as primary—this is what distinguishes slavery from all other forms of dependency and involuntary labour."[5]

My objection to these definitions is not that I do not consider slaves to be property objects. The problem, rather, is that to define slavery *only* as the treatment of human beings as property fails as a definition, since it does not really specify any distinct category of persons. Proprietary claims and powers are made with respect to many persons who are clearly not slaves. Indeed any person, beggar or king, can be the object of a property relation. Slaves are no different in this respect.

If we must use the property concept (an approach I prefer to avoid because of the inevitable confusions), we need to be more specific. We must show not simply that slaves are a category of persons treated as property objects, but as Moses Finley cogently demonstrates, that they are a *subcategory* of human proprietary objects.[6] The fact that we tend not to regard "free" human beings as objects of property— legal things—is merely a social convention. To take the most obvious example, an American husband is part of the property of his wife. We never express it this way, of course, for it sounds quite ghastly. Nevertheless, in actual and sociological terms a wife has all sorts of claims, privileges, and powers in the person, labor power, and earnings of her husband—as every third husband in America has painfully discovered in the divorce courts.[7] We need hardly add that husbands also have proprietary claims and powers in their wives, powers that they all too frequently exercise with naked violence.

These examples also reveal the speciousness of the ownership concept in definitions of slavery. It is often contended that a person does not own his or her spouse, whereas a master does own his slave. This distinction, however, is an exercise in semantics. If we do not accept the Roman and civil law conception of absolute ownership, then ownership, stripped of its social and emotional rhetoric, is simply another name for property; it can only mean claims and powers vis-à-vis other persons with respect to a given thing, person, or action. This is what a master possesses with respect to his slave; it is also exactly what a person possesses with respect to his or her spouse, child, employee, or land. The fact that a man does not say he "owns" his wife, or that she is part of his property, is purely conventional, as it is conventional for a master to say that he "owns" his slave, or that the slave is part of his property. To be sure, this convention is subjectively meaningful though objectively spurious. But the subjective meaning of the convention is an aspect of the slave's lack of honor. It is *impolite* to say of one's spouse or one's debtor that they are part of one's property. With slaves politeness is unnecessary.

Another fallacy that we can quickly dispose of is the common definition of a slave as someone without a legal personality. "The conventional legal explanation of personality," writes G. B. J. Hughes, "is that a person in law is an entity which may be the bearer of rights and duties."[8] Even if we rephrase the words "rights" and "duties" in realist terms—the *stricto sensu*, for example, of the technical terminology of Hohfeld—we find that the idea of the slave as someone without a legal personality has no basis in legal practice. It is a fiction found only in western societies, and even there it has been taken seriously more by legal philosophers than by practicing lawyers. As a legal fact, there has never existed a slaveholding society, ancient or modern, that did not recognize the slave as a person in law. All we need to do to demonstrate this is to examine the legal response in slaveholding societies to the delicts of slaves: in all cases the slave is held legally and morally responsible.

Many modern students of slavery, in failing to see that the definition of the slave as a person without a legal personality is a fiction, have found irresistible a popular form of argument that amounts to a red herring. The argument has a standard formula. The scholar, usually not very well informed about comparative legal practice, declares as a legal fact that the slave is defined and treated by the slaveholding class as a person without legal or moral personality. He then digs into his data and comes up with "proof" that the slave is indeed treated as a person in law—for is he not punished for his crimes? and are there not laws restricting the powers of the master? Thus there is, we are told, a fundamental problem posed by slavery, the so-called conflict between the treatment of the slave as a thing and as a human being. The formula ends with some ringing piece of liberal rhetoric to the effect that human dignity is irrepressible: "You may define a person as a thing," goes the flourish, "but you cannot treat him as one" (or some such pious statement). The whole formula is, of course, a piece of irrelevance. No legal code I know has ever attempted to treat slaves as anything other than persons in law. The irrelevance, I might add, springs from the confusion of jurisprudence with law. It is unfortunate that most students of slavery tend to be as knowledgeable about jurisprudence as they are ignorant of law.

Closely related to the definition of slavery as property rights in man is the view, held by some Marxists, that slavery is distinctive in that slaves are the only group of persons who constitute disposable capital—the only group of persons in whom capital is invested and who can be bought and sold on the market.[9] The first part of this claim can be quickly discarded. One need only cite that whole branch of modern economics known as the study of human capital to indicate its speciousness. When any firm, ancient or modern, invests funds in the training of persons whose skilled labor it later hopes to exploit for profit, it is doing nothing other than investing capital in persons.

More deserving of attention is the claim that only slaves are capable of being bought and sold. This claim, however, is also incorrect on purely empirical grounds. On the one hand, in the vast majority of premodern slaveholding societies there was usually a prohibition on the sale of all slaves beyond the second generation. The houseborn slave was considered so intimate and close a member of the household, or when not in the household so special a dependent, that masters would rather go into debt or pawn one of their free dependents than sell that slave. Indeed, such an act was usually considered so dishonorable that it resulted in a severe loss of face and prestige by the master. Nor was this always left to the sanction of public opinion. In many highly developed slave systems it was forbidden by law to sell a slave of the third or later generation.

On the other hand—and perhaps more tellingly—there were many societies in which "free" (or at any rate definitely nonslave) persons were capable of being sold. In imperial and modern China up to the early part of the present century, for example, it was common practice to sell certain categories of nonslave persons such as concubines and children—especially girls. In imperial China a distinction was always drawn between the continued "honorable" status of these individuals and the dishonored slaves, and it was a serious offense to sell such a person without making her status known to the purchaser.[10] The sale of concubines, and even daughters, continued into the 1940s.[11] (It is probable too that in early Rome children were sold into nonslave statuses.[12])

More important is the practice of bride sale all over traditional Africa and other parts of the world, where bride-price is an essential part of all marital transactions. Western anthropologists, compensating for earlier racist interpretations, have bent so far backward in denying the commercial aspect of these transactions that they have positively distorted the truth. But as anthropologist Robert F. Gray has demonstrated,[13] this overcompensation by liberal anthropologists, however laudable, completely misses the point. Both African men and women regard the exchange of brides as a sale—in addition, of course, to recognizing its other, equally important social and emotional functions. The women, in particular, make it clear that they take pride in the amount of goods or money paid for them and in no way feel that they have been demeaned by the fact that they were sold. The only source of humiliation would be the eventuality that a very low bride-price had been paid for them. These women would be universally horrified to learn that their sale in any way implied that they were slaves.

It is tempting to interpret the strong distaste for the sale of free persons as a peculiarly Western concern, but even this would be wrong. For it is a fact that in what is reputedly one of the world's most advanced societies—the contemporary United States—certain categories of persons annually are put up for auction and sold to the highest bidder. I refer to professional athletes, especially football stars. While the terms of the transaction differ, there is no substantive difference in the sale of a football idol such as Joe Namath by his proprietors, the New York Jets, to the Los Angeles Rams, and the sale of a slave by one proprietor to another. Namath would no doubt be as amazed and distressed as the betrothed bride of Africa to learn that his sale implied anything slavelike about him. (So, no doubt, would be the millions of Americans who count themselves among his fans.)

What do professional American athletes and the brides of tribal Africa have in common that makes it absurd for us to call them slaves in spite of the fact that they are bought and sold? Before answering this question, let me dispose of two popular though erroneous explanations. It is commonly thought that what is purchased in the case of a slave transaction is the "raw body" of the slave, whereas in the case of athletes, employees, and tribal wives not their bodies but their services are purchased or hired. This distinction has subjective meaning, but it makes no sense in physical or economic terms. When one buys or hires a person's labor, by implication one purchases the person's body for the negotiated period. There is no such thing as a disembodied service, only the discreet willingness to suspend all disbelief in such disembodiment. Present-day employers, it is true, do not demand of potential employees that they stand naked on an auction block being prodded and inspected by the employers and their physicians. But when an employer requires a medical certificate from a worker or professional athlete before hiring him, he is not only soliciting the same kind of information as a slavemaster inspecting his

latest cargo of bodies, he is betraying the inherent absurdity of the distinction between "raw bodies" and the services produced by such bodies. There is certainly an
important difference in the way the information is gathered, but the difference has
to do with respect for the employee, recognition of his dignity and honor; it is in no
way a confirmation of the fiction that there is a real difference between hiring a
person's body and hiring his services. . . .

A second common error is the assumption that all nonslave persons have a
choice in the sale and withdrawal of their services, whereas slaves do not. This might
usefully distinguish slaves from most wage earners, but not from other forms of
bonded laborers. Serfs, indentured servants, peons, and debt-bondsmen had no say in
the purchase and sale of their labor. Nor for that matter did contracted professional
athletes in the United States up until 1975 (not if they wanted to remain professional athletes). As late as 1970 the Supreme Court of the United States upheld, in
the Curt Flood case, the notorious reserve clause that enabled proprietors to sell and
buy athletes against their will. In addition to his antitrust claim, Flood made three
other arguments in support of his case, one of them being that "the reserve system is
a form of peonage and involuntary servitude in violation of the antipeonage statutes
and the Thirteenth Amendment."[14] Many sportswriters directly compare the reserve
clause to slavery, Alex Ben Block's comment on the issue being typical: "After the
Civil War settled the slavery issues, owning a ball club was the closest one could
come to owning a plantation."[15] The reserve clause has been defined as "a rule (or
agreement between all clubs) that the baseball services of each player are in effect
the permanent property, unless assigned, of the team holding the player's contract."[16]

Although the sale of a player is often euphemistically referred to as the sale of
his "contract," the expressed views of players, proprietors, and sportswriters alike
leave us in no doubt that it is the player's body and services that are sold. Typical of
the proprietors' attitude is that of Philip K. Wrigley, chewing gum magnate and
owner of the Chicago Cubs. In 1938 Wrigley hired a researcher to investigate the
reflexes of his players, and he later commented on the experiment as follows: "We
figured if we could measure the physical characteristics and reflexes of an established player, we could test prospects and know what to look for. If you want
to make the best knives in the world you buy the finest steel. You can go out and
spend $250,000 for a ballplayer and he may not be able to cut butter."[17] Just as
significant is the fact that the Internal Revenue Service accepts as legitimate
accounting practice the depreciation of players "over their estimated useful life in
computing taxable income."[18]

American professional athletes, then, are depreciating proprietary assets in
whom capital is heavily invested, who may be bought and sold like any other object
of property. They now have a say in their sale and purchase, but until December
1975 their bodies when used to secure a livelihood in their chosen occupation (for
many, the only occupation they knew) were part of the permanent assets of their
proprietors. As professional athletes they had no voice whatever in their sale and
purchase, nor in the price paid for them.

And yet these professional athletes are not slaves, and were not even during the
era of the reserve clause. Why is this? What, in other words, are the real differences
between slaves and nonslaves who are nonetheless salable even against their will?
The first difference is the relative power of the parties concerned and the origins of

their relationship. The proprietor's power is limited by the fact that nonslaves always possess some claims and powers themselves vis-à-vis their proprietor. This power has its source not only in central authorities (where they exist) but in a person's claims on other individuals. Even in early Rome where the pater familias had enormous power over his wife and children, the father could not kill the children without justification and "a wife in manu remained very much under the jurisdiction of her blood-relatives."[19] The slavemaster's power over his slave was total. Furthermore with nonslaves the proprietor's powers, however great, were usually confined to a specific range of activities; with slaves, the master had power over all aspects of his slave's life.

The power relationship also differs in its origins. The crucial difference here, however, lies not in the fact that nonslaves always had some choice in initiating the relationship but in the fact that only slaves entered the relationship as a substitute for death. Serfs and peons, for example, were obliged to enter and remain in the relationship with their lords as a result of the latter's monopoly of the means of production.

Slaves also differ from contracted athletes and bond servants in their alienation from all ties of natality and in their lack of honor and publicly recognized repute. As indicated earlier, it is the latter that partially dictates the necessity for the fiction of disembodied labor.

While the constituent elements of slavery are the same for all kinds of social orders, the fact remains that this specific configuration of elements will be understood differently in different socioeconomic systems. Any attempt to understand comparatively the nature of slavery, or any other social process, if it fails to take account of such contextual variations, must remain of limited value.

1. For a review of ancient and modern definitions up to the 1930s see G. Landtman, *The Origin of the Inequality of the Social Classes* (London: Routledge & Kegan Paul, 1938), pp. 228–229.
2. *History of Slavery and Serfdom* (London: Black, 1895), p. 265
3. *Slavery as an Industrial System* (The Hague: Martinus Nijhoff, 1910), p. 6 and chap. 1, passim.
4. *Report to the League of Nations Advisory Committee of Experts on Slavery,* Geneva, April 5, 1938, vol. 6, p. 16.
5. "Slavery as an Institution, Open and Closed Systems," in James L. Watson, ed., *Asian and African Systems of Slavery* (Oxford: Basil Blackwell, 1980), p. 809.
6. M. I. Finley, *Ancient Slavery and Modern Ideology* (New York: Viking Press, 1980), pp. 73–75.
7. In *Life and Labor in the Old South* (Boston: Little, Brown, 1963), p. 160.
8. *Jurisprudence,* p. 442.
9. See, for example, Barry Hindess and Paul Q. Hirst, *Pre-Capitalist Modes of Production* (London: Routledge & Kegan Paul, 1975), pp. 109–177. For a critique of these authors' theoretical views on slavery, see Orlando Patterson, "Slavery and Slave Formations," *New Left Review* 117 (1979): 49–52.
10. Wang Yi-T'ung, "Slaves and Other Comparable Social Groups during the Northern Dynasties (386–618)," *Harvard Journal of Asiatic Studies* 16 (1953): 313–314.
11. Olga Lang, *Chinese Family and Society* (New Haven: Yale University Press, 1946), pp. 259–260. For a more recent discussion see James L. Watson, "Transactions in People: The Chinese Market in Slaves, Servants, and Heirs," in Watson, *Asian and African Systems of Slavery,* pp. 223–250.

12. On the sale of children into slavery see Alan Watson, *Rome of the XII Tables* (Princeton, N.J.: Princeton University Press, 1975), p. 44; on the "strange provision" see p. 45.
13. "Sonjo Bride-Price and the Question of African 'Wife Purchase,'" in E. E. Le Clair, Jr., and H. K. Schneider, eds., *Economic Anthropology* (New York: Holt, Rinehart and Winston, 1968), pp. 259–282.
14. Michael S. Jacobs and Ralph K. Winter, Jr., "Antitrust Principles and Collective Bargaining by Athletes: Of Superstars in Peonage," *Yale Law Journal* 81 (1971): 3.
15. "So You Want to Own a Ball Club," *Forbes,* April 1, 1977, p. 37. Cited in D. Stanley Eitzen and George H. Sage, *The Sociology of American Sports* (Dubuque, Iowa: Wm. C. Brown Co., 1978), p. 188.
16. Jacobs and Winter, "Antitrust Principles," p. 2.
17. Dan Kowel, *The Rich Who Own Sport* (New York: Random House, 1977), pp. 19–20. See also the reference to Vida Blue as "The property of Oakland through 1978," p. 134.
18. See Roger Noll, ed., *Government and the Sports Business* (Washington, D.C.: Brookings Institution, 1974), pp. 3–4 and p. 217.
19. Watson, *Rome of the XII Tables,* p. 38.

The Legal Basis for Mastery

EUGENE D. GENOVESE

When Mao Tse-tung told his revolutionary army, "Political power grows out of the barrel of a gun," he stated the obvious, for as Max Weber long before had observed as a matter of scientific detachment, "The decisive means for politics is violence." This viewpoint does not deny an ethical dimension to state power; it asserts that state power, the conquest of which constitutes the object of all serious political struggle, represents an attempt to monopolize and therefore both discipline and legitimize the weapons of violence.

One of the primary functions of the law concerns the means by which command of the gun becomes ethically sanctioned. But if we left it at that, we could never account for the dignity and élan of a legal profession in, say, England, that has itself become a social force; much less could we account for the undeniable influence of the law in shaping the class relations of which it is an instrument of domination. Thus, the fashionable relegation of law to the rank of a superstructural and derivative phenomenon obscures the degree of autonomy it creates for itself. In modern societies, at least, the theoretical and moral foundations of the legal order and the actual, specific history of its ideas and institutions influence, step by step, the wider social order and system of class rule, for no class in the modern Western world could rule for long without some ability to present itself as the guardian of the interests and sentiments of those being ruled.

The idea of "hegemony," which since Gramsci has become central to Western Marxism, implies class antagonisms; but it also implies, for a given historical epoch, the ability of a particular class to contain those antagonisms on a terrain in which its legitimacy is not dangerously questioned. . . . Ruling classes differ, and each must rule differently. But all modern ruling classes have much in common in their attitude toward the law, for each must confront the problem of coercion in such a way as to minimize the necessity for its use, and each must disguise the extent to which state power does not so much rest on force as represent its actuality. . . .

In southern slave society, as in other societies, the law, even narrowly defined as a system of institutionalized jurisprudence, constituted a principal vehicle for the hegemony of the ruling class. Since the slaveholders, like other ruling classes, arose and grew in dialectical response to the other classes of society—since they were molded by white yeomen and black slaves as much as they molded them— the law cannot be viewed as something passive and reflective, but must be viewed as an active, partially autonomous force, which mediated among the several classes and compelled the rulers to bend to the demands of the ruled. The slave- holders faced an unusually complex problem since their regional power was em- bedded in a national system in which they had to share power with an antagonistic northern bourgeoisie. . . .

The slaveholders as a socio-economic class shaped the legal system to their interests. But within that socio-economic class—the class as a whole—there were elements competing for power. Within it, a political center arose, consolidated itself, and assumed a commanding position during the 1850s. The most advanced fraction of the slaveholders—those who most clearly perceived the interests and needs of the class as a whole—steadily worked to make their class more conscious of its nature, spirit, and destiny. In the process it created a world-view appropriate to a slaveholders' regime.

For any such political center, the class as a whole must be brought to a higher understanding of itself—transformed from a class-in-itself, reacting to pressures on its objective position, into a class-for-itself, consciously striving to shape the world in its own image. Only possession of public power can discipline a class as a whole, and through it, the other classes of society. The juridical system may become, then, not merely an expression of class interest, nor even merely an expression of the willingness of the rulers to mediate with the ruled; it may become an instrument by which the advanced section of the ruling class imposes its viewpoint upon the class as a whole and the wider society. The law must discipline the ruling class and guide and educate the masses. To accomplish these tasks it must manifest a degree of evenhandedness sufficient to compel social conformity; it must, that is, validate itself ethically in the eyes of the several classes, not just the ruling class. Both crim- inal and civil law set standards of behavior and sanction norms that extend well beyond strictly legal matters. The death penalty for murder, for example, need not arise from a pragmatic concern with deterrence, and its defenders could justifiably resist psychological arguments. It may arise from the demand for implementation of a certain idea of justice and from the educational requirement to set a firm standard of right and wrong. "The Law," as Gramsci says, "is the repressive and negative aspect of the entire positive civilising activity undertaken by the State."

The law acts hegemonically to assure people that their particular consciences can be subordinated—indeed, morally must be subordinated—to the collective judgment of society. It may compel conformity by granting each individual his right of private judgment, but it must deny him the right to take action based on that judgment when in conflict with the general will. Those who would act on their own judgment as against the collective judgment embodied in the law find them- selves pressed from the moral question implicit in any particular law to the moral question of obedience to constituted authority. It appears mere egotism and anti-social behavior to attempt to go outside the law unless one is prepared to attack the entire legal system and therefore the consensual framework of the body politic.

The white South shaped its attitude toward its slaves in this context. With high, malicious humor, William Styron has his fictional T. R. Gray explain to Nat Turner how he, a mere chattel, can be tried for the very human acts of murder and insurrection:

> "... The point is that *you* are *animate* chattel and animate chattel is capable of craft and connivery and wily stealth. You ain't a wagon, Reverend, but chattel that possesses moral choice and spiritual volition. Remember that well. Because that's how come the law provides that animate chattel like you can be tried for a felony, and that's how come you're goin' to be tried next Sattidy."
>
> He paused, then said softly without emotion: "And hung by the neck until dead."

Styron may well have meant to satirize Judge Green of the Tennessee Supreme Court, who declared in 1846, "A slave is not in the condition of a horse." The slave, Judge Green continued, is made in the image of the Creator: "He has mental capacities, and an immortal principle in his nature that constitute him equal to his owner, but for the accidental position in which fortune has placed him. . . . The laws . . . cannot extinguish his high born nature, nor deprive him of many rights which are inherent in man." The idea that chattels, as the states usually defined slaves, could have a highborn nature, complete with rights inherent in man, went down hard with those who thought that even the law should obey the rules of logic.

Four years before Judge Green's humane observations, Judge Turley of the same court unwittingly presented the dilemma. "The right to obedience . . ." he declared in *Jacob (a Slave) v. State,* "in all lawful things . . . is perfect in the master; and the power to inflict any punishment, not affecting life or limb . . . is secured to him by law." The slave, being neither a wagon nor a horse, had to be dealt with as a man, but the law dared not address itself direct to the point. Had the law declared the slave a person in a specific class relationship to another person, two unpleasant consequences would have followed. First, the demand that such elementary rights as those of the family be respected would have become irresistible in a commercialized society that required the opposite in order to guarantee an adequate mobility of capital and labor. Second, the slaveholders would have had to surrender in principle, much as they often had to do in practice, their insistence that a slave was morally obligated to function as an extension of his master's will. However much the law generally seeks to adjust conflicting principles in society, in this case it risked undermining the one principle the slaveholders viewed as a *sine qua non.*

Yet, as Styron correctly emphasizes in the words he gives to T. R. Gray, the courts had to recognize the humanity—and therefore the free will—of the slave or be unable to hold him accountable for antisocial acts. Judge Bunning of Georgia plainly said, "It is not true that slaves are only chattels . . . and therefore, it is not true that it is not possible for them to be prisoners. . . ." He did not tell us how a chattel (a thing) could also be nonchattel in any sense other than an agreed-upon fiction, nor did he wish to explore the question why a fiction should have become necessary. Since much of the law concerns agreed-upon fictions, the judges, as judges, did not have to become nervous about their diverse legal opinions, but as slaveholders, they could not avoid the prospect of disarray being introduced into their social philosophy. Repeatedly, the courts struggled with and tripped over the slave's humanity. Judge Hall of North Carolina, contrary to reason, nature, and the opinion of his fellow judges, could blurt out, *en passant,* "Being slaves, they had no will of their own. . . ." If so, then what of the opinion expressed by the State Supreme Court of Missouri: "The power of the master being limited, his responsibility is proportioned accordingly"?

The high court of South Carolina wrestled with the conflicting principles of slave society and came up with an assortment of mutually exclusive answers. Judge Waites, in *State v. Cynthia Simmons and Lawrence Kitchen* (1794): "Negroes are under the protection of the laws, and have personal rights, and cannot be considered on a footing only with domestic animals. They have wills of their own—capacities to commit crimes; and are responsible for offences against society." The court in *Fairchild v. Bell* (1807): "The slave lives for his master's service. His time, his labor, his comforts, are all at the master's disposal." Judge John Belton O'Neall in *Tennent v. Dendy* (1837): "Slaves are our most valuable property. . . . Too many guards cannot be interposed between it and violent unprincipled men. . . . The slave ought to be fully aware that his master is to him . . . a perfect security from injury. When this is the case, the relation of master and servant becomes little short of that of parent and child." But in Kentucky, the high court had pronounced in 1828: "However deeply it may be regretted, and whether it be politic or impolitic, a slave by our code is not treated as a person, but *(negotium)* a thing, as he stood in the civil code of the Roman Empire." But one year later we hear: "A slave has volition, and has feelings which cannot be entirely disregarded." And again in 1836: "But, although the law of this state considers slaves as property, yet it recognizes their personal existence, and, to a qualified extent, their natural rights."

The South had discovered, as had every previous slave society, that it could not deny the slave's humanity, however many preposterous legal fictions it invented. That discovery ought to have told the slaveholders much more. Had they reflected on the implications of a wagon's inability to raise an insurrection, they might have understood that the slaves as well as the masters were creating the law. The slaves' action proceeded within narrow limits, but it realized one vital objective: it exposed the deception on which the slave society rested—the notion that in fact, not merely in one's fantasy life, some human beings could become mere extensions of the will of another. The slaves grasped the significance of their victory with deeper insight than they have usually been given credit for. They saw that they had few rights at law and that those could easily be violated by the whites. But even one right, imperfectly defended, was enough to tell them that the pretensions of the master class could be resisted. Before long, law or no law, they were adding a great many "customary rights" of their own and learning how to get them respected.

The slaves understood that the law offered them little or no protection, and in self-defense they turned to two alternatives: to their master, if he was decent, or his neighbors, if he was not; and to their own resources. Their commitment to a paternalistic system deepened accordingly, but in such a way as to allow them to define rights for themselves. For reasons of their own the slaveholders relied heavily on local custom and tradition; so did the slaves, who turned this reliance into a weapon. If the law said they had no right to property, for example, but local custom accorded them private garden plots, then woe to the master or overseer who summarily withdrew the "privilege." To those slaves the privilege had become a right, and the withdrawal an act of aggression not to be borne. The slaveholders, understanding this attitude, rationalized their willingness to compromise. The slaves forced themselves upon the law, for the courts repeatedly sustained such ostensibly extralegal arrangements as having the force of law because sanctioned by time-honored practice. It was a small victory so far as everyday protection was concerned, but not so small psychologically; it gave the slaves some sense of having rights of their own and also made them more aware of those rights withheld. W. W. Hazard of Georgia ran the risk of telling his slaves about their legal rights and of stressing the legal limits of his own power over them. He made it clear that he had an obligation to take care of them in their old age, whereas free white workers had no such protection, and argued deftly that their being whipped for insubordination represented a humane alternative to the practice of shooting soldiers and sailors for insubordination. His was an unusual act, but perhaps not so risky after all. He may have scored a few points while not revealing much they did not already know. . . .

"It is remarkable at first view," wrote George Fitzhugh, the proslavery ideologue of Virginia, "that in Cuba, where the law attempts to secure mild treatment to the slave, he is inhumanely treated; and in Virginia, where there is scarce any law to protect him, he is very humanely governed and provided for." This self-serving sermon, with its exaggeration and its kernel of truth, became standard fare for the apologists for slavery and has won some support from subsequent historians. The slaveholders did not intend to enforce their severe legislation strictly and considered it a device to be reserved for periods of disquiet and especially for periods of rumored insurrectionary plots. In practice this easy attitude confirmed the direct power of the master. For example, although state or local laws might forbid large meetings of slaves from several plantations, the planters normally permitted religious services or balls and barbecues unless they had some reason to fear trouble. The local authorities, generally subservient to the planters, usually looked the other way. Thus in Ascension Parish, Louisiana, the local ordinance declared: "Every person is prohibited from permitting in his negro quarters any other assemblies but those of his slaves and from allowing his slaves to dance during the night." Enforcement of such an edict would have required that masters constantly punish their slaves, who were not to be denied, and thereby ruin the morale of their labor force. Planters who agreed to such an edict had either let themselves be swept away by some momentary passion or intended it for emergency enforcement. The laws of most states also forbade teaching slaves to read and write. Most slaveholders obeyed these laws because they thought them wise, not because they expected punishment of violators. In many of the great planter families various individuals, especially the white children, taught slaves to read. Some slaveholders violated the laws against giving slaves guns to hunt with, although they no doubt screened the beneficiaries with care. The law existed as a resource to provide means for meeting any emergency and to curb permissive masters. But the heart of the slave law lay with the master's prerogatives and depended upon his discretion. In this sense alone did practice generally veer from statute.

A slaveholding community did not intervene against a brutal master because of moral outrage alone; it intervened to protect its interests. Or rather, its strong sense of interest informed its moral sensibilities. "Harmony among neighbors is very important in the successful management of slaves," wrote a planter in an article directed to his own class. A good manager among bad ones, he explained, faces a hopeless task, for the slaves easily perceive differences and become dissatisfied. It does no good, wrote another, to enforce discipline on your plantation if the next planter does not. These arguments cut in both directions. They called for strict discipline from those who tended to be lax and for restraint from those who tended to be harsh.

What the law could not accomplish, public opinion might. A brutal overseer threatened by arrest could be made to understand that, however his trial might turn out, the community would welcome his departure. J. H. Bills reported from one of his plantations in Mississippi: "A jury of inquest was held yesterday over the body of a negro fellow, the property of the John Fowler estate, whose verdict was, I understand, that he came to his death by a blow given him on the head by Mahlon Hix a few days before. Hix left the country this morning."

A more difficult question concerned atrocities by respected masters. When in Richmond, Virginia, Fredrika Bremer heard some slaveholders talking about a rich neighbor who treated his slaves savagely. They condemned him, but had nevertheless accepted an invitation to his party. When questioned, they explained that they did not wish to offend his wife and daughters. Miss Bremer thought that his money and power had played a part in their decision. She noted a five-year sentence handed down on a master for barbarously killing a favorite house slave. When the entire community expressed outrage at the crime and approved the prison term, she concluded that that was about what it took to provoke a meaningful reaction.

Ex-slaves from various parts of the South recalled community interventions and moral pressure on cruel masters. Hagar Lewis of Texas said that her master filed charges against some neighbors for underfeeding and excessive whipping. A. M. Moore, an educated preacher from Harrison County, Texas, added, "I've known courts in this county to fine slaveowners for not feeding and clothing their slaves right." George Teamoh of Virginia recalled that his mistress gave runaways from cruelty refuge on her place. Lou Smith of South Carolina recalled a slave's slipping off to tell white neighbors that his master had savagely whipped a slave and left him bleeding. The neighbors forced the master to have the slave attended by a doctor. And others testified that brutal masters had constant trouble from irate fellow slaveholders, none of whom, however, seemed willing to take direct action unless something atrocious had occurred.

Cruel and negligent masters did not often face trial. Some did, primarily because of the efforts of other slaveholders. A slaveholder in certain states could be convicted on circumstancial evidence alone, if the decision in *State of Louisiana v. Morris* (1849) may be taken as a guide. Even then, no conviction was likely without an aroused public opinion. These convictions, inadequate as they were, reminded the community of what was expected of individual behavior.

Fortunately for the slaves, in many communities one or two souls among the slaveholders ran the risks of personal retaliation to keep an eye on everyone else's plantations. Captain J. G. Richardson of New Iberia, Louisiana, made no few enemies by compelling prosecution of delinquent fellow slaveholders, and others like him cropped up here and there. The private papers of the slaveholders, as well as their public efforts, suggest that they could become enraged at local sadists and would take action in the extreme cases.

Moral suasion and active intervention had limits. Much cruelty occurred because average masters lost their tempers—something any other master had to excuse unless he saw himself as a saint who could never be riled—and little could be done about someone who stopped short of atrocities as defined by other slave-holders and who did not much care about his neighbors' criticism. Yet moral pressure, if it could not prevent savages from acting savagely, did set a standard of behavior to which men who cared about their reputations tried to adhere.

Although we do not have a thorough study of the place of the slave law in the southern legal system and of the relationship of the southern legal system as a whole to that of the United States and Western Europe, tentative appraisals must be risked if much sense is to be made out of the broader aspects of the master-slave relationship. Two questions in particular present themselves: the general character of the southern legal system; and the relationship between the legal status of the slave and his position in what appears to many to have been extralegal practice.

The two questions merge. The dichotomy, made current by Ulrich Bonnell Phillips, of a decisive distinction between law and practice or custom, requires critical examination. W. E. B. Du Bois's comment on the proslavery apologetics to which such a distinction has sometimes been applied says enough on the level on which he chose to leave the matter:

> It may be said with truth that the law was often harsher than the practice. Nevertheless, these laws and decisions represent the legally permissible possibilities, and the only curb upon the power of the master was his sense of humanity and decency, on the one hand, and the conserving of his investment on the other. Of the humanity of large numbers of Southern masters there can be no doubt.

The frontier quality of much of the Old South inhibited the growth of strong law-enforcement agencies, but this quality itself cannot be separated from the geographic advance of slave society. The plantation system produced an extensive pattern of settlement, relative to that of the Northwest, and resulted in the establishment of a multitude of separate centers of power in the plantations themselves. At the same time, the nonplantation areas found themselves developing as enclaves more or less detached from the mainstream of southern society. Thus, whereas the frontier steadily passed in the free states and even the formative stages of civilization rested on a certain civic consciousness, it not only passed less rapidly in the slave states but actually entrenched itself within the civilization being built. This process imparted a higher degree of apparent lawlessness—of the extralegal settlement of personal disputes—to southern life. Its spirit might be illustrated by the advice given to Andrew Jackson by his mother: "Never tell a lie, nor take what is not your own, nor sue anybody for slander or assault and battery. *Always settle them cases yourself!*"

This "violent tenor of life," to use an expression Johan Huizinga applied to late medieval Europe, provided one side of the story; the intrinsic difficulty of developing a modern legal system in a slave society provided another. Southerners considered themselves law-abiding and considered northerners lawless. After all, southerners did not assert higher-law doctrines and broad interpretations of the Constitution. Rather, as Charles S. Sydnor has argued, they understood the law in a much different way and professed to see no contradiction between their code of honor, with its appeal to extralegal personal force, and a respect for the law itself. Notwithstanding some hypocrisy, their view represented a clumsy but authentic adjustment to the necessity for a dualistic, even self-contradictory, concept of law prefigured in the rise of a rational system of law in European civilization.

At first glance, the legal history of Western Europe represents an anomaly. The law arose in early modern times on rational rather than traditional, patrimonial, or charismatic foundations, however many elements of these remained. As such, it assumed an equality of persons before the law that could only have arisen from the social relationships introduced by the expansion of capitalism and the spread of bourgeois, marketplace values, although to a considerable extent it derived from Roman tradition. Max Weber's distinction between "capitalism in general" and "modern capitalism," however suggestive, cannot resolve the apparent contradiction.

As Weber clearly understood, the ruling class of Roman society, and therefore the society itself, rested on slave-labor foundations. We do not have to follow Rostovtzeff, Salvioli, and others in projecting an ancient capitalism or a cycle of capitalisms in order to establish a firm link between ancient and modern civilization in Western Europe, as manifested in the continuity of legal tradition. Slavery as a mode of production creates a market for labor, much as capitalism creates a market for labor-power. Both encourage commercial development, which is by no means to be equated with capitalist development (understood as a system of social relations within which labor-power has become a commodity). Ancient slave society could not, however, remove the limits to commercial expansion—could not raise the marketplace to the center of the society as well as the economy—for its very capitalization of labor established the firmest of those limits. The modern bourgeoisie, on the other hand, arose and throve on its ability to transform labor-power into a commodity and thereby revolutionize every feature of thought and feeling in accordance with the fundamental change in social relations. It thereby created the appearance of human equality, for the laborer faced the capitalist in a relation of seller and buyer of labor-power—an ostensibly disembodied commodity. The relationship of each to the other took on the fetishistic aspect of a relationship of both to a commodity—a thing—and cloaked the reality of the domination of one man by another. Although ancient slavery did not create a market for labor-power, it did, by creating a market for human beings and their economic products, induce a high level of commercialization that, together with the successful consolidation of a centralized state, combined to bequeath a system of law upon which modern bourgeois society could build. The rise of capitalism out of a seigneurial society in the West owed much to cultural roots that that particular kind of seigneurialism had in a long slaveholding past.

The slave South inherited English common law as well as elements and influences from continental Roman and Germanic communal and feudal law. But by the time the slave regime underwent consolidation, the legal system of the Western world had succumbed to a bourgeois idea of private property. The southern slaveholders had been nurtured on that idea but also had to draw upon earlier traditions in order to justify their assimilation of human beings to property. In so doing, they contradicted, however discreetly, that idea of property which had provided the foundation for their class claims.

The slaveholders could not simply tack the idea of property in man onto their inherited ideas of property in general, for those inherited ideas, as manifested in the bourgeois transformation of Roman law and common law, rested precisely upon a doctrine of marketplace equality within which—however various the actual practice for a protracted period of time—slavery contradicted first principles. The southern legal system increasingly came to accept an implicit duality: a recognition of the rights of the state over individuals, slave or free, and a recognition of the rights of the slaveholders over their slaves. Since the slaveholders' property in man had to be respected, the state's rights over the slaveholders as well as the slaves had to be circumscribed. At first glance, this arrangement appears simple enough: considered abstractly, a system in which the state, representing above all the collective will of the slaveholding class, could lay down rules for the individual slaveholders, who would, however, have full power over their chattels. But the slaves, simply by asserting their humanity, quickly demolished this nice arrangement. The moral, not to mention political, needs of the ruling class as a whole required that it interpose itself, by the instrument of state power, between individual masters and their slaves. It is less important that it did so within narrow bounds than that it did so at all. The resultant ambiguity, however functional in quiet times, ill prepared the South to meet the test of modern war.

Even in peacetime the slaveholders had to pay dearly for their compromises. Among other things, as Charles S. Sydnor saw and as Robert Fogel and Stanley Engerman have reflected on further, the reintroduction of precapitalist elements into the legal system weakened the economic organization and business capacity of the planters. These questions await a full exploration at other hands.

The immediate concern is with the effect of the imposed duality created by the reintroduction as well as the continuation of precapitalist ideas of power and property into an inherited system of bourgeois-shaped rational jurisprudence. This momentous reintroduction was effected with some ease because the idea of the state's having a monopoly of the legal means of coercion by violence had had only a brief history—roughly, from the conquest of state power by the bourgeoisies of England and Holland during the seventeenth century and of France at the end of the eighteenth. Nor had traditional ideas simply disappeared. Not only from the Left, but more powerfully from the Right, they continued to do battle within even the most advanced capitalist countries.

The slaveholders fell back on a kind of dual power: that which they collectively exercised as a class, even against their own individual impulses, through their effective control of state power; and that which they reserved to themselves as individuals who commanded other human beings in bondage. In general, this duality appears in all systems of class rule, for the collective judgment of the ruling class, coherently organized in the common interest, cannot be expected to coincide with the sum total of the individual interests and judgments of its members; first, because the law tends to reflect the will of the most politically coherent and determined fraction, and second, because the sum total of the individual interests and judgments of the members of the ruling class generally, rather than occasionally, pulls against the collective needs of a class that must appeal to other classes for support at critical junctures. But the slaveholders' problem ran much deeper, for the idea of slavery cannot easily be divorced from the idea of total power—of the reduction of one human being to the status of an extension of another's will—which is phenomenologically impossible, and more to the point, as Judge Ruffin had to face, politically impossible as well. Repeatedly, the slaveholders' own legal apparatus had to intervene, not primarily to protect the slaves from their masters, but to mediate certain questions among contending manifestations of human action. In so doing, it discredited the essential philosophical idea on which slavery rested and, simultaneously, bore witness to the slaves' ability to register the claims of their humanity.

Confronted with these painful and contradictory necessities, the slaveholders chose to keep their options open. They erected a legal system the implications of which should have embarrassed them and sometimes did; and then they tried to hold it as a reserve. They repeatedly had to violate their own laws without feeling themselves lawbreakers. The slave laws existed as a moral guide and an instrument for emergency use, although the legal profession and especially the judges struggled to enforce them as a matter of positive law; wherever possible, the authority of the master class, considered as a perfectly proper system of complementary plantation law, remained in effect. But since no reasonable formula could be devised to mediate between counterclaims arising from the two sides of this dual system, much had to be left outside the law altogether. . . .

For the slaves, two major consequences flowed from the ambiguities of the system. First, they constantly had before them evidence of what they could only see as white hypocrisy. An ex-slave commented on the antimiscegenation laws and their fate at the hands of the white man: "He made that law himself and he is the first to violation." No respect for the law could easily rise on such a foundation. Since the slaves knew that the law protected them little and could not readily be enforced even in that little, the second consequence followed. For protection against every possible assault on their being they had to turn to a human protector—in effect, a lord. They had to look to their masters for protection against patrollers, against lynching, against the strict enforcement of the law itself, as well as against hunger and physical deprivation. And they had to look to some other white man to shield them against a harsh or sadistic master. Thus, the implicit hegemonic function of the dual system of law conquered the quarters. But not wholly and not without encouraging a dangerous misunderstanding.

As the masters saw, the working out of the legal system drove the slaves deeper into an acceptance of paternalism. As the masters did not see, it did not drive them into an acceptance of slavery as such. On the contrary, the contradictions in the dual system and in the slave law per se, which had developed in the first place because of the slaves' assertion of their humanity, constantly reminded the slaves of the fundamental injustice to which they were being subjected. Paternalism and slavery merged into a single idea to the masters. But the slaves proved much more astute in separating the two; they acted consciously and unconsciously to transform paternalism into a doctrine of protection of their own rights—a doctrine that represented the negation of the idea of slavery itself.

Slave Property as Property Owners

PHILIP D. MORGAN

Perhaps the most distinctive and central feature of slave life in the low-country region of South Carolina and Georgia was the task system. In Lewis C. Gray's words, "Under the task system the slave was assigned a certain amount of work for the day, and after completing the task he could use his time as he pleased." However, under the gang system, prevalent in most Anglo-American plantation societies, "slaves were worked in groups under the control of a driver or leader. . . . [and] the laborer was compelled to work the entire day. . . ." The significance of this peculiar labor arrangement for those who operated it—particularly the use slaves made of "their time" to produce goods and gain access to property—has never before been systematically explored. This is the aim of the present essay.

The most obvious advantage of the task system to the slaves was the flexibility it permitted them in determining the length of the working day. The nearly universal lament that we hear whenever ex-slaves reminisce is that labor under slavery was "exhausting and unremitting." Working from sunup to sundown "was the pervasive reality." Ex-slaves from the low country recall a different reality. Listen to Richard Cummings, a former field hand: ". . . a good active industrious man would finish his task sometimes at 12, sometimes at 1 and 2 oclock and the rest of the time was his own to use as he pleased." Or to Scipio King, another former field hand: "I could save for myself sometimes a whole day if I could do 2 tasks in a day then I had the next day to myself. Some kind of work I could do 3 tasks in a day." Or to the ex-slave cooper who remembered "hav[ing] from midday till night— sometimes from 3 o'clock and sometimes later" to work on his own behalf. Or, finally, to the former slave driver who recalled seeing men split two hundred rails a day, "and in that way have a day for themselves." But perhaps the most impressive feat of task labor must be reserved for the former field hand who reckoned he could sometimes finish his task by 9 o'clock in the morning if, as he put it, "I began just before day and worked in the marsh and light ground." Exhausting as task labor undoubtedly was, its prime virtue was that it was not unremitting.

Angrier voices occasionally make themselves heard above the swelling choruses of praise. One ex-slave voiced a criticism which, if general, would have undermined the main advantage of the system. Harry Porter, a former field slave, remembered that if the slaves on his plantation "got through early or half an hour before sundown . . . [their master] would give them more next day." During harvest time or other periods of comparable urgency the temptation to increase the work load must have been hard for planters to resist. And yet Frederick Law Olmsted identified one pertinent reason why few planters succumbed: "In nearly all ordinary work," Olmsted observed, "custom has settled the extent of the task, and it is difficult to increase it." If these customs were systematically ignored, Olmsted continued, the planter simply increased the likelihood "of a general stampede to the 'swamp.'" Another complaint was less against the task system itself than against its incomplete application. One former slave remembered that slaves sometimes "had no task but worked by the day, then they worked till 5 oclock." Olmsted witnessed a group of low-country women "working by the day" rather than by task; and his observations once again explain its relative infrequency. The women, he noted, were "keeping steadily, and it seemed sullenly, on at their work," but they cleared only a quarter of the ground that would have been accomplished in task work. To work "steadily" was just not the low-country way. Indeed, more than one low-country ex-slave was unable to recall a single planter "who worked his hands from sun to sun."

A less tangible, but no less real, reason for the attachment of slaves to the task-ing system was the sense of personal responsibility that it inculcated. Planters cer-tainly tried to "create responsibility," as one put it, by offering the same task of ground to a slave throughout the season. In that way, "Where a negro knows that the task he is working is to be worked by him the next time he goes over the field, he is induced, in order to render the next working as light as possible, to work it well as [at] first." Olmsted was impressed by the results of this policy. The laborer under the task system, he noted, "works more rapidly, energetically, and, within narrow limits, with much greater use of discretion, or skill, than he is often found to do elsewhere. By assuming responsibility for his task, the slave had to be treated responsibly. He was not to be called away from his task: this would be tantamount to an invasion of his "customary privileges," one planter explained. Put another way, one former slave recalled how "his master used to come in the field, and tell the overseer not to balk we, if we got done soon to let us alone and do our own work as we pleased." This sense of personal responsibility, this quasi-proprietorial attitude that the system encouraged, may well explain one of the most distinctive responses of low-country slaves when confronted with freedom. It is graphically captured in the exchange that occurred in 1866 between a woman field hand and a plantation agent who had apparently overstepped his authority. She "ordered me out of her task," the agent reported, "saying if I come into her Task again she would put me in the ditch." An army officer who inspected another lowland plantation was "hooted at" and told by the freedmen that "they wanted nothing to do with white men." Without in any way suggesting that slavery was a beneficent school in which slaves gained a valuable education, perhaps a low-country master was close to the mark (closer than he realized) when he suggested that, under the task system, the slaves had "learnt in many instances to govern themselves and to govern each other . . . ."

A sharply felt sense of personal responsibility was allied to a recognition of the merits of collective solidarity. A task system could conceivably encourage an indi-vidualistic, not to mention competitive, ethic; low-country slaves, on the other hand seem on the whole to have valued the relative freedom it permitted for pooling resources when necessary. One planter recalled witnessing "with much pleasure the husband assisting the wife after he has finished his own task, and sometimes I have seen several members of a family in like manner, unite in aiding those who have been less fortunate than themselves in accomplishing their tasks." Speaking to the same point, but less romantically, James R. Sparkman reckoned "it is customary (and never objected to) for the more active and industrious hands to assist those who are slower and more tardy in finishing their daily task." Even less romantically, Richard Mack, an ex-slave interviewed in the 1930s, remembered that when he had "done all my task, and I help[ed] others with their task so they wouldn't get whipped . . . ." The first few years of freedom could conceivably have seen an over-throw of any preexisting communal straitjacket. Instead, observers were astonished at the solid front presented by the low-country freedmen. "It is really wonderful," noted one army commander in January 1866, "how unanimous they are; communi-cating like magic, and now holding out, knowing the importance of every day in regard to the welfare of the next crop, thinking that the planters will be obliged to come to their terms."

The merits of collective solidarity could also be experienced in familial form. Once tasks were completed, slaves could work in groups of their own choosing. Many ex-slaves recall that family groups were by far the most preferred units. Susan Bennett, a former slave, remembered how she and her husband had worked "together on our own works after we got through our tasks"; George Gould and his wife, both former slaves, "put their labor together" after completing their tasks; Prince Wilson, an ex-slave from Chatham County, Georgia, recollected how his family of nine had "all worked together and all worked at task work and raised [their own] corn in that way." Toney Elliott had resided on a different plantation from his wife when he was a slave, but he recalled how "my wife and myself raised this corn and rice together. We both worked by task and when I had done my task I went over to her house and we both worked together." A neighbor added that Toney Elliott's son also helped his father; in fact, the neighbor noted with some surprise, the son worked only for his father and mother because he "had a master that didn't put his boys into the field until they were 15 or 16 years old." In other words, slave kin groups and families in the low country could function as significant *economic* units for at least a part of the working day.

Another facet of this collective solidarity can be detected in the reaction of the freedmen to their former drivers. Throughout the South the authority of the driver generally evaporated once freedom came. Many an ex-slave, interviewed in the 1930s, testified to the hatred felt by field hands towards these men. Although a loss of the driver's prestige occurred in the low country—Edward S. Philbrick reckoned that the driver's influence was reduced to "a cypher"—a more ambivalent response, traceable perhaps to the special role of the driver in a task system, can also be discerned. The special role of the driver in the low country stemmed from his role as "the second Master," as one former slave put it, whose function was not to wield a whip over a line of gang slaves but, rather, to allocate tasks, to ensure that they were satisfactorily performed, and to fulfill other managerial duties. Furthermore, in some respects, the driver was seen to be at a disadvantage for having, as one ex-slave put it, "no task-work and [having] no time of his own." By way of compen-sation, low-country drivers were entitled to receive a certain amount of help in tending their own crops.

The task system was, in other words, the yardstick by which most work in the low country was measured. It bound all slaves together. Thus, the unusual spectacle of field hands rallying behind their former drivers, which occurred in the low coun-try in the immediate postemancipation years, becomes a little more explicable. When a white agent ordered a "Headman" to "take his hoe and work under the con-tract with the rest," he found himself facing the fury of a number of field hands; when he returned with a party of soldiers, he had to beat another hasty retreat under a barrage of blows from the women laborers. In one labor contract drawn up between a Georgia planter and thirty-four freedmen, the freedmen agreed to pay out of their share of the crop an extra cash sum to their foreman. This contract is a testimonial to the respect with which at least some foremen were held.

One final feature of this collective solidarity was the sense of pride that freedmen obviously felt for their forebears. Slave complements on low-country plantations were not only large but also unusually stable. This, together with the autonomy permitted under the task system, fostered a sense of collective identity. The sense of respect felt by Ben Horry, an ex-slave interviewed in the 1930s, for his ancestors' accomplishments is made in resounding terms: "All them rice field been nothing but swamp. Slavery people cut kennel (canal) and dig ditch through the raw swamp." An even more emphatic memorial is provided by a low-country resident in 1866: "They often speak of the Relations upon the Lands that their Fathers and Mothers cleared, those Swamps and Marshes, and Made them the Fruitful Rice Fields they are." A sense of collective esteem, communal solidarity, and personal responsibility went hand in hand among low-country slaves and freedmen.

The task system was characterized by, and indeed encouraged, a number of traits—an ability to lengthen or shorten the working day, a sense of personal responsibility, a commitment to and economic underpinning for the slave family, and attitudes of collective solidarity and communal worth. All these features manifested themselves, and in one sense reached their fullest expression, in the ability of low-country slaves to accumulate property. An investigation of this subject is the focus for the remainder of this essay.

Mid-nineteenth-century evidence exists by which it is possible to assess, however, imprecisely, the scale and range of property-owning by slaves. It takes the form of depositions and supporting testimony submitted to the Southern Claims Commission from former slaves who could prove both their loyalty and their loss of property to Federal troops. Frank W. Klingberg, the author of the standard monograph on the work of the commission, may well have been correct, in general terms, when he stated that "A very small number of claims were filed by former slaves, for the obvious reason that during the war years they were virtually a propertyless class." But this statement is inaccurate for the low-country region of South Carolina and Georgia. The settled or allowed claims from Liberty County, Georgia, amounted to ninety-two, of which eighty-nine were from ex-slaves. There were an additional sixty-one settled claims from ex-slaves in the neighboring counties of Chatham, Georgia, and Beaufort, South Carolina. As it is, the settled claims from the low-country region come overwhelmingly from ex-slaves; but if, as Klingberg suggests, most claims filed by former slaves were disallowed for lack of clear title, the disproportion between white and black claims would be greatly magnified.

. . . [A]n awareness of the hurdles that had to be overcome before a claim could even be submitted, not to mention settled, makes the list of ex-slave claimants more impressive. To find a competent attorney and to be able to pay him (most freedmen had to employ a succession of attorneys) were major obstacles. Overcoming the ridicule and opposition of neighboring whites must have tested the determination of many an aspiring claimant. One ex-slave refused to call his former master as a witness in his claim "because he always was a great Rebel and now tries to cry down this claims business and tells people that they never will get nothing." Just being available when the commissioners came to the neighborhood was not necessarily a simple matter. One freedwoman, acting as a witness in another's claim, mentioned in passing that Federal troops had taken her buggy, potatoes, and poultry but that she had submitted no claim, for "when they were putting in claims, I had the rheumatism and couldn't go."

The historical value of these claims is enhanced because in them the authentic voice of the slave (or rather, the recently freed slave) can be heard, not recalling experiences some sixty or seventy years after the event but immediately and pointedly. These claim depositions are not simply matter-of-fact inventories of lost property but personal, moving statements. They combine a touching concern for detail (names of purchasers, prices paid, and dates of purchase); a dash of pride (one freedman referred to having raised stock "ever since I had sense"; another to having raised "fowls almost as soon as I could walk"; and a third claimed that "some slaves had more property than the crackers"); and an occasional display of emotion (Lydia Brown "cried when they took [my property]. I know I was foolish but I couldn't help it. I was very glad to see them come; but I didn't think they would take my things"); while the overall flavor was salty and direct (the appearance of William Tecumseh Sherman's troops was likened, among other things, to a pack of "ravenous wolves [that] didn't say howdy" and to "a flock of blackbirds only you could not scare them").

An analysis of these claims—and for this the Liberty County, Georgia, claims will serve as the sample—provides as detailed a survey as one can ever expect of the amount and variety of property owned by slaves on the eve of emancipation. Virtually all the Liberty County ex-slave claimants had apparently been deprived of a number of hogs and a substantial majority listed corn, rice, and fowls among their losses. In addition, a surprising number apparently possessed horses and cows, while buggies or wagons, beehives, peanuts, fodder, syrup, butter, sugar, and tea were, if these claims are to be believed, in the hands of at least some slaves. The average cash value (in 1864 dollars) claimed by Liberty County former slaves was $357.43, with the highest claim totaling $2,290 and the lowest $49.

Before passing to a more detailed analysis of these claims, a pertinent question needs to be addressed. Can a person who is owned himself "own" property in any meaningful sense? A partial answer to this question is supplied by the claim process itself. Many ex-slaves were, after all, reimbursed for their loss of property, which constitutes one test of the validity of their titles. On average, the freedmen received 40 percent of the asserted value of their claims. But this, in turn, raises the question of why the commissioners discounted almost two-thirds of most freedmen's claims. The answer does not generally lie in exaggerated claims (although some undoubtedly were) or in disputed titles but, rather, in the construction put on the term "army supply." Virtually all claims for buggies, fowls, beehives, clothing, and crockery were automatically disregarded because these items were not considered to be legitimate army supplies. Though the commissioners and some planters often took issue with the values attached to the ex-slaves' property, rarely did they dispute the fact of possession. In fact, the testimony of whites is impressive in its support of the details of many freedmen's claims. Raymond Cay, Sr., a Liberty County planter, knew that slaves owned cattle on George Howe's plantation because he had himself purchased cattle from them; a slave's ownership of a buggy was proved when the county postmaster and his wife admitted to hiring it on Sundays; and one master even acknowledged paying taxes for one of his slaves who possessed horses, cattle, and a buggy.

While conceding that slaves in some sense possessed property, it may be argued that this property was held only on the sufferance of the master. In the final analysis, could not the master always expropriate all the property supposedly owned by the slave? Many ex-slaves addressed this question and, not surprisingly, showed a keen understanding of it. Some were exceedingly forthright and blunt about the matter: Hercules LeCount stressed that his master "did not own or even claim a cents worth of . . . [his property]"; Prince Wilson asserted that he was "the only one who has any legal right to the property"; and Henry Stephens "never heard of a master's claiming property that belonged to his slaves." When one witness was asked to address directly the proposition that a horse claimed by a slave in fact belonged to his master, he emphatically refuted the suggestion by stating "what was his'n [that is, the slave's] was his'n." One former bondsman, who, as a slave, was married to a free black woman, made the interesting claim that she "could own and hold property the same as slaves were allowed by their masters to hold property." Some slaves obviously believed that their titles to property were more, rather than less, secure because it was held, as one freedman put it, "by [the] master's protection." Others were prepared to admit the de facto nature of their property ownership, but this did little to diminish their assertiveness. Joseph Bacon admitted that "legally the property was his [master's] but a master who would take property from his slaves would have a hard time"; his master, he averred, "never interfered with me and my property at all." Toney Elliott, after emphasizing that "our masters had nothing to do with our property any more than I had with their's," described how, when his master died, "some of the young heirs begrudged me my hogs because I had so many more than they did and wanted to take it, but they didn't and could not because it was mine and they knew it was mine." He recognized that "they could have taken it and I could not have helped myself legally"; but such an eventuality was obviously unthinkable. Thus, while virtually all slaves were extremely assertive about their de facto rights, some were willing to concede their lack of legal title. Others were not willing to concede that much.

If one accepts, then, that the property (or at least some of it) listed in these claims actually belonged to the slaves, what can this information tell us? Most conspicuous perhaps is the sheer amount of property claimed by some slaves. Paris James, a former slave driver, was described by a neighboring white planter as a "substantial man before the war [and] was more like a free man than any slave." James claimed, among other things, a horse, eight cows, sixteen sheep, twenty-six hogs, and a wagon. Another slave driver, according to one of his black witnesses, lived "just like a white man except his color. His credit was just as good as a white man's because he had the property to back it." Although the commissioners of claims were skeptical about his alleged loss of twenty cows (as they explained, "Twenty cows would make a good large dairy for a Northern farmer"), his two white and three black witnesses supported him in his claim. Other blacks were considered to be "more than usually prosperous," "pretty well off," and "hardworking and moneysaving," unremarkable characterizations perhaps but surprising when the individuals were also slaves. Alexander Steele, a carpenter by trade and former house servant in Chatham County, Georgia, submitted a claim for $2,205 based on the loss of his four horses, mule, a silver watch, two cows, a wagon, and large quantities of fodder, hay, and corn. He had been able to acquire these possessions by "tradeing" for himself for thirty years; he had had "much time of . . . [his] own" because his master "always went north" in the summer months. He took "a fancy . . . [to] fine horses," a whim he was able to indulge when he purchased "a blooded mare," from which he raised three colts. He was resourceful enough to hide his livestock on Onslow Island when Sherman's army drew near, but the Federal troops secured boats and took off his prized possessions. Three white planters supported Steele in his claim; indeed, one of them recalled that before the war he had made an offer of $300 for one of Steele's colts, an offer that Steele refused.

The ownership of horses was not, however, confined to a privileged minority of slaves. Among the Liberty County claimants, almost as many ex-field hands claimed horses as did former drivers and skilled slaves. This evidence supplies a context for the exchange recorded by Frederick Law Olmsted when he was being shown around the plantation of Richard J. Arnold in Bryan County, Georgia. Olmsted noticed a horse drawing a wagon of "common fieldhand negroes" and asked his host if he usually let the slaves have horses to ride to church.

> "Oh, no; that horse belongs to the old man."
> "Belongs to him! Why, do they own horses?"
> "Oh, yes; William (the House servant) owns two, and Robert, I believe, has three now; that was one of them he was riding."
> "How do they get them?"
> "Oh, they buy them."

Although a few freedmen recalled that former masters had either prohibited horse ownership among slaves or confined the practice to drivers, most placed the proportion of horse owners on any single plantation at between 15 and 20 percent. A former slave of George Washington Walthour reckoned that "In all my master's plantations there were over 30 horses owned by slaves . . . . I think come to count up there were as many as 45 that owned horses—he would let them own any thing they could if they only did his work." Nedger Frazer, a former slave of the Reverend Charles Colcock Jones, recalled that on one of his master's plantations (obviously Arcadia, from Frazer's description) there were forty working hands, of whom five owned horses; and on another (obviously Montevideo) there were another ten hands out of fifty who owned horses. This, in turn, supplies a context for an interesting incident that occurred within the Jones "family" in 1856. In that year Jones, after much soul-searching, sold one of his slave families, headed by Cassius, a field hand. Jones, a man of integrity, then forwarded Cassius the balance of his account, which amounted to $85, a sum that included the proceeds from the sale of Cassius's horse. Perhaps one freedman was not exaggerating when he observed in 1873 that "there was more stock property owned by slaves before the war than are owned now by both white and black people together in this county."

The spectacular claims and the widespread horse ownership naturally catch the eye, but even the most humdrum claim has its own story to tell. Of particular interest for this essay, each contains a description of how property was accumulated. The narrative of John Bacon can stand as proxy for many such accounts: "I had a little crop to sell and bought some chickens and then I bought a fine large sow and gave $10.00 for her. This was about ten years before the war and then I raised hogs and sold them till I bought a horse. This was about eight years before freedom. This was a breeding mare and from this mare I raised this horse which the Yankees took from me." This was painstaking accumulation: no wonder one freedman referred to his former property as his "laborment." And yet, occasionally, the mode of procurement assumed a slightly more sophisticated cast. Some slaves recalled purchasing horses by installment; some hired additional labor to cultivate their crops; two slaves (a mill engineer and a stockminder) went into partnership to raise livestock; and a driver lent out money at interest.

But whatever the mode of accumulation, the ultimate source, as identified by virtually all the ex-slaves, was the task system. Even slaves who had escaped field labor attributed their acquisition of property to this form of labor organization. Thus, a former wagoner was able to work on his own behalf, he recalled, because he was tasked; a waiting man explained that "if . . . [he] was given Morning work and . . . got thro' before 12 oclock . . . [he] was allowed to go" and produce for himself; and a dairy woman was able to acquire her possessions because she "worked and earned money outside her regular task work." For field hands, of course, this advantage was universally recognized. Provided a slave had "a mind to save the time," one former slave pointed out, he could take advantage of the task system to produce goods and acquire possessions. Joseph James, a former field hand, emphatically underlined the connection between tasking and property owning: all low-country slaves "worked by tasks," he noted, "and had a plenty of time to work for themselves and in that way all slaves who were industrious could get around them considerable property in a short time."

What all this suggests is that by the middle of the nineteenth century it is correct to speak of a significant internal economy operating within a more conventional low-country economy. According to the depositions of the freedmen this internal economy rested on two major planks. The first concerns the degree to which some slaves engaged in stock raising. One white planter, testifying on behalf of a freedman, recalled that "a good many" slaves owned a number of animals; he then checked himself, perhaps realizing the impression that he was creating, and guardedly stated that "What I mean was they were not allowed to go generally into stock raising." And yet some slaves seem to have been doing just that. One ex-slave spoke of raising "horses to sell"; another claimed to have raised fourteen horses over a period of twenty-five to thirty years, most of which he had sold; and one freedwoman named the purchasers, all of whom were slaves, of the nine horses that she had raised.

The other major foundation upon which this internal economy rested was the amount of crop production by slaves. Jeremiah Evarts observed that the slaves in Chatham County, Georgia, had "as much land as they can till for their own use." The freedmen's recollections from all over the low country support this statement. A number of ex-slaves reckoned that they had more than ten acres under cultivation, though four or five acres was the norm; and one freedman pointed out that low-country slaves "were allowed all the land they could tend without rent." The proprietorial attitude that this independent production encouraged is suggested in one freedman's passing comment that, when he was a slave, he used to work in his "own field" after completing his task.

Through the raising of stock and the production of provisions, together with the sale of produce from woodworking, basketmaking, hunting, and fishing, slaves were able to draw money into their internal economy. Some of these exchanges were regarded as legitimate, and their scale can occasionally be glimpsed. Robert Wilson Gibbes, for example, knew of an individual slave who received $120 from his master for his year's crop of corn and fodder; Richard J. Arnold owed his slaves $500 in 1853 when Olmsted visited him. Other exchanges were regarded as illegitimate, and the scale of these transactions remain clouded in obscurity. One freedman spoke of being about to sell the fruits of his three-acre crop "to a man in Tatnall County" when the plundering Federal troops dashed his hopes; another ex-slave spoke of taking his corn to Riceboro in exchange for tobacco. The recipients of such exchanges were, according to Richard Dennis Arnold, waxing fat on the proceeds. He noted that "These little shops [of Savannah] afford an ever ready market where the demand is always equal to the supply." As a result, he added, these shopkeepers "often acquire large fortunes." He cited one "man who commenced one of these negro shops with perhaps not fifty dollars of capital, some thirteen years [ago] . . . ," and in 1850 "bought at public outcry some wharf property for which he paid $19,000." Similarly, Daniel Elliott Huger Smith reckoned that "the keepers of the smaller grocery shops" in Charleston "made a good profit" from trading with slaves. Thus, while produce and livestock were constantly being bartered by slaves ("swapping" was rife, according to the freedmen) one observer of the mid-nineteenth-century low country was undoubtedly correct when he noted that "In a small way a good deal of money circulated among the negroes, both in the country and in the towns."

The autonomy of this internal economy is further indicated by the development of a highly significant practice. By the middle of the nineteenth century, if not before, slave property was not only being produced and exchanged but also inherited. The father of Joseph Bacon bequeathed him a mare and left all his other children $50 each. Samuel Elliott claimed a more substantial legacy. His father "had 20 head of cattle, about 70 head of hogs—Turkeys Geese Ducks and Chickens a Plenty— he was foreman for his master and had been raising such things for years. When he died the property was divided among his children and we continued to raise things just as he had been raising." Property was also bequeathed to less immediate kin. Two freedmen recalled receiving property from their grandfathers; another inherited a sow from his cousin; and William Drayton of Beaufort County, South Carolina, noted that when his father died he "left with his oldest brother, my uncle, the means or property he left for his children"; and Drayton bought a mule "by the advice of my uncle who had the means belonging to me." There were rules governing lines of descent: one woman claimant emphasized that she had not inherited any of her first husband's property because she had borne him no children; rather, the property went to his son by a former marriage. The ability to bequeath wealth and to link patrimony to genealogy serves to indicate the extent to which slaves created autonomy for themselves while they were still enslaved.

Slave property rights were recognized not only across generations but also across proprietorial boundaries. Some slaves employed guardians to facilitate the transfer of property from one plantation to another. Thus, when Nancy Bacon, belonging to John Baker, inherited cattle from her deceased husband, who had belonged to a Mr. Walthour, she employed her second cousin, Andrew Stacy, a slave on the Walthour plantation, to take charge of the cattle and drive them over to her plantation. According to Stacy, Mr. Walthour "didn't object to my taking them . . . [and] never claimed them." The way slaves took advantage of divided ownership is suggested by Diana Cummings of Chatham County, Georgia. Her husband's master, she explained, "allowed him to sell but mine didn't," so Diana marketed her crops and stock through her husband and received a part of the proceeds. On her husband's death she received all his property for, as she put it, her "entitle" (surname) was then the same as her husband's. She had since changed it through remarriage to Sydney Cummings, but, she noted, "He has no interest in [the] property [being claimed]."

By the middle of the nineteenth century the ownership of property by low-country slaves was relatively extensive and had assumed relatively sophisticated dimensions. By way of conclusion, the scale and significance of this phenomenon needs to be assessed as precisely as the evidence will admit. As far as scale is concerned, the proportion of slaves who possessed sizable amounts of property will, of course, never be known, although it is possible to report estimates of horse ownership on some plantations. Moreover, those freedmen who claimed property were not, on the face of it, an unrepresentative group. And yet, for a slave to take advantage of the opportunities inherent in a task system required consistent physical effort. Presumably, the young, the sick, and the aged were very largely excluded from these opportunities. Even those who were not excluded on these grounds may have been unwilling to endure or assume the attendant physical strains. William Gilmore suggests as much when he likened Raymond Cay's slaves to the "five wise and five foolish" and disparaged those who "slept and slumbered the time away."

Much more frequent, however, are the claims of ex-slaves that "almost all had property" or that "Every man on the place had property. . . . Our master allowed us everything except guns." White planters concurred in this view. One planter from Chatham County, Georgia, recollected that "people generally throughout the country permitted their servants to own hogs, and cattle, and other property to a certain extent. I knew a good many who had one, two, or even four cows. . . . There may have been some plantations were the owners did not allow them to own property, but none such in my knowledge." But perhaps the best witnesses are the outsiders. R. B. Avery, the special agent investigating freedmen claims, reported that Somerset Stewart was "poor in slavery times"—not the sort of characterization one would expect of a slave. At the same time, Avery confirmed Stewart's claim to a horse, for which he was allowed $90. If a "poor" slave could own a horse, then property ownership must have been extensive indeed. Rufus Saxton's discovery in the early 1860s that low-country slaves "delight in accumulating" would appear fully justified.

The ownership of property by low-country slaves had a number of short-term consequences. First, the particular conjunction of task system and domestic economy that characterized the lives of low-country slaves afforded a measure of autonomy unusual in New World plantation societies. The low-country slaves worked without supervision in their private endeavors, and even their plantation work was loosely superintended. Second, the private economic activities of the slaves necessarily involved them in a whole range of decision-making, ranging from the planting of a crop to the purchase of an article of consumption. These calculations fed individual initiative and sponsored collective esteem. Third, when laboring in their own plots, slaves could work in cooperative units of their own choice, and these generally took the form of family groups. In addition, low-country slaves not only accumulated wealth in this way, they bequeathed it, which in turn strengthened the family unit. . . .

F U R T H E R   R E A D I N G

Ira Berlin and Philip D. Morgan, eds., *Cultivation and Culture: Labor and the Shaping of Slave Life in the Americas* (1993).

Ira Berlin and Philip D. Morgan, eds., *The Slaves' Economy: Independent Production by Slaves in the Americas* (1991).

John W. Blassingame, *The Slave Community: Plantation Life in the Ante-Bellum South* (1972).

Robert William Fogel, *Without Consent or Contract: The Rise and Fall of American Slavery* (1992).

Eugene D. Genovese, *From Rebellion to Revolution: Afro-American Slave Revolts in the Making of the Modern World* (1979).

Eugene D. Genovese, *Roll, Jordan, Roll: The World the Slaves Made* (1974).

Al-Tony Gilmore, ed., *Revisiting Blassingame's* The Slave Community: *The Scholars Respond* (1978).

Vincent Harding, *There is a River: The Black Struggle for Freedom in America* (1981).

Norrece T. Jones, Jr., *Born a Child of Freedom, yet a Slave: Mechanisms of Control and Strategies of Resistance in Antebellum South Carolina* (1990).

Charles Joyner, *Down by the Riverside: A South Carolina Slave Community* (1984).

Allan Kulikoff, *Tobacco and Slaves: The Development of Southern Cultures in the Chesapeake, 1680–1800* (1986).

Melton McLaurin, *Celia, a Slave* (1992).

Clarence L. Mohr, *On the Threshold of Freedom: Masters and Slaves in Civil War Georgia* (1986).

Leslie Howard Owens, *This Species of Property: Slave Life and Culture in the Old South* (1976).

Loren Schweninger, *Black Property Owners in the South, 1790–1915* (1990).

Mark M. Smith, *Mastered by the Clock: Time, Slavery, and Freedom in the American South* (1997).

The Roots of Resistance:
Slave Cultures
and Communities

An inherent danger in accepting the "logic of slavery,"—that the slavemaster's will to absolute power over the slave was achieved in reality—is that it necessarily renders what African-American novelist Ralph Ellison has called "a drained image of humanity." It is no accident that portrayals of slavery as extreme and un-relenting brutality tend also to discount any possibility for slave family life or com-munity. The slave becomes an abstract object and not a living, breathing, loving person. It is also difficult to imagine how such a creature could summon the moral and psychological resources necessary to resist slavery, or to survive in freedom after emancipation. Indeed, it was precisely such a portrait of the slave as a pliant, childlike "Sambo" that historian Stanley Elkins rendered several decades ago when he compared slavery to Nazi concentration camps. Indeed, the veritably ex-plosive growth in scholarship on slavery in the decades that followed was largely in response to Elkins's dour portrait.

What that scholarship uncovered was extensive evidence of the deep human re-sources, individual and institutional, that slaves managed to acquire despite the harshness and brutality of the slave regime. Slaves lived in families even though their marital and parental relations had no support in law and could be and were broken at the master's whim. Slaves developed autonomous religious beliefs and shadow re-ligious institutions despite difficulties posed by white opposition and surveillance. Slaves formed communities that provided mutual support and sustenance in the face of the arbitrary brutalities of their condition, even though by the logic of slavery they should have looked only to their masters for succor and not to each other.

Questions remain, however, about how to evaluate and account for such behaviors and institutions, on the one hand, while giving adequate weight to the horror and brutality of slavery, on the other hand. How does one strike a balance between these imperatives? What meaning could "community" really have in the context of enslavement? To what extent were there means by which slaves could create an alternative life and culture to what the logic of slavery predicted?

245

D O C U M E N T S

The first set of documents describe—one by a newspaper reporter, the second by an abolitionist—how a fugitive slave mother kills her child rather than see the child returned to slavery. Among contemporary abolitionists this incident became a cause célèbre and the mother a heroine; the story received a much more morally ambiguous treatment, however, in Toni Morrison's novel, *Beloved* (1987). In the second set of documents, two former Virginia slaves describe strong slave women who resisted the slave regime. In the third set former slave women describe their widely varying experiences of courtship and marriage. The seven letters from slave women to their husbands in the fourth set reveal the affection and attachments formed despite the fact that such unions had no legal basis or civil recognition. The fifth set consists of letters by Martin Lee and Hawkins Wilson that show how the strength of kinship attachments, especially to children, endured separations caused by slavery and the war that destroyed it. The sixth set of documents features letters from a black Union soldier determined to reclaim his children from their owner. The three folk-tales that make up the seventh set of documents suggest something of the humor and cunning, as well as the moral anarchy that were prominent in the slaves' secular view of the world. The two spirituals that make up the final set of documents reflect the strong faith that sustained the slaves' sacred world-view.

1. Margaret Garner, a Slave Mother, Kills Her Child to Prevent Reenslavement, 1856

City News

Arrest of Fugitive Slaves

A Slave Mother Murders her Child rather than see it Returned to Slavery

Great excitement existed throughout the city the whole of yesterday, in consequence of the arrest of a party of slaves, and the murder of her child by a slave mother, while the officers were in the act of making the arrest. A party of seventeen slaves escaped from Boone and Kenton counties, in Kentucky, (about sixteen miles from the Ohio,) on Sunday night last, and taking with them two horses and sled, drove that night to the Ohio river, opposite to Western Row, in this city. Leaving the horses and sled standing there, they crossed the river on foot on the ice.

Five of them were the slaves of Archibald K. Gaines, three of John Marshall, both living in Boone county, a short distance beyond Florence, and six of Levi F. Daugherty, of Kenton county. We have not learned who claims the other three.

About 7 o'clock this morning the masters and their agents arrived in pursuit of their property. They swore out a warrant before J. L. Pendery, Esq., U.S. Commissioner, which was put into the hands of Deputy U.S. Marshal Geo. S. Bennet, who obtained information that they were in a house belonging to a son of Jo. Kite, the third house beyond Millcreek. The son was formerly owned in the neighborhood from which they had escaped and was bought from slavery by his father.

From *The Cincinnati Daily Gazette,* January 29, 1856, and *The Black Book,* ed. Middleton Harris (New York: Random House, 1974), 10.

About 10 o'clock the Deputy U.S. Marshall proceeded there with his posse, including the slave owners and their agent and Major Murphy, a Kentuckian, and a large slave holder. Kite was called out and agreed to open the door, but afterwards refused, when two Kentucky officers, assisted by some of the Deputy Marshals forced it, whereupon the young negro man Simon, the father of the children, fired a revolver three times before he was overpowered. By one of these shots special Marshal John Patterson, who raised his arm to reach the pistol, had two of his fingers of his right hand shot off, the ball afterwards striking his lip.

In the house were found four adults, viz: old Simon and his wife, and young Simon and his wife and four children of the latter, the oldest near six years and the youngest a babe of about nine months. One of these, however, was lying on the floor dying its head cut almost entirely off. There was also a gash about four inches long in the throat of the eldest, and a wound on the head of the other boy.

The officers state that when they questioned the boys about their wounds they said the folks threw them down and tried to kill them.

The young woman, Peggy, and her four children belonged to Marshall, and her husband and the old man Simon and the old woman Mary to Gaines. Old Simon and Mary are the parents of young Simon.

The other nine of the party, we were informed, were put upon the cars yesterday, by a director of the underground railway, and furnished with through tickets.

Those arrested in Kite's house, were taken to the U.S. Court Rooms about 12 o'clock, and guarded there until 3 o'clock, when Commissioner Pendery came and opened his Court.

Gaines appeared to claim his negroes. Marshall was represented by his son, but as he had no power of attorney from his father, the case was postponed until 9 o'clock this morning, in order to give him time to supply this omission.

The fugitives were then taken to the Hammond street station house to be kept over night. The Marshal attempted to get a hack to carry them there, but the crowd frightened all the hackmen that were called so that they declined. They were afraid their carriages would be broken by the mob.

About an hour after they were taken there, Mr. Gaines came along with the dead body of the murdered child. He was taking it to Covington for interment that it might rest in ground consecrated to slavery.

About 3 o'clock a habeas corpus was issued by Judge Burgoyne, and put into the hands of Deputy Sheriff Jeff. Buckingham. He went down to the Hammond street Station House, accompanied by a posse, and took possession of the fugitives. Deputy Marshall Bennet refused at first to give them up, but at length, after consulting with Mayor Farran, came and agreed to compromise by permitting them to be lodged for safe keeping in the county jail. During the debate, Lieut. Hazen, who has charge of the Hammond street Station House, refused to admit the gentleman who swore out the habeas corpus. When Gaines, the master, came along he was freely admitted, and this gentleman walked in behind him, but was siezed [sic] by Lieut. Hazen and put out.

Deputy Sheriff Buckingham having put the fugitives in a 'bus, got in himself, and directed it to be driven to the jail, but Mr. Bennet jumped on the box and ordered the driver to drive to the U.S. Court Rooms. Here another fuss ensued, and Bennet, by the assistance of special Marshals, run the fugitives up into his office.

But Buckingham sent for Sheriff Brashears and a large force, and by these they were re-taken and finally lodged in the county jail about 8 o'clock last evening.

They are now in the custody of the Sheriff, and it is said will not be forthcoming to attend Commissioner Pendery's Court this morning.

Judge Burgoyne, after issuing the writ, started to Columbus. It is presumed he will be back at 11 o'clock this morning, the hour at which the writ is returnable.

The Inquest on the Dead Child

Coroner Menzies held an inquest yesterday afternoon on the body of the murdered slave child. Its throat appeared to have been cut by a single stroke of a knife, and it died a few minutes after the arrest. Mr. Sutton, who lives next door to Kite's, testified that after the other slaves were arrested by the officers, Mr. Gaines, the master, took this child and was in the act of carrying it off, when objections were made to it being removed before an inquest was held. He at length surrendered it to Mr. Sutton, in whose arms it died.

The inquest was not concluded, but will be resumed at 9 o'clock this morning, at the Coroner's office.

The Object of the Habeas Corpus

It is said that it can be proven that these slaves have frequently been in Ohio in company with their masters, and the question will be raised before Judge Burgoyne on the trial of the Habeas Corpus, whether such bringing them into a free State has not rendered them free.

A Visit to the Slave Mother Who Killer Her Child

Last Sabbath, after preaching in the city prison, Cincinnati, through the kindness of the Deputy Sheriff, I was permitted to visit the apartment of that unfortunate woman, concerning whom there has been so much excitement during the last two weeks.

I found her with an Infant in her arms only a few months old, and observed that it had a large bump on its forehead. I inquired the cause of the injury. She then proceeded to give a detailed account of her attempt to kill her children.

She said, that when the officers and slave-hunters came to the house in which they were concealed, she caught a shovel and struck two of her children on the head, and then took a knife and cut the throat of the third, and tried to kill the other,—that if they had given her time, she would have killed them all—that with regard to herself, she cared but little; but she was unwilling to have her children suffer as she had done.

I inquired if she was not excited almost to madness when she committed the act. No, she replied, I was as cool as I now am; and would much rather kill them at once, and thus end their sufferings, than have them taken back to slavery, and be murdered piece-meal. She then told the story of her wrongs. She spoke of her days of suffering, of her nights of unmitigated toll, while the bitter tears coursed their way down her cheeks, and fell in the face of the innocent child as it looked smiling up, little conscious of the danger and probable suffering that awaited it.

As I listened to the facts, and witnessed the agony depicted in her countenance, I could not but exclaim, Oh, how terrible is irresponsible power, when exercised over intelligent beings! She alludes to the child that she killed as being free from all trouble and sorrow, with a degree of satisfaction that almost chills the blood in one's veins; yet she evidently possesses all the passionate tenderness of a mother's love. She is about twenty-five years of age, and apparently possesses an average amount of kindness, with a vigorous intellect, and much energy of character.

The two men and the two other children were in another apartment, but her mother-in-law was in the same room. She says she is the mother of eight children, most of whom have been separated from her; that her husband was once separated from her twenty-five years, during which time she did not see him; that could she have prevented it, she would never have permitted him to return, as she did not wish him to witness her sufferings, or be exposed to the brutal treatment that he would receive.

She states that she has been a faithful servant, and in her old age she would not have attempted to obtain her liberty; but as she became feeble, and less capable of performing labor, her master became more and more exacting and brutal in his treatment, until she could stand it no longer; that the effort could result only in death, at most—she therefore made the attempt.

She witnessed the killing of the child, but said she neither encouraged nor discouraged her daughter-in-law,—for under similar circumstances she should probably have done the same. The old woman is from sixty to seventy years of age, has been a professor of religion about twenty years, and speaks with much feeling of the time when she shall be delivered from the power of the oppressor, and dwell with the Savior, "where the wicked cease from troubling, and the weary are at rest."

Three slaves (as far as I am informed) have resided all their lives within sixteen miles of Cincinnati. We are frequently told that Kentucky slavery is very innocent. If these are its fruits, where it exists in a mild form, will some one tell us what we may expect from its more objectionable features? But comments are unnecessary.

P.S. Bassett.
Fairmont Theological Seminary,
Cincinnati, (Ohio,) Feb. 12, 1856.

2. Descriptions of Two Women Outlaws, c. 1850s

Interview with Lorenzo L. Ivy

Runaways! Lawd, yes, dey had plenty of runaways. Dere was two kin's of runaways—dem what hid in de woods an' dem what ran away to free lan'. Mos' slaves jes' runaway an' hide in de woods for a week or two an' den come on back. My grandmother lived in de woods. Dey say her people treated her lak a dog. In fac' dey treat her so bad she often come down to our place. After a while dey tell some

---

From interviews with Lorenzo L. Ivy and West Turner in Charles L. Perdue, Jr., Thomas E. Barden, and Robert K. Phillips, eds., *Weevils in the Wheat: Interviews with Virginia Ex-Slaves* (1976), 153–289. Copyright © 1976 by the Rector and Visitors of the University of Virginia [The University of Virginia Press].

one to tell her to come on home. Dey warn' goin' beat her anymore. She go on back fo' a while.

Dey sol' slaves heah an everywhere. I've seen droves of Negroes brought in heah on foot goin' Souf to be sol'. Each one have an old tow sack on his back wif everythin' he's got in it. Over de hills dey come in lines reachin' as far as you kin see. Dey walk in double lines chained tergether in twos. Dey walk 'em heah to de railroad an' ship 'em Souf lak cattle. Truely, son, de haf has never been tol'.

I know a lot more I kin tell you some other time. I'll tell you; I'll write it out. Jes' sen' me an envelope lak you said an' I'll write it all down an' sen' it to you. Be good.

Interview with West Turner

Ant Sallie ain't sayed nothin' but de nex' mornin' she ain't nowhere 'bout. Finally Marsa come down to de quarters an' git my pa an' ast him whar was Ant Sallie. Pa say he don' know nothin' 'bout her. Marsa didn' do nothin' to pa, but he knowed pa was lyin' 'cause he done heard dat pa been feedin' Ant Sallie in de night time. Well, pa used to put food in a pan 'neath de wash bench 'side de cabin, an' it was so dark Ant Sallie come on inside to eat it.

I was layin' on de pallet listenin' to her an' pa whisperin' an' jus' den dere come abangin' on de do'. It was wedged shut an' dar was ole Marsa bangin'. "Come on out dere Sallie," he yelled. "I know you is in dere." Didn't nobody say nothin'. Den I heard ole Marsa yellin' fo' all de niggers an' tellin' em to come dere an' catch Sallie else he gonna whup 'em all. Dey all come, too, and gathered 'round de do'. Pa didn't know what to do. But Ant Sallie ain't ketched yet. She grabbed up a scythe knife f'om de corner an' she pulled de chock out dat do' an' come out a-swingin.' An' dose niggers was glad cause dey didn't want to catch her. An' Marsa didn't dare tetch her.

She cut her way out, den turned roun' and backed off into de woods, an' ole Marsa was just screamin' an' cussin' an' tellin' her one minute what he's gonna do when he ketch her an' de nex' minute sayin' he gonna take her back in de big house ef she stay. I was peekin' out de slip of de winder, an' de las' I saw was Ant Sallie goin' into de bushes still swingin' dat scythe. Didn't no one foller her neither.

3. Descriptions of Love and Courtship in Slavery

I walk with Jim to de gate and stood under de honeysuckle dat was smelling so sweet. I heard de big ol' bullfrogs a' croakin' by de river and de whippoorwills a-hollerin' in de woods. Dere was a big yellow moon, and I reckon Jim did love me. Anyhow he said so and asked me to marry him and he squeezed my hand. I told him I'd think it over and I did and de next Sunday I told him dat I'd have him.

He ain't kissed me yet but he asked my mammy for me. She says dat she'll have to talk to me and let him know. Well all dat week she talks to me, tellin' me how serious gettin' married is and dat it last a powerful long time. I tells her dat I knows it but dat I am ready.

"Courtship," in Dorothy Sterling, ed., *We Are Your Sisters: Black Women in the Nineteenth Century* (New York: Norton, 1984), 33–35. Copyright © 1984 by Dorothy Sterling.

On Sunday night Mammy tells Jim dat he can have me and you ought to seed dat black boy grin. He comes to me without a word and he picks me up out dat chair and dere in de moonlight he kisses me right before my mammy who am a-cryin'.

I married when I was 14 years old. So help me God, I didn't know what marriage meant. I had an idea when you loved de man, you an' he could be married an' his wife had to cook, clean up, wash an' iron for him was all. I slept in bed he on his side an' I on mine for three months an' dis aint no lie. He never got close to me 'cause mama had sed, "Don't let no body bother yo' principle, 'caus dat wuz all yo' had." I 'bey my mama, an' tol' him so, and I said to go an' ask mama an' ef she sed he could get close to me hit was alright. An' he an' I went together to see and ask mama. Den mama said "Come here chillun," and she began telling me to please my husband, an' 'twas my duty as a wife, dat he had married a pu'fect lady.

I was a housemaid and my mammy run de kitchen. They say I was a pretty gal then, face shiny like a ginger cake, and hair straight and black as a crow. One springtime de flowers git be blooming, de hens to cackling, and de guineas to patarocking. Sam come along when I was out in de yard wid de [white] baby. He fust talk to de baby, and I asked him if de baby wasn't pretty. He say, "Yes, but not as pretty as you is, Louisa." I looks at Sam, and dat kind of foolishness wind up in a weddin'.

My mammy stay on wid de same marster 'til I was grown, dat is fifteen, and Thad got to lookin' at me, meek as a sheep and dumb as a calf. I had to ask dat nigger, right out, what his 'tentions was, befo' I get him to bleat out dat he love me. Him name Thad Guntharpe. I glance at him one day at de pigpen when I was sloppin' de hogs, I say: "Mr. Guntharpe, you follow me night and mornin' to dis pigpen; do you happen to be in love wid one of these pigs? If so, I'd like to know which one 'tis; then sometime I come down here by myself and tell dat pig 'bout your 'fections." Thad didn't say nothin; but just grin. Him took de slop bucket out of my hand and look at it, put upside down on de ground, and set me down on it; then he fall down dere on de grass by me and warm my fingers in his hands. I just took pity on him and told him mighty plain dat he must limber up his tongue and say what he mean, wantin' to visit them pigs so often. Us carry on foolishness 'bout de little boar shoat pig and de little sow pig, then I squeal in laughter over how he scrouge so close; de slop bucket tipple over and I lost my seat. Dat ever remain de happiest minute of my eighty-two years.

My first husband—nice man; den he sold off to Florida—neber hear from him 'gain. Den I sold up here. Massa want me to breed; so he say "Violet you must take some nigger here."

Den I say, "No, Massa, I can't take any here." Well den, Missis, he go down Virginia, and he bring up two niggers—and Missis say, "One ob dem's for you Violet;" but I say, "No, Missis, I can't take one ob dem, 'cause I don't lub 'em." By-and-by, Massa he buy tree more, and den Missis say, "Now, Violet, ones dem is for you." I say "I do' no—maybe I can't lub one dem neider;" but she say "You must hab one ob dese." Well, so Sam and I we lib along two year—he watchin my ways and I watchin his ways. At last, one night, we was standin' by de wood-pile togeder, and de moon bery shine, and I do' no how 'twas, Missis, he answer me, he want a wife, but he didn't know where he get one. I say, "Plenty girls in G." He say, "Yes—but maybe I shan't find any I like so well as you." Den I say maybe he wouldn't like my ways 'cause I'se an ole woman, and I hab four children; and anybody marry me must be jest kind to dem children as dey was to me, else I couldn't lub him. Well, so we went on from one ting to anoder, till at last we say we'd take one anoder, and so we've libed togeder eber since—and I's had four children by him—and he never slip away from me nor I from him.

We just takes one anoder—we asks de white folks' leave, and den takes one anoder. Some folks dey's married by de book; but den, what's de use? Dere's my fus husband, we'se married by de book, and he sold way off to Florida, and I's here. Dey do what dey please wid us, so we jest make money for dem.

We didn't have no preacher when we married. My Marster said, "Now you and Lewis wants to marry and there ain't no objections so go on and jump over the broom stick together and you is married." That was all there was to it. I lived on with my white folks and he lived on with his and kept comin' to see me jest like he had done when he was a courtin'. He never brought me any presents 'cause he didn't have no money to buy them with, but he was good to me and that was what counted.

4. Letters Showing Relations Between Slave Husbands and Wives, 1840–1863

Dear Husband: Richmond, Virginia, October 27, 1840

This is the third letter that I have written to you, and have not received any from you. I think very hard of it. The trader has been here three times to look at me. I wish that you would try to see if you can get any one to buy me. If you don't come down here this Sunday, perhaps you wont see me any more. Give my love to them all, and to your mother in particular, and to aunt Betsey, and all the children, tell Jane and Mother they must come down a fortnight before Christmas. I wish to see you all, but I expect I never shall—never no more.

I remain your Dear and affectionate Wife,
Sargry Brown

Sargry Brown's husband never received her appeal; it was found in the Dead Letter Office in Washington, D.C. Louisa and Archer Alexander had better luck. Both slaves belonging to the Hollman family, they had been married for thirty years when Archer ran away during the Civil War. He kept in touch with his wife until he was able to engineer her escape.

"Letters from Slave Women," in Dorothy Sterling, ed., *We Are Your Sisters: Black Women in the Nineteenth Century* (New York: Norton, 1984), 44–47. Copyright © 1984 by Dorothy Sterling.

Dear Husband:

Naylor's Store [Missouri]
November 16, 1863

I received your letter yesterday, and lost no time in asking Mr. Jim if he would sell me, and what he would take for me. He flew at me, and said I would never get free only at the point of the Baynot, and there was no use in ever speaking to him any more about it. I don't see how I can ever get away except you get soldiers to take me from the house, as he is watching me night and day. He is always abusing Lincoln, and calls him an old Rascoll. He is the greatest rebel under heaven. It is a sin to have him loose. He says if he had hold of Lincoln he would chop him up into mincemeat. I had good courage all along until now but now I am almost heart broken. Answer this letter as soon as possible.

I am your affectionate wife,
Louisa Alexander

Harriet Newby, a Virginia slave, was about forty years old when she wrote to her husband, Dangerfield Newby. Freed by his white father, he was working in the North and trying to raise money to buy Harriet and their six children.

Dear Husband:

Brentville, [Virginia,] April 22d, 1859

I received your letter today, and it gives much pleasure to here from you, but was sorry to [hear] of your sikeness; hope you may be well when you receive this. I wrote to you several weeks ago, and directed my letter to Bridge Port, but I fear you did not receive it, as you said nothing about it in yours. I wrote in my last letter that Miss Virginia had a baby—a little girl. I had to nurse her day and night. Dear Dangerfield, you cannot imagine how much I want to see you. Com as soon as you can for nothing would give more pleasure than to see you. It is the greatest Comfort I have is thinking of the promist time when you will be here. The baby commenced to crall to-day it is very delicate. Nothing more at present, but remain

your affectionate wife
Harriet Newby

Dear Husband:

Brentville, [Virginia,] August 16, 1859

Your letter came duly to hand and it gave me much pleasure to here from you, and especely to here you are better of your rhumatism. I want you to buy me as soon as possible, for if you do not get me some body else will. Dear Husband you [know] not the trouble I see; the last two years has been like a trouble dream. It is said Master is in want of money. If so, I know not what time he may sell me, and then all my bright hopes of the futer are blasted, for their has been one bright hope to cheer me in all my troubles, that is to be with you. If I thought I shoul never see you this earth would have no charms for me. Do all you can for me, witch I have no doubt you will. The children are all well. The baby cannot walk yet. It can step around everything by holding on. I must bring my letter to a Close as I have no newes to write. You mus write soon and say when you think you can come.

Your affectionate wife,
Harriet Newby

Two months after the above letter was written, Dangerfield Newby returned to
Virginia with John Brown and his men. He was killed in the attack on Harpers Ferry.
After Harriet Newby's letters were found on his body, she was sold to the Deep South.

When Emily Saunders (1815–76) married Adam Plummer (1819–1905) in 1841,
they were Maryland house servants belonging to different masters. Every Saturday
night Adam walked eight miles to see his wife, returning to his owner in time for work
on Monday. After Emily's owner died in 1851, she and their older children were
purchased by residents of Washington, D.C., fifteen miles from Adam's home. Adam
was able to visit his family every second week until 1855 when Emily's owner moved
to a farm near Baltimore. After that, he was seldom permitted to visit more than twice
a year, at Christmas and Easter. It was then that husband and wife began to corre-
spond. Emily dictated her letters to her mistress or to a white seamstress in the
household. A selection from her letters follows.

Ellicott Mills, Maryland,
My Dear Plummer: April 20, 1856

I want you to let me know why you wrote me so troubled a letter. I was very
sorry to hear that you should say you and I are parted for life, and am very troubled
at it. I don't think I can stand it long. What do you mean? Does your master say he
will not let you come any more? Or what is the reason you say we are parted for
life? I can't think it is your wish to give me up for another wife.

I want you to write me about my two children, if they are well and comfortable,
and how mother is. Saunders said today "My Pappy is coming to bring me a hat and a
pair of boots to go to church with." I want to have the baby baptized and I want to
know if you can come, when you will be able to do so, and I will wait until you come.

The baby has her chills come back on her now and then. The other children are
all well, and Henry sends his love to his father. I have been quite well, and have no
trouble but the one great trouble, the want to see you sometimes. God bless and
keep you!

Your affectionate wife,
Emily Plummer

Ellicott Mills, Maryland,
My Deare Husband: September 18, 1860

I recived you kind letter and was very much oblige to you for what you sent
me. The fridy night after i rote to you i was confined with too babys one was a boy
and the other a girl every body that see them says they are the fines chrilden they
every sar. When mother came and scene them she was delited. I am as well as can
bee expected. The chrilden ar all well and join me in love to you from your wife

Emily Plummer

Ellicott City, Maryland,
My ever dear Husband: August 19, 1861

I have been hoping each day to hear from you. We are all well. The babies
grow and improve rapidly. They can almost walk. And Papa, Saunders is not with

me, he is hired to Miss Eliza Dorsey, as house servant, is doing very well. He and all the children are so anxious to see you.

I think each day I cannot longer wait for a visit from you. My heart aches at the thought of this long and painful separation. I dream of you and think you are once more with me, but wake to find myself alone and so wretchedly unhappy.

Could you come up early some Sunday morning to breakfast? Do try this plan, my dear husband, and let me hear from you soon, that you will come, but under any circumstances write very frequently. It is our next great pleasure to seeing your kind face, and hearing your voice of affection.

Your truly affectionate wife,
Emily Plummer

Set free in 1863, Emily Plummer joined her husband, to live with him for the rest of her life. Their happiness was marred only by the absence of their oldest daughter, Sarah Miranda. Sold South in 1861, she had last written to them from New Orleans.

5. Martin Lee and Hawkins Wilson, Two Ex-Slaves, Seek to Reunite with Their Children After Emancipation, 1866, 1867

Letter by Martin Lee

Florence Ala December 7the 1866

Dear Sir   I take the pleashure of writing you A fue lins hoping that I will not ofende you by doing so   I was raised in your state and was sold from their when I was 31 years olde   left wife one childe Mother Brothers and sisters   My wife died about 12 years agoe and ten years agoe I Made money And went back and bought My olde Mother and she lives with Me   Seven years agoe I Maried again and commence to by Myself and wife for two thousande dollars and last Christ∂mas I Made the last pay Ment and I have made Some little Money this year and I wish to get my Kinde All with me and I will take it as a Greate favor if you will help me to get them by sending me a order to Carey with me to the agent of Monroe walton County Georgia   I was out their last weeke and Got My daughter And hear childern but I could not Get My Sisters Son   she is live and well   there is a Man by the name of Sebe—Burson that ust to one them and he will not let me or his Mother have the boy   he says he has the boy bound to him and the law in our State is that a childe cannot be bounde when the[y] have Mother father brother sistter uncl or Aunt that can take care of them but I went to the Agent and he says the boy has not ben bounde to him his county and if I will Give him 25 dollars he will deliver the boy to me but I think that to harde and I hope you will Sende me a order that I can cary to Mr Arnel so I May be Able to Get him without that much Money   I would not Minde paying him 5 dollars and I think that far [*fair*]   I live 3 hunderde and 25 miles from Monroe Ande it will cost me 3 hunderde dollars to Get them to Alabama   pleas

From "Afro-American Families in the Transition from Slavery to Freedom," ed. Ira Berlin et al., *Radical History Review*, 42 (1988), 102–103.

answer this as soon as you get it and pleas dont sende to Georgia untill I goe   it
Might Make it against me   answer this to me and I will let you know the time I will
starte and I can get their in 2 days   pleas do the best you can for Me and I remain
yours a Servent And will untill death

Martin Lee

Letter by Hawkins Wilson

[Galveston, Tex.] May 11th, 1867—

Dear Sir, I am anxious to learn about my sisters, from whom I have been separated
many years— I have never heard from them since I left Virginia twenty four years
ago— I am in hopes that they are still living and I am anxious to hear how they are
getting on— I have no other one to apply to but you and am persuaded that you
will help one who stands in need of your services as I do— I shall be very grateful
to you, if you oblige me in this matter— One of my sisters belonged to Peter
Coleman in Caroline County and her name was Jane— Her husband's name was
Charles and he belonged to Buck Haskin and lived near John Wright's store in the
same county—She had three children, Robert, Charles and Julia, when I left—
Sister Martha belonged to Dr Jefferson, who lived two miles above Wright's
store— Sister Matilda belonged to Mrs. Botts, in the same county— My dear
uncle Jim had a wife at Jack Langley's and his wife was named Adie and his oldest son was named Buck and they all belonged to Jack Langley— These are all my
own dearest relatives and I wish to correspond with them with a view to visit them
as soon as I can hear from them— My name is Hawkins Wilson and I am their
brother, who was sold at Sheriff's sale and used to belong to Jackson Talley and
was bought by M. Wright, Boydtown C.H. You will please send the enclosed letter
to my sister Jane, or some of her family, if she is dead— I am, very respectfully,
your obedient servant,

Hawkins Wilson—

[Enclosure]
Dear Sister Jane, Your little brother Hawkins is trying to find out where you are
and where his poor old mother is— Let me know and I will come to see you— I
shall never forget the bag of buiscuits you made for me the last night I spent with
you— Your advice to me to meet you in heaven has never passed from my mind
and I have endeavored to live as near to my God, that if He saw fit not to suffer us
to meet on earth, we might indeed meet in Heaven— I was married in this city on
the 10th March 1867 by Rev. Samuel Osborn to Mrs. Martha White, a very intelligent and lady-like woman— You may readily suppose that I was not fool enough
to marry a Texas girl— My wife was from Georgia and was raised in that state and
will make me very happy— I have learned to read, and write a little— I teach Sunday School and have a very interesting class— If you do not mind, when I come, I
will astonish you in religious affairs— I am sexton of the Methodist Episcopal
Church colored— I hope you and all my brothers and sisters in Virginia will stand
up to this church; for I expect to live and die in the same— When I meet you, I
shall be as much overjoyed as Joseph was when he and his father met after they

had been separated so long— Please write me all the news about you all— I am writing tonight all about myself and I want you to do likewise about your and my relations in the state of Virginia— Please send me some of Julia's hair whom I left a baby in the cradle when I was torn away from you— I know that she is a young lady now, but I hope she will not deny her affectionate uncle this request, seeing she was an infant in the cradle when he saw her last— Tell Mr. Jackson Talley how-do-ye and give my love to all his family, Lucy, Ellen and Sarah— Also to my old playmate Henry Fitz who used to play with me and also to all the colored boys who, I know, have forgotten me, but I have not forgotten them— I am writing to you tonight, my dear sister, with my Bible in my hand praying Almighty God to bless you and preserve you and me to meet again— Thank God that now we are not sold and torn away from each other as we used to be— we can meet if we see fit and part if we like— Think of this and praise God and the Lamb forever— I will now present you a little prayer which you will say every night before you go to sleep— Our father who art in heaven &c, you will know what the rest is— Dear sister, I have had a rugged road to travel, since I parted with you, but thank God, I am happy now, for King Jesus is my Captain and God is my friend. He goes before me as a pillar of fire by night and a cloud by day to lead me to the New Jerusalem where all is joy, and happiness and peace— Remember that we have got to meet before that great tribune God— My reputation is good before white and black. I am chief of all the turnouts of the colored people of Galveston— Last July 1866, I had the chief command of four thousand colored people of Galveston— So you may know that I am much better off, than I used to be when I was a little shaver in Caroline, running about in my shirt tail picking up chips— Now, if you were to see me in my fine suit of broadcloth, white kid gloves and long red sash, you would suppose it was Gen. Schofield marching in parade uniform into Richmond— The 1st day of May, 1867, I had 500 colored people, big and little, again under my command— We had a complete success and were complimented by Gen. Griffin and Mr. Wheelock the superintendent of the colored schools of Texas— We expect to have a picnic for the Sunday School soon— I am now a grown man weighing one hundred and sixty odd pounds— I am wide awake and full of fun, but I never forget my duty to my God— I get eighteen dollars a month for my services as sexton and eighteen dollars a week outside— I am working in a furniture shop and will fix up all your old furniture for you, when I come to Virginia if you have any— I work hard all the week— On Sunday I am the first one in the church and the last to leave at night; being all day long engaged in serving the Lord; teaching Sunday School and helping to worship God— Kind sister, as paper is getting short and the night is growing old and I feel very weak in the eyes and I have a great deal to do before I turn in to bed and tomorrow I shall have to rise early to attend Sunday School, I must come to a conclusion— Best love to yourself and inquiring friends— Write as quickly as you can and direct to Hawkins Wilson care of Methodist Episcopal church, colored, Galveston, Texas— Give me your P. Office and I will write again— I shall drop in upon you some day like a thief in the night.— I bid you a pleasant night's rest with a good appetite for your breakfast and no breakfast to eat— Your loving and affectionate brother—

Hawkins Wilson

6. Spotswood Rice, an Ex-Slave Soldier, Seeks to Protect His Children, 1864

[Benton Barracks Hospital, St. Louis, Mo., September 3, 1864]

My Children   I take my pen in hand to rite you A few lines to let you know that I have not forgot you and that I want to see you as bad as ever   now my Dear Children I want you to be contented with whatever may be your lots   be assured that I will have you if it cost me my life   on the 28th of the mounth. 8 hundred White and 8 hundred blacke solders expects to start up the rivore to Glasgow and above there thats to be jeneraled by a jeneral that will give me both of you   when they Come I expect to be with them and expect to get you both in return.   Dont be uneasy my children   I expect to have you.   If Diggs dont give you up this Government will and I feel confident that I will get you   Your Miss Kaitty said that I tried to steal you   But I'll let her know that god never intended for man to steal his own flesh and blood.   If I had no cofidence in God I could have confidence in her   But as it is If I ever had any Confidence in her I have none now and never expect to have   And I want her to remember if she meets me with ten thousand soldiers she [will?] meet her enemy   I once [*thought*] that I had some respect for them but now my respects is worn out and have no sympathy for Slaveholders.   And as for her cristianantty I expect the Devil has Such in hell   You tell her from me that She is the frist Christian that I ever hard say that aman could Steal his own child especially out of human bondage

You can tell her that she can hold to you as long as she can   I never would expect to ask her again to let you come to me because I know that the devil has got her hot set against that that is write   now my Dear children I am a going to close my letter to you   Give my love to all enquiring friends   tell them all that we are well and want to see them very much and Corra and Mary receive the greater part of it you sefves   and dont think hard of us not sending you any thing   I you father have a plenty for you when I see you   Spott & Noah sends their love to both of you   Oh! My Dear children how I do want to see you

[Spotswood Rice]

[Benton Barracks Hospital, St. Louis, Mo., September 3, 1864]

I received a leteter from Cariline telling me that you say I tried to steal to plunder my child away from you   now I want you to understand that mary is my Child and she is a God given rite of my own and you may hold on to hear as long as you can but I want you to remembor this one thing that the longor you keep my child from me the longor you will have to burn in hell and the qwicer youll get their   for we are now makeing up a bout one thoughsand blacke troops to Come up tharough and wont to come through Glasgow and when we come wo be to Copperhood rabbels and to the Slaveholding rebbels for we dont expect to leave them there root neor branch   but we thinke how ever that we that have Children in the hands of

From Ira Berlin and Leslie S. Rowland, eds., *Families and Freedom: A Documentary History of African-American Kinship in the Civil War Era* (1997), 195–197. Copyright © 1997 by Ira Berlin and Leslie S. Rowland.

you devels we will trie your [vertues?] the day that we enter Glasgow   I want you to understand kittey diggs that where ever you and I meets we are enmays to each orthere   I offered once to pay you forty dollers for my own Child but I am glad now that you did not accept it   Just hold on now as long as you can and the worse it will be for you   you never in you life befor I came down hear did you give Children any thing not eny thing whatever not even a dollers worth of expencs   now you call my children your pro[*per*]ty   not so with me   my Children is my own and I expect to get them and when I get ready to come after mary I will have bout a powrer and autheirty to bring hear away and to exacute vengencens on them that holds my Child   you will then know how to talke to me   I will assure that and you will know how to talk rite too   I want you now to just hold on to hear if you want to   iff your conchosence tells thats the road go that road and what it will brig you to kittey diggs   I have no fears about geting mary out of your hands   this whole Government gives chear to me and you cannot help your self

Spotswood Rice

7. Three Folktales Show How to Cope with Powerlessness, 1860s

Rabbit Teaches Bear a Song

Br'er Rabbit. . . . This rabbit an' Bear goin to see a Miss Reyford's daughter. N'Br'er Rabbit been killin' Miss Reyford's hogs. Miss Reyford didn't know he was killin' her hogs. She said to him, "If you tell me who been killin' my hogs I'll give you my daughter." N' so he said he'd go an' find out. He went to Mr. Bear an' said, "They's some ladies down here an' they're givin' a social. Y'know, you have a wonderful voice, an' they want you to sing a bass solo." So Bear he felt real proud an' he said, "All right." So Rabbit said, "I'm gonna try to train your voice. Now you just listen to me an' do everything I tell you." So Bear said, "All right." So Rabbit said, "Now I'm gonna sing a song. Listen to me. When I say these lines:

> "Who killed Mr. Reyford's hogs,
> Who killed Mr. Reyford's hogs?"

you just sing back:

> "Nobody but me."

So Brer Rabbit started singing:

> "Who killed Mr. Reyford's hogs,
> Who killed Mr. Reyford's hogs?"

The Bear answered back:

> "Nobody but me."

Rabbit said, "That's right, Br'er Bear, that's fine. My, but you got one fine voice." So ol' Bear he felt real good, 'cause Rabbit flatterin' him, tellin' him that his voice

From Langston Hughes and Arna Bontemps, eds., *The Book of Negro Folklore* (New York: Dodd, Mead, 1958), 3, 12, 20–23.

was such a wonderful one. So they went up there to Miss Reyford's party an' pretty soon Rabbit an' Bear commence to sing. Rabbit sang:

> "Who killed Mr. Reyford's hogs,
> Who killed Mr. Reyford's hogs?"

an' Bear sang out:

> "Nobody but me."

The Fox and the Goose

One day a Fox was going down the road and saw a Goose. "Good morning, Goose," he said; and the Goose flew up on a limb and said, "Good-morning, Fox."

Then the Fox said, "You ain't afraid of me, is you? Haven't you heard of the meeting up at the hall the other night?"

"No, Fox. What was that?"

"You haven't heard about all the animals meeting up at the hall! Why, they passed a law that no animal must hurt any other animal. Come down and let me tell you about it. The hawk mustn't catch the chicken, and the dog mustn't chase the rabbit, and the lion mustn't hurt the lamb. No animal must hurt any other animal."

"Is that so!"

"Yes, all live friendly together. Come down, and don't be afraid."

As the Goose was about to fly down, way off in the woods they heard a "Woo-wooh! woo-wooh!" and the Fox looked around.

"Come down, Goose," he said.

And the Dog got closer. "Woo-wooh!"

Then the Fox started to sneak off; and the Goose said, "Fox, you ain't scared of the Dog, is you? Didn't all the animals pass a law at the meeting not to bother each other any more?"

"Yes," replied the Fox as he trotted away quickly, "the animals passed the law; but some of the animals round here ain't got much respec' for the law."

T'appin (Terrapin)

It was famine time an' T'appin had six chillun. Eagle hide behin' cloud an' he went crossed de ocean an' go gittin' de palm oil; got de seed to feed his chillun wid it. T'appin see it, say "hol' on, it har' time. Where you git all dat to feed your t'ree chillun? I got six chillun, can't you show me wha' you git all dat food?" Eagle say, "No, I had to fly 'cross de ocean to git dat." T'appin say, "Well, gimme some o' you wings an' I'll go wid you." Eagle say, "A' right. When shall we go?" T'appin say, "Morrow mornin' by de firs cock crow." So 'morrow came but T'appin didn' wait till mornin'. T'ree 'clock in de mornin' T'appin come in fron' Eagle's house say, "Cuckoo—cuckoo—coo." Eagle say, "Oh, you go home. Lay down. 'Taint day yit." But he kep' on, "Cuckoo—cuckoo—coo." An bless de Lor' Eagle got out, say, "Wha' you do now?" T'appin say, "You put t'ree wings on this side an' t'ree on udda side." Eagle pull out six feathers an' put t'ree on one side an' t'ree on de udda. Say, "Fly, le's see." So T'appin commence to fly. One o' de wings fall out. But T'appin said, "Da's all right, I got de udda wings. Le's go." So dey flew an' flew; but when dey got over de ocean all de eagle wings fell out. T'appin about to fall in de water.

Eagle went out an' ketch him. Put him under his wings. T'appin say, "Gee it stink here." Eagle let him drop in ocean. So he went down, down, down to de underworl'. De king o' de underworl' meet him. He say, "Why you come here? Wha' you doin' here? T'appin say, "King, we in te'bul condition on de earth. We can't git nothin' to eat. I got six chillun an' I can't git nothin' to eat for dem. Eagle he on'y got t'ree an' he go 'cross de ocean an' git all de food he need. Please gimme sumpin' so I kin feed my chillun." King say, "A' right, a' right," so he go an' give T'appin a dipper. He say to T'appin, "Take dis dipper. When you want food for your chillun say:

> Bakon coleh
> Bakon cawbey
> Bakon cawhubo lebe lebe."

So T'appin carry it home an' go to de chillun. He say to dem, "Come here." When dey all come he say:

> Bakon coleh
> Bakon cawbey
> Bakon cawhubo lebe lebe.

Gravy, meat, biscuit, ever'ting in de dipper. Chillun got plenty now. So one time he say to de chillun, "Come here. Dis will make my fortune. I'll sell dis to de King." So he showed de dipper to de King. He say:

> Bakon coleh
> Bakon cawbey
> Bakon cawhubo lebe lebe.

Dey got somet'ing. He feed ev'ryone. So de King went off, he call ev'ryboda. Pretty soon ev'ryboda eatin'. So dey ate an' ate, ev'ryt'ing, meats, fruits, all like dat. So he took his dipper an' went back home. He say, "Come, chillun." He try to feed his chillun; nothin' came. (You got a pencil dere, ain't you?) When it's out it's out. So T'appin say, "Aw right, I'm going back to de King an' git him to fixa dis up." So he went down to de underworl' an' say to de King. "King, wha' de matter? I can't feeda my chilun no mora." So de King say to him, "You take dis cow hide an' when you want somepin' you say:

> Sheet n oun
> n-jacko
> nou o quaako.

So T'appin went off an' he came to cross roads. Den he said de magic:

> Sheet n oun
> n-jacko
> nou o quaako.

De cowhide commence to beat um. It beat, beat. Cowhide said, "Drop, drop." So T'appin droup an' de cowhide stop beatin'. So he went home. He called his chillun in. He gim um de cowhide an' tell dem what to say, den he went out. De chillun say:

> Sheet n oun
> n-jacko
> nou o quaako.

De cowhide beat de chillun. It say, "Drop, drop." Two chillun dead an' de others sick. So T'appin say, "I will go to de King." He calls de King, he call all de people. All de people came. So before he have de cowhide beat, he has a mortar made an' gits in dere an' gits all covered up. Den de King say:

> Sheet n oun
> n-jacko
> nou o quaako.

So de cowhide beat, beat. It beat everyboda, beat de King too. Dat cowhide beat, beat right t'roo de mortar wha' was T'appin an' beat marks on his back, an' da's why you never fin' T'appin in a clean place, on'y under leaves or a log.

8. Two Slave Spirituals Express Values and Hopes

I've Got a Home in the Rock, Don't You See?

I've got a home in the rock,
    don't you see?
I've got a home in the rock,
    don't you see?
Just between the earth and skies,
I behold my Savior's side,
I've got a home in the rock,
    don't you see?
Swing low, chariot, in the east
    don't you see?
Swing low, chariot, in the east
    don't you see?
Let God's people have some peace,
I've got a home in the rock,
    don't you see?

Swing low, chariot, in the west,
    don't you see?
Swing low, chariot, in the west,
    don't you see?
Let God's people have some rest,
I've got a home in the rock,
    don't you see?

Come along, Moses, don't get lost,
    don't you see?
Come along, Moses, don't get lost,
    don't you see?

From *Lyrics of the Afro-American Spiritual: A Documentary Collection* by Erskine Peters, pp. 85, 359–396. Copyright © 1993 by Erskine Peters. Published by Greenwood Press.

Stretch your rod and come across;
I've got a home in the rock,
                    don't you see?

Heard a mighty rumbling in the ground,
                    don't you see,
Heard a mighty rumbling in the ground,
                    don't you see?
Must be Satan passing 'round;
I've got a home in the rock,
                    don't you see?

My God is a Man of War

My God He is a Man—a Man of war,
My God He is a Man—a Man of war,
My God He is a Man—a Man of War,
An' the Lord God is His name.

He tol' Noah to build an ark,
By His Holy plan;
He tol' Moses to lead the children,
From Egypt to the Promised Lan'.

Long befo' the flyin' clouds,
Befo' the heavens above,
Befo' creation ever was made,
He had redeemin' lov.

He made the sun an' moon an' stars,
To rule both day an' night;
He placed them in the firmament,
An' tol' them to give light.

He made the birds of the air,
An' made the earth aroun';
He made the beasts of the field,
An' made the serpents on the groun'.

 # E S S A Y S

In the first essay, University of Maryland historians Ira Berlin and Leslie Rowland argue forcefully that slave kinship networks not only remained strong despite the pressures of the slave system but provided resources for the enslaved to resist the brutality of their enslavement. Rutger's historian Deborah Gray White's essay, focusing on women's roles as slave laborers and nurturers within the household, argues that slave women created strong networks among themselves that enabled them to make a decisive contribution to sustaining the slave community as a whole. Lawrence W. Levine of Berkeley and George Mason University challenges the conventional view of slave trickster tales. The idea that the trickster was the slave, using cunning to overcome the more powerful master, is too simple argues Levine. Many tales designed to socialize children to survive the harshness of slavery exhibit an arbitrary violence and anarchic moral universe that suggests that the trickster figure sometimes is not the slave but the master.

Slave Communities Are Grounded in Family and Kinship

IRA BERLIN AND LESLIE S. ROWLAND

From the beginning of African slavery in mainland North America, black people understood their society in the idiom of kinship. During the long years of bondage, African-American families transmitted African culture from the Old World to the New, socialized the young and succored the old, buffered relations with masters and mistresses, and served as engines of resistance to an oppressive regime. Early on, African-American slaves extended the bonds of kinship beyond the boundaries of individual households, uniting family members who were forced to live apart by the circumstances of their enslavement. The language of kinship expressed a broad range of mutual obligations. Slaves addressed each other as brothers and sisters, uncles and aunts, conferring the status of kin on men and women who were unrelated by blood or marriage. By the middle of the eighteenth century, kinship ideology and practices had extended to the larger African-American community. For most slaves, familial and communal relations were one.

Yet in many respects, the African-American family was the most fragile of institutions. The slave regime of the American South gave slaves little room to develop a family life. Slaves' marriages had no legal standing; their unions were mere couplings whose issue, like the slaves' labor, belonged to their owners. In the eyes of the law, slaves could not be husbands and wives, fathers and mothers. Slave parents had no rights to their children, who—like themselves—were the owner's property. Since the owner's rights were preeminent, slave parents lacked authority to discipline their children or sustain their aged parents. Among slaves, kinship ties were simple fictions that no one need respect, certainly not the slaveowner.

Backed by the power of the state and a monopoly of legal force, slaveowners projected themselves as the fictive fathers and mothers of the slave community. It was the owners—who preferred the titles "master" and "mistress" precisely because of their domestic connotations—rather than their fathers and mothers of birth, to whom slave children were taught to defer and whom they were expected to love. It was the owners who fed, clothed, and sheltered slave children and who established the regulations and articulated the values that would govern their lives. As if to confirm this harsh reality, slaveowners often contradicted and superseded slave parents in matters of disciplining and directing slave children. Indeed, slave children regularly saw slaveholders chastise their parents, a chilling lesson about the source of domestic—as well as plantation—governance and authority.

Often the slaveholders' commitment to their own preeminence took the insidious form of manipulating the slaves' desire for a modicum of domestic security. From the owners' perspective, regular family relations made slaves less rebellious, inasmuch as domestic ties gave them something to protect. No threat was more effective in bringing an unruly slave to heel than the intimation that failure to yield to the owner's wishes would mean sale, separation, and the permanent loss of loved ones. Furthermore, domestic stability appeared to promote the growth of the slave population, adding to the slaveholders' wealth. By allowing slaves to establish family ties, slaveholders strengthened the plantation regime.

Much as slaveowners likened themselves to concerned, even loving parents and found their own interests served by domestic regularity in the slave quarter, they understood that the business of domination was a brutal one. The lash, the paddle, the branding iron, and the stocks were necessities, since slaves continually resisted their rule. Slaveholders also acknowledged that at times they—or at least some of their number—overstepped the bounds needed to gain obedience. Some did so out of anger, some out of lust, and some from the perverse pleasure of brutalizing men and women they considered barely human. While many owners deplored such barbarism and worked to eliminate it, even the fiercest defenders of the slave regime recognized the unfortunate reality.

The slaveholders' interest in encouraging family connections in the quarter was also compromised by decisions to sell or transfer slaves. Such decisions might be the calculated result of a reorganization of plantation production or a hasty response to financial crisis; they might derive from an owner's death or from a determination to punish an intractable slave. Whatever the cause, such transfers—mere property transactions in the plantation account book—inevitably fragmented families.

Few slaves escaped the pain of forcible separation from their kin, especially during the nineteenth century. The spread of cotton cultivation across the Lower South resulted in the removal or sale of some one million slaves from their homes in the seaboard states, deeply disrupting the civilization that black people had established in the aftermath of their forced exodus from Africa. The westward migration tore black families asunder, as households and sometimes whole communities dissolved under the pressure of the cotton revolution. In the older states of the Upper South, few slaves could expect to see their children grow to maturity; in the newer states of the Lower South, many slaves had neither siblings, parents, nor grandparents in residence.

Within the plantation, slaveholders had innumerable means at their disposal to disrupt slaves' domestic life. Rations could be allotted and clothing dispersed in ways that created envy and competition among kin, work could be assigned that left parents no time to tend to infant children, older children could be removed from their parents to labor in the Big House, and parents could be ridiculed and shamed before their children. But perhaps the most detested manifestation of the slaveholders' power was the usurpation of the marriage bed and the sexual violation of young people, particularly young women.

Slavery thus played havoc with the domestic lives of slaves. The inability of parents to protect their children and to provide for loved ones eroded their domestic authority and their capacity to impart their own values to their offspring. In like manner, the slaves' inability to hold—rather than be—property and the resulting absence of a system of legal inheritance denied the slave family a material base and eroded long-term loyalties. The owners' power stunted generational ties within the slave community, as slaves were dealt from master to master and from plantation to plantation like so many cards in a game of chance.

Slaves resisted the reduction of their domestic life to a mere extension of the owner's will, refusing, as best they could, to allow their most intimate and treasured relationships to be hostage to their owner's whim. Like the slaveholders, slaves recognized that the struggle for "mastery" literally began at home and understood that only their ability to govern families of their own would free them from their owner's claim. Thus, in the teeth of the slaveholder's power—and the state's authority, which buttressed that power—slaves entered into conjugal unions, established families, and articulated values that contradicted those of the owners or selectively appropriated the owners' values to their own advantage. Ultimately the slave family became the primary bulwark against the master's rule. It sowed the seeds of the destruction of chattel bondage.

Slaves based their family life on the marriage compact. They courted according to customs of their own choosing and selected partners according to rules of their own making—rarely, for example, marrying first cousins or other close kin, a practice that was common among the slaveholding class. Once married, most slave husbands and wives honored their vows with lifelong fidelity. Their unions were broken more often by death or forcible separation than by desertion or mutual agreement. Within the slave household, husbands and wives played distinct and complementary roles, which—although frequently strained by the realities of chattel bondage and sometimes disrupted by violence—enriched the material and emotional lives of both partners. To supplement the owner's dole, husbands hunted and fished and crafted furniture, shoes, and tools, and wives fashioned their own wares as quilters, weavers, and seamstresses. Together they worked gardens and provision grounds, kept barnyard animals, made pottery, and wove baskets. Sometimes they sold their produce and handicrafts to fellow slaves, to their owners, or to other free people. Slave men and women thus divided some tasks within the household and shared others, creating their own sexual division of labor.

The division of labor within the household was never fixed, however, for the slave family was not a static institution. The roles of men and women within the family changed over time, and differed from place to place, depending on the demands of particular crops, the size of the unit on which slaves resided, the possibility of joint residence, and, of course, the intrusive power of the master and mistress.

Most slave children were born into two-parent households, generally with the help of a slave midwife. The slave community condemned some relationships as illegitimate, although it rarely shamed women who bore children out of wedlock and almost never failed to accept those children. Nonetheless, censure of some relationships affirmed the legitimacy of others and attested to the central function of the slave family. Slave parents—often in direct conflict with their owners—took responsibility for their children from birth. They named them, nurtured them through infancy, guided them through childhood, and led them through the various—and dangerous—rites of passage whereby children became "hands" and took their place in the owners' kitchens, workshops, and fields. By tutoring their children in the complex etiquette necessary to survive in the violent and exploitative world of slavery, slave parents clarified the differences between masters and parents. In passing to manhood or womanhood, slave children became members of both the plantation community and the slave community, but—from their parents' perspective—there could be no doubts as to where loyalty should rest. In this they were remarkably successful: Many slaves named their children after their parents, grandparents, aunts, and uncles; few named them after their owners.

Husbands and wives divided the labor of childrearing among themselves. Much turned on the question of residence, for while many slave husbands and wives shared the same cabin, others—in some places, a majority—belonged to different owners and resided miles apart. But whether parents lived together or not, most of the responsibilities of childrearing fell to mothers. Fathers also played an important role in the lives of slave children, and perhaps to strengthen the more distant tie, children were more often named for their fathers than their mothers.

Still, sale, death, and divided residence limited the ability of husbands and wives to shepherd their progeny to adulthood. To ensure that their children would be raised in accordance with their wishes, slave parents called on other members of their community. Slaves understood that at any time they might be required to assume the role of mother or father, aunt or uncle, for a child to whom they were unconnected by blood or marriage. Children sold from one plantation were generally adopted into the households on another. Such fosterage, moreover, was not limited to long-term separations, but might be initiated as a result of short-term illness or the seasonal absence of a parent. In recognition of the large roles played by fictive kin, slaves invested such men and women with the titles of "aunt" and "uncle," esteemed appellations within the slave quarter. Large-scale fosterage and fictive kinship knit community and household together, making them one.

Slaves nurtured these connections in various ways. Although they could legally hold no property, they nonetheless developed systems of gifting and inheritance, which, like the customs that regulated courtship and mate selection, existed outside the owner's purview and the state's laws. The generational transfer of property was small by any measure—a quilt, a few sticks of furniture, a treasured tool or cooking pot, but often included barnyard animals like chickens and hogs. These tokens not only held enormous emotional value but also gave young people "a start," enabling them to reproduce the household economies that enriched their parents' life.

Slaves recognized that their owners had an interest in maintaining a modicum of family stability on the plantation. They manipulated to their own benefit the slave-owners' belief that regular family relations made for good business. Slaves thus turned the owners' self-interest against them in petitioning to reside with a spouse, to visit an ailing relative, or to celebrate a wedding in the quarter. When they could, they reinforced the slaveowners' understanding that productivity and social peace required that slave family life be undisturbed by meddling from above. They made the point by objecting violently to such interference. Slaveholders came to appreciate that the greatest source of flight and other disorder was the division of families.

Slaves valued their family ties. Marriage was a joyous occasion, as was the birth of a child—which represented renewed hope that the next generation would live to celebrate the "Day of Jubilee" when all would be free at last. Severance of the bonds of kinship was a grievous loss. Slaves reserved their harshest judgment against their owners not for insufficient food, shabby clothing, inadequate shelter, overwork, or even gratuitous violence but for playing havoc with their families. Slaves never forgot the husbands and wives, mothers and fathers, brothers and sisters, and other kin who were sold away. Many slaves carried in their minds detailed genealogies that reached back generations, sometimes to an African root. That familial root, which nurtured people of African descent through the years of bondage, also shaped their vision of a future in freedom.

The slave family reflected the basic contradiction of an institution that defined men and women as property, a contradiction that has divided historians considering slave family life. Reflecting on the legal constraints and the asymmetry of power between master and slave, many have concluded that the slave family was of little consequence. To argue otherwise, they maintain, denies the brutal reality of slavery. Although these scholars concede that some men and women may have tried to create a meaningful domestic life under barbarous conditions, their efforts were doomed to failure. Such heroic struggles might be admired, but to presume that they succeeded was romantic fantasy purveyed by either softheaded sentimentalists or unabashed apologists for southern slavery. Wrapping themselves in the mantle of realism, these historians see the glass as half empty. They emphasize the violent, destructive character of chattel bondage and the damage it inflicted on black people.

For other scholars, the glass was half full. Recognizing the horrific circumstances of slaves' domestic life, these historians are impressed by the dense web of family ties slaves spun and the system of values they created in contradistinction to that of their owners. Reflecting on what slaves created in practice, such historians deny the charges of romanticism or apology. Instead, they claim for themselves the banner of realism, maintaining that actions rather than laws are a better test of historical reality. While not denying the brutality of slavery, these historians measure the slaves' achievement not only by what they did but also by what they did with what they had. To them, the slave family was neither romantic vision nor sentimentalist sop, but the central reality of African-American life.

Was the glass half empty or half full or perhaps both? . . .

Gender Roles and Gender Identity in Slave Communities

DEBORAH GRAY WHITE

In his 1939 study of the black family in America, sociologist E. Franklin Frazier theorized that in slave family and marriage relations, woman played the dominant role. Specifically, Frazier wrote that "the Negro woman as wife or mother was the mistress of her cabin, and, save for the interference of master and overseer, her wishes in regard to mating and family matters were paramount." He also insisted that slavery had schooled the black woman in self-reliance and self-sufficiency and that "neither economic necessity nor tradition had instilled in her the spirit of subordination to masculine authority." The Frazier thesis received support from other social scientists, including historians Kenneth Stampp and Stanley Elkins, both of whom held that slave men had been emasculated and stripped of their paternity rights by slave masters who left control of slave households to slave women. In his

Deborah Gray White, "Female Slaves: Sex Roles and Status in the Antebellum Plantation South," *Journal of Family History,* 8 (Fall 1983), 248–261. Copyright © 1983 by Sage Publications, Inc. Reprinted by permission of Sage Publications, Inc.

infamous 1965 national report, Daniel Patrick Moynihan lent further confirmation to the Frazier thesis when he alleged that the fundamental problem with the modern black family was the "often reversed roles of husband and wife," and then traced the origin of the "problem" back to slavery.

Partly in response to the criticism spawned by the Moynihan Report, historians reanalyzed antebellum source material, and the matriarchy thesis was debunked. For better or worse, said historians Robert Fogel and Stanley Engerman, the "dominant" role in slave society was played by men. Men were dominant, they said, because men occupied all managerial and artisan slots, and because masters recognized the male head of the family group. From historian John Blassingame we learned that by building furnishings and providing extra food for their families, men found indirect ways of gaining status. If a garden plot was to be cultivated, the husband "led" his wife in the family undertaking. After a very thoughtful appraisal of male slave activities, historian Eugene Genovese concluded that "slaves from their own experience had come to value a two-parent, male-centered household, no matter how much difficulty they had in realizing the ideal." Further tipping the scales toward patriarchal slave households, historian Herbert Gutman argued that the belief that matrifocal households prevailed among slaves was a misconception. He demonstrated that children were more likely to be named after their fathers than mothers, and that during the Civil War slave men acted like fathers and husbands by fighting for their freedom and by protecting their wives and children when they were threatened by Union troops or angry slaveholders.

With the reinterpretation of male roles came a revision of female roles. Once considered dominant, slave woman were now characterized as subordinated and sometimes submissive. Fogel and Engerman found proof of their subordinated status in the fact that they were excluded from working in plow gangs and did all of the household chores. Genovese maintained that slave women's "attitude toward housework, especially cooking, and toward their own femininity," belied the conventional wisdom "according to which women unwittingly helped ruin their men by asserting themselves in the home, protecting their children, and assuming other normally masculine responsibilities." Gutman found one Sea Island slave community where the black church imposed a submissive role upon married slave women.

In current interpretations of the contemporary black family the woman's role has not been "feminized" as much as it has been "deemphasized." The stress in studies like those done by Carol Stack and Theodore Kennedy is not on roles per se but on the black family's ability to survive in flexible kinship networks that are viable bulwarks against discrimination and racism. These interpretations also make the point that black kinship patterns are not based exclusively on consanguineous relationships but are also determined by social contacts that sometimes have their basis in economic support.

Clearly then, the pendulum has swung away from the idea that women ruled slave households, and that their dominance during the slave era formed the foundation of the modern day matriarchal black family. But how far should that pendulum swing? This paper suggests that we should tread the road that leads to the patriarchal slave household and the contemporary amorphous black family with great caution. It suggests that, at least in relation to the slave family, too much emphasis has been placed on what men could not do rather than on what women could do and did. What follows is not a comprehensive study of female slavery, but an attempt to reassess Frazier's claim that slave women were self-reliant and self-sufficient through an examination of some of their activities, specifically their work, their control of particular resources, their contribution to their households and their ability to cooperate with each other on a daily basis. Further, this paper will examine some of the implications of these activities, and their probable impact on the slave woman's status in slave society, and the black family.

At the outset a few points must be made about the subject matter and the source material used to research it. Obviously, a study that concentrates solely on females runs the risk of overstating woman's roles and their importance in society. One must therefore keep in mind that this is only one aspect, although a very critical one, of slave family and community life. In addition, what follows is a synthesis of the probable sex role of the average slave woman on plantations with at least twenty slaves. In the process of constructing this synthesis I have taken into account such variables as plantation size, crop, region of the South, and the personal idiosyncrasies of slave masters. Finally, in drawing conclusions about the sex role and status of slave women, I have detailed their activities and analyzed them in terms of what anthropologists know about women who do similar things in analogous settings. I took this approach for two reasons. First information about female slaves cannot be garnered from sources left by slave women because they left few narratives, diaries or letters. The dearth of source material makes it impossible to draw conclusions about the slave woman's feelings. Second, even given the ex-slave interviews, a rich source material for this subject, it is almost impossible to draw conclusions about female slave status from an analysis of their individual personalities. Comments such as that made by the slave woman, Fannie, to her husband Bob, "I don't want no sorry nigger around me," perhaps says something about Fannie, but not about all slave women. Similarly, for every mother who grieved over the sale of her children there was probably a father whose heart was also broken. Here, only the activities of the slave woman will be examined in an effort to discern her status in black society.

Turning first to the work done by slave women, it appears that they did a variety of heavy and dirty labor, work which was also done by men. In 1853, Frederick Olmsted saw South Carolina slaves of both sexes carting manure on their heads to the cotton field where they spread it with their hands between the ridges in which cotton was planted. In Fayetteville, North Carolina, he noticed that women not only hoed and shovelled but they also cut down trees and drew wood. The use of women as lumberjacks occurred quite frequently, especially in the lower South and Southwest, areas which retained a frontier quality during the antebellum era. Solomon Northup, a kidnapped slave, knew women who wielded the ax so perfectly that the largest oak or sycamore fell before their well-directed blows. An Arkansas ex-slave remembered that her mother used to carry logs. On Southwestern plantations women did all kinds of work. In the region of the Bayou Boeuf women were expected to "plough, drag, drive team, clear wild lands, work on the highway," and do any other type of work required of them. In short, full female hands frequently did the same kind of work as male hands.

It is difficult, however, to say how often they did the same kind of field work, and it would be a mistake to say that there was no differentiation of field labor on Southern farms and plantations. The most common form of differentiation was that women hoed while men plowed. Yet, the exceptions to the rule were so numerous as to make a mockery of it. Many men hoed on a regular basis. Similarly, if a field had to be plowed and there were not enough male hands to do it, then it was not unusual for an overseer to command a strong woman to plow. This could happen on a plantation of twenty slaves or a farm of five.

It is likely, however, that women were more often called to do the heavy labor usually assigned to men after their childbearing years. Pregnant women, and sometimes women breastfeeding infants, were usually given less physically demanding work. If, as recent studies indicate, slave women began childbearing when about twenty years of age and had children at approximately two and a half year intervals, at least until age thirty-five, slave women probably spent a considerable amount of time doing tasks which men did not do. Pregnant and nursing women were classified as half-hands or three-quarter hands and such workers did only some of the work that was also done by full hands. For instance, it was not unusual for them to pick cotton or even hoe, work done on a regular basis by both sexes. But frequently, they were assigned to "light work" like raking stubble or pulling weeds, which was often given to children and the elderly.

Slave women might have preferred to be exempt from such labor, but they might also have gained some intangibles from doing the same work as men. Anthropologists have demonstrated that in societies where men and women are engaged in the production of the same kinds of goods and where widespread private property is not a factor, participation in production gives women freedom and independence. Since neither slave men nor women had access to, or control over, the products of their labor, parity in the field may have encouraged equalitarianism in the slave quarters. In Southern Togo, for instance, where women work alongside their husbands in the field because men do not alone produce goods which are highly valued, democracy prevails in relationships between men and women.

But bondswomen did do a lot of traditional "female work" and one has to wonder whether this work, as well as the work done as a "half-hand" tallied on the side of female subordination. In the case of the female slave, domestic work was not always confined to the home, and often "woman's work" required skills that were highly valued and even coveted because of the place it could purchase in the higher social echelons of the slave world. For example, cooking was definitely "female work" but it was also a skilled occupation. Good cooks were highly respected by both blacks and whites, and their occupation was raised in status because the masses of slave women did not cook on a regular basis. Since field work occupied the time of most women, meals were often served communally. Female slaves therefore, were, for the most part, relieved of this traditional chore, and the occupation of "cook" became specialized.

Sewing too was often raised above the level of inferior "woman's work." All females at one time or another had to spin and weave. Occasionally each woman was given cloth and told to make her family's clothes, but this was unusual and more likely to happen on small farms than on plantations. During slack seasons women probably did more sewing than during planting and harvesting seasons, and pregnant women were often put to work spinning, weaving and sewing. Nevertheless, sewing could be raised to the level of a skilled art, especially if a woman sewed well enough to make the white family's clothes. Such women were sometimes hired out and allowed to keep a portion of the profit they brought their master and mistress.

Other occupations which were solidly anchored in the female domain, and which increased a woman's prestige, were midwifery and doctoring. The length of time and extent of training it took to become a midwife is indicated by the testimony of Clara Walker, a former slave interviewed in Arkansas, who remembered that she trained for five years under a doctor who became so lazy after she had mastered the job that he would sit down and let her do all the work. After her "apprenticeship" ended she delivered babies for both slave and free, black and white. Other midwives learned the trade from a female relative, often their mother, and they in turn passed the skill on to another female relative.

A midwife's duty often extended beyond delivering babies, and they sometimes became known as "doctor women." In this capacity they cared for men, women, and children. Old women, some with a history of midwifery and some without, also gained respect as "doctor women." They "knowed a heap about yarbs [herbs]," recalled a Georgia ex-slave. Old women had innumerable cures, especially for children's diseases, and since plantation "nurseries" were usually under their supervision, they had ample opportunity to practice their art. In sum, a good portion of the slave's medical care, particularly that of women and children, was supervised by slave women.

Of course, not all women were hired-out seamstresses, cooks, or midwives; a good deal of "female work" was laborious and mundane. An important aspect of this work, as well as of the field work done by women, was that it was frequently done in female groups. As previously noted, women often hoed while men plowed. In addition, when women sewed they usually did so with other women. Quilts were made by women at gatherings called, naturally enough, "quiltins." Such gatherings were attended only by women and many former slaves had vivid recollections of them. The "quiltin's and spinnin' frolics dat de women folks had" were the most outstanding remembrances of Hattie Anne Nettles, an Alabama ex-slave. Women also gathered, independent of male slaves, on Saturday afternoons to do washing. Said one ex-slave, "they all had a regular picnic of it as they would work and spread the clothes on the bushes and low branches of the tree to dry. They would get to spend the day together."

In addition, when pregnant women did field work they sometimes did it together. On large plantations the group they worked in was sometimes known as the "trash gang." This gang, made up of pregnant women, women with nursing infants, children and old slaves, was primarily a female work gang. Since it was the group that young girls worked with when just being initiated into the work world of the plantation, one must assume that it served some kind of socialization function. Most likely, many lessons about life were learned by twelve-year-old girls from this group of women who were either pregnant or breastfeeding, or who were grandmothers many times over.

It has been noted that women frequently depended on slave midwives to bring children into the world; their dependence on other slave women did not end with childbirth but continued through the early life of their children. Sometimes women with infants took their children to the fields with them. Some worked with their children wrapped to their backs, others laid them under a tree. Frequently, however, an elderly woman watched slave children during the day while their mothers worked in the field. Sometimes the cook supervised young children at the master's house. Mothers who were absent from their children most of the day, indeed most of the week, depended on these surrogate mothers to assist them in child socialization. Many ex-slaves remember these women affectionately. Said one South Carolinian: "De old lady, she looked after every blessed thing for us all day long en cooked for us right along wid de mindin'."

Looking at the work done by female slaves in the antebellum South, therefore, we find that sex role differentiation in field labor was not absolute but that there was differentiation in other kinds of work. Domestic chores were usually done exclusively by women, and certain "professional" occupations were reserved for females. It would be a mistake to infer from this differentiation that it was the basis of male dominance. A less culturally biased conclusion would be that women's roles were different or complementary. For example, in her overview of African societies, Denise Paulme notes that in almost all African societies, women do most of the domestic chores, yet they lead lives that are quite independent of men. Indeed, according to Paulme, in Africa, "a wife's contribution to the needs of the household is direct and indispensable, and her husband is just as much in need of her as she of him." Other anthropologists have suggested that we should not evaluate women's roles in terms of men's roles because in a given society, women may not perceive the world in the same way that men do. In other words, men and women may share a common culture but on different terms, and when this is the case, questions of dominance and subservience are irrelevant. The degree to which male and female ideologies are different is often suggested by the degree to which men and women are independently able to rank and order themselves and cooperate with members of their sex in the performance of their duties. In societies where women are not isolated from one another and placed under a man's authority, where women cooperate in the performance of household tasks, where women form groups or associations, women's roles are usually complementary to those of men, and the female world exists independently of the male world. Because women control what goes on in their world, they rank and order themselves vis à vis other women, not men, and they are able to influence decisions made by their society because they exert pressure as a group. Ethnographic studies of the Igbo women of Eastern Nigeria, the Ga women of Central Accra in Ghana, and the Patani of Southern Nigeria confirm these generalizations. Elements of female slave society—the chores done in and by groups, the intrasex cooperation and dependency in the areas of child care and medical care, the existence of high echelon female slave occupations—may be an indication, not that slave women were inferior to slave men, but that the roles were complementary and that the female slave world allowed women the opportunity to rank and order themselves and obtain a sense of self which was quite apart from the men of their race and even the men of the master class.

That bondswomen were able to rank and order themselves is further suggested by evidence indicating that in the community of the slave quarters certain women were looked to for leadership. Leadership was based on either one or a combination of factors, including occupation, association with the master class, age, or number of children. It was manifested in all aspects of female slave life. For instance, Louis Hughes, an escaped slave, noted that each plantation had a "forewoman who . . . had charge of the female slaves and also the boys and girls from twelve to sixteen years of age, and all the old people that were feeble." Bennett H. Barrow repeatedly lamented the fact that Big Lucy, one of his oldest slaves, had more control over his female slaves then he did: "Anica, Center, Cook Jane, the better you treat them the worse they are. Big Lucy, the Leader, corrupts every young negro in her power." When Elizabeth Botume went to the Sea Islands after the Civil War, she had [as] a house servant a young woman named Amy who performed her tasks slowly and sullenly until Aunt Mary arrived from Beaufort. In Aunt Mary's presence the obstreperous Amy was "quiet, orderly, helpful and painstaking."

Another important feature of female life, bearing on the ability of women to rank and order themselves independently of men, was the control women exercised over each other by quarreling. In all kinds of sources there are indications that women were given to fighting and irritating each other. From Jesse Belflowers, the overseer of the Allston rice plantation in South Carolina, Adele Petigru Allston learned that "mostly mongst the Woman," there was "goodeal of quarling and disputing and telling lies." Harriet Ware, a northern missionary, writing from the Sea Islands in 1863 blamed the turmoil she found in black community life on the "tongues of the women." The evidence of excessive quarreling among women hints at the existence of a gossip network among female slaves. Anthropologists have found gossip to be a principal strategy used by women to control other women as well as men. Significantly, the female gossip network, the means by which community members are praised, shamed, and coerced, is usually found in societies where women are highly dependent on each other and where women work in groups or form female associations.

In summary, when the activities of female slaves are compared to those of women in other societies a clearer picture of the female slave sex role emerges. It seems that slave women were schooled in self-reliance and self-sufficiency but the "self" was more likely the female slave collective than the individual slave woman. On the other hand, if the female world was highly stratified and if women cooperated with each other to a great extent, odds are that the same can be said of men, in which case neither sex can be said to have been dominant or subordinate.

There are other aspects of the female slave's life that suggest that her world was independent of the male slave's and that slave women were rather self-reliant. It has long been recognized that slave women did not derive traditional benefits from the marriage relationship, that there was no property to share and essential needs like food, clothing, and shelter were not provided by slave men. Since in almost all societies where men consistently control women, that control is based on male ownership and distribution of property and/or control of certain culturally valued subsistence goods, these realities of slave life had to contribute to female slave self-sufficiency and independence from slave men. The practice of "marrying abroad," having a spouse on a different plantation, could only have reinforced this tendency, for as ethnographers have found, when men live apart from women, they cannot control them. We have yet to learn what kind of obligations brothers, uncles, and male cousins fulfilled for their female kin, but it is improbable that wives were controlled by husbands whom they saw only once or twice a week. Indeed "abroad marriages" may have intensified female intradependency.

The fact that marriage did not yield traditional benefits for women, and that "abroad marriages" existed, does not mean that women did not depend on slave men for foodstuffs beyond the weekly rations, but since additional food was not guaranteed, it probably meant that women along with men had to take initiatives in supplementing slave diets. So much has been made of the activities of slave men in this sphere that the role of slave women has been overlooked. Female house slaves, in particular, were especially able to supplement their family's diet. Mary Chesnut's maid Molly made no secret of the fact that she fed her offspring and other slave children in the Confederate politician's house. "Dey gets a little of all dat's going," she once told Chesnut. Frederick Douglass remembered that his grandmother was not only a good nurse but a "capitol hand at catching fish and making the nets she caught them in." Eliza Overton, an ex-slave, remembered how her mother stole, slaughtered, and cooked one of her master's hogs. Another ex-slave was not too bashful to admit that her mother "could hunt good ez any man." Women, as well as men, were sometimes given the opportunity to earn money. Women often sold baskets they had woven, but they also earned money by burning charcoal for blacksmiths and cutting cordwood. Thus, procuring extra provisions for the family was sometimes a male and sometimes a female responsibility, one that probably fostered a self-reliant and independent spirit.

The high degree of female cooperation, the ability of slave women to rank and order themselves, the independence women derived from the absence of property considerations in the conjugal relationship "abroad marriages," and the female slave's ability to provide supplementary foodstuffs are factors which should not be ignored in considerations of the character of the slave family. In fact, they conform to the criteria most anthropologists list for that most misunderstood concept—matrifocality. Matrifocality is a term used to convey the fact that women *in their role as mothers* are the focus of familial relationships. It does not mean that fathers are absent; indeed two-parent households can be matrifocal. Nor does it stress a power relationship where women rule men. When *mothers* become the focal point of family activity, they are just more central than are fathers to a family's continuity and survival as a unit. While there is no set model for matrifocality, Smith has noted that in societies as diverse as Java, Jamaica, and the Igbo of eastern Nigeria, societies recognized as matrifocal, certain elements are constant. Among these elements are female solidarity, particularly in regard to their cooperation within the domestic sphere. Another factor is the economic activity of women which enables them to support their children independent of fathers *if they desire to do so or are forced to do so*. The most important factor is the supremacy of the mother-child bond over all other relationships.

Female solidarity and the "economic" contribution of bondswomen in the form of medical care, foodstuffs, and money has already been discussed; what can be said of the mother-child bond? We know from previous works on slavery that certain slaveholder practices encouraged the primacy of the mother-child relationship. These included the tendency to sell mothers and small children as family units, and to accord special treatment to pregnant and nursing women and women who were exceptionally prolific. We also know that a husband and wife secured themselves somewhat from sale and separation when they had children. Perhaps what has not been emphasized enough is the fact that it was the wife's childbearing and her ability to keep a child alive that were the crucial factors in the security achieved in this way. As such, the insurance against sale which husbands and wives received once women had borne and nurtured children heads the list of female contributions to slave households.

In addition to slaveowner encouragement of close mother-child bonds there are indications that slave women themselves considered this their most important relationship. Much has been made of the fact that slave women were not ostracized by slave society when they had children out of "wedlock." Historians have usually explained this aspect of slave life in the context of slave sexual norms which allowed a good deal of freedom to young unmarried slave women. However, the slave attitude concerning "illegitimacy" might also reveal the importance that women, and slave society as a whole, placed on the mother role and the mother-child dyad. For instance, in the Alabama community studied by Charles S. Johnson in the 1930s, most black women felt no guilt and suffered no loss of status when they bore children out of wedlock. This was also a community in which, according to Johnson, the role of the mother was "of much greater importance than in the more familiar American family group." Similarly, in his 1956 study of the black family in British Guyana, Smith found the mother-child bond to be the strongest in the whole matrix of social relationships, and it was manifested in a lack of condemnation of women who bore children out of legal marriage. If slave women were not ostracized for having children without husbands, it could mean that the mother-child relationship took precedence over the husband-wife relationships.

The mystique which shrouded conception and childbirth is perhaps another indication of the high value slave women placed on motherhood and childbirth. Many female slaves claimed that they were kept ignorant of the details of conception and childbirth. For instance, a female slave interviewed in Nashville, noted that at age twelve or thirteen, she and an older girl went around to parsley beds and hollow logs looking for newborn babies. "They didn't tell you a thing," she said. Another ex-slave testified that her mother told her that doctors brought babies, and another Virginia ex-slave remembered that "people was very particular in them days. They wouldn't let children know anything." This alleged naiveté can perhaps be understood if examined in the context of motherhood as a *rite de passage*. Sociologist Joyce Ladner found that many black girls growing up in a ghetto area of St. Louis in the late 1960s were equally ignorant of the facts concerning conception and childbirth. Their mothers had related only "old wives tales" about sex and childbirth even though the community was one where the mother-child bond took precedence over both the husband-wife bond and the father-child bond. In this St. Louis area, having a child was considered the most important turning point in a black girl's life, a more important *rite de passage* than marriage. Once a female had a child all sorts of privileges were bestowed upon her. That conception and childbirth were cloaked in mystery in antebellum slave society is perhaps an indication of the sacredness of motherhood. When considered in tandem with the slave attitude toward "illegitimacy," the mother-child relationship emerges as the most important familial relationship in the slave family.

Finally, any consideration of the slave's attitude about motherhood and the expectations which the slave community had of childbearing women must consider the slave's African heritage. In many West African tribes the mother-child relationship is and has always been the most important of all human relationships. To cite one of many possible examples, while studying the role of women in Ibo society, Syvia Leith-Ross asked an Ibo woman how many of ten husbands would love their wives and how many of ten sons would love their mothers. The answer she received demonstrated the precedence which the mother-child tie took: "Three husbands would love their wives but seven sons would love their mothers."

When E. Franklin Frazier wrote that slave women were self-reliant and that they were strangers to male slave authority he evoked an image of an overbearing, even brawny woman. In all probability visions of Sapphire danced in our heads as we learned from Frazier that the female slave played the dominant role in courtship, marriage and family relationships, and later from Elkins that male slaves were reduced to childlike dependency on the slave master. Both the Frazier and Elkins theses have been overturned by historians who have found that male slaves were more than just visitors to their wive's cabins, and women something other than unwitting allies in the degradation of their men. Sambo and Sapphire may continue to find refuge in American folklore but they will never again be legitimized by social scientists.

However, beyond the image evoked by Frazier is the stark reality that slave women did not play the traditional female role as it was defined in nineteenth-century America, and regardless of how hard we try to cast her in a subordinate or submissive role in relation to slave men, we will have difficulty reconciling that role with the plantation realities. When we consider the work done by women in groups, the existence of upper echelon female slave jobs, the intradependence of women in childcare and medical care; if we presume that the quarreling or "fighting and disputing" among slave women is evidence of a gossip network and that certain women were elevated by their peers to positions of respect, then what we are confronted with are slave women who are able, within the limits set by slaveowners, to rank and order their female world, women who identified and cooperated more with other slave women than with slave men. There is nothing abnormal about this. It is a feature of many societies around the world, especially where strict sex role differentiation is the rule.

Added to these elements of female interdependence and cooperation were the realities of chattel slavery that decreased the bondsman's leverage over the bondswoman, made female self-reliance a necessity, and encouraged the retention of the African tradition which made the mother-child bond more sacred than the husband-wife bond. To say that this amounted to a matrifocal family is not to say a bad word. It is not to say that it precluded male-female cooperation, or mutual respect, or traditional romance and courtship. It does, however, help to explain how African-American men and women survived chattel slavery.

The Slaves' World-View Revealed in Their Stories

LAWRENCE W. LEVINE

For the historian interested in slave culture, the use of folk tales parallels that of songs and folk beliefs. Although few black tales were collected until the decades following the Civil War, their distribution was so widespread throughout the South, their content so similar, and their style and function so uniform that it is evident they

Lawrence W. Levine, *Black Culture and Black Consciousness: Afro-American Folk Thought from Slavery to Freedom.* Copyright © 1977 Oxford University Press, Inc. Used by permission of Oxford University Press, Inc.

were not a sudden post-emancipation creation. "All over the South the stories of Br'er Rabbit are told," Octave Thanet reported in 1892. "Everywhere not only ideas and plots are repeated, but the very words often are the same; one gets a new vision of the power of oral tradition." The variations in patterns of mobility, educational and vocational opportunities, cultural expression, and life styles brought about by emancipation produced inevitable changes in black folklore. . . . Still, throughout the remainder of the nineteenth century—and well into the twentieth—the large body of slave tales remained a vital and central core of Afro-American expression.

As with other aspects of their verbal art, slaves established in their tales important points of continuity with their African past. This is not to say that slave tales in the United States were necessarily African. Scholars will need more complete indices of African tale types and motifs than now exist before they can determine the origin of slave tales with any definitiveness. Comparison of slave tales with those guides to African tales that do exist reveals that a significant number were brought directly from Africa; a roughly similar percentage were tales common in both Africa and Europe, so that, while slaves may have brought the tale type with them, its place in their lore could well have been reinforced by their contact with whites; and, finally, a third group of tales were learned in the New World both through Euro-American influence and through independent creation.

Unfortunately, extended debate concerning the exact point of origin of these tales has taken precedence over analysis of their meaning and function. Cultural continuities with Africa were not dependent upon importation and perpetuation of specific folk tales in their pristine form. It was in the place that tales occupied in the lives of the slaves, the meaning slaves derived from them, and the ways in which slaves used them culturally and psychically that the clearest resemblances with their African past could be found. Thus, although Africans brought to the New World were inevitably influenced by the tales they found there and frequently adopted white tale plots, motifs, and characters, what is most important is not the mere fact of these borrowings but their nature. Afro-American slaves did not borrow indiscriminately from the whites among whom they lived. A careful study of their folklore reveals that they tended to be most influenced by those patterns of Euro-American tales which in terms of functional meaning and aesthetic appeal had the greatest similarity to the tales with deep roots in their ancestral homeland. Regardless of where slave tales came from, the essential point is that, with respect to language, delivery, details of characterization, and plot, slaves quickly made them their own and through them revealed much about themselves and their world. . . .

Although the range of slave tales was narrow in neither content nor focus, it is not surprising or accidental that the tales most easily and abundantly collected in Africa and among Afro-Americans in the New World were animal trickster tales. Because of their overwhelmingly paradigmatic character, animal tales were, of all the narratives of social protest or psychological release, among the easiest to relate both within and especially outside the group.

The propensity of Africans to utilize their folklore quite consciously to gain psychological release from the inhibitions of their society and their situation . . . needs to be reiterated here if the popularity and function of animal trickster tales is to be understood. After listening to a series of Ashanti stories that included rather elaborate imitations of afflicted people—an old woman dressed in rags and covered with sores, a leper, an old man suffering from the skin disease yaws—which called forth roars of laughter from the audience, the English anthropologist R. S. Rattray suggested that it was unkind to ridicule such subjects. "The person addressed replied that in everyday life no one might do so, however great the inclination to laugh might be. He went on to explain that it was so with many other things: the cheating and tricks of priests, the rascality of a chief—things about which every one knew, but concerning which one might not ordinarily speak in public. These occasions gave every one an opportunity of talking about and laughing at such things; it was 'good' for every one concerned, he said." Customs such as these led Rattray to conclude "beyond a doubt, that West Africans had discovered for themselves the truth of the psychoanalysts' theory of 'repressions,' and that in these ways they sought an outlet for what might otherwise become a dangerous complex."

Certainly this was at the heart of the popularity of animal trickster tales. Whether it is accurate to assert, as Rattray has done, that the majority of "beast fables" were derived from the practice of substituting the names of animals for the names of real individuals whom it would have been impolitic or dangerous to mention, there can be no question that the animals in these tales were easily recognizable representations of both specific actions and generalized patterns of human behavior. "In the fable," Léopold Senghor has written, "the animal is seldom a totem; it is this or that one whom every one in the village knows well: the stupid or tyrannical or wise and good chief, the young man who makes reparation for injustice. Tales and fables are woven out of everyday occurrences. Yet it is not a question of anecdotes or of 'material from life.' The facts are images and have paradigmatic value." The popularity of these tales in Africa is attested to by the fact that the Akan-speaking peoples of the West Coast gave their folk tales the generic title *Anansesem* (spider stories), after the spider trickster Anansi, whether he appeared in the story or not, and this practice was perpetuated by such New World Afro-American groups as the South American Negroes of Surinam who referred to all their stories, whatever their nature, as *Anansitori,* or the West Indian blacks of Curaçao who called theirs *Cuenta de Nansi.*

For all their importance, animals did not monopolize the trickster role in African tales; tricksters could, and did, assume divine and human form as well. Such divine tricksters as the Dahomean Legba or the Yoruban Eshu and Orunmila did not survive the transplantation of Africans to the United States and the slaves' adaptation to Christian religious forms. Human tricksters, on the other hand, played an important role in the tales of American slaves. By the nineteenth century, however, these human tricksters were so rooted in and reflective of their new culture and social setting that outside of function they bore increasingly little resemblance to their African counterparts. It was in the animal trickster that the most easily perceivable correspondence in form and usage between African and Afro-American tales can be found. In both cases the primary trickster figures of animal tales were weak, relatively powerless creatures who attain their ends through the application of native wit and guile rather than power or authority: the Hare or Rabbit in East Africa, Angola, and parts of Nigeria; the Tortoise among the Yoruba, Ibo, and Edo peoples of Nigeria; the Spider throughout much of West Africa including Ghana, Liberia, and Sierra Leone; Brer Rabbit in the United States.

In their transmutation from their natural state to the world of African and Afro-American tales, the animals inhabiting these tales, though retaining enough of their natural characteristics to be recognizable, were almost thoroughly humanized. The world they lived in, the rules they lived by, the emotions that governed them, the status they craved, the taboos they feared, the prizes they struggled to attain were those of the men and women who lived in this world. The beings that came to life in these stories were so created as to be human enough to be identified with but at the same time exotic enough to allow both storytellers and listeners a latitude and freedom that came only with much more difficulty and daring in tales explicitly concerning human beings.

This latitude was crucial, for the one central feature of almost all trickster tales is their assault upon deeply ingrained and culturally sanctioned values. This of course accounts for the almost universal occurrence of trickster tales, but it has not rendered them universally identical. The values people find constraining and the mechanisms they choose to utilize in their attempts at transcending or negating them are determined by their culture and their situation. "It is very well to speak of 'the trickster,'" Melville and Frances Herskovits have noted, "yet one need but compare the Winnebago trickster [of the North American Indians] . . . with Legba and Yo in Dahomey to find that the specifications for the first by no means fit the second." The same may be said of the slave trickster in relation to the trickster figures of the whites around them. Although animal trickster tales do not seem to have caught a strong hold among American whites during the eighteenth and the first half of the nineteenth century, there were indigenous American tricksters from the tall, spare New Englander Jonathan, whose desire for pecuniary gain knew few moral boundaries, to the rough roguish confidence men of southwestern tales. But the American process that seems to have been most analogous in function to the African trickster tale was not these stories so much as the omnipresent tales of exaggeration. In these tall tales Americans were able to deal with the insecurities produced by forces greater than themselves not by manipulating them, as Africans tended to do, but by overwhelming them through the magnification of the self epitomized in the unrestrained exploits of a Mike Fink or Davy Crockett. "I'm . . . half-horse, half-alligator, a little touched with the snapping turtle; can wade the Mississippi, leap the Ohio, ride upon a streak of lightning, and slip without a scratch down a honey locust; can whip my weight in wildcats, . . . hug a bear too close for comfort, and eat any man opposed to Jackson," the latter would boast.

It is significant that, with the exception of the stories of flying Africans, mythic strategies such as these played almost no role in the lore of nineteenth-century slaves; not until well after emancipation do tales of exaggeration, with their magnification of the individual, begin to assume importance in the folklore of Afro-Americans. Nor did the model of white trickster figures seem to have seriously affected the slaves, whose own tricksters remained in a quite different mold—one much closer to the cultures from which they had come. In large part African trickster tales revolved around the strong patterns of authority so central to African cultures. As interested as they might be in material gains, African trickster figures were more obsessed with manipulating the strong and reversing the normal structure of power and prestige. Afro-American slaves, cast into a far more rigidly fixed and certainly a more alien authority system, could hardly have been expected to neglect a cycle of tales so ideally suited to their needs.

This is not to argue that slaves in the United States continued with little or no alteration the trickster lore of their ancestral home. The divergences were numerous: divine trickster figures disappeared; such important figures as Anansi the spider were at best relegated to the dim background; sizable numbers of European tales and themes found their way into the slave repertory. But we must take care not to make too much of these differences. For instance, the fact that the spider trickster retained its importance and its Twi name, Anansi, among the Afro-Americans of Jamaica, Surinam, and Curaçao, while in the United States Anansi lived only a peripheral existence in such tales as the Aunt Nancy stories of South Carolina and Georgia, has been magnified out of proportion by some students. "The sharp break between African and American tradition," Richard Dorson has written, "occurs at the West Indies, where Anansi the spider dominates hundreds of cantefables, the tales that inclose songs. But no Anansi stories are found in the United States." The decline of the spider trickster in the United States can be explained by many factors from the ecology of the United States, where spiders were less ubiquitous and important than in either Africa or those parts of the New World in which the spider remained a central figure, to the particular admixture of African peoples in the various parts of the Western Hemisphere. Anansi, after all, was but one of many African tricksters and in Africa itself had a limited influence. Indeed, in many parts of South America where aspects of African culture endured overtly with much less alteration than occurred in the United States, Anansi was either nonexistent or marginal.

What is more revealing than the life or death of any given trickster figure is the retention of the trickster tale itself. Despite all of the changes that took place, there persisted the mechanism, so well developed throughout most of Africa, by means of which psychic relief from arbitrary authority could be secured, symbolic assaults upon the powerful could be waged, and important lessons about authority relationships could be imparted. Afro-Americans in the United States were to make extended use of this mechanism throughout their years of servitude.

In its simplest form the slaves' animal trickster tale was a cleanly delineated story free of ambiguity. The strong assault the weak, who fight back with any weapons they have. The animals in these tales have an almost instinctive understanding of each other's habits and foibles. Knowing Rabbit's curiosity and vanity, Wolf constructs a tar-baby and leaves it by the side of the road. At first fascinated by this stranger and then progressively infuriated at its refusal to respond to his friendly salutations, Rabbit strikes at it with his hands, kicks it with his feet, butts it with his head, and becomes thoroughly enmeshed. In the end, however, it is Rabbit whose understanding of his adversary proves to be more profound. Realizing that Wolf will do exactly what he thinks his victim least desires, Rabbit convinces him that of all the ways to die the one he is most afraid of is being thrown into the briar patch, which of course is exactly what Wolf promptly does, allowing Rabbit to escape.

This situation is repeated in tale after tale; the strong attempt to trap the weak but are tricked by them instead. Fox entreats Rooster to come down from his perch, since all the animals have signed a peace treaty and there is no longer any danger: "I don't eat you, you don' boder wid me. Come down! Le's make peace!" Almost convinced by this good news, Rooster is about to descend when he thinks better of it and tests Fox by pretending to see a man and a dog coming down the road. "Don' min' fo' comin' down den," Fox calls out as he runs away. "Dawg ain't got no sense, yer know, an' de man got er gun." Spotting a goat lying on a rock, Lion is about to surprise and kill him when he notices that Goat keeps chewing and chewing although there is nothing there but bare stone. Lion reveals himself and asks Goat what he is eating. Overcoming the momentary paralysis which afflicts most of the weak animals in these tales when they realize they are trapped, Goat saves himself by saying in his most terrifying voice: "Me duh chaw dis rock, an ef you dont leff, wen me done . . . me guine eat you."

At its most elemental, then, the trickster tale consists of a confrontation in which the weak use their wits to evade the strong. Mere escape, however, does not prove to be victory enough, and in a significant number of these tales the weak learn the brutal ways of the more powerful. Fox, taking advantage of Pig's sympathetic nature, gains entrance to his house during a storm by pleading that he is freezing to death. After warming himself by the fire, he acts exactly as Pig's instincts warned him he would. Spotting a pot of peas cooking on the stove, he begins to sing:

> Fox and peas are very good,
> But Pig and peas are better.

Recovering from his initial terror, Pig pretends to hear a pack of hounds, helps Fox hide in a meal barrel, and pours the peas in, scalding Fox to death.

In one tale after another the trickster proves to be as merciless as his stronger opponent. Wolf traps Rabbit in a hollow tree and sets it on fire, but Rabbit escapes through a hole in the back and reappears, thanking Wolf for an excellent meal, explaining that the tree was filled with honey which melted from the heat. Wolf, in his eagerness to enjoy a similar feast, allows himself to be sealed into a tree which has no other opening, and is burned to death. "While eh duh bun, Buh Wolf bague an pray Buh Rabbit fuh leh um come out, but Buh Rabbit wouldnt yeddy [hear] um." The brutality of the trickster in these tales was sometimes troubling ("Buh Rabbit . . . hab er bad heart," the narrator of the last story concluded), but more often it was mitigated by the fact that the strong were the initial aggressors and the weak really had no choice. The characteristic spirit of these tales was one not of moral judgment but of vicarious triumph. Storytellers allowed their audience to share the heartening spectacle of a lion running in terror from a goat or a fox fleeing a rooster; to experience the mocking joy of Brer Rabbit as he scampers away through the briar patch calling back to Wolf, "Dis de place me mammy fotch me up,—dis de place me mammy fotch me up"; to feel the joyful relief of Pig as he turns Fox's song upside down and chants:

> Pigs and peas are very good,
> But Fox and peas are better.

Had self-preservation been the only motive driving the animals in these stories, the trickster tale need never have varied from the forms just considered. But Brer Rabbit and his fellow creatures were too humanized to be content with mere survival. Their needs included all the prizes human beings crave and strive for; wealth, success, prestige, honor, sexual prowess. Brer Rabbit himself summed it up best in the tale for which this section is named:

> De rabbit is de slickest o' all de animals de Lawd ever made. He ain't de biggest, an' he ain't de loudest but he sho' am de slickest. If he gits in trouble he gits out by gittin' somebody else in. Once he fell down a deep well an' did he holler and cry? No siree. He

set up a mighty mighty whistling and a singin', an' when de wolf passes by he heard him an' he stuck his head over an' de rabbit say, "Git 'long 'way f'om here. Dere ain't room fur two. Hit's mighty hot up dere and nice an' cool down here. Don' you git in dat bucket an' come down here." Dat made de wolf all de mo' onrestless and he jumped into the bucket an' as he went down de rabbit come up, an' as dey passed de rabbit he laughed an' he say, "Dis am life; some go up and some go down."

There could be no mistaking the direction in which Rabbit was determined to head. It was in his inexorable drive upward that Rabbit emerged not only as an incomparable defender but also as a supreme manipulator, a role that complicated the simple contours of the tales already referred to.

In the ubiquitous tales of amoral manipulation, the trickster could still be pictured as much on the defensive as he was in the stories which had him battling for his very life against stronger creatures. The significant difference is that now the panoply of his victims included the weak as well as the powerful. Trapped by Mr. Man and hung from a sweet gum tree until he can be cooked, Rabbit is buffeted to and fro by the wind and left to contemplate his bleak future until Brer Squirrel happens along. "This yer my cool air swing," Rabbit informs him. "I taking a fine swing this morning." Squirrel begs a turn and finds his friend surprisingly gracious: "Certainly, Brer Squirrel, you do me proud. Come up here, Brer Squirrel, and give me a hand with this knot." Tying the grateful squirrel securely in the tree, Rabbit leaves him to his pleasure—and his fate. When Mr. Man returns, "he take Brer Squirrel home and cook him for dinner."

It was primarily advancement not preservation that led to the trickster's manipulations, however. Among a slave population whose daily rations were at best rather stark fare and quite often a barely minimal diet, it is not surprising that food proved to be the most common symbol of enhanced status and power. In his never-ending quest for food the trickster was not content with mere acquisition, which he was perfectly capable of on his own; he needed to procure the food through guile from some stronger animal. Easily the most popular tale of this type pictures Rabbit and Wolf as partners in farming a field. They have laid aside a tub of butter for winter provisions, but Rabbit proves unable to wait or to share. Pretending to hear a voice calling him, he leaves his chores and begins to eat the butter. When he returns to the field he informs his partner that his sister has just had a baby and wanted him to name it. "Well w'at you name um?" Wolf asks innocently. "Oh, I name um Buh Start-um," Rabbit replies. Subsequent calls provide the chance for additional assaults on the butter and additional names for the nonexistent babies: "Buh Half-um," "Buh Done-um." After work, Wolf discovers the empty tub and accuses Rabbit, who indignantly denies the theft. Wolf proposes that they both lie in the sun, which will cause the butter to run out of the guilty party. Rabbit agrees readily, and when grease begins to appear on his own face he rubs it onto that of the sleeping wolf. "Look, Buh wolf," he cries, waking his partner, "de buttah melt out on you. Dat prove you eat um." "I guess you been right," Wolf agrees docilely, "I eat um fo' trute." In some versions the animals propose a more hazardous ordeal by fire to discover the guilty party. Rabbit successfully jumps over the flames but some innocent animal—Possum, Terrapin, Bear—falls in and perishes for Rabbit's crime.

In most of these tales the aggrieved animal, realizing he has been tricked, desperately tries to avenge himself by setting careful plans to trap Rabbit, but to no avail.

Unable to outwit Rabbit, his adversaries attempt to learn from him, but here too they fail. Seeing Rabbit carrying a string of fish, Fox asks him where they came from. Rabbit confesses that he stole them from Man by pretending to be ill and begging Man to take him home in his cart which was filled with fish. While riding along, Rabbit explains, he threw the load of fish into the woods and then jumped off to retrieve them. He encourages Fox to try the same tactic, and Fox is beaten to death, as Rabbit knew he would be, since Man is too shrewd to be taken in the same way twice.

And so it goes in story after story. Rabbit cheats Brer Wolf out of his rightful portion of a cow and a hog they kill together. He tricks Brer Fox out of his part of their joint crop year after year "until he starved the fox to death. Then he had all the crop, and all the land too." He leisurely watches all the other animals build a house in which they store their winter provisions and then sneaks in, eats the food, and scares the others, including Lion, away by pretending to be a spirit and calling through a horn in a ghostly voice that he is a "better man den ebber bin yuh befo." He convinces Wolf that they ought to sell their own grandparents for a tub of butter, arranges for his grandparents to escape so that only Wolf's remain to be sold, and once they are bartered for the butter he steals that as well.

The many tales of which these are typical make it clear that what Rabbit craves is not possession but power, and this he acquires not simply by obtaining food but by obtaining it through the manipulation and deprivation of others. It is not often that he meets his match, and then generally at the hands of an animal as weak as himself. Refusing to allow Rabbit to cheat him out of his share of the meat they have just purchased, Partridge samples a small piece of liver and cries out, "Br'er Rabbit, de meat bitter! Oh, 'e bitter, bitter! bitter, bitter! You better not eat de meat," and tricks Rabbit into revealing where he had hidden the rest of the meat. "You is a damn sha'p feller," Partridge tells him. "But I get even wid you." Angry at Frog for inviting all the animals in the forest but him to a fish dinner, Rabbit frightens the guests away and eats all the fish himself. Frog gives another dinner, but this time he is prepared and tricks Rabbit into the water. "You is my master many a day on land, Brer Rabbit," Frog tells him just before killing and eating him, "but I is you master in the water."

It is significant that when these defeats do come, most often it is not brute force but even greater trickery that triumphs. Normally, however, the trickster has more than his share of the food. And of the women as well, for sexual prowess is the other basic sign of prestige in the slaves' tales. Although the primary trickster was occasionally depicted as a female—Ol' Molly Hare in Virginia, Aunt Nancy or Ann Nancy in the few surviving spider stories—in general women played a small role in slave tales. They were not actors in their own right so much as attractive possessions to be fought over. That the women for whom the animals compete are frequently the daughters of the most powerful creatures in the forest makes it evident that the contests are for status as well as pleasure. When Brer Bear promises his daughter to the best whistler in the forest, Rabbit offers to help his only serious competitor, Brer Dog, whistle more sweetly by slitting the corners of his mouth, which in reality makes him incapable of whistling at all. If Rabbit renders his adversaries figuratively impotent in their quest for women, they often retaliate in kind. In the story just related, Dog chases Rabbit, bites off his tail, and nothing more is said about who wins the woman. . . .

In the best known and most symbolically interesting courting tale, Rabbit and Wolf vie for the favors of a woman who is pictured as either equally torn between her two suitors or leaning toward Wolf. Rabbit alters the contest by professing surprise that she could be interested in Wolf, since he is merely Rabbit's riding horse. Hearing of this, Wolf confronts Rabbit, who denies ever saying it and promises to go to the woman and personally refute the libel as soon as he is well enough. Wolf insists he go at once, and the characteristic combination of Rabbit's deceit and Wolf's seemingly endless trust and gullibility allows Rabbit to convince his adversary that he is too sick to go with him unless he can ride on Wolf's back with a saddle and bridle for support. The rest of the story is inevitable. Approaching the woman's house Rabbit tightens the reins, digs a pair of spurs into Wolf, and trots him around crying, "Look here, girl! what I told you? Didn't I say I had Brother Wolf for my riding-horse?" It was in many ways the ultimate secular triumph in slave tales. The weak doesn't merely kill his enemy: he mounts him, humiliates him, reduces him to servility, steals his woman, and, in effect, takes his place.

Mastery through possessing the two paramount symbols of power—food and women—did not prove to be sufficient for Rabbit. He craved something more. Going to God himself, Rabbit begs for enhanced potency in the form of a larger tail, greater wisdom, bigger eyes. In each case God imposes a number of tasks upon Rabbit before his wishes are fulfilled. Rabbit must bring God a bag full of blackbirds, the teeth of a rattlesnake or alligator, a swarm of yellowjackets, the "eyewater" (tears) of a deer. Rabbit accomplishes each task by exploiting the animals' vanity. He tells the blackbirds that they cannot fill the bag and when they immediately prove they can, he traps them. He taunts the snake, "dis pole *swear* say you ain't long as him." When Rattlesnake insists he is, Rabbit ties him to the stick, ostensibly to measure him, kills him, and take his teeth. Invariably Rabbit does what is asked of him but finds God less than pleased. In some tales he is chased out of Heaven. In others God counsels him, "Why Rabbit, ef I was to gi' you long tail aint you see you'd 'stroyed up de whol worl'? Nobawdy couldn' do nuttin wid you!" Most commonly God seemingly complies with Rabbit's request and gives him a bag which he is to open when he returns home. But Rabbit cannot wait, and when he opens the bag prematurely "thirty bull-dawg run out de box, an' bit off Ber Rabbit tail again. An' dis give him a short tail again."

The rabbit, like the slaves who wove tales about him, was forced to make do with what he had. His small tail, his natural portion of intellect—these would have to suffice, and to make them do he resorted to any means at his disposal—means which may have made him morally tainted but which allowed him to survive and even to conquer. In this respect there was a direct relationship between Rabbit and the slaves, a relationship which the earliest collectors and interpreters of these stories understood well. Joel Chandler Harris, as blind as he could be to some of the deeper implications of the tales he heard and retold, was always aware of their utter seriousness. "Well, I tell you dis," Harris had Uncle Remus say, "ef deze yer tales wuz des fun, fun, fun, en giggle, giggle, giggle, I let you know I'd a-done drapt um long ago." From the beginning Harris insisted that the animal fables he was collecting were "thoroughly characteristic of the negro," and commented that "it needs no scientific investigation to show why he selects as his hero the weakest and most harmless of all animals, and brings him out victorious in contests with the bear, the wolf, and the fox."

Harris' interpretations were typical. Abigail Christensen noted in the preface to her important 1892 collection of black tales: "It must be remembered that the Rabbit represents the colored man. He is not as large nor as strong, as swift, as wise, nor as handsome as the elephant, the alligator, the bear, the deer, the serpent, the fox, but he is 'de mos' cunnin' man dat go on fo' leg' and by this cunning he gains success. So the negro, without education or wealth, could only hope to succeed by stratagem." That she was aware of the implications of these strategies was made evident when she remarked of her own collection: "If we believe that the tales of our nurseries are as important factors in forming the characters of our children as the theological dogmas of maturer years, we of the New South cannot wish our children to pore long over these pages, which certainly could not have been approved by Froebel." In that same year Octave Thanet, in an article on Arkansas folklore, concluded, "Br'er Rabbit, indeed, personifies the obscure ideals of the negro race.... Ever since the world began, the weak have been trying to outwit the strong; Br'er Rabbit typifies the revolt of his race. His successes are just the kind of successes that his race have craved."

These analyses of the animal trickster tales have remained standard down to our own day. They have been advanced not merely by interpreters of the tales but by their narrators as well. Prince Baskin, one of Mrs. Christensen's informants, was quite explicit in describing the model for many of his actions:

> You see, Missus, I is small man myself; but I aint nebber 'low no one for to git head o' me. I allers use my sense for help me 'long jes' like Brer Rabbit. 'Fo de wah ol' Marse Heywood mek me he driber on he place, an' so I aint hab for work so hard as de res'; same time I git mo' ration ebery mont' an' mo' shoe when dey share out de cloes at Chris'mus time. Well, dat come from usin' my sense. An' den, when I ben a-courtin' I nebber 'lowed no man to git de benefit ob me in dat. I allers carry off de purties' gal, 'cause, you see, Missus, I know how to play de fiddle an' allers had to go to ebery dance to play de fiddle for dem.

More than half a century later, William Willis Greenleaf of Texas echoed Baskin's admiration: "De kinda tales dat allus suits mah fancy de mo'es' am de tales de ole folks used to tell 'bout de ca'iens on of Brothuh Rabbit. In de early days Ah heerd many an' many a tale 'bout ole Brothuh Rabbit what woke me to de fac' dat hit tecks dis, dat an' t'othuh to figguh life out—dat you hafto use yo' haid fo mo'n a hat rack lack ole Brothuh Rabbit do. Ole Brothuh Rabbit de smaa'tes' thing Ah done evuh run 'crost in mah whole bawn life."

This testimony—and there is a great deal of it—documents the enduring identification between black storytellers and the central trickster figure of their tales. Brer Rabbit's victories became the victories of the slave. This symbolism in slave tales allowed them to outlive slavery itself. So long as the perilous situation and psychic needs of the slave continued to characterize large numbers of freedmen as well, the imagery of the old slave tales remained both aesthetically and functionally satisfying. By ascribing actions to semi-mythical actors, Negroes were able to overcome the external and internal censorship that their hostile surroundings imposed upon them. The white master could believe that the rabbit stories his slaves told were mere figments of a childish imagination, that they were primarily humorous anecdotes depicting the "roaring comedy of animal life." Blacks knew better. The trickster's exploits, which overturned the neat hierarchy of the world in which he was forced to live, became their exploits; the justice he achieved, their justice; the strategies he employed, their strategies. From his adventures they obtained relief; from his triumphs they learned hope.

To deny this interpretation of slave tales would be to ignore much of their central essence. The problem with the notion that slaves completely identified with their animal trickster hero whose exploits were really protest tales in disguise is that it ignores much of the complexity and ambiguity inherent in these tales. This in turn flows from the propensity of scholars to view slavery as basically a relatively simple phenomenon which produced human products conforming to some unitary behavioral pattern. Too frequently slaves emerge from the pages of historians' studies either as docile, accepting beings or as alienated prisoners on the edge of rebellion. But if historians have managed to escape much of the anarchic confusion so endemic in the Peculiar Institution, slaves did not. Slaveholders who considered Afro-Americans to be little more than subhuman chattels converted them to a religion which stressed their humanity and even their divinity. Masters who desired and expected their slaves to act like dependent children also enjoined them to behave like mature, responsible adults, since a work force consisting only of servile infantiles who can make no decisions on their own and can produce only under the impetus of a significant other is a dubious economic resource, and on one level or another both masters and slaves understood this. Whites who considered their black servants to be little more than barbarians, bereft of any culture worth the name, paid a fascinated and flattering attention to their song, their dance, their tales, and their forms of religious exercise. The life of every slave could be altered by the most arbitrary and amoral acts. They could be whipped, sexually assaulted, ripped out of societies in which they had deep roots, and bartered away for pecuniary profit by men and women who were also capable of treating them with kindness and consideration and who professed belief in a moral code which they held up for emulation not only by their children but often by their slaves as well.

It would be surprising if these dualities which marked the slaves' world were not reflected in both the forms and the content of their folk culture. In their religious songs and sermons slaves sought certainty in a world filled with confusion and anarchy; in their supernatural folk beliefs they sought power and control in a world filled with arbitrary forces greater than themselves; and in their tales they sought understanding of a world in which, for better or worse, they were forced to live. All the forms of slave folk culture afforded their creators psychic relief and a sense of mastery. Tales differed from the other forms in that they were more directly didactic in intent and therefore more compellingly and realistically reflective of the irrational and amoral side of the slaves' universe. It is precisely this aspect of the animal trickster tales that has been most grossly neglected.

Although the vicarious nature of slave tales was undeniably one of their salient features, too much stress has been laid on it. These were not merely clever tales of wish-fulfillment through which slaves could escape from the imperatives of their world. They could also be painfully realistic stories which taught the art of surviving and even triumphing in the face of a hostile environment. They underlined the dangers of acting rashly and striking out blindly, as Brer Rabbit did when he assaulted the tar-baby. They pointed out the futility of believing in the sincerity of the strong, as Brer Pig did when he allowed Fox to enter his house. They emphasized the necessity of comprehending the ways of the powerful, for only through such understanding could the weak endure. This lesson especially was repeated end-lessly. In the popular tales featuring a race between a slow animal and a swifter opponent, the former triumphs not through persistence, as does his counterpart in the Aesopian fable of the Tortoise and the Hare, but by outwitting his opponent and capitalizing on his weaknesses and short-sightedness. Terrapin defeats Deer by placing relatives along the route with Terrapin himself stationed by the finish line. The deception is never discovered, since to the arrogant Deer all terrapins "am so much like anurrer you cant tell one from turrer." "I still t'ink Ise de fas'est runner in de worl'," the bewildered Deer complains after the race. "Maybe you air," Terrapin responds, "but I kin head you off wid sense." Rabbit too understands the myopia of the powerful and benefits from Mr. Man's inability to distinguish between the animals by manipulating Fox into taking the punishment for a crime that Rabbit himself commits. "De Ole Man yent bin know de diffunce tween Buh Rabbit an Buh Fox," the storyteller pointed out. "Eh tink all two bin de same animal." For black slaves, whose individuality was so frequently denied by the whites above them, this was a particularly appropriate and valuable message.

In many respects the lessons embodied in the animal trickster tales ran directly counter to those of the moralistic tales [which slaves also told]. Friendship, held up as a positive model in the moralist tales, was pictured as a fragile reed in the trick-ster tales. In the ubiquitous stories in which a trapped Rabbit tricks another animal into taking his place, it never occurs to him simply to ask for help. Nor when he is being pursued by Wolf does Hog even dream of asking Lion for aid. Rather he tricks Lion into killing Wolf by convincing him that the only way to cure his ailing son is to feed him a piece of half-roasted wolf liver. The animals in these stories seldom ask each other for disinterested help. Even more rarely are they caught per-forming acts of altruism—and with good reason. Carrying a string of fish he has just caught, Fox comes upon the prostrate form of Rabbit lying in the middle of the road moaning and asking for a doctor. Fox lays down his fish and hurries off to get help—with predictable results: "Ber Fox los' de fish. An 'Ber Rabbit got de fish an' got better. Dat's de las' of it." Brer Rooster learns the same lesson when he un-selfishly tries to help a starving Hawk and is rewarded by having Hawk devour all of his children.

Throughout these tales the emphasis on the state of perpetual war between the world's creatures revealed the hypocrisy and meaninglessness of their manners and rules. Animals who called each other brother and sister one moment were at each others throats the next. On his way to church one Sunday morning, Rabbit meets Fox and the usual unctuous dialogue begins. "Good-mornin', Ber Rabbit!" Fox sings out. "Good-mornin', Ber Fox!" Rabbit sings back. After a few more pleas-antries, the brotherliness ends as quickly as it had begun and Fox threatens: "Dis is my time, I'm hungry dis mornin'. I'm goin' to ketch you." Assuming the tone of the weak supplicant, Rabbit pleads: "O Ber Fox! leave me off dis mornin'. I will sen' you to a man house where he got a penful of pretty little pig, an' you will get yer brakefus' fill." Fox agrees and is sent to a pen filled not with pigs but hound dogs who pursue and kill him. Reverting to his former Sabbath piety, Rabbit calls after the dogs: "Gawd bless yer soul! dat what enemy get for meddlin' Gawd's people when dey goin' to church." "I was goin' to school all my life," Rabbit mutters to himself as he walks away from the carnage, "an learn every letter in de book but *d*, an' D was death an' death was de en' of Ber Fox."

Such stories leave no doubt that slaves were aware of the need for role playing. But animal tales reveal more than this; they emphasize in brutal detail the irrationality and anarchy that rules Man's universe. In tale after tale violence and duplicity are pictured as existing for their own sake. Rabbit is capable of acts of senseless cruelty performed for no discernible motive. Whenever he comes across an alligator's nest "didn' he jes scratch the aigs out fur pure meaness, an' leave 'em layin' around to spile." In an extremely popular tale Alligator confesses to Rabbit that he doesn't know what trouble is. Rabbit offers to teach him and instructs him to lie down in the broom grass. While Alligator is sleeping in the dry grass, Rabbit sets it on fire all around him and calls out: "Dat's trouble, Brer 'Gator, dat's trouble youse in." Acts like this are an everyday occurrence for Rabbit. He sets Tiger, Elephant, and Panther on fire, provokes Man into burning Wolf to death, participates in the decapitation of Raccoon, causes Fox to chop off his own finger, drowns Wolf and leaves his body for Shark and Alligator to eat, boils Wolf's grandmother to death and tricks Wolf into eating her. These actions often occur for no apparent reason. When a motive is present there is no limit to Rabbit's malice. Nagged by his wife to build a spring house, Rabbit tricks the other animals into digging it by telling them that if they make a dam to hold the water back they will surely find buried gold under the spring bed. They dig eagerly and to Rabbit's surprise actually do find gold. "But Ole Brer Rabbit never lose he head, that he don't, and he just push the rocks out the dam, and let the water on and drown the lastest one of them critters, and then he picks up the gold, and of course Ole Miss Rabbit done get her spring house." It is doubtful, though, that she was able to enjoy it for very long, since in another tale Rabbit coolly sacrifices his wife and little children in order to save himself from Wolf's vengeance.

Other trickster figures manifest the identical amorality. Rabbit himself is taken in by one of them in the popular tale of the Rooster who tucked his head under his wing and explained that he had his wife cut his head off so he could sun it. "An' de rabbit he thought he could play de same trick, so he went home an' tol' his ol' lady to chop his head off. So dat was de las' of his head." All tricksters share an incapacity for forgetting or forgiving. In a North Carolina spider tale, Ann Nancy is caught stealing Buzzard's food and saves herself only by obsequiously comparing her humble lot to Buzzard's magnificence, stressing "how he sail in the clouds while she 'bliged to crawl in the dirt," until he takes pity and sets her free. "But Ann Nancy ain't got no gratitude in her mind; she feel she looked down on by all the creeters, and it sour her mind and temper. She ain't gwine forget anybody what cross her path, no, that she don't, and while she spin her house she just study constant how she gwine get the best of every creeter." In the end she invites Buzzard to dinner and pours a pot of boiling water over his head, "and the poor old man go baldheaded from that day." At that he was lucky. When Rabbit's friend Elephant accidentally steps on Rabbit's nest, killing his children, Rabbit bides his time until he catches Elephant sleeping, stuffs leaves and grass in his eyes, and sets them on fire. Hare, unable to forgive Miss Fox for marrying Terrapin instead of himself, sneaks into her house, kills her, skins her, hangs her body to the ceiling, and smokes her over hickory chips.

The unrelieved violence and brutality of these tales can be accounted for easily enough within the slave-as-trickster, trickster-as-slave thesis. D. H. Lawrence's insight that "one sheds one's sicknesses in books" is particularly applicable here. Slave tales which functioned as the bondsmen's books were a perfect vehicle for the channelization of the slaves' "sicknesses": their otherwise inexpressible angers, their gnawing hatreds, their pent-up frustrations. On one level, then, the animal trickster tales were expressions of the slaves' unrestrained fantasies: the impotent become potent, the brutalized are transformed into brutalizers, the undermen inherit the earth. But so many of these tales picture the trickster in such profoundly ambivalent or negative terms, so many of them are cast in the African mold of not depicting phenomena in hard-and-fast, either-or, good-evil categories, that it is difficult to fully accept Bernard Wolfe's argument that it is invariably "the venomous American slave crouching behind the Rabbit." Once we relax the orthodoxy that the trickster and the slave are necessarily one, other crucial levels of meaning and understanding are revealed.

"You nebber kin trus Buh Rabbit," a black storyteller concluded after explaining how Rabbit cheated Partridge. "Eh all fuh ehself; an ef you listne ter him tale, eh gwine chat you ebry time, an tell de bigges lie dout wink eh yeye." Precisely what many slaves might have said of their white masters. Viewed in this light, trickster tales were a prolonged and telling parody of white society. The animals were frequently almost perfect replicas of whites as slaves saw them. They occasionally worked but more often lived a life filled with leisure-time activities: they fished, hunted, had numerous parties and balls, courted demure women who sat on verandas dressed in white. They mouthed lofty platitudes and professed belief in noble ideals but spent much of their time manipulating, oppressing, enslaving one another. They surrounded themselves with meaningless etiquette, encased themselves in rigid hierarchies, dispensed rewards not to the most deserving but to the most crafty and least scrupulous. Their world was filled with violence, injustice, cruelty. Though they might possess great power, they did not always wield it openly and directly but often with guile and indirection. This last point especially has been neglected; the strong and not merely the weak could function as trickster. Jenny Proctor remembered her Alabama master who was exceedingly stingy and fed his slaves badly: "When he go to sell a slave, he feed that one good for a few days, then when he goes to put 'em up on the auction block he takes a meat skin and greases all around that nigger's mouth and makes 'em look like they been eating plenty meat and such like and was good and strong and able to work." . . .

Slave tales are filled with instances of the strong acting as tricksters: Fox asks Jaybird to pick a bone out of his teeth, and once he is in his mouth, Fox devours him; Buzzard invites eager animals to go for a ride on his back, then drops them to their deaths and eats them; Wolf constructs a tar-baby in which Rabbit almost comes to his end; Elephant, Fox, and Wolf all pretend to be dead in order to throw Rabbit off guard and catch him at their "funerals"; Fox tells Squirrel that he had a brother who could jump from the top of a tall tree right into his arms, and when Squirrel proves he can do the same, Fox eats him. Tales like these, which formed an important part of the slaves' repertory, indicate that the slave could empathize with the tricked as well as the trickster. Again the didactic function of these stories becomes apparent. The slaves' interest was not always in being like the trickster but often in avoiding being like his victims from whose fate they could learn valuable lessons. Although the trickster tales could make a mockery of the values preached by the moralistic tales—friendship, hard work, sincerity—there were also important lines of continuity between the moralistic tales and the trickster stories. Animals were taken in by the trickster most easily when they violated many of the lessons of the moralistic tales: when they were too curious, as Alligator was concerning trouble; too malicious, as Wolf was when he tried to kill Rabbit by the most horrible means possible; too greedy, as Fox and Buzzard were when their hunger for honey led to their deaths; overly proud and arrogant, as Deer was in his race with Terrapin; unable to keep their own counsel, as Fox was when he prematurely blurted out his plans to catch Rabbit; obsessed with a desire to be something other than what they are, as the Buzzard's victims were when they allowed their desire to soar in the air to overcome their caution.

The didacticism of the trickster tales was not confined to tactics and personal attributes. They also had important lessons to teach concerning the nature of the world and of the beings who inhabited it. For Afro-American slaves, as for their African ancestors, the world and those who lived in it were pictured in naturalistic and unsentimental terms. The vanity of human beings, their selfishness, their propensity to do anything and betray anyone for self-preservation, their drive for status and power, their basic insecurity, were all pictured in grim detail. The world was not a rational place in which order and justice prevailed and good was dispensed. The trickster, as Louise Dauner has perceived, often functioned as the eternal "thwarter," the symbol of "the irrational twists of circumstance." His remarkably gullible dupes seldom learned from their experience at his hands any more than human beings learn from experience. There was no more escape from him than there is escape from the irrational in human life. The trickster served as agent of the world's irrationality and as reminder of man's fundamental helplessness. Whenever animals became too bloated with their power or importance or sense of control, the trickster was on hand to remind them of how things really were. No animal escaped these lessons; not Wolf, not Lion, not Elephant, indeed, not the trickster himself. Throughout there is a latent yearning for structure, for justice, for reason, but they are not to be had, in this world at least. If the strong are not to prevail over the weak, neither shall the weak dominate the strong. Their eternal and inconclusive battle served as proof that man is part of a larger order which he scarcely understands and certainly does not control.

If the animal trickster functioned on several different symbolic levels—as black slave, as white master, as irrational force—his adventures were given coherence and continuity by the crucial release they provided and the indispensable lessons they taught. In the exploits of the animal trickster, slaves mirrored in exaggerated terms the experiences of their own lives. . . .

It can be argued that by channelizing the bondsmen's discontent, reducing their anxieties, and siphoning off their anger, slave tales served the master as well as the slave. In a sense of course they did, and the fact that tales and songs were often encouraged by the masters may indicate a gleaning of this fact on their part as well. But in terms of the values they inculcated, the models of action they held up for emulation, the disrespect and even contempt they taught concerning the strong, the psychic barriers they created against the inculcation of many of the white world's values, it would be difficult to maintain that they should be viewed primarily as a means of control. What the tales gave to the masters with one hand they more than took back with the other. They encouraged trickery and guile; they stimulated the search for ways out of the system; they inbred a contempt for the powerful and an admiration for the perseverance and even the wisdom of the undermen; they constituted an intragroup lore which must have intensified feelings of distance from the world of the slaveholder.

. . . The slaves' ready identification with animals in their tales revealed not merely a strategy for disguising their inner emotions from the whites but also a tendency to see themselves as part of a unified world in which Man, beasts, spirits, even inanimate objects, were a natural part of the order of things. Slave tales no less than slave songs or folk beliefs were fashioned within this world view and derived much of their substance and meaning from it. Equally revealing is the similar emphasis both spirituals and tales placed upon the need for the assertion of the weak against the strong and the belief that although the latter may control the earth their power is neither irrevocable nor permanent. This dynamic faith in the possibilities of transcendence and the certainties of change made the expression of a tragic sense as rare among Afro-American slaves as it was among their African ancestors. . . .

Aesthetically, slaves undoubtedly derived great pleasure from all forms of their folk culture. Functionally, however, these divergent levels of expression operated in very different ways and served distinct needs. Viewed in isolation they each reveal only one aspect of the slaves' consciousness. But slaves did not experience or create the various parts of their folk culture in isolation. On any given evening slaves might transcend their temporal situation by singing their sacred songs of hope, attempt to control it by putting into practice one or more of their varied store of folk beliefs, and understand it and its immediate imperatives by reciting some of their tales. All three were essential parts of the slaves' life. Their sum did not add up merely to an instrument which allowed slaves to survive their situation, but more importantly it added up to a cultural *style*. Perhaps at no other point in United States history is the term *Afro-American* a more accurate cultural designation than when it is applied to black Americans in the mid-nineteenth century. The essence of their thought, their world view, their culture, owed much to Africa, but it was not purely African; it was indelibly influenced by the more than two hundred years of contact with whites on American soil, but it was not the product of an abject surrender of all previous cultural standards in favor of embracing those of the white master. This syncretic blend of the old and the new, of the African and the Euro-American, resulted in a style which in its totality was uniquely the slaves' own and defined their expressive culture and their world view at the time of emancipation.

FURTHER READING

Steven E. Brown, "Sexuality and the Slave Community," *Phylon,* 42 (1981), 1–10.
Margaret Washington Creel, *A Peculiar People: Slave Religion and Community-Culture Among the Gullahs* (1988).

Angela Davis, "Reflections on the Black Woman's Role in the Community of Slaves," *Black Scholar,* 3 (1971), 2–15.

Sharla Fett, " 'It's a Spirit in Me': Spiritual Power and the Healing Work of African American Women in Slavery," in Susan Juster and Lisa MacFarlane, eds., *A Mighty Baptism: Race, Gender, and the Creation of American Protestantism* (1996).

Elizabeth Fox-Genovese, *Within the Plantation Household: Black and White Women in the Old South* (1988).

Herbert G. Gutman, *The Black Family in Slavery and Freedom, 1750–1925* (1975).

Peter Kolchin, "Reevaluating the Antebellum Slave Community: A Comparative Perspective," *Journal of American History,* 1983, 70 (3): 579–601.

Paul Lachance, "Use and Misuse of the Slave Community Paradigm," *Canadian Review of American Studies* [Canada], 17 (1986), 449–458.

Anne Patton Malone, *Sweet Chariot: Slave Family and Household Structure in Nineteenth-Century Louisiana* (1992).

Michael Mullin, *Africa in America: Slave Acculturation and Resistance in the American South and the British Caribbean, 1736–1831* (1992).

John T. O'Brien, "Factory, Church, and Community: Blacks in Antebellum Richmond," *Journal of Southern History,* 44 (November 1978), 509–536.

Stephanie J. Shaw, "Mothering Under Slavery in the Antebellum South," in Evelyn Nakano Glenn, ed., *Mothering: Ideology, Experience, and Agency* (1994).

Brenda E. Stevenson, *Life in Black & White: Family and Community in the Slave South* (1996).

Sterling Stuckey, *Slave Culture: Nationalist Theory and the Foundations of Black America* (1987).

Thomas L. Webber, *Deep like the Rivers: Education in the Slave Quarter Community, 1831–1865* (1978).

Deborah Gray White, *Ar'n't I a Woman? Female Slaves in the Plantation South* (1985).

John White, "Veiled Testimony: Negro Spirituals and the Slave Experience," *Journal of American Studies* [Great Britain], 17 (1983), 251–263.

David K. Wiggins, "The Play of Slave Children in the Plantation Community of the Old South, 1820–1860," in N. Ray Hiner and Joseph M. Hawes, eds., *Growing Up in America: Childhood in Historical Perspective* (1985).

CHAPTER
8

Free Blacks Confront the "Slave Power": The Meaning of Freedom in a Slave Society

Being a free Negro in a society organized to support racial slavery was an anomalous status, in the North as well as in the South. Free blacks were legally free but not accorded full civil rights and freedom of movement. They were natives of American soil but not fully accepted as American citizens. The fact that most black people were held in bondage and that bondage was defended as their "natural" condition undercut any claims to respect or equal treatment that blacks who were legally free might make. These anomalies produced tensions and conflicts within northern free black communities.

Racially yoked to their enslaved brothers and sisters, free blacks alternated between struggles to abolish slavery and the impulse to emigrate to a more hospitable place. Some sought to merge the two responses, seeing redemption for the race and the possible economic destruction of slavery in whatever success African-American emigrants to Africa might have in building a modern civilization. Others rejected this course as a betrayal of an American destiny for African Americans as well as of the members of their race who were still enslaved. As the prospects for abolishing slavery through either Garrisonian "moral suasion" or political and legal measures grew bleak in the 1850s, northern free blacks grew more impatient with the pace of change and more open to taking violent steps to free their enslaved brethren, especially those who were fugitives in the North.

Despite the oppression they faced, free blacks managed to build viable communities and institutions, such as newspapers, churches, and mutual aid societies. Some of them accumulated considerable wealth, property, and education. Most devoted their energies and fortunes to the abolitionist cause and to "uplifting" the race. Many also identified with and supported the other progressive reform movements of their era, including women's rights, temperance, and the moral improvement of civil society. In their speeches and behavior began a tradition that would reach well into the twentieth century: the idea that the moral respectability, noteworthy achievements, and material success of each individual member of the race enhanced the opportunities and recognition accorded to all members of the race.

D O C U M E N T S

The first document is excerpted from the famous speech by a free black abolitionist, Henry Highland Garnet, challenging the pacifist tradition of the Garrisonian wing of the movement; he calls on slaves to resist their masters. The second document reflects a schism among northern free blacks; Frederick Douglass strongly challenges the emigration schemes of Garnet and other prominent free black leaders. In the third document Frederick Douglass's daughter, Rosetta, paying homage to her mother, describes the home life of her parents, with the stress and strain Douglass's activism entailed. In the fourth document Charlotte Forten, a young free black woman, makes entries in her personal diary describing her reaction to a celebrated trial and return to slavery from Boston of a fugitive, Anthony Burns. This was one of several cases tried under the Fugitive Slave Act of 1850, to which abolitionists responded by organizing daring rescues to free the defendants. The next document, a militant speech by Frederick Douglass, reflects the growing militancy and impatience among black abolitionists in particular at a moment when all three branches of the federal government seemed adamantly opposed to the antislavery cause. The final document is an account by Richard Winsor, speaking at the fiftieth anniversary celebration of Oberlin College, of the dramatic rescue of John Price, an adolescent fugitive living in the town of Oberlin, Ohio. Interestingly, Winsor, a white English-born graduate of Oberlin, gives no hint of the prominent role black Oberlin students and free black residents of the town played in this rescue. Other evidence shows that the antislavery crowd that gathered at Wellington, the site of the rescue, was mostly black, and twelve of the thirty-seven persons indicted for violating the 1850 Fugitive Slave Act in this case were black, including some future African-American political leaders.

1. Henry Highland Garnet Urges Slaves to Resist, August 1843

Brethren and Fellow Citizens:

Your brethren of the north, east, and west have been accustomed to meet to-gether in National Conventions, to sympathize with each other, and to weep over your unhappy condition. In these meetings we have addressed all classes of the free, but we have never until this time, sent word of consolation and advice to you. We have been contented in sitting still and mourning over your sorrows, earnestly hoping that before this day, your sacred Liberties would have been restored. But, we have hoped in vain. Years have rolled on, and tens of thousands have been borne on streams of blood, and tears, to the shores of eternity. While you have been op-pressed, we have also been partakers with you; nor can we be free while you are enslaved. We therefore write to you as being bound with you.

"Speech by Henry Highland Garnet," in *The Black Abolitionist Papers*, ed. C. Peter Ripley, Jeffrey S. Rossback, associate editor. Chapel Hill: University of North Carolina Press (1985).

Many of you are bound to us, not only by the ties of common humanity, but we are connected by the more tender relations of parents, wives, husbands, children, brothers and sisters, and friends. As such we most affectionately address you.

Slavery has fixed a deep gulf between you and us, and while it shuts out from you the relief and consolation which your friends would willingly render, it afflicts and persecutes you with a fierceness which we might not expect to see in the fiends of hell. . . .

SLAVERY! How much misery is comprehended in that single word. What mind is there that does not shrink from its direful effects! Unless the image of God is obliterated from the soul, all men cherish the love of Liberty. The nice discerning political economist does not regard the sacred right, more than the untutored African who roams in the wilds of Congo. Nor has the one more right to the full enjoyment of his freedom than the other. In every man's mind the good seeds of Liberty are planted, and he who brings his fellow down so low, as to make him contented with a condition of slavery, commits the highest crime against God and man. Brethren, your oppressors aim to do this. They endeavor to make you as much like brutes as possible. When they have blinded the eyes of your mind—when they have embittered the sweet waters of life—when they have shut out the light which shines from the word of God—then, and not till then has American slavery done its perfect work.

TO SUCH DEGREDATION IT IS SINFUL IN THE EXTREME FOR YOU TO MAKE VOLUNTARY SUBMISSION. The divine commandments, you are in duty bound to reverence, and obey. If you do not obey them you will surely meet with the displeasure of the Almighty. He requires you to love him supremely, and your neighbor as yourself—to keep the Sabbath day holy—to search the Scriptures—and bring up your children with respect for his laws, and to worship no other God but him. But slavery sets all these at naught, and hurls defiance in the face of Jehovah. The forlorn condition in which you are placed does not destroy your moral obligation to God. You are not certain of Heaven, because you suffer yourselves to remain in a state of slavery, where you cannot obey the commandments of the Sovereign of the universe. If the ignorance of slavery is a passport to heaven, then it is a blessing, and a curse, and you should rather desire its perpetuity than its abolition. God will not receive slavery, nor ignorance, nor any other state of mind, for love, and obedience to him. Your condition does not absolve you from your moral obligation. The diabolical injustice by which your Liberties are cloven down, NEITHER GOD NOR ANGELS, OR JUST MEN COMMAND YOU TO SUFFER FOR A SINGLE MOMENT. THEREFORE IT IS YOUR SOLEMN AND IMPERATIVE DUTY TO USE EVERY MEANS, BOTH MORAL, INTELLECTUAL, AND PHYSICAL, THAT PROMISE SUCCESS. . . .

Brethren, it is as wrong for your lordly oppressors to keep you in slavery, as it was for the man thief to steal our ancestors from the coast of Africa. You should therefore now use this same manner of resistance, as would have been just in our ancestors, when the bloody footprints of the first remorseless soul thief was placed upon the shores of our fatherland. The humblest peasant is as free in the sight of God, as the proudest monarch that ever swayed a scepter. Liberty is a spirit sent out from God, and like its great Author, is no respecter of persons.

Brethren, the time has come when you must act for yourselves. It is an old and true saying, that "if hereditary bondsmen would be free, they must themselves strike the blow." You can plead your own cause, and do the work of emancipation better than any other. . . . Look around you, and behold the bosoms of your loving wives, heaving with untold agonies! Hear the cries of your poor children! Remember the stripes your fathers bore. Think of the torture and disgrace of your noble mothers. Think of your wretched sisters, loving virtue and purity, as they are driven into concubinage, and are exposed to the unbridled lusts of incarnate devils. Think of the undying glory that hangs around the ancient name of Africa—and forget not that you are native-born American citizens, and as such, you are justly entitled to all the rights that are granted to the freest. Think how many tears you have poured out upon the soil which you have cultivated with unrequited toil, and enriched with your blood; and then go to your lordly enslavers, and tell them plainly, that YOU ARE DETERMINED TO BE FREE. Appeal to their sense of justice, and tell them that they have no more right to oppress you, than you have to enslave them. Entreat them to remove the grievous burdens which they have imposed upon you, and to remunerate you for your labor. Promise them renewed diligence in the cultivation of the soil, if they will render to you an equivalent for your services. Point them to the increase of happiness and prosperity in the British West Indies, since the act of Emancipation. Tell them in language which they cannot misunderstand, of the exceeding sinfulness of slavery, and of a future judgement, and of the righteous retributions of an indignant God. Inform them that all you desire, is FREEDOM, and that nothing else will suffice. Do this, and forever after cease to toil for the heartless tyrants, who give you no other reward but stripes and abuse. If they then commence the work of death, they, and not you, will be responsible for the consequences. You had far better all die—*die immediately*, than live slaves, and entail your wretchedness upon your posterity. If you would be free in this generation, here is your only hope. However much you and all of us may desire it, there is not much hope of Redemption without the shedding of blood. If you must bleed, let it all come at once—rather, *die freemen, than live to be slaves*. It is impossible, like the children of Israel, to make a grand Exodus from the land of bondage. THE PHAROES ARE ON BOTH SIDES OF THE BLOOD-RED WATER! You cannot remove en masse, to the dominions of the British Queen—nor can you pass through Florida, and overrun Texas, and at last find peace in Mexico. The propagators of American slavery are spending their blood and treasure, that they may plant the black flag in the heart of Mexico, and riot in the halls of the Montezumas. . . .

We do not advise you to attempt a revolution with the sword, because it would be INEXPEDIENT. Your numbers are too small, and moreover the rising spirit of the age, and the spirit of the gospel, are opposed to war and bloodshed. But from this moment cease to labor for tyrants who will not remunerate you. Let every slave throughout the land do this, and the days of slavery are numbered. You cannot be more oppressed than you have been—you cannot suffer greater cruelties than you have already. RATHER DIE FREEMEN, THAN LIVE TO BE SLAVES. Remember that you are THREE MILLIONS.

It is in your power so to torment the God-cursed slaveholders, that they will be glad to let you go free. If the scale was turned and black men were the masters, and white men the slaves, every destructive agent and element would be employed to lay the oppressor low. Danger and death would hang over their heads day and night. Yes, the tyrants would meet with plagues more terrible than those of Pharaoh. But you are a patient people. You act as though you were made for the special use of these devils. You act as though your daughters were born to pamper the lusts of your masters and overseers. And worse than all, you tamely submit, while your lords tear your wives from your embraces, and defile them before your eyes. In the name of God we ask, are you men? Where is the blood of your fathers? Has it all run out of your veins? Awake, awake; millions of voices are calling you! Your dead fathers speak to you from their graves. Heaven, as with a voice of thunder, calls on you to arise from the dust.

Let your motto be RESISTANCE! RESISTANCE! RESISTANCE! No oppressed people have ever secured their Liberty without resistance. What kind of resistance you had better make, you must decide by the circumstances that surround you, and according to the suggestion of expediency. Brethren, adieu. Trust in the living God. Labor for the peace of the human race, and remember that you are three millions.

2. Frederick Douglass Opposes Free Black Emigration, September 1851

It is my purpose to occupy but a few moments of the meeting on this subject, as I know you are anxious to hear our other friend (Mr. Scoble) from England.

In listening to the remarks of our friend from Jamaica, I was struck with the similarity of the reasons given by him for the emigration of colored persons from this country, to those which are given, but with very different motives, by the agents of the American Colonization Society—a society which ever has and, I hope, ever will receive the utter detestation of every colored man in the land. I know that our friend (Mr. A[nderson]) will find it difficult to appreciate the reasons which induce the free colored people of these states to insist upon remaining here. He sees us, a suffering people, hemmed in on every side by the malignant and bitter prejudice which excludes us from nearly every profitable employment in this country, and which, as he has well said, has led several of the states to legislate for our expulsion.

In the extremity of our need, he comes to us in the spirit of benevolence, I believe, and holds out to us the prospect of a better country, the prospect of a home, where none shall molest or make us afraid. And he will think it strange that we do not accept of his benevolent proffer, and welcome him in his mission of mercy and good will towards us. And yet we must say that such a welcome cannot be given by the colored people of this country without stabbing their own cause to the vitals, without conceding a point which every black man should feel that he must die for rather than yield, and that is, that the prejudice and the mal-administration toward us in this country are invincible to truth, invincible to combined and virtuous effort for their overthrow. We must make no such concession.

Sir, the slaveholders have long been anxious to get rid of the free colored person of this country. They know that where we are left free, blacks though we are, thick-skulled as they call us, we shall become intelligent, and moreover, that as we become intelligent, in just that proportion shall we become an annoyance to them in their slaveholding. They are anxious therefore to get us out of the country. They

"The Free Negro's Place Is in America: An Address Delivered in Buffalo, New York, on 18 September 1851," in *The Frederick Douglass Papers: Series One, Speeches, Debates and Interviews,* ed. John Blassingame (New Haven: Yale University Press), 2:338–341.

know that a hundred thousand intelligent, upright, industrious and persevering black men in the northern states must command respect and sympathy, must encircle themselves with the regard of a large class of the virtue-loving, industry-loving people of the north, and that whatever sympathy, whatever respect they are able to command must have a reflex influence upon slavery. And, therefore, they say "*out with them,*" let us get rid of them!

For my part, I am not disposed to leave, and, I think, our friend must have been struck with the singular kind of applause at certain sayings of his, during the address—an applause that seemed to come from the galleries, from the door, and from that part of the house that does not wish to be mixed up with the platform. Straws show which way the wind blows (applause). I fancied, too, that when our friend was portraying the blessings that would result from our removal from this land to Jamaica, that delightful visions were floating before the minds of those gentlemen in the distance. (Great applause.)

Now sir, I want to say on behalf of any negroes I have the honor to represent, that we *have* been with, still *are* with you, and *mean* to be with you *to the end.* (Cheers.) It may seem ungrateful, but there are some of us who are resolved that you shall not get rid of your colored relations. (Immense applause.) Why should we not stay with you? Have we not a right here? I know the cry is raised that we are out of our native land, that this land is the land of the white man; that Africa is the home of the negro, and not America.

But how stands the matter? I believe that simultaneously with the landing of the pilgrims, there landed slaves on the shores of this continent, and that for two hundred and thirty years and more we have had a foothold on this continent. We have grown up with you, we have watered your soil with our tears, nourished it with our blood, tilled it with our hard hands. Why should we not stay here? We came when it was a wilderness, and were the pioneers of civilization on this continent. *We* levelled your forests, *our hands* removed the stumps from your fields, and raised the first crops and brought the first produce to your tables. We have been with you, are still with you, have been with you in adversity, and by the help of God will be with you in prosperity. (Repeated applause.)

There was a time when certain learned men of this country undertook to argue us out of existence. Professor *Grant* of New York reckoned us of a race belonging to a by-gone age, which, in the progress of the human family, would become perfectly extinct. Yet we do not die. It does seem that there is a Providence in this matter. Chain us, lash us, hunt us with bloodhounds, surround us with utter insecurity, render our lives never so hard to be borne, and yet we do live on—smile under it all and are able to smile. Amid all our afflictions there is an invincible determination to stay right here, because a large portion of the American people desire to get rid of us. In proportion to the strength of their desire to have us go, in just that proportion is the strength of our determination to stay, and in staying we ask nothing but justice. We have fought for this country, and we only ask to be treated as well as those who fought against it. We are American citizens, and we only ask to be treated as well as you treat aliens. And you will treat us so yet.

Most men assume that we cannot make progress here. It is not true sir. That we can make progress in the future is proved by the progress we have already made. Our condition is rapidly improving. Sir, but a few years ago, if I attempted to ride on the railroad cars in New England, and presumed to take my seat in the cars with white persons, I was dragged out like a beast. I have often been beaten until my hands were blue with the blows in order to make me disengage those hands from the bench on which I was seated. On every railroad in New England this was the case. How is it now? Why, a negro may ride just where he pleases, and there is not the slightest objection raised, and I have very frequently rode over those same roads since, and never received the slightest indignity on account of my complexion.

Indeed the white people are becoming more and more disposed to associate with the blacks. I am constantly annoyed by these pressing attentions. (Great laughter.) I used to enjoy the privilege of an entire seat, and riding a great deal at night, it was quite an advantage to me, but sometime ago, riding up from Geneva, I had curled myself up, and by the time I had got into a good snooze, along came a man and lifted up my blanket. I looked up and said, "pray do not disturb me, I am a black man." (Laughter.) "I don't care who the devil you are, only give me a seat," was the reply. (Roars of laughter.) I tell you the white people about here are beginning "to don't care who the devil you are." If you can put a dollar in their way, or a seat under them, they don't care who the devil you are. But I will not detain you longer, I know you are anxious to hear our friend from England.

3. Rosetta Douglass Desribes Her Father and Mother at Home, 1851–1853

She had brought with her sufficient goods and chattels to fit up comfortably two rooms in her New Bedford home—a feather bed with pillows, bed linens, dishes, knives, forks and spoons, besides a well filled trunk of wearing apparel for herself. She had previously sold one of her feather beds to assist in defraying the expenses of the flight from bondage. The early days in New Bedford were spent in daily toil, the wife at the wash board, the husband with saw, buck and axe. After the day of toil they would seek their little home of two rooms and the meal of the day that was most enjoyable was the supper nicely prepared by mother. Father frequently spoke of the neatly set table with its snowy white cloth—coarse tho' it was.

Father built a nice little cottage in Lynn, Mass., and moved his family there, previously to making his first trip to Europe. It was then that mother with four children struggled to maintain the family amid much that would dampen the courage of many a young woman of to-day. I had been taken to Albany by my father as a means of lightening the burden for mother. Abigail and Lydia Mott, cousins of Lucretia Mott, desired to have the care of me.

During the absence of my father, mother sustained her little family by binding shoes. Mother was a recognized co-worker in the A.S. Societies of Lynn and Boston. There was a weekly gathering of the women to prepare articles for the Annual A.S. Fair held in Faneuil Hall, Boston. At that time mother would spend the week in attendance having charge, in company of a committee of ladies, over

From Dorothy Sterling, ed., *We Are Your Sisters: Black Women in the Nineteenth Century* (New York: Norton, 1984), 133–135, 137. Copyright © 1984 by Dorothy Sterling.

the refreshments. It became the custom of the ladies of the Lynn society for each to take their turn in assisting mother in her household duties on the morning of the day that the sewing circle met so as to be sure of her meeting with them. It was mother's custom to put aside the earnings from a certain number of shoes she had bound as her donation to the A.S. cause. Being frugal and economic she was able to put by a portion of her earnings for a rainy day.

During [my father's] absence abroad, he sent, as he could, support for his family, and on his coming home he supposed there would be some bills to settle. One day while talking over their affairs, mother arose and quietly going to the bureau drawer produced a Bank book containing deposits of her own earnings—and not a debt had been contracted during his absence.

The greatest trial, perhaps, that mother was called upon to endure was the leaving her Massachusetts home for Rochester where father established the "North Star." The atmosphere in which she was placed lacked the genial cordiality that greeted her in Massachusetts. There were only the few that learned to know her, for she drew around herself a certain reserve, after meeting her new acquaintances that forbade any very near approach to her.

She watched with a great deal of interest and no little pride the growth in public life of my father, and in every possible way that she was capable aided him by relieving him of all the management of the home as it increased in size and in its appointments. It was her pleasure to know that when he stood up before an audience that his linen was immaculate and that she had made it so, for, no matter how well the laundry was done for the family, she must with her own hands smooth the tucks in father's linen and when he was on a long journey she would forward at a given point a fresh supply.

Father was mother's honored guest. He was from home so often that his home comings were events that she thought worthy of extra notice. Every thing was done to add to his comfort.

Perhaps no other home receive under its roof a more varied class of people than did our home. From the highest dignitaries to the lowliest person, bond or free, white or black, were welcomed, and mother was equally gracious to all. During her wedded life of forty-five years, she was the same faithful ally, guarding as best she could every interest connected with my father, his lifework and the home.

4. Charlotte Forten Protests the Trial of a Fugitive Slave, 1854

Thursday, May 25, 1854. Did not intend to write this evening, but have just heard of something which is worth recording;—something which must ever rouse in the mind of every true friend of liberty and humanity, feelings of the deepest indignation and sorrow. Another fugitive from bondage has been arrested; a poor man, who for two short months has trod the soil and breathed the air of the "Old Bay

From *A Free Negro in the Slave Era: The Journal of Charlotte L. Forten*, ed. Ray Allen Billington (New York: Collier Books, 1961), 43–46. Copyright ©1953 by The Dryden Press, Inc.

State," was arrested like a criminal in the streets of her capital, and is now kept strictly guarded,—a double police force is required, the military are in readiness; and all this done to prevent a man, whom God has created in his own image, from regaining that freedom with which, he, in common with every other human being, is endowed. I can only hope and pray most earnestly that Boston will not again disgrace herself by sending him back to a bondage worse than death; or rather that she will redeem herself from the disgrace which his arrest alone has brought upon her. . . .

Friday, May 26, 1854.   Had a conversation with Miss [Mary] Shepard about slavery; she is, as I thought, thoroughly opposed to it, but does not agree with me in thinking that the churches and ministers are generally supporters of the infamous system; I believe it firmly. Mr. Barnes, one of the most prominent of the Philadelphia clergy, who does not profess to be an abolitionist, has declared his belief that "the American church is the bulwark of slavery." Words cannot express all that I feel; all that is felt by the friends of Freedom, when thinking of this great obstacle to the removal of slavery from our land. Alas! that it should be so. . . .

Saturday, May 27.   . . . Returned home, read the Anti-Slavery papers, and then went down to the depot to meet father, he had arrived in Boston early in the morning, regretted very much that he had not reached there the evening before to attend the great meeting at Faneuil Hall. He says that the excitement in Boston is very great; the trial of the poor man takes place on Monday. We scarcely dare to think of what may be the result; there seems to be nothing too bad for these Northern tools of slavery to do. . . .

Tuesday, May 30.   Rose very early and was busy until nine o'clock; then, at Mrs. Putnam's urgent request, went to keep store for her while she went to Boston to attend the Anti-Slavery Convention. I was very anxious to go, and will certainly do so to-morrow; the arrest of the alleged fugitive will give additional interest to the meetings, I should think. His trial is still going on and I can scarcely think of anything else; read again to-day as most suitable to my feelings and to the times, "The Run-away Slave at Pilgrim's Point," by Elizabeth B. Browning; how powerfully it is written! how earnestly and touchingly does the writer portray the bitter anguish of the poor fugitive as she thinks over all the wrongs and sufferings that she has endured, and of the sin to which tyrants have driven her but which they alone must answer for! It seems as if no one could read this poem without having his sympathies roused to the utmost in behalf of the oppressed.—After a long conversation with my friends on their return, on this all-absorbing subject, we separated for the night, and I went to bed, weary and sad.

Wednesday, May 31.   . . . Sarah [Remond] and I went to Boston in the morning. Everything was much quieter—outwardly than we expected, but still much real indignation and excitement prevail. We walked past the Court-House, which is now lawlessly converted into a prison, and filled with soldiers, some of whom were looking from the windows, with an air of insolent authority which made my blood boil, while I felt the strongest contempt for their cowardice and servility. We went to the meeting, but the best speakers were absent, engaged in the most arduous and untiring efforts in behalf of the poor fugitive; but though we missed the glowing eloquence of Phillips, Garrison, and Parker, still there were excellent speeches made, and our hearts responded to the exalted sentiments of Truth and Liberty which were uttered. The exciting intelligence which occasionally came in relation to the trial, added fresh zeal to the speakers of whom Stephen Foster and his wife were the principal. The latter addressed, in the most eloquent language, the women present, entreating them to urge their husbands and brothers to action, and also to give their aid on all occasions in our just and holy cause.—I did not see father the whole day; he, of course, was deeply interested in the trial.—Dined at Mr. Garrison's; his wife is one of the loveliest persons I have ever seen, worthy of such a husband. At the table, I watched earnestly the expression of that noble face, as he spoke beautifully in support of the non-resistant principles to which he has kept firm; his is indeed the very highest Christian spirit, to which I cannot hope to reach, however, for I believe in "resistance to tyrants," and would fight for liberty until death. We came home in the evening, and felt sick at heart as we passed through the streets of Boston on our way to the depot, seeing the military as they rode along, ready at any time to prove themselves the minions of the south.

Thursday, June 1st. . . . The trial is over at last; the commissioner's decision will be given to-morrow. We are all in the greatest suspense; what will that decision be? Alas! that any one should have the power to decide the right of a fellow being to himself! It is thought by many that he will be acquitted of the *great crime* of leaving a life of bondage, as the legal evidence is not thought sufficient to convict him. But it is only too probable that they will sacrifice him to propitiate the South, since so many at the North dared oppose the passage of the infamous Nebraska Bill.—Miss Putnam was married this evening. Mr. Frothingham performed the ceremony, and in his prayer alluded touchingly to the events of this week; he afterwards in conversation with the bridegroom, (Mr. Gilliard), spoke in the most feeling manner about this case;—his sympathies are all on the right side. The wedding was a pleasant one; the bride looked very lovely; and we enjoyed ourselves as much as is possible in these exciting times. It is impossible to be happy now.

Friday, June 2. Our worst fears are realized; the decision was against poor Burns, and he has been sent back to a bondage worse, a thousand times worse than death. Even an attempt at rescue was utterly impossible; the prisoner was completely surrounded by soldiers with bayonets fixed, a cannon loaded, ready to be fired at the slightest sign. To-day Massachusetts has again been disgraced; again has she shewed her submission to the Slave Power; and Oh! with what deep sorrow do we think of what will doubtless be the fate of that poor man, when he is again consigned to the horrors of Slavery. With what scorn must that government be regarded, which cowardly assembles thousands of soldiers to satisfy the demands of slaveholders; to deprive of his freedom a man, created in God's own image, whose sole offense is the color of his skin! And if resistance is offered to this outrage, these soldiers are to shoot down American citizens without mercy; and this by the express orders of a government which proudly boasts of being the freeest [sic] in the world; this on the very soil where the Revolution of 1776 began; in sight of the battle-field, where thousands of brave men fought and died in opposing British tyranny, which was nothing compared with the American oppression of to-day. In looking over my diary, I perceive that I did not mention that there was on the Friday night after the man's arrest, an attempt made to rescue him, but although it failed, on account of there not being men enough engaged in it, all honor should be given to those who bravely made the attempt. I can write no more. A cloud seems hanging over me, over all our persecuted race, which nothing can dispel.

5. Frederick Douglass Urges Resistance
to Oppression, 1857

. . . The general sentiment of mankind is that a man who will not fight for himself, when he has the means of doing so, is not worth being fought for by others, and this sentiment is just. For a man who does not value freedom for himself will never value it for others, or put himself to any inconvenience to gain it for others. Such a man, the world says, may lie down until he has sense enough to stand up. It is useless and cruel to put a man on his legs, if the next moment his head is to be brought against a curbstone.

A man of that type will never lay the world under any obligation to him, but will be a moral pauper, a drag on the wheels of society, and if he too be identified with a peculiar variety of the race he will entail disgrace upon his race as well as upon himself. The world in which we live is very accommodating to all sorts of people. It will cooperate with them in any measure which they propose; it will help those who earnestly help themselves, and will hinder those who hinder themselves. It is very polite, and never offers its services unasked. Its favors to individuals are measured by an unerring principle in this—viz., respect those who respect themselves, and despise those who despise themselves. It is not within the power of unaided human nature to persevere in pitying a people who are insensible to their own wrongs and indifferent to the attainment of their own rights. The poet was as true to common sense as to poetry when he said,

Who would be free, themselves must strike the blow.

. . . I know, my friends, that in some quarters the efforts of colored people meet with very little encouragement. We may fight, but we must fight like the Sepoys of India, under white officers. This class of Abolitionists don't like colored celebrations, they don't like colored conventions, they don't like colored antislavery fairs for the support of colored newspapers. They don't like any demonstrations whatever in which colored men take a leading part. They talk of the proud Anglo-Saxon blood as flippantly as those who profess to believe in the natural inferiority of races. Your humble speaker has been branded as an ingrate, because he has ventured to stand up on his own right and to plead our common cause as a colored man, rather than as a Garrisonian. I hold it to be no part of gratitude to allow our white friends to do all the work, while we merely hold their coats. Opposition of the sort now referred to is partisan opposition, and we need not mind it. The white people at large will not largely be influenced by it. They will see and appreciate all honest efforts on our part to improve our condition as a people.

Let me give you a word of the philosophy of reform. The whole history of the progress of human liberty shows that all concessions yet made to her august claims have been born of earnest struggle. The conflict has been exciting, agitating, all-absorbing, and for the time being, putting all other tumults to silence. It must do this or it does nothing. If there is no struggle there is no progress. Those who profess to favor freedom and yet deprecate agitation are men who want crops without plowing

From *The Voice of Black America: Major Speeches by Negroes in the United States* ed. Philip Foner (New York: Simon & Schuster 1972), 198–201.

up the ground; they want rain without thunder and lightning. They want the ocean without the awful roar of its many waters.

This struggle may be a moral one, or it may be a physical one, and it may be both moral and physical, but it must be a struggle. Power concedes nothing without a demand. It never did and it never will. Find out just what any people will quietly submit to and you have found out the exact measure of injustice and wrong which will be imposed upon them, and these will continue till they are resisted with either words or blows, or with both. The limits of tyrants are prescribed by the endurance of those whom they oppress. In the light of these ideas, Negroes will be hunted at the North and held and flogged at the South so long as they submit to those devilish outrages and make no resistance, either moral or physical. Men may not get all they pay for in this world, but they must certainly pay for all they get. If we ever get free from the oppressions and wrongs heaped upon us, we must pay for their removal. We must do this by labor, by suffering, by sacrifice, and if needs be, by our lives and the lives of others.

Hence, my friends, every mother who, like Margaret Garner, plunges a knife into the bosom of her infant to save it from the hell of our Christian slavery, should be held and honored as a benefactress. Every fugitive from slavery who, like the noble William Thomas at Wilkes Barre, prefers to perish in a river made red by his own blood to submission to the hell hounds who were hunting and shooting him should be esteemed as a glorious martyr, worthy to be held in grateful memory by our people. The fugitive Horace, at Mechanicsburgh, Ohio, the other day, who taught the slave catchers from Kentucky that it was safer to arrest white men than to arrest him, did a most excellent service to our cause. Parker and his noble band of fifteen at Christiana, who defended themselves from the kidnapers with prayers and pistols, are entitled to the honor of making the first successful resistance to the Fugitive Slave Bill. But for that resistance, and the rescue of Jerry and Shadrack, the man hunters would have hunted our hills and valleys here with the same freedom with which they now hunt their own dismal swamps.

There was a important lesson in the conduct of that noble Krooman in New York the other day, who, supposing that the American Christians were about to enslave him, betook himself to the masthead and with knife in hand said he would cut his throat before he would be made a slave. Joseph Cinque, on the deck of the *Amistad*, did that which should make his name dear to us. He bore nature's burning protest against slavery. Madison Washington who struck down his oppressor on the deck of the *Creole*, is more worthy to be remembered than the colored man who shot Pitcairn at Bunker Hill.

6. Oberlin Graduate Rev. Richard Winsor Describes the Rescue of a Fugitive Slave, 1858

How John Price was rescued at Wellington has for years been a wonder; but it has often afforded me great pleasure in a distant land to relate the incidents of that hour to many an interested listener.

On the day in which he was kidnapped, hearing a commotion in the square, I made the remark to a friend, "I must see what the matter is."

Richard Winsor, "How John Price Was Rescued," in *The Oberlin Jubilee, 1833–1883*, ed. William Gay Ballantine (Oberlin, Ohio: E. J. Goodrich, 1883), 251–255.

In a moment I was on the spot, and found that John Price, a boy who had been in my little Sabbath-school, was kidnapped. All was commotion; old men and young were ready to start to the rescue.

Two men, whom I knew, were just seating themselves in a buggy. I said, "I go with you," and holding three rifles in my hand, we drove through the crowd of students and citizens who had assembled in the square, and taking off my hat, I said, "I am going to rescue John Price." Immediately shout on shout and cheer on cheer went up from the assembly, and on we went. Some had already set out, taking what weapons they could find, and all hurrying toward Wellington; but our buggy passed everything. That nine miles between Oberlin and Wellington was made in quicker time than the same distance was ever made by me before by horse and buggy.

It was Mrs. Ryder's horse, and she had said, "If necessary, spare not the life of my beast, but rescue the boy."

It was the purpose of the Kentucky kidnappers to reach Wellington to take the five o'clock train that afternoon to go South, in which event we, no doubt, should have lost our prize.

We reached Wellington, and found the kidnappers, with the boy, in the garret of the hotel. An immense crowd was fast gathering, and hundreds of pro-slavery men, willing to show their loyalty to the Fugitive Slave Act of 1850, had gathered at the hotel to protect the man-stealers.

Wishing to enter the hotel, we procured the services of the constable, so as to do it legally, and then Mr. Scrimgeour, our tutor, Mr. Watson and myself, led by the constable, proceeded to enter the hotel; but as I had a rifle in my hand, I was not at first permitted to enter, while the former two were. I told the crowd of men keeping the door that I must and would go in, as I had authority to do it whereupon they said, "No arms can be admitted"; but I said, "Well then, take the rifle, if you choose. I must go." They took the weapon, which they bent over a brick wall. I went into the house and up into the garret, or attic, where the boy was. Troops had been telegraphed for to Cleveland, and the aim of the pro-slavery crowd was to detain us and prevent the few anti-slavery men from getting the boy away before the troops came. But the five o'clock train came in; no troops were there. Watson, Scrimgeour, and the constable left the garret. The two Kentuckians, with drawn pistols, the boy and myself, were left alone, and the door fastened by a rope inside, held by the two men. I found that now some of our students had reached the garret and stood outside the door. I took John Price over to the other end of the room. The two kidnappers presented their pistols, and dared me to touch that boy; but I said I thought I should, and then took him aside and asked him whether he wished to go back home to Oberlin. He said he did. The sun was just setting, and in the light of the rays that fell upon the floor of a closet, I wrote on a slip of paper a line to let the students outside know our position within. I put that note up the sleeve of my coat and went to the door that was held fast and tight by the kidnappers. There was a stone pipe-hole in the wall, and taking a chair near by, I stood upon it, and hearing the voice of Lincoln outside, I said, "Lincoln, give me your hand," and out from my coat-sleeve dropped the note into Lincoln's hand (Lincoln tells me he still has that slip of paper). Immediately the door, by a sudden jerk, came open wide enough to permit the students to thrust in the muzzles of their guns, which kept the door from being closed on their fingers, and then with a united pull the door came wide open. But the two great Kentuckians rushed into the doorway, quite filling the space between the door-posts, and a warm contest in words ensued.

At this juncture, I took the boy, putting his arms around my waist and telling him to keep his head close to my back between my shoulders. I stood beside his captors, and pushing my head and shoulders little by little forward, as if listening to the warm debate, keeping the boy at my back, I gave a sudden lurch, passed out with my prize, went through that crowd down the long flight of stairs into a buggy that was in waiting for me, and was off before they knew I had gone. The boy was taken care of overnight, and soon passed on to far-away friends.

At Oberlin noble hearts were anxiously waiting to learn the result of the hour. "Sim Bushnell" was able to go to one side of the town while I went to the other to relate the glad news that John Price was rescued—the Lord had given success.

After this, followed the imprisonment of many of our good people. While within these prison walls for the eighty-five days, men's hearts were moved, as was my own, when I stood a youth and saw Burns conveyed between a double line of armed soldiers through the city of Boston back to slavery. Every house-top in the line of march, every window, every door-step, was filled with eager spectators, thousands thronged the olden city as oft they were not wont to do.

Then to my young heart State Street became a Roman altar, the sacrifice on which was brightly burning, when from our midst at Oberlin a youth was stolen.

Into that prison, during our stay, there poured a stream of living souls; old man and maiden, mother and son, patriot and statesman, sat in our midst in that upper room, and tears rolled down the cheeks of many a sire as we related the story of the day. From the far West, from the distant North, from Canada, from the East, and even from the South, came thousands to hear and to see for themselves, to sympathize and to become strong in their purposes, more fervent than ever, more resolute to rise up and stand against the great curse of American civilization.

One could not see these thousands of noble men and women visiting us in that prison and notice the deep sadness in which they hung their heads for very shame for America's name without perceiving that hearts were moved in this nation as nothing heretofore had ever moved them, and that patriots were being made ready for the war that was so soon to follow.

Nothing in the history of the country so prepared it to apprehend and to do away with the evil, slavery, as the influence that went forth from that prison to leaven the whole people, and which so prepared them for the great conflict that was to do away for ever with what was called "the right of man in man."

E S S A Y S

In the first essay, Emma Jones Lapansky of Temple University develops a revealing portrait of the successes and vulnerabilities of America's premier antebellum free black community. Principally organized around the Bethel A.M.E. Church and its ancillary institutions, the members of this community achieved individual as well as collective successes that challenged white racial stereotypes, and in turn attracted white racial violence. In the second essay, James and Lois Horton of George Washington University explore the complex problems free black men confronted in trying to achieve respect and recognition in a slave society. Most free black leaders identified with the progressive reform movements of their day, which often embraced ideals of male behavior that eschewed violence. Yet, increasingly, violence seemed the only option not only for destroying slavery but for claiming their own "manhood" rights.

The Roots of Resistance in Free Black Communities

EMMA JONES LAPANSKY

In August 1834, a mob of white Philadelphians launched a massive three-day attack on a nearby black community. This riot, the first in a series of such anti-black incidents in Philadelphia, was finally quelled by some 300 special constables and militia. However, before peace was restored, one black church had been destroyed, another defaced, and scores of black people had been injured, at least one fatally so. The incident, one of many examples of violence in Jacksonian America, attracted attention, both from contemporary reporters and subsequent investigators. While observers often cited general unrest to explain such urban violence, modern historians have had more success in isolating specific community concerns that were potential causes of racial disturbances. They have subjected the riots to close scrutiny. Who were the rioters (by age, occupation, social background, etc.)? How were they organized, how mobilized, how viewed by society, how punished?

Historians who have recently examined patterns of riots and rioters in western society over the last four centuries have reached some generalizations valid for Philadelphia's 1830s anti-black riots. First, they have concluded that the terms "riot" and "mob" carry connotations that are too suggestive of lack of direction and purpose—that often so-called "mob" action is actually a violent statement of a quite specific political objective. Second, these historians have agreed that the rioters often were not simply representing the ideas of a narrow minority but, in fact, felt "legitimate" because they reflected concerns held by a wide section of a community, including not just the "rabble" but rather the "respectable" and even the well-to-do. Third, the riots of the 1830s and 1840s have been represented as the last violent gasp of a western society making a lurching transition from government by unbridled human passion to government of laws administered by "professionals."

Using these generalizations as a beginning point, other investigators have sought to isolate more specifically the dynamics of certain types of disturbances in antebellum American cities. Usually these investigators have followed the formula set forth by David Grimsted on Jacksonian riots: that they had "obvious roots in both the psychology of . . . [their] participants and their socioeconomic situation." In the case of anti-black rioting the analyses have sought to identify the characteristics which separate those individuals who engaged in anti-black mob action from those who did not, and the investigators have generally concluded that certain elements of white society felt "threatened" by free blacks. While the thrust of such investigations is not to be disputed, they usually have paid little attention to the possibility that unique qualities and actions among the riot victims may give us further insight into the dynamics of racial violence. . . .

The Philadelphia black community makes a particularly interesting case study. It was not "typical"; but it was atypical in ways that tended to produce a good deal of measurable evidence of the tension between blacks and whites. The most important

Emma Jones Lapansky, "'Since They Got Those Separate Churches': Afro-Americans and Racism in Jacksonian Philadelphia," *American Quarterly*, 32 (Spring 1980), pp. 54–78. © 1980 The American Studies Association. Reprinted by permission of the John Hopkins University Press.

characteristic of the Philadelphia black community is that it was a visible presence. In 1830 its 15,000 members made it America's largest northern urban black population. Moreover, though this community represented less than 10 percent of the total city population, it reflected a 30 percent increase over the city's black population of 1820. Hence, though the number of blacks in Philadelphia was not large, black and white Philadelphians perceived an ever-increasing number of dark faces in their midst.

The Philadelphia black community was also visible because, compared to other black communities, it was economically well off. This was due partly to the progress of several decades of freedom, partly to Quaker philanthropy, and partly to the in-migration of some exceptionally talented and energetic ex-slaves. An 1838 census concluded that the aggregate wealth of the community was $977,500, or about $270 per household. Even by nineteenth-century standards this did not mean the community was wealthy, but the distribution of that wealth is significant for an understanding of both the internal dynamics of the black community and its relationships with the larger community. While a great majority of black households had no real property and only negligible personal property, the wealthiest tenth of the population controlled 70 percent of the community's wealth. Stated another way, the black community might be seen as some 14,000 poor people juxtaposed to upwards of 1,000 economically "substantial" black citizens. Indeed, a survey published in 1845 listed six Afro-Americans among the city's several dozen wealthiest people. Moreover, two of these wealthy Afro-Americans had inherited their money, and could not be dismissed as self-made *nouveau riche*. For the black community this economic disparity meant that a noticeable minority stood out, economically and socially, from the majority. For the white community it meant the visibility of Afro-Americans who seemed to differ from upper-class or middle-class whites only in the incidental aspect of color.

The black community of Philadelphia was spatially stable and had been so for many years. In the 1790s Bethel African Methodist Episcopal Church had been established at 6th and Lombard Streets. Since then Afro-Americans had increasingly anchored their "turf," setting up a number of institutions—schools, insurance companies, masonic lodges, and several additional churches within a few blocks of Bethel. As early as 1811, a black neighborhood was identifiable at the southern edge of the city, near Bethel Church, and by 1830, this neighborhood, while not devoid of whites, had become more heavily black and was expanding to the west. Though Afro-Americans and their institutions were to be found in all parts of the city and its suburbs, there was, then, an early, clearly defined intellectual, social, and economic focus for the Negro community at the southern edge of the city.

This stability in the black community was enhanced by increasingly cosmopolitan contacts after 1820. Beginning in 1827 with *Freedom's Journal*, America's first black newspaper, black Philadelphia always had a distribution office for the black newspapers, as well as for Garrison's *Liberator* (usually located in the neighborhood near Bethel). In addition to this formal mechanism of communication, informal connections between prominent black Philadelphians and the world outside black Philadelphia were well established and expanding through the 1820s. Francis Johnson, a musician in demand at white "society" parties all over Pennsylvania and New York, was in a position to bring the news and tastes of the outside world home to his fellow black Philadelphians. Likewise, noted black caterers like Robert Boggle had some intimacy with such white Philadelphia power figures as Nicholas Biddle.

Black abolitionists, carrying out their organizing activities, traveled widely and met frequently with their wealthy and powerful patrons. Such people returned to the black community bursting with the news of their travels and of the support of their white friends. Typical was this report by John Bowers of a stopover in a Lancaster, Pennsylvania hotel enroute from an abolitionist meeting in Harrisburg:

> . . . I finished my breakfast . . . I rose and the [white abolitionist] friends in company (which they certainly were) gave the landlord to understand . . . that if I could not sit there, they would not . . . thus proving to the colored men, and to the world, that they were not abolitionists in word, but in deed, and determined to carry out those principles which they profess.

Such contacts of professional service and social reform with the white upper classes brought black Philadelphians comfortable incomes and information about the lives, values, and tastes of white leaders. These contacts also brought access to powerful allies in times of need. On more than one occasion a black individual's personal, medical, or legal crises were eased by the intervention of a powerful white friend.

Many of the characteristics of the Philadelphia black community were apparent in other urban black communities in some measure and combination. In New York, for example, black leaders could draw on the resources of wealthy white abolitionists like the Tappan brothers. What made the Philadelphia community unique was that its size, wealth, stability, and access to resources in the white community were older and more pronounced than in other cities, and that it had a number of wealthy blacks as well as access to wealthy whites. If racial tensions were connected to any of these characteristics, then, these tensions should be evident in Philadelphia. Hence, Philadelphia becomes a laboratory in which to explore the interaction between mechanisms within the antebellum black community and the white communities with which it shared the city. For the white communities in Philadelphia, black people constituted a presence not easily ignored.

To black people their spokesmen had double status: they were prominent in local black affairs, but they were "national" leaders as well. Numerous enough and informed enough to encompass a range of tastes, the black neighborhood at the south of the city had, for example, not one but two masonic lodges and a half-dozen different churches to accommodate the diversity within the black community. All of this added up to a highly visible group of upwardly mobile black people, to be emulated by other blacks, to be carefully and suspiciously watched by groups of whites.

White contemporaries perceive the concerns of Philadelphia blacks in terms of some of their own primary tensions: the pressing problem of economic competition, the emotional issues of "amalgamation" (cross-racial mating) and of blacks' aspirations for upward social mobility, the heightened aggressiveness of blacks in the economic sphere, and the increased belligerence of their social and political style and rhetoric.

On the question of economic competition, the white working-class community was vocal. A commission appointed to investigate the causes of the 1834 riot reported:

> Among the causes which originated the late riots, are two . . . An opinion prevails, especially among white laborers, that certain portions of our community, prefer to employ colored people, whenever they can be had, to the employing of white people;

and that, in consequence of this preference, many whites, who are able and willing to work, are left without employment, while colored people are provided with work, and enabled comfortably to maintain their families; and thus many white laborers, anxious for employment, are kept idle and indigent. Whoever mixed in the crowds and groups, at the late riots, must so often have heard those complaints, as to convince them, that . . . they . . . stimulated many of the most active among the rioters. . . .

Occupational competition was certainly at the top of the list of working-class whites' concerns, but the question of amalgamation was equally important. Nor was this latter a concern only of the working classes. Among upper-class whites, there was some annoyance over the rumor that wealthy black sailmaker James Forten "was ambitious . . . and strove for a respectable platform for [his family]; and to this end it was said of him that he coveted to wed his daughter to a whiter species at some sacrifice to his fortune." Liberal Quakers themselves, while supporting black "progress," were conservative in their estimate of the appropriate limits of social intercourse with blacks.

Reform[er]s concerned with promoting public morality toward black people were joined in their disapproval of racial intermixing by others more interested in protecting the purity of immorality. The publisher of a guide to the city's brothels questioned the limit of decorum in racial taboos:

> . . . There is a brothel occupied by a swarm of yellow girls, who promenade up and down Chestnut Street . . . and strange to say, they meet with more custom [*sic*] than their fairer skinned rivals. . . . There is no accounting for taste, however, and we have no objection to a white man hugging a negro wench to his bosom, providing his stomach is strong enough. . . .

Statements ranging from curiosity to annoyance at the possibilities of "race mixing" were frequent among Philadelphia whites, and one riot, that of 1849, focused on the destruction of a prosperous little tavern, in the neighborhood near Bethel Church, which was owned by a mulatto man and his wife. However, since numerous less prominent but no less interracial bars, gambling houses, and brothels in the neighborhood were left untouched, it is worth speculating that it was, perhaps, intermarriage for the purpose of upward mobility that was abhorred by the riotous whites, and not necessarily amalgamation per se. In any case, "race mixing" in the nineteenth-century city, and its meanings for different groups of whites and blacks, is a subject that bears further inquiry. Job competition and amalgamation were but portions of a larger issue, that of blacks' rising aspirations and designs for upward mobility that threatened to jostle the established social order. Even before the significant anti-black riots of the 1830s, a white Philadelphia historian expressed the widespread resentment against blacks' new values and aspirations:

> In the olden time, dressy blacks and dandy coloured beaux and belles, as we now see them issuing from their proper churches, were quite unknown. Their aspirings and little vanities have been growing since they got those separate churches. Once they submitted to the appellation of servants, blacks, or negroes, but now they require to be called coloured people, and among themselves, their common call of salutation is—gentlemen and ladies.

Ironically, "those separate churches," symbolizing black arrogance to many whites, were the result of whites' own unchristian attitudes toward their black brothers. In the 1790s, Philadelphia blacks had rebelled against segregated seating in racially mixed churches, and withdrew to their own institutions.

With the exception of their masonic lodges (the leadership of which was frequently drawn from the leaders of the church), the black community had developed no other major public arena by 1830. Whereas in the white community church leadership was frequently drawn from among people who were leaders in other spheres, in the black community the separate church had become and remained *the* arena for developing leadership skills.

Furthermore, to fill a vacuum, the churches had expanded their jurisdiction to include political and social, as well as religious concerns. The absence of alternative networks through which leadership might emerge (political, professional, or commercial) meant that this church leadership and its values became synonymous with the values of the entire black community. The church, then, served as both the training ground and the operating base for religious leaders such as Bethel's pastor, Richard Allen, who in turn were seen by many whites and blacks as the black community's secular leaders as well. For white rioters to attack the black church was to strike at the seat of the black community's organizational strength, while simultaneously aiming at one of the symbols of black arrogance.

While this issue of symbols was not as immediate as job competition, it was no less important, and many aspects of the tangible issues cannot be fully understood without also comprehending the importance of such symbols. For example, recent analysis has shown that many anti-black rioters were not in direct economic competition with black workers, that the occupations for which they were trained were ones in which blacks did not participate. Clearly, something more was at work here than simply a matter of white workers being replaced at their jobs by black workers.

Some insight into the hidden agenda in the labor controversy may be drawn from the newspaper passage quoted earlier that describes white frustration that "colored people are . . . enabled comfortably to maintain their families." At issue was not so much specific jobs as the fact that whites were jobless while blacks lived comfortably—that, in fact, sometimes blacks' comfort was had from the income of poorer whites. Thus, it is not surprising that one of the targets of the 1834 rioters, in the early stages of the riot when choice of targets appears to have been most selective, was the son of wealthy black Philadelphian James Forten, owner of a country estate and a carriage—and several rental properties occupied by less well-off whites.

Available evidence of the Philadelphia riots does not provide conclusive proof that the more well-to-do blacks and their property were preferred targets. Nevertheless, certain patterns that emerged lend weight to the argument that this was so. For example, in the 1834 riot many victims were robbed of their valuables—silver, watches, etc.—items which the poor would have been less likely to possess (or to convince authorities that they possessed). An additional indication that the better-off blacks made more appealing targets is to be found in the fact that of the more than three dozen houses destroyed in the second night of this rioting, many were "substantial brick ones," from which fine furniture was thrown into the streets and destroyed, while many more easily destroyed frame houses, owned by blacks in the same streets, were left untouched.

These choices of targets suggest resentment of the "have nots" specifically against the "haves." So too does the casualty of the third night of this rioting. A group of whites, claiming to have been fired upon from a house *near* the black masonic lodge, destroyed the lodge building, citing it as a place where blacks would gather, rather than attacking the *house* from which the alleged shots originated. Similar insight may be drawn from the descriptions of the kinds of people who were assaulted in the 1834 riot. Contemporaries expressed some outrage that the mob attacked "old, confiding and unoffending" blacks. Yet this outrage is more comprehensible if one substitutes the words "middle-aged, respectable, and hardworking" for the description of these victims, one of whom was reportedly a one-time servant of George Washington. It then begins to appear that individuals, groups, and property which represented economic and social "success" and "respectability" were prime targets for rioters' resentments.

It seems also significant that some of the attackers had actually crossed the city, passing other concentrations of Afro-Americans, in order to reach the south end where the greatest concentration, not just of black people, but also of their organizations, was to be found. Equally informative were the continuing complaints that blacks could find work when whites could not, and the repeated reports of blacks being assaulted *at their work.*

The visibility of affluent Negroes, and the resentment of them by struggling whites, was apparent not only in the printed sources of the day, but also in stage and iconographic caricature in which the Philadelphia Negro was portrayed as the prototype of the "uppity nigger." In the late 1820s, a caricaturist, Edward Clay, introduced a series of cartoons entitled "Life in Philadelphia," many of which poked fun at the activities and aspirations of upwardly mobile blacks in the city. Clay, a professional man himself, ignored the doings of the lower-class and working-class blacks, who by far outnumbered the tiny elite which he chose to ridicule. Instead, he concentrated on the attempts of the black upper classes to set themselves apart from the masses, and on their conspicuous consumption of the material goods and social values associated with upper-class whites. He ridiculed their strivings by pointing to their adoption of values of family heritage, their cultivation of music, romance languages, and the arts, and to their tendency to adopt the latest style in dress and furnishings. These caricatures, capturing as they did the essence of black "society" in Philadelphia, were immensely popular both in Philadelphia and in England where they were copied and augmented by other cartoonists over the next several decades.

Conspicuous consumption and other elements of the lifestyle of the class of Philadelphia Afro-Americans represented was a topic of general discussion for both blacks and whites of the day. Whites' comments indeed suggested the reactions expected of a class "threatened" from below: annoyance at the audacity of the lower classes in stepping out of their "places." Typical was this comment from the same historian quoted earlier on the subject of "dressy blacks and dandy coloured beaux":

> As a whole, they show an overwhelming fondness for display and vainglory in processions . . . and in the pomp and pageantry of Masonic . . . societies . . . With the kindest feelings for their race, judicious men wish then wiser conduct. . . .

Typical also is this satire of black social life, published in the Pennsylvania *Gazette*:

> A joke of no ordinary magnitude was enacted last night, by getting up a Coloured Fancy Ball, at the Assembly-Room. . . . Carriages arrived, with *ladies* and *gentlemen* of colour, dressed in "character" in the most grotesque style. . . .
> It is worthy of remark, that many of the coaches containing these sable divinities were attended by white coachmen and *white footmen*. It is indeed high time that some

serious attention was paid to the conduct and pursuits of the class of persons alluded to, and it may be well to inquire if matters progress at this rate how long it will be before masters and servants change places.

Settled securely in the city of 1830, what were the concerns of black leaders? How did they interpret the dynamics of the racist attacks? What did they see as the most effective response to the rising frequency and virulence of such attacks after 1830? Did they passively accept this as the reality of their world? Did they seek simply to escape? Did they launch or consider counterattacks? And, ultimately, how effective were their strategies in reducing the hostility against them; in protecting them from its ravages; and in helping them to progress toward the place they sought in society?

Commentary by contemporary Afro-Americans on the subject of lifestyles shed some light on goals and values as seen from within the black community. Concerned with acceptability to the larger white society, black leaders admonished their constituents to make life choices that would convince whites of their suitability for responsible citizenship. To this end, one of the early Philadelphia meetings of the national Convention of Free People of Color—a group established in the early 1830s to address the problems of free blacks and, in later years, the problems of enslaved brothers as well—adopted a resolution advocating that the designation "African" be dropped from the titles of black organizations. Instead, the fact that black people were colored *Americans* should be stressed. To this end also, they gravitated toward values which they felt would establish them as "respectable" in wider American society. An 1837 statement of goals written by a Philadelphia black leader bears the unmistakable mark of liberal Quaker influence:

> . . . We shall advocate the cause of peace, believing that whatever tends to the destruction of human life is at variance with the precepts of the Gospel. . . . We shall endeavor to promote education with sound morality, not that we shall become "learned and mighty," but "great and good." . . . We shall advocate temperance in all things, and total abstinence from all alcoholic liquors. We shall advocate a system of economy, not only because luxury is injurious to individuals, but because its practice exercises an influence on society, which in its very nature is sinful.

Frugality, temperance, religion, and education, they argued, would be the keys that would result in the respectability that would open the doors of American society to black people.

Among this list of goals of the elites in the black community, perhaps the most important was education. But why? In a society where few people were formally educated, and in which the highly educated Negro was frequently frustrated by lack of opportunities to exercise his talents, how would education help them become "great and good"? For the leaders of this community the purpose of education seemed to be two-fold. For one thing, it would keep black youths off the streets, where their presence and idleness would reinforce whites' perception that Negroes were aimless, undisciplined, and untrainable. Hence the statement by one black leader that education inspired ambition, "the cornerstone of all human greatness . . . without which we become nothing—nay, we become awful nuisances to society."

Equally important, educational institutions would provide the medium for socializing black youth and ex-slaves into the temperate, "orderly" lifestyle that leaders felt was so essential to their acceptance in the larger society:

. . . the age in which we live is fastidious in its taste. It demands eloquence, figure, rhetoric, and pathos; plain, honest, common sense is no longer attracting. . . . the means of ameliorating our condition . . . is by a strict attention to education. We find that those men who have ever been instrumental in raising a community into respectability, have devoted their best and happiest years to this important object, have lived laborious days and restless nights; made a sacrifice of ease, health, and social joys and terminated their useful career in poverty, with the only consoling hope that they had done justice to their fellow men, and should in their last hours of triumphant prospect lie down on the bed of fame and live to future ages. . . .

As an accompaniment to practical education, black elites enjoyed a wide range of curricular "extras," designed to add an "eloquence" to their lives that was frequently publicized by white and black alike. Edward Clay and his followers satirized this "society," but an anonymous writer—probably a black Philadelphian named Joseph Willson—produced a more serious document on upper-class black social life. Willson in 1841 published a book describing the lifestyles of what he termed "the higher classes of colored society," mentioning "parlors . . . carpeted and furnished with sofas, sideboards, cardtables, mirrors, . . .and in many instances, . . . a piano forte," where, in prearranged formal visits, black women trained in "painting, instrumental music, singing . . . and . . . ornamental needlework" visited with each other. Their men—home from concerts, lectures, or meetings of literacy, debating, and library association gatherings at their meeting halls—sometimes joined their women, bringing news of the lectures and debates they had heard or engaged in. The topics of these meetings ranged from treatises on ancient Rome to studies of medicine, but the most frequent subjects related to the plight of blacks in America. Jacob White, destined to become a public school administrator in the years after the Civil War, was one young member of this social circle whose debating skills, at one point, were turned to a defense—before a black audience—of slavery as beneficial because it brought Africans in touch with civilization.

Rivaling the commitment to education was the Philadelphia black leaders' concern for frugality and temperance—a concern which sometimes led to a delicate balancing act against the desire for "eloquence . . . and rhetoric." An article in the black newspaper *Freedom's Journal* denounced the Pennsylvania *Gazette's* satire of a black "fancy ball" in Philadelphia, and cautioned Afro-Americans about the damaging image of such balls:

> The obloquy and contempt which have heretofore been heaped upon us, as a body, for our much and continual dancing, will, we hope, cause many who are persons of reflection, to think some upon the propriety of spending so many valuable hours in this amusement. While we are no advocates of dancing, we do not consider it criminal to indulge in it, occasionally, once or twice a year.

The writer went on to distinguish the "we [who] don't believe in balls" from the "few who do" and expressed the concern that these latter "should not be cause to ridicule a whole society."

Black newspapers frequently carried articles exhorting their readers to live disciplined, frugal lives and set before them numerous biographies—from Toussaint L'Overture to Paul Cuffe—of black leaders who had contributed to the progress of the race by so doing. In their statements black leaders expressed this commitment to sober consumption but in actuality they seemed to live well, making up in "style" and "culture" what they denied themselves in frivolity. Abolitionists who visited black Philadelphians' homes commented—some with disapproval—on the sumptuousness they found there. And Joseph Willson described the homes of Philadelphia's black elite as "present[ing] an air of neatness and [having] the evidences of comfort . . . quite astonishing when compared with their limited advantages for securing them. . . ." But Willson goes on to make the point that people do not seem to be living beyond their means: ". . . unlike fashionable people of other communities, they live mostly within their incomes . . . and hence . . . they manage to maintain even appearances."

Such "even appearances" in the lives of black elites must have been particularly annoying to whites in less stable positions: the displaced skilled laborers who participated in the riots. Though it was not black competition, but rather new technology and new work routines that actually caused skilled whites' job displacement, "upper-class" blacks were an acceptable target for frustration, whereas upper-class whites were not.

Bruce Laurie, in this study of antebellum Philadelphia working-class whites' lifestyles and values, has suggested that among certain segments of society (the same segments that would have been involved in the riots) there was a strong resistance to temperance and punctuality—what Laurie terms the "new morality" or "new respectability"—that was necessary for the coming regimentation of the industrial work day. Such an interpretation adds the potential for yet another dimension to anti-black violence, for the recipe of frugality, temperance, religion, and education—seasoned with "eloquence"—advocated by black leaders must have given added spice to the taste of anti-black hatred in the mouths of white rioters.

Hence, the virulent attack of the black temperance parade, which triggered the race riot of 1842, emerges as something more than simple racial violence. If blackness was injury, black temperance added insult to it. Before the riot was over, a black meeting hall, erected by and named for Stephen Smith, a wealthy black merchant, was destroyed. Nor was this destruction the result of random violence, for the local authorities, pinpointing the hall as a potential target, had set up a guard around the building. Nevertheless, it and a neighboring black church were destroyed by the crowd, and a third building, a brick structure erected as a temperance, meeting hall by the black community, was ordered destroyed by municipal authorities lest its presence incite more unrest.

Few participants in anti-black riots were every prosecuted, and this fact was not lost on black leaders. An article in the *Colored American* newspaper spelled out one Afro-American's perception that the black upper classes presented a target partly because the white upper classes were unavailable:

> Abolition is a mere pretext for these outbreakings. The same class of vagabonds who mob abolitionists, would as readily mob . . . the aristocracy could they do it with the same impunity.

Though these leaders understood that they were the scapegoats of American society, still they continued to pursue the only strategy they could conceive: to convince that society of the Afro-American's respectability. They were proud of their restraint and their independence. They were quick to take offense to any disparagement of their character, and they responded with lengthy protestations of their temperance and industry. One such refutation, published in a white newspaper in 1832, pointed to the large number of colored benevolent societies and the fact that none of the societies' members had ever been convicted in the court as evidences of the respectable nature of the black community.

These groups, pleased with their capacity to care for blacks both inside and outside their membership, noted how few black people were in the almshouses and then went on to point out that "in Philadelphia, far from burdening the whites with the support of . . . [black] paupers, . . . [black people's] taxes, over and above the support of their own poor, furnish funds for the support of *white* paupers."

A significant segment of the black elite was, then, concerned with whites' perception of the Negro. This group was committed to education and frugal, temperate living, with the intent of "rendering harmless, false and exaggerated accounts of our degraded condition by living consistent, orderly and moral lives."

A small minority of Philadelphia blacks, however, grew frustrated with shaping its rhetoric and its policies to suit the tastes of a white public. Some resorted to direct confrontations with local authorities—a fact which was noted as one of the "causes" of the 1834 riots:

> The other cause . . . [of rioting] is the conduct of certain portions of the colored people, when any of their members are arrested as fugitives from justice. It has too often happened, that . . . the colored people have not relied on the wisdom and justice of the judiciary, . . . or on the active and untiring exertions of benevolent citizens. . . . but they have . . . forcibly attempted the rescue of prisoners. . . .

While some took to physical force, others confined their anger to a growing belligerence in their public statements. Though forced to recognize that white allies might desert their cause if the black community exhibited too much radical spirit, these dissenters had come to understand that the elite's stride toward "respectability" had been, at best, minimally effective in bringing about significant change in the lives of most black people. As the national black organizations inched away from total commitment to pacifism and lost some of their zeal for temperance as a pressing issue for Afro-Americans, a few Philadelphia leaders reluctantly followed, with blistering statements against white slaveholders, and even some mild protest of the hypocrisy of some abolitionists. A few blacks as well as whites criticized the bold ones who indulged in such "measures denunciatory" of the white community, claiming such measures were ineffectual and self-defeating. Yet some black leaders, disgruntled at the slowness of progress, became increasingly verbal about their exasperation as mid-century approached. Scattered among the exhortations to black Americans to improve themselves there began to creep a note of admonition toward the white world as well. Typical was this statement, made by one black leader:

> On the one hand we see arrayed against us unblushing impiety, unholy pride, grovelling sinful prejudice, and a short-sighted worldly policy . . . *the unholy alliance must capitulate.* . . .

If one response of Afro-Americans to increased racism was the redoubling of efforts to prove themselves respectable, and another was the increase in the belligerent tone of rhetoric, yet a third expression of disillusionment, frustration, and fear was to flee Philadelphia altogether—a response that contemporary observers felt to be part of the design of the rioters:

> It is notorious indeed, a fact not to be concealed or disputed, that the "object" of the most active among the rioters, was a destruction of the property, and injury to the persons, of the colored people, with intent, as it would seem to induce or compel them to remove from this district . . .

It was possible, of course, that one individual might do all three: step up efforts to be "respectable," increase the amount of anger expressed in public statements, and leave the city. Those who left went to places as close as New Jersey and as far away as West Africa. But one of the more interesting developments in the black community through the 1830s and 1840s was the number of people who chose the first two alternatives, but rejected—in fact, reversed—the third; that is, the number of vocal and militant abolitionists who moved from outside the black neighborhood or outside of Philadelphia into the area that was experiencing the riots.

While we cannot discount the external pressure (from the city's white communities) to "ghettoize" the black community, it is worth noticing that by 1850, a number of black leaders with substantial economic power had left other neighborhoods— neighborhoods untouched by riots—and bought residences in the area in which resided black churches, newspapers, etc. Since in 1850, all the neighborhoods of the city still had some black residents, including some black homeowners, it would seem unlikely that those black owners who moved from other neighborhoods into the riot area did so solely because of force—or at least unlikely that they were driven out of the old neighborhood simply because they were black.

By 1850, leading families of Cassey, Ayres, Forten, and Parrot were joined in the neighborhood near Bethel by the Gloucester, Bustill, Stephen Smith, Florin, and White families, each with taxable property worth from $500 to $12,000. These families were typically composed of two working parents—e.g., a tailor or baker father and a teacher or seamstress mother—who had one or more children in the local black schools. Seven of the thirteen black schools were located in this neighborhood, and none of the other schools were grouped so closely together. These people's names appeared frequently as organizers of local meetings, signers of petitions, or representatives on boards of black organizations.

From this group and this neighborhood came a disproportionately large number of the public statements of the black community in the years 1834–1850 when anti-black rioting was at its peak in Philadelphia. The concerns they voiced for action within the black community were handed down to the next generation of leaders, many of whom were their biological as well as their spiritual children, for Bustills, Fortens, Whites, Stills, and many other black leaders through the Civil War and late nineteenth century were second, if not third generation organizers in the black community.

The strategy of respectability, adopted in the 1830s by the majority of the influential black leaders, was the strategy carried on by the younger group of leaders that drew together in the Bethel neighborhood in the wake of the riots. The full import of the fact that the white community seemed to grow more hostile in proportion to the success of these goals seems to have been lost on these leaders. Yet each of the five major riots against the black community between 1834 and 1849 resulted not only in generalized mayhem, but also in the destruction of at least one of these symbols of group "success": churches, meeting halls, outstanding black leaders' property. In 1834 it was a masonic hall and a church: several substantial brick houses in 1835: in 1838—in addition to Pennsylvania Hall itself—rioters burned the Quaker Shelter for Colored Orphans and another black church: the temperance parade in 1842 occasioned the destruction of two meeting halls and yet another church: and in 1849 an interracial tavern went up in smoke. An examination of other inhabitants who shared the neighborhood adds further weight to the argument that the rioters chose their targets with some purpose, for all along small streets that rippled the area, rioters bypassed seats of gambling and prostitution—some of them interracial—to reach homes and meeting places of "unoffending" blacks.

The differences of style and opinion between the respectable and the unrespectable within the black community are of use in gaining insight into the relationship of the total black community to the equally varied white community. Some progress has recently been made in describing objective characteristics that differentiated various levels of material progress among antebellum urban blacks. Sometimes these intrablack dynamics had a dramatic effect on black-white relations. One example of what might be called a "domino" effect of intrablack tensions may be seen in the riot that occurred in the summer of 1835. A group of blacks, reflecting the widespread acceptance of the black community's adoption of "Americanization" values, ridiculed the manners and clothing of a West Indian servant, teasing him for his "African" ways and unstylish clothing. The servant, much upset, petitioned his master for better clothing. When the master refused, the servant beat him. A race riot ensured, which, like the one before it, was aimed at the property of comfortable black people. Presenting the image of colored Americans as separate in style and dress from Africans was a highly emotional issue within some segments of the black community—important enough to inspire public ridicule and destroy at least one servant's social restraint.

Out of an examination of the black community then, the anti-black riots of the 1830s and 1840s are given another dimension—a dimension born not only out of the peculiarities of Philadelphia's white communities but also out of the unique qualities of the black community. While the white mobs were expressing their frustration at their own social immobility, black people, for their part, were concerned with publicly exhibiting the proof of their progress toward the "respectable" life. This set of dynamics proved mutually antagonistic. Within this setting, Philadelphia's black leaders continued to focus on three goals: economic security, physical safety, and social status. With respect to the first goal, they achieved some measure of success by 1830, accentuated by the fact that a few Afro-Americans achieved some economic power, and that in times of crisis both black and white wealth could be called in for support. After 1830, when changes in the geographic integration of the city, heightened competition for work, and the rise of trade guilds that excluded blacks eroded the gains made in the early years of the century, Philadelphia's black leaders still had no choice but to continue agitation for economic opportunities.

On the second goal, physical security, the tactic adopted by the black community was even less successful. Since the upper-class whites whom black leaders saw as their national allies were themselves hated by working-class whites, black leaders' choices of allies had the effect of reinforcing their position of being attractive targets for anti-upper class, as well as anti-black, attack.

It is interesting that no major black leader conceived of a cross-racial political union among the working classes. Until well into the 1840s, black leaders steered clear of political organization completely, and their huddling together helped in forming the ghetto that made it unnecessary to attack anymore; now they could simply be isolated.

If the effectiveness of the first two strategies was limited, in the third, the pursuit of status, blacks found their goals even more thwarted. For here black leaders found that they were alone. White working people hated the idea of upward mobility in an economic way, white elites supported it only as long as it stayed within certain limits—as long as it avoided measures "denunciatory" of themselves, or attempts at intermarriage. The 1838 decision of the state legislature to rescind black suffrage suggests that the rioters were indeed "legitimized" by the approval of the larger white community, as it is "respectable" citizens and not criminals who are most likely to exercise this kind of political power. The 1830s and 1840s were a critical time for Afro-Americans in a northern city. All-black organizations, only a generation or so old found themselves working out policies and goals under the tremendous pressure of generally tumultuous urban situations in which they were under physical and psychological attack. It was too soon in the development of Afro-American organizational life for the group to move toward recognizing that its own sets of values differed from those of the major society it sought to enter. It was too soon to have accumulated the experience that might later tell them that inclusion in American society required fundamental change— not just within the black community, but in the entire political and class structure of American society.

Black leaders, then, adjusted their tactics and goals to the realities of their city as it moved into the Civil War. They gave up physical competition for city space and retreated to the safety of their own neighborhood, with its supportive institutions and services. Likewise, they gave up their commitment to some of the causes of white liberals, such as temperance. A few expatriated, foregoing hope of acceptance in America at all. Most, however, continued their use of their "separate churches" and lodges to cultivate and promote their leaders and their pursuits of respectability and acceptability. And on the issue of "amalgamation" they were silent. Continued resentment against the abolitionists and against blacks as the "cause" of the disruption of Civil War far outweighed the gains possible through the old strategies of preparing for full inclusion in American society by living "respectably." And though riots and rioters gradually disappeared from American cities as legitimate extralegal tools of public discipline, rioting against blacks remained acceptable. But the black churches and masonic lodges remained under the leadership of the children of leaders steeped in the values of frugality, temperance, respectability, and "Americanization." As they moved into the twentieth century, such leaders found themselves more and more out of touch with a constituency that could no longer see the use of such values.

A generalized racism in the context of the riot atmosphere of the mid-nineteenth century might well have been sufficient to engender both the riots and the rioters without any "provocation" from within the black community. Nevertheless, an examination of inner dynamics may help to keep us aware that interracial tensions are a complex phenomenon.

Manhood and Womanhood in a Slave Society

JAMES OLIVER HORTON AND LOIS E. HORTON

In his autobiography, Frederick Douglass recalled his confrontation with the slave breaker Covey as the first step on his escape to freedom. After regular beatings from Covey, to whom he had been hired, he had run away, and then returned to face certain and severe punishment. This time, though, the adolescent slave resisted, and the two became locked in a two-hour struggle that left both exhausted. Young Frederick was not subdued, and Covey never beat him again. This successful resistance changed the slave: "My dear reader this battle with Mr. Covey . . . was the turning point in my life as a slave . . . I was nothing before; I was a man now." It was natural for Douglass to express his new-found power in terms of manhood, as power, independence, and freedom were often thought of as traits reserved for men in nineteenth-century America. To be a man was to be free and powerful.

Although the American man in the nineteenth century could choose from a variety of gender ideals, virtually all the combinations of characteristics, values, and actions constituting each ideal included self-assertion and aggression as key elements. Aggression, and sometimes sanctioned violence, was a common thread in American ideals of manhood. Charles Rosenberg believes that two masculine ideals exemplified the choices open to nineteenth-century men, the *Masculine Achiever* and *Christian Gentleman*. The Masculine Achiever ideal was closely associated with the rapid economic growth of the nineteenth century. As the rise of the market economy disrupted local relationships and tied formerly isolated communities to distant economic affiliations, this ideal provided American men with a dynamic model of behavior. The man of action was unencumbered by sentiment and totally focused on advancement, the quintessential individualist and the self-styled ruthless competitor. He was the rugged individual succeeding in the world of commercial capitalism.

The Christian Gentleman ideal arose in reaction to the Masculine Achiever and threats to traditional values and relationships. Eschewing self-seeking behavior and heartless competition in the commercial world, this gentler ideal stressed communal values, religious principles, and more humanitarian action. It was a natural outgrowth of the religious revival that blossomed under the Second Great Awakening of the early nineteenth century and stressed self-restraint and Christian morality. Christian Gentlemen were not expected to be passive. Dynamic and aggressive action was assumed, but in the name of moral values and self-sacrifice, not personal greed.

"Violence, Protest, and Identity: Black Manhood in Antebellum America," by James Oliver Horton and Lois E. Horton. From *Free People of Color: Inside the African American Community* by James Oliver Horton, copyright © 1993 by the Smithsonian Institution. Used by permission of the publisher.

E. Anthony Rotundo argues that an additional ideal emerged among northern males in the nineteenth century—the *Masculine Primitive*. This ideal stressed dominance and conquest through harnessing the energy of primitive male instincts and savagery lurking beneath the thin veneer of civilization. This was a more physically aggressive ideal, based on the natural impulses of man's most primitive state, and violence was its confirming feature. Although Rotundo sees this ideal as influential among northern men by the middle of the nineteenth century, southern historians have found a strikingly similar ideal in the South throughout the eighteenth and nineteenth centuries. Bertram Wyatt-Brown and Grady McWhiney describe the violence in defense of honor sanctioned by even the most genteel southerners. Elizabeth Fox-Genovese notes the simultaneous existence of gentility and savagery: "Southern conventions of masculinity never abandoned the element of force or even brutality . . . This toleration of male violence responded to the perceived exigencies of governing a troublesome people . . . " The behaviors believed necessary for managing the slave system were incorporated into the gender ideals for all southern white men.

Black men growing up as slaves in southern society had an especially complex gender socialization. The gender ideals of white southern society overlaid the foundations of African cultural expectations and the intentional socialization imposed on slaves. The dual and contradictory genteel and savage images applied to southern white manhood paralleled characteristics whites imagined black men possessed. The happy, contented Sambo stereotype slaveholders wanted to believe existed was placed alongside the brute, savage Negro they feared. Slaveholders tried to cultivate a slave approximation of the Christian Gentlemen ideal, typified by Harriet Beecher Stowe's Uncle Tom, all the while dreading the emergence of the barbaric Masculine Primitive. Thomas R. Dew argued in 1832 that Africans were by nature savage and that it was only the civilizing influence of slavery that restrained their brutish nature. According to William Drayton, another nineteenth-century apologist for slavery, only slavery checked the "wild frenzy of revenge, and the savage lust for blood" natural to the African and dramatically apparent in the Haitian Revolution. In 1858 Thomas R. R. Cobb alleged that once removed from the domesticating influence of slavery, Haitian blacks "relapsed into barbarism."

Ever watchful for any outward signs of rebellion, white southerners went to great lengths to suppress black aggression and assertiveness. As one former slave recalled, "Every man [was] called boy till he [was] very old, then the more respectable slaveholder call[ed] him uncle." Actions expected of white men were condemned in black men. No black man could defend his family from a white attacker, "let him be ever so drunk or crazy," without fear of drastic reprisal. Yet a black man under the orders of white authority could legitimately use his strength against a white person. A slave directed by his overseer could strike a white man for "beating said overseer's pig."

"A slave can't be a man," proclaimed former slave Lewis Clarke. Slavery was designed to make it impossible for a man to freely express his opinions and make his own decisions. Yet many slave men asserted aspects of manhood even under the most difficult circumstances. William Davis refused to be whipped by his overseer. When the white man realized he could not administer the beating alone, he ordered three "athletic fellows" to assist him, but Davis served notice that he would not be taken easily. "Boys, I am only a poor boy and you are grown men, but if either of you touch me, I'll kill one of you . . . ," he warned. Davis was not whipped.

Slave men found many ways to assert themselves. Even the threat of self-assertion could be effective. One man reported that he avoided being sold at auction by meeting the gaze of prospective buyers directly as they inspected him, an obvious sign of a hard-to-handle slave. Another stopped his master from beating slave children by standing beside them, glaring at the master as he began punishment. Among the slaves, men who refused to submit to the master's authority were accorded respect. Those who submitted too easily to the master's authority lost respect. "Them as won't fight," reported Lewis Clarke, "is called Poke-easy." How could a man be both manly and a slave? A central theme in the abolitionists' attacks on slavery was that it robbed men of their manhood. The widely used anti-slavery emblem was a manacled slave kneeling in the supplication, "Am I not a man and brother?"

David Walker, a free black North Carolinian who migrated to Boston, gained national attention and raised southern fears by urging slaves to prove their manhood, to rise up and take their freedom by force if necessary. His call to arms was issued in partial answer to Thomas Jefferson's suggestions that African Americans were an inferior species and could not be granted freedom. Walker asserted that the African American could not be domesticated like an animal and could never be held in slavery against his will. He goaded black men to action by rhetorically wondering how so many could be enslaved: "Are we Men!! How we could be so submissive to a gang of men, whom we cannot tell whether they are as good as ourselves or not, I never could conceive." Blacks, he wrote, must not wait for either God or slaveholders to end slavery. "The man who would not fight . . . to be delivered from the most wretched, abject and servile slavery, that ever a people was afflicted with since the foundation of the world . . . ought to be kept with all his children or family, in slavery or in chains to be butchered by his cruel enemies."

In his *Appeal* David Walker called upon the memory of the successful Haitian Revolution in 1804 as proof of the power of unity and manliness. "One thing which gives me joy," he wrote of the Haitians, "is, that they are men who would be cut off to a man before they would yield to the combined forces of the whole world." Black men demonstrated in Haiti, Walker contended, that "a groveling, servile and abject submission to the lash of tyrants" is not the African man's natural state. Walker believed that slaves could transform themselves into men through aggressive action. "If ever we become men," he said, "we must assert ourselves to the full."

In his call to action, Walker claimed the physical superiority of black men. "I do declare," he wrote, "that one good black can put to death six white men." The assertion that slaves were stronger and better in combat than their masters was not new. It became part of the racial folklore of the period and was often cited in conjunction with rumors of slave uprisings. Yet this declaration posed problems for African Americans. The use of violence to assert manhood tended to reinforce white stereotypes of the "brutish African nature" only restrained by slavery.

Despite David Walker's mysterious death in 1831, his advocacy of the use of violence as an acceptable tactic for the acquisition of freedom and equality, what were increasingly referred to as *manhood rights*, remained an important position among blacks throughout the antebellum period. At the time that Walker wrote his

Appeal, the American imagination was captured by Greek revolutionaries seeking independence from Turkey, by rising Polish discontent with their Russian masters, and the revolutions in Latin America that, in 1826, brought the abolition of slavery to the former Spanish colonies. Thus he drew on more than the distant models of the American Revolution and the revolt in Haiti. He was undoubtedly aware that freedom was being sought through violence abroad and that revolutionary armies in Latin America included black soldiers bearing arms supplied by the Haitian government.

Walker was not alone in using international illustrations to attack slavery or in considering the prospect of slave revolt. In 1825 in his commencement address at Bowdoin College, John Russwurm, one of the first African Americans to graduate from an American college, assailed the institution, taking as his paradigm the establishment of Haitian independence. Later, as coeditor of *Freedom's Journal*, Russwurm speculated that if the federal government would stop providing protection for slaveholders, slaves might very well settle the question of slavery themselves. Ohio judge Benjamin Tappan shocked an acquaintance by inquiring rhetorically "whether the slave has not a resort to the most violent measures, if necessary, in order to maintain his liberty? And if he has the least chance of success, are we not, as rational and consistent men, bound to justify him?" Historian Merton Dillon asserts that most antislavery proponents of the time accepted the right of slaves to strike for their liberty.

The 1830s brought a new, more forceful critique of violent means in the fight against slavery as William Lloyd Garrison began publishing his newspaper, the *Liberator*, in Boston. His commitment to immediate emancipation for slaves and civil rights for free blacks was popular among African Americans who had worked toward these ends for decades with only marginal assistance from white reformers. Garrison was a nonresister—a pacifist opposed to cooperating with any government built on slavery and compromise with slaveholders. His pacifism led him to oppose government that forced citizens to participate directly or indirectly in violence, through, for example, war, imprisonment, or capital punishment. He opposed voting or participating in politics, and condemned the use of violence even to achieve freedom. The route to manhood, he believed, was through strength of character and principled action. In the pages of the *Liberator* he rejected Walker's call for slave revolt, and although he praised Walker personally, Garrison made clear that "we do not preach rebellion—no, but submission and peace." His stand on the use of violence by slaves was complex. He considered slaves "more than any people on the face of the earth" justified in the use of force and compared slave revolt to the American Revolution in the justice of its cause, but a just cause, Garrison believed, was no justification for violence.

Garrison's strong commitment to nonviolence and his philosophy of nonresistance entered the continuing debate within black society over violent and nonviolent means for the abolition of slavery. African Americans had been influenced by arguments for nonviolence early in the colonial era. Quakers, some of their first allies, were pacifists. Blacks who became Friends often wrestled with the question of the practicality of nonviolence for a people violently deprived of their rights. Yet blacks were obliged to "become convinced of [Quaker] principles" in order to be accepted into the society. During the War of 1812, black Quaker David Mapps of

Little Egg Harbor, New Jersey, demonstrated his pacifist principles and refused to transport cannon balls aboard his schooner, explaining, "I cannot carry thy devil's pills that were made to kill people."

Although black Quakers were strongly committed to nonviolence, most African Americans expressed a great deal more ambivalence on this issue. At the opposite extreme from the Quakers, many continued to agree with David Walker that violence was the surest route to freedom and manhood. Some opposed the use of violence on practical grounds, others wrestled with moral issues and searched for alternative ways to assert themselves and to achieve dignity without the use of force. Garrison and his philosophy had become the center of this debate by the 1830s, but the debate was over means, not ends. All blacks agreed that freedom and equality were the goals, and most continued to equate these with manhood.

Speaking to a gathering of black Bostonians in 1831, black activist Maria W. Stewart echoed Walker's call to black men to assert their manhood: O ye fearful ones, throw off your fearfulness . . . If you are men, convince [whites] that you possess the spirit of men." Yet hers was not a call to violence. She called forth the "sons of Africa" to show their bravery, their intelligence, and their commitment to serving their community. "But give the man of color an equal opportunity . . . from the cradle to manhood, and from manhood to grave, and you would discover a dignified statesman, the man of science, and the philosopher."

Maria Stewart urged a version of the Masculine Achiever ideal of manhood that incorporated achievement, autonomy, and "intensive competition for success in the marketplace." Her ideal, however, was not completely individualistic. The object of success in the masculine competition was to prove black men the equals of other men. It was also important, according to Stewart, that successful men become assets to the black community and contribute to the struggle of black people. Even though Stewart was a friend and co-worker of Garrison, her appeal was not incontrovertibly nonviolent. The heroes she called upon to inspire black men to the competition included the black soldiers of the American Revolution and the War of 1812—and David Walker.

Garrison agreed that bondage and discrimination denied human dignity and pledged his efforts to combat these destructive forces. He was a pacifist, but his philosophy and style was neither passive nor apologetic. As he began the *Liberator*, Garrison promised to speak clearly and forcefully in words that could not be misunderstood. He was unequivocal in his opposition to slavery, but he also believed he had a responsibility to free blacks in the North. He dedicated himself and his paper to work for their "moral and intellectual elevation, the advancement of [their] rights, and the defense of [their] character." Less than two months after beginning publication, Garrison felt his venture had already met with success. He reported: "Upon the colored population in the free states, it has operated like a trumpet call. They have risen in their hopes and feelings to the perfect stature of men. . . ."

Garrison's conception of manhood, characterized by intellectual achievement personal dignity, and moral responsibility, was shared by many abolitionists, whose underlying antislavery motivation was religious. It had particular appeal for black abolitionists, who felt they carried the added burden of disproving the claims of black inferiority advanced by Jefferson and the proslavery interests. Yet even among black Garrisonians there was some ambivalence regarding total reliance on the pacific means of moral suasion. A widely circulated poem composed by the intellectual black abolitionist Charles L. Reason illustrates this ambivalence, Reason's poem, entitled "The Spirit Voice: or Liberty Calls to the Disfranchised," is filled with martial images but comes to a decidedly nonviolent conclusion. He wrote:

> Come! rouse ye brothers, rouse! a peal now breaks,
> From lowest island to our gallant lakes,
> 'Tis summoning you, who long in bonds have lain,
> To stand up manful on the battle plain,
> Each as a warrior, with his armor bright,
> Prepared to battle in a bloodless fight.

Respect for Garrison and his work kept many black abolitionists from openly questioning reliance on moral suasion, even when they harbored doubts about its effectiveness. Some Garrisonians, of course, were committed to nonviolence on principle; others saw it as a practical strategy. Throughout the 1830s and early 1840s, the small band of antislavery crusaders was continually under attack. Mobs broke up their meetings, attacked them in the streets, and occasionally set fire to their lecture halls and homes. Slaveholders posted rewards for the most notorious abolitionists, dead or alive. In the face of such opposition, taking the principled stance of moral suasion had the additional practical benefit of attracting adherents while avoiding inflaming even more violent reactions.

Yet some continued to proclaim the rights of slaves to take their freedom "like men." One of the most radical and elaborate schemes for the forcible abolition of slavery came from a white sixty-year-old politician, Jabez Delano Hammond, a jurist and former U.S. congressman from Cherry Valley, New York. In 1839 Hammond proposed that abolitionists sponsor military academies in Canada and Mexico that would train blacks in military arts and sabotage. The trainees would then be set loose in the South to commit terrorist acts and to encourage and lead slave rebellions. Referring to these infiltrators as potentially "the most successful Southern missionaries," Hammond explained that such steps were necessary because "the only way in which slavery at the South can be abolished is by force."

Many black reformers were also growing impatient with moral suasion as the primary weapon against slavery and moral elevation as the surest route to progress for free blacks. Peter Paul Simons spoke for a growing minority in 1839 when he challenged the efficacy of moral reform. Instead of lessening the hold of slavery and prejudice on blacks, he believed, it had encouraged timidity and self-doubt. African Americans do not suffer from lack of moral elevation, he argued. "There is no nation of people under the canopy of heaven, who are given more to good morals and piety than we are." He contended that blacks suffered from a lack of direct "physical and political" action. They lacked confidence in one another, he said, and were thus likely to depend on the leadership of whites, a not-so-subtle reference to the willingness of many blacks to follow Garrison's lead. His argument continued, charging that black children learned passive acceptance not manly action and leadership from parental examples. Action must be the watchword: "This we must physically practice, and we will be in truth an independent people."

Although Simons stopped short of endorsing a David Walker–style call for violence in this pursuit of self-confident independence, his statements did signal the move toward a more aggressive posture. He was not alone. Many who worked most closely with fugitive slaves or on behalf of free blacks kidnapped into slavery were among those least able to accept the doctrine of nonviolence. Black abolitionist David Ruggles, an officer of the New York Committee of Vigilance, had never been totally committed to nonresistance. As early at 1836 he wrote that in dealing with slave hunters and kidnappers, "Self-defense is the first law of nature." Gradually Ruggles grew more impatient with the slow pace of antislavery and civil rights progress. In the summer of 1841, he addressed a meeting of the American Reform Board of Disfranchised Commissioners, a New York protest group of which he was a founding member. In strident tones he rallied the group to action and explained that "in our cause" words alone would not suffice. "Rise brethren rise!" he urged the distant slaves. "Strike for freedom or die slaves!"

Two years later at the Buffalo meeting of the National Negro Convention, twenty-seven-year-old black abolitionist minister Henry Highland Garnet echoed David Walker's exhortation, urging black men to act like men. Addressing himself to the slaves, he used provocative and incendiary language. "It is sinful in the extreme," he admonished, "for you to make voluntary submission." As Walker had accepted the necessity for a man to use violence in the assertion of his manhood, so Garnet concluded that "there is not much hope of Redemption without the shedding of blood." Black men must not shrink from bloody confrontation—there was no escape. A mass exodus was not an option for African Americans, he argued. The solution must be found in America, and it might well be violent. "If you must bleed, let it come at once, rather, die freemen than live to be slaves." Garnet did not urge a revolution. "Your numbers are too small," he observed. But all slaves should immediately "cease to labor for tyrants who will not remunerate you." He assumed, however, that violence would be the inevitable result of this tactic. And when it came, he instructed, "Remember that you are THREE MILLIONS."

As Maria Stewart had done a decade earlier, Garnet used black heroes as a standard for manhood, and he found contemporary black men wanting. Questioning the commitment of his fellows to the assertion of manhood, Garnet cut to the heart of masculine pride. "You act as though your daughters were born to pamper the lusts of your masters and overseers," he charged. Garnet continued forcefully: "And worst of all, you timidly submit while your lords tear your wives from your embraces and defile them before your eyes. In the name of God, we ask, are you men? Where is the blood of your fathers? Has it all run out of your veins?" Here Garnet drew upon one of the most powerful justifications for the link between physical prowess and masculinity in American gender ideals—the responsibility of men to protect their families. This responsibility was an important part of all male ideals in the society. Even those most committed to the Christian Gentleman ideal, even the most fervent black nonresisters had great difficulty arguing that nonviolence was the only recourse when one's family was in physical danger. Garnet's charge to the slaves forcefully affected the black and white abolitionists and observers in his audience as he evoked the universal images of manhood.

Garnet's speech split the convention; debate was heated. Ardent Garrisonians Frederick Douglass and Charles Lenox Remond spoke against endorsing his sentiments. They pointed to the bloody retribution slaves and free blacks, especially those in the border states, might suffer should the convention support such a radical call to violence. Although there was substantial support for Garnet's message, by a narrow margin the convention refused to endorse his words. For the time being the black Garrisonians remained convinced and had successfully blocked the open embrace of violent means.

A commitment to nonviolence and a sense of the dangers the relatively powerless slaves faced continued to prevent most blacks from urging slaves to gain their freedom through physical force. Many black abolitionists had been slaves and were intimately familiar with the dangers involved. Even Frederick Douglass, who recounted the story of attaining his manhood through physical confrontation, was aware of the risks and continued to be reluctant to sanction calls for slave rebellion. A news story he printed in his paper in the late 1840s illustrated the horrors of slavery and made the point that resistance could be deadly:

> Wm. A. Andrews, an overseer of J. W. Perkins, Mississippi attempted to chastise one of the negro boys who seized a stick and prepared to do battle. The overseer told the boy to lay the stick down or he would shoot him; he refused, and the overseer then fired his pistol, and shot the boy in the face, killing him instantly. The jury of inquest found the verdict, "that the said Wm. A. Andrews committed the killing in self-defense."

In the 1840s Garrisonian nonresistance came under fire from many quarters. There was a split in the abolition movement at the start of the decade, and many of those committed to political antislavery cast their lot with the newly formed Liberty party. Among white abolitionists there was also growing intolerance of what some saw as Garrison's unreasoned radicalism, not only attacking slavery but also condemning the Constitution, the entire federal government, and the national political system. Further, some criticized his support of women's rights as an unnecessary complication that made abolition even less palatable to the general public and threatened to blunt the central thrust of the movement. This fear was reinforced when feminist Abby Kelley was elected to be the first female member of the business committee of the Garrisonian-dominated American Anti-Slavery Society. Opposition groups sprang up to challenge this and other Garrisonian organizations.

This debate between those who favored political participation and those who opposed it split the black abolitionist ranks. Despite their ambivalence, most black Bostonians remained personally loyal to Garrison. New York's *Colored American* attempted to remain neutral, but many black New Yorkers sided with the political abolitionists. Blacks in several northern states faced the curtailment or loss of their voting rights. The vote was an instrument of males' political power, and blacks viewed disenfranchisement as symbolic emasculation. Garrison himself conceded that where rights were in jeopardy, black voters should vote in self-defense.

The debate was short lived among blacks, and even Boston blacks openly took part in electoral politics by the mid-1840s. There were Liberty party announcements inserted in the pages of the *Liberator*, and by 1848 the paper reported on meetings at which African Americans in Boston discussed the formation of an auxiliary to the Liberty party. William Cooper Nell, one of the most loyal of the black Garrisonians, allowed his name to be put into nomination as Free-Soil party candidate for the 1850 Massachusetts legislature.

By the mid-nineteenth century, Garrisonians were also reassessing their stand on nonviolence. Among African Americans almost all reservations about the appropriateness of violence in the struggle against slavery were wiped away by the passage of the federal Fugitive Slave Law of 1850. This measure, which made it easier for fugitives to be captured and for free blacks to be kidnapped into slavery, was seen as a direct blow against all African Americans. It generated a strongly militant reaction even among those who had favored nonviolence. Charles Lenox Remond, who had opposed Garnet's call to arms in the early 1840s, a decade later demanded defiance of the law, protection of all fugitives, and the withholding of federal troops should the southern slaves rise against their masters.

Douglass, who had joined Remond in voting against Garnet, published a novella in 1853 in which slaves killed the captain of a slave ship and a slave owner. In an editorial entitled "Is It Right and Wise to Kill a Kidnapper?" published in *Frederick Douglass' Paper* a year later, he was even more forthright. Violence, even deadly violence, was justifiable when used to protect oneself, one's family, or one's community. At a community meeting in Boston, Nell cautioned African Americans to be watchful for kidnappers. If confronted, he urged them to defend themselves.

The defection from nonviolence was not limited to African Americans. Boston journalist Benjamin Drew suggested that when the government supported oppression, violence against the state might be reasonable. Pacifist minister Samuel J. May and five fugitive slaves stood before an antislavery convention in Syracuse. In surprising tones for the longtime Garrisonian, May asked, "Will you defend [these fugitives] with your lives?" The audience threw back the answer: "Yes!"

Most plans of action were far less offensive. New vigilance committees were formed to protect the safety of fugitives, and already established committees redoubled their efforts, publicly vowing that no slave would be taken. This was a manly pursuit it was said, for every "slavehunter who meets a bloody death in his infernal business, is an argument in favor of the manhood of our race." Yet not all blacks viewed violent confrontation with slave catchers as the route to manliness. Former slave Philip Younger, who sought refuge in Canada in the 1850s, wrote that even more than in the free states, Canada offered a black man self-respect and dignity. "It was a hardship at first," he reported, "but I feel better here—more like a man—I know I am—than in the States."

Some reformers, such as New York's Gerrit Smith, were critical of men who protected themselves and their families by escaping to Canada, viewing this as a cowardly act. Black abolitionist William Whipper took offense when Smith published such criticism, considering it a slur on the bravery of all black men. Whipper offered a combative reply, saying that he could not understand Smith's attack, considering that African Americans were leaving "a country whose crushing influence . . . aims at the extinction of [their] manhood." Reactions to the Fugitive Slave Law of 1850 ranged from flight to confrontation—different, but each an assertion of personal dignity.

The rising anger at the attack by the "slave power" through its influence over the federal government went beyond militancy to an interest in military preparedness. The Negro Convention in Rochester in 1853 called for the removal of all restrictions on black enlistment in state militia. Sixty-five Massachusetts blacks petitioned their state legislature, demanding that a black military company be chartered. The right to bear arms for their state, they contended, was part of their "rights as men." Their petition was rejected, but a black military company called the Massasoit Guard was formed in Boston in 1854. The unit took its name, their second choice, from a powerful seventeenth-century Indian chief. Most would have preferred the name Attucks, in honor of the black revolutionary hero Crispus Attucks, but the name had already been taken by two other black miliary companies, the Attucks Guards of New York and the Attucks Blues of Cincinnati. Before the decade ended, there were several black military units in northern cities. Binghamton, New York, named its company after black abolitionist Jermain Loguen, an associate of John Brown, and Harrisburg, Pennsylvania, formed the Henry Highland Garnet Guards. Thus during the 1850s, black men armed themselves, poised to strike against slavery and to re-affirm their manhood through military action.

The opinion in the Dred Scott decision in 1857, which declared that African Americans were not citizens of the United States, further inflamed antigovernment sentiment, as it placed African Americans in an even more perilous position. In-creasing militancy and the continuing formation of black military companies led white abolitionist John Brown to believe that substantial numbers of northern free blacks might join a military attack on slavery. He was wrong; in 1859 only five blacks and sixteen whites (three of whom were Brown's sons) joined his attack on the federal arsenal at Harpers Ferry, Virginia. Despite the depth of their antislavery feeling, anger, and frustration, African Americans were not ready to join a private venture that seemed doomed to failure.

Within two years Brown's private war assumed national proportions. Although Lincoln firmly proclaimed preservation of the Union as his sole Civil War aim, northern blacks were convinced that abolition would be its outcome. Their imme-diate offer of service was refused, even though more than eighty-five hundred men had joined black militia units by the fall of 1861. Two years later, however, with U.S. casualties mounting and the nation bogged down in a protracted war, the gov-ernment reversed itself and began active recruitment of African American troops. Black abolitionists became energetic recruiters. Jermain Loguen, William Wells Brown, Martin R. Delany, Garnet, and Douglass were among those who encouraged black men to provide their services to the forces of the United States. Victories in the abolition and civil rights struggles during the antebellum period had enhanced their self-image, and most viewed the war as another opportunity to prove themselves to a skeptical white populace. "The eyes of the whole world are upon you, civilized man everywhere waits to see if you will prove yourselves . . . Will you vindicate your manhood?" challenged the *Weekly Anglo-African* in 1863. African Americans hoped that the war would do more than end slavery. Dignity awaited the black man who would "get an eagle on his button, a musket on his shoulder, and the star-spangled banner over his head." Black men marched off to win freedom for slaves and respect and equality for those already free. War was the culmination of the aggressiveness emphasized in much of the resistance to slavery. It celebrated the instincts necessary for survival and reinforced the violence of the Masculine Primitive ideal.

Given the realities of life for African Americans under slavery or in freedom during the antebellum period the irony of using the term *manhood* to apply to the assertion of dignity or the acquisition of freedom is striking. All black people were aware that such action respected no lines of gender. Yet both black men and women used the term. Maria Stewart, David Walker, and Henry Highland Garnet used appeals to manhood to incite blacks to action, but it was not clear whether black women were included. Did calls for slave resistance include women? Were they expected to be "manly"?

Black women's resistance to slavery paralleled black men's, running the gamut from trickery and feigning illness to escape and physical confrontation. Women's physical prowess was acknowledged and often admired within the slave community. Silvia Dubois was proud of the strength that enabled her to run a ferryboat better than any man on the Susquehanna River. As a child she endured her mistress' brutality, but when grown to five feet ten inches tall and weighing more than two hundred pounds, Silvia finally exacted her retribution by severely beating her mistress. After intimidating white spectators who might have subdued her, she picked up her child and made her escape from slavery.

Woman's right advocate and abolitionist Sojourner Truth often spoke with pride of her ability while a slave to do the work of any man. She did not find her strength or her six-foot frame incompatible with being a woman. Nor did Frederick Douglass question the appropriateness of one slave woman's refusal to be beaten and her physical ability to stand her ground against any disbelieving master. When Douglass was resisting Covey, a slave woman named Caroline was ordered to help restrain him. Had she done so, Douglass believed her intervention would have been decisive, because "she was a powerful woman and could have mastered me easily . . . " Thus only because a women defied her master was Douglass able to assert his manhood.

For black women no less than black men, freedom and dignity were tied to assertiveness, even to the point of violence. Slavery blurred distinctions between the gender expectations in black society and reinforced the broader economic and political roles provided to black women by their African heritage. Slavery attempted to dehumanize the slave without regard to gender. Both men and women resisted in concert with others and through the force of their individual personalities; dignity and respect could be achieved by remarkable individuals of both sexes. In freedom, black women protected themselves and their families from slave catchers and kidnappers. They were also aggressive wage earners, providing substantial portions of their household income. Scholars have described the independence and economic autonomy of women in precolonial West and Central Africa. As women's spheres and traits became increasingly differentiated from men's in nineteenth-century America, the experience and traditions of black women led them to depart from American gender expectations.

There was no ideal in American society encompassing the experience or honoring the heritage of black women. Perhaps the closest was the notion identified by Ronald W. Hogeland as *Radical Womanhood*, which allowed women a public role. But even this most extreme norm was not sufficient. It accepted the separation of feminine and masculine capabilities, granting moral superiority to women but reserving intellectual and physical power to men.

Accepting masculine traits as the opposite of feminine traits was one of many ways black men sought to establish and define themselves as men in the face of assaults by slavery and racial discrimination. Gender comparisons in Western society were carefully controlled to favor men, limiting women's sphere. Here black people participated in the ongoing effort in nineteenth-century America to construct gender roles in what Hogeland argued was a male-initiated attempt "not conceived of essentially to improve the lot of women, but [implemented] for the betterment of men." The argument set forth by black minister J. W. C. Pennington in opposition to the ordination of women into the African Methodist Episcopal Church illustrates this point. Pennington contended that women were unsuited for "all the learned professions, where mighty thought and laborious investigation are needed," because as "the weaker sex" they were "incapacitated for [them] both physically and mentally."

The force of prevailing gender conventions outside the black community led some to promote gender expectations totally inappropriate for black women's lives. In the face of solid evidence to the contrary, several blacks, such as abolitionist Charles B. Ray, argued that the proper place for women was in the home, as "daughters are destined to be wives and mothers—they should, therefore, be taught to . . . manage a house, and govern and instruct children." Even Douglass, who spoke at the Seneca Falls Convention in 1848 in favor of women's right to vote, asserted in that same year that "a knowledge of domestic affairs, in all their relations is desirable—nay, essential, to the complete education of every female . . . A well regulated household, in every station of society, is one of woman's brightest ornaments—a source of happiness to her and to those who are dependent upon her labors of love for the attractions of home and its endearments." Although this may have been an appropriate ideal for many white middle- and upper-class women of the time, it was unrealistic for white working women, and even more unrealistic for black women. Most black women did become wives and mothers, but for many their knowledge of domestic affairs was necessarily applied in someone else's home in exchange for wages to help support their families.

Of all the techniques for bolstering black manhood, this was the most internally destructive. It demanded that women affirm their own inferiority in order to uphold the superiority of their men. Not that every African American accepted these gender images, many did not, but they nevertheless became touchstones for gender conventions within black society. Moreover, women faced sanctions for disregarding them, for to do so was viewed as furthering the aims and continuing the effects of slavery, depriving black men of their manhood.

There were women who recognized the dangerous consequences of counterpoising male and female traits, but only the boldest voices were raised in opposition. One of those voices was Sojourner Truth's. In the aftermath of the Civil War, when Congress debated the Fifteenth Amendment and related legislation providing the franchise to black men but not to women, she warned of the dangers inherent in such a move: "I feel that I have a right to have just as much as a man . . . if colored men get their rights and not colored women theirs, the colored men will be masters over the women, and it will be just a bad as before."

 F U R T H E R   R E A D I N G

Adele Logan Alexander, *Ambiguous Lives: Free Women of Color in Rural Georgia, 1789–1879* (1991).

Ira Berlin, *Slaves Without Masters: The Free Negro in the Antebellum South* (1975).

William Cheek and Aimee Lee Cheek, *John Mercer Langston and the Fight for Black Freedom, 1829–1865* (1989).

Leonard P. Curry, *The Free Black in Urban America, 1800–1850: The Shadow of the Dream* (1981).

Kimberly S. Hanger, *Bounded Lives, Bounded Places: Free Black Society in Colonial New Orleans, 1769–1803* (1997).

Theodore Hershberg, "Free Blacks in Antebellum Philadelphia: A Study of Ex-Slaves, Freeborn, and Socioeconomic Decline," *Journal of Social History*, 5 (1971–1972), 183–209.

Peter P. Hinks, "Frequently Plunged into Slavery: Free Blacks and Kidnapping in Antebellum Boston," *Historical Journal of Massachusetts,* 20 (1992), 16–31.

Peter P. Hinks, *To Awaken My Afflicted Brethren: David Walker and the Problem of Antebellum Slave Resistance* (1997).

James Oliver Horton and Lois E. Horton, *In Hope of Liberty: Culture, Community, and Protest Among Northern Free Blacks, 1700–1860* (1997).

Thomas N. Ingersoll, "Free Blacks in a Slave Society: New Orleans, 1718–1812," *William and Mary Quarterly*, 3rd Series, 48 (1991), 173–200.

Michael P. Johnson and James L. Roark, *Black Masters: A Free Family of Color in the Old South* (1984).

Whittington B. Johnson, *Black Savannah, 1788–1864* (1996).

Larry Koger, *Black Slaveowners: Free Black Slave Masters in South Carolina, 1790–1860* (1995).

Leon F. Litwack, *North of Slavery: The Negro in the Free States, 1790–1860* (1961).

Waldo E. Martin, *The Mind of Frederick Douglass* (1984).

Gary Nash, *Forging Freedom: The Formation of Philadelphia's Black Community, 1720–1840* (1988).

Nell Irvin Painter, *Sojourner Truth: A Life, a Symbol* (1996).

Benjamin Quarles, *Black Abolitionists* (1969).

Gayle T. Tate, "Political Consciousness and Resistance Among Black Antebellum Women," *Women and Politics*, 3 (1993), 67–89.

William Toll, "Free Men, Freedmen, and Race: Black Social Theory in the Gilded Age," *Journal of Southern History*, 44 (1978), 571–596.

Shane White, *Somewhat More Independent: The End of Slavery in New York City, 1770–1810* (1995).

Carol Wilson, *Freedom at Risk: The Kidnapping of Free Blacks in America, 1780–1865* (1994).

Carol Wilson, " 'The Thought of Slavery Is Death to a Free Man': Abolitionists' Response to the Kidnapping of Free Blacks," *Mid-America*, 74 (1992), 105–124.

Civil War and Emancipation

Although the 1850s was a decade of discouragement and setbacks for the abolitionist cause, it ended with the revolutionary violence of John Brown's assault on the federal arsenal at Harpers Ferry, which presaged the violent end of slavery. Brown's intent was to rally a slave insurrection, but it never materialized. Rather the election of Abraham Lincoln and southern secession precipitated a sectional war that at first studiously evaded an abolitionist purpose. Slaves responded not with violence but with something more akin to what W. E. B. Du Bois would later call "a general strike." Pouring into Union lines by the tens of thousands, fugitives from slavery forced the Lincoln administration's hand. Within months of the outbreak of war they were declared "contraband of war," comparable to any other war supplies that would not be returned to their owners to support the Confederate military. A little over a year later the Union made emancipation a more explicit tool in the war to suppress the rebellion. With the subsequent enlistment of blacks—southern slaves and northern freemen— into the ranks of the Union army and navy, John Brown's vision came close to being realized. Fittingly enough, the former slaves, now soldiers, marched off to war to the strains of the "Battle Hymn of the Republic," better known as "John Brown's Body."

Any assessment of the African-American role in the destruction of slavery has implications for an understanding of both slavery and emancipation. That blacks would seize the time to resist their masters put a lie to lingering racial stereotypes and the notion that they had internalized a slavish personality. That blacks spilled blood to gain their freedom and save the Union gave them a claim on the nation to fulfill emancipation's implicit promise of complete freedom and equality. Much, then, was at stake in how the history of that conflict and of the African-American role in it was written.

 D O C U M E N T S

In the first document, Captain C. B. Wilder describes the first, spontaneous reactions to the outbreak of war by slaves near Union lines in the Virginia tidewater region. The second document is a deposition by an ex-slave and Union veteran from Louisiana, describing one of the maroon or runaway communities formed by fugitive slaves deep in rebel-held territory. Even those slaves who did not escape their master's plantation recognized the challenges the war posed to their master's authority, and some began to assert claims to better working conditions and even wages, as revealed in accounts making up the third document. The photographs of Private Hubbard Pryor of the 44th U.S. Colored Infantry visually capture the transformation wrought when a lowly slave became a proud soldier. Heroic and harrowing tales of wartime escapes from slavery are related by free black abolitionist and missionary Charlotte Forten in the fifth document. In the sixth, Forten describes the celebration of the Emancipation Proclamation held in the very heart of the Confederacy. Running through her account is the assumption common among blacks that the future fate and destiny of the race depends on their own efforts in support of the war and their willingness to fight for their freedom. One of the songs they sang, the final document, prefigures the "freedom songs" of the liberation struggles to come a century later.

1. Captain C. B. Wilder, a Civil War Relief Worker, Describes Flight from Slavery, 1863

[Fortress Monroe, Va.,] May 9, 1863.

Question How many of the people called contrabands, have come under your observation?

Answer Some 10,000 have come under our control, to be fed in part, and clothed in part, but I cannot speak accurately in regard to the number. This is the rendezvous. They come here from all about, from Richmond and 200 miles off in North Carolina   There was one gang that started from Richmond 23 strong and only 3 got through.

. . . .

Q In your opinion, is there any communication between the refugees and the black men still in slavery?

A Yes Sir, we have had men here who have gone back 200 miles.

Q In your opinion would a change in our policy which would cause them to be treated with fairness, their wages punctually paid and employment furnished them in the army, become known and would it have any effect upon others in slavery?

A Yes—Thousands upon Thousands. I went to Suffolk a short time ago to enquire into the state of things there—for I found I could not get any foot hold to make things work there, through the Commanding General, and I went to the Provost Marshall and all hands—and the colored people actually sent a deputation to me one morning before I was up to know if we put black men in irons and sent them off to Cuba to be sold or set them at work and put balls on their legs and whipped them, just as in slavery; because that was the story up there, and they were frightened and didn't know what to do. When I got at the feelings of these people I found they were not afraid of the slaveholders. They said there was nobody on the plantations but women and they were not afraid of them   One woman came through 200 miles in Men's clothes. The most valuable information we received in regard to the Merrimack and the operations of the rebels came from the colored people and they got no credit for it. I found hundreds who had left their wives and families behind. I asked them "Why did you come away and leave them there?" and I found they had heard these stories, and wanted to come and see how it was. "I am going back again after my wife" some of them have said

"Testimony by the Superintendent of Contrabands at Fortress Monroe, Virginia, Before the American Freedmen's Inquiry Commission," in *Freedom: A Documentary History of Emancipation, 1861–1867, Series 1, Vol. 1: The Destruction of Slavery*, eds. Ira Berlin et al. (Cambridge, U.K.: Cambridge University Press, 1985), 88–90. Copyright © 1985 by Cambridge University Press.

"When I have earned a little money" "What as far as that?" "Yes" and I have had them come to me to borrow money, or to get their pay, if they had earned a month's wages, and to get passes. "I am going for my family" they say. "Are you not afraid to risk it?" "No I know the Way" Colored men will help colored men and they will work along the by paths and get through. In that way I have known quite a number who have gone up from time to time in the neighborhood of Richmond and several have brought back their families; some I have never heard from. As I was saying they do not feel afraid now. The white people have nearly all gone, the blood hounds are not there now to hunt them and they are not afraid, before they were afraid to stir. There are hundreds of negroes at Williamsburgh with their families working for nothing. They would not get pay here and they had rather stay where they are. "We are not afraid of being carried back" a great many have told us and "if we are, we can get away again" Now that they are getting their eyes open they are coming in. Fifty came this morning from Yorktown who followed Stoneman's Cavalry when they returned from their raid. The officers reported to their Quartermaster that they had so many horses and fifty or sixty negroes. "What did you bring them for" "Why they followed us and we could not stop them." I asked one of the men about it and he said they would leave their work in the field as soon as they found the Soldiers were Union men and follow them some-times without hat or coat. They would take [the] best horse they could get and every where they rode they would take fresh horses, leave the old ones and follow on and so they came in. I have questioned a great many of them and they do not feel much afraid; and there are a great many courageous fellows who have come from long dis-tances in rebeldom. Some men who came here from North Carolina, knew all about the Proclamation and they started on the belief in it; but they had heard these stories and they wanted to know how it was. Well, I gave them the evidence and I have no doubt their friends will hear of it. Within the last two or three months the rebel guards have been doubled on the line and the officers and privates of the 99th New York be-tween Norfolk and Suffolk have caught hundreds of fugitives and got pay for them.

Q Do I understand you to say that a great many who have escaped have been sent back?

A Yes Sir, The masters will come in to Suffolk in the day time and with the help of some of the 99th carry off their fugitives and by and by smuggle them across the lines and the soldier will get his $20. or $50.

2. Corporal Octave Johnson, a Union Soldier, Describes His Escape from Slavery During the War, 1864

[New Orleans February? 1864]

Deposition of Octave Johnson, Corporal Co. C, 15th Regt. Corps d'Afrique.

I was born in New Orleans; I am 23 years of age; I was raised by Arthur Thiboux of New Orleans; I am by trade a cooper; I was treated pretty well at

"Testimony by a Corporal in a Louisiana Black Regiment Before the American Freedmen's Inquiry Commission," in *Freedom: A Documentary History of Emancipation, 1861–1867, Series 1, Vol. 1: The Destruction of Slavery*, eds. Ira Berlin et al. (Cambridge, U.K.: Cambridge University Press, 1985), 217. Copyright © 1985 by Cambridge University Press.

home; in 1855 master sold my mother, and in 1861 he sold me to S. Contrell of St. James Parish for $2,400; here I worked by task at my trade; one morning the bell was rung for us to go to work so early that I could not see, and I lay still, because I was working by task; for this the overseer was going to have me whipped, and I ran away to the woods, where I remained for a year and a half; I had to steal my food; took turkeys, chickens and pigs; before I left our number had increased to thirty, of whom ten were women; we were four miles in the rear of the plantation house; sometimes we would rope beef cattle and drag them out to our hiding place; we obtained matches from our friends on the plantation; we slept on logs and burned cypress leaves to make a smoke and keep away mosquitoes; Eugene Jardeau, master of hounds, hunted for us for three months; often those at work would betray those in the swamp, for fear of being implicated in their escape, we furnished meat to our fellow-servants in the field, who would return corn meal; one day twenty hounds came after me; I called the party to my assistance and we killed eight of the bloodhounds; then we all jumped into Bayou Faupron; the dogs followed up and the alligators caught six of them; "the alligators preferred dog flesh to personal flesh;" we escaped and came to Camp Parapet, where I was first employed in the Commissary's office, then as a servant to Col. Hanks; then I joined his regiment.

3. John C. P. Wederstrandt and I. N. Steele, Two Slaveholders, Lose Control of Their Slave Labor, 1862, 1865

Statement of John C. P. Wederstrandt

New Orleans [*La.*] Sept. 19. 1862.

Sir   In obedience to an order of Col J N French Provost Marshall, I respectfully submit the following statement—

On Monday last, while on a visit to my plantation, I was startled at the dawn of day by the announcement of my brother in law Mr Smith the manager of the place, that the negroes were in a state of insurection, some of them refusing to work—   Proceeding immediately to the Cabin Yard, I found them gathered in different groups & on enquiry learned, that some of them would not work at all, & others wanted wages, I informed them, I should not pay them wages, & being excited by their ingratitude & not wishing to feed and clothe those who would not work. & to avoid any difficulty, as my sister and her four small children were on the place, I said that it was better to part in peace & go off quietly & that I did not

John C. P. Wederstrandt to Provost Marshall, in Ira Berlin et al., eds., *Free At Last: A Documentary History of Slavery, Freedom, and the Civil War* (1992), 72–73. Copyright © 1992 by The New Press. "A Kentucky Slaveholder to the Superintendent of the Organization of Black Troops," in *Freedom: A Documentary History of Emancipation, 1861–1867, Series 1, Vol. 1: The Destruction of Slavery*, eds. Ira Berlin et al. (Cambridge, U.K.: Cambridge University Press, 1985), 616. Copyright © 1985 by Cambridge University Press.

wish to lay eyes on them again, & they went away   I never drove any of them off the plantation, or told them according to the expression of Genl Dow to shift for themselves—   So far from it, I sent a written notice to the rice planters below, forbidding them to employ them under the pains & risks of the law, in regard to employment of runaway slaves   about twenty five of them left the plantation, some of them remained & went to work the next day—

On the 17th inst one of the revolted named Auguste, demanded from the overseer his gun, & not being able to find it endeavoured to get possession of the overseer's. In reply to Mr Smith's question, "If he had a pass," he said Genl Dow had given him his free papers which he produced, & said moreover that Genl Dow had told him all the people were free & that he, (Auguste) had come for what belonged to him—   My brother in law, the overseer, and myself, knowing him to be a dangerous man, determined to bring him to the city & have the whole subject properly investigated—   I started with him in my buggy, Mr Smith & the overseer on horseback—accompanyed me a short distance and returned—   His language was very offensive,   among other things he said that he wished to go to Virginia, meaning thereby that he wished to enlist—   I succeeded with some assistance in securing him in the jail of St Bernard—

Considering this boy as one of the ring-leaders & a dangerous character on the plantation, I thought it best to remove him, & leave it to the Provost Marshal to dispose of him as it may seem best—   There are about twenty negroes with free papers from Genl Dow, a great burthen to the place; a heavy tax on me & a bad example to the other negroes—

Under this anamolous state of affairs, I pray that the Governor & Provost Marshall, will take the necessary steps to examine into this affair, & send an officer to verify this statement. & see into the condition of things on the plantation, that a suitable protection be afforded my sister and her children, that the negroes may be informed how far the emancipation of Genl Dow may be valid, & the future conduct of the place & themselves, may be put upon such a footing & will restore peace & good order—   I am very respectfully your obt

John C. P. Wederstrandt

Statement of I. N. Steele

Lexington [*Ky.*] April 1st 1865

Kind sir: I have a black Boy, or rather, a mulatto, who has refused to serve me any longer, and affirms that he is as free as I am. Said Boy has done me only one days work since Christmas. He is 49 years old, about five feet ten in., high; and a very stout, able bodied Boy. I wish to enlist him into the service; and being some distance from home, and anxious to join my family, I will be under lasting obligations to you; if you will instruct your recruiting officer, Porteus P. Bielby (at Lexington) immediately to have him arrested and enlisted.

Said Boy is in the vicinity of Hutchison's station nine miles from Lexington on the Covington R.R.   Yours very Respectfully,

I. N. Steele

4. Private Hubbard Pryor as a Slave and as a Union Soldier, c. 1864

Enclosed in Colonel R. D. Mussey to Major C. W. Foster, October 10, 1864, M-750 1864, Letters Received, ser. 360, Colored Troops Division, RG 94. Reprinted from *Freedom: A Documentary History of Emancipation, 1861–1867, Series 1, Vol. 1: The Destruction of Slavery,* eds. Ira Berlin et al. (Cambridge, U.K.: Cambridge University Press, 1985), 217. Copyright © 1985 by Cambridge University Press.

5. Slave Fugitives Tell Their Stories to Charlotte Forten, 1863

Monday, February 2.   Have just heard to-night of the return of the 1st Regt. They came back with laurels—and Secesh prisoners. Have heard no particulars, but am *glad,* emphatically glad to know that they come back completely successful. That is grand, glorious! In the joy of my heart sat down and wrote a congratulatory note, to my dear friend Dr. R. [ogers]. I know how rejoiced he must be. Thank God that he and the noble Col. [Higginson] have come back safe.

Saturday, February 7.   One day this week Tina, an excellent woman from Pala-wana came in, and told us a very interesting story about two girls, one about ten and the other fifteen, who having been taken by their master up into the country about the time of the "Gun Shoot," determined to try to get back to their parents who had been left on this island. They stole away at night, and travelled through woods and swamps, for two days without eating. Sometimes their strength w'ld fail and they w'ld sink down in the swamps, and think they c'ld go no further, but they had brave little hearts, and struggled on, till at last they reached Port Royal Ferry. There they were seen by a boat-load of people who had also made their escape. The boat was too full to take them but the people, as soon as they reached these islands, told the father of the children, who immediately hastened to the Ferry for them. The poor little creatures were almost wild with joy, despite their exhausted state, when they saw their father coming to them. When they were brought to their mother she fell down "jus' as if she was dead" as Tina expressed it. She was so overpowered with joy. Both children are living on Balta now. They are said to be very clever. I want to see the heroic little creatures.

Another day, one of the black soldiers came in and gave us *his* account of the Expedition. No words of mine, dear A.[,] can give you any account of the state of exaltation and enthusiasm that he was in. He was eager for another chance at "de Secesh." I asked him what he w'ld do if his master and others sh'ld come back and try to reenslave him. "I'd fight un Miss, I'd fight un till I turned to dust!" He was especially delighted at the ire which the sight of the black troops excited in the minds of certain Secesh women whom they saw. These vented their spleen by calling the men "baboons dressed in soldiers' clothes, and telling them that they ought to be at work in their masters' rice swamps, and that they ought to be lashed to death." "And what did you say to them?" I asked. "Oh, miss, we only tell us 'Hole your tongue, and dry up,! You see we wusn't feared of *dem, dey cldn't hurt us now.* Whew! didn't we laugh to see dem so mad!" The spirit of resistance to the Secesh is strong in these men.

6. Charlotte Forten Describes the Celebration of Emancipation in the Heart of the Confederacy, January 1, 1863

Thursday, New Year's Day, 1863.   The most glorious day this nation has yet seen, *I* think. I rose early—an event here—and early we started, with an old borrowed carriage and a remarkably slow horse. Whither were we going? thou wilt ask, dearest A.

Brenda Stevenson, ed., *The Journals of Charlotte Forten Grimké* (1988), 444–45. Copyright © 1988 by Oxford University Press, Inc.

Brenda Stevenson, ed., *The Journals of Charlotte Forten Grimké* (1988), 428–432. Copyright © 1988 by Oxford University Press, Inc.

To the ferry; thence to Camp Saxton, to the celebration. From the ferry to the camp the "Flora" took us. How pleasant it was on board! A crowd of people, whites and blacks, and a band of music—to the great delight of the negroes. Met on board Dr. [Solomon] and Mrs. Peck and their daughters, who greeted me most kindly. Also Gen. S.[axton]'s father whom I like much, and several other acquaintances whom I was glad to see. We stopped at Beaufort, and then proceeded to Camp Saxton, the camp of the 1st Reg.[iment] S.[outh] C.[arolina] Vol[unteer]s. The "Flora" c'ld not get up to the landing, so we were rowed ashore in a row boat. . . . The meeting was held in a beautiful grove, a live-oak grove, adjoining the camp. It is the largest one I have yet seen; but I don't think the moss pendants are quite as beautiful as they are on St. Helena. As I sat on the stand and looked around on the various groups, I thought I had never seen a sight so beautiful. There were the black soldiers, in their blue coats and scarlet pants, the officers of this and other regiments in their handsome uniforms, and crowds of lookers-on, men, women and children, grouped in various attitudes, under the trees. The faces of all wore a happy, eager, expectant look. The exercises commenced by a prayer from Rev. Mr. [James H.] Fowler, Chaplain of the Reg. An ode written for the occasion by Prof. [John] Zachos, originally a Greek, now Sup.[erintendent] of Paris Island, was read by himself, and then sung by the whites. Col. H.[igginson] introduced Dr. [William] Brisbane in a few elegant and graceful words. He (Dr. B.[risbane]) read the President's Proclamation, which was warmly cheered. Then the beautiful flags presented by Dr. [George] Cheever's Church were presented to Col. H.[igginson] for the Reg. in an excellent and enthusiastic speech, by Rev. Mr. [Mansfield] French. Immediately at the conclusion, some of the colored people—of their own accord sang "My Country Tis of Thee." It was a touching and beautiful incident and Col. Higginson, in accepting the flags made it the occasion of some happy remarks. He said that *that* tribute was far more effecting than any speech he c'ld make. He spoke for some time, and all that he said was grand, glorious. He seemed inspired. Nothing c'ld have been better, more perfect. And Dr. R.[ogers] told me afterward that the Col. was much affected. That tears were in his eyes. He is as Whittier says, truly a "sure man." The men all admire and love him. There is a great deal of personal magnetism about him, and his kindness is proverbial. After he had done speaking he delivered the flags to the color-bearers with a few very impressive remarks to them. They each then, Prince Rivers, and Robert Sutton, made very good speeches indeed, and were loudly cheered. Gen. Saxton and Mrs. Gage spoke very well. The good Gen. was received with great enthusiasm, and throughout the morning— every little while it seemed to me three cheers were given for him. A Hymn written I believe, by Mr. Judd, was sung, and then all the people united with the Reg. in singing "John Brown." It was grand. During the exercises, it was announced that [John C.] Fremont was appointed Commander-in-Chief of the Army, and this was received with enthusiastic and prolonged cheering. But as it was picket news, I greatly fear that it is not true.

    . . . The Dress Parade—the first I have ever seen—delighted me. It was a brilliant sight—the long line of men in their brilliant uniforms, with bayonets gleaming in the sunlight. The Col. looked splendid. The Dr. said the men went through the drill remarkably well. It seemed to me nothing c'ld be more perfect. To me it was a grand triumph—that black regiment doing itself honor in the sight of the white officers, many of whom, doubtless "came to scoff." It was typical of what the race, so long down-trodden and degraded will yet achieve on this continent. . . .

7. A Freedom Song from the Civil War Era

Who'll Join the Union?

Oh, hallelujah, Oh, hallelujah,
Oh, hallelujah, Lord,
Who'll join the Union?

My lovely brethren, how ye do?
Who'll join the Union?
Oh, does your love continue true?
Who'll join the Union?
Ever since I have been newly born;
Who'll join the Union?
I love to see-a God's work go on;
Who'll join the Union?

If you want to catch that heavenly breeze,
Go down in the valley upon your knees,
Go bend your knees right smooth with the ground,
And pray to the Lord to turn you around.

Say, if you belong to the Union band,
Then here's my heart, and here's my hand,
I love you all both bond and free,
I love you if you don't love me.

Now if you want to know of me,
Just who I am, and a-who I be,

I'm a child of God with my soul set free,
For Christ has bought my liberty.

Oh, hallelujah, Oh, hallelujah,
Who'll join the Union?

E S S A Y S

In the first essay Vincent Harding muses over the ironic position African Americans found themselves in during the Civil War: although convinced that the destruction of slavery was divinely ordained, in the ambivalence and racial hostility of the northern white agents of that destruction they found cause to be ambivalent themselves. Southern slaves, in contrast, took immediate and forceful action, deserting their slave posts to seek refuge behind Union lines and eventually enlisting to fight their former masters. The final irony, Harding observes, is that history recognized their ambivalent emancipators rather than their own actions as the instrument of slavery's destruction. In the second essay, by examining slave escape and rescue initiatives in one state, Clarence L. Mohr shows how they were rooted in strong ties of kinship and community that the slave regime had not broken. They reflected a view of the war at once pragmatic and idealistic, as Georgia slaves accepted help where they found it but ultimately relied on themselves. Such initiatives prepared them eventually to join in the Union military struggle as soldiers and sailors and to attempt to forge independent black communities in the postwar era.

Soldiers of God's Wrath

VINCENT HARDING

Although the destruction of the oppressors God may not be effected by the oppressed, yet the Lord our God will surely bring other destructions upon them—for not infrequently will he cause them to rise up against one another, to be split and divided, and to oppress each other, and sometimes to open hostilities with sword in hand.

DAVID WALKER, 1829

On certain stark and bloody levels, a terrible irony seemed to be at work. For those who interpreted the events of their own times through the wisdom and anguish of the past, the guns of Charleston certainly sounded like the signal for the fulfillment of David Walker's radical prophecies. Here at last was the coming of the righteous God in judgment, preparing to bring "destructions" upon America. Here was the divine culmination of the struggle toward freedom and justice long waged by the oppressed black people. From such a vantage point, the conflict now bursting out was the ultimate justification of the costly freedom movement, a welcome vindication of the trust in Providence. And yet the war was not simply an ally. Like all wars, it brought with it a train of demoralizing, destructive elements, deeply affecting even those persons and causes which seemed to be its chief beneficiaries. In the case of black people, the guns broke in upon their freedom struggle at many levels, diverted and diffused certain of its significant radical elements, and became a source of profound confusion and disarray among its most committed forces. This was especially the case where independent radical black struggle for justice and self-determination was concerned.

Part of the ironic confusion of the Civil War was lodged in the very tradition of David Walker's divine vengeance. In a sense, it was also the tradition of Frederick Douglass's beneficent Providence, of Sojourner Truth's living God, and Henry Garnet's Sovereign of the Universe. In fact, hundreds of thousands of black people, north and south, believed unwaveringly that their God moved in history to deliver his people, and they had been looking eagerly, praying hourly, waiting desperately for the glory of the coming of the Lord. For them, all the raucous, roaring guns of Charleston Harbor and Bull Run, of Antietam and Fort Pillow, of Shiloh and

Murfreesboro and Richmond were the certain voice of God, announcing his judgment across the bloody stretches of the South, returning blood for blood to the
black river. Then came the critical, human judgment: because the white South was
holding millions of black people in bondage while the white North officially held
none, the North was designated—with no little fear and trembling—as the force
through which God was working his righteous, liberating purpose, the obvious side
for black men to join.

But the North was also the federal government, which had repeatedly turned
its various faces against black people, denying their citizenship rights and eliciting
a mounting storm of black fury, widespread civil disobedience, attempts at insurrection. The North was the state legislatures of the section, with their unjust laws
and acts of disfranchisement against their often unwanted black residents. The
North was the merchants and the mobs, the school boards and the white farmers.
Just yesterday this North, this government, this guarantor of the rights of white
slaveholders, had inspired powerful black radical analysis and action. Now, with
the firing of a thousand guns—which the North had not initiated—this North was
transformed into the instrument of God. With this confused and confusing transformation, the power of black resistance to the real North was subverted. Thus war—
so often the supreme honer and harshener of men—in fact blunted and softened
much black radicalism. For as the armies reeled their fear-drunken, honor-drunken,
pain-drunken ways across the land, and battered their lives against the hills and
mountains, against the visions that Prophet Nat and David Walker had seen, they
released the revolutionary tension, distorted the terrible beauty, stymied temporarily the movement toward radical, self-reliant, independent black struggle.

To see the meaning of this irony more clearly, one must remember that David
Walker had envisioned two distinct possibilities for the final destruction of slavery,
racism, and exploitation in America. One was that God would send a black Messiah
to lead his people in a righteous crusade against the whole of white, slaveholding,
slavery-supporting American society. The second was that the two equally guilty
Northern and Southern sections would rise up in civil war, carrying out a sanguinary
judgment upon each other with black people on hand, waiting, as the independent,
righteous remnant. In those same vision-swept days, Nat Turner had seen only the
first shattering possibility: white and black apocalyptic armies, battling each other
for victory. Both visions of the end presumed independent black forces, arrayed
against the total white-created evil of American society.

Prior to the outbreak of hostilities, the tension in the black community increased
as it recognized that the vast majority of white America, represented by its government, was not only prepared to live with slavery, but was opposed to the full development of any black people's rights anywhere. It was this reality which helped to drive
the John Copelands to Harpers Ferry, pressed the Martin Delanys to West Africa, sent
thousands of others to Canada. But in 1861 the guns of Charleston shattered the tension, broke into the visions, confused the emerging hard radical analysis.

When the war broke out, black men and women were convinced that it had to
destroy slavery. Especially in the North, this inner certainty flooded their consciousness, buoyed up their hopes. Now it appeared that God was providing a way
out of the darkness of slavery and degradation, a way which would release some of
the frightening tension of the previous decade. Because they wanted a way out so

desperately, because it was hard to be driven by a fierce urgency, fearsome to experience the personal honing in spite of one's own softer and blunter ways, the children of Africa in America clutched at a solution which would not cause them to be driven into the depths of radicalism. For they must have realized that the chances were good that they might not survive without being seriously, unpredictably transformed. Therefore, when the guns began, black people shunted aside the knowledge of certain fierce realities.

In that mood their men surged forward to volunteer for service in the Union cause, repressing bitter memories. In spite of their misgivings, disregarding the fact that it was not the North which had initiated this righteous war, they offered their bodies for the Northern cause, believing that it was—or would be—the cause of black freedom. If the excited, forgetful young volunteers sought justification, they could find it in the *Anglo-African:* "Talk as we may, we are concerned in this fight and our fate hangs upon its issues. The South must be subjugated, or we shall be enslaved. In aiding the Federal government in whatever way we can, we are aiding to secure our own liberty; for this war can end only in the subjugation of the North or the South." When hard pressed, the journal, like the young men it encouraged, knew very well the nature of the "liberty" they had found so far in the unsubjugated North, and the writer admitted that the North was not consciously fighting for black rights. However, the *Anglo-African* chose to see a power beyond the councils of the North: "Circumstances have been so arranged by the decrees of Providence, that in struggling for their own nationality they are forced to defend our rights."

That was the key to the diverting force of the war as it met the river of struggle. Men and women chose to believe that some mysterious movement of the Divine was among them, forcing a recalcitrant white America; against its will and desire, to fight for the rights of black men. It was a strange theodicy, but it reigned in black America. In January 1862, when the eloquent black physician John Rock announced the doctrine to his black and white abolitionist audience at the Massachusetts Anti-Slavery Society, he drew loud cheers and applause: "I think I see the finger of God in all this. Yes, there is the hand-writing on the wall: *Break every yoke, and let the oppressed go free. I have heard the groans of my people, and am come down to deliver them.*" He too was forced to admit that the government was not intentionally abolitionist, but he was certain that God would break through anyway. "While fighting for its own existence," said Rock, the federal government had been "obliged to take slavery by the throat, and sooner or later *must* choke her to death."

Following such strange turnings of history, and such inspired readings of the writings on the wall, black men ran to volunteer. At the outset of hostilities, in Boston and throughout the North they pledged to "organize themselves immediately into drilling companies, to become better skilled in the use of fire-arms; so that when we shall be called upon by the country, we shall be better prepared to make a ready and fitting response." This was the same Boston and Cincinnati and Chicago where black men had only recently been arming themselves against the courts and the laws and the people. But now God had spoken in the guns.

Early in the war black men were eager not only to participate in the righteous work of the federal government, but to serve their state governments as well. In May 1861 a number of free black men in Pennsylvania offered to go down into the South to try to provoke slave rebellions, but the governor refused to sanction it. (This was, of course, the same Pennsylvania which had readily extradited to Virginia one of John Brown's white followers to be tried and executed.) Following the voices which said that God, in his mysterious ways, had chosen white racist forces to bring about black freedom, black men continued to offer their services to federal and state governments for military duty. These Northern governments, perversely ignorant of any special ordination by Providence, refused the black volunteers. Afro-Americans could serve as laborers and cooks, doing all the dirty and menial work of the armed forces, but any large-scale arming of these freedom-hungry people seemed out of the question. So in the early period of the war, with very few exceptions (often the light-skinned children of Africa), the black volunteers were refused. In their official language, the government refusals were only a more polite form of the essential message which many white people of the streets shouted, and sang in doggerel:

> To the flag we are pledged, all its foes we abhor
> And we ain't for the nigger, but we are for the war.

This sentiment was totally compatible with the history of the North, and the Union leaders were as yet unprepared to try to create any new black-white relations. Abraham Lincoln had not seen the visions which possessed the black people of the North. He had not yet rightly measured "the judgements of the Lord," the movements of Providence. Instead, he was still trapped in his own obsession with saving the white Union at all costs, even the cost of continued black slavery. Sensitively attuned to the feelings of whites, Lincoln believed that the arming of black people would strike deep chords of fear among whites, especially among his tender allies in the "loyal" slave states of Delaware, Maryland, Kentucky, and Missouri. Perhaps of even more importance, he knew that accepting the help of black troops in quelling the Southern rebellion carried with it the moral responsibility of facing their demands for citizenship rights; Lincoln was still convinced that blacks and whites could not live peaceably as equal citizens in the United States. So the black men were refused, and when their eager volunteer companies stubbornly insisted on drilling and marching in the streets and fields of the North, in many cities they were actually attacked by the whites.

Finally such rejection, humiliation, and persecution gave some black people pause for thought, threw their minds back into the recent terrors of the 1850s, suggested again the possibility of other ways in the struggle. One black man put the essential question to all these eager volunteers: "Is this country ready and anxious to initiate a new era for downtrodden humanity, that you now so eagerly propose to make the sacrifice of thousands of our ablest men to encourage and facilitate the great work of regeneration?" Then he answered his own question: "No! No! . . . Our policy must be neutral, ever praying for the success of that party determined to initiate first the policy of justice and equal rights." Obviously, the North had made no such decision.

The same message appeared in a letter from Troy, New York, to the *Anglo-African,* signed by one who called himself "Ivanhoe," who urged black men not to volunteer even if invited: "And suppose we were invited, what duty would we then owe to ourselves and our posterity? We are in advance of our fathers. They put confidence in the word of the whites only to feel the dagger of slavery driven still deeper into the heart. . . . We are not going to re-enact that tragedy. Our enslaved brethren must be made freedmen. . . . We of the North must have all the rights which white men enjoy; until then we are in no condition to fight under the flag [which] gives us no protection."

These were echoes of H. Ford Douglas, voices searching toward an independent black position, lives still impelled toward treason. But these were not the dominant voices of the years of war. In spite of rebuffs the overwhelming call was still to join forces with the North, to proclaim the white Republican leaders as divinely ordained allies in a struggle which only yesterday had carried black people to open defiance of the government, but which now sought desperately to join that same government in its ambiguous forced march toward black freedom. This meant joining the Sewards, the Trumballs, the Greeleys, and the Lincolns, and the white supremacy they unashamedly professed. It meant helping to build the rapidly expanding forces of the industrialists, railroad owners, land speculators, and bankers as they transformed the face of America. God was using most unusual vessels, and it was a most confusing time. Delany cried out: "In God's name, must we ever be subordinate to those of another race? . . . Have we no other destiny in prospect as an inheritance for our children? It is for us to determine whether or not this shall be so." And Delany remained in America to follow the wavering hand of the Divine, to erode his own sense of destiny.

And what of the South? What of those sometimes God-obsessed black believers who had long lifted their cries for deliverance in songs and shouts, in poetry filled with rich and vibrant images? Did they sense the coming of Moses now? Was this finally the day of the delivering God, when he would set his people free? Did they hear Nat Turner's spirit speaking in the guns? Did they believe he was calling them to freedom through all the lines of skirmishers who left their blood upon the leaves? Did they have any difficulty knowing which of the white armies was Pharaoh's?

The answers were as complex as life itself. In many parts of the nation and the world there had been predictions that secession, disunion, and war would lead to a massive black insurrection which would finally vindicate Turner and Walker, and drown the South in blood. Such predictions were made without knowledge of the profound racism and fear which pervaded the white North, and certainly without awareness of the keen perceptions of black people in the South. For most of the enslaved people knew their oppressors, and certainly realized that such a black uprising would expose the presence of Pharaoh's armies everywhere. To choose that path to freedom would surely unite the white North and South more quickly than any other single development, making black men, women, and children the enemy— the isolated, unprepared enemy. For anyone who needed concrete evidence, Gen. George B. McClellan, the commander of the Union's Army of the Ohio, had supplied it in his "Proclamation to the People of Western Virginia" on May 26, 1861: "Not only will we abstain from all interferences with your slaves, but we will, with an iron hand, crush any attempt at insurrection on their part."

So, heeding their own intuitive political wisdom, the black masses confirmed in their actions certain words which had recently appeared in the *Anglo-African.* Thomas Hamilton, the editor, had heard of Lincoln's decision to countermand an emancipation order issued by one of his most fervent Republican generals, John C. Fremont, in Missouri. Hamilton predicted: "The forlorn hope of insurrection among the slaves may as well be abandoned. They are too well informed and too *wise* to court destruction at the hands of the combined Northern and Southern armies—for the man who had reduced back to slavery the slaves of rebels in Missouri would order the army of the United States to put down a slave insurrection in Virginia or Georgia." He was right, of course, and the enslaved population was also right. Therefore, instead of mass insurrection, the Civil War created the context for a vast broadening and intensifying of the self-liberating black movement which had developed prior to the war. Central to this black freedom action, as always, was the continuing series of breaks with the system of slavery, the denials of the system's power, the self-emancipation of steadily increasing thousands of fugitives. Thus, wherever possible, black people avoided the deadly prospects of massive, sustained confrontation, for their ultimate objective was freedom, not martyrdom.

As the guns resounded across the Southern lands, the movement of black folk out of slavery began to build. Quickly it approached and surpassed every level of force previously known. Eventually the flood of fugitives amazed all observers and dismayed not a few, as it sent waves of men, women, and children rushing into the camps of the Northern armies. In this overwhelming human movement, black people of the South offered their own responses to the war, to its conundrums and mysteries. Their action testified to their belief that deliverance was indeed coming through the war, but for thousands of them it was not a deliverance to be bestowed by others. Rather it was to be independently seized and transformed through all the courage, wisdom, and strength of their waiting black lives.

This rapidly increasing movement of black runaways had been noted as soon as the reality of Southern secession had been clearly established. Shortly after the guns of April began to sound in Charleston harbor, large companies of fugitives broke loose from Virginia and the Carolinas and moved toward Richmond. Again, one day in Virginia in the spring of 1861, a black fugitive appeared at the Union-held Fortress Monroe. Two days later eight more arrived, the next day more than fifty, soon hundreds. The word spread throughout the area: there was a "freedom fort," as the fugitives called it, and within a short time thousands were flooding toward it. Similarly, in Louisiana two families waded six miles across a swamp, "spending two days and nights in mud and water to their waists, their children clinging to their backs, and with nothing to eat." In Georgia, a woman with her twenty-two children and grandchildren floated down the river on "a dilapidated flatboat" until she made contact with the Union armies. In South Carolina, black folk floated to freedom on "basket boats made out of reeds," thus reviving an ancient African craft. A contemporary source said of the black surge toward freedom in those first two years of the war: "Many thousands of blacks of all ages, ragged, with no possessions, except the bundles which they carried, had assembled at Norfolk, Hampton, Alexandria and Washington. Others . . . in multitudes . . . flocked north from Tennessee, Kentucky, Arkansas, and Missouri."

This was black struggle in the South as the guns roared, coming out of loyal and disloyal states, creating their own liberty. This was the black movement toward a new history, a new life, a new beginning. W. E. B. Du Bois later said, "The whole move was not dramatic or hysterical, rather it was like the great unbroken swell of the ocean before it dashes on the reefs." Yet there was great drama as that flowing movement of courageous black men and women and children sensed the movement of history, heard the voices of God, created and signed their own emancipation proclamations, and seized the time. Their God was moving and they moved with him.

And wherever this moving army of self-freed men and women and children went, wherever they stopped to wait and rest and eat and work, and watch the movements of the armies in the fields and forests—in all these unlikely sanctuaries, they sent up their poetry of freedom. Some of them were old songs, taking on new meaning:

> Thus said the Lord, Bold Moses said
> Let my people go
> If not I'll smite your first-born dead
> Let my people go.
> No more shall they in bondage toil
> Let my people go.

But now there was no need to hide behind the stories of thousands of years gone by, now it was clearly a song of black struggle, of deliverance for their own time of need. Now the singers themselves understood more fully what they meant when they sang again:

> One of dese mornings, five o'clock
> Dis ole world gonna reel and rock,
> Pharaoh's Army got drownded
> Oh, Mary, don't you weep.

They were part of the drowning river. Out there, overlooking the battlefields of the South, they were the witnesses to the terrible truth of their own songs, to the this-worldliness of their prayers and aspirations. Remembering that morning in Charleston harbor, who could say they were wrong? "Dis ole world gonna reel and rock. . . ."

Every day they came into the Northern lines, in every condition, in every season of the year, in every state of health. Children came wandering, set in the right direction by falling, dying parents who finally knew why they had lived until then. Women came, stumbling and screaming, their wombs bursting with the promise of new and free black life. Old folks who had lost all track of their age, who knew only that they had once heard of a war against "the Redcoats," also came, some blind, some deaf, yet no less eager to taste a bit of that long-anticipated freedom of their dreams. No more auction block, no more driver's lash, many thousands gone.

This was the river of black struggle in the south, waiting for no one to declare freedom for them, hearing only the declarations of God in the sound of the guns, and moving.

By land, by river, creating their own pilgrim armies and their own modes of travel, they moved south as well as north, heading down to the captured areas of the coast of South Carolina. *Frederick Douglass's Monthly* of February 1862 quoted the report of a *New York Times* correspondent in Port Royal: "Everywhere I find the same state of things existing; everywhere the blacks hurry in droves to our lines; they crowd in small boats around our ships; they swarm upon our decks; they hurry to our officers from the cotton houses of their masters, in an hour or two after our guns are fired. . . . I mean each statement I make to be taken literally; it is not garnished for rhetorical effect." As usual, black people were prepared to take advantage of every disruption in the life of the oppressing white community. When they heard the guns, they were ready, grasping freedom with their own hands, walking to it, swimming to it, sailing to it—determined that it should be theirs. By all these ways, defying masters, patrols, Confederate soldiers, slowly, surely, they pressed themselves into the central reality of the war.

And the songs continued to rend the air, bursting with new meaning, pointing with every word and note toward freedom, filled with a hope and wonder only the captives could know:

> Slavery chain done broke at last!
> Broke at last! Broke at last!
> Slavery chain done broke at last!
> Gonna praise God till I die!

It was a magnificent hope, a commitment purchased with blood; but its ardor could not conceal the fact that the paradoxical war had thrust certain ironies into the Southern struggle for freedom as well. On the one hand, the rapid flow of black fugitives was a critical part of the challenge to the embattled white rulers of the South; by leaving, they denied slavery's power and its profit. But much of their movement out of slavery carried them into the camps of the Union troops, brought them harshly against the incongruous reality of the white North as God's saving agent.

Roaring past and over one set of dams, the black community of escape soon discovered, in the cruelties and racism of the Union camps, yet another set of obstacles to their freedom. For at levels that in those days men dared not explore too fully, the deliverers often seemed to be the enemy. In many places the desperate, weary, uncertain fugitives were mistreated, abused, or chased away by Union soldiers. In some cases the deliverers even returned them to their owners. Still, the black flood did not abate. So while enslaved black people initially took their freedom into their own hands because they had no other apparent options, they were almost immediately forced to entrust that freedom to the hesitant white hands of the armies and leaders of the North. Thus, instead of again connecting with the Northern black movement, they were largely halted in the camps of the federal government, thereby depriving both the Northern and Southern movements of the needed impetus to take them into the next period, when the nature and extent of that hard-won freedom would be viciously questioned and attacked. (Some black fugitives partially avoided the contradiction, but not the problem, by moving far beyond the Union lines, refusing to stop until they reached Canada or Mexico.)

Nevertheless, during the war's first years many variations on the fugitive theme were reported. "A Southern planter wrote a friend in New York that four of his runaway slaves had returned voluntarily after a spell of 'Yankee freedom.' But several months later he complained bitterly that the same four had run away again—this time taking with them two hundred other slaves." Many persons who could not or would not leave their immediate areas joined the struggle in other ways. Shortly after the outbreak of the war, blacks in Georgetown, South Carolina, were jailed for joyously singing:

> We'll soon be free,
> We'll soon be free;
> We'll soon be free,
> When de Lord will call us home.

For the white authorities, the last line could in no way ease the meaning of the song.

Arson continued, too. In May 1861 a dozen ships were burned while at anchor in New Orleans. According to a newspaper correspondent from that area, nobody in the city felt any doubt that the black captives of the area (and probably some of their aggressive free companions) had done the work. That was also the general opinion in Charleston later that same year, when a massive fire swept the city, destroying six hundred buildings and causing seven million dollars in damage. And when, in the fall of 1861, Union gunboats arrived at Beaufort, South Carolina, and many whites fled the city, blacks from the countryside poured into the town to ransack and destroy white property. Meanwhile runaway blacks also served as spies and saboteurs for the Union military forces. One audacious group of families under the leadership of a skilled black harbor pilot, Robert Smalls, actually commandeered and sailed the *Planter,* a Confederate coastal supply ship, past the unwitting Southern keepers of the Charleston harbor batteries and delivered it—and themselves—into Union hands at Beaufort harbor, Smalls' home town.

Although the mass insurrection that men had expected did not take place, in the early years of the war more limited risings were reported in many parts of the South. In Mississippi several plots were supposedly planned to explode on July 4, 1861—that day of black irony; by the end of the summer, some forty black men had been hanged in the Natchez area for their part in the movement. In the same year an attempt at a smaller insurrection led to the hanging of two black men and one woman in northern Arkansas. In South Carolina, whites became suspicious of an increasing number of black funerals and followed a group of mourners to a cemetery, "where it was discovered that the coffin contained arms which were being removed and hidden in a vault." Real mourning followed when "nineteen of the most 'intelligent' conspirators were executed." As for the border states, there too the movement continued unabated, in spite of their special status: In December 1861 some sixty enslaved blacks marched through New Castle, Kentucky, "singing political songs and shouting for Lincoln"; we are told that no one dared stop them.

As the war spread into the South, the black outlyers often found themselves in a crucial and sensitive position. Many of them stepped up their activities against the weakened plantation areas, and successfully resisted patrols sent to capture or destroy them. Some developed strange alliances with white Confederate deserters; together, the two groups created troublesome guerrilla forces in several places behind the Confederate lines. For the blacks, many of whom had always considered themselves at war with Southern society, this was a logical development in their struggle.

Nevertheless, beyond outlyers, arsonists, and insurrectionaries, in the South the major black resistance and struggle was focused in the relentless movement of the self-liberated fugitives into the Union lines. Without speeches, laws, or guns, literally, insistently, with bold force, often organized and led by the trusted black slave drivers, they inserted their bodies into the cauldron of the war. All the denials of Lincoln and his government, all the doggerel of the white Northern population, could not stop them from their own dramatic proclamation, their own announcement that they were at the heart of this conflict. By the end of the spring of 1862, tens of thousands were camped out in whatever areas the Northern armies had occupied, thereby making themselves an unavoidable military and political issue. In Washington, D.C., the commander-in-chief of the Union armies had developed no serious plans for the channeling of the black river. Consequently, in the confusion which all war engenders, his generals in the field made and carried out their own plans. They were badly strapped for manpower, and the black fugitives provided some answers to whatever prayers generals pray. The blacks could relieve white fighting men from garrison duties. They could serve as spies, scouts, and couriers in the countryside they knew so well. They could work the familiar land, growing crops for the food and profit of the Union armies. But as the war dragged on and Northern whites lost some of their early enthusiasm, many Union commanders saw the black men among them primarily as potential soldiers. Many of the black men were eager to fight, but Lincoln was still not prepared to go that far.

Nevertheless, some Union commanders like Gen. David Hunter in South Carolina were again issuing their own emancipation proclamations and beginning to recruit black soldiers. In places like occupied New Orleans it was the unmanageable and threatening movement of the blacks themselves which placed additional pressures on the Union's leader. Reports were pouring into Washington which told not only of the flood of fugitives, but of black unrest everywhere. Black men were literally fighting their way past the local police forces to get themselves and their families into the union encampments. There was word of agricultural workers killing or otherwise getting rid of their overseers, and taking over entire plantations. Commanders like Gen. Ben Butler warned that only Union bayonets prevented widespread black insurrection. (In August 1862, to preserve order and satisfy his need for manpower, Butler himself had begun to recruit black troops in New Orleans, beginning with the well-known Louisiana Native Guards.) The dark presence at the center of the national conflict could no longer be denied. Lincoln's armies were in the midst of a surging movement of black people who were in effect freeing themselves from slavery. His generals were at once desperate for the military resources represented by the so-called contrabands, and convinced that only through military discipline could this volatile, potentially revolutionary black element be contained. As a result, before 1862 was over, black troops were being enlisted to fight for their own freedom in both South Carolina and Louisiana.

In Washington, Congress was discussing its own plans for emancipation, primarily as a weapon against the South, hoping to deprive the Confederacy of a major source of human power and transfer it into Union hands. Their debates and imminent action represented another critical focus of pressure on the President. While Lincoln continued to hesitate about the legal, constitutional, moral, and military aspects of the matter, he was also being constantly attacked in the North for his conduct of the war. The whites were weary and wanted far better news from the fronts. The blacks were angry about his continued refusal to speak clearly to the issue of their people's freedom and the black right to military service. In the summer of 1862 Frederick Douglass declared in his newspaper: "Abraham Lincoln is no more fit for the place he holds than was James Buchanan. . . . The country is destined to become sick of both [Gen. George B.] McClellan and Lincoln, and the sooner the better. The one plays lawyer for the benefit of the rebels, and the other handles the army for the benefit of the traitors. We should not be surprised if both should be hurled from their places before this rebellion is ended. . . . The signs of the times indicate that the people will have to take this war into their own hands." But Frederick Douglass was not one to dwell on such revolutionary options. (Besides, had he considered what would happen to the black cause, if the white "people" really did take the war into their own hands?) Fortunately, by the time Douglass's words were published, he had seen new and far more hopeful signs of the times.

In September 1862 Abraham Lincoln, in a double-minded attempt both to bargain with and weaken the South while replying to the pressures of the North, finally made public his proposed Emancipation Proclamation. Under its ambiguous terms, the states in rebellion would be given until the close of the year to end their rebellious action. If any did so their captive black people would not be affected; otherwise, the Emancipation Proclamation would go into effect on January 1, 1863, theoretically freeing all the enslaved population of the Confederate states and promising federal power to maintain that freedom.

What actually was involved was quite another matter. Of great import was the fact that the proclamation excluded from its provisions the "loyal" slave states of Missouri, Kentucky, Delaware, and Maryland, the anti-Confederate West Virginia Territory, and loyal areas in certain other Confederate states. Legally, then, nearly one million black people whose masters were "loyal" to the Union had no part of the emancipation offered. In effect, Lincoln was announcing freedom to the captives over whom he had least control, while allowing those in states clearly under the rule of his government to remain in slavery. However, on another more legalistic level, Lincoln was justifying his armies' use of the Confederates' black "property," and preparing the way for an even more extensive use of black power by the military forces of the Union. Here, the logic of his move was clear, providing an executive confirmation and extension of Congress's Second Confiscation Act of 1862: once the Emancipation Proclamation went into effect, the tens of thousands of black people who were creating their own freedom, and making themselves available as workers in the Union camps, could be used by the North without legal qualms. Technically, they would no longer be private property, no longer cause problems for a President concerned about property rights.

It was indeed a strange vessel that the Lord had chosen, but black folk in the South were not waiting on such legal niceties. Not long after the preliminary proclamation, an insurrectionary plot was uncovered among a group of blacks in Culpepper County, Virginia. Some were slaves and some free, and the message of their action carried a special resonance for South and North alike, and perhaps for the President himself. For a copy of Lincoln's preliminary proclamation was reportedly found among the possessions of one of the conspirators. Though at least seventeen of the group were executed, their death could not expunge the fact that they had attempted to seize the time, to wrest their emancipation out of the hands of an uncertain President. On Nat's old "gaining ground" they had perhaps heard the voice of his God and, forming their own small army, were once again searching for Jerusalem.

Such action symbolized a major difference in the movement of the Southern and Northern branches of the struggle. In the South, though most of the self-liberating black people eventually entered the camps, or came otherwise under the aegis of the Northern armies, they were undoubtedly acting on significant, independent initiatives. During the first years of the war, the mainstream of the struggle in the South continued to bear this independent, self-authenticating character, refusing to wait for an official emancipation.

In such settings black hope blossomed, fed by its own activity. Even in the ambiguous context of the contraband communities the signs were there. In 1862–63, in

Corinth, Mississippi, newly free blacks in one of the best of the contraband camps organized themselves under federal oversight, and created the beginnings of an impressive, cohesive community of work, education, family life, and worship. They built their own modest homes, planted and grew their crops (creating thousands of dollars of profit for the Union), supported their own schools, and eventually developed their own military company to fight with the Union armies. It was not surprising, then, that black fugitives flocked there from as far away as Georgia. Nor was it unexpected that, in 1863, federal military plans demanded the dismantling of the model facility. Nevertheless, the self-reliant black thrust toward the future had been initiated, and Corinth was only one among many hopeful contraband communities.

Such movement, and the vision which impelled it, were integral aspects of the freedom struggle in the South. Meanwhile, to aid that struggle, by 1863 Harriet Tubman had entered the South Carolina war zone. Working on behalf of the Union forces, she organized a corps of black contrabands and traveled with them through the countryside to collect information for army raids, and to urge the still-enslaved blacks to leave their masters. Apparently the intrepid leader and her scouts were successful at both tasks, though Tubman complained that her long dresses sometimes impeded her radical activities.

In the North the situation was somewhat different. Word of Lincoln's anticipated proclamation had an electrifying effect on the black community there, but at the same time further removed the focus from the black freedom-seizing movement in the South. The promised proclamation now gave the Northerners more reason than ever to look to others for release, to invest their hope in the Union cause. Now it seemed as if they would not need to be isolated opponents of an antagonistic federal government. Again, because they wanted to believe, needed to hope, yearned to prove themselves worthy, they thought they saw ever more clearly the glory of the coming; before long, in their eyes the proclamation was clothed in what appeared to be almost angelic light. As such, it became an essentially religious rallying point for the development of a new, confusing mainstream struggle: one which, nervous and excited, approached and embraced the central government and the Republican Party as agents of deliverance. Doubts from the past were now cast aside, for their struggle was unquestionably in the hands of Providence and the Grand Army of the Republic. The voice of God was joined to that of Abraham Lincoln.

The way for the full merger was prepared in November 1862, when the putative effects of the Dred Scott decision were essentially annulled. The unexpectedly harsh exigencies of war, the reluctance of whites to fight, the pressure from his generals, the unpredictable freedom activities of blacks in the South, and the constant demands from Northern black leaders—all had combined to convince Lincoln that the North must finally enlist black troops in the federal armies. Of course, it would be somewhat embarrassing to call upon noncitizens and nonaliens to fight and die for the Union and for rights they did not have. So, near the end of November, Attorney General Edward Bates issued an official advisement, saying in part: "Free men of color, if born in the United States, are citizens of the United States." That war-created statement became the first federal admission of black citizenship. A little more than a month later, the Emancipation Proclamation was announced, followed by the first official national recruitment of black troops. Taken together, these three events—rising out of the bitter agonies and unexpected duration of the civil conflict, and inspired in large part by the powerful presence of tens of thousands of Southern blacks who had created their own emancipation—placed the bloody imprimatur of black struggle upon the federal government's pursuit of victory.

Many white persons in the North and in the border states reacted against this obvious change in the war aims of the Union. Some regular army men resigned from the federal service rather than fight for "the niggers." White Northern newspapers warned against an inundation of newly freed blacks, increasing public antipathy. Most whites, like almost every people in the midst of war, simply adjusted themselves to the new situation—so long as it did not touch them too closely—maintaining a continuous, sullen hostility to black people which periodically broke out into violence. Earlier, Sen. Lyman Trumbull of Illinois had spoken accurately for the white Northern majority when he said, "Our people want nothing to do with the negro." Indeed, according to the powerful Republican leader, his own constituents were expressing alarm about the precipitate movement toward black emancipation and were saying, "We do not want them set free to come in among us."

On the other hand, from a certain legal point of view it could be argued that the Emancipation Proclamation set free no enslaved black people at all. Since by December 31, 1862, no Confederate state had accepted Lincoln's invitation to return to the fold with their slaves unthreatened, and since Lincoln acknowledged that he had no real way of enforcing such a proclamation within the rebellious states, the proclamation's power to set anyone free was dubious at best. (Rather, it confirmed and gave ambiguous legal standing to the freedom which black people had already claimed through their own surging, living proclamations.)

Indeed, in his annual address to Congress on December 1, 1862, Lincoln had not seemed primarily concerned with the proclamation. Instead, he had taken that crucial opportunity to propose three constitutional amendments which reaffirmed his long-standing approach to national slavery. The proposed amendments included provisions for gradual emancipation (with a deadline as late as 1900), financial compensation to the owners, and colonization for the freed people. In other words, given the opportunity to place his impending proclamation of limited, immediate emancipation into the firmer context of a constitutional amendment demanding freedom for all enslaved blacks, Lincoln chose another path, one far more in keeping with his own history.

But none of this could dampen the joy of the black North. Within that community, it was the Emancipation Proclamation of January 1, 1863, which especially symbolized all that the people so deeply longed to experience, and its formal announcement sent a storm of long-pent-up emotion surging through the churches and meeting halls. It was almost as if the Northern and Southern struggles had again been joined, this time not through wilderness flights, armed resistance, and civil disobedience, but by a nationwide, centuries-long cord of boundless ecstasy. In spite of its limitations, the proclamation was taken as the greatest sign yet provided by the hand of Providence. The river had burst its boundaries, had shattered slavery's dam. It appeared as if the theodicy of the Northern black experience was finally prevailing. For the freedom struggle, especially in the South, had begun to overwhelm the white man's war, and had forced the President and the nation officially to turn their faces toward the moving black masses. Wherever black people could assemble, by themselves or with whites, they came together to lift joyful voices of thanksgiving, to sing songs of faith, to proclaim, "Jehovah hath triumphed, his people are free." For them, a new year and a new era had been joined in one.

On the evening of December 31, 1862, Frederick Douglass was in Boston attending one of the hundreds of freedom-watch-night services being held across the North in anticipation of the proclamation. That night, a line of messengers had been set up between the telegraph office and the platform of the Tremont Temple, where the Boston meeting was being held. After waiting more than two hours in agonized hope, the crowd was finally rewarded as word of the official proclamation reached them. Douglass said: "The effect of this announcement was startling beyond description, and the scene was wild and grand. Joy and gladness exhausted all forms of expression, from shouts of praise to sobs and tears . . . a Negro preacher, a man of wonderful vocal power, expressed the heartfelt emotion of the hour, when he led all voices in the anthem, 'Sound the loud timbrel o'er Egypt's dark sea, Jehovah hath triumphed, his people are free.'"

Such rapture was understandable, but like all ecstatic experiences, it carried its own enigmatic penalties. Out of it was born the mythology of Abraham Lincoln as Emancipator, a myth less important in its detail than in its larger meaning and consequences for black struggle. The heart of the matter was this: while the concrete historical realities of the time testified to the costly, daring, courageous activities of hundreds of thousands of black people breaking loose from slavery and setting themselves free, the myth gave the credit for this freedom to a white Republican president. In those same times when black men and women saw visions of a new society of equals, and heard voices pressing them against the American Union of white supremacy, Abraham Lincoln was unable to see beyond the limits of his own race, class, and time, and dreamed of a Haitian island and of Central American colonies to rid the country of the constantly accusing, constantly challenging black presence. Yet in the mythology of blacks and whites alike, it was the independent, radical action of the black movement toward freedom which was diminished, and the coerced, ambiguous role of a white deliverer which gained pre-eminence.

In a sense, then, it was these ecstatic Emancipation Proclamation meetings which provided the first real shaping of the unlikely message that the God of the black community had used Abraham Lincoln as his primary agent of freedom—Abraham Lincoln, rather than those many, many thousands of Afro-Americans who had lived and died through blood baptism in the river. In the development of black struggle and black radicalism in America, the consequences of this mythology lasted long and created many difficulties. . . .

The Slaves Strike for Freedom

CLARENCE L. MOHR

The collapse of slavery in Georgia has traditionally been identified with General William Tecumseh Sherman's devastating march from Atlanta to the sea during the autumn of 1864. According to some estimates as many as nineteen thousand bondsmen fled to freedom behind Sherman's advancing columns, thereby inflicting a crippling blow upon Georgia slavery if not on southern independence itself.

"Before Sherman: Georgia Blacks and the Union War Effort, 1861–1864," by Clarence L. Mohr. From *Journal of Southern History*, XLV (August 1979), 331–352. Copyright © 1962 by the Southern Historical Association. Reprinted by permission of the Managing Editor.

In reality, however, Sherman's march to the sea represented the end rather than the beginning of black defections from Confederate Georgia. The most revealing escapes occurred earlier in the war and involved black people on or near the Georgia seaboard. Unlike the thousands of Negroes who followed Sherman's conquering army to Savannah, blacks reaching Union lines earlier in the war were usually the instruments of their own deliverance. The timing and method of their escape efforts were matters of conscious choice, and their decision to strike out for liberty meant risking recapture, punishment, and even death in case of failure. By looking for patterns in these early escapes and by examining the statements and actions of successful fugitives one can learn much about the culture, values, and aspirations of black Georgians on the eve of emancipation.

Escape from the seaboard became possible early in 1862 when northern naval and military forces bloodlessly captured Georgia's deserted Sea Islands. Ignoring an intense campaign of anti-Yankee atrocity stories, local blacks immediately began making their way to Union-held territory. Hard-pressed sailors in the South Atlantic Blockading Squadron gave the refugees protection and assistance but recorded their arrival rather haphazardly. Consequently, only a small fraction (perhaps 25 percent) of the slaves and free Negroes who fled Georgia during this early period were mentioned in official documents.

The disparity between actual and reported incidents of escape is illustrated by population data from a settlement of black refugees on St. Simons Island near the mouth of the Altamaha River. Established by the Union navy in March 1862, the St. Simons settlement (officially designated a "colony") was only one of several locations to which escaped slaves from Georgia were taken. In the space of some nine months the island's black population grew from none to nearly 600, but during this same period the total number of black escapees reported by military and naval commanders on station off the Georgia coast was only 144, or about a fourth of the black population of St. Simons alone. By the most conservative estimates, then, commands of individual blockading vessels failed to record some 70 to 80 percent of the Georgia fugitives who passed through their hands.

Whether or not this ratio remained constant throughout the thirty months preceding Sherman's invasion is uncertain. If it did and if three out of four black escapees went unreported, then the 561 Georgia slaves and free Negroes known to have reached Union lines from December 1861 through October 1864 would represent a total of 2,000 to 2,500 actual escapees. If one assumes, on the other hand, that the volume of escapes declined and the efficiency of reporting increased markedly after 1862, an estimate of 1,000 black refugees for the entire period would still be well within reason.

Whatever the precise number of refugees may have been, enough escapes were reported to reveal clear trends in several key areas. For purposes of analysis, escape efforts may, at the outset, be separated into two basic categories: (1) those conceived and initiated by blacks without initial Union assistance (hereafter designated "black initiated" escapes) and (2) those occurring during Union coastal or river raids (hereafter designated "rescues"). Out of a total of fifty-six reported escape incidents some forty-two fall within the first category. These "black-initiated" efforts involved 290 individuals, or roughly 45 percent of the 650 known Georgia fugitives. The volume and frequency of black-initiated escape efforts varied considerably over time. Whereas "rescue" incidents simply mirrored the pace of Union military operations along Georgia's coast, black-initiated efforts were concentrated most heavily during the first nine to twelve months after the arrival of Federal blockading vessels. The number of such incidents declined slowly throughout 1863 and dwindled to almost nothing after the first three months of 1864.

This pattern suggests that logistical factors were of central importance in determining the rate of black escapes. There was, for example, no perceptible increase in escape attempts following the issuance of the final Emancipation Proclamation in January 1863. To most black Georgians freedom was a condition rather than a theory, and in Georgia, as in neighboring South Carolina, Negroes who reached the Sea Islands were virtually free from the moment of their arrival. What varied in Georgia was not the desire of black people for liberty but their physical opportunity to obtain it. Black-initiated escapes were most numerous in 1862 because the number of blacks near the Georgia seaboard was larger then than at any subsequent period of the war. By 1863 nearly all coastal planters had moved their slaves well inland to areas where escape was difficult if not impossible. The impressment of 1,500 black laborers to work on Savannah's defenses in the summer of 1862 further increased the pool of potential escapees, while the Union navy's black settlement on St. Simons Island offered tangible proof of northern willingness to grant fugitives a sanctuary.

The size and composition of escape groups were even more revealing than their frequency. In antebellum days the typical runaway episode involved a young, healthy male traveling northward alone. The fugitive's major physical obstacle was distance, and the most crippling psychological barrier he faced was the pain of abandoning home, friends, and family. This picture changed drastically, however, when Union blockading forces reached Georgia's coast in 1862. With freedom then as close as the Union-controlled Sea Islands, escaping ceased to be a solitary endeavor. Adult men continued to lead or participate in most defections, but statistics reveal a clear trend toward collective escape efforts involving family groups or, occasionally, plantation communities.

Relevant information is available for a total of forty-two separate black-initiated escape incidents involving some 290 people. Thirty-two of the escapees fled Georgia alone or in company with one other person; 249 of the remaining 258 black fugitives (some 86 percent of the total) reached or attempted to reach the Sea Islands in groups of three or more. Although the specific age and sexual makeup of these groups was seldom recorded, surviving evidence suggests that most of the large parties included women and children as well as men. In 1862, for example, the black refugee population on St. Simons Island grew from 26 men, 6 women, and 9 children in late March to 60 men, 16 women, and 13 children by mid-April. When abolitionist clergyman Mansfield French visited the island in July a total of 52 black children were presented for baptism during one afternoon service. Susie King Taylor, an ex-slave from Savannah, recalled that by the time she left St. Simons in October a majority of its 600 inhabitants were women and children.

Strict policing made mass escapes more difficult in 1863, but black families continued to flee. In July "two or three families" of free Negroes from Darien, Georgia, reached Union lines together with "four slaves whom they owned." Nineteen blacks from Samuel N. Papot's plantation near Savannah were less successful in October, when their boat was captured by Confederate pickets. Approximately one-third of the would-be escapees in this group were men, the rest women and children. In late

December 1863 thirteen black fugitives from McIntosh County, Georgia, were taken aboard the U.S.S. *Fernandina* in St. Catherines Sound. The leader of the party was a twenty-seven-year-old slave named Cain, who, like most of the escapees, had formerly belonged to William King. Accompanying Cain was the twenty-two-year-old woman Bella and her six-year-old son Romeo, the twenty-five-year-old woman Lizzie and her four children (Joseph, Sam, Eve, and Martha, aged twelve years, four years, two years, and five months respectively), and finally the thirty-two-year-old woman Sallie with her four children (Fannie, Joseph, Emma, and Ben, who ranged in age from eleven years to seven months). Early in 1864 Cain left the *Fernandina* to rescue his relatives from the vicinity of Sunbury, Georgia. He returned on January 7, along with ex-slave Sam, bringing the forty-five-year-old woman Grace, her five children (Judy, Elizabeth, Phoebe, Victoria, and James), her son-in-law Charley, and her grandchildren (Arphee, Virginia, Clarissa, and Edward).

Under the best of circumstances black-initiated escape efforts were risky, a fact graphically illustrated by the failure of some eighty-nine Georgia fugitives to reach Union lines. From a purely pragmatic standpoint the lone young black man probably continued to stand the best chance of escape throughout most of the war. By including women, children, or old people in escape parties, therefore, black Georgians repeatedly showed their willingness to place family and group loyalty above individual self-interest. A typical episode occurred in September 1862 following the successful escape of twenty-three slaves from plantations on both sides of the Savannah River. The main party paddled their way to freedom in a large canoe, but two men, one woman, and a child failed to reach the boat on time and were left behind to face pursuers. A Georgia planter reported the grim outcome in a private letter. Overtaken while fording a creek, the group refused to stop, whereupon "Bob, who was leading, was shot in the leg and immediately taken. Peter was also fired at and fell" but fled deeper into the marshes in a "wounded condition." After a "pursuit of 3 or 4 miles" the woman and child "became exhausted" and surrendered but refused to reveal the hiding place of their wounded companion.

More successful escapes also underscored the importance of family ties among Georgia's black refugees. An abolitionist officer from Massachusetts recalled three or four brothers in a black family named Wilson who planned a daring escape from the interior of Georgia. Leaving their youngest brother behind to look after an aged mother, the other men, in company with their sister and her children, fled downriver in a log dugout. Before reaching the coast the boat came under heavy fire from Confederate pickets, who wounded every male occupant of the open craft. Despite their injuries the men eventually completed the voyage and reached the safety of Federal gunboats. Even more striking was the case of a seventy-year-old Georgia black woman, who, after failing in one escape attempt, assembled her twenty-two children and grandchildren on an abandoned flatboat and drifted forty miles down the Savannah River to freedom. When rescued by a Union vessel "the grandmother rose to her full height, with her youngest grandchild in her arms, and said only, 'My God! are we free?' "

If family commitments shaped the pattern of wartime escape efforts they also influenced the nature and scope of black support for the Union cause. Nowhere was the importance of family ties more evident than in the realm of actual military service. Northern recruiters discovered early that the prospect of securing the freedom of friends and relatives was a powerful inducement for blacks to join Union ranks. Or, taking the opposite viewpoint, blacks soon discovered that the Union army offered an effective vehicle for rescuing family members still held in bondage. Thomas Wentworth Higginson, who commanded numerous black Georgians in the famous First South Carolina Volunteers, candidly admitted that his soldiers "had more to fight for than [did] the whites. Besides the flag and the Union, they had home and wife and child." A northern official who spent the summer and fall of 1862 with Georgia blacks on St. Simons Island fully confirmed this judgment. In early October he attended a Negro "war meeting" at St. Helena village, where several speakers including one black man addressed an assembly of ex-slaves:

> They were asked to enlist for pay, rations and uniform, to fight for their country, for freedom and so forth, but not a man stirred. But when it was asked them to fight for themselves, to enlist to protect their wives and children from being sold away from them, and told of the little homes which they might secure to themselves and their families in after years, they all rose to their feet, the men came forward and said "I'll go," the woman shouted, and the old men said "Amen."

Family considerations were clearly uppermost in the minds of many black Georgians as they embarked on their first combat mission in November 1862. At the staging area on St. Catherines Island the former bondsmen "needed no 'driver's lash' . . . for they were preparing to go up Sapelo River, along whose banks on the beautiful plantations, were their fathers, mothers, brothers, sisters, wives and children. Weeks and months before some of the men had left those loved ones, with a promise to return . . ." if the way were opened. A white observer who accompanied the expedition up river found it "very affecting" to see the soldiers gaze "intensely [at] the colored forms on land," frequently calling out such things as "Oh, masir, my wife and chillen lib dere" or "dere, dere my brodder." When the ships were unable to take away slaves from certain plantations the disappointment of relatives on board was acute and virtually "inexpressible (except by sighs)."

Some black Georgians were unwilling to risk such disappointments and took the business of rescuing friends and relatives into their own hands. One of the first to adopt this self-help philosophy was ex-slave March Haynes, who functioned unofficially within the military command structure of the Department of the South. Described as "a pure, shrewd, brave efficient man," Haynes was literate and had worked as a stevedore and river pilot in antebellum Savannah. "Comprehending the spirit and scope of the war," Haynes began smuggling Georgia fugitives into Union lines shortly after the fall of Fort Pulaski in April 1862. When white suspicions against him became too great, he fled Savannah with his wife but continued his rescue efforts from the Sea Islands. Although the term "commando" did not exist in the military vocabulary of the 1860s, Haynes' activities fit neatly under this modern rubric. General Quincy Adams Gillmore of the Tenth Army Corps recognized the value of Haynes's services and "furnished him with whatever he needed in his perilous missions," including a "staunch, swift boat, painted a drab color, like the hue of the Savannah River." Allowed to "select such negroes to assist him as he thought proper," Haynes landed repeatedly "in the marshes below Savannah" and entered the city under cover of darkness. Sheltered and supplied by local blacks, he sometimes remained for several days collecting "exact and valuable information" on the strength and location of Confederate defenses. He also made night reconnaissances "up the creeks along the Savannah, gathering information and bringing away boat-loads of negroes." On one expedition Haynes was shot in the leg by Confederate pickets and in April 1863 was apparently arrested and temporarily jailed by Savannah authorities.

Liberating friends and relatives was only one of many motives for black enlistment in the Union ranks. Nearly all Negro soldiers shared a basic hatred of bondage and a desire to strike out directly at the slave system. Undoubtedly, some ex-slaves viewed military service as an opportunity both to demonstrate personal courage and to consummate the process of self-emancipation by meeting white southerners in battle. Yet even the most dedicated abolitionists admitted that black attitudes toward former masters were ambivalent and complex. Upon reaching the Sea Islands in 1862, for instance, Colonel Higginson "expected to find a good deal of the patriarchal feeling" among local Negroes but discovered instead a very different and more discriminating attitude. Many former slaves did indeed claim "to have had kind owners and some expressed great gratitude to them for particular favors received" during slavery. To these same black people, however, the central fact of being owned was "a wrong which no special kindness could right." Thus, whatever their feelings toward individual whites, they looked upon the mass of slaveholders as their "natural enemies." Confederate observers like Mrs. James Sanchez of Florida confirmed the existence of a generalized hostility toward slaveholders among black escapees. In early 1863, while traveling to Georgia under a flag of truce, Mrs. Sanchez was detained briefly at Union-occupied Fort Pulaski. "The negroes there were far more insolent than the [white] soldiers," she reported. The blacks "took great pleasure in insulting the whites; cursing the 'd—n rebel secesh women and men' and laughing in their faces."

Such racial antagonisms often went hand in hand with personal grievances against former owners. Higginson mentions several black Georgians who seethed with anger over slave experiences and whose desire for revenge steeled their courage on the battlefield. For some bondsmen the war was quite literally an extension of earlier rebellious activities. The theory that black defection to Federal lines acted as a "safety valve" against slave uprisings within the Confederacy finds at least partial confirmation in the career of a militant black runaway named Nat. Owned by a planter in Glynn County, Georgia, Nat left his master some time in 1860 and remained at large for the next four years. By the summer of 1862 he had reached St. Simons Island, where he engaged in operations somewhat similar to those of March Haynes. Described by white Savannahians as a "notorious runaway . . . and rascal," Nat was ultimately accused of killing one white civilian and two Confederate soldiers. In his most daring wartime exploit he led six other black men some thirty miles up the Altamaha River to rescue their wives and children from bondage. In the course of the expedition he fought off white attackers twice and exchanged gunfire with a Confederate river patrol. Even after most black refugees had been moved to Port Royal, Nat remained on St. Simons and soon joined forces with another slave rebel named Harvey. Denounced on the mainland as "spies, murderers, incendiaries and thieves," the pair survived until June 1864, when both fell victim to a shotgun-wielding southern soldier. At the time of Nat's death Georgia whites held him responsible for the escape of from seventy to a hundred slaves from the coastal counties.

Whether or not they were rebels before the war, Georgia's black soldiers were ready to redress past wrongs if the opportunity arose. During the 1862 Sapelo River expedition, for example, black troops singled out the plantation of Captain William Brailsford for a special retaliatory attack. Brailsford, a wealthy cotton planter, known for his flamboyance and fiery temper, had succeeded Georgia slave trader Charles Augustus Lafayette Lamar as captain of the Savannah Mounted Rifles in 1861. By July of the following year he was actively engaged in a campaign to recapture slaves from the Georgia Sea Islands. After Union officers refused his request to return black fugitives from St. Simons, Brailsford descended on St. Catherines Island with thirty armed men in October 1862, killing two black refugees and capturing four others.

The memory of this attack was still fresh in the minds of black soldiers as they ascended the Sapelo early the next month. Even without the St. Catherines raid Brailsford would probably still have been a marked man, for on board the Union gunboats were several of Brailsford's former slaves, including Sam Miller, who had been whipped severely by the hot-tempered planter for refusing to betray another escapee. Since Brailsford's plantation was also a major Confederate picket station Union officers agreed after "full consultation" to destroy the place during their retreat. Landing after sunset the black troops routed a strong force of defenders and pushed inland nearly half a mile, burning cabins, outbuildings, and finally the Brailsford mansion itself. When interviewed immediately after the attack, morale among the black soldiers was high. Some spoke of having "grown three inches," while Sam Miller said simply, "I feel a heap more of a man."

If the alliance between Georgia blacks and the Union military was cemented with blood, it was also constructed upon the shifting foundation of pragmatic self-interest. Throughout most of the war the aims and goals of northern commanders corresponded neatly with individual priorities and racial or group loyalties of black refugees. So long as this community of interest existed black allegiance to the Stars and Stripes remained strong. When Federal policies ceased to be mutually beneficial, however, black cooperation and white benevolence declined proportionately. The process was visible on St. Simons Island during the spring and summer of 1862 when naval authorities set out to make the black colony self-supporting. Shortly after the first blacks were landed on St. Simons in March Commander Sylvanus W. Godon decided they should "procure their own living from the land . . ." and ordered them also "to plant cotton and thus . . . become of use to themselves." By mid-April some eighty acres of corn plus additional fields of potatoes and beans were under cultivation, and in late May Godon reported triumphantly that "Thus far the Government has not spent a dollar on these people. . . ." Actually, the government probably did more than just break even, for by late July St. Simons's black residents had planted three hundred acres of food crops and picked 25,000 pounds of valuable Sea Island cotton.

The navy's agricultural achievement fell considerably short of being a genuine cooperative effort. Godon quickly discovered that black refugees showed "a great dislike to do the work they have been accustomed to . . ." under slavery. Toiling daily in the abandoned plantation fields seemed "to make their condition the same as before," and appointing an ex-slave to direct the work accomplished little because even the black foreman needed "pushing" and "indulges his men too much away from the care of fields. . . ." Ultimately, Godon's solution to the problem was simple and direct. "Where work is neglected my rule has been to stop off the ration of beef or something else," he wrote in late June; adding "and I have also placed men in irons for punishment."

If Godon's heavy-handed methods produced results, they did little to build black trust in the motives of the Federal officials. Confidence was further eroded by the navy's inability to shield the St. Simons settlement from Confederate attack. Naval officers did their best to protect the island, but black refugees seemed more impressed by the flintlock muskets they received for self-defense than by the navy's good intentions. In May 1862 a large Confederate force actually landed on St. Simons but was repulsed at the last moment by fire from a newly arrived Union gunboat. The island's black residents took the lesson to heart, and when a second rebel attack occurred in August the ex-slaves seized the initiative.

Ironically, the second Confederate landing on St. Simons coincided almost exactly with the arrival of some thirty-eight black soldiers from Port Royal, who were all that remained of General David Hunter's recently disbanded Negro regiment. Still lacking any official military status, the troops and their white commander Charles T. Trowbridge were eager for a chance to prove themselves in battle. Grabbing their knapsacks and cartridge boxes "with alacrity," the men came ashore only to discover that twenty-five local blacks were already armed and in pursuit of the invaders. According to one writer the action was "entirely a spontaneous thing." No white man accompanied the local defenders, who were commanded, instead, by two of their own number, John Brown and Edward Gould. Overtaking the invaders in a swamp, the ex-slaves fought a brief engagement and suffered several casualties including their leader John Brown, who was killed.

The August encounter was not the end of local defense efforts on St. Simons. When Captain Trowbridge's company left the island in early November, shortly before being mustered into Union service, the seventy or so black men who remained behind took further precautions against attack. "Immediately they organized a guard on each plantation, appointed their own sergeant or leader, and guarded the island day and night" until its evacuation five weeks later. The men met for drill each afternoon at Thomas Butler King's plantation, where assignments for night guard duty were also made. Even during this final period the defenders did not rely on government support and received neither clothing, pay, nor rations.

Elsewhere along the Georgia coast conditions were much the same. When Confederate forces attacked St. Catherines Island in 1862 they were fired on by six black men, armed like the St. Simons defenders with flintlock muskets. On Cumberland Island during this same period armed blacks clashed with both Confederate raiding parties and unsympathetic Union naval officers, who came to the aid of R. Stafford, a white slaveowner who had remained on the island. The Stafford incident occurred in early September when a number of the planter's former slaves returned from nearby Fernandina, Florida, in company with other escaped bondsmen. Many of the blacks had obtained guns, and they took up residence on Stafford's plantation "refusing to submit to any control, killing the cattle and overrunning the private dwelling with arms and clubs in their hands. . . ." Naval officers declared the blacks in "a state of mutiny" and sent an armed party of marines to Stafford's assistance. Apparently determined to maintain slavery even inside Union lines, Lieutenant

Commander William Talbot Truxtun reported the arrest of nine Negroes "belonging to Mr. Stafford and said to be dangerous." Truxtun placed the men in irons but later released them "at their own request and at the desire of their master (who gives up all claim to them). . . ." Significantly, the black prisoners did not actually go free but were retained on board Truxtun's vessel as part of the crew. Approximately a month after this brush with the Union navy Negroes on Cumberland Island were attacked by a company of Confederate cavalrymen. The encounter was brief but resulted in the capture of twelve blacks, who were returned to slavery on the Georgia mainland.

Episodes like that on Cumberland Island make the zealous self-defense efforts of Georgia escapees more readily understandable. They had learned in antebellum days to take freedom where they found it and to guard it tenaciously. If, as Willie Lee Rose argues, "Getting out of the master's power was the essence of freedom . . ." for most blacks, then preventing the master's return in either actual or surrogate form was a logical response to wartime conditions along Georgia's coast.

There was, of course, a more positive side to black life on the Sea Islands. One Georgia escapee recalled that the St. Simons colony consisted of numerous small settlements "just like little villages." Despite fear of Confederate attack, women and children were free to move about at will and engage in social activities forbidden during slavery. On St. Simons, Sapelo, St. Catherines, Ossabaw, and elsewhere agricultural operations centered around food production and were apparently conducted on both a collective and an individual basis. The ex-slaves combined subsistence farming with limited cash transactions in ways which harkened back to their previous commercial dealings in the rural South. They frequently sold vegetables and poultry to the crews of nearby warships, and the women took in sailors' washing to earn extra money. On St. Simons schools were conducted for black children and adults during 1862. Both literate fugitives and white naval personnel served as teachers, and navy surgeons treated the sick and elderly on some islands.

Initially, at least, conditions on the Sea Islands were fairly conducive to stable family life. In July 1862 the Reverend Mansfield French found blacks on St. Simons eager to formalize their marriage vows "in the most public and solemn manner" possible. The abolitionist clergyman performed numerous marriages and also baptized black children. On these occasions the extended kinship patterns evolved during slavery were clearly visible. Candidates for baptism lined up in two rows. "On . . . [the] right stood a father and mother, with five children; then a mother with so many of her children as she could rescue from Slavery; and then perhaps, a father, with the two or three children, and their grandmother, in the place of the poor mother, who had been sold." In the left line "were children presented by [distant] relatives or strangers, the parents being sold . . ." or not yet escaped from slavery. The Reverend Mr. French genuinely wished to protect black family ties, but he was also a leading advocate of Negro military service. During the summer of 1862 the two objectives were not necessarily incompatible. French could not have known that in the later stages of the war callous Union conscription policies would wrench many black fathers away from their wives and children, thereby achieving what southern slave markets had failed to accomplish.

Although Sea Island refugees showed a strong desire for autonomy and independence, open confrontations between blacks and Union forces were rare. From the outset Georgia escapees showed a general willingness to aid the northern war effort within reasonable limits. Virtually all refugees shared whatever military information they possessed at the time of their escape, and many offered their services in more tangible form. The quality of military intelligence received from ex-slaves was usually high. Black estimates of Confederate troop strength sometimes proved unreliable, but escapees furnished accurate and detailed information on the ironclad warships under construction in savannah harbor as well as up-to-date reports on the movements of potential blockade runners. In the course of the war black defections stripped the Confederate navy's Savannah Squadron of numerous highly competent river and coastal pilots, while the Union navy benefited both from the escapee's services and from the Confederate navy's resulting weakness.

Among the first black pilots to reach Union lines was Isaac Tatnall, who escaped in December 1861 from the packet *St. Mary's* in Savannah harbor. Valued at $1,500 and hired by his master for $35.00 per month, Tatnall had piloted vessels along the entire length of the Georgia coast and could navigate the Savannah River even at night. Union naval officers found he could "be perfectly relied upon," and he remained aboard warships off Georgia as late as 1863. Another 1861 escapee was the slave Brutus, who proved to be "quite familiar with the rivers and creeks between Savannah City and Tybee Island." Captain (later General) Quincy A. Gillmore placed "great reliance on Brutus' statement" after learning that "everything he said of Big Tybee Inlet, was verified with remarkable accuracy. . . ." Other additions to the Navy's pilot force during 1862 and 1863 included the slave Cassius, who claimed to be "a good pilot" by virtue of his experiences as "fireman on one of the small steamers used for inland navigation . . ."; an unnamed slave, who worked on a Rebel tugboat in the Ogeechee River; and, finally even the black pilot from the Confederate blockade runner *Nashville.* "These men risk their lives to serve us . . . [and] make no bargains about their remuneration . . . ," wrote Union admiral Samuel Francis Du Pont early in 1862. The pay differential was amply demonstrated by the fact that two years later black pilots serving under Du Pont earned from $30 to $40 per month, only a fraction of the salaries paid their white counterparts in the same squadron and less than half of the $100 per mcnth received by Moses Dallas, one of the few black pilots serving the Confederate navy at that time.

Despite equally unattractive pay rates the Union army also received its full share of Georgia recruits. Particularly valuable were the services of Abraham [or Abram] Murchison, a literate slave preacher from Savannah, who helped initiate the first recruiting efforts among black refugees on Hilton Head Island, South Carolina, in early 1862. After a private interview with General David Hunter, Murchison called a meeting of all black males on April 7, where the prospect of military service was first broached to the former bondsmen. Murchison addressed this meeting, explaining with "clearness and force . . . the obligations and interests" which should induce blacks to take up arms for the Union. A New York *Times* correspondent reported that Murchison's language on occasion "rose to eloquence . . ." as he described "the labors, hardships and dangers, as well as the advantages of soldier life. . . ." At the conclusion of his address 105 recruits were enrolled, and within a week the number of volunteers had reached 150.

Perhaps because of age, Murchison did not join the army himself but remained on Hilton Head throughout the war, serving as the religious and secular leader of local blacks. A Baptist during slavery, Murchison was formally ordained by Union army chaplains and reportedly baptized more than a thousand freedmen in Port Royal harbor during the war. By 1864 he had also become a pivotal figure in the self-governing black village of Mitchelville, where under army auspices he exercised the powers of magistrate. At night the village was off limits to all whites, and the black soldiers of the provost guard were placed under Murchison's control to make arrests for disorderly conduct. When Mitchelville residents held their first election in 1865 two black Georgians headed the ticket. March Haynes, the daring spy and commando, was elected marshal, while Abraham Murchison assumed the duties of recorder.

The men Murchison had helped recruit in April 1862 formed the nucleus of General Hunter's ill-fated black regiment which, as mentioned earlier, survived only in the form of a thirty-eight-man company sent to St. Simons Island. In November 1862 this hardy remnant, augmented by thirty to forty Georgia recruits from St. Simons, was mustered into service as Company A of the First South Carolina Volunteers. Company E was also composed largely of refugees from St. Simons, and black Georgians were scattered throughout the rest of the regiment. The mandatory conscription of Sea Island Negroes begun in 1863 ensured that Georgia bondsmen would ultimately find their way into all the black regiments raised in the Department of the South. Recruiting for Colonel James Montgomery's Second South Carolina regiment occurred mostly in Florida, but during June 1863 a special draft for the Third South Carolina Volunteers was conducted at Ossabaw Island and Fort Pulaski, Georgia, as well as at Fernandina, Florida, near Georgia's southern border. This regiment, which was soon consolidated with the embryonic Fourth and Fifth South Carolina Volunteers to form the Twenty-first United States Colored Troops, numbered slightly over three hundred men until December 1864, when its ranks were filled by black Georgians who had followed General Sherman to Savannah.

In addition to purely military training the army provided some blacks with valuable leadership experience and allowed many others to begin or expand their formal education. Much of the educational work was carried on by literate ex-slaves like Sergeant Edward King of Darien, Georgia, and his young wife Susie, who also served the regiment as nurse and laundress. Although involved in no decisive military campaigns, the "First South" nonetheless acquitted itself well in numerous raids and partisan expeditions from the Edisto River to the St. Johns. Perhaps most important, the black troops' solid performance under close public scrutiny paved the way for slave enlistments throughout the South.

Students of both slavery and Reconstruction can gain valuable insights from the wartime behavior of Georgia's black refugees. Viewed from an antebellum perspective the escape and subsequent military service of many black Georgians underscore the importance of slave family ties and simultaneously cast doubt on the depth of black commitment to the paternalist ethic. On the pivotal questions of how southern bondsmen viewed the nature of the war and the meaning of emancipation the Georgia experience is particularly revealing. Some black fugitives may, as Joel R. Williamson argues, have "fled not so much to freedom as away from slavery," but the weight of surviving evidence suggests that most participants in well-planned and deliberately executed efforts to escape had a far more definite concept of liberty. From the outset blacks on the Sea Islands adopted a pragmatic stance which defined freedom in terms of immediate and tangible realities; family stability, physical security, freedom of movement, the right to determine one's own work and living arrangements, and the opportunity for education were apparently central concerns for numerous Georgia escapees.

To recognize that newly freed blacks had a clear sense of priorities is not necessarily to argue that their view of postemancipation life was sophisticated or fully defined. In certain realms black behavior was little more than an extension of familiar slave survival strategies altered or reshaped in the crucible of wartime chaos and uncertainty. There can be little doubt, however, that for the thousands of freedmen who took possession of Georgia's coastal and Sea Island region under the auspices of General Sherman's famous Field Order 15 much more was ultimately at stake than the simple issue of landownership. At its most elemental level the Georgia freedmen's ill-fated struggle for political power and economic independence can probably best be understood as a quest for collective autonomy, tempered by a largely defensive impulse toward racial separatism. In this broad objective, as well as in regard to more specific goals, the freedmen of 1865 shared much in common with those black Georgians who seized their liberty before the coming of Sherman.

F U R T H E R   R E A D I N G

David Walker's Appeal, in Four Articles; Together with a Preamble, to the Concerned Citizens of the World, but In Particular, and Very Expressly, to Those of the United States of America, third and last edition, revised and published by David Walker, 1830; reprint, Baltimore: Black Classics Press, 1993, p. 23.

Ira Berlin, Wayne Durrell, Steven F. Miller, Leslie S. Rowland, and Leslie Schwalm, " 'To canvass the nation': the War for Union Becomes a War for Freedom," *Prologue: Journal of the National Archives* 20 (1988), 227–247.

Ira Berlin, Barbara J. Fields, Steven F. Miller, Joseph P. Reidys and Leslie S. Rowland, eds. *Slaves No More: Three Essays on Emancipation and the Civil War* (1992).

Eric Foner, "The Meaning of Freedom in the Age of Emancipation," *Journal of American History,* 81 (1994), 435–460.

Eric Foner, "Rights and the Constitution in Black Life During the Civil War and Reconstruction," *Journal of American History,* 74 (1987), 863–883.

Joseph T. Glatthaar, *Forged in Battle: The Civil War Alliance of Black Soldiers and White Officers* (1990).

Winthrop D. Jordan, *Tumult and Silence at Second Creek: An Inquiry into a Civil War Slave Conspiracy,* rev. ed. (1995).

James M. McPherson, "Who Freed the Slaves?" *Proceedings of the American Philosophical Society,* 139 (1995), 1–10.

Clarence L. Mohr, *On the Threshold of Freedom: Masters and Slaves in Civil War Georgia* (1986).

Joseph P. Reidy, *From Slavery to Agrarian Capitalism in the Cotton Plantation South: Central Georgia, 1800–1880* (1992).

C. Peter Ripley, *Slaves and Freedmen in Civil War Louisiana* (1976).

Willie Lee Rose, *Rehearsal for Reconstruction: The Port Royal Experiment* (1967).

CHAPTER
10

The Work of Reconstruction

What determined the conditions under which former slaves remade themselves as
a free people? What aspirations did they articulate, and what initiatives did they
take? What determined their success or failure in those initiatives or in achieving
those aspirations?

For 4 million newly freed men, women, and children throughout the South,
1865 was a year of tremendous excitement, hope, and expectation, and, at the same
time, a year of enormous effort to make a living, secure families, and protect rights.
One former slave, Violet Guntharpe, captured the essence of the terms of emancipation when she said, "Us had no education, no land, no mule, no cow, not a pig, nor
a chicken, to set up housekeeping." Three centuries of slavery in the United States
had been ended with no compensation to the enslaved. Lacking any economic resources or political power, how could freedpeople remake their lives? In the first
days and months after the Confederate surrender, in various ways formerly enslaved people tried on their new freedom. For some this meant removing themselves
from the place where they had been enslaved, finding new homes, or just moving
about to express or test their freedom. For others it meant staying where they had
lived all their lives, claiming as their own the land on which they previously toiled
without reward. For still others it meant building their first public church for the
congregation of people with whom they had worshiped in secret during slavery or
claiming title to the churches they had built with their own monies and labor, the
titles to which were held by whites. For most it meant looking for and they hoped,
reuniting with family members.

In areas that Union forces had occupied during the war, various experiments
with creating free lives and new economics were already underway. There, as elsewhere, former slaves, former masters, Freedmen's Bureau agents, Union army
officers, northern missionary teachers, and others brought their own understandings
of freedom into the post–Civil War world. Their various antebellum and Civil War
experiences fundamentally shaped these understandings. Even so, the Emancipation
Proclamation, Union success in the Civil War and ratification of the Thirteenth
Amendment to the Constitution, formally terminating slavery, all gave ex-slaves not
only the expectation of freedom but also the expectation that the federal government
would guarantee their freedom.

Many local and state governments were reorganized as they had been before the
war; leading secessionists assumed their former positions in civil life. The Bureau
of Refugees, Freedmen and Abandoned Lands (Freedmen's Bureau), authorized by

368

Congress in March 1865, had branches and agents throughout the former Confederacy. Ex-slaves' reliance on bureau agents became all the more important after May 1865 when President Andrew Johnson proposed a plan of reconstruction that would pardon southern rebels and return their confiscated lands if they swore allegiance to the Union. Buoyed by Johnson's leniency, former Confederates worked to restore as much of the antebellum social order as possible, including passing a series of restrictive laws aimed not merely at maintaining a racial hierarchy but also ensuring a dependable supply of black labor. Historians have collectively named these the Black Codes of 1865 and 1866.

In what ways could ex-slaves expect life to be different after emancipation? What would it take to guarantee real freedom? Who would be their allies in these struggles?

D O C U M E N T S

If ex-slaves thought freedom would immediately accompany emancipation, the events of the first few weeks and months of Union occupation soon disabused them of such ideas. In the first two documents, addressed to President Andrew Johnson, ex-slaves set forth their credentials as loyal citizens, question the restoring of the old order, and call the question as to which side the federal government would be on. The first document, delivered directly to the president at the White House in June 1865 by a committee of freedmen representing the communities of Richmond and Manchester, Virginia, met with immediate success. Within a week the former Confederate mayor was removed from office, two of the Freedmen's Bureau agents who had refused to aid the freedpeople were reassigned; and pass laws they objected to were rescinded. The second document issues from freedmen of Edisto Island, South Carolina, who in January 1865 had taken possession of land confiscated by General William T. Sherman. Learning that this ownership had been reversed and the land on which they had settled would be returned to its former owners, they demanded to know what freedom can mean if it is coupled with economic dependence, especially dependence on the same men who only days and months previous had held them as slaves. Contrast the understandings of freedom in these two petitions with Captain Charles Soule's characterization in the third document. Soule, who had captained a black regiment during t'ıe war, draws on his very pessimistic understanding of what it meant to be a free white laboring man in the 1860s to try to interpret the aftermath of emancipation.

At the heart of ex-slaves' struggles were issues of labor and family. In the fourth document, a share-wages contract, notice the conditions under which these Arkansas men and women were to labor and the terms by which they were to be paid. Charles Raushenberg, a Georgia bureau agent, in the fifth document, argues the need for continued federal oversight. Notice particularly his recounting of the differing interpretations that plantation owners and laborers put on the share-wages contract.

Most enslaved people had known, if not firsthand then certainly through close acquaintances, the horror of the thousands of sales, migrations, and inheritances that separated family members. Even for those fortunate enough to locate their loved ones after the Civil War, the reconstruction of the family was often not easily achieved. In the sixth document, Elizabeth Botume, a northern schoolteacher working in South Carolina at the end of the war, recalls the efforts of freedpeople to find their scattered families and the hard decisions many had to make. Sarah Jones submitted the seventh document, a letter from her cousin Dave Waldrop, to Freedmen's Bureau officials with her request for government transportation for her and her three children to join Waldrop's family in Florida. Bureau officials, desirous of preventing dependency on government assistance, often welcomed such requests to help families reunite if there was evidence as Waldrop's letter provided, of economic support after relocation.

The final two documents suggest the horrors and the possibilities that faced freedpeople as they made their way into U.S. citizenship. For many African Americans their assumption of their rights came with the high price of violent recrimination. Harriet Hernandes's testimony in the eighth document is but one of the hundreds of accounts collected by a U.S. Senate committee investigating Ku Klux Klan activities throughout the South; Hernandes offers a view into how family and work decisions were politicized in the Reconstruction era. The ninth document is a portrait of the first men of African descent to be elected to serve in Congress.

1. African Americans in Richmond, Virginia, Petition President Andrew Johnson, 1865

MR. PRESIDENT: We have been appointed a committee by a public meeting of the colored people of Richmond, Va., to make known to your Excellency, as our best friend, the wrongs as we conceive them to be, by which we are sorely oppressed.

We represent a population of more than 20,000 colored people, including Richmond and Manchester, who have ever been distinguished for their good behavior as slaves and as freemen, as well as for their high moral and Christian character; more than 6,000 of our people are members in good standing of Christian churches, and nearly our whole population constantly attend divine service. Among us there are at least 2,000 men who are worth from $200 to $500; 200 who have property valued at from $1,000 to $5,000, and a number who are worth from $5,000 to $20,000. None of our people are in the alms-house, and when we were slaves the aged and infirm who were turned away from the homes of hard masters, who had been enriched by their toil, our benevolent societies supported while they lived, and buried when they died, and comparatively few of us have found it necessary to ask for Government rations, which have been so bountifully bestowed upon the unrepentant Rebels of Richmond.

The law of Slavery severly [sic] punished those who taught us to read and write, but, notwithstanding this, 3,000 of us can read, and at least 2,000 can read and write, and a large number of us are engaged in useful and profitable employment on our own account.

During the whole of the Slaveholders' Rebellion we have been true and loyal to the United States Government; privately and collectively we have sent up our prayers to the Throne of Grace for the success of the Union cause. We have given aid and comfort to the soldiers of Freedom (for which several of our people, of both sexes, have been severely punished by stripes and imprisonment). We have been their pilots and their scouts, and have safely conducted them through many perilous adventures, while hard-fought battles and bloody fields have fully established the indomitable bravery, the loyalty and the heroic patriotism of our race.

We rejoiced with exceeding great joy at the fall of Richmond and the termination of the war, which we supposed broke the last fetter of the American slave. When the triumphant Union army entered the City of Richmond we alone gave it a cordial welcome, receiving it with hearts bursting with joy and thanksgiving; and when our late beloved and martyred President made his *entreé* [sic] into our city

New York Tribune, June 17, 1865, p. 1.

we alone hailed his advent with enthusiastic cheers of acclamation, and of all the citizens of Richmond we alone, with a few solitary exceptions, wear the exterior badges of mourning, as truthful expressions of our grief for his untimely death; and it is, therefore, with sorrowing hearts that we are compelled thus to acquaint your Excellency with our sad disappointment, for our present condition is, in many respects worse than when we were slaves, and living under slave law. Under the old system, we had the *protection* of our masters, who were financially interested in our physical welfare. That protection is now withdrawn, and our old masters have become our enemies, who seek not only to oppress our people, but to thwart the designs of the Federal Government and of benevolent Northern associations in our behalf. We cannot appeal to the laws of Virginia for protection, for the old negro laws still prevail, and besides, the oath of a colored man against a white man will not be received in any of our State Courts: so that we have nowhere to go for protection and justice but to that power which made us free. . . .

In the city of Richmond, the military and police authorities will not allow us to walk the streets by day or night, in the regular pursuit of our business or on our way to church, without a *pass*, and passes do not in all cases protect us from arrest, insult, abuse, violence and imprisonment, against which we have thus far had no protection or redress. Men have not only been arrested in the street, but the police, in conjunction with the Provost Guards, have entered our dwellings and workshops, and have taken men from the work-bench and put them into prison because they had no pass, or because they would not recognize the pass presented as genuine or sufficient.

In numerous instances our people have been driven from their old homes, or have sought employment elsewhere, when justice to themselves and their families, demanded that they should make such a change; and many of these people have been rudely arrested, thrust into prison, and hired out by miliary authority for the most insignificant sums. A number of men who have been employed upon plantations have visited Richmond in search of long-lost wives and children, who had been separated by the cruel usages of Slavery. Wives, too, are frequently seen in our streets, anxiously inquiring for husbands who had been sold away from them, and many of these people, who ignorantly supposed that the day of passes had passed away with the system which originated them, have been arrested, imprisoned and hired out without their advice or consent, thus preventing the reunion of long estranged and affectionate families. . . .

. . . [H]owever sad our hearts may be over the present state of our affairs, we have lost none of our faith in or love for the Union, or for yourself as its Chief Magistrate, and therefore, as oppressed, obedient and loving children, we ask your protection, and upon the loyalty of our hearts and the power of our arms you may rely with unbounded confidence; and in conclusion, let us respectfully remind your Excellency of that sublime motto once inscribed over the portals of an Egyptian temple, *"Know all ye who exercise power, that God hates injustice!"*

FIELDS COOK.   RICHARD WELLS.
WALTER SNEAD.   WM. WILLIAMSON
PETER WOOLFOLK.   T. MORRIS CHESTER.
NELSON HAMILTON.

Richmond Va., June 10, 1865.

2. Freedmen of Edisto Island, South Carolina, Demand Land, 1865

To the President of these United States. We the freedmen Of Edisto Island South Carolina have learned From you through Major General O O Howard commissioner of the Freedmans Bureau. with deep sorrow and Painful hearts of the possibility of government restoring These lands to the former owners. We are well aware Of the many perplexing and trying questions that burden Your mind. and do therefore pray to god (the preserver of all, and who has through our Late and beloved President (Lincoln) proclamation and the war made Us A free people) that he may guide you in making Your decisions. and give you that wisdom that Cometh from above to settle these great and Important Questions for the best interests of the country and the Colored race: Here is where secession was born and Nurtured   Here is where we have toiled nearly all Our lives as slaves and were treated like dumb Driven cattle. This is our home, we have made These lands what they are. we were the only true and Loyal people that were found in posession of these Lands. we have been always ready to strike for Liberty and humanity yea to fight if needs be To preserve this glorious union. Shall not we who Are freedman and have been always true to this Union have the same rights as are enjoyed by Others? . . . are not our rights as A free people and good citizens of these United States To be considered before the rights of those who were Found in rebellion against this good and just Government (and now being conquered) come (as they Seem) with penitent hearts and beg forgiveness For past offences and also ask if thier lands Cannot be restored to them   are these rebellious Spirits to be reinstated in thier *possessions* And we who have been abused and oppressed For many long years not to be allowed the Privilige of purchasing land But be subject To the will of these large Land owners? God forbid, Land monoploy is injurious to the advancement of the course of freedom, and if Government Does not make some provision by which we as Freedmen can obtain A Homestead, we have Not bettered our condition.

We have been encouraged by Government to take Up these lands in small tracts, receiving Certificates of the same—we have thus far Taken Sixteen thousand (1600) acres of Land here on This Island. We are ready to pay for this land When Government calls for it, and now after What has been done will the good and just government take from us all this right and make us Subject to the will of those who have cheated and Oppressed us for many years   God Forbid!

We the freedmen of this Island and of the State of South Carolina—Do therefore petition to you as the President of these United States, that some provisions be made by which Every colored man can purchase land. and Hold it as his own. We wish to have A home if It be but A few acres without some provision is Made our future is sad to look upon. yess our Situation is dangerous. we therefore look to you In the trying hour as A true friend of the poor and Neglected race. for

Ira Berlin, Steven Hahn, Steven F. Miller, Joseph P. Reidy, and Leslie S. Rowland, "The Terrain of Freedom: The Struggle over the Meaning of Free Labor in the U.S. South," *History Workshop*, no. 22 (Autumn 1986), 128–129.

protection and Equal Rights. with the privilege of purchasing A Homestead—A Homestead right here in the Heart of South Carolina.

. . . May God bless you in the Administration of your duties as the President Of these United States is the humble prayer Of us all—

In behalf of the Freedmen
Henry Bram
Committee   Ishmael. Moultrie.
yates. Sampson

3. Captain Charles Soule, Northern Army Officer, Lectures Ex-Slaves on the Responsibilities of Freedom, 1865

To the Freed People of Orangeburg District.

You have heard many stories about your condition as freemen. You do not know what to believe: you are talking too much; waiting too much; asking for too much. If you can find out the truth about this matter, you will settle down quietly to your work. Listen, then, and try to understand just how you are situated.

You are now free, but you must know that the only difference you can feel yet, between slavery and freedom, is that neither you nor your children can be bought or sold. You may have a harder time this year than you have ever had before; it will be the price you pay for your freedom. You will have to work hard, and get very little to eat, and very few clothes to wear. If you get through this year alive and well, you should be thankful. Do not expect to save up anything, or to have much corn or provisions ahead at the end of the year. You must not ask for more pay than free people get at the North. There, a field hand is paid in money, but has to spend all his pay every week, in buying food and clothes for his family and in paying rent for his house. You cannot be paid in money,—for there is no good money in the District,—nothing but Confederate paper. Then, what can you be paid with? Why, with food, with clothes, with the free use of your little houses and lots. You do not own a cent's worth except yourselves. The plantation you live on is not yours, nor the houses, nor the cattle, mules and horses; the seed you planted with was not yours, and the ploughs and hoes do not belong to you. Now you must get something to eat and something to wear, and houses to live in. How can you get these things? By hard work—and nothing else, and it will be a good thing for you if you get them until next year, for yourselves and for your families. You must remember that your children, your old people, and the cripples, belong to you to support now, and all that is given to them is so much pay to you for your work. If you ask for anything more; if you ask for a half of the crop, or even a third, you ask too much; you wish to get more than you could get if you had been

Ira Berlin, Steven Hahn, Steven F. Miller, Joseph P. Reidy, and Leslie S. Rowland, "The Terrain of Freedom: The Struggle over the Meaning of Free Labor in the U.S. South," *History Workshop*, no. 22 (Autumn 1986), 120–123.

free all your lives. Do not ask for Saturday either; free people everywhere else work Saturday, and you have no more right to the day than they have. If your employer is willing to give you part of the day, or to set a task that you can finish early, be thankful for the kindness, but do not think it is something you must have. When you work, work hard. Begin early at sunrise, and do not take more than two hours at noon. Do not think, because you are free you can choose your own kind of work. Every man must work under orders. The soldiers, who are free, work under officers, the officers under the general, and the general under the president. There must be a head man everywhere, and on a plantation the head man, who gives all the orders, is the owner of the place. Whatever he tells you to do you must do at once, and cheerfully. Never give him a cross word or an impudent answer. If the work is hard, do not stop to talk about it, but do it first and rest afterwards. . . .

There are different kinds of work. One man is a doctor, another is a minister, another a soldier. One black man may be a field hand, one a blacksmith, one a carpenter, and still another a house-servant. Every man has his own place, his own trade that he was brought up to, and he must stick to it. . . .

You do not understand why some of the white people who used to own you, do not have to work in the field. It is because they are rich. If every man were poor, and worked in his own field, there would be no big farms, and very little cotton or corn raised to sell; there would be no money, and nothing to buy. Some people must be rich, to pay the others, and they have the right to do no work except to look out after their property. It is so everywhere, and perhaps by hard work some of you may by-and-by become rich yourselves.

Remember that all your working time belongs to the man who hires you: therefore you must not leave work without his leave not even to nurse a child, or to go and visit a wife or husband. When you wish to go off the place, get a pass as you used to, and then you will run no danger of being taken up by our soldiers. . . .

Do not think of leaving the plantation where you belong. If you try to go to Charleston, or any other city, you will find no work to do, and nothing to eat. You will starve, or fall sick and die. Stay where you are, in your own homes, even if you are suffering. There is no better place for you anywhere else.

You will want to know what to do when a husband and wife live on different places. Of course they ought to be together, but this year, they have their crops planted on their own places, and they must stay to work them. At the end of the year they can live together. Until then they must see each other only once in a while. . . .

Do not grumble if you cannot get as much pay on your place as some one else, for on one place they have more children than on others, on one place the land is poor, on another it is rich; on one place Sherman took everything, on another, perhaps, almost everything was left safe. One man can afford to pay more than another. Do not grumble, either, because the meat is gone or the salt hard to get. Make the best of everything, and if there is anything which you think is wrong, or hard to bear, try to reason it out: if you cannot, ask leave to send one man to town to see an officer. Never stop work on any account, for the whole crop must be raised and got in, or we shall starve. . . .

. . . Remember that even if you are badly off, no one can buy or sell you . . .

4. A Share-Wages Contract, 1865

State of Arkansas
County of Ouachita

This indenture made and entered into this the 26th day of December AD1865 between H. C Cleaver & Brs of the first part & Isaac Squash; Caroline his wife and Counsel, Cato, Churchill, F[ur]ney, Isah, Epsey and Minerva his children, of the second part witneseth.

Firstly, That the said parties of the first part for and in consideration of twelve (12) months labor to be well and faithfully rendered by the parties of the second part. beginning on the 1st day of January AD1866 & ending on the 31st day of December AD1866. agree to furnish.

1st Land. team and all necessary farming utencels for planting and cultivating the crop for 1866,

2d Good and sufficient rations to be furnished by the week.

3d House rent and fuel free of cost.

4th All necessary attention when sick except when the skill of a physician is necessary.

Secondly, That at the close of the year 1866, the parties of the 1st part are to deliver to the parties of the 2d part one fourth (¼) of the crop of corn and cotton made and saved upon the plantation cultivated by the parties of the 1st part, the parties of the second part agreeing to accept this in lieu of other wages,

Thirdly, That the parties of the 1st part, exempt the old gentleman Isaac and his wife Caroline, of the 2d part from labor in the plantation and furnish the said Isaac with land upon which to make a garden plant potatoes &c but his wife Caroline is to do the cooking and washing for the other seven hands,

Fourthly that no night work be required of the said parties of the second part except such as the necessities of the plantation absolutely demand,

Fifthly, That one hour will be allowed during the winter months for dinner, and two (2) hours and a half during the months of June July and August.

Sixthly, That for and in consideration of one fourth (¼) of the crop of corn & cotton to be delivered to the parties of the 2d part by the said parties of the 1st part at the close of the year 1866, the parties of the 2d part agree,

1st To make good, faithful and obedient servants,

2d To, rise at day break, each one to feed and take care of the stock assigned to him, to eat our breakfast, and be ready for work at the signal to be given at half an hour by sun,

3d To enter into no general conversation during work hours.

4th To have one Dollar deducted for disobedience—neglect of duty and leaving without permission being considered acts of disobedience.

5th To raise no live stock without special contract with the parties of the 1st part of this contract,

---

Labor Contracts, ser. 263, Arkansas Assistant Commissioner, Records of the Bureau of Refugees, Freedmen, and Abandoned Lands, National Archives, Washington, D.C.; filed as A-2493 in Freedmen and Southern Society Project files, University of Maryland, College Park.

6th To be charged with all Apples peaches and Melons and all other products of the farm taken by us without permission of our employers,

7th To receive no visitors during work hours,

8th To suffer dismissal for repeating acts of *insolence, swearing* or *indecent* and *unseemly* language to or in the presence of our employers or their families, or for qurrelling and fighting so as to disturb the peace of the plantation, the like penalty shall be suffered,

9th To be charged for all wilful abuse of stock, breaking of tools and throwing away gear,

10th To render cheerful and willing performance of duty,

11th To feed the stock on sunday,

12th To look after and study the interest of our employers, to inform of anything going amiss, to be peaceable orderly and pleasant, to discourage theft &c

13th In case of any controversy with our employers in regard to contract or to regulations we agree to submit it to the Agent of the Freedmen's Bureau of this county,

In testimony whereof we have herewith set our hands and affixed our seals, day and date above writen

H C Cleaver & Bro.

5. Charles Raushenberg, a Freedmen's Bureau Agent, Reports from Georgia, 1867

Office of Agent Bur. R. F. A Lds.
Division of Cuthbert
Cuthbert, Ga. Novbr. 14, 1867

Lieut O. H. Howard
Sub.Asst Commnr Bur R. F. A. Lds
Albany, Ga.

Sir,

In obedience to the instructions received from you I have the honor to submit this Report on the General Condition of Affairs in my division.

When I entered upon my duties as Agent in this Division the Bureau of R. F. A Lds seemed to be generally considered by the community, a substitute for overseers and drivers and to take up and return run away laborers and to punish them for real or imaginary violations of contract by fines, imprisonment and some times by corporeal punishment. . . .

The idea that a planter or employer of any kind should in case of dissatisfaction with his freedmen, instead of driving him of[f] often without paying him his wages, first establish a complaint before the Bureau and let that tribunal decide wether [sic] a sufficient violation of contract existed to justify the discharge of the

Lawanda Cox and John H. Cox, eds., *Reconstruction, the Negro, and the New South* (New York: Harper & Row, 1973), 339–347.

laborer or not, was then considered quite unreasonable; while every employer thought it perfectly proper that a Bureau agent, when notified of a freedmans leaving his employment should immediately issue an order for the arrest of the same and have him brought back—in chains if possible. The fairness of the principle that either party must submit its complaints to the Bureau for adjustment and that the white man can not decide the case a priori and only use the agent of the bureau as his executive organ and that employer as well as employee must submit to its decision wether [sic] the laborer ought to be discharged or ought to remain is just beginning to gain ground amongst both races. . . . The common bulk of the population is just beginning to suspect that nothing else but what is justice and equity to a white man under certain circumstances would be justice and equity to a negro under the same circumstances. . . .

The number of complaints made at this office is very large and increasing continually as the time of settlements is drawing nearer. The white man complains generally that the freedman is lazy, impudent and unreliable, that he will not fulfill his contract any further than it suits his convenience . . . ; the freedman on the other hand generally complains that the white man has made him sign a contract, which he does not understand to mean what the white man says it does mean. . . .

The majority of complaints that have been made at this Office by both races have found their origin in contracts, where freedmen received as compensation for their labor a certain share in the crop. The majority of the plantations in my division were worked under such contracts. The freedman claims under such contracts frequently that he has no other work to do but to cultivate and gather the crop, that being a partner in the concern he ought to be allowed to exercise his own judgment in the management of the plantation, that he ought to be permitted to loose time, when it suits his convenience to do so and when according to his judgement his labor is not needed in the field, that he ought to have a voice in the manner of gathering and dividing the corn and cotton and in the ginning, packing and selling of the latter product—while the employer claims that the labor of the employee belongs to him for the whole year, that he must labor for him six days during the week and do all kinds of work required of him wether [sic] directly connected with the crop or not, that he must have the sole and exclusive management of the plantation and that the freedman must obey his orders and do all work required as if he was receiving money wages, the part of the crop standing in the place of money, that the laborer must suffer deduction for lost time, that if he does not work all the time for him, he is not bound to furnish him provisions all the time, that the crop must be gathered, divided and housed to suit the convenience and judgement of the employer and that the share of the employee must be held responsible for what he has received in goods & provisions during the year. Taking in consideration that often quite a number of freedmen are employed on one plantation under such a contracts [sic], who frequently not only become discontented with the employer but with each other, accusing each other of loosing time unnecessarily and of not working well enough to be entitled to an equal share in the crop, it is easily understood to what amount of implicated difficulties, and vexatious [sic] questions these contracts furnish the material.

. . . [A]s it is I consider [contracts of that kind] inimical to the maintenance of good order discipline and success on plantations and productive of ill will and hatred between the parties concerned. . . .

My conviction is that plain labor contracts for wages for the year, one half of the wages paid every month or every quarter, the other half to be forfeited if the freedman fails to comply, are the most practicable contracts that can be made. They cause frequent & therefore fairer settlements, showing the freedman oftener what he consumes and how much is left to him, prompting him to economy on the one hand and cheering him up to increased energy if he finds himself saving money and, giving very little cause for difficulties and troubles. . . .

The freedman like other human beings thinks and studies more about his rights and privileges than his duties and obligations and his ignorance and deficient capacity to comprehend and reason cause him to invariably overrate the extent of the former and to underrate that of the later, hence he often claims an independence and freedom of action, which it justly incompatible with the faithful performance of his duties as a laborer and servant. . . .

While the colored people have thus erred, . . . the white themselves as a mass . . . have failed to treat them with justice, kindness and forbearance. . . . Employers generally are exacting and tyrannical not disposed to forbear, to reason or to exhort but require implicit obedience and unconditional submission and try very frequently to accomplish by revolting harshness and unscrupulous overbearance, what a universally mild and kind but firm and just treatment should accomplish. They yet act the masters.—The freedman in his new condition is not willing to bear that kind of treatment. . . .

The political excitement and the election troubles between the employer and employee have, I am sorrow [sic] to say, perceptibly increased the already existing antagonism between the two races in my division and particularly in Cuthbert. They have no confidence to [sic] each other whatever and the freedpeople generally look almost upon every white man here as an enemy, they are defiant & challenging and many really insulting in their language and conduct. . . . The whites have made threats & have used imprudent language on the streets and every now and then the paper contains an article calculated to hurt feelings. The general voting of the colored people for the colored candidates and their radical ticket has called into existence an association amongst the whites of Randolph undoubtedly for the purpose of controlling hereafter the colored vote. . . . [F]rom all I can learn, they threaten or rather pledge themselves not to employ a colored man, who is not a friend to the white people, which undoubtedly means one that will not vote their way.

The present aspect of the two races in their relations to each other therefore warrants no expectation that they will get along amically with each other for any length of time but insures the belief that after the removal of the military authority the freedmen when allowed to exercise all the rights & privileges of citizens with their want of knowledge and experience in business and law, will generally fail to obtain justice from the hands of the white race in the daily relations of life as well as in the courts. They would generally come out the loosers [sic], factors liens and mortgages being pushed in before their claims, frequently before they even suspected a danger of any loss, would yearly take away thousands of Dollars of their wages, all kinds of frauds would be practiced on them in making contracts, all kinds of impediments and obstacles would be put in the way of their complaints even reaching the courts and when there they would often fail to receive the necessary attention. . . .

The Judges of the County Courts of my counties have, since I have been in office, promptly acted on all cases referred to them and no palpable act of neglect of duty or injustice has come to my knowledge on the part of the officers of the Courts. The causes, why freedmen fail so often to get redress for wrongs practiced on them and are unjustly found guilty appears to me less owing to the conduct of the officers of the courts, then to the indifference and trickery of lawyers and the partial and prejudiced spirit of Juries. The freedmen need friends, who will espouse their cause and who will show them the way to justice, they need attornies [sic] who are not afeared of injuring their popularity by pleading for them and who will conscientiously fulfil their whole duty towards them, when their clients, and they need good and conscientious men of their own race on the Juries. . . .

The educational progress of the colored people in this division is of late origin but of very fair promise. One educational association exists and is in good working order in each one of my counties at Cuthbert, Lumpkin and Georgetown and the people generally seem to be fully aware of the great importance of this subject and have now for some time been contributing regularly for the maintenance of their schools. Young and old are anxious to learn, in some instances almost to the neglect of other duties.

. . . Encouragement and aid in the building of schoolhouses is much needed at all these places. . . .

I apprehend little danger but what the growing generation of the freedpeople will generally have a common education & will be able to read, write and cypher and to take care of themselves pretty well. . . .

As a mass the freedpeople are easier governed by Bureau authority than any other and the large majority of the freedpeople in my division, I am convinced, look upon the Freedmans Bureau as an institution where they will receive full justice. . . .

I have the honor to remain

Very respectfully
Your ob'd't serv't
Ch. Raushenberg
Agent etc &

6. Elizabeth Botume, a Northern Schoolteacher, Remembers a Husband and Wife Reunion, c. 1865

Much of our spare time—if by any stretch of the imagination we could be supposed to have spare time—was employed in writing letters for the freed people. . . .

These epistles were sent to every nook and corner of the Confederacy, hunting for lost members of scattered families. . . .

Just after the surrender of Charleston an old woman came to me "fur read one letter" which had just arrived. When I opened these letters I always looked first to see from whom they came. This said, "My dear mother."

"Well, Sarah, who do you think wrote this?"

Elizabeth Hyde Botume, *First Days Amongst the Contrabands* (Boston: Lee and Shepard Publishers, 1893), 143–156.

"I 'spects it's William, ma'am. Him's wid de soldiers in Virginny."

"But have you no other sons?"

"You 'member, ma'am, I bin telling you de oder day de rebels catch my biggest boy an' hang him for a spy. An' Martin, the next boy, been sell off by de secesh, an' de Lord knows where him is ef him living."

"This letter is from Martin, Sarah."

The old woman dropped her head upon her knees, and began to rock forward and back, exclaiming, —

"T'ank ye, good Massa! T'ank ye, good Massa! O blessed Jesus! You is berry good, berry good! . . .

"Oh! I is satisfied, ma'am. Martin is alive. But read de letter, please, missis."

It was the same story, daily and hourly repeated. As soon as our troops took possession of Charleston the slave boy, now a free man, turned with his whole heart and soul to his wife and child and his mother. . . .

These people had a marvellous way of tracing out the missing members of their families, and inflexible perseverance in hunting them up.

"Where is Martin's wife!" I asked.

"Don't you know, ma'am? She is Jane Ferguson."

"Why, Sarah! Jane has taken another husband!" I exclaimed. . . .

"Never mind, ma'am. Jane b'longs to Martin, an' she'll go back to him. Martin been a sickly boy, an' de secesh treat him too bad, an' we never 'specs him to lib t'rough all."

Just then Jane came in.

"Bless de Lord, gal!" said Sarah. "Martin is alive an' coming back to we."

"What will you do now, Jane?" I asked. "You have got another husband."

She drew herself up, and said deliberately,—"Martin Barnwell is my husband, ma'am. I am got no husband but he. W'en de secesh sell him off we nebber 'spect to see each odder more. He said 'Jane take good care of our boy, an' w'en we git to hebben us will lib togedder to nebber part no more.' You see, ma'am, w'en I come here I had no one to help me."

"That's so," chimed in the mother. "I tell you, missis, it been a hard fight for we."

"So Ferguson come," continued Jane, "an' axed me to be his wife. I told him I never 'spects Martin *could* come back, but if he did he would be my husband above all others. An' Ferguson said, 'That's right, Jane;' so he cannot say nothing, ma'am."

"But supposing he *does* say something, and is not willing to give you up, Jane?"

"Martin is my husband, ma'am, an' the father of my child; and *Ferguson is a man.* He will not complain. And we had an understanding, too, about it. And now, please, ma'am, to write a letter for me to Ferguson,—he was with the Thirty Fourth Regiment. I want to treat the poor boy well."

I wrote the letter word for word as she dictated. It was clear and tender, but decided. Ferguson was not quite so ready to give her up as she expected. He wrote,— "Martin has not seen you for a long time. He *cannot* think of you as I do. O Jane! do not go to Charleston. Come to Jacksonville. I will get a house and we will live here. Never mind what the people say. Come to me, Jane."

I read the letter to her. It was evidently written by the chaplain, who sympathized with *his client.*

"Will you please, ma'am, write a letter yourself for me? Tell him, I say I'm sorry he finds it so hard to do his duty. But as he does, I shall do mine, an' I shall always pray de Lord to bless him."

"Shall I sign your name, Jane?"

"No, ma'am. I shall never write to him no more. But tell him I wish him well."

Soon after this Martin came and claimed his wife and child, who gladly clung to him.

7. Dave Waldrop, a Florida Freedman, Seeks to Reunite His Family, 1867

Milton Fla June the 18th 1867.

Dear Cousin   I received word last week that you wer not doing very well in Montgomery and that times there wer very hard there   Now Sarah if you will come down here to me I will take care of you and your children and you and children shall never want for anything as long as I have anything to help you with   Come down and I will have a place for you and your three children for I Know that it is hard enough for a woman to get along that has a husband to help her and one that has not I do not Know how they do to get living these times   Cousin I want you to be shure and come down if you posibly can and stay here as long as you want to   if it is three or four year it will not make a bit of differance to me   Sarah you must excuse this paper and ill writen letter and bad composition for I am in a great hurry and have not much time to write for I have to go to away   But I shall look for you down here   Please come down and make your home here with my family   Kate and the children send you there love and best Respects and are wanting you to come down as they want to see you very bad   your friends sends there Respects to you

I shall bring this to a close hoping this will find you well in health if not doing well   And I want to see you as soon as I can

No more at this time   Farewell from your Cousin

Dave Waldrop

8. Harriet Hernandes, a South Carolina Woman, Testifies Against the Ku Klux Klan, 1871

Spartanburgh, South Carolina, *July* 10, 1871.

Harriet Hernandes (colored) sworn and examined.

Question. How old are you?
Answer. Going on thirty-four years.
Question. Where do you live?

Ira Berlin and Leslie S. Rowland, eds., *Families and Freedom: A Documentary History of African-American Kinship in the Civil War Era* (New York: New Press, 1997), 230-231.

42nd Congress, 2nd Session, S.R. 41, pt. 4, *Testimony Taken by the Joint Select Committee to Inquire into the Condition of Affairs in the Late Insurrectionary States, South Carolina*, Vol. 2 (GPO, 1872), 585–590.

Answer. Down toward Cowpens' Furnace, about nineteen miles from here.

Question. Are you married or single?

Answer. Married.

Question. Did the Ku-Klux come to your house at any time?

Answer. Yes, sir; twice.

Question. Go on and tell us about the first time; when was it?

Answer. The first time was after last Christmas. When they came I was in bed. They hallooed, "Hallo!" I got up and opened the door; they came in; they asked who lived there; I told them Charley Hernandes. "Where is he?" they said. Says I, "I don't know, without he is at the Cowpens; he was beating ore there." Says he, "Have you any pistol here?" Says I, "No, sir." Says he, "Have you any gun?" Says I, "No, sir." He took on, and says he, "Your husband is in here somewhere, and damn him, if I see him I will kill him." I says, "Lord o'mercy, don't shoot in there; I will hold a light under there, and you can look." I held a light, and they looked. They told me to go to bed; I went to bed. Two months after that they came again.

Question. How many men were there at that first visit?

Answer. Eight.

Question. How were they dressed?

Answer. All kinds of form; but the first ones that came would not look me in the face, but just turned their backs to me, for they knew I would know them.

Question. Had they disguises?

Answer. Yes; horns and things over their faces; but still, that did not hinder me from knowing them if these things were off.

Question. Did you know any of them?

Answer. I did not know any of the first ones, to say truthful, but the last ones I did know.

Question. Had the first ones arms—guns or pistols?

Answer. Yes, sir; they had their guns and pistols. They came with a long gun, and told me they were going to shoot my damned brains out it I did not tell where my husband was.

Question. What time of night was it?

Answer. Away between midnight and day.

Question. How long had your husband lived there?

Answer. We have been living there three years, now.

Question. Is he a mechanic or laboring man?

Answer. He is a laboring man.

Question. He was working at the furnace?

Answer. Yes, sir.

Question. Go on to the second time; you say it was two months afterward?

Answer. Yes; just exactly two months; two months last Saturday night when they were at our house. . . . They came in; I was lying in bed. Says he, "Come out here, sir; come out here, sir!" They took me out of bed; they would not let me get out, but they took me up in their arms and toted me out—me and my daughter Lucy. He struck me on the forehead with a pistol, and here is the scar above my eye now. Says he, "Damn you, fall!" I fell. Says he, "Damn you get up!" I got up. Says he, "Damn you get over this fence!" and he kicked me over when I went to get over; and then he went on to the brush pile, and they laid us right down there, both together. They laid us down twenty yards apart, I reckon. They had dragged and beat us along. They struck me right on the top of my head, and I thought they had killed me; and I said, "Lord o'mercy, don't, don't kill my child!" He gave me a lick on the head, and it liked to have killed me; I saw stars. He threw my arm over my head so I could not do anything with it for three weeks, and there are great knots on my wrist now.

Question. What did they say this was for?

Answer. They said, "You can tell your husband that when we see him we are going to kill him." They tried to talk outlandish.

Question. Did they say why they wanted to kill him?

Answer. They said, "He voted the radical ticket, didn't he?" I said "Yes," that very way. . . .

Question. Had your husband any guns or pistols about his house?

Answer. He did not have any there at all. If he had, I reckon they would have got them.

Question. How old is your daughter?

Answer. She is fifteen.

Question. Is that the one they whipped?

Answer. Yes, sir.

Question. Is this all you know about it?

Answer. I know the people that came.

Question. Who were they?

Answer. One was Tom Davis, and there was Bruce Martin and his two sons. There are only four that I knew. There were only six that came that last night.

Question. When did your husband get back home?

Answer. He went back yesterday.

Question. When did he get back home after this whipping? He was not at home, was he?

Answer. He was lying out; he couldn't stay at home, bless your soul!

Question. Did you tell him about this?

Answer. O, yes.

Question. What caused him to lie out?

Answer. They kept threatening him. They said if they saw him anywhere about they would shoot him down at first sight. . . .

Question. Had he been afraid for any length of time?

Answer. He has been afraid ever since last October. He has been lying out. He has not laid in the house ten nights since October.

Question. Is that the situation of the colored people down there to any extent?

Answer. That is the way they all have to do—men and women both.

Question. What are they afraid of?

Answer. Of being killed or whipped to death.

Question. What has made them afraid?

Answer. Because men that voted radical tickets they took the spite out on the women when they could get at them.

Question. How many colored people have been whipped in that neighborhood?

Answer. It is all of them, mighty near. I could not name them all.

Question. Name those you remember.

Answer. Ben Phillips and his wife and daughter; Sam Foster; and Moses Eaves, they killed him—I could not begin to tell all—Ann Bonner and her daughter, Manza Surratt and his wife and whole family, even the least child in the family, they took it out of bed and whipped it. They told them if they did that they would remember it.

Question. You have seen those people that were whipped?

Answer. Yes, sir; and I have seen the marks on them, too.

Question. How do colored people feel in your neighborhood!

Answer. They have no satisfaction to live like humans, no how. . . .

Question. What do the colored people do for their safety?

Answer. They lie out all night.

Question. Is that generally the case?

Answer. Yes, sir; some families down there say they don't think they can get tamed to the house in five years.

Question. Does this fear extend to women and children and whole families?

Answer. Yes, sir; they just whipped all. I do not know how bad they did serve some of them. They did them scandalous; that is the truth—they did them scandalous. . . .

Question. Were those that came the second time the same as those that came the first time?

Answer. No, sir.

Question. How do you know?

Answer. I knew they were not.

Question. How do you know?

Answer. Because those that came the last time lived right at us in about a mile and a half, or worked right in that neighborhood; and ever since we have been there nigh them they can't face me, can't look at me . . . and these here wanted me to work for them a good while, and I could not work for them then. . . .

Question. You say one of the last six was Tom Davis?

Answer. Yes, sir.

Question. Was he disguised?

Answer. Yes, sir.

Question. What had he on?

Answer. His horns and a long blue coat. He was the one that told them to lay us down, and then just jumped right on the top of my head.

Question. Could you see his face?

Answer. Not all of it. I had just seen him the day before. . . .

Question. It was a pretty bold fellow that came that way?

Answer. Yes, sir; that was one of Martin's sons . . . both were along.

Question. What are their names?

Answer. Romeo and Tine.

Question. Which one was it?

Answer. I think it was Romeo. . . .

Question. . . . [W]hat was the reason why you thought it was Romeo?

Answer. Because that family wanted me to work for them and I could not work for them; I was working for another man.

Question. How long was that time when they wanted you to work before this whipping?

Answer. Not more than a month.

Question. Before the last visit?

Answer. Yes, sir.

Question. What took place that you could not work?

Answer. My husband rented some land and I had to come home.

Question. Did they get mad?

Answer. Yes, sir.

Question. What did they say?

Answer. They said they were going to have me Ku-Kluxed. . . .

Question. Who was present?

Answer. Only old Missus Williams, and she said, "Harriet, you'll be Ku-Kluxed for that."

Question. Who is she?

Answer. She is a white woman. It was her son I was to work for. He wanted me to work for him.

Question. What is his name?

Answer. Augustus Williams.

Question. I thought it was the Martins you had the trouble with?

Answer. They were the ones that whipped me. I thought it was Mr. Williams that held the horses.

Question. You said the Martins wanted you to work for them and you could not?

Answer. Yes, sir, all the family; they were all kin.

Question. And when you could not work for them they said they would have you Ku-Kluxed?

Answer. Yes, sir.

Question. Who said that, Bruce Martin?

Answer. Yes, sir.

Question. Was Mrs. Williams there?

Answer. Yes, sir.

Question. She heard them say that?

Answer. Yes, sir.

Question. They were bold enough to say before you and Mrs. Williams that you would be Ku-Kluxed?

Answer. Yes, sir, that I would be Ku-Kluxed. . . .

Question. You think the Martins did this for the reason that they were so mad because you would not work for them, that they Ku-Kluxed you?

Answer. Yes, sir; they got so mad that they could not stand it.

Question. Are they white people?

Answer. Yes, sir.

Question. How did you know Tine Martin?

Answer. By his size and his ways and all. . . .

Question. What did they do, that you knew them?

Answer. Their father was there. . . . One took hold of one arm of my little child and the other took the other arm, and I said, "Lord, don't kill my child;" and he knocked me down with the pistol and said, "Damn you, fall! Damn you, get up!" and I went to get up and he said, "Damn you, get over the fence;" and when I tried to get over he kicked me over, and I knew the horses.

Question. What horses?

Answer. One big black and four big sorrels and a mule. There were two of the Martins, and I reckon they had borrowed a mule of Gus Williams.

Question. Did you talk to him about it?

Answer. No, sir; if I told them I believed it was them they would have come the next night and killed me.

Question. Did you know the mule?

Answer. I knew it; it was Gus Williams's mule. He must have been holding the horses. He must have known that I would have known him if I had touched him almost.

Question. Did not the Martins know that you would recognize the horses?

Answer. I don't know. . . .

Question. Is there any justice of the peace up there? Have you any squires?

Answer. I know there was a squire named Blackwell.

Question. You could have come here and made complaint?

Answer. But I was afraid.

Question. Afraid of what?

Answer. Afraid of the Ku-Klux.

Question. What Ku-Klux?

Answer. Of the Martins.

Question. Why are you not afraid of them now?

Answer. I am; I am afraid to go back home.

Question. Are you going home?

Answer. I don't know whether I shall go back or not.

9. Elected Representatives, 1872

This 1872 Currier and Ives print depicts the black men who served in the Forty-first and Forty-second Congresses of the United States. From left to right they are: Sen. Hiriam R. Revels of Mississippi; Rep. Benjamin S. Turner of Alabama; Rep. Robert C. De Large of South Carolina; Rep. Josiah T. Walls of Florida; Rep. Jefferson F. Long of Georgia; Rep. Joseph H. Rainey of South Carolina; and Rep. Robert Brown Elliott of South Carolina.

These first Congressmen came from a variety of backgrounds. Revels, Elliott, and De Large were born free: Elliott in Boston or England and Revels and De Large in North Carolina and South Carolina respectively. The other four were born enslaved, although Rainey's father purchased their whole family's freedom in the

Library of Congress, Prints and Photographs Division; Eric Foner, *Freedom's Lawmakers: A Directory of Black Officeholders During Reconstruction*, rev. ed. (Baton Rouge: Louisiana State University Press, 1996).

US Senator H R REVELS of Mississippi   BENJ S TURNER M C of Alabama   JOSIAH T WALLS M C of Florida   JOSEPH H RAINY M C of S Carolina   R BROWN ELLIOT M C of S Carolina

ROBERT C DE LARGE M C of S Carolina   JEFFERSON H LONG M C of Georgia

THE FIRST COLORED SENATOR AND REPRESENTATIVES.
In the 41ˢᵗ and 42ⁿᵈ Congress of the United States.

mid-1840s, and Turner, while still enslaved, ran his own hotel and livery stable, accumulating considerable wealth. Their relations to the Confederate and Union forces suggest the range of experiences that black men had during the Civil War. De Large was employed by the Confederate Navy, while Rainey, impressed into work on Confederate fortifications, fled to Bermuda with his wife, returning only at the conclusion of the war. Walls, impressed into labor in the Confederate Army, was captured by Union forces and sent North where he enlisted in the 3d U.S. Colored Infantry, with which he returned South to fight the Confederacy. Revels served the Union forces as an army chaplain.

E S S A Y S

The first essay, by the late historian Herbert G. Gutman, recounts the ways ex-slaves throughout the South took responsibility for providing for their own education and that of their children. Gutman argues against the tendency to view aspirations for education as a middle-class value, noting the ways in which the desires and work for these schools were rooted in black working-class cultural values. In the second essay, Julie Saville, a historian at the University of Chicago, recounts the numerous ways ex-slaves in South Carolina sought to take charge of their economic lives in the post–Civil War era and especially how their struggles to define themselves as free workers were entwined with their struggles for political and family rights. In the final essay, Elsa Barkley Brown, who teaches history, women's studies, and African-American studies at the University of Maryland, explores the little-researched area of black women's political activities after the Civil War. Through the lens of women's activities she argues for understanding how ex-slaves—male and female— developed their understandings of political rights in ways that were profoundly different from those being championed by their white Republican allies. Collectively, what do these essays suggest about the challenges that faced ex-slaves, the resources they could draw on in their struggles, and their prospects for success?

Schools for Freedom

HERBERT G. GUTMAN

"The Principle of schools, of education," said James T. White, a black delegate to the 1868 Arkansas Constitutional Convention, "is intended to elevate our families." The role former slaves and other blacks such as White (an Indiana-born minister and Union Army veteran) played in bringing schools to their children offers a rare insight into the values of the black community as it emerged from slavery. Blacks voluntarily paid school tuition, purchased schoolbooks, hired, fed, boarded, and protected teachers, constructed and maintained school buildings, and engaged in other costly (and sometimes dangerous) activities to provide education for their children. To expect such sustained efforts from men and women fresh to freedom, poor by any material standard, and entirely without political power is, perhaps, much to ask. But evidence disclosing such efforts is indeed abundant.

The former slaves themselves, not the schools per se, remain the center of this study. Historians of American (and particularly Southern) education have reconstructed in close detail the work of Northern white schoolteachers and missionaries in the postbellum South. While making it clear that articulate freedmen and freedwomen enthusiastically welcomed education for their children, the existing literature—even by "revisionist" historians of the Reconstruction—emphasizes the energy sympathetic Northern whites expended in helping freedpeople establish schools. In actual fact, the former slaves themselves played the central role in building, financing, and operating these schools, a fact that adds to our understanding of the family sensibilities and parental concerns of these men and women. It also indicates some of the ways in which reciprocal obligations operated beyond the immediate family and bound together former slaves living in rural and urban communities.

Postwar educational efforts by blacks built on a firm base of educational activism during slavery. Scattered but nevertheless convincing evidence reveals that secret slave schools had existed in a number of antebellum Southern cities. A black woman named Deveaux began a secret school in Savannah, Georgia, in 1835 and taught in the same room for the next thirty years. After the war, a visitor talked with her (she still taught in that room but to "the children of the better class of the colored people") and learned how she had eluded "for more than a quarter of a century the most constant and lynx-eyed vigilance of the slaveholders of her native city." She was not alone in this work. . . .

Herbert G. Gutman, "Schools for Freedom: The Post-Emancipation Origins of Afro-American Education," in Herbert G. Gutman, *Power and Culture: Essays on the American Working Class,* ed. Ira Berlin (New York: Pantheon Books, 1987), 260–280, 285–293, 296.)

. . . Southern cities with secret schools included Richmond, Virginia, where an unnamed black woman managed such a place for slaves, and Augusta, Georgia, where Edwin Purdy, a black clergyman, started a school in "a small room of his house" in the middle of the Civil War. Soon discovered, Purdy paid a $50 fine, suffered sixty lashes, and was sentenced to prison for an undisclosed time (friends, apparently whites, won his release after twelve days). . . .

The efforts of blacks to educate themselves expanded greatly during the Civil War, especially in locales that fell to the Union Army. "One of the first acts of the Negroes, when they found themselves free," observed the American Freedmen's Inquiry Commission, "was to establish schools at their own expense. A pay school—the first school for wartime runaways—was opened in Alexandria, Virginia, on September 1, 1861, by two black women. Later that month, one of them joined Mrs. Mary Smith Peake, the daughter of an English father and a free black woman who had taught at an antebellum Hampton, Virginia, school (and had her black stepfather among her pupils), to start a second contraband school at Fortress Monroe, Virginia. White teachers did not work with the Alexandria contrabands until October 1862. By that time, blacks managed three other schools. Before the war's end, at least sixteen other black men and women taught or directed Alexandria schools for runaway slaves. By April 1863, about 2,000 former slaves had congregated in Alexandria and 400 children attended their schools. "The first demand of these fugitives when they come into the place," observed a *New York Evening Post* correspondent, "is that their children may go to school." "Another surprising fact," he went on, "is that the poor negro women had rather toil, earn and pay one dollar per month for their children's education, than to permit them to enter a charity school." The contraband blacks also built, by voluntary labor, a school worth about $500, and later enlarged and improved it, making it "well lathed and plastered."

But there was more to establishing a school than bricks and mortar. At the start, a dispute over whether white or black teachers should be "the superintendents" threatened this Alexandria school's future. The blacks called a meeting. "I wish you could have been at that meeting," reported North Carolina fugitive slave Harriet Jacobs, who had come to Virginia to teach. "Most of the people were slaves until quite recently, but they talked sensibly and . . . put the question to a vote in quite parliamentary style. The result was a decision that the colored teachers should have charge of the school." The school opened in January 1864 with 75 pupils; two months later, it had 225, and the following August it was "the largest school and schoolhouse in the city." Once it had opened, blacks maintained their support. "My table in the school room," an early Hampton teacher reported, "is loaded, morning and noon, with oranges, lemons, apples, figs, candies, and other sweet things too numerous to mention." Such gift-giving was common in many parts of the South. . . .

Schools grew with the arrival of the federal army. . . .

North Carolina contrabands knew their first school in the spring of 1862, taught by a white man in the New Bern African Methodist Episcopal Church. Army officers also gave a Baptist missionary two Beaufort churches in which to teach. He found them "very filthy and sadly out of repair," but Beaufort blacks soon agreed to raise funds for their improvement. A Sabbath collection produced $84.88 ("to my surprise," said the white missionary), and in five weeks the blacks had gathered $200. In the winter and spring of 1863, New Bern blacks also established their own small schools. A *New York Tribune* reporter visited a school near the Camp Trent contraband "huts" built by the former slaves. "In one of the huts," he related, "a school was in progress, kept by a black man. He has thirty scholars, who he told me were learning quite fast. He himself has a fair education; could read, write, and cypher. He had learned all this, while a slave, from a schoolboy." Later that year, New Bern had twenty-four teachers, three blacks among them. James O'Hara, a West Indian mulatto, ran a "self-supported school." O'Hara's institution, New Bern's "most advanced colored school," included among its subjects "Geography, Grammar, and Arithmetic."

In *Rehearsal for Reconstruction,* Willie Lee Rose fully described the schooling given South Carolina Sea Island blacks by Yankee missionaries and schoolteachers. Sea Island blacks contributed mightily to that effort. A white Boston Baptist clergyman started Beaufort's first school in early January 1862. "Both teachers and pupils are negroes," said one report. This school, called "the Billaird Hall school," had four black "assistant" teachers: Paul Johnson, Thomas Ford, Peter Robinson, and Ephraim Lawrence, "themselves not far advanced but able to read and spell one-syllabled words." Missionaries spent an hour each day giving them special instruction, and a weekly contribution of five cents from each pupil (both boys and girls attended the school) helped pay their salary. The five-cent contribution, a white teacher wrote, "is cheerfully made, but not enforced in exceptional cases of orphanage or extreme poverty." Sixteen pupils attended the first day; two months later, school enrollment had reached 101. Indeed, three of every five Beaufort youths regularly attended the wartime schools.

Beaufort was the only town of size on the Sea Islands, but schools also flourished in rural areas, some maintained by Northern benevolent societies like the National Freedmen's Relief Association (which had established twenty-two schools by 1864) and others by the blacks themselves. A former slave woman named Hettie (she had "stolen a knowledge of letters from time to time") began a day school in March 1863 and kept up her work after the Edisto blacks became war refugees on St. Helena's Island. Even before that time, white missionary-teachers arrived at the Smith plantation to find that "the children were all assembled by Cuffy, and he was teaching them when we went in." . . .

In other places, Sea Island parents shared in the supervision of the schools. Northern teachers encouraged St. Helena's blacks to form visiting committees to help manage that island's school. One person from each plantation served on the committee, which Robert Chaplin headed. The school visiting committee did its work every Friday. . . . Chaplin, then seventy-three, composed the report that went North, explaining that the committee visited the schools to "see that everything go regular among the children" and to help the teacher "so far as our understanding goes." All books and property that belong to the school," he added, "is in our charge."

Farther west, blacks exhibited the same concern for wartime schooling. When Union Army recruiters first arrived in Nashville, Tennessee, they found that blacks had started "without any assistance" schools in which more than 800 children "received instruction from teachers paid by their parents—the slaves but just emancipated." . . . A Nashville bookseller remarked that he had "sold more spelling books in a short time than he has done for years." The first school had opened in the fall of 1862 in the First Colored Baptist Church. Its teacher was Daniel Wadkins, an antebellum free black whose school for free black children had twice been closed by worried whites in the 1850s. By the fall of 1863, several schools had "sprung up, taught by colored people who have got a little learning somehow." Students paid between one and two dollars each month. By the summer of 1864, the schools had "become so numerous, and the attendance so large, that all open opposition to them has ceased." That year, more black than white Nashville children attended school, and some black students established "schools on their own as soon as they were able to read." . . .

Between April 1865 and the advent of Radical Reconstruction two years later, educational opportunities for blacks expanded dramatically throughout the South, thanks in part to the work of Northern benevolent societies and the newly established Freedmen's Bureau. But as during the war, initiative often rested with the blacks themselves. The process can best be examined in . . . Virginia, South Carolina . . . and Georgia.

The general public and private policies that affected the education of blacks deserve brief notice. Except for Florida, where the legislature imposed a special education tax on blacks, no Southern state made provision to educate the former slaves. In establishing the Freedmen's Bureau, Congress did not include funds for education in 1865; not until the summer of 1866 did the federal government authorize the bureau to spend half a million dollars for the rental, construction, and repair of schoolhouses. Some additional money for the education of former slaves came from funds appropriated by several Northern states to purchase black substitutes in the South and thereby help to fill draft quotas. Bureau policies and shortage of funds obliged the former slaves to take the initiative in establishing schools, and in this they were encouraged by the Northern benevolent societies. The New England Freedmen's Aid Society, for example, only offered funds to blacks who erected, repaired, and cared for schools, furnished board for teachers, and paid small tuition fees. Edward Everett Hale explained the guiding assumptions shared by many who managed these benevolent societies: "The policy . . . has not been to make these people beggars. . . . The black people know they must support themselves, as they have always done." Hale admitted that such policies assured "suffering" but went on: "Where is there not suffering in this world? We have never said that the black man's life should be raised above suffering. We have said that he should be free to choose between inevitable hardships. This promise we perform."

In fact, blacks did not wait for state authorization, the advent of the bureau, or the advice of Northern societies to establish schools in 1865 and 1866. In the late fall of 1865, John W. Alvord, superintendent of education for the Freedmen's Bureau, toured the South. Everywhere he traveled, he informed General O. O. Howard, the bureau commissioner, he found "a class of schools got up and taught by colored people, rude and imperfect, but still groups of persons, old and young, *trying* to learn." They lacked "the patience to wait for the coming of a white teacher." Alvord estimated that the South knew "at least five hundred" such schools, many of them never before visited "by any white man." "In the absence of other teaching," he said, "they are determined to be self-taught. . . . In truth, these spontaneous efforts of the colored people would start up everywhere if books could be sent them."

Virginia and South Carolina blacks typified the early postwar concern for education. Richmond and Charleston deserve special attention. Quite different in many ways (Richmond, for example, had more black factory workers than any other American city), both cities had fallen to the Union Army just before the war's end. It should be kept in mind that schooling for blacks in these and other Southern places was entirely voluntary. No external compulsion forced the former slaves to attend school or to contribute to the success of educational institutions. A school for Richmond blacks started in mid-April at the First African Baptist Church, and 1,025 students (50 of them sixteen or older) showed up. Their enthusiasm for schooling stunned one observer: "I never before imagined it possible for an uneducated class to have such zeal of earnestness for schools and books. . . ." On a visit to Richmond in 1866, William Hepworth Dixon, the editor of the London *Athenaeum,* agreed, noting that the city had forty black schools. . . . None of this came easily. "Many of our children" explained a Quaker teacher, "have been driven from their homes because they came to school; and, in some instances, *whole families* have been turned into *the streets* because they were represented in the school-room."

In these early months, "by far the largest proportions of Richmond children" paid for "their books, slates, etc." . . . That winter individual black children, most from families living on the edge of poverty, contributed to or collected for a "fuel fund" to heat their schools in sums ranging from two cents to one dollar. When the Second Baptist Church burned in March 1866 (some suspected "rebel malice"), it also meant the destruction of an important school facility. "All were for action," said a leader of the affected blacks. They hired rooms to continue the school and planned to rebuild a brick building. . . .

Charleston blacks took similar initiatives. Schools there opened in early March 1865 and immediately served (in separate rooms and on separate floors) between 200 and 300 white and 1,200 black students. At least that number of black students waited for additional school places. A *New York Tribune* correspondent noted that "the loyal white people—the Irish and German population"—allowed their children to attend school with the freed blacks but would not "tolerate" mixed classes. Five days after the schools opened, James Redpath, their superintendent, counted forty-two teachers, nearly all local residents and twenty-five of them blacks. At first, whites were not permitted to teach the black children. "Some of the colored teachers," said George Newcomb, "passed a good examination, and will, I doubt not, prove excellent." "Colored South Carolinians" also taught in the night schools. These teachers included women "very light in complexion" and members of "the aristocracy of the colored community," who, a white teacher noted, were "advanced enough to pursue intelligently all the common branches of English education." Among them was Miss Weston, an "accomplished and talented colored lady" once jailed "for teaching a little school." Early in 1867, several young Charleston black men ("most of them, though quite well educated, had never taught before") quit that city to spread literacy in "the country districts." A reverse process brought black teachers to Charleston: the Old Zion Church School included on its staff women graduates of the Philadelphia Institute for Colored Youth. . . .

Charleston blacks did not just staff their schools and fill them with their children. They purchased books and, after a time, paid "a school tax." . . .

Letters sent by teachers working for Northern benevolent societies help illuminate Virginia blacks' educational activities. Just after the war, Farmville blacks applied at Petersburg for a teacher, and despite some threats of violence, a school started and remained open two years later. . . . Three teachers started Petersburg schools in May 1865: chased from their first building, they taught 200 students next in a railroad station; when a tobacco company claimed that place, the school was moved to a warehouse. Less than a year later, Petersburg and its vicinity counted twenty-two schools and 2,769 registered pupils. . . .

Official Freedmen's Bureau reports for 1866 and early 1867 fill in the Virginia picture. The bureau took notice of 136 teachers in January 1866 and 225 twelve months later. By March 1867, the number had risen to 278 (81 of them blacks). In January 1866, Rolzo M. Manly, then superintendent of the bureau's Virginia schools, reported: "Every week since the first of October, new schools have been opened in some part of the State. It has been essentially a period of organization." Manly did not give much credit to resident whites, claiming that "practically all our progress, with rare exceptions, is in the face of actual opposition." "Milder modes of resistance" included "refusing the use of all churches or vestries which the whites can possibly control, refusing to rent room or charging exorbitant rates, refusing to board teachers, forbidding colored tenants sending their children to school on pain of being turned out of doors." "The more forcible forms of resistance," Manly felt, "such as mobs and conflagrations, are restrained by occasional hints from the military arms." Later that same year, Manly added that "in more than a score of places, the colored people have erected schoolhouses with their own hands, and employed either some poor white person, or someone of their own people, who has some small attainments, as a teacher. . . . They lack books, and have not a penny of money, their wages of the farm being received in the form of food and clothing." . . .

The detailed letters of two white Quaker teachers in Danville, Eunice Congdon and George Dixon, allow us to examine with greater precision the ways Virginia blacks sustained schools for their children and protected white teachers. Eunice Congdon and another white woman teacher arrived in Danville to teach early in the fall of 1865. . . . By early February 1866, the Danville teachers had enrolled 299 day-school pupils and employed "a young colored girl to assist" in "the lowest division."

The Danville school taught more than reading and writing. In 1866, blacks crowded densely into it to hear the Civil Rights Bill of 1866 read and discussed. Miss Congdon called the discussion "rich and significant beyond description." Another time, the Northern teachers distributed seeds to Danville blacks. And when some black men formed a voluntary association called "The Mechanics' Society for Mutual Aid," they met in the schoolhouse and their president asked Miss Congdon to "send North and get for him the book containing the names of the different *trades,* coming under the head of mechanics." Such community efforts suggest that schools had become more than mere educational institutions. And for that reason, among others, they provoked bitter opposition.

Opposition by whites to the Danville school increased after the Union Army withdrew from the town. The school remained there, however, owing to the courage displayed by Eunice Congdon, George Dixon, and Danville blacks. When Condgon fell ill, Dixon, who was then teaching English in Greensboro, North Carolina, came to help. Soon after his arrival, a white man attacked Eunice Congdon. . . . A Union Army officer later learned that the man had planned to kill Miss Congdon, plunder the place, and then "set fire to the buildings." Threats against Miss Congdon were overheard in the streets. "A white woman," Dixon insisted, "told a colored chid she need not go to school on Monday morning, because Miss Eunice would be dead." Danville blacks protected the teacher and the school. Dixon explained: "The colored men are kind in coming to keep a watch in the dead of night, but we are fearful of their coming in collision with the citizens, and blood being shed, as they will bring firearms with them and feel very desperate." "The colored people are our friends," Congdon confirmed. "They guard us every night." . . . Miss Congdon herself left Danville after the school year ended. "The first day school," she explained, "will be continued by four colored men whom we have initiated." More than this, other blacks promised to protect school property and records. When the Danville school closed for the summer, it had a full enrollment: 237 children had registered for its day classes.

Evidence also abounds of the black zeal for education in rural South Carolina. The Sea Island schools established during the war continued, and still received aid from local blacks. Blacks at Edgerly and Union Point joined together to build a new schoolhouse. "The island has gone wild to have a school on every plantation," reported Laura Towne from Port Royal in November 1865. Enthusiasm did not wane in the next two years. When Elizabeth Botume opened a schoolhouse at the Old Fort Plantation, some men came unannounced to "white-wash the interior of the building." . . .

Throughout South Carolina, blacks pressed for schools and contributed to their success, and their efforts deserve particular notice because, unlike Sea Island blacks, they had not experienced wartime contact with Northern soldiers, missionaries, and school teachers. . . .

. . . [I]n northeastern South Carolina, a rich cotton region that was home to nearly a third of the state's former slave population, Benjamin Franklin Whittemore— an Amherst College graduate, Methodist clergyman, and former Union Army chaplain—supervised education . . . for the Freedmen's Bureau between 1865 and 1867. Despite their economic troubles and local white opposition, he reported that black men and women contributed handsomely to their children's education. They moved an old "Confederate building" ten miles from Florence to Darlington to start the district's first school. By April 1866 six schools existed, and a month later eleven. Northern soldiers had burned a Marion schoolhouse, so its teacher met classes in the woods.

Summerville got its school sometime before July. Two white women offered two acres of land for $200 as school property. Local blacks, many among them poor and destitute, crowded into an army barracks they used as a church to agree that if the Northern societies paid for the land and the government supplied lumber, they would build a school to open in October. "A good carpenter," Dan Meyers, spoke first: "I is a plain man and alers does what I agree, and I say that I will stan' by the good work till it's done finished." Another black man boomed: "I is a good carpenter; I has no children of my own to send to the school; but I want to see the house build, and I gives two weeks work for it." Others offered their labor, and some, including young boys, gave small sums of money. In all, $60 was raised and twelve weeks of labor pledged. "The women," enthused schoolteacher Esther Hawkes, did "their part, offering to board or lodge the workmen as they best could." "These destitute people," she mused, "living, some of them, in rude huts made of mud and palmetto, one might suppose that all their interest was necessary [just] to keep them from starving. . . ." But this was only the start. By October, the burned Marion school had been rebuilt ($200); Darlington black men and women gave their labor and money for a school ($500); Simmonsville blacks ditched and fenced and then built a home for the teacher ($150); Sumter blacks moved a building forty miles and then reconstructed it ($250). Lynchburg blacks also moved and repaired a building ($150), and so did those in Florence ($350). In Camden, black muscle and money meant a new schoolhouse ($800), and Camden blacks also rented an old building for $30 a month. Schoolhouses also went up on the Mulberry Plantation ($100) and in Springville ($100).

In Camden, most blacks worked crops on contract and saw no cash until they had gathered the full crop. Teachers, however, did not suffer discomfort. "They furnish us with beds, bedding, and furniture for our rooms free, though they do not pay the rent," reported one teacher. "They sell articles to teachers at under price, and bring in gratuitously articles of food. The girls at the night school have made me some presents." "There is no lack of 'a disposition to do all in their power *now*,' " the teacher added. "Indeed I think they *have* done it." The obstacles faced by these former South Carolina slaves seeking education for themselves and their children, however, should not be obscured by this enthusiasm. In June 1867, Darlington residents appealed to Boston's mayor: "We are on the eve of Starvation. . . ." Between September 1866 and January 1867, Camden blacks raised $120 to pay the school rent, heat the school building, and furnish the schoolteachers's rooms. "They have performed *all they have promised*," reported Jane Smith from Sumter. "They were to pay a certain sum toward the erection of their church which they have done. They were to whitewash it, to buy a bell, build a belfry, furnish lamps, lumber for the pulpit, and several comforts for the teachers. All this, *they have done*." Overall, South Carolina blacks had done much to educate themselves. For the entire state in the year starting July 1866, $106,797.73 was expended to educate South Carolina blacks. Northern societies gave $65,087.01, while the Freedmen's Bureau advanced $24,510.72. South Carolina blacks contributed cash to the amount of $17,200.00 (16 percent), and more in kind and labor. Only where poverty prevented such self-help efforts did blacks request assistance. . . .

Still the efforts of [of other southern blacks] pale in comparison with those of Georgia blacks. Between 1865 and 1867, black people in Georgia did more to educate their children than those in any other Southern state. When white missionary teachers arrived in Atlanta, they found that two former slaves, James Tate and Grandison Daniels, had started a small school in an old church building. . . . In Augusta, illiterate blacks filled a meeting place and helped pick a committee to aid the white teachers. That committee raised more than $100 and received promises of more money. Augusta blacks also repaired a schoolroom in an old Confederate shoe shop. . . . A school opened on June 12: 500 children showed up the first day and 100 more came in the days that followed . . . Richard R. Wright started learning in a Cuthbert school in 1865. It "scarcely had one of its sides covered or weather-boarded," Wright remembered. "It was about twenty by thirty. . . . The house was packed as tightly with dusky children as a sardine box. . . ." (In Atlanta, Wright's second schoolhouse was "an abandoned box car.") . . . Newton blacks held their first classes in a kitchen.

Georgia blacks made phenomenal advances in educating their children in 1866 and 1867. A March 1866 survey found fifty-two black schools in ten Georgia cities and towns. In a four-month period (December 1865 to March 1866), blacks in seven of these places contributed $5,060 in cash for their schools, causing a Northern missionary to note that "the benevolent efforts among the Freedmen *themselves* for their education are considerable." One of every three Georgia teachers (102 men and women in all) received funds from that state's blacks. Schools existed in out-of-the-way Georgia places. Rome and Marietta had black teachers, and the Rome teacher held his classes "in a church with no windows." Tuition payments supported other black teachers in small Dalton, Deep Valley, Cartersville, and Red Clay schools. . . .

Opposition from hostile whites, especially in 1866, made the work of these blacks and their few white allies especially difficult. Two former Confederate soldiers taught Elberton and McDonough blacks until pressure from white mobs forced them to seek bureau protection. From Henry County came "frequent complaints" to federal officials "that the inhabitants attacked the scholars and teachers of freedom schools—stoned them on the way home and threatened to 'kill every d——d nigger white man' who upheld the establishment and continuation of the 'nigger schools.'" A black teacher in Newman was so harassed that he quit that place. Despite these troubles, twenty-one Georgia schools remained open in the summer of 1866. The Freedmen's Bureau supported three of them, and the freed men and women the rest. More than 2,000 children attended these summer schools. Overall, the number of school[s] increased from 79 in June 1866 to 147 in December 1866 and then to 232 in June 1867. Enrollment jumped from 2,755 to 13,263. Blacks contributed much to these schools; during the 1867 winter quarter, they paid $7,224 in tuition. In June 1867, a bureau report showed that 45 percent of the schools and 23 percent of the pupils were entirely supported by the freedmen themselves. In part, these successes derived from the organization of the Georgia Educational Association in January 1866. But its work cannot be understood without first examining events in Savannah between December 1864 and January 1866.

Prodded by James Lynch, a missionary for the African Methodist Episcopal Church, Savannah blacks entered on a massive program of school organization in the years immediately following the war. Lynch himself deserves notice. Born in 1839 to a Baltimore free black father and a slave mother, Lynch drove a delivery wagon as a boy to help his father's mercantile business, attended a New Hampshire college, preached for a time in Indiana and then in Illinois, and helped to edit the AME's *Christian Recorder.* When Union troops entered the slave South, he followed as one of the African Methodist Episcopal Church's first missionaries. He labored for a time among the South Carolina Sea Island blacks. In late 1864, he taught a St. Helena's Island school sponsored by the National Freedman's Relief Association. . . .

General William T. Sherman's army had conquered the city [of Savannah, Georgia] in December 1864, and Savannah blacks . . . quickly set up their own schools. "I hurried here," Lynch wrote in early January, "expecting much to do, [and] I have not been disappointed." . . . [C]lergy and church officials met on January 12, 1865, with General Sherman and Secretary of War Edwin M. Stanton, to promise their support for the Union, to press for land and protection for the freedpeople, and to spark the Savannah educational effort. Twenty men, Lynch among them, talked with Stanton and Sherman. Four had been born free; three each had gained their freedom either through manumission or by self-purchase; and nine had been slaves until Sherman's arrival in Georgia. . . .

Even before they met with Stanton and Sherman, Savannah's "principal colored men" had formed the Savannah Educational Association and started schools for their children. Help came from Lynch and three white missionaries, John Alvord, Mansfield French, and William Richardson. In either late December or early January, Savannah blacks filled Campbell's church to overflowing; hundreds could not gain admission. . . . Lynch, Alvord, and French spoke, calling for the establishment of schools for former slaves. Lynch asked that the local clergy remain afterwards and assured Alvord that "persons could be found among the colored people who would teach [the] schools if organized." He proved true to his word.

Later that day, the cleric Abraham Burke, a Georgia slave who had purchased his freedom sometime in the 1840s, moved that the governing boards and clergy of Savannah's black churches constitute the Savannah Educational Association. A second mass meeting, in early January, heard members propose the names of teachers and saw a constitution adopted requiring all members to pay three dollars a year and twenty-five cents each month in dues. A resolution invited the cooperation and support of the American Missionary Association, and its representative promised such aid. Contributions were then solicited from the crowd, and a white observer reported to the secretary of the American Missionary Association that . . . "Men and women . . . came to the table with a *grand rush*—much like the charge of union soldiers on a rebel battery! Fast as their names could be written by a swift penman, the Greenbacks were laid upon the table in sums from one to ten dollars, until the pile footed up the round sum of *seven hundred* and *thirty dollars* as the cash receipts of the meeting."

Soon after, Lynch and Alvord examined prospective teachers and found fifteen suitable black teachers, ten women and five men. "The teachers," Lynch said, "are the best educated among our people here." . . . Monthly salaries ranged from $35 each for two principals to $15 each for the women teachers, so that the SEA's monthly wage bill came to $300.

Local Union Army officers (Lynch found General John Geary, the federal commander in Savannah, "*sincerely* willing to encourage anything that will elevate the freed men") gave the Savannah Educational Association four buildings for schoolrooms, including Oglethorpe Medical College and Bryan's Slave Mart, a three-story building that fronted on Market Square and had till nearly that day served as a meeting place for slave traders and owners. . . . A few days later, the schools opened. About 500 children gathered in the First African Baptist Church's lecture room to parade to their new schoolrooms. An observer felt that the street procession excited "feeling and interest second only to that of Gen. Sherman's army." "Such a gathering of Freedmen's sons and daughters that proud city had never seen before," said this same witness. "Many of the people rushed to doors and windows of their houses, wondering what these things could mean! *This* they were told is in *onward march of freedom."*

. . . Soon after their schools started, they [the Savannah blacks] encountered . . . trouble. . . . It came from the American Missionary Association. S. W. Magill, a missionary, arrived in Savannah to head the association's educational work and schemed to subvert what the local blacks had started. "However good men [they] might be," he said of the Savannah Educational Association leadership clergy, "they know nothing about education." None had "much more in the way of education than [the] ability to read & write & cypher a little." . . . "I fear," he wrote of the Savannah black clergy, "they will be jealous & sullen if I attempt to place t[he] management in t[he] hands of our white teachers. But this must be done in order to make [the] sch[ools] effective for good."

. . . Magill had quite specific complaints. Leaders of the Savannah Educational Association expected to hire white teachers only as "assistants" and hoped the American Missionary Association would lend financial support. "The whole thing in this aspect of it is preposterous," Magill warned. When he first met with the Savannah Educational Association's executive committee, he learned that it controlled four school buildings, had already enrolled 600 pupils, and had appointed fifteen "colored teachers." More than this, his request that the Savannah blacks allow him to start a school for adults did not get a prompt reply. They "gave me the cold shoulder," complained Magill. The entire operation disturbed him: former slaves and free blacks had preempted his mission. "Here," he moaned, "instead of finding a clear field to work in, we find it preoccupied by this radically defective organization."

Magill pressured vigorously for a federal appointment as the head of Savannah's educational work. Even after Savannah blacks allowed him to use a building for his school, he remained dissatisfied and urged the American Missionary Association to withhold promised funds and not to praise the Savannah blacks too excessively in print. A letter dated February 16 (which, incidentally, noted that Savannah's blacks had already raised perhaps $1,000 for their schools) explained that when he took over he would "be obliged to relieve many of their teachers, some of whom are not professors of religion, and are very lavish in the use of the strap & to diminish the salaries of others, some of whom receive from $25 to $35 per month" Magill expected "trouble," but promised to "proceed with great caution and kindness."

The zealous evangelical finally had his way, as Union officials appointed him to supervise the government's educational efforts in the city. Magill soon reported that the executive committee of the Savannah Educational Association had surrendered the principle of "excluding white control." Magill seemed pleased. Managing Savannah's black schools, after all, required "more head than these colored people yet have." Another Northern white cleric, a visitor to Savannah, made the same point somewhat differently. "They have several interesting schools of their own starting and maintaining there," J. W. Fowler reported in June 1865. He found the black clergy and teachers "gifted with a large share of common sense," but worried because "their expression is very bad" and urged that some Savannah black children be sent North to live in the homes of refined whites and study there to become teachers and ministers.

Despite their defeat, Savannah blacks continued to support their own schools. Financial help came from the New England Freedmen's Aid Society after prodding by William C. Gannett, who visited Savannah in the spring of 1865 and thought the Savannah Educational Association's leaders "men of real ability and intelligence" who had "a natural and praiseworthy pride in keeping their educational institutions in their own hands." "What they desire," he observed, "is assistance without control." By late July 1865, Savannah blacks had spent more than $20,000 for salaries and other educational costs. Crude estimates fixed the number of school-age children in Savannah at 1,600, and three-quarters of them were in school. When the schoolteachers Harriet Jacobs and her daughter arrived in mid-December to work in the schools, they found nineteen of them "principally sustained by the colored people." Another visit to Savannah about that same time convinced John Alvord that the Savannah Educational Association had improved over the year. But he worried over its fiscal condition: "Their association is now, with the high price of everything, falling in debt." In March 1866, Savannah still had eight schools, the largest with 300 students. Savannah blacks boasted of their schools, calling them "self-supporting" and insisting that such was "the only true road to honor and distinction." Alvord agreed. He accepted as "fact" that such "self-made efforts may not be perfect" nor "perhaps as good as those taught by men and women from the north." But Alvord pointed out that the Savannah blacks had revealed "a vitality *within themselves*," showed that "*opportunity* will induce *development*," and made it clear that black people "are not always to be dependent on white help and Government charity."

Savannah's blacks did more than start schools on their own in and near their city. In January 1866, together with other Georgia blacks and some friendly whites, they founded the Georgia Educational Association to encourage the state's former slaves to form local associations that would build schools supported "entirely by the colored people." At first the Georgia Educational Association advanced political as well as educational objectives, but at an October 1866 convention attended by blacks from more than fifty counties it renounced its political role and, while defending equal rights under the law, restricted its work to educational matters. By then, the association had established county organizations in different places in the state. Augusta had five subassociations, each with its own officers and a special school committee to "establish the schools and employ and pay the teachers. The scholars pay the expenses. All persons are allowed to attend the schools." The association, however, suffered for want of funds, and John E. Bryant, a Maine-born Union Army Officer, and others pleaded for help from the North: $7,000 would sustain its work so well that the Georgia Educational Association would "never need further assistance from friends outside of the State." . . . [The association] helped Georgia blacks organize schools and pressured for a free public school system that would serve whites as well as blacks. When the Radical Constitutional Convention met in 1868, more than half the members of the Georgia Educational Association's state executive board served as delegates. These blacks helped draw up a constitutional provision that assured free public education to black as well as white children. Their work between 1865 and 1868 had prepared them well for this task. . . .

Blacks throughout the South voluntarily built and sustained schools in ways similar to those in Virginia, South Carolina, . . . and Georgia. Although their work cannot be detailed here, John Alvord's published semiannual reports allow a brief summary of that work before 1868. His reports contain serious flaws but nevertheless retain general value. In the fall of 1865, school attendance, as a percentage of all children eligible to attend ranged from 43 percent in New York State to 93 percent in Boston. That same fall, 41 percent of eligible white children and 75 percent of eligible black children attended District of Columbia schools. An equally high percentage of black children attended the Memphis (72 percent) and Virginia (82 percent) schools. In the three years following the war, General O. O. Howard estimated that nearly one-third of black children over the entire South had some formal education. Not all of these former slaves and free blacks studied with Yankee schoolmarms. In December 1866, 37 percent of teachers in the South known to the bureau were blacks. The percentage increased to over 40 in June 1867, and was even higher a year later. The bureau noted in June 1868 that 2,291 men and women were teaching blacks, and that 990 (43 percent) of them were blacks.

In the fall of 1866, moreover, blacks sustained in full or in part the operation of at least half of the Arkansas, Florida, Georgia, Kentucky, Louisiana, Maryland, and Texas schools. In five states (Alabama, North Carolina, South Carolina, Tennessee, and Virginia), between 25 percent and 49 percent of the schools received financial support from resident blacks. Six months later, at least half of the schools in ten Southern states received assistance from black parents and in six states (Arkansas, Delaware, Kentucky, Louisiana, Mississippi, and Texas) at least three of every four schools were partially financed in this way. . . . The significance of these financial payments can best be realized by comparing the dollars paid in by blacks for tuition with the money expended by the Freedmen's Bureau between January 1 and June 30, 1867. . . . In two states, Alabama and Florida, blacks paid in less than $25 for every $100 spent by the bureau, but in seven others, tuition payments ranged between $25.00 and $49.99 for every $100 of federal money. Tennessee blacks paid in $59.20 and Georgia blacks $77.20. In two states, Kentucky ($131.20) and Louisiana ($178.80), resident blacks, nearly all former slaves there as elsewhere, put more money into the schools that the bureau itself.

Innumerable obstacles, which should not be minimized, hampered the voluntary efforts made by former slaves to educate their children before the start of Radical Reconstruction and the coming of free public education to the South. But neither should these difficulties be emphasized so as to divert our attention from the extraordinary energy and social purpose revealed by these men and women. Theirs was a magnificent effort. We study it in detail because of what it tells about important and little-understood historical processes. In examining how men and women fresh to freedom built and sustained schools, we find much more than simply a desire for schooling. It is inconceivable, for example, that former Memphis slaves would have paid more than $5,000 in tuition between November 1864 and June 1865 without preexisting notions of parental . . . responsibility and kin obligation. Yet it is erroneous to find in their quest for education "proof" that the former slaves held "middle-class" values. The ways in which former slaves built and sustained schools, for example, were quite alien to the "middle class." Yankee shopkeepers and successful artisans favored education, but did not move buildings ten miles and then reconstruct them as schoolhouses. Ohio and Indiana farmers paid school taxes, but did not stand guard over teachers threatened with violence. Former slaves did. The freedpeople's early post-emancipation craving for and defense of schooling for themselves, and especially for their children, rested in good part of values and aspirations known among them as slaves. "The daily job of living did not end with enslavement," the anthropologist Sidney Mintz comments, "and the slaves could and did create viable patterns of life, for which their pasts were pools of available symbolic and material resources." That was true for the blacks after emancipation, too. . . .

Not all the schools freedpeople established between 1861 and 1867 succeeded. The poverty of most Southern blacks, the early decline in interest (and in money and teachers) on the part of Northern benevolent societies, the federal government's shifting policies, and white violence closed many schools. Teachers everywhere noticed the strains that poverty caused among schoolchildren and their parents. Near Darlington, South Carolina (where former slaves had done so much to build schools in 1866 and 1867), a teacher said that students came to school "very badly dressed and barefooted, though the winter has been very cold and the ground frozen." Farm laborers there had been offered one-third of the crop (hardly enough "to keep their families from starvation"), and many suffered "for food." "The best of the women get only four or five dollars a month," she added, "and work for nothing but their poor and scanty food." These observations were made by Frances A. Keigh, who had been a student at the new Darlington black school two years before, in 1866. Now she was a teacher.

Another black teacher, Harriet Jacobs, had returned to her Southern birthplace to teach. A single sentence in her narrative, published in 1861, explains why she, a fugitive slave, and so many other Southern blacks had done so much to bring education to their children and those of other former slaves so soon after their emancipation. "There are no bonds so strong," Jacobs insisted, "as those which are formed by suffering." Slaves and freed blacks did not forget the sacrifices they had made for one another. . . . It was because of the daily efforts of many . . . blacks in the American South between 1861 and 1868 that black and white schoolteachers were able to spread literacy among their children.

Defining Free Labor

JULIE SAVILLE

. . . The politicization of former slaves remains a remarkable feature of a politically vibrant era. Underlying the course of Reconstruction was a simultaneous transformation of petty commodity production in the Old North and of slave society in the Old South. In the "old-issue" free states of the North, wage earners mounted their first nationwide movements to redefine the standing of labor in the Republic. In the "new-issue" free states below the Mason-Dixon line, emancipated workers also took into the arena of party politics demands that joined political and economic reconstruction. In South Carolina, the transformation of work under a "free

Reprinted by permission from *Slavery and Abolition, Vol. 12, No. 3* published by Frank Cass & Company, 900 Eastern Avenue, Ilford, Essex, England. Copyright Frank Cass & Co. Ltd.

labor" regimen drove forward local movements of "grassroots reconstruction." Freedpeople reorganized their household and community life in attempts to shape the character of evolving postwar wage relationships. Those concrete struggles were the seeds of the popular movements that coursed through the South Carolina countryside in the wake of emancipation. In them lay the making of a vigorous labor movement ready to seize suffrage rights conferred by Radical Reconstruction in order to bring the terms of agricultural employment under popular control.

Ex-slaves' agrarian movements drew initial force from the outcome of antebellum struggles to shape the power relations implicit in daily work routines. In the freedpeople's view, slavery had not died intestate. Rather, they expected to inherit intact whatever improvements of condition their struggles as slaves had garnered. It seems clear that many nineteenth-century slaves produced and independently managed a marketable surplus—comprised of food crops and occasionally of the plantation staple, in addition to barnyard fowl and swine—which their owners did not appropriate outright. Such supplements to the guaranteed, if scant, weekly allowances were the product of combinations of nighttime overwork, Sunday labor, toil on recognized holidays, and exertion to complete assigned tasks in less time than most slaves normally required. In the state's rice and cotton producing regions alike, time for such labor had been augmented when slaveowners set aside certain days during planting season and harvest or portions of Saturdays for all slaves to tend "their" crops. At emancipation, therefore, many slaves claimed ownership of a largely perishable property rooted in a fragile network of customary rights.

Like the mass of servile workers in the age of emancipation, former slaves in South Carolina expected their freedom to be founded on the possession of land. The varying character of ex-slaves' early claims to land reflects the influence of both antebellum circumstance and wartime military events. Freedpeople who had lived as slaves on the sea islands below St. Helena Sound that were early occupied and continuously held be federal forces claimed *particular* lands. Wartime auctions of plantations forfeited for non-payment of taxes under the federal Direct Tax Act of 1862 threatened to sever them from the region's large, quasi-village settlements on which their kinship and networks of social organization converged. The wartime claims to land voiced by Port Royal's longtime residents typically referred to "home land"—land that was, as a former slave and church elder from St. Helena island explained, "rich wid de sweat ob we face and de blood ob we back;" land where "we born" and where rested "we parents" graves. By war's end, it was a steadily dwindling proportion of ex-slaves in the sea islands who still resided on their home plantations. An almost continuous wartime incursion of fugitives climaxed in the winter of 1864–65, when some 15,000 Georgia slaves reached the coast in the wake of Sherman's army. Their arrival forced the Union general to issue his famous Field Order 15, aptly characterized by James S. Allen as "the most far-reaching step taken toward the distribution of land from above."

Sherman's land grants were as singular as they were temporary. In the fall of 1865, an Edisto island freedmen's committee protested President Andrew Johnson's restoration of lands embraced by Sherman's order. Embellishing ex-slaves' wartime claims to land, the Edisto committee delineated a victorious Union's obligations to its supporters in the state where, the committee pointed out, "secession was born and Nurtured." Land, the committee's petition to Andrew Johnson insisted, constituted a franchise by which free men "always . . . true to this Union" rightfully defended themselves against the burden of servitude. On the Carolina coast, ex-slaves' early claims to land were therefore a compound of birthright, indemnification, and enfranchisement.

Freedpeople's desire for land, however ardent, was a landmark of social experience, not an *idée fixe*. For three years, from federal occupation of the entire state to the assembly of the first legislature elected under the Reconstruction acts, the convocation of federal or local assemblies—with the notable exception of the reconvened 1865 legislature—stimulated an endemic hunger for land to assume more open expression. By the onset of congressional reconstruction in 1867, former slaves had also begun to pioneer tactics of collective action premised on grudging acknowledgment that theirs would be a landless emancipation. More than chimera, less than aim, freedpeople's expectation of a government distribution of land came to reside in a murky realm, dimly charted by rumor, grim fear, or faint prospect. By contrast, collective efforts to regulate agricultural employment were clear and direct. Such tactics had, by 1867, begun to supplant expectations of a federal distribution of plantation lands.

Free labor work arrangements constrained, when they did not erode outright, the wide array of localized, idiosyncratic customs by which slaves had gained access to land and created time for domestic production. Owners of men had found that slave workers' production of a marketable surplus complemented their goal to render their plantations self-sufficient. Lords of acres, on the other hand, tried to hold freed employees' non-plantation work to the production of daily necessities. The change was most stark in lowcountry districts. There, antebellum planters' seasonal absenteeism and widespread reliance on drivers to supervise cultivation of the regional staples of rice and long-staple cotton had supported the relative success with which one of the most densely concentrated slave populations in the United States gained intermittently independent management of their working time and community life.

After emancipation, lowcountry planters exploited their possession of land to restrict freedpeople's domestic production. To the approximately forty people working on his Hilton Head island cotton plantation, the Northern planter E. T. Wright in 1865 allowed "one acre [of provision lands] to every *four* [acres of cotton lands] they cultivate for me." Freedmen on the Jehossee island rice plantation of former governor William Aiken, who in 1866 had been permitted to plant as much land as they could tend without interfering with their daily labor, found that in 1867 Aiken's contract allowed them to cultivate but half an acre of rice land and further required that they sow on their supplemental tracts only rice distinct from the plantation's commercially superior golden seed. Some planters attracted workers by initially offering fairly large household plots only to reduce the plots in subsequent planting years. William Hazzard, for example, attracted workers to his Santee river estates in 1867 by offering 5 acres to each household. The next year, Hazzard's contract offered but a single acre of rice land. Such postwar regulations reflect the extent to which emancipation had transformed the antebellum relationship between plantation labor and domestic production.

Nuances of cultivation colored lowcountry freedmen's responses to the postwar impasse. Workers in rice cultivation, where periodic flooding diminished the intensity of field cultivation during the growing season, elaborated sexual divisions of labor in order to expand household production. The men of the household performed the work required by contracts, while women assumed chief responsibility for tending the supplemental tracts that freedmen exacted in exchange for their labor on plantation lands. Sea island cotton workers, facing their crops more constant demands for hoeing throughout the growing season, adopted the classic peasant tactic of claiming time from obligations to landlords in order to expand household production. In return for labor on a specified number of "contract days"—usually two or three in the early postwar period—sea island cotton workers acquired the right to reside on and cultivate supplemental tracts of plantation lands.

Such alterations gave labor and time devoted to domestic production new political significance. Although ex-slaves in the lowcountry continued to tend the old provision grounds, few postwar planters mistook the freedpeople's efforts for attempts to retain or restore antebellum practices. From the outset, it was clear that freedpeople did not seek to work provision grounds and gardens under constraints that the work loads of slavery had imposed. Edward Barnwell Heyward, who in 1867 planted Combahee river rice lands inherited from his father, found the expanded domestic production of the new order incompatible with the old labor regimen:

> The women appear most lazy, merely because they are allowed the opportunity. They wish to stay in the house, or in the garden all the time. If you chide them, they say "Ehch! Massa, ain't I mus mind de fowl, and look a' me young corn aint I must watch um," and to do this the best hands on the place will stay at home all day and every day, and litterally do nothing.

The independence that ex-slaves in the lowcountry attempted to anchor in household divisions of labor or contractual guarantees of time proved less an alternative to wage labor than local adjuncts of the wage relationship. Formal restrictions on provision acreage, an 1866 fence law that prohibited open grazing on the sea islands, and requirements that workers perform additional labor services for the use of farm implements and draft animals curtailed domestic production. A committee of freed men in Georgetown district identified contractual requirements that "they must not have poltry of eny kind a beast or anamal of eny kind, the[y] must not plant a seed of eny kind for themselves" among features that rendered postwar work arrangements "to[o] intollarable to comply worst than slavery."

The small slaveholding sector of interior farming districts presented ex-slaves with circumstances of residence and labor in 1865 that made their agenda upon emancipation differ from that of freedpeople on coastal plantations. Slaves owned by the small planters and middling farmers scattered in Piedmont districts had seldom lived in the same place among all members of their immediate families. The dispersion of kin among neighboring slaveowners was common. Freedpeople often needed to reclaim even those family members who lived no more than a few miles away. Under such circumstances, asserting claims to particular persons preceded claims to particular lands.

Political overtones attended the reconstitution of families in the wake of emancipation. The consolidation of household animated those challenges to the master's authority which had reposed in slaves' networks of kin associations. Kinship provided the primary means by which freedpeople on small places first articulated resistance to postwar work arrangements.

The reconstitution of families brought to the fore challenges to the master's personal sovereignty that lurked behind abolition. Ties of blood and marriage carried social obligations that ex-slaves readily defended. Family members assumed primary responsibility for defending one of their own against the corporal punishment that freedpeople generally pronounced the most patent violation of their new condition. Heads of reconstituted families served as the chief bargaining agents in negotiating work arrangements with employers; relatives accompanied each other to Freedmen's Bureau posts to demand redress or carried complaints on a relative's behalf. Wielding a solidarity initially expressed in the idiom of kinship, the reconstituted family became an immediate agency for defending common rights.

The reunion of once scattered families introduced into the plantation's work force new residents, who strained ex-masters' personal authority. Masters' dominion over particular slaves was not easily attached to the new arrivals. Into the domain of power that masters had characterized as "my family white and black," newcomers intruded the long suppressed, alien claims or a competing kinship. Where freed men came to work at the "wife place," landowners found them a troublesome presence. John Smith, a farmer in Richland district, was certain that the arrival of the freedman Ephraim, who joined his wife and child on Smith's place sometime during 1865, hastened rejection of the 1866 contract:

> I am influenced to believe that Ephraim was in instrumental [sic] in his Brother in law Simon leaving me as he (Ephraim) told them that they had [not] entered into a written contract and were not bound. To use Ephraims own words to his brother in law Thomas, he Ephraim said to Thomas that he would suck sorrow thro his teeth if he remained on the place.

Emancipation thus intensified the political significance of slaves' extended networks of kinship. Reconstitution of family households was a precondition for the establishment of a domestic economy through whose development freedpeople pursued economic independence. It was their kinship to other ex-slaves that freedpeople customarily tapped in order to forge resistance to postwar work arrangements, reaching for a shield that at times had held at bay the intrusive intimacy of daily contact with a resident owner.

Like their counterparts in coastal plantation districts, ex-slaves in interior cotton districts gained the right to cultivate tracts on their own account in addition to the still undivided arable lands which they most often worked on shares. Such allotments at times antedated emancipation; the practice may have become more widespread in response to slaves' wartime demands. Certainly, by the end of the war, the arrangement appeared widely in the interior. An officer whose command embraced Barnwell and Orangeburg districts noted in November 1865 that crops raised by freedpeople included "produce, on small lots, assigned to them for their benefit."

The postwar allocation of additional plots intensified rather than reconciled contradictions between the regimen of free labor and freedpeople's pursuit of domestic production. Interior cotton planters typically allotted marginal tracts encrusted with usages not compatible with ex-slaves' intent to develop them as the material base of their households. Planters brooked no interference in prior customs which governed the use of marginal lands. Aiken landowner, John Seigler, for example, allotted a tract of land to the freedman Stephen Marshall. The landowner nevertheless refused to turn his hogs out of the field that Marshal had planted in potatoes.

"Open range" grazing and common pasturage rights practiced by landowners on marginal tracts wreaked predictable havoc on freedpeople's crops. Defense of crops planted on marginal tracts drew ex-slaves and landowners into assaults and counterattacks that threatened to engulf all crops, stock, and buildings found on the premises. Freedman Billy Kincaide's determination to protect his corn patch against depredations by the stock of his Fairfield district employer climaxed when he set his dog on the planter's grazing cows and gave the overseer's mare a beating to which Kincaide's employer attributed her death. When the overseer shot the dog, Kincaide's rage coursed through the cotton fields—where he chopped down growing plants, swept up plantation stock—all of which he threatened to kill before the end of the year, and left his employer "afraid to lie Down at night not knowing but [my] house may be on fire before the morning." Conflicting land uses are perhaps most apparent in specialized plantation regions of the Piedmont because the allotments on which ex-slaves staked their production of a marketable household surplus had initially been carved from marginal tracts rather than from improved acreage.

Of course, a deeper antagonism underlay landowners' and ex-slaves' disputes over marginal lands. Their competing land uses were not easily reconciled when freedpeople were attempting to bring marginal tracts into more regular cultivation precisely in order to escape full-time employment on a landowner's more intensively cultivated fields. As wage laborers, freedpeople encountered a form of exclusive use rights even on common lands. Ex-slaves' resistance to the dependent terms to which planters held their employees' use of marginal tracts strained the network of less than absolute property rights in which marginal lands were enmeshed. Pitched battles stemming from competing uses of marginal lands helped push Piedmont planters toward agreements to sub-divide improved arable lands into units for household cultivation.

By the onset of Radical reconstruction, freedpeople in lowcountry and interior districts alike had attempted to expand domestic production in the face of landlessness. The ensuing conflicts were just opening skirmishes in agricultural workers' long postwar efforts to regulate the terms of their employment. Such early disputes did not, however, lack significance for later contests. From early struggles emerged the specific crop mixes, constraints on subsistence production, interposition of landowners' power in freedmen's elaboration of spheres of familial prerogative, and increasingly absolute rights of property with which planters stocked an arsenal to define the social character of wage relations. The planter's measures were also early targets of freedmen's rural associations—the quasi-military marching companies that flowered in the wake of congressional reconstruction to mount public campaigns to regulate wage rates and tenure arrangements. Early postwar reconstructions of work primed freedpeople for the further work of reconstruction.

The Labor of Politics

ELSA BARKLEY BROWN

After emancipation, African American women, as part of black communities throughout the South, struggled to define on their own terms the meaning of freedom. Much of the literature on Reconstruction-era African American women's political history has focused on the debates at the national level over the Fifteenth Amendment, which revolved around the question of whether the enfranchisement of African American men or the enfranchisement of women should take precedence. Such discussions, explicitly or not, contribute to a political framework that assumes democratic political struggles in the late-nineteenth-century United States were waged in pursuit of constitutional guarantees of full personhood and citizenship. A careful investigation of the actions of African American women between 1865 and 1880, however, leads one to question that framework. Historians seeking to reconstruct the post–Civil War political history of African American women have first to determine whether the conceptualizations of republican representative government and liberal democracy, which are the parameters of such a discussion, are the most appropriate ones for understanding southern black women's search for freedom—even political freedom—following the Civil War. . . .

The institutions that ex-slaves developed give testament to the fact that their vision of freedom was not merely an individual one or, as historian Thomas C. Holt has put it, "that autonomy was not simply personal" but "embraced familial and community relationships as well." . . . African Americans throughout the South in the post–Civil War period emphatically articulated their understanding that freedom and autonomy could not be independently achieved. . . .

This understanding of autonomy was shared by those who had been slave and those who had been free. In fact, the whole process of emancipation may have, at least momentarily, reaffirmed the common bonds of ex-slave and formerly free, for, despite their individual freedom in law, "freedom" in actuality did not come to free black men and women until the emancipation of slaves. Thus their own personal experiences confirmed for formerly free men and women as well as ex-slaves the limitations of personal autonomy and affirmed the idea of collective autonomy.

The vision of social relations that [many southern African Americans] articulated was not the traditional nineteenth-century notion of possessive individualism whereby society is merely an aggregation of individuals, each of whom is ultimately responsible for her/himself. In this individual autonomy, "whether one eats or starves depends solely on one's individual will and capacities." According to liberal ideology, it is the self-regulating impersonality of contractual relations that makes social relations just. Such a notion of freedom and social responsibility was diametrically opposed to the one that undergirded [southern] black institutional developments . . . in the post–Civil War period, where the community and each individual in the community were ultimately responsible for every other person. Whether one eats or starves in this setting depends on the available resources within the community as a whole. Individuals must each do their part and are free

---

Reprinted by permission from Elsa Barkley Brown.

to make decisions about their lives, but ultimately it is the resources of the whole that determine the fate of the individual. . . .

It is a striking example of the different vision held by white Freedmen's Bureau officials throughout the South that they regarded this ethos of mutuality as one of the negative traits that had to be curtailed in the process of preparing freedpeople for life in a liberal democratic society. One South Carolina bureau agent, John DeForest, lamented the tendency among freedpeople to assume obligations to "a horde of lazy relatives and neighbors, thus losing a precious opportunity to get ahead on their own." A case in point was Aunt Judy, who, though supporting herself and her children on her meager income as a laundress, had "benevolently taken in, and was nursing, a sick woman of her own race. . . . The thoughtless charity of this penniless Negress in receiving another poverty-stricken creature under her roof was characteristic of the freedmen. However selfish, and even dishonest, they might be, they were extravagant in giving." As historian Jacqueline Jones has pointed out, De Forest's notion that the willingness to share constituted a "thoughtless" act was a product of assumptions "that a 'rational' economic being would labor only to enhance her own material welfare." The different vision of African American women, and of freedpeople in general, posed a persistent problem for northern white men and women, who consistently sought to reeducate and assimilate freedpeople . . . by introducing a different cultural world view as a means of imposing a different economic and political world view as well.

Recent historical explorations of the transition from slavery to freedom have provided substantial evidence that the economic vision of many African American women and men differed fundamentally from that imposed even by freedpeople's most supportive white allies. . . .

. . . If an understanding of the different world views from which African Americans and Euro-Americans operated in the post–Civil War South is necessary to analyze work, family, and community behavior, then a similar understanding is also fundamental to an analysis of the political position of African American women in this same time period. Relatively little has been written about southern black women's participation in Reconstruction-era politics. . . . The few efforts . . . have failed to consider the possibility of a radically different political world view in the African American community. . . .

The Reconstruction Act of 1867 required all the former Confederate states, except Tennessee, to hold constitutional conventions. Black men were enfranchised for the delegate selection and ratification ballots. In Virginia, Republican ward clubs elected delegates to the party's state convention, where a platform was to be adopted. On 1 August, the day the Republican state convention opened in Richmond, thousands of African American men, women, and children absented themselves from their employment and joined the delegates at the convention site, First African Baptist Church. Tobacco factories, lacking a major portion of their workers, were forced to close for the day. This pattern persisted whenever a major issue came before the state and city Republican conventions held during the summer and fall of 1867 or the state constitutional convention which convened in Richmond from December 1867 to March 1868. A *New York Times* reporter estimated that "the entire colored population of Richmond" attended the October 1867 local Republican convention where delegates to the state constitutional convention were nominated.

Noting that female domestic servants composed a large portion of those in attendance, the correspondent reported: "as is usual on such occasions, families which employ servants were forced to cook their own dinners, or content themselves with a cold lunch. Not only had Sambo gone to the Convention, but Dinah was there also."

It is important to note that these men and women did not absent themselves from work just to be onlookers at the proceedings. Rather, they intended to be active participants. They assumed as equal a right to be present and participate as the delegates themselves, a fact they made abundantly clear at the August 1867 Republican state convention. Having begun to arrive four hours before the opening session, African American women and men had filled the meeting place long before the delegates arrived. Having shown up to speak for themselves, they did not assume delegates had priority—in discussion or in seating. Disgusted at the scene, as well as unable to find seats, the conservative white Republican delegates removed to the Capitol Square to convene an outdoor session. That was quite acceptable to the several thousand additional African American men and women who, unable to squeeze into the church, were now able to participate in the important discussions and to vote down the proposals of the conservative faction.

Black Richmonders were also active participants throughout the state constitutional convention. A *New York Times* reporter commented on the tendency for the galleries to be crowded "with the 'unprivileged,' and altogether black." At issue was not just these men's and women's presence but also their behavior. White women, for example, certainly on occasion sat in the convention's gallery as visitors silently observing the proceedings; these African Americans, however, participated from the gallery, loudly engaging in the debates. At points of heated controversy, black delegates turned to the crowds as they made their addresses on the convention floor, obviously soliciting and relying upon mass participation. Outside the convention hours, mass meetings were held to discuss and vote on the major issues. At these gatherings vote was either by voice or by rising, and men, women, and children voted. These meetings were not mock assemblies; they were important gatherings at which the community made plans for freedom. The most radical black Republican faction argued that the major convention issues should actually be settled at these mass meetings with delegates merely casting the community's vote on the convention floor. Though this did not occur, black delegates were no doubt influenced by the mass meetings in the community and the African American presence in the galleries, both of which included women.

Black Richmonders were, in fact, operating in two political arenas—an internal and an external one. Though these arenas were related, they each proceeded from different assumptions, had different purposes, and therefore operated according to different rules. Within the internal political process women were enfranchised and participated in all public forums—the parades, rallies, mass meetings, and conventions themselves. Richmond is not atypical in this regard.

It was the state constitutional convention, however, that would decide African American women's and men's status in the political process external to the African American community. When the Virginia convention began its deliberations regarding the franchise, Thomas Bayne, a black delegate from Norfolk, argued the inherent link between freedom and suffrage and contended that those who opposed universal suffrage were actually opposing the freedom of African American people. . . . In rejoinder, E. L. Gibson, a conservative white delegate, enunciated several principles of republican representative government. Contending that "a man might be free and still not have the right to vote," Gibson explained the fallacy of assuming that this civil right was an inherent corollary to freedom: If the right were inherent then it would belong to both sexes and to all from "the first moment of existence" and to foreigners immediately. This was "an absurdity too egregious to be contemplated." And yet this "absurd" notion of political rights was in practice in the Richmond black community, where males and females voted without regard to age and the thousands of rural migrants who came into Richmond suffered no waiting period but immediately possessed the full rights of the community. What was absurd to Gibson and most white men—Republican or Democrat—was obviously quite rational to many black Richmonders. Two different conceptions of freedom and public participation in the political process were in place.

Gibson's arguments relied on several assumptions which were by then basic to U.S. democracy. First[,] . . . some persons were not capable, that is, not "fit" to exercise political liberty. . . .

. . . [Second,] even those with political liberty—as indicated by the right of suffrage—were not equally capable of political decision making. Thus the majority of the people, including the majority of those with suffrage, were expected to leave political decision making to those more qualified. Such political assumptions required that an individual, having once achieved freedom, hand over to others the responsibilities and rights of preserving her/his freedom. In fact, late-nineteenth-century assumptions concerning republican representative government required that the majority of people be passive in their exercise of freedom for the proper operation of democracy. Suffrage granted people not the right to participate in political decision making but the right to participate in choosing political decision-makers. Having become accustomed to this political process by now, we often act as if the two are synonymous. Freedpeople knew they were not.

In a frequently noted observation on women in Reconstruction-era politics, Elizabeth Botume, a northern white teacher in Beaufort, South Carolina, made clear that the political view many white northerners tried to impose was consistent with a particular economic view, too:

> Most of the field-work was done by the women and girls; their lords and masters were much interrupted in agricultural pursuits by their political and religious duties. When the days of "*conventions*" came, the men were rarely at home; but the women kept steadily at work in the fields. As we drove around, we saw them patiently "cleaning up their ground," "listing," "chopping down the old cotton stalks and hoeing them under," gathering "sedge" and "trash" from the riverside, which they carried in baskets on their heads, and spread over the land. And later, hoeing the crops and gathering them in.
>
> We could not help wishing that since so much of the work was done by the colored women—raising the provisions for their families, besides making and selling their own cotton, they might also hold some of the offices held by the men. I am confident they would despatch business if allowed to go to the polls; instead of listening and hanging around all day, discussing matters of which they knew so little, they would exclaim,—
> "Let me vote and go; I've got work to do."

Botume's analysis hinged on several assumptions: that adoption of habits of thrift and diligence were the factors that qualified one for suffrage; that voting equaled political participation; and that "'listening and hanging around all day, discussing matters," were not important forms of political participation. Botume, like so many northern allies, thought free black people were to earn the rights of freedom by adopting the proper habits of responsibility and industry. Her lament was that these African American women, who had been "reconstructed" in that sense, were not rewarded by the franchise. Central to her complaint about African American women's disfranchisement is her exasperation at African American men's assumption that political rights included the right to participate in political discussions (and thereby political decision making). She believed these industrious women, having come to exercise their proper economic role, would also adopt their appropriate role in the political system and would properly exercise the suffrage. They would vote and get on back to work rather than hang around engaging in political issues which, she thought, neither they nor the men had capacity to understand. Botume would leave it to others more capable to make the important political decisions. Thus even the slight support southern black women mustered among white northerners for their enfranchisement came in a context that would have preferred to leave them far less active in the political process than they had been in the most immediate post–Civil War days.

The history of African American women's political involvement in South Carolina and elsewhere leaves one dubious about Botume's predictions regarding how black women would exercise the franchise. Nevertheless, Botume's observations do point to the fact that in the end only men obtained the legal franchise. The impact of this decision is neither inconsequential nor fully definitive. African American women were by law excluded from the political arena external to their community. Yet this does not mean that they were not active in that arena—witness Richmond women's participation in the Republican and the constitutional conventions.

Southern black men and women debated the issue of woman suffrage in both the external and internal political arenas, with varying results. Delegates to the South Carolina convention, 56 percent of whom were black, adopted a constitution that included "male" as a qualification for voting, despite a stirring argument for woman suffrage from William J. Whipper, a black delegate from Beaufort. Nevertheless, a significant proportion of South Carolina's Reconstruction-era black elected officials favored woman suffrage or were at least open to a serious discussion of the issue. It was the South Carolina House of Representative, which was 61 percent black, that allowed Louisa Rollin to speak on the floor of the assembly in support of woman suffrage in March 1869. Several black male representatives argued in favor of the proposal then and again two years later, when Lottie Rollin led a woman suffrage rally at the state capital. In March 1872 Beverly Nash, state senator, and Whipper, then state representative, joined with other delegates to propose a woman suffrage amendment to the state constitution. Alonzo J. Ransier, U.S. congressman from South Carolina and later the state's first black lieutenant governor, presented his argument on the floor of the U.S. House of Representatives in 1874: "until [women as well as men have the right to vote] the government of the United States cannot be said to rest upon the 'consent of the governed.'" According to historian Rosalyn Terborg-Penn, Ransier, who was president of the South Carolina Woman's Rights Association, was widely supported by his black South Carolinian colleagues. In fact, six of the eight black men who represented

South Carolina in the U.S. Congress during the Reconstruction era supported woman suffrage.

The question of woman suffrage was a subject of discussion in other southern legislative chambers as well. It was often raised by white men to demonstrate the absurdity of black delegates' argument for the inherent right of suffrage. Black delegates, even when they rejected woman suffrage, were far more likely to treat it as a matter for serious discussion. If not, as they often did, expressing support, black delegates were far more likely to express at least ambivalence rather than firm conviction of the absurdity of woman electorates . . . [I]t is clear that serious discussion of woman suffrage in southern legislative chambers during the Reconstruction era seemed to depend upon a strong African American representation.

The debate over woman's suffrage occurred in the internal arena as well, with varying results. In Nansemond County, Virginia, a mass meeting held that women should get the legal franchise; in Richmond while a number of participants in a mass meeting held for female suffrage, the majority opinion swung against it. But the meaning of that decision was not as straightforward as it may seem. The debate as to whether women should be given the vote in the external political arena occurred in internal political arena mass meetings where women participated and voted not just before and during *but also after* the negative decision regarding legal enfranchisement. This mass meeting's decision maintained the status quo in the external community; ironically enough, the status quo in the internal community was maintained as well—women continued to have a vote. Both African American men and women clearly operated within two distinct political systems. . . .

Focusing on formal disfranchisement, however, obscures the larger story. . . .

In Richmond and throughout the South exclusion from legal enfranchisement did not prevent African American women from affecting the vote and the political decisions. They organized political societies such as the Rising Daughters of Liberty which actively engaged in the political campaigns by educating the community on the issues, raising funds for the candidates, and getting out the vote. Coal miners' wives living outside Manchester, Virginia, played a similar role through the United Daughters of Liberty. Mississippi freedwomen placed themselves in potentially dangerous positions by wearing Republican campaign buttons during the 1868 election. In some instances the women walked "all the way to town, as many as twenty or thirty miles," to "buy, beg, or borrow one, and thus equipped return and wear it openly in defiance of . . . master, mistress, or overseer" and sometimes of husband as well. Domestic servants also risked job and perhaps personal injury by wearing their buttons to work. "To refuse neglect, or lack the courage to wear that badge . . . amounted almost to a voluntary return to slavery," according to many freedwomen and freedmen.

Black women initially took an active role in the South Carolina political meetings. Those disfranchised women whom Botume imagined would vote and go home, not involving themselves in political discussion, displayed a particular insistence on continued *public* political activity. The assumptions that underlay these women's activities are instructive. Laura Towne, a northern white teacher, tells us it was the white Republicans who first announced to the freedpeople that "women and children ought to stay at home on such occasions." Yet it does not appear to be merely the presence of females that disturbed these white men, for they quickly made it clear that Towne, of course, was welcome. Their announcement was meant to exclude "outsiders who were making some noise." Probably because of protests or disregard of the exclusion notice, the white Republicans modified their initial ban to state that "the *females* can come or not as they choose, . . . but the meeting is for men voters." It was clearly the women's failure to take the position of passive observers that was being censured. Some black men took their cue, one even using the occasion to prompt women to "'stay at home and cut grass,' that is, hoe the corn and cotton fields—clear them of grass!" while the men were at the political meetings.

Even though they were excluded from further participation in the Republican meetings by the late 1860s, African American women in South Carolina, Louisiana, and elsewhere were still attending the meetings in the 1870s. Although women were never elected delegates, it does appear that occasionally women were sent to the political meetings on behalf of their community. Lucy McMillan, a South Carolina widow, reported that her attendance at a political meeting was the result of community pressure: "They all kept at me to go. I went home and they quizzed me to hear what was said, and I told them as far as my senses allowed me."

Women's presence at these meetings was often anything but passive. In the violent political atmosphere of the last years of Reconstruction, they had an especially important—and dangerous—role. While the men participated in the meeting, the women guarded the guns—thus serving in part as the protectors of the meeting. This was not a symbolic or a safe role in a time when "men are shot at, hunted down, trapped and held till certain meetings are over, and intimidated in every possible way." During the violent times of late Reconstruction, African American women in South Carolina were reported "in arms, carrying axes or hatchets in their hands hanging down at their sides, their aprons or dresses half-concealing the weapons." One clergyman, contending African Americans could defend themselves if necessary, noted that "80,000 black men in the State . . . can use Winchesters and 2000,000 black women . . . can light a torch and use a knife." At times women as well as men actually took up arms. In 1878 Robert Smalls, attacked by redshirts while attempting to address a Republican meeting in Gillisonville, sought refuge and later reported that "every colored man and woman seized whatever was at hand—guns, axes, hoes, etc., and ran to the rescue." Some of these women probably had double incentive as the redshirts had "slap[ped] the faces of the colored women coming to the meeting."

African American women took the political events to heart and took dramatic steps to make their political sentiments known. They also expressed their outrage when the political tide turned against their interests. Alabama women, reportedly, "were converted to Radicalism long before the men and almost invariably used their influence strongly for the purpose of the League." South Carolina Democrats believed African American women to be "the head and fount of the opposition." . . .

African American women in South Carolina and elsewhere understood themselves to have a vital stake in African American men's franchise. The fact that only men had been granted the vote did not mean that only men should exercise that vote. Women reportedly initiated sanctions against men who voted Democratic. One South Carolina witness reported that "no mens were to go to the polls unless their wives were right alongside of them; some had hickory sticks; some had nails—four nails drive in the shape of a cross—and dare their husbands to vote any other than the Republican ticket." In the highly charged political atmosphere of the late 1870s it was no small matter for these women to show up at the election site carrying weapons. Armed Democrats patrolled the polling areas, and Republicans were often "driven from the polls with knives and clubs. Some of them were badly wounded." We might wonder whether the weapons the women carried were for use on their husbands or on the Democratic opponents, but in either case these women very publicly declared their stake in their husband's vote.

Black Republican politicians throughout the South took women's participation seriously and publicly encouraged them to abstain from sexual relations with any man who voted Democratic. Some women left their Democratic husbands. Engaged women were encouraged to postpone the wedding until after the election when they could obtain assurance that their future husband was not a Democrat. In Alabama women banded together in political clubs to enforce these sanctions collectively. Some politicians also endorsed women's use of weapons to influence their husbands' vote. It is likely that, rather than initiating these actions on the part of African American women, Republican legislators merely recognized and endorsed actions initiated by the women themselves. These examples all suggest that African American women and men understood the vote as a collective, not an individual, possession and, furthermore, that African American women, unable to cast a separate vote, viewed African American men's vote as equally theirs. Their belief that the franchise should be cast in the best interest of both was not the nineteenth-century patriarchal notion that men voted on behalf of their wives and children. By the latter assumption, women had no individual wills; rather, men operated in women's best interest because women were assumed to have no right of input. African American women assumed the political rights that came with being a member of the community, even though they were not granted the political rights they thought should come with being citizens of the state.

The whole sense of the ballot as collectively owned is most eloquently presented by Violet Keeling, a tobacco worker who testified in February 1884 before a Senate committee investigating the violence in the previous year's elections in Danville, Virginia. Assenting in her husband's decision not to vote in that election for fear he might be killed, she made it clear that she would not, however, assent in his or anyone else's voting Democratic: "as for my part, if I hear of a colored man voting the Democratic ticket, I stay as far from him as I can; I don't have nothing in the world to do with him. . . . No, sir; I don't 'tallow him to come in my house." Asked why she should "have such a dislike to a colored man that votes the Democratic ticket," she replied:

> I think that if the race of colored people that has got no friends nohow, and if they don't hang together they won't have none while one party is going one way and another the other. I don't wish to see a colored man sell himself when he can do without. Of course we all have to live, and I always like to have a man live even if he works for 25 cents a day, but I don't want to see him sell himself away. . . . I think if a colored man votes the Democratic ticket he has always sold himself. . . . If I knew a colored man that voted the Democratic ticket to come to my house, I would tell him to go somewhere else and visit.

Asked "suppose your husband should go and vote a Democratic ticket," she responded: "I would just picke up my clothes and go to my father's, if I had a father, or would go to work for 25 cents a day."

Violet Keeling clearly articulated the notion that a black man could not exercise his vote only in his own behalf. If he sold his vote, he sold hers. The whole issue of the ostracism of black Democrats reveals very clearly the assumptions regarding suffrage that were operative throughout African American communities. Black Democrats were subject to the severest exclusion: disciplined within or quite often expelled from their churches; kicked out of mutual benefit societies; not allowed to work alongside others in the fields of accepted leadership positions at work or in the community. Ministers were dismissed from their churches or had their licenses to preach revoked; teachers who voted Democratic found themselves without pupils. Democrats' children were not allowed in schools. And, perhaps the most severe sanction of all, black Democrats found themselves unaided at time of death of a family member. Women participated in all of these actions as well as in the mobs that jeered, jostled, and sometimes beat black Democrats or rescued those who were arrested for such behavior. In fact, women were often reported to be the leaders of such mob involvements. . . .

From the perspective of liberal democratic political ideology, these activities might be perceived as "unconscionable" "interference with the [individual voter's] expression of . . . political preference." But African Americans in the post–Civil War South understood quite clearly that the actions of one member of the community affected, and in this instance endangered, all others in that community. Thus they understood there was no such thing as an individual action or a "possessive individual," owing nothing to society. . . . It was that sense of suffrage as a collective, not an individual, possession that was the foundation of much of women's political activities.

. . . This is not to suggest that African American women did not desire the vote or that they did not often disagree with the actions taken by some black men. One should, however, be careful about imposing presentist notions of gender equality on these women. Clearly for them the question was not an abstract notion of individual gender equality but rather one of community. That such a vision might over time lead to a patriarchal conception of gender roles is not a reason to dismiss the equality of its inception.

Women's presence at the polls was not just a negative sanction; it was also a positive expression of the degree to which they understood the men's franchise to be a new political opportunity for themselves as well as their children. They reinforced this idea of black men's voting as a new freedom which they had all achieved by turning the occasion into a public festival and celebration, bringing lemonade and gingercakes and spending the day at the polls. Of course, the principal reason for the group presence at the polls was protection. The tendency for "crowds" of freedmen to go to the polls together was seen by their white contemporaries and by some historians as evidence that they were forced to vote the Republican ticket or that they did not take seriously the franchise but instead saw election day as an opportunity for a picnic or other entertainment. Henderson Hamilton Donald, for example, noting that freedmen "always voted in companies," found this behavior "odd and sometimes amusing." Yet his own description suggests the real meaning: "When distances were great, crowds of them under leaders went to the polling places a day in advance and *camped out like soldiers on the march.*" Women and children often went along, their presence reflecting their excitement about the franchise but also their understanding of the dangers involved in voting. Women may have gone for additional protection of the voters, like those women in South Carolina who carried weapons, or to avoid potential danger to those left alone in the countryside while the men were gone. But, in any case, the necessity for a group presence at the polls reinforced the sense of collective enfranchisement. What may have been chiefly for protection was turned into festivity as women participated in a symbolic reversal of the meaning of the group presence.

African American women throughout the South in the Reconstruction era assumed *publicly* the right to be active participants in the political process long after they had been formally removed—and they did so, in part, through their husbands. They operated out of an assumption that his vote was theirs. Unlike many northern white middle-class women, southern black women in the immediate post–Civil War era did not base their political participation in justifications of superior female morality or public motherhood. They did not need to; their own cultural, economic, and political traditions provided rationale enough—"autonomy was not simply personal."

One of the ramifications of liberal democratic political theory is that our notion of politics is severely circumscribed. In a context where only certain persons have the rights and abilities to participate fully, the *formal* political process takes on an exclusivity and sanctity all its own. Historians operating from this perspective often ascribe the totality of politics to the formal political arena. . . . But these women's actions were fundamentally *political.* That African American women did not operate inside the formal political process does not negate the intensely political character of their actions. These actions represented a continuous significant political participation on their part. Black women, therefore, were hardly confined (even without the franchise or elective office) to a private sphere. They were certainly not confined to any less bloody sphere.

African American women understood "that freedom meant above all the right to participate in the process of creating it." Being denied this right in the external political arena and having this right increasingly circumscribed in the internal arena as well, these women created their own political expression, thus inventing the power their freedom required. Their actions were not merely a grievance against their own lack of political rights or lack of rights of the black community but, more importantly, a critique of the absence of freedom and democracy, as they understood it, in the society at large. By their actions and assumptions they challenged the fundamental assumptions of the U.S. political process itself. . . .

Ultimately northern and southern white men may have denied African American women the freedom fully to shape their own lives in the post–Civil War era. But we, trapped in our own mental prisons, have denied them their freedom as well, insisting instead that they accept our very limited and pessimistic vision of human possibilities. . . . Just as African American women, as part of black communities throughout the South, struggled in the post–Civil War era to catch, that is, to make real, their vision of freedom, we, as historians, must now struggle to catch, that is, to understand, their vision of freedom. In the process we need not only to refine our base of information but also to reconstruct our frameworks, creating new ones that allow us to interpret these women's lives in ways that do justice to their vision of freedom.

FURTHER READING

James Anderson, *The Education of Blacks in the South, 1860–1935* (1988).

Kathleen C. Berkeley, "'Colored Ladies Also Contributed': Black Women's Activities from Benevolence to Social Welfare, 1866–1896," in Walter J. Fraser, Jr., R. Frank Saunders, Jr., and Jon L. Wakelyn, eds., *The Web of Southern Social Relations: Women, Family, and Education* (1985).

Ira Berlin, Barbara J. Fields, Steven F. Miller, Joseph P. Reidy, and Leslie S. Rowland, eds., *Free at Last: A Documentary History of Slavery, Freedom, and the Civil War* (1992).

Ira Berlin, Barbara J. Fields, Steven F. Miller, Joseph P. Reidy, and Leslie S. Rowland, eds., *Slaves No More: Three Essays on Emancipation and the Civil War* (1992).

Ira Berlin and Leslie S. Rowland, eds., *Families and Freedom: A Documentary History of African-American Kinship in the Civil War Era* (1997).

W. E. Burghardt Du Bois, *Black Reconstruction in America* (1935).

Eric Foner, *Freedom's Lawmakers: Directory of Black Office Holders During Reconstruction* (1996).

Eric Foner, *Reconstruction: America's Unfinished Revolution, 1863–1877* (1980).

Thavolia Glymph and John Kushma, eds. *Essays on the Postbellum Southern Economy* (1985).

Reginald F. Hildebrand, *The Times Were Strange and Stirring: Methodist Preachers and the Crisis of Emancipation* (1995).

Sharon Ann Holt, "Making Freedom Pay: Freedpeople Working for Themselves, North Carolina, 1865–1900," *Journal of Southern History*, 60 (May 1994), 229–262.

Thomas C. Holt, *Black over White: Negro Political Leadership in South Carolina During Reconstruction* (1977).

Thomas C. Holt, "'An Empire over the Mind': Emancipation, Race, and Ideology in the British West Indies and the American South," in J. Morgan Kousser and James McPherson, eds., *Region, Race, and Reconstruction: Essays in Honor of C. Vann Woodward* (1982).

Gerald David Jaynes, *Branches Without Roots: Genesis of the Black Working Class in the American South, 1862–1882* (1986).

Jacqueline Jones, *Labor of Love, Labor of Sorrow: Black Women, Work, and the Family from Slavery to the Present* (1985).

Lawrence Levine, *Black Culture and Black Consciousness: Afro-American Folk Thought from Slavery to Freedom* (1977).

Leon F. Litwack, *Been in the Storm So Long: The Aftermath of Slavery* (1979).

Edward Magdol, *A Right to the Land: Essays on the Freedmen's Community* (1977).

Robert C. Morris, *Reading, 'Riting, and Reconstruction: The Education of Freedmen in the South, 1861–1870* (1981).

Donald G. Nieman, *Promises to Keep: African Americans and the Constitutional Order, 1776 to the Present* (1991).

Claude F. Oubre, *Forty Acres and a Mule: The Freedmen's Bureau and Black Landownership* (1973).

Linda M. Perkins, "The Black Female American Missionary Association Teacher in the South, 1861–1870," in Jeffrey J. Crow and Flora J. Hatley, eds., *Black Americans in North Carolina and the South* (1984).

Howard N. Rabinowitz, ed., *Southern Black Leaders of the Reconstruction Era* (1982).

Peter J. Rachleff, *Black Labor in the South: Richmond, Virginia*, 1865–1890 (1984).

Armstead L. Robinson, "Plans Dat Comed from God: Institution Building and the Emergence of Black Leadership in Reconstruction Memphis," in Orville Vernon Burton and Robert C. McMath, Jr., eds., *Toward a New South? Studies in Post–Civil War Southern Communities* (1982).

Julie Saville, *The Work of Reconstruction: From Slave to Wage Laborer in South Carolina*, 1860–1870 (1994).

James D. Schmidt, *Free to Work: Labor Law, Emancipation, and Reconstruction*, 1815–1880 (1998).

Leslie A. Schwalm, *A Hard Fight for We: Women's Transition from Slavery to Freedom in South Carolina* (1997).

Rebecca Scott, "The Battle over the Child: Child Apprenticeship and the Freedmen's Bureau in North Carolina," *Prologue*, 10 (Summer 1978), 101–113.

Alrutheus Ambush Taylor, *The Negro in the Reconstruction of Virginia* (1926).

Allen W. Trelease, *White Terror: The Ku Klux Klan Conspiracy and Southern Reconstruction* (1971).

Theodore Branter Wilson, *The Black Codes of the South* (1965).

Major Problems in American History Series
Titles Currently Available

CPSIA information can be obtained
at www.ICGtesting.com
Printed in the USA
FFOW01n1249120718
47397752-50530FF